Common Admission Test

CAT - MBA Entrance Exam

Latest Edition
Practice Kit

12 Tests
12 Topic-Wise Test

Topic Wise Chapters with Questions

✓ Thoroughly Revised and Updated

✓ Detailed Analysis of all MCQs

Title	: Common Admission Test CAT - MBA Entrance Exam
Author Name	: Mr. Rohit Manglik
Published By	: EduGorilla Community Pvt. Ltd.
Publishers Address	: 12/651, First Floor Opp. Arvindo Park, Near Jama Masjid, Indira Nagar, Lucknow, Uttar Pradesh-226016, India

Copyright EduGorilla

ISBN : 978-93-55563-68-2

First Edition

Disclaimer EduGorilla

Compiled and created by EduGorilla Community Pvt. Ltd

Printed By EduGorilla Community Pvt. Ltd.

ROHIT MANGLIK
CEO, EduGorilla

Dear Applicants,

People say *"Success comes to those who work hard."* But I've seen people working hard for their exams day in and day out for marginal success. While others succeed in their examinations by putting in just half the work. So are they God Gifted? No! I believe that it's because they work *smart* and not just *hard*. Similarly, for your exams, you should strategize your preparation so as to increase the likelihood of success. Well with EduGorilla get ready to increase your *chances of selection* in your exam by *16x*.

EduGorilla helps you in not only working *hard* but also working in a *smart and strategic* manner. With EduGorilla's preparation package, you get a chance to make your exam preparation easy, and a fun learning path towards selection. Finding the right path to your preparations can be difficult if you don't know in which direction to head. Don't worry, we have you covered! EduGorilla will be your guide to success in your journey. With our Preparation Package, you can prepare strategically and beat the exam in just one attempt.

EduGorilla's Preparation Package includes-

- **Test Series**
- **Books**

Our preparation package is handcrafted as per the latest changes, expert opinions, and students' discretion. Thus, enabling you to get through each stage of the selection process for your exam.

Our Books are designed by the teachers and experts of the respective exam with a combined 150+ years of experience; to provide you with easy, efficient, and effective learning. Our books are smart, in the sense that not only do they give you the answers to the questions but also provide similar questions for practice.

EduGorilla's competent Test Series gives you real-time experience and confidence through which you can clear your offline or online exam in just one attempt. We currently host 83,000+ mock tests for 1,440+ competitive and academic exams.

Thus, EduGorilla misses no chance to assist you in your preparation and covers all stages of the exam, so that you don't have to look anywhere else.

We provide complete preparation packages for defense, banking, teaching, and other National & State-Level exams. Hence, it doesn't matter which exam you aspire to because you will reach your success.

ALL THE BEST !

Let EduGorilla be your Guide to Success.

Rohit Manglik,
Founder and CEO, EduGorilla

INTRODUCTION

EduGorilla focuses on guiding students to succeed in their examinations. With that in mind, our book, titled "Common Admission Test : CAT - MBA Entrance Exam", has been drafted through the collective efforts of our distinguished experts with 150+ years of combined experience. This book consists of questions that are created following the latest changes in the syllabus and exam pattern. We compiled the book on the basis of questions that are most likely to appear in the . Through EduGorilla's "Common Admission Test : CAT - MBA Entrance Exam" your chances of success will increase 16x.

EduGorilla does this through our Complete Preparation Package. This package consists of well-conceptualized and structured content in the form of questions that are tailor-made according to your needs and will help you practice for exams in a smart way by pinpointing all the necessary information. It also provides hints and solutions, along with a smart answer sheet for your self-evaluation. You can assess your shortcomings and work accordingly on areas that may require more of your attention.

EduGorilla promises to help you succeed in your examination and accomplish your dream goals. We believe in our aspirants and see them at the top of the merit list. And the first step towards the top is to start preparing with us. EduGorilla's "Common Admission Test : CAT - MBA Entrance Exam" includes the following attributes.

➤ Well-Researched Content

➤ Top-Notch Quality

➤ Detailed Answers and Analysis

➤ Smart Answer Sheet

➤ Exam Relevant Questions

Therefore, EduGorilla fortifies your preparation and makes it durable enough to help you stand tall and beat the examination.

TABLE OF CONTENTS

Q.1 A sum of Rs. 12200 is to be repaid in three equal annual installments. If the rate of interest is 25%, compounded annually, then the value of each installment?

A. Rs. 6450   **B.** Rs. 5950   **C.** Rs. 6600   **D.** Rs. 6250

Q.2 Rocky lent a sum of Rs.100 at simple interest of 6% p.a. for the first month, 12% p.a. for the second month, 24% p.a. for the third month, and so on. Find the total amount of interest earned at the end of one year.

A. Rs. 2145
B. Rs. 2130.5
C. Rs. 2047.5
D. Rs. 2095.6

Q.3 Ram saves Rs.60,000 at the beginning of each year and puts the money in a bank, That pays 10% annual compound interest, What would be the total saving of Ram at the end of 4 years?

A. Rs.3,06,400
B. Rs.2,96,306
C. Rs.2,40,000
D. Rs.3,06,306

Q.4 Mohan deposit certain amount in bank saving account for 6 year which give simple interest of $x\%$ annually and invest same principle in fix deposit for 2 year which gives interest rate 10% and compounded annually, total interest he get from saving account to fix deposit in the ratio of $6:7$, if bank provide $(x+3)\%$ rate annually on saving account deposit, then difference of interest arise Rs. 7,500 between saving account and fix deposit after respective time period, what amount he invest in fix deposit?

A. Rs.40,000
B. Rs.50,000
C. Rs.70,000
D. Rs.60,000

Q.5 The fare of a royal train between two stations increases at the rate of 25% per month at simple interest and the number of passengers decreases at the rate of 10% per month compounded monthly. If the present fare per person and the total fare charged by the train are Rs. 1000 and Rs. 2500000 respectively, then find the total fare earned by the train authority after 2 months.

A. Rs. 3037000
B. Rs. 3037500
C. Rs. 3030000
D. Rs. 3000000

Q.6 From a class of 50 students, some students were selected randomly for the republic day parade but the condition was that the number should be either multiple of 2 or multiple of 5. The average weight of all the students who were not selected was 56 kg and the average weight of all the students who were selected was 58 kg. What was the average weight (in kg) of the class?

A. 57.8   **B.** 57.2   **C.** 56.9   **D.** 57.6

Q.7 A can do a work in 24 days, B can do the same work in 48 days and C can do the same work in 72 days. Unfortunately, B could not become part of the work so the work was completed by A and C only, so in this case how much more money is

earned by A than the previous situation, if the total amount distributed to them in both the cases was 4400 rupees.

A. Rs. 600   **B.** Rs. 700   **C.** Rs. 800   **D.** Rs. 900

Q.8 A company hires 25 people and all the people can complete the work in 60 days. But seeing their disinterest, the company hires 10 more persons after every 5 days. Then how many days before the work will be finished?

A. 45 days   **B.** 60 days   **C.** 15 days   **D.** 30 days

Q.9 A, B and C can complete a work in 20, 24 and 30 days respectively. All three of them starts together but after 4 days A leaves the job and B left the job 6 days before the work was completed. C completed the remaining work alone. In how many days was the total work completed?

A. 10   **B.** 12   **C.** 14   **D.** 16

Q.10 A man, a woman, and a boy can do a work in 20, 30, and 40 days respectively. How many women are required to finish the remaining task in 1 day if to finish twice of work 5 boys and 4 men worked for 4 days and then left?

A. 24   **B.** 25   **C.** 23   **D.** 21

Q.11 Two workers Samrat and Kamlesh started working together and completed the work in 18 days and when Samrat worked thrice as efficiently and then Kamlesh worked with half his efficiency it will take same time to finish the work. Calculate the time taken by Samrat to finish the work alone.

A. 45   **B.** 80   **C.** 90   **D.** 70

Q.12 In an election, 80% of the people casted their votes and 45% of the voters who casted votes are employed and 66.67% of employed voters are engineers. Find the percentage of non-engineers among total voters?

A. 12%   **B.** 24%   **C.** 50%   **D.** 76%

Q.13 In an election, there are two parties A and B involved. 18% of the total votes were invalid and the ratio of votes received by A and B is 5 : 3. If the number of votes polled in favor of B was 615, then find the total number of votes polled.

A. 3000   **B.** 2400   **C.** 2600   **D.** 2000

Q.14 What will be the percentage change in the volume of a cuboid if its length increases by 57.13%, breadth decreases by 41.66%, and height decrease by 46.66%?

A. 57.13%
B. −41.66%
C. −51.11%
D. 104.54%

Q.15 A shopkeeper marked his article 80% above the cost price and sold it after giving a discount of 25%. Had he given a discount of 13% he would have earned Rs 378 more. Find the cost price of the article?

A. Rs 1250   **B.** Rs 1650   **C.** Rs 1850   **D.** Rs 1750

Q.16 Aman marked his goods price at 24% above the cost price. He sold half the stock at the marked price, one quarter at a discount of 30% on the marked price and the rest at a discount of 48% on the marked price. His total gain is:

A. 2.34%   B. 2.00%   C. 3.82%   D. 2.82%

Q.17 A shopkeeper gives a discount of 28% on the marked price of article P and selling price of article Q is $33\frac{1}{3}\%$ more than the selling price at article P, if shopkeeper made 20% profit on article Q and selling price of article P was Rs 200 less than the cost price of article Q, then find the cost price of article P, which shopkeeper sold at a profit of 20%?

A. 1500   B. 2200   C. 2200   D. 2850

Q.18 A started business in 2010 with Rs. 75,000. In 2011, B joined him with Rs. 45,000, in year 2012 they both invested an additional amount of Rs. 25,000 each at the end of 3 years they earned a profit of Rs. 43800, Find A's share in the profit?

A. 40,000   B. 45,000   C. 30,000   D. 50,000

Q.19 The ratio of cost price of two articles is 4 : 9. The articles are marked up by 40% and and 15% respectively and the ratio of their Marked price is 112 : 207.If the discount of 12.5% and 11.11% is given respectively the profit earned on first article is Rs.270. What is the profit earned on second article?

A. Rs.40   B. Rs.150   C. Rs.60   D. Rs.80

Q.20 The cost price of a smartphone is Rs. 44040 . Mukesh purchases 5 such smartphones and adds in an extra cost for installing newly licensed software whose cost is $\left(\frac{1}{8}\right)^{th}$ of cost price of each smartphone. He sells the first smartphone at Rs. 35000 and still made a profit of 20% on the whole deal by selling smartphones at the average price required to maintain the profit. One such smartphone was sold to Seema who in turn traded her new phone for an old phone whose cost was Rs. 50000. Find loss incurred by Seema in this whole deal.

A. Rs. 15567.5   B. Rs. 17587.6
C. Rs. 32548.5   D. Rs. 28458.5

Q.21 A mixture of 343 litres of wine and water is to be distributed in the ratio of 5 : 2. How much more water (In litres) should be added so that the new mixture contains wine and water in the ratio of 5 : 3?

Q.22 In a mixture, the ratio of alcohol and water is 6 : 5. When 22 liters mixture are replaced by water, the ratio becomes 9 : 13. Find the quantity of alcohol (In litres) after replacement.

Q.23 A vessel contains 2.5 liters of water and 10 liters of milk. 20% of the contents of the vessel are removed. To the remaining contents, x liters of water is added to reverse the ratio of water and milk. Then y liter of milk is added again to reverse the ratio of water and milk. Find y.

Q.24 In a mixture, there is 63 litres of water and 77 litres of milk. Some quantity of the mixture is taken out. After that 16 litres of water and 4 litres of milk are added in to the mixture, so that quantity of water and milk are the same in the mixture. Find the total quantity of mixture when some amount of mixture taken out.

Q.25 If the 20 liters mixture of milk and water contains 60% milk. If x liter of milk is added then the mixture contains 80% milk. Now if 40% mixture is emptied into another flask. Find the remaining quantity of milk in the remaining mixture.

A. 19.2 liters   B. 16.2 liters
C. 14.2 liters   D. 21.2 liters

Q.26 A swimmer swims from point A against a current for 8 minutes and then swims backwards in favor of the current for next 8 minutes and comes to the point B. If AB = 200 meter, then what is the speed of the current (in kmph)?

A. 1.50 km /hr   B. 0.75 km/hr
C. 1.0 km/hr   D. 2.25 km/hr

Q.27 Two trains pass each other on parallel lines. Each train is 100 meters long. When they are going in the same direction, the faster one takes 60 seconds to pass the other completely. If they are going in opposite directions they pass each other completely in 10 seconds. Find the speed of the slower train in km/h.

A. 26 km/h   B. 18 km/h
C. 48 km/h   D. None of these

Q.28 Ravi is riding his bike with a speed 80 km/hr on the road which is along to a railway track on which Rajdhani Express having length 250 meters is running with a speed of 90 km/hr. Suddenly Ravi saw that there is sparking in the train's generator coach which is just on the right side of Ravi. At which speed Ravi ride his bike so that he inform the driver of the train at 54th second.

A. $\frac{250}{3}$ km/hr   B. $\frac{320}{3}$ km/hr
C. $\frac{290}{3}$ km/hr   D. $\frac{270}{3}$ km/hr

Q.29 A thief started running from point X at a speed of $20\ km/hr$, after running for 30 minutes, when he watched the police at the distance of $400\ m$ coming from opposite direction at the speed of $30\ km/hr$, he turned and started running at $25\ km/hr$ in the same direction as of police. After how much distance from point X police will catch the thief?

A. $2m$ B. $8m$ C. $2\ km$ D. $8\ km$

Q.30 A person during a bike ride covers 45 mins at speed of $45kmph$, another 45 mins at $60kmph$ and next 30 mins at $90\ kmph$ speed. Find the average speed of man during the entire journey.

A. 61.875   B. 60.5   C. 75.32   D. 45

Q.31 430 fruits have been distributed in a school among 45 people consisting of boys, girls and teachers. The total fruits given to boys, girls and teachers are in the ratio 12 : 15 : 16. But the fruits received by each boy, girl and teacher are in the ratio 6 : 5 :4. Find what each boy, girl and teacher receives?

A. 10, 9, 8   B. 25, 37, 120
C. 12, 10, 8   D. 13, 14, 20

Q.32 The ratio of the present age of Chinky and Minky is 4 : 5 and the present age of Chinky's mother is $\frac{9}{2}$ times Minky's age

5 years ago and the present age of Minky's mother is $\frac{7}{3}$ times of Chinky's age after 3 years. If after 15 years the average age of Minky's mother and Chinky's mother is 55, then find the Difference between Chinky's and Minky's present age.

A. 3 years   B. 2 years   C. 4 years   D. 5 years

Q.33 The ratio of the prices of two mobiles I-phone 9 and I-phone X was 13 : 20 last year. In current year, the prices are drop by 10% of I-phone 9 and that of I-phone X by Rs. 20,000. If their prices are now in the ratio 117 : 160. Find the price of I-phone 9 in last year.

A. Rs. 56,000   B. Rs. 65,000
C. Rs. 75,000   D. Rs. 57,000

Q.34 A bank offers the business loan at simple interest, rate of interest for 1st 2 years is 8% for the next 3 years it is 10% and for the period beyond 5 years it is 12.5% per annum. If a person took the loan of Rs. $20\,L$ and paid Rs. $36.7\,L$ after some years. Find the number of years after which he repaid the loan:

Q.35 Raghav took a loan at the compound interest at a rate of 37.5% per annum for 3 years if the compound interest paid by him in 3rd year is Rs. 7260 then find the principal.

Q.36 A sum of Rs. 10000 is divided into two parts such that the simple interest on first part for 1 year 3 months at the rate of $6\frac{2}{3}\%$ per annum is half the simple interest on the second part for 13 years 4 months at the rate of $1\frac{2}{13}\%$ per annum then what is the difference between two parts?

Q.37 Rs. 1200 amount to Rs. 1632 in 4 years at a certain rate of SI. If the rate of interest increases by 1% each year then what will be the amount if the same is invested for the same period?

Q.38 Varshika purchases a dress for Rs. 3200 but the shop had another paying option of Rs. 1000 as a down payment and two equal monthly installments of Rs. 1200 each. Find the rate of interest in the installment scheme.

A. $\frac{100}{3}\%$ B. 65%   C. $\frac{5\cdot00}{12}\%$ D. 75%

Q.39 Karan calculates the average of his marks in five subjects. By mistake, he writes a number of two subjects as the reverse of original marks thereby increasing the average by 27 marks. If the incorrect numbers are in the ratio $13:10$, what is the sum of the original numbers? (The marks awarded are from 01, 02 ... to 99)

Q.40 $A, B, C, D,$ and E are five persons. The weight of $A, B,$ and C is 90%, 112% and 94% respectively of the average weight of all five. The ratio of the weight of D and E is $6:11$. The difference between the weight of D and E is $75\,kg$. What is the average weight of all five persons?

Q.41 In a group of 140 people $\frac{1}{5}$ are males, $\frac{1}{4}$ of remaining are females and rest are children. If the average weight of children is $30\,kg$ and the average weight of females is twice the average weight of C, Also the average weight of males is 1.5 times the average age of F. The average weight of whole group is?

Q.42 The weight of Varun, Rahul and Priyanka in 2011 was is in the ratio 6: $5:7$. In 2016 weight of Varun became 150%, weight of Rahul became 160% and the weight of Priyanka increased by $\frac{300}{7}\%$ as compared to their weight in 2011. If the average increase in their weight is $7.2\,kg$, what is the difference between the weight of Varun in 2016 and the weight of Priyanka in 2011?

A. $5.0\,kg$ B. $4.8\,kg$ C. $5.2\,kg$ D. $4.6\,kg$

Q.43 A and B together can complete a task in 1.2 days. However, if A works alone, completes half the job and leaves and then B works alone and completes the rest of the work, it takes 2.5 days in all to complete the work. If B is more efficient than A, how days would it have taken B to do the work by herself?

Q.44 50 employees in a company can complete a work in 23 days. They start work together and after every 5 days, 5 employees more join them. Then in how much time work will be completed?

A. $25 days$ B. $15 days$ C. $20 days$ D. $30 days$

Q.45 A can plough a square field of side $10\,m$ in 10 hours and that can be done by B in 5 hours. In how much time a new field having 50% larger side and square in shape is ploughed if A and B plough together?

A. $10 hours$ B. $7.5 hours$
C. $6.5 hours$ D. $15 hours$

Q.46 Two workers Samrat and Kamlesh started working together and completed the work in 18 days and when Samrat worked thrice as efficiently and then Kamlesh worked with half his efficiency it will take same time to finish the work. Calculate the time taken by Samrat to finish the work alone.

Q.47 In an institute, 60% of the students are boys and the rest are girls. Further 15% of the boys and 7.5% of the girls are getting a fee waiver. If the number of those getting a fee waiver is 90, find the total number of students getting 50% concessions if it is given that 50% of those not getting a fee waiver are eligible to get half fee concession?

Q.48 Out of total students in class X^{th} $66\frac{2}{3}\%$ are in section A and remaining are in section B. If 50 students from section A are shifted to section B, then total students in section A becomes 50% of total students. If 40 students from section B are shifted to section A, then the total students in section B becomes what per cent of total students in class X^{th} ?

A. 32%   B. 40%   C. 20%   D. 30%

Q.49 The cost price of item A is equal to the cost price of item B. If the market price of item A is Rs after increased by 60% of its cost price and the market price of B is Rs 600 after increased by 50% of its cost price. The difference between the selling price of item B and item A is Rs if a 10% of discount given on the market price of both the items.

A. 680,80   B. 640, 36   C. 540, 28   D. 720, 240

Q.50 A trader purchases a book and a pen for Rs. 526 . He sells them making a profit of 12% on the book and 16% on the pen. He earns a profit of Rs. 74. The difference between the cost prices of the pen and the book is equal to:

Q.51 If two successive discounts, each of 20% on the marked price of an article, are equal to a single discount of Rs. 331.20, then the marked price (in Rs.) of the article is:

Q.52 A shopkeeper sold two toys for Rs. 990 each. On the first toy he gained 10% and on the second he lost 10%. Find the total percentage gain or loss.

[RRB (NTPC), 2020]

A. 10% Loss   B. 10% Gain
C. 1% Loss   D. 1% Gain

Q.53 The weight of Kanye, Ashton and Justin is in the ratio $10 : 9 : 12$. Which of the following statements is not true?

A. $\left(\frac{1}{3}\right)$ of Ashton's weight $+ \left(\frac{1}{4}\right)$ of Justin's weight $= \left(\frac{3}{5}\right)$ of Kanye's weight.

B. $\left(\frac{7}{3}\right)$ of Ashton's weight $- \left(\frac{3}{2}\right)$ of Kanye's weight $= \left(\frac{1}{2}\right)$ of Justin's weight.

C. $\left(\frac{3}{5}\right)$ of Kanye's weight $= \left(\frac{2}{3}\right)$ of Ashton's weight.

D. $\left(\frac{8}{5}\right)$ of Kanye's weight $+ \left(\frac{3}{4}\right)$ of Justin's weight $= \left(\frac{10}{3}\right)$ of Ashton's weight.

Q.54 The income of A and B is in the ratio $7 : 8$ and that of B and C is $4 : 3$. The ratio of savings of A and C is $4 : 3$ and the difference between the savings of B and C together to the savings A is Rs. 32,000 . Find the salary of B (In rupees) if it is given their expenditure is equal.

Q.55 Pavan gave 20% and 30% of his salary to his two friends Chandan and Lakshman. Chandan and Lakshman spend 40% and 50% of their money respectively. What is the ratio between the amount left with Chandan and Lakshman together and the amount left with Pavan?

A. $50 : 27$ B. $6 : 25$ C. $25 : 6$ D. $27 : 50$

Q.56 The monthly incomes of A and B are in the ration $3 : 5$ and the ratio of their savings is $2 : 3$If the income of B is equal to three times the savings of A, then what is the ratio of the expenditures of A and B ?

A. $8 : 15$ B. $7 : 11$ C. $5 : 8$ D. $5 : 7$

Q.57 A sum of Rs. 3200 was to be divided between A, B, C and D in the ratio 4:6:7:3. But by mistake, it was divided in the ratio $3 : 5 : 6 : 2$ As a result, who got $16\frac{2}{3}\%$ less than her due?

[SSC MTS, 2019]

A. B   B. C   C. D   D. A

Q.58 If $(a + b) : (b + c) : (c + a) = 7 : 6 : 5$ and $a + b + c = 27$ then what will be the value of $\frac{1}{a} : \frac{1}{b} : \frac{1}{c}$?

A. $4 : 3 : 6$ B. $3 : 2 : 4$ C. $3 : 4 : 2$ D. $3.6 : 4$

Q.59 A person divides a certain amount among his three sons in the ratio of $3 : 4 : 5$. If he had divided this amount in the ratio of $\frac{1}{3}, \frac{1}{4}, \frac{1}{5}$ his son, who had got the lowest share earlier, would get Rs. 1188 more. Find the amount (in Rs).

Q.60 A alone can complete a work in 12 days and B alone can complete the same work in 15 days. If they finish the work together and received Rs. 3600. Then find the share of A.

A. Rs. 1200   B. Rs. 3000   C. Rs. 1500   D. Rs. 2000

// Smart Answer Sheet //

Correct — Indicates percentage of students who answered questions correctly.

Skipped — Indicates percentage of students who skipped questions.

Q.	Ans.	Correct / Skipped	Q.	Ans.	Correct / Skipped	Q.	Ans.	Correct / Skipped	Q.	Ans.	Correct / Skipped	Q.	Ans.	Correct / Skipped
1	D	45.95 % / 32.69 %	13	D	63.88 % / 31.51 %	25	A	29.75 % / 67.03 %	37	1704	45.45 % / 47.88 %	49	B	69.91 % / 30.06 %
2	C	40.46 % / 53.15 %	14	C	48.59 % / 41.56 %	26	B	52.14 % / 33.32 %	38	D	52.67 % / 43.0 %	50	18	12.33 % / 75.2 %
3	D	57.96 % / 40.89 %	15	D	40.84 % / 51.69 %	27	D	63.65 % / 32.56 %	39	26	52.84 % / 36.32 %	51	920	54.39 % / 40.46 %
4	B	52.19 % / 35.89 %	16	D	41.34 % / 42.59 %	28	B	52.39 % / 42.77 %	40	125	49.44 % / 45.77 %	52	C	22.19 % / 76.04 %
5	B	48.93 % / 32.85 %	17	A	63.83 % / 35.13 %	29	D	69.7 % / 30.06 %	41	48	63.6 % / 34.31 %	53	D	56.95 % / 39.06 %
6	B	28.79 % / 69.72 %	18	C	52.55 % / 33.43 %	30	A	29.96 % / 67.55 %	42	B	47.32 % / 44.99 %	54	64000	30.72 % / 68.93 %
7	D	52.76 % / 40.8 %	19	C	53.0 % / 34.17 %	31	C	47.18 % / 38.26 %	43	2	13.72 % / 83.63 %	55	D	28.79 % / 70.35 %
8	D	30.04 % / 69.18 %	20	A	55.55 % / 40.42 %	32	A	54.9 % / 45.02 %	44	C	26.16 % / 71.14 %	56	A	52.81 % / 34.98 %
9	C	56.2 % / 36.88 %	21	49	11.74 % / 75.67 %	33	B	53.92 % / 30.45 %	45	B	68.97 % / 30.99 %	57	C	60.66 % / 37.24 %
10	D	32.44 % / 67.4 %	22	36	60.01 % / 39.81 %	34	8	62.75 % / 30.06 %	46	90	13.89 % / 69.76 %	58	A	20.58 % / 70.81 %
11	C	67.76 % / 30.94 %	23	120	55.35 % / 41.86 %	35	10240	25.65 % / 71.63 %	47	330	41.48 % / 31.43 %	59	6768	46.89 % / 42.62 %
12	A	41.91 % / 56.78 %	24	120	58.36 % / 32.51 %	36	400	15.41 % / 74.16 %	48	C	27.18 % / 67.21 %	60	D	62.13 % / 31.52 %

Performance Analysis

Avg. Score (%)	48.89%
Toppers Score (%)	71.67%
Your Score	

//Hints and Solutions//

1. Given,

Principal Amount = Rs. 12200

Rate of interest $= 25\%$

Three equal annual instalment means (Time)=3 years

$$A = P \times \left(1 + \frac{R}{100}\right)^n$$

Here,

$A = $ Amount

$P = $ Principal Amount

$R = $ Rate of interest

$n = $ time in year

$$I_A = I \times \left(1 + \frac{R}{100}\right)^t$$

Here,

$I_A = $ Instalment Amount

$I = $ Instalment

$R = $ Rate of interest

$t = (n-1)$ year, $(n-2)$ year,

Here, $n = $ time in years

We know that:

$$A = P \times \left(1 + \frac{R}{100}\right)^n \quad \text{.....(1)}$$

Put all the given values in equation (1)

$$A = 12200 \times \left(1 + \frac{25}{100}\right)^3$$

$$= 12200 \times \left(1 + \frac{1}{4}\right)^3$$

$$= 12200 \times \left(\frac{5}{4}\right)^3$$

$$= 12200 \times \frac{125}{64}$$

Now,

Let the instalment be Rs.y

Instalment Amount (I_A) for three years means $= (n-1)$ year $+$

$(n-2)$ year $+(n-3)$ year

We know that —

$$(I_A) \text{ for } (n-1) \text{ year } = 1 \times \left(1 + \frac{R}{100}\right)^n \quad \text{.....(2)}$$

Put all the given values in equation (2) then we get

$$(I_A) \text{ for } (n-1) \text{ year } = y \times \left(1 + \frac{25}{100}\right)^2$$

$$= y \times \left(1 + \frac{1}{4}\right)^2$$

$$= y \times \left(\frac{5}{4}\right)^2$$

$$= \frac{25y}{16}$$

Similarly,

$$I_A \text{ for } (n-2) \text{ year } = y \times \left(1 + \frac{25}{100}\right)^1$$

$$= y \times \left(1 + \frac{1}{4}\right)$$

$$= y \times \frac{5}{4}$$

$$= \frac{5y}{4}$$

Now,

$$I_A \text{ for } (n-3) \text{ year}$$

$$= y \times \left(1 + \frac{25}{100}\right)^0$$

$$= y \times 1$$

$$= y$$

Instalment Amount (I_A) for three years $= \frac{25y}{16} + \frac{5y}{4} + y$

$$= \frac{(25y + 20y + 16y)}{16}$$

$$= \frac{61y}{16}$$

Now,

We equate the Amount (A) \\& Instalment Amount (I_A)

$$12200 \times \frac{125}{64} = \frac{61y}{16}$$

$$\Rightarrow 200 \times \frac{125}{4} = y$$

$$\Rightarrow y = 50 \times 125$$

$$\Rightarrow y = 6250$$

$\therefore$ The Value of each instalment will be Rs. 6250.

Hence, the correct option is (D).

2. Given,

Principal $=$ Rs. 100

Rate of Interest for 1st month $= 6\%$

Interest $= \dfrac{6}{12}$

Interest for second month $= \dfrac{12}{12}$

The interest earned for the successive months is in the form of geometric progression.

Rs. $\dfrac{6}{12}$, Rs. $\dfrac{12}{12}$, Rs. $\dfrac{24}{12}$ …..

$a = $ Rs. $\dfrac{6}{12}, r = \dfrac{\left(\frac{12}{12}\right)}{\left(\frac{6}{12}\right)} = 2$, where a is the first term and r is the

common ratio of the series

$\therefore$ Sum of series $= \dfrac{a(r^n - 1)}{r - 1}$

$= \dfrac{\frac{6}{12}(2^{12} - 1)}{2 - 1}$

$= \dfrac{1}{2}(4096 - 1)$

$= $ Rs. 2047.5

The total amount of interest earned at the end of one year is Rs. 2047.5.

Hence, the correct option is (C).

3. Given,

Ram saves Rs. 60,000 at the beginning of each year and puts the money in a bank.

Rate of compound interest $= 10\%$ annually

Time $= 4$ year

Compound interest is interest on interest.

$$A = P \times \left(1 + \dfrac{R}{100}\right)^T$$

$A = $ Final amount

$P = $ Initial amount

$R = $ Rate of interest

$T = $ Time

First year deposit in bank Rs. 60,000

After 1 year Amount $= 60000 \times \left(1 + \dfrac{10}{100}\right)^1$

After 2 year Amount $= 60000 \times \left(1 + \dfrac{10}{100}\right)^2$

After 3 year Amount $= 60000 \times \left(1 + \dfrac{10}{100}\right)^3$

After 4 year Amount $= 60000 \times \left(1 + \dfrac{10}{100}\right)^4$

Total amount after 4 year $= 60000 \times 1.1 \times \{1 + 1.1 + (1.1)^2 + (1.1)^3\}$

$= 66000 \times (1 + 1.1 + 1.21 + 1.331)$

$= 66000 \times 4.641$

$= $ Rs. $3,06,306$

$\therefore$ Total saving of Ram at the end of 4 years is Rs. $3,06,306$.

Hence, the correct option is (D).

4. Given,

Amount deposit in saving account $= $ Amount deposit in fix deposit

Saving account on simple interest $= x\%$ annually

Period of time for which deposited in saving account $= 6$ year

Fix deposit on compound interest $= 10\%$ annually

Period of time for which deposited in fix deposit $= 2$ year

Total interest he get from saving account : Total interest get on fix deposit in the ratio of $= 6:7$

If bank provide $(x + 3)\%$ rate annually on saving account deposit, then difference of interest arise Rs.7,500 between saving account and fix deposit after respective time period.

When annually interest rate $x\%$ given for 2 year compound interest than effective interest for two year is $= x + x + \left(\dfrac{x^2}{100}\right)$

When different interest getting on same principal, then amount of interest also in ratio of effective interest $\%$ ratio.

(Amount deposit in saving account = Amount deposit in fix deposit), means both deposit are 100% individually.

Effective simple interest on saving account for 6 year with $x\%$ interest rate $= (6 \times x)\%$

Effective compound interest on fix deposit for 2 year with $10\% = 10 + 10 + \dfrac{(10 \times 10)}{100} = 21\%$

Total interest he get from saving account : Total interest get on fix deposit in the ratio of $= 6x : 7x$

$7x = 21\%$

$6x = 18\%$ (effective interest for 6 year of simple interest)

Rate of interest for simple interest $x\% = \dfrac{18}{6} = 3\%$

If bank provide $(x + 3)\%$ rate annually on saving account deposit, then difference of interest arise Rs. 7,500 between saving account and fix deposit after respective time period.

Now, bank provide $(3 + 3)\%$ simple interest annually on saving account

$\Rightarrow$ New simple interest annually on saving account $= 6\%$

Effective interest occur on saving account for 6 year $= 6 \times 6 = 36\%$

Difference of interest between saving account and fix deposit after

respective time period $= 36 - 21 = 15\%$

$\because$ Difference of interest arise Rs. $7,500 = 15\%$

And Amount of Mohan invest in fix deposit $= 100\%$

Amount of Mohan invest in fix deposit $= \left(\dfrac{7,500}{15}\right) \times 100$

$\Rightarrow$ Rs. 50,000

$\therefore$ Amount of Mohan invest in fix deposit is Rs. 50,000

Hence, the correct option is (B).

5. Given,

Present fare per person = Rs. 1000

Total fare charged by the train $=$ Rs. 2500000

The fare of a royal train between to stations increases at the rate of 25% per month at simple interest.

The number of passenger decreases at the rate of 10% per annum compounded monthly.

$$S.I = \frac{P \times R \times T}{100}$$

$$A = P\left(1 - \frac{r}{100}\right)^2$$

Where, $A = $ Number of passengers after 2 months and $P = $ Current fare of the train.

Present number of passenger in the train $= \dfrac{2500000}{1000} = 2500$

Increased amount of fare per person $= 1000 + 1000 \times 25 \times \dfrac{2}{100}$

= Rs. 1500

Number of passenger after 2 months $= 2500\left(1 - \dfrac{10}{100}\right)^2$

$= 2025$

So, the total amount earned by the train authority $= 2025 \times 1500$ = Rs. 3037500

Hence, the correct option is (B).

6. Given,

The total number of students is 50 and the number of selected students should be either multiple of 2 or 5.

The average weight of students who were not selected = 56 kg

The average weight of students who were selected = 58 kg

Total students whose number was multiple of 2 = 25

Total students whose number was multiple of 5 = 10

Total students whose number was multiple of 5 and 2 both i.e., of 10 = 5

Total students whose number was either multiple of 2 or multiple of 5 = (25 + 10 − 5)

= 30

It means, 30 students were selected and 20 students were not selected.

According to question,

The sum of the weight of all the students = (56 × 20 + 58 × 30) kg

= 2860 kg

The average weight of all the students $= \dfrac{2860}{50}$

= 57.2 kg

Hence, the correct option is (B).

7. Given:

A can do a work in 24 days, B can do the same work in 48 days and C can do the same work in 72 days.

Calculation:

In the first case

A can do the work in 24 days

B can do the work in 48 days

C can do the work in 72 days

$\Rightarrow$ the ratio of their efficiency will be A : B : C = $\dfrac{1}{24} : \dfrac{1}{48} : \dfrac{1}{72} = 6 : 3 : 2$

$\Rightarrow$ A will get $\dfrac{6}{(6+3+2)} = \dfrac{6}{11}$ of the total amount which will be equal to Rs. 2400

But in the second case only A and C work

$\Rightarrow$ the efficiency of A : C = $\dfrac{1}{24} : \dfrac{1}{72} = 3 : 1$

So A will get now $\dfrac{3}{(1+3)} = \dfrac{3}{4}$th of the total amount which will be Rs. 3300

$\therefore$ Extra money earned by A = Rs. (3300 - 2400) = Rs. 900

Hence, the correct option is (D).

8. Given:

Total number of hired people = 25

25 people can complete the work in 60 days.

The company hires 10 more persons after every 5 days.

Formula:

Total work = total employees × total time

Calculation:

Total number of hired people = 25

25 people can complete the work in 60 days.

Total work = 25 × 60 = 1500 units

So work done by 25 people in first 5 days = 25 × 5 = 125 units

The company hires 10 more persons after every 5 days.

Now total number of people = 25 + 10 = 35

So work done by 35 people in next 5 days = 35 × 5 = 175 units

Again in next five days, total number of people = 35 + 10 = 45

So work done by 45 people in next 5 days = 45 × 5 = 225 units

Again in next five days, total number of people = 45 + 10 = 55

So work done by 55 people in next 5 days = 55 × 5 = 275 units

Again in next five days, total number of people = 55 + 10 = 65

So work done by 65 people in next 5 days = 65 × 5 = 325 units

Again in next five days, total number of people = 65 + 10 = 75

So work done by 75 people in next 5 days = 75 × 5 = 375 units

Total work that done = 125 + 175 + 225 + 275 + 325 + 375 = 1500 units

Thus the total work is done.

Now time taken by people to complete work = 5 + 5 + 5 + 5 + 5 + 5 = 30 days

Number of days before the work will be finished = 60 − 30 = 30 days

∴ The work will be finished before 30 days.

Hence, the correct option is (D).

9. Given:

Time is taken by A to complete a work = 20 days

Time is taken by B to complete a work = 24 days

Time is taken by C to complete a work = 30 days

Formula Used:

Total work = Efficiency × Total time taken

Calculation:

The LCM for 20, 24, 30 is 120.

Total work = 120 units

The efficiency of A = $\dfrac{120}{20}$ = 6 units/day

The efficiency of B = $\dfrac{120}{24}$ = 5 units/day

The efficiency of C = $\dfrac{120}{30}$ = 4 units/day

The efficiency of A + B + C = 6 + 5 + 4

= 15 units/day

The efficiency of B + C = 5 + 4

= 9 units/day

A, B, C work together for first 4 days = 15 × 4 = 60 units

Remaining work = 120 - 60

= 60 units

B left the work 6 days before completion

So, C completed the remaining work in last 6 days = 4 × 6 = 24 unit

Middle work = Total work - First work - last work

The B and C complete the work in middle days = 120 - 60 - 24 = 36 units

Time taken by B and C to do the middle days work = $\dfrac{36}{9}$ = 4 days

Total Time taken to complete the work = 4 + 4 + 6 = 14 days

∴ In 14 days the total work completed was completed.

Hence, the correct option is (C).

10. Given:

Time is taken by a man to do the work = 20 days

Time is taken by a woman to do the work = 30 days

Time is taken by a boy to do the work = 40 days

Formula:

Total work = Efficiency × Time is taken

Calculation:

Let the total work be x units

The efficiency of a man = $\dfrac{x}{20}$

The efficiency of a woman = $\dfrac{x}{30}$

The efficiency of a boy = $\dfrac{x}{40}$

So the efficiency of 4 men = 4 × $\left(\dfrac{x}{20}\right)$ = $\dfrac{x}{5}$

Now efficiency of 5 boys = 5 × $\left(\dfrac{x}{40}\right)$ = $\dfrac{x}{8}$

The total efficiency of 4 men and 5 boys = $\left(\frac{x}{5}\right) + \left(\frac{x}{8}\right) =$ $\frac{13x}{40}$

Now the work is done by 4 men and 5 boys in 4 days.

$\Rightarrow 4 \times \left(\frac{13x}{40}\right)$ units

$= \frac{13x}{10}$ units

Remaining work = 2x - initial work

$= 2x - \left(\frac{13x}{10}\right) = \frac{7x}{10}$

So the remaining work is done in 1 day by women.

Now the number of women = $\left(\dfrac{remaining\ work}{efficiency\ of\ a\ woman}\right)$

$\Rightarrow \dfrac{\left(\frac{7x}{10}\right)}{\left(\frac{x}{30}\right)} = 21$ women

∴ Need 21 women assist to complete work in 1 day.

Hence, the correct option is (D).

11. Given:

Time taken by Samrat and Kamlesh to do the work together = 18 days

Calculation:

Let the time taken by Samrat and Kamlesh to do the work alone be x and y respectively.

Then, Samrat's and Kamlesh's 1 day work = $\frac{1}{x}$ and $\frac{1}{y}$ respectively

Total work = $\left(\frac{1}{x}\right) + \left(\frac{1}{y}\right) = \frac{1}{18}$ ----(i)

Samrat worked thrice as efficiently and then Kamlesh worked with half his efficiency it will take same time to finish the work.

Samrat's 1 day work = $\frac{3}{x}$

Kamlesh's 1 day work = $\frac{1}{2y}$

Time taken by them to finish the work = 18 days

Total work = $\frac{3}{x} + \frac{1}{2y} = \frac{1}{18}$ ----(ii)

Multiplying (i) by 3 and subtracting (ii) by (i),

$\frac{3}{x} + \frac{3}{y} - \frac{3}{x} - \frac{1}{2y} = \frac{3}{18} - \frac{1}{18}$

$\Rightarrow \frac{3}{y} - \frac{1}{2y} = \frac{1}{9}$

$\Rightarrow y = \frac{45}{2}$

Putting the value of y in (ii), we get

$\Rightarrow \frac{3}{x} + \frac{1 \times 2}{2 \times 45} = \frac{1}{18}$

$\Rightarrow \frac{3}{x} = \frac{1}{18} - \frac{1}{45}$

$\Rightarrow \frac{3}{x} = \frac{5-2}{45}$

$\Rightarrow \frac{3}{x} = \frac{3}{90}$

$\Rightarrow x = 90$

∴ Time taken by Samrat to finish the work alone is 90 days.

Hence, the correct option is (C).

12. Given:

80% of the people casted their votes

45% of the voters who casted votes are employed

66.67% of employed voters are engineers

Let the total number of voters be 100

80% of the voters casted their votes

$\left(\frac{80}{100}\right) \times 100 = 80$

80 people casted their votes

45% of 80 = $\left(\frac{45}{100} \times 80\right) = 36$

36 voters were employed

Among employed voters 66.67% are engineers

$\Rightarrow 36 \times 66.67\% = 24$

24% voters were the engineer

Number of non − engineers among total voters = 36 − 24 = 12

∴ Required percentage = $\frac{12}{100} \times 100 = 12\%$

Hence, the correct option is (A).

13. Given:

The ratio of votes received by A and B = 5 : 3

Invalid vote = 18% of total votes

Votes received by B = 18%

Let the total number of votes polled be x

18% of votes were invalid, so remaining votes = 0.82x

The ratio of votes received by A and B = 5 : 3

Let the number of votes received by A and B be 5y and 3y respectively

According to the question,

$\Rightarrow 3y = 615$

$\Rightarrow y = 205$

$\Rightarrow 5y = 5 \times 205 = 1025$

⇒ Votes received by A = 1025

Now total votes received by A and B = 1025 + 615 = 1640

Now,

⇒ 0.82x = 1640

⇒ x = 2000

∴ Total number of votes polled = 2000

Hence, the correct option is (D).

14. Given,

Increase in length $57.13\% = \dfrac{4}{7}$

Decrease in breadth $41.66\% = \dfrac{5}{12}$

Decrease in height $46.66\% = \dfrac{7}{15}$

Let initial length, breadth and height as $7x, 12y, 15z$ respectively.

Increase in length $= 7x \times \dfrac{4}{7} = 4x$

Decrease in breadth $= 12y \times \dfrac{5}{12} = 5y$

Decrease in height $= 15z \times \dfrac{7}{15} = 7z$

Final length $= 7x + 4x = 11x$

Final breadth $= 12y - 5y = 7y$

Final breadth $= 15z - 7z = 8z$

Initial volume $= 7x \times 12y \times 15z = 1260xyz$

Final volume $= 11x \times 7y \times 8z = 616xyz$

Percentage change $= \left\{ \dfrac{(\text{ Final volume - Initial volume })}{\text{Initial Volume}} \right\} \times 100$

$= \left\{ \dfrac{(616xyz - 1260xyz)}{1260xyz} \right\} \times 100$

$= \left(-\dfrac{644xyz}{1260} \right) \times 100$

$= -51.11\%$

∴ Percentage change in the volume of a cuboid is -51.11%.

Hence, the correct option is (C).

15. Given:

A shopkeeper marked his article 80% above the cost price.

A shopkeeper sells at discount of 25%.

Formula Used:

MP $= \dfrac{100 + Marked\ up\%}{100} \times$ CP

SP $=$ MP $\times \dfrac{100 - discount\%}{100}$

Let the Cost price of the article be x

Then, the Marked price $= \dfrac{100 + 80}{100} \times x = 1.8x$

Then, the Selling price of the article $= 1.8x \times \dfrac{100 - 25}{100} = 1.35x$

According to the question,

The new Selling price of the article $= 1.8x \times \dfrac{100 - 13}{100} = 1.566x$

Difference in selling price = 378

⇒ 1.566x - 1.35x = 378

⇒ 0.216x = 378

⇒ x = 1750

Therefore, the cost price of the article is Rs 1750.

Hence, the correct option is (D).

16. Let, the cost price of goods be Rs. 100 and total stock be N.

So, the total cost of all goods $= \dfrac{100}{N}$

⇒ Marked price of goods $= 100 + 100 \times \left(\dfrac{24}{100} \right) =$ Rs. 124

Given, he sold half of the stock at Rs. 124

⇒ Total Selling price of $\dfrac{N}{2}$ goods $= 130 \times \left(\dfrac{N}{2} \right) = 65N$

Selling price of another $\dfrac{N}{4}$ goods $= (70\%$ of $124 = 86.8$

Total selling price $\dfrac{N}{4}$ goods $= 86.8 \times \left(\dfrac{N}{4} \right) = 21.7N$

Selling price of another $\dfrac{N}{4}$ goods $= (52\%$ of $124 = 64.48I)$

Total selling price $\dfrac{N}{4}$ goods $= 64.48 \times \left(\dfrac{N}{4} \right) = 16.12N$

Total selling price $= 65N + 21.7N + 16.12N = 102.82N$

Gain percentage $= \left[\dfrac{(S.p - C.p)}{C.p} \right] \times 100$

$= \left[\dfrac{(102.82N - 100N)}{100N} \right] \times 100$

$= 2.82\%$

∴ He has 2.82% of gain.

Hence, the correct option is (D).

17. Discount on article P = 28%

Profit percent on article P = Profit percent on article Q = 20%

CP (article Q) – SP (article P) = Rs. 200

$$SP = \frac{(100+x)}{100} \times CP \quad [x = \text{profit percent}]$$

$$SP = \frac{(100-y)}{100} \times MP \quad [y = \text{discount percent}]$$

Let MP of article of P be 100x.

$$SP \text{ of article P} = 100x \times \frac{(100-28)}{100} = 72x$$

$$SP \text{ of article Q} = 72x \times \frac{4}{3} = 96x$$

$$CP \text{ of article Q} = \frac{96x}{120} \times 100 = 80x$$

CP of article P = 72x/120 × 100 = 60x

According to the question,

80x – 72x = 200

$$\Rightarrow x = \frac{200}{8}$$

$\Rightarrow$ x = 25

∴ CP of article P = 60 × 25 = Rs. 1500

Hence, the correct option is (A).

18. Given:

In year 2010 A invests Rs. 75000

In year 2011 A's capital value is same for the whole year = Rs. 75000

In year 2012 A invests an additional amount of Rs. 25000 so total amount invested is Rs. 100000

In case of B; B joined in year 2011 with Rs. 45000

In year 2012 he also invests an additional amount of Rs. 25000 so total amount invested = is Rs. 70000

(Profit)$_A$: (Profit)$_B$

(share × Time)$_A$: (share × Time)$_B$

(Profit)$_A$: (Profit)$_B$

[75000 × 12 + 75000 × 12 + (75000 + 25000) × 12] : [45000 × 12 + (25000 + 45000) ×12]

(1800 + 1200) : (540 + 840)

50 : 23

$$A's \text{ share} = \frac{50}{(50 + 23)} \times 43800$$

$\Rightarrow$ Rs. 30,000

Hence, the correct option is (C).

19. The ratio of cost price of two articles is $4 : 9$

$\Rightarrow$ Let the cost price of first article $= 4x$

The cost price of second article $= 9x$

The articles are marked up by 40% and 15% respectively

$$\Rightarrow \text{Marked price of first article} = 4x \times \left(\frac{140}{100}\right) = 5.6x$$

$$\text{Marked price of second article} = 9x \times \left(\frac{115}{100}\right) = 10.35x$$

The ratio of their Marked price is $112 : 207$

$$\Rightarrow \text{Marked price of first article} = 112y$$

$$\text{Marked price of second article} = 207y$$

$$\therefore 5.6x = 112y$$

$$\Rightarrow x = 20y$$

According to question,

$$\text{Selling price of first article} = 112y \times \left(\frac{7}{8}\right) = 98y$$

$$\text{Profit} = 98y - 4x = 270$$

$$\Rightarrow 98y - 80y = 270$$

$$\Rightarrow 18y = 270$$

$$\Rightarrow y = 15$$

$$\therefore x = 20 \times 15 = 300$$

$$\Rightarrow \text{Cost price of second article} = 300 \times 9 = 2700$$

$$\text{Marked price of second article} = 2700 \times \left(\frac{115}{100}\right) = 3105$$

$$\text{Selling price of second article} = 3105 \times \left(\frac{8}{9}\right) = 2760$$

$$\therefore \text{Profit earned} = 2760 - 2700 = 60$$

∴ The profit earned on second article is Rs. 60.

Hence, the correct option is (C).

20. Given,

C.P. of smartphones $=$ Rs. 44040

Number of smartphones (N) $= 5$

$$\text{Software} = \left(\frac{1}{8}\right)^{th} \text{ of C.P.}$$

First Smart phone $=$ Rs. 35000

Overall profit $= 20\%$

Trade $=$ Rs 50000

$$S.P. = C.P. \times \left(1 + \frac{Profit\%}{100}\right)$$

C.P. of five phones $= 5 \times 44040$

C.P. of 5 phones $=$ Rs. 220200

Cost of software $= \dfrac{44040}{8}$

= Rs. 5505

Total C.P. $=$ Rs. $220200 +$ Rs 27525

Total C.P. $=$ Rs. 247725

Actual S.P. $=$ Rs. $247725 \times (1 + 0.20)$

Actual S.P. $=$ Rs. 297270

Rs. $297720 - 35,000 = 262270$

Avg price S.P. required $=$ Rs. 65567.5

Seema purchased at Rs. 65567.5

Loss of Seema $=$ Rs. 15567.5

Loss incurred by Seems is Rs. 15567.5.

Hence, the correct option is (A).

21. The initial quantity of mixture = 343 litres

Initial ratio of mixture = 5 : 2

The final ratio of mixture = 5 : 3

Let initial quantity of wine and water be 5x and 2x.

5x + 2x = 343

$\Rightarrow$ 7x = 343

$\Rightarrow$ x = 49

Initial quantity of wine = 5x

= 5 × 49

= 245 litres

Initial quantity of sugar = 2x

= 2 × 49

= 98 litres

Let the water to be added in new mixture be x litres.

According to the question,

$\dfrac{245}{(98+x)} = \dfrac{5}{3}$

$\Rightarrow$ 245 × 3 = 5(98 + x)

$\Rightarrow$ 735 = 490 + 5x

$\Rightarrow$ 5x = 245

$\Rightarrow$ x = 49 litres

$\therefore$ The quantity of water added is 49 litres.

Hence, the correct answer is 49.

22. Given:

Alcohol : Water = 6 : 5

22 liters mixture are replaced by water.

Let alcohol = 6x and water = 5x

In 21 liter mixture, alcohol = $\left(\dfrac{6}{11}\right) \times 22 = 12$ liter

And water = $\left(\dfrac{5}{11}\right) \times 22 = 10$ liter

According to the question,

(6x - 12) : (5x - 10 +22) = 9 : 13

$\Rightarrow$13(6x - 12) = 9(5x + 12)

$\Rightarrow$ 78x - 156 = 45x + 108

$\Rightarrow$ 78x - 45x = 108 + 156

$\Rightarrow$ 33x = 264

$\Rightarrow$ x = 8

So, alcohol after replacement = 6 × 8 -12 = 36 liter

$\therefore$ The quantity of alcohol after the replacement is 36 liter.

Hence, the correct answer is 36.

23. Given:

The initial quantity of water in vessel $= 2.5$ liters

And the initial quantity of milk in vessel $= 10$ liters

The ratio of milk and water $= 10 : 2.5$

$= 4 : 1$

Amount of mixture removed $= \left(\dfrac{20}{100}\right) \times (10 + 2.5)$

$= \left(\dfrac{1}{5}\right) \times 12.5$

$= 2.5$ litres

Amount of milk removed $= 2.5 \times \left(\dfrac{4}{5}\right) = 2$ litres

Amount of water removed $= 2.5 \times \left(\dfrac{1}{5}\right) = 0.5$ litres

Now, After adding x litres of water the ratio of milk and water get reversed,

$\dfrac{(10-2)}{(2.5-0.5+x)} = \dfrac{1}{4}$

$\Rightarrow \dfrac{8}{(2+x)} = \dfrac{1}{4}$

$\Rightarrow 8 \times 4 = 2 + x$

$\Rightarrow x = 32 - 2$

$\Rightarrow x = 30$

Now, Quantity of water $= (2.5 - 0.5 + 30)$ liters $= 32$ liters

And, Quantity of milk $= (10 - 2)$ liters $= 8$ liters

Then, After adding y litres of milk the ratio of milk and water get reversed,

$$\frac{(8+y)}{32} = \frac{4}{1}$$

$$\Rightarrow 8 + y = 32 \times 4$$

$$\Rightarrow 8 + y = 128$$

$$\Rightarrow y = 120$$

$\therefore$ The value of y is 120 .

Hence, the correct answer is 120.

24. Given:

Total quantity of mixture $= 63 + 77 = 140$ litres

Let quantity of mixture taken out be a litres.

Percentage Quantity of water in mixture $= \frac{63}{140} \times 100 = 45\%$

Percentage quantity of alcohol in mixture $= \frac{77}{140} \times 100 = 55\%$

Quantity of water in mixture after addition $= 63 - a \times \frac{45}{100} + 16$

Quantity of milk in mixture after addition $= 77 - a \times \frac{55}{100} + 4$

Then,

$$63 - a \times \frac{45}{100} + 16 = 77 - a \times \frac{55}{100} + 4$$

$$\Rightarrow a = 20$$

$\therefore$ Total quantity of mixture after 20 litres of mixture taken out $= 140 - 20 = 120$ litres

Hence, the correct answer is 120.

25. Given:

Quantity of mixture = 20 liters

Concentration of milk = 60%

So, the ratio of milk and water = 3 : 2

The quantity of milk and water be 12 liters and 8 liters.

According to the question,

After adding x liter milk,

Quantity of milk after addition = (12 + x) liters

Quantity of water after addition = 8 liters

$\because$ The mixture contains 80% milk, water is 20%.

20% mixture = 8 liters

100% mixture = 40 liters

The difference between the quantity of the mixture is due to the addition of x liter milk = 40 - 20 = 20 liters

$\therefore$ x = 20 liters

Final quantity of milk = 12 + 20 = 32 liters

Final quantity of water = 8 liters

Final Ratio of milk and water = 32 : 8

$\therefore$ The final ratio of milk and water in the mixture is 4 : 1.

If 40% mixture is emptied into another flask,

Then quantity of remaining mixture = 60% × 40 = 24 liters

$\therefore$ The remaining quantity of milk in the remaining mixture $= \frac{4}{5} \times 24 = 19.2$ liters

Hence, the correct option is (A).

26. Given:

Man swimmer swims from point A against a current for 8 minutes.

Man Swims backwards in favor of the current for next 8 minutes and comes to the point B.

Distance between A and B = 200 m

$$\text{Speed} = \frac{Distance}{Time}$$

Speed upstream = (x + y) km/hr

Speed downstream = (x – y) km/hr

Where x and y are speed of boat and speed of stream respectively.

Let speed of swimmer be x km/hr and speed of current be y km/hr

$\Rightarrow$ Downstream speed = (x + y) km/hr

$\Rightarrow$ Upstream speed = (x – y) km/hr

Downstream distance covered in 8 minutes by swimmer = (x + y) $\times \frac{8}{60}$ km

Upstream distance covered in 8 minutes by swimmer = (x – y) $\times \frac{8}{60}$ km

$$\Rightarrow 2\frac{(x + y)}{15} - 2\frac{(x - y)}{15} = \frac{200}{1000}$$

$$\Rightarrow \frac{(2x + 2y - 2x + 2y)}{15} = \frac{1}{5}$$

$\Rightarrow 4y = 3$

$\Rightarrow y = 0.75$ km/hr

$\therefore$ Speed of stream = 0.75 km/hr

Hence, the correct option is (B).

27. Let speeds of the faster train and that of the slower train be S1 and S2 (m/s) respectively.

When they go in the same direction,

Hint: When two long objects cross each other,

The distance travelled by them = Sum of the lengths of both objects

Relative speed = S1 - S2,

Distance travelled = 100 + 100 = 200 meters,

Distance = Speed × Time,

200 = (S1 - S2) × 60,

$\Rightarrow$ S1 - S2 = $\dfrac{200}{60}$ = $\dfrac{10}{3}$ m/s   .....(i)

When they go in opposite directions,

Relative speed = S1 + S2,

200 = (S1 + S2) × 10,

$\Rightarrow$ (S1 + S2) = 20 m/s   .....(ii)

Solving, equations (i) and (ii) we get,

S1 = $\dfrac{70}{6}$ m/s = $\dfrac{70}{6} \times \dfrac{18}{5}$ km/h = 42 km/h,

S2 = $\dfrac{50}{6}$ m/s = $\dfrac{50}{6} \times \dfrac{18}{5}$ km/h = 30 km/h

So, speed of the slower train = 30 km/h.

Hence, the correct option is (D).

28. Given:

Ravi's speed before incident = 80 km/hr

Speed of train = 90 km/hr

Length of the train = 250 meters

Formula used:

Speed = $\dfrac{Distance}{Time}$

Let Ravi increases the speed of the bike by x km/hr

Now, the speed of the bike is (80 + x) Km/hr

$\Rightarrow$ The relative speed of bike with respect to the train = [(80 + x) - 90]

$\Rightarrow$ (x - 10) Km/hr

Now, according to question

250 = (x - 10) × $\dfrac{5}{18}$ × 54

$\Rightarrow$ x - 10 = $\dfrac{250}{15}$

$\Rightarrow$ x = $\dfrac{80}{3}$

$\Rightarrow$ Increased speed of bike = Speed of bike + Increased speed of bike by Ravi just after seeing the fault in the train

$\Rightarrow$ Increased speed of bike = 80 + $\dfrac{80}{3}$

$\Rightarrow$ $\dfrac{320}{3}$ km/hr

$\therefore$ The required speed of the bike just after seeing the fault in the train is $\dfrac{320}{3}$ km/hr.

Hence, the correct option is (B).

29. Given,

Speed of thief before watching the police $= 20 \; km/hr$

Speed of thief after watching the police $= 25 \; km/hr$

Distance between police and thief $= 400 \; m$

We know that, Speed $= \dfrac{Distance}{Time}$

If speed of body A is $x \; m/s$ and speed of body B is $y \; m/s$ then

Relative speed of two bodies moving in same direction

$= (x - y) m/s$

Relative speed of two bodies moving in opposite direction

$= (x + y) m/s$

In 20 minutes, thief covered the distance from point

$X = 20 \times$

$= 10 \; km$

Relative speed of police with respect to thief

$= (30 - 25) km/hr$

$= 5 \; km/hr$

Time taken by police to cover $400 \; m$ or $0.4 \; km = \dfrac{0.4}{5} hr$

$= 0.08 hr$

Distance covered by the thief in $0.08 hr = 25 \times 0.08 = 2 \; km$

Distance from Point $X = (10 - 2) km$

$= 8 \; km$

$\therefore$ Police will catch the thief at $8 \; km$ from point X.

Hence, the correct option is (D).

30. As per given data-

A person travels $45 mins$ at speed of $45 kmph$.

So, he travels $\dfrac{3}{4}$ hrs at a speed of $45 kmph$

$\therefore$ Distance covered by person $=$ speed of bike x time traveled

$\Rightarrow$ Distance covered by person $= 45 \times \frac{3}{4}$

$\Rightarrow$ Distance covered by person $= \frac{135}{4} \, km$ ... (1)

Next he travels 45 mins at $60 \, kmph$

So, he travels $\frac{3}{4}$ hrs at a speed of $60 \, kmph.$

$\therefore$ Distance covered by man $=$ speed of bike $\times$ time traveled

$\Rightarrow$ Distance covered by man $= 60 \times \frac{3}{4}$

$\Rightarrow$ Distance covered by person $= 45 \, km$...... (2)

Then he travels 30 mins at $90 kmph$

So, he travels $0.5 hrs$ at a speed of $90 kmph.$

$\therefore$ Distance covered by person $=$ speed of bike $\times$ time traveled

$\Rightarrow$ Distance covered by person $= 90 \times 0.5$

$\Rightarrow$ Distance covered by person $= 45 \, km.$ .. (3)As per given data-

A person travels $45 mins$ at speed of $45 kmph.$

So, he travels $\frac{3}{4}$ hrs at a speed of $45 kmph$

$\therefore$ Distance covered by person $=$ speed of bike x time traveled

$\Rightarrow$ Distance covered by person $= 45 \times \frac{3}{4}$

$\Rightarrow$ Distance covered by person $= \frac{135}{4} \, km$ ... (1)

Next he travels 45 mins at $60 \, kmph$

So, he travels $\frac{3}{4}$ hrs at a speed of $60 \, kmph.$

$\therefore$ Distance covered by man $=$ speed of bike $\times$ time traveled

$\Rightarrow$ Distance covered by man $= 60 \times \frac{3}{4}$

$\Rightarrow$ Distance covered by person $= 45 \, km$...... (2)

Then he travels 30 mins at $90 kmph$

So, he travels $0.5 hrs$ at a speed of $90 kmph.$

$\therefore$ Distance covered by person $=$ speed of bike $\times$ time traveled

$\Rightarrow$ Distance covered by person $= 90 \times 0.5$

$\Rightarrow$ Distance covered by person $= 45 \, km.$ .. (3)

From above we can see the total distance traveled by person is $\frac{135}{4+45+45} = 123.75 kms$

& total time taken to travel $= 0.75 + 0.75 + 0.5 = 2 hrs.$

$\therefore$ Average speed of person $=$ Total distance travelled/Time taken

Average speed of person $= \frac{123.75}{2}$

$\therefore$ Average speed of person $= 61.875 \, kmph$

$\therefore$ Person ride bike at average speed of $61.875 kmph.$

Hence, the correct option is (A).

31. Given,

Total fruits = 430, and total people = 45

Ratio of personal shares = 6 : 5 : 4

Ratio of the total sweets = 12 : 15 : 16

Ratio of boys, girls and teachers $= \frac{12}{6} : \frac{15}{5} : \frac{16}{4}$

$= 2 : 3 : 4$

Sum of these ratios = 2 + 3 + 4 = 9

Number of boys $= \frac{45}{9} \times 2 = 10$

Number of girls $= \frac{45}{9} \times 3 = 15$

Number of teachers $= \frac{45}{9} \times 4 = 20$

Now, divide 430 fruits in the ratio of 12 : 15 : 16

Now,

The number of the fruits received by boys $= \frac{430}{43} \times 12 = 120$ fruits.

The Number of fruits received by girls $= \frac{430}{43} \times 15 = 150$ fruits.

The number of the fruits received by boys $= \frac{430}{43} \times 12 = 160$ fruits.

Now,

Each boy's share $= \frac{120}{10} = 12$ fruits

Each girl's share $= \frac{150}{15} = 10$ fruits

Each teacher's share $= \frac{160}{20} = 8$ fruits.

The required number is 12, 10, 8.

Hence, the correct option is (C).

32. Given,

The ratio of the present age Chinky and Minky = 4 : 5

The present age of Chinky's mother $= \frac{9}{2} \times$ Minky's age 5 years ago

The present age of Minky's mother $= \dfrac{7}{3} \times$ Chinky's age after 3 year

Divide the age according to the ratio.

Average Age $= \dfrac{\text{Sum of total age}}{\text{Total person}}$

Let the present age of Chinky be $4x$ and Minky be $5x$

5 year ago Minky's age $= 5x - 5$

The present age of Chinky's mother $= \left(\dfrac{9}{2}\right) \times$ Minky's age 5 years ago

So, the present age of Chinky's mother $= \left(\dfrac{9}{2}\right) \times (5x - 5)$

$= \dfrac{(45x - 45)}{2}$

After 15 years, Chinky's mother age $= \dfrac{(45x - 45)}{2} + 15$

$= \dfrac{(45x - 15)}{2}$

Chinky's age after 3 years $= 4x + 3$

The present age of Minky's mother $= \left(\dfrac{7}{3}\right) \times$ Chinky's age after 3 year

So, the present age of Minky's mother $= \left(\dfrac{7}{3}\right) \times (4x + 3)$

$= \left(\dfrac{28x}{3}\right) + 7$

After 15 years, Minky's mother age $= \left(\dfrac{28x}{3}\right) + 7 + 15$

$= \dfrac{28x + 66}{3}$

Total age of Chinky's mother and Minky's mother after 15 years
$= \dfrac{(45x - 15)}{2} + \dfrac{(28x + 66)}{3}$

$= \dfrac{(135x - 45 + 56x + 132)}{6}$

$= \dfrac{(191x + 87)}{6}$

Average age of Chinky's mother and Minky's mother after 15 years $= \dfrac{\text{Sum of total age}}{\text{Total person}}$

$= \dfrac{(191x + 43)}{(6 \times 2)}$

$\Rightarrow \dfrac{(191x + 87)}{12} = 55$

$\Rightarrow 191x = 573$

$\Rightarrow x = 3$

The present age of Chinky $= 4x = 4 \times 3 = 12$

The present age of Minky $= 5x = 5 \times 3 = 15$

The Difference between Chinky's and Minky's present age $= 15 - 12 = 3$ years

The Difference between Chinky's and Minky's present age is 3 years.

Hence, the correct option is (A).

33. Given,

Ratio of the prices of two mobiles I-phone 9 and I-phone X last year was 13 : 20.

In current year, I-phone 9 price drops by 10% and I-phone X price drop by Rs. 20,000

Now, ratio of the price of two mobiles I - phone 9 and I - phone X is 117 : 160.

Let the I-phone 9 and I-phone X price last year was $13x$ and $20x$.

For current year Prices drop by 10% of I-phone $9 =$
$[(13x) - \left(\dfrac{13x}{10}\right)]$

$= \dfrac{117x}{10}$

Current year price of I -phone X $= (20x - 20000)$

According to question:

$[\dfrac{\left(\frac{117x}{10}\right)}{(20x - 20000)}] = \left(\dfrac{117}{160}\right)$

$\Rightarrow [\left(\dfrac{117x}{(200x - 200000)}\right] = \left(\dfrac{117}{160}\right)$

$\Rightarrow [\dfrac{x}{(200x - 200000}] = \dfrac{1}{160}$

$\Rightarrow 200x - 200000 = 160x$

$\Rightarrow 40x = 200000$

$\Rightarrow x = 5000$

Last year I-phone price is Rs. 65000 (i.e. 13×5000).

Hence, the correct option is (B).

34. Given:

The rate of interest for 1st 2 years is 8%

For the next 3 years it is 10%

For the period beyond 5 years it is 12.5%

Principal $=$ Rs $20\,L$

Amoun paid $= Rs\,36.7\,L$

Amount $= P + SI$

Simple Interest, SI $= \dfrac{P \times R \times T}{100}$

Where $\mathbf{P} \rightarrow$ Principal, $\mathbf{R} \rightarrow$ rate of interest, $T \rightarrow$ time

Total $SI = A - P = 36.7\,L - 20L$

Total $SI = 16.7\,L$

SI for first 2 years $= 20\,L \times 2 \times \dfrac{8}{100} = 3.2\,L$

SI for next 3 years $= 20\,L \times 3 \times \dfrac{10}{100} = 6\,L$

So, total SI for the first 5 years $= 9.2\,L$

Then, the rest of the interest is obtained at the rate of 12.5%

Remaining interest $= 16.7\,L - 9.2\,L = 7.5\,L$

SI for next N years $= 20\,L \times N \times 12.5\% = 7.5\,L$

$N = 7.5\,L \times \dfrac{8}{20}\,L \quad \left(12.5\% \rightarrow \dfrac{1}{8}\,in \text{ fraction }\right)$

$N = 3$

That is, total years $= 2 + 3 + 3 = 8$ years.

Hence, the correct answer is 8 years.

35. Given:

Rate of interest $= 37.5\%$

Fraction value of $37.5\% = \dfrac{3}{8}$

Time $= 3$ years

3rd -year Compound interest $= 7260$

If the fraction value of rate is $\dfrac{1}{x}$ then let the principal be x^2 for 2 years and x^3 for three years interest.

Let the fraction value of rate of interest be $\dfrac{1}{x}$

Let the principal be x^3

Then from the slab method it is given by

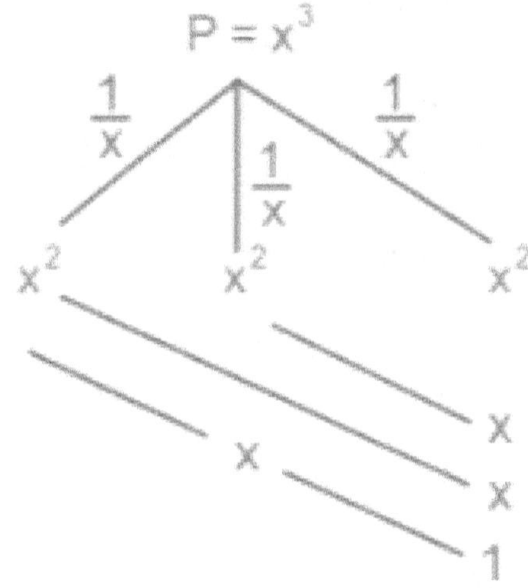

Here principal $= (8)^3 = 512$

Interest for the 3rd year $= \left(\dfrac{3}{8}\right) \times 512 + 2 \times \left(\dfrac{3}{8}\right) \times$

$192 + \left(\dfrac{3}{8}\right) \times 72 = 363$ units

Now, 363 units $=$ Rs. 7260

$\Rightarrow 1$ unit $=$ Rs. 20

$\Rightarrow 512$ units

$= 20 \times 512$

$=$ Rs. 10240

$\therefore$ principal amount is Rs. 10240

Hence, the correct answer is 10240.

36. Given:

Total amount = Rs. 10000

The simple interest on first part for 1 year 3 months at the rate of $6\dfrac{2}{3}\%$ per annum is half the simple interest on the second part for 13 years 4 months at the rate of $1\dfrac{2}{13}\%$ per annum.

Formula:

$$S.I = \dfrac{P \times R \times T}{100}$$

$$A = P\left(1 + R \times \dfrac{T}{100}\right)$$

Calculation:

Let the first part be Rs. x

And let the second part be Rs. $(10000 - x)$

The simple interest on first part $= x \times \dfrac{20}{3} \times \dfrac{1.25}{100} = \dfrac{x}{12}$

And the simple interest on second part

$$= \frac{(10000-x)\times\frac{15}{10}\times\frac{10}{2}}{100} = \frac{2(10000-x)}{13}$$

According to question,

$$\text{The simple interest on first part} = \frac{\text{The simple interest on second part}}{2}$$

$$\Rightarrow \frac{x}{12} = \frac{2(10000-x)}{13} \times \frac{1}{2}$$

$$\Rightarrow 13x = 120000 - 12x$$

$$\Rightarrow 25x = 12000$$

$$\Rightarrow x = 4800$$

So, the first part $=$ Rs. 4800

And the second part $= 10000 - 4800 =$ Rs. 5200

So, the required difference $= 5200 - 4800 =$ Rs. 400

Hence, the correct answer is 400.

37. Given:

Principal $=$ Rs. 1200

Amount $=$ Rs. 1632

Time $= 4$ years

Formula:

$$SI = \frac{P \times R \times T}{100}$$

Calculation:

Let the rate of interest be $R\%$

$$1632 - 1200 = \frac{1200 \times R \times 4}{100}$$

$$\Rightarrow R = 9\%$$

For 1st year, $R = 9\%$

$$\Rightarrow \text{Interest} = \frac{1200 \times 9 \times 1}{100} = 108$$

For 2 nd year, $R = 10\%$

$$\Rightarrow \text{Interest} = \frac{1200 \times 10 \times 1}{100} = 120$$

For 3 rd year, $R = 11\%$

$$\Rightarrow \text{Interest} = \frac{1200 \times 11 \times 1}{100} = 132$$

For 4 th year, $R = 12\%$

$$\Rightarrow \text{Interest} = \frac{1200 \times 12 \times 1}{100} = 144$$

$\Rightarrow$ Total interest in 4 year

$$= 108 + 120 + 132 + 144 = 504$$

$\therefore$ Amount after 4 years $= 1200 + 504 = 1704$

Hence, the correct answer is 1704.

38. Given:

Cost $=$ Rs. 3200

Down payment = Rs. 1000

Installments = Rs. 1200 each

Calculation:

Let the rate percent be $R\%$ per annum

Total payment due to installment $= 2400 + 1000 = 3400$

Interest amount $= 3400 - 3200 = 200$

So, Principal for the 1st month $=$ Rs. $(3200 - 1000)$

$=$ Rs. 2200

So, Simple interest for 1 st month $= 2200 \times \frac{R}{100} \times \frac{1}{12}$ — (i)

Now, Principal for the 2nd month $=$ Rs. $(2200 - 1200)$

$=$ Rs. 1000

So, Simple interest for 2 nd month $= 1000 \times \frac{R}{100} \times \frac{1}{12}$ -(ii)

So, According to the question

$$2200 \times \frac{R}{100} \times \frac{1}{12} + 1000 \times \frac{R}{100} \times \frac{1}{12} = 200$$

$$\Rightarrow 3200 \times \frac{R}{1200} = 200$$

$$\Rightarrow R=\frac{200 \times 1200}{3200}$$

$$\Rightarrow R = 75\%$$

Hence, the correct option is (D).

39. Given,

Total number of subjects $= 5$

The incorrect ratio $= 13:10$

Increase in marks $= 27$

Total marks increase $= 5 \times 27$

$$= 135$$

Let the original number be ab and xy.

Their reverse order is ba and yx.

As the rest of the numbers remain the same the increase is only in the two numbers

So,

$$ba + yx - ab - xy = 135$$

$$\Rightarrow 10b + a + 10y + x - (10a + b + 10x + y) = 135$$

$$\Rightarrow 9(b - a) + 9(y - x) = 135$$

$$\Rightarrow (b - a) + (y - x) = 15$$

The sum of the difference of the digits of the two numbers is 15.

Multiplying both 13 and 10 by a number like $5, 6, 7, 8$, etc we will get:

$$13 \times 7 = 91$$

$$10 \times 7 = 70$$

91,70 as the only combination where the sum of the difference of digits is $15 (9 - 1 + 7 - 0)$

The original numbers are 19 and 07 and their sum $= 19 + 7 = 26$

Hence, the correct answer is 26.

40. Given:

The weight of A, B, and C is $90\%, 112\%$, and 94% respectively of the average weight of all five.

The ratio of the weight of D and $E = 6:11$

The difference between the weight of D and $E = 75\ kg$

Let the average weight of all five $= 100k$

So, weight of $A = 90k$

$$B = 112k$$

$$C = 94k$$

Let the weight of D is d and that of E is e.

Then,

$$100k = \frac{90k + 112k + 94k + d + e}{5}$$

$$d + e = 204k$$

$$d:e = 6:11$$

$$\Rightarrow d = \frac{6}{17} \times 204k$$

$$= 72k$$

$$\Rightarrow e = 132k$$

$$\text{Difference} = 132k - 72k$$

$$= 60k$$

According to question,

$$60k = 75$$

So, $k = \dfrac{75}{60}$

$$= 1.25$$

The average weight of all the five persons $= 100 \times 1.25$

$$= 125\ kg$$

Hence, the correct answer is 125.

41. Given:

$$\text{Average} = \frac{\text{sum of all the observations}}{\text{Total number of observations}}$$

Let the number of males, females and children be M, F and C respectively.

$$M + F + C = 140$$

Number of males $= \dfrac{1}{5} \times 140 = 28$

Number of females $= \dfrac{(140 - 28)}{4} = 28$

Number of children $= 140 - 28 - 28 = 84$

Average weight of children $= 30\ kg$

Sum of weights of children $=$ no. Of children x avg. Weight

$$\Rightarrow 84 \times 30$$

$$\Rightarrow 2520\ kg$$

Average weight of females $= 2(30) = 60\ kg$

Sum of weights of females $=$ no. Of females x avg. Weight $\Rightarrow$ $28 \times 60 = 1680\ kg$

Average weight of male $= 1.5(60) = 90\ kg$

Sum of weights of males $=$ no. Of males x avg. Weight $\Rightarrow$ $28 \times 90 = 2520\ kg$

Average of whole group $= \dfrac{(2520 + 1680 + 2520)}{140} = 48\ kg$

Hence, the correct answer is 48.

42. Given,

The weight of Varun, Rahul and Priyanka in 2011 was is in the ratio $6:5:7$

In 2011, let the weight of Varun, Rahul, and Priyanka be $6k, 5k$, and $7k$.

In 2016 weight of Varun became 150%, the weight of Rahul became 160% and the weight of Priyanka increased by $\dfrac{300}{7}\%$ i.e., it became $\dfrac{1000}{7}\%$.

So, the new weight of Varun $= \dfrac{150}{100} \times 6k$

$$= 9k$$

Weight of Rahul $= \dfrac{160}{100} \times 5k$

$= 8k$

Weight of Priyanka $= \dfrac{\left(\frac{1000}{7}\right)}{100} \times 7k$

$= 10k$

There is a change in the weight of each of them by $3k$. So the change in average weight would also be $3k$.

$3k = 7.2\ kg$

$\Rightarrow k = 2.4\ kg$

Difference between Varun's weight in 2016 and Priyanka's weight in $2011 = 9k - 7k$

$= 2k$

$2k = 2 \times 2.4$

$= 4.8\ kg$

Hence, the correct option is (B).

43. Let, A can complete the task in $= x$ days

B can complete the task in $= y$ days

According to the question,

$\dfrac{1}{x} + \dfrac{1}{y} = \dfrac{1}{1.2}$

$\Rightarrow x + y = \dfrac{xy}{1.2} \quad \dots \text{(i)}$

A completes half the job in $= \dfrac{x}{2}$ days and B completes half the job in $= \dfrac{y}{2}$ days

$\Rightarrow \dfrac{x}{2} + \dfrac{y}{2} = 2.5$

$\Rightarrow x + y = 5 \quad \dots \text{(ii)}$

From (i) and (ii), we get,

$\dfrac{xy}{1.2} = 5$

$\Rightarrow xy = 6$

$\Rightarrow X = \dfrac{6}{y} \quad \dots \text{(iii)}$

From (ii) and (iii) we get,

$\dfrac{6}{y} + y = 5$

$\Rightarrow 6 + y^2 = 5y$

$\Rightarrow y^2 - 3y - 2y + 6 = 0$

$\Rightarrow y(y - 3) - 2(y \times 3) = 0$

$\Rightarrow (y - 3)(y - 2) = 0$

$\Rightarrow y = 3 \text{ or } 2$

For $y = 3, x = \dfrac{6}{3} = 2$

For $y = 2, x = \dfrac{6}{2} = 3$

$\because B$ is more efficient than A

$\therefore$ B take less days than A

$\therefore B$ would take 2 days to complete the task.

Hence, the correct answer is 2.

44. Given:

Total employees $= 50$

Time is taken by 50 employees to complete work $= 23$ days

After every 5 days, 5 employees more join them.

Formula:

Total work $=$ Total employees $\times$ Total time

Calculation:

Total employees $= 50$

Time is taken by 50 employees to complete work $= 23$ days

Then total work $= 50 \times 23 = 1150$ units

So work that done in the first 5 days by 50 employees $= 5 \times 50 = 250$ units

After every 5 days, 5 employees more join them.

After 5 days total employees $= 50 + 5 = 55$

So work that done in next 5 days by 55 employees $= 5 \times 55 = 275$ units

Again after 5 days total employees $= 55 + 5 = 60$

So work that done in next 5 days by 60 employees $= 5 \times 60 = 300$ units

Again after 5 days total employees $= 60 + 5 = 65$

So work that done in next 5 days by 65 employees $= 5 \times 65 = 325$ units

Total work that done $= 250 + 275 + 300 + 325 = 1150$ units

Thus the total work is done.

Now time taken by employees to complete work $= 5 + 5 + 5 + 5 = 20$ days

$\therefore$ In 20 days the work will be completed.

Hence, the correct option is (C).

45. Given:

Length of the side of square-shaped field $= 10\ m$

Time taken by A to plough the field $= 10$ hours

Time taken by B to plough the field $= 5$ hours

Percentage increase in the side of the new square-shaped field = 50%

Formula:

Area of Square $= (\text{ side })^2$

Work efficiency $= \dfrac{(\text{ Total Work })}{(\text{ Total time})}$

Calculation:

Area of the field to be ploughed $= (\text{ side })^2 = 100\ m^2$

The efficiency of A to plough the field $= \dfrac{(\text{Area of field })}{(\text{Total Time})} =$

$\dfrac{100}{10} = 10\ m^2/\text{ hour} \quad -(1)$

The efficiency of B to plough the field $= \dfrac{(\text{ Ares of field })}{(\text{Total Time})} =$

$\dfrac{100}{5} = 20\ m^2/\text{ hour} \quad -(2)$

Length of side of new field $= 10 + \left[10 \times \left(\dfrac{50}{100}\right)\right] = 10 + 5 = 15\ m$

Area of new field $= (\text{ side })^2$

$= 15^2$

$= 225\ m^2$

Colletive efficiency of A and $B = (10 + 20)m^2/\text{ hour}$ $-(By \text{ adding (1) and (2))}$

$= 30\ m^2/\text{ hour}$

Total time taken by A and B to plough together $=$

$\dfrac{(\text{Ares of field})}{(\text{Collective efficiency of } A \text{ and } B)}$

$= \dfrac{225}{30}$

$= 7.5\text{ hours}$

$\therefore A$ and B will take 7.5 hours to plough the new field.

Hence, the correct option is (B).

46. Given:

Time taken by Samrat and Kamlesh to do the work together $= 18$ days

Calculation:

Let the time taken by Samrat and Kamlesh to do the work alone be x and y respectively.

Then, Samrat's and Kamlesh's 1 day work $= \dfrac{1}{x}$ and $\dfrac{1}{y}$ respectively

Total work $= \left(\dfrac{1}{x}\right) + \left(\dfrac{1}{y}\right) = \dfrac{1}{18} - (i)$

Samrat worked thrice as efficiently and then Kamlesh worked with half his efficiency it will take same time to finish the work

Samrat's 1 day work $= \dfrac{3}{x}$

Kamlesh's 1 day work $= \dfrac{1}{2y}$

Time taken by them to finish the work $= 18$ days

Total work $= \dfrac{3}{x} + \dfrac{1}{2y} = \dfrac{1}{18} \quad - (ii)$

Multiplying (i) by 3 and subtracting (ii) by (i),

$\dfrac{3}{x} + \dfrac{3}{y} - \dfrac{3}{x} - \dfrac{1}{2y} = \dfrac{3}{18} - \dfrac{1}{18}$

$\Rightarrow \dfrac{3}{y} - \dfrac{1}{2y} = \dfrac{1}{9}$

$\Rightarrow y = \dfrac{45}{2}$

Putting the value of y in (ii), we get

$\Rightarrow \dfrac{3}{x} + \dfrac{1 \times 2}{2 \times 45} = \dfrac{1}{18}$

$\Rightarrow \dfrac{3}{x} = \dfrac{1}{18} - \dfrac{1}{45}$

$\Rightarrow \dfrac{3}{x} = \dfrac{5-2}{45}$

$\Rightarrow \dfrac{3}{x} = \dfrac{3}{90}$

$\Rightarrow x = 90$

$\therefore$ Time taken by Samrat to finish the work alone is 90 days.

Hence, the correct answer is 90.

47. Let us assume there are 100 students in the institute.

Then, number of boys $= 60$

And, number of girls $= 40$

Further, 15% of boys get fee waiver $= 9$ boys

7.5% of girls get fee waiver $= 3$ girls

Total $= 12$ students who gets fee waiver

But, here given 90 students are getting fee waiver. So we compare $12 = 90$

So, $1 = \dfrac{90}{12}$

$= 7.5$

Now number of students who are not getting fee waiver $= 51$ boys and 37 girls

50% concession $= 25.5$ boys and 18.5 girls (i.e. total 44)

So, required students $= 44 \times 7.5$

$= 330$

Hence, the correct answer is 330.

48. Given:

In class Xth

$66\dfrac{2}{3}\%$ are in section A and remaining are in section B.

Case 1: 50 students from section A are shifted to section B then total students in section A becomes 50% of total students.

Case 2: 40 students from section B are shifted to section A.

Percentage

Let the students in class Xth be x.

Then students in section A

$\Rightarrow 66\dfrac{2}{3}\% \times x = \dfrac{2x}{3}$

Students in section B

$\Rightarrow x - \dfrac{2}{3}x = \dfrac{x}{3}$

Now according to question,

50 students from section A are shifted to section B then total students in section A becomes 50% of total students.

$\Rightarrow \dfrac{x}{3} + 50 = \dfrac{x}{2}$

$\Rightarrow \dfrac{x}{2} - \dfrac{x}{3} = 50$

$\Rightarrow x = 300$

$\Rightarrow$ Number of students in section $A = 200$

$\Rightarrow$ Number of students in section $B = 100$

Now,

40 students from section B are shifted to section A.

$\Rightarrow$ Students in section $A = 200 + 40 = 240$

$\Rightarrow$ Students in section $A = 100 - 40 = 60$

$\therefore$ Required percentage $= \left(\dfrac{60}{300}\right) \times 100 = 20\%$

Hence, the correct option is (C).

49. Given:

Cost price of item A is equal to the cost price of item B

MP of item $A = 160\%$ of CP

MP of item $B = 150\%$ of CP

Calculation:

Marked price of item B is 600 after increased by 50%

CP of item B,

$\Rightarrow CP \times \dfrac{150}{100} = 600$

Cost price of item $B =$ Rs. 400

CP of $A = CP$ of B

$\Rightarrow$ Marked price of item $A = 400 \times \dfrac{160}{100}$

MP of item $A =$ Rs. 640

MP of item $B =$ Rs. 600

Selling price of item A and item B after giving 10% discount

SP of Item $A = 640 \times \dfrac{90}{100} = 576$

SP of Item $B = 600 \times \dfrac{90}{100} = 540$

$\Rightarrow$ Difference between selling price of item A and item

$B = 576 - 540$

$\Rightarrow$ Rs. 36

Hence, the correct option is (B).

50. Let the cost price of book $=$ Rs. a

Let the cost price of pen $=$ Rs. b

As per the question, $a + b = 526 \dots (1)$

Selling price of book $= \left(\dfrac{112}{100}\right)a$

Selling price of pen $= \left(\dfrac{116}{100}\right)b$

Total selling price $= \left(\dfrac{112a}{100}\right) + \left(\dfrac{116b}{100}\right)$

Profit earned $=$ Rs. 74

Total Selling price $= 526 + 74 =$ Rs. 600

$\Rightarrow \left(\dfrac{112a}{100}\right) + \left(\dfrac{116b}{100}\right) = 600$

$\Rightarrow 112a + 116b = 60000 \dots (2)$

By multipling (1) by 112

$\Rightarrow 112a + 112b = 58912 ....(3)$

By subtracting (3) and (2)

$\Rightarrow 4b = 1088$

$\Rightarrow b = 272$

$\therefore$ Cost Price of pen $=$ Rs. 272

$\Rightarrow$ Cost price of Book $= 526 - 272$

$=$ Rs. 254

Required difference $= 272 - 254$

$=$ Rs. 18

Hence, the correct answer is 18.

51. Given:

Each discount $= 20\%$

Single discount $=$ Rs. 331.20

As we know,

Using the concept of percentage.

Let the MP is Rs. x.

1st discount at $MP = (100 - 20)\%$ of x

$\Rightarrow 1^{st}$ discount $= 80\%$ of x

$\Rightarrow 1^{st}$ dicount $= \dfrac{80}{100} \times x$

$\Rightarrow 1^{st}$ dicount $= 0.8x$

2nd discount $= (100 - 20)\%$ of $0.8x$

$\Rightarrow 2^{nd}$ discount $= 80\%$ of $0.8x$

$\Rightarrow 2^{nd}$ dicount $= \dfrac{80}{100} \times 0.8x$

$\Rightarrow 2^{nd}$ dicount $= 0.8 \times 0.8x$

$\Rightarrow 2^{nd}$ dicount $= 0.64x$

Equivalent discount $= x - 0.64x$

$\Rightarrow 331.20 = 0.36x$

$\Rightarrow x = \dfrac{331.20}{0.36}$

$\Rightarrow x =$ Rs. 920

$\therefore$ The marked price of an article is Rs. 920 .

Hence, the correct answer is 920.

52. Given:

Selling price of two toys $=$ Rs. 990 each

Increase/ Decrease $\% = 10\%$

As we know,

Loss $\% = (CP - SP) \times \dfrac{100}{CP}$

SP (selling price) $=$ Cost Price $(CP) \times \dfrac{(100 + \text{Profit} \backslash\%)}{100}$

$SP = \dfrac{CP(100 - lnoss\%)}{100}$

Total SP of both toy is $= 990 + 990$

$=$ Rs. 1980

CP of the first toy he gained 10%

$= 990 \times \dfrac{100}{(100 + 10)}$

$=$ Rs. 900

CP of the second toy he loss 10%

$= \dfrac{990 \times (100)}{(100 - 10)}$

$=$ Rs. 1100

Total $CP = 900 + 1100$

$=$ Rs. 2000

Loss $= CP > SP$

Loss $\% = (2000 - 1980) \times \dfrac{100}{2000} = 1\%$

$\therefore$ Loss percent $= 1\%$

Hence, the correct option is (C).

53. Let the weight of Kanye, Ashton and Justin be $10x''$, $9x'$ and $12x'$

Case 1:

$\left(\dfrac{1}{3}\right)$ of Ashton's weight $+ \left(\dfrac{1}{4}\right)$ of Justin's weight $= \left(\dfrac{3}{5}\right)$ of Kanye's weight

$\Rightarrow \left(\dfrac{1}{3}\right) \times 9x + \left(\dfrac{1}{4}\right) \times 12x = \left(\dfrac{3}{5}\right) \times 10x$

$\Rightarrow 3x + 3x = 6x$, which is true.

Case 2:

$\left(\dfrac{7}{3}\right)$ of Ashton's weight $- \left(\dfrac{3}{2}\right)$ of Kanye's weight $= \left(\dfrac{1}{2}\right)$ of Justin's weight

$\Rightarrow \left(\dfrac{7}{3}\right) \times 9x - \left(\dfrac{3}{2}\right) \times 10x = \left(\dfrac{1}{2}\right) \times 12x$

$\Rightarrow 21x - 15x = 6x$, which is true.

Case 3:

$\left(\dfrac{3}{5}\right)$ of Kanye's weight $= \left(\dfrac{2}{3}\right)$ of Ashton's weight

$\Rightarrow \left(\dfrac{3}{5}\right) \times 10x = \left(\dfrac{2}{3}\right) \times 9x$

$\Rightarrow 6x = 6x$, which is true.

Case 4:

$\left(\dfrac{8}{5}\right)$ of Kanye's weight $+ \left(\dfrac{5}{4}\right)$ of Justin's weight $= \left(\dfrac{10}{3}\right)$ of Ashton's weight

$\Rightarrow \left(\dfrac{8}{5}\right) \times 10x + \left(\dfrac{5}{4}\right) \times 12x = \left(\dfrac{10}{3}\right) \times 9x$

$\Rightarrow 16x + 15x = 30x$, which is not true.

Hence, the correct option is (D).

54. Given,

The income of A and B is in the ratio $7:8$

The income of B and C is $4:3$.

The ratio of savings of A and C is $4:3$

The difference between the savings of B and C together to the savings A is Rs. 32,000 .

Income of A, B and C is $7x, 8x, 6x$

Let their expenditure be y

Income = Expenditure + Saving

Savings of $A = 7x - y$

Savings of $C = 6x - y$

Ratio of $A : B = 7:8$

Ratio of $B : C = 4:3$

Now equating ratios of B we get

B: $C \times 2 = 8:6$

A: $B:C = 7:8:6$

$\Rightarrow$ Ratio of saving A and $C = \dfrac{(7x-y)}{(6x-y)} = \dfrac{4}{3}$

$\Rightarrow 21x - 3y = 24x - 4y$

$\Rightarrow y = 3x$

$\Rightarrow$ Saving of $A = 7x - 3x = 4x$

$\Rightarrow$ Saving of $B = 8x - 3x = 5x$

$\Rightarrow$ Saving of $C = 6x - 3x = 3x$

Difference between the savings of B and C together to the savings

A is 32,000

$\Rightarrow (5x + 3x) - (4x) = 32,000$

$\Rightarrow 4x = 32,000$

$\Rightarrow x = 8000$

$\therefore$ Income of $B = 8x = 8 \times 8000$

Rs. 64, 000

Hence, the correct answer is 64000.

55. Given:

The amount that Pavan gives to Chandan $= 20\%$

The amount that Pavan gives to Lakshman $= 30\%$

Chandan and Lakshman spend 40% and 50% of their money,

Let, the salary of Pavan be x.

The amount that Pavan gives to Chandan $= 20\%$ of $x = \left(\dfrac{20}{100}\right) \times x = \dfrac{x}{5}$

The amount that Chandan spent $= 40\%$ of $\left(\dfrac{x}{5}\right) = \left(\dfrac{40}{100}\right) \times \left(\dfrac{x}{5}\right) = \dfrac{2x}{25}$

Amount left with Chandan $= \left(\dfrac{x}{5}\right) - \left(\dfrac{2x}{25}\right) = \dfrac{3x}{25}$

The amount that Pavan gives to Lakshman $= 30\%$ of $x = \left(\dfrac{30}{100}\right) \times x = \dfrac{3x}{10}$

The amount that Lakshman spent $= 50\%$ of $\left(\dfrac{x}{4}\right) = \left(\dfrac{50}{100}\right) \times \left(\dfrac{3x}{10}\right) = \dfrac{3x}{20}$

Amount left with Lakshman $= \left(\dfrac{3x}{10}\right) - \left(\dfrac{3x}{20}\right) = \dfrac{3x}{20}$

The total amount that left with Chandan and Lakshman

$= \left(\dfrac{3x}{25}\right) + \left(\dfrac{3x}{20}\right) = \dfrac{27x}{100}$

Now the amount left with Pavan

$= x - \left(\dfrac{x}{5}\right) - \left(\dfrac{3x}{10}\right) = \dfrac{5x}{10} = \dfrac{x}{2}$

Now to find the ratio between the amount left with Chandan and Lakshman together and the amount left with Pavan

$=$ The total amount that left with Chandan and Lakshman : the amount left with Pavan

$= \dfrac{27x}{100} : \dfrac{x}{2}$

$= 27 : 50$

$\therefore$ The ratio between the amount left with Chandan and Lakshman together and the amount left with Pavan is $27:50$.

Hence, the correct option is (D).

56. Given:

Monthly incomes of A and B are in the ratio $= 3:5$

The ratio of their savings $= 2:3$

The income of $B = 3 \times$ Savings of A

As we know,

Income $=$ Savings $+$ Expenditure

Let the monthly income of A and B be 300 and 500 and the savings be $2x$ and $3x$ respectively

$\Rightarrow 500 = 3 \times 2x$

$\Rightarrow 500 = 6x$

$\Rightarrow x = \dfrac{250}{3}$

Expenditure of $A = $ Income of A - Savings of A

$= 300 - 2 \times \left(\dfrac{250}{3}\right)$

$= \dfrac{(900-500)}{3}$

$= \dfrac{400}{3}$

Expenditure of $B = $ Income of B - Savings of B

$= 500 - 3 \times \left(\dfrac{250}{3}\right)$

$= 500 - 250$

$= 250$

Ratio of expenditure of A and $B = \dfrac{\left(\frac{400}{3}\right)}{250}$

$= \dfrac{400}{750}$

$= \dfrac{8}{15}$

$\therefore$ The ratio of the expenditures of A and B is $8:15$.

Hence, the correct option is (A).

57. Correct ratio of A, B, C and $D = 4x:6x:7x:3x$

$4x + 6x + 7x + 3x = 3200$

$20x = 3200$

$x = \dfrac{3200}{20} = 160$

Share of $A = 4 \times 160 = 640$

Share of $B = 6 \times 160 = 960$

Share of $C = 7 \times 160 = 1120$

Share of $D = 3 \times 160 = 480$

Wrong ratio of A, B, C and $D = 3x:5x:6x:2x$

$3x + 5x + 6x + 2x = 3200$

$16x = 3200$

$x = \dfrac{3200}{16} = 200$

Wrong share of $A = 3 \times 200 = 600$

Wrong share of $B = 5 \times 200 = 1000$

Wrong share of $C = 6 \times 200 = 1200$

Wrong share of $D = 2 \times 200 = 400$

A got less than her due $= \left[\dfrac{(640-600)}{640}\right] \times 100 = 6.25\%$

B got less than her due $= \left[\dfrac{(960-1000)}{960}\right] \times 100 = 4.16\%$

C got less than her due $= \left[\dfrac{(1120-1000)}{1120}\right] \times 100 = 7.14\%$

D got less than her $due = \left[\dfrac{(480-400)}{480}\right] \times 100 = 16\%$

Hence, the correct option is (C).

58. Given,

$(a + b):(b + c):(c + a) = 7k:6k:5k$

$\Rightarrow (a + b + c) \times 2 = 18k$

$\Rightarrow (a + b + c) = 9k$

$\Rightarrow 9k = 27$

$\Rightarrow k = 3$

$\Rightarrow a + b = 21 \ldots.. \text{(i)}$

$\Rightarrow b + c = 18 \ldots \text{(ii)}$

$\Rightarrow c + a = 15 \ldots. \text{(iii)}$

Adding equation (i) and (iii).

$a + b + c + a = 21 + 15$

$\Rightarrow 2a + b + c = 36$

Putting the value of $b + c$ from equation (ii),

$\Rightarrow 2a + 18 = 36$

$\Rightarrow 2a = 36 - 18$

$\Rightarrow 2a = 18$

$\Rightarrow a = 9$

Putting the value of a in equation (i),

$\Rightarrow 9 + b = 21$

$\Rightarrow b = 21 - 9$

$\Rightarrow b = 12$

Putting the value of b in equation (ii),

$\Rightarrow 12 + c = 18$

$\Rightarrow c = 18 - 12$

$\Rightarrow c = 6$

$\therefore a = 9, b = 12, c = 6$

$\Rightarrow \dfrac{1}{a} : \dfrac{1}{b} : \dfrac{1}{c} = \dfrac{1}{9} : \dfrac{1}{12} : \dfrac{1}{6}$

$\Rightarrow \dfrac{1}{a} : \dfrac{1}{b} : \dfrac{1}{c} = 4 : 3 : 6$

Hence, the correct option is (A).

59. Given:

A person divides a certain amount among his three sons in the ratio $= 3 : 4 : 5$

If he had divided this amount in the ratio $= \dfrac{1}{3} : \dfrac{1}{4} : \dfrac{1}{5}$

The person who had got the lowest share earlier would get Rs. 1188 more

Let money get by first, second and third son be $3x, 4x$ and $5x$ respectively

Total share $= 3x + 4x + 5x = 12x$

Here first son got minimum share $= 3x$

If person had divided total amount in the ratio $= \dfrac{1}{3} : \dfrac{1}{4} : \dfrac{1}{5}$

LCM of 3,4 and $5 = 60$

Ratio of First, second and third

$= \left(\dfrac{1}{3}\right) \times 60 : \left(\dfrac{1}{4}\right) \times 60 : \left(\dfrac{1}{5}\right) \times 60 = 20 : 15 : 12$

Share of first student $= \left(\dfrac{12x}{47}\right) \times 20$

$= \dfrac{240x}{47}$

According to the question,

$\Rightarrow \left(\dfrac{240x}{47}\right) - (3x) = 1188$

$\Rightarrow \dfrac{(240x - 141x)}{47} = 1188$

$\Rightarrow \dfrac{99\pi}{47} = 1188$

$\Rightarrow x = 12 \times 47$

$\Rightarrow x = 564$

Total amount $= 12x$

$= 12 \times 564$

$= $ Rs. 6768

$\therefore$ The total amount is Rs. 6768 .

Hence, the correct answer is 6768.

60. Given,

A alone can complete a work in $= 12$ days

B alone can complete the same work in $= 15$ days

As we know,

Wages are distributed into efficiency ratio.

Efficiency is inversely proportional to time.

Time ratio of A and $B = 12 : 15 = 4 : 5$

Efficiency ratio of A and $B = 5 : 4$

According to the question,

$5 + 4 = 9$ units

$\Rightarrow 9$ units $= 3600$

$\Rightarrow 1$ unit $= 400$

$\Rightarrow 5$ units $= 5 \times 400 = $ Rs. 2000

$\therefore$ Share of A is Rs. 2000 .

Hence, the correct option is (D).

Q.1 In the binomial expansion of $\left(\sqrt[3]{2} + \frac{1}{\sqrt[3]{3}}\right)^n$, the ratio of the 7th term from the beginning to the 7th term from the end is $1:6$, then the value of n is:

A. 13   **B.** 16   **C.** 9   **D.** 23

Q.2 Find the middle terms in the expansion of $\left(2x + \frac{1}{x}\right)^5$.

A. 80

B. $\frac{80}{x}$

C. $80x$ and $\frac{40}{x}$

D. $80x$ and $\frac{80}{x}$

Q.3 Find out the value of n in the expansion $\left(5 + \frac{x}{7}\right)^n$, where x^{10} and x^{11} are equal.

A. 75   **B.** 110   **C.** 395   **D.** 225

Q.4 In the expansion of $\left(\sqrt{x} + \frac{1}{3x^2}\right)^{10}$ the value of constant term (independent of x) is:

A. 5   **B.** 8   **C.** 45   **D.** 90

Q.5 Term independent of x in the expansion of $\left(x - \frac{1}{3x^2}\right)^9$ is:

A. $^9C_3\left(\frac{-1}{3}\right)^3$

B. $^9C_6\left(\frac{-1}{3}\right)^6$

C. $^9C_3\left(\frac{1}{3}\right)^3$

D. $^9C_6\left(\frac{1}{3}\right)^6$

Q.6 Find the coefficient of x^{11} in the expansion of $\left(x^3 - \frac{1}{x^4}\right)^{13}$:

A. -143   **B.** -572   **C.** 143   **D.** 715

Q.7 The co-efficient of y in the expansion of $\left(y^2 + \frac{c}{y}\right)^5$ is?

A. $10c^3$ **B.** $20c^3$ **C.** $10c$ **D.** $20c$

Q.8 What is the sum of the coefficients of first and last terms in the expansion of $(1+x)^{2n}$, where n is a natural number?

[UPSC NDA, 2021]

A. 1   **B.** 2   **C.** n **D.** $2n$

Q.9 The term independent of x in $\left(2x - \frac{1}{2x^2}\right)^{12}$ is:

A. $^{12}C_4 \times 2^4$

B. $^{12}C_4 \times 3^4$

C. $^{12}C_8$

D. $-^{12}C_6$

Q.10 6th term in expansion of $\left(2x^2 - \frac{1}{3x^2}\right)^{10}$ is:

A. $^{10}C_5\left(\frac{2}{3}\right)^5$

B. $-^{10}C_5\left(\frac{2}{3}\right)^5$

C. $-^{10}C_6\left(\frac{2}{3}\right)^6$

D. None of these

Q.11 A number 727X44 is divisible by 88. Find the value of X.

A. 3   **B.** 4   **C.** 2   **D.** 1

Q.12 Find the remainder when $(585)^3 \times (1197)^{999} \times 2188$ is divided by 23.

A. 10   **B.** 3   **C.** 2   **D.** 4

Q.13 When $(77^{77} + 77)$ is divided by 78, the remainder is:

A. 75   **B.** 74   **C.** 77   **D.** 76

Q.14 Find the remainder the number $(2^{18} + 5)$ is divided by 9.

A. 5   **B.** 4   **C.** 6   **D.** 1

Q.15 If p and q are positive integers and (p–q) is an even number, then (p^2-q^2) will always be divisible by:

A. 4   **B.** 6   **C.** 12   **D.** 8

Q.16 Numbers 11284 and 7655, when divided by a certain number of three digits, leave the same remainder. Find that number of 3 digits and their sum.

A. 191 & 11   **B.** 911 & 11

C. 181 & 10   **D.** 811 & 10

Q.17 How many numbers are there from 200 to 800 which are neither divisible by 5 nor by 7?

A. 411   **B.** 410   **C.** 407   **D.** 413

Q.18 There are T number of total factors of Number N = 64 × 3125 × 343 × 343 × 10000000. Among them there are E number of Even factors. Find the Value of T + E.

A. 2477   **B.** 2403   **C.** 2457   **D.** 2467

Q.19 Factorise:

$$10x^2 - 18x^3 + 14x^4$$

A. $2x^2(7x^2 - 9x + 5)$

B. $x^2(7x^2 - 9x + 5)$

C. $2x^3(7x^2 - 9x + 5)$

D. $2x^2(x^2 - 9x + 5)$

Q.20 What will you get on dividing $(x^2 - 25) + (x + 5)$ by $(x - 4)$?

A. $x + 4$ **B.** $x - 5$ **C.** $x - 4$ **D.** $x + 5$

Q.21 Which of the following are the factors of $120 + x^2 - 22x$?

A. $(x + 10), (x - 12)$

B. $(x + 10), (x + 12)$

C. $(x - 10), (x + 12)$

D. $(x - 10), (x - 12)$

Q.22 Factorise:

$$a^2 - (2a + 3b)^2$$

A. $-(a + 3b)(a + b)$

B. $-3(a + 3b)(a + b)$

C. $-3(a + b)(a + b)$

D. $-2(a + 3b)(a + b)$

Q.23 Factorise: $2a^2 + bc - 2ab - ac$

A. $(a - 2b)(2a - c)$

B. $(a + b)(2a - c)$

C. $(a - b)(2a - c)$

D. $(a - b + c)$

Q.24 Factorise:

$$a^3 + 2a^2 - a - 2$$

A. $(a-1)(a-2)(a+1)$
B. $(a+1)(a+2)(a+1)$
C. $(a-1)(a+2)(a+1)$
D. $(2a+1)(a+2)(a+1)$

Q.25 Which of the following represents the factorised form of $72m^2n - 50n^3$?

A. $(18m+n)(19m-n)$
B. $(25m+16n)(25m-16n)$
C. $2n(6m+5n)(6m-5n)$
D. $(6m+5n)(6m-5n)$

Q.26 What is the value of $\frac{1}{1+\sqrt{2}} + \frac{1}{\sqrt{2}+\sqrt{3}} + \frac{1}{\sqrt{3}+\sqrt{4}} + \cdots + \frac{1}{\sqrt{99}+\sqrt{100}}$?

[Indian Military Academy (IMA), 2020]

A. 1
B. 5
C. 9
D. 10

Q.27 What will come in the place of question mark (?).

$$(25)^{7.5} \times (5)^{2.5} \div (125)^{1.5} = 5^?$$

A. 8.5
B. 13
C. 16
D. 17.5

Q.28 The value of $\left(\frac{9^2 \times 18^4}{3^{16}}\right)$ is $=?$

A. $\frac{3}{2}$
B. $\frac{4}{9}$
C. $\frac{16}{81}$
D. $\frac{32}{243}$

Q.29 Find the value of $(x-y)$, if $(3^5)^x \div (9)^{2x-1} = 243$ and $(5)^{x-2y} \times (5)^{x+y} = 625$.

A. 0
B. 1
C. 2
D. 3

Q.30 Find the value

of $\sqrt{72 + \sqrt{72 + \sqrt{72 + \sqrt{72 + - - - \infty}}}}$.

A. 9
B. 8
C. 18
D. 36

Q.31 $\frac{1}{1+x^{(b-a)}+x^{(c-a)}} + \frac{1}{1+x^{(a-b)}+x^{(c-b)}} + \frac{1}{1+x^{(b-c)}+x^{(a-c)}} = ?$

A. 0
B. 1
C. x^{a-b-c}
D. 2

Q.32 Evaluate- $\sqrt{20 - \sqrt{20 - \sqrt{20 - \ldots \ldots \infty}}}$.

A. 4
B. 5
C. 20
D. None of these

Q.33 If $\sqrt{4624} = 68$, then the value of:

$$\sqrt{46.24} + \sqrt{0.4624} + \sqrt{0.004624}$$

A. 7.548
B. 7.854
C. 7.458
D. 7.648

Q.34 Simplify the following expression.

$$\left(\frac{4^{-2}\times3^2}{4\times3^{-4}}\right)^{\frac{1}{3}} \times \frac{4^{-3}\times3^3}{4^{-4}\times3^6}$$

A. $\frac{1}{9}$
B. $\frac{1}{12}$
C. $\frac{1}{3}$
D. $\frac{27}{16}$

Q.35 $\sqrt{5} + \sqrt{12 - 2\sqrt{35}}$ is equal to?

A. $\sqrt{5}$
B. $\sqrt{3}$
C. $\sqrt{7}$
D. $\sqrt{7} + \sqrt{5}$

Q.36 Find the unit digit of $(28^{144} + 33^{168})$.

A. 5
B. 6
C. 7
D. 8

Q.37 Unit digit of the multiplication of $(2023)^{2023}$ is:

A. 3
B. 9
C. 7
D. 1

Q.38 Let x = $(433)^{24} - (377)^{38} + (166)^{54}$. What is the units digit of x?

A. 7
B. 6
C. 8
D. 9

Q.39 If x = $(164)^{169} + (333)^{337} - (727)^{726}$, then what is the units digit of x?

A. 5
B. 9
C. 7
D. 8

Q.40 What is the unit digit in the expansion of 67^{32}?

[Indian Military Academy (IMA), 2021]

A. 1
B. 3
C. 7
D. 9

Q.41 What is the unit digit of $(217)^{413} \times (819)^{547} \times (414)^{624} \times (342)^{812}$?

A. 2
B. 4
C. 6
D. 8

Q.42 How many 3-digit positive integers, with digits a, b and c exist such that a < b and c < b? Assume that a is in hundred's place, b is in ten's place, c is in unit's place and a is a non-zero digit.

A. 450
B. 240
C. 364
D. 648

Q.43 Positive numbers 1 to 55, inclusive are placed in 5 groups of 11 numbers each. What is the maximum possible average of the medians of the 5 groups?

A. 34
B. 28
C. 35
D. 38

Q.44 $n^2 + 5n + 6$ is a multiple of 6. n is natural number less than 100. How many values can n take?

A. 33
B. 65
C. 66
D. 67

Q.45 How many numbers with distinct digits are possible product of whose digits is 28?

A. 6
B. 4
C. 8
D. 12

Q.46 Which is the digit at unit place of the product $(5^{41} \times 7^{69} \times 3^{57})$?

A. 7
B. 5
C. 3
D. 1

Q.47 Find the unit digit of $(144^{23} + 67^3)$.

A. 1
B. 3
C. 5
D. 7

Q.48 Find the smallest number which is divisible by 5, 7, 8 and leaves the remainder 4. It is also given that number is completely divisible by 13.

A. 4484
B. 5044
C. 4204
D. 4764

Q.49 If a number 42x73y is divisible by 72, then the value of (5x - 3y) is:

A. 7   **B.** 8   **C.** 10   **D.** 11

Q.50 If 257x8 is divisible by 11, what will be the value of x?

A. 0   **B.** 2   **C.** 5   **D.** 1

Q.51 The term independent of x in $\left(x^2 - \dfrac{1}{x^3}\right)^{10}$ is:

A. $^{10}C_5$ **B.** $^{10}C_3$ **C.** $^{10}C_2$ **D.** $^{10}C_4$

Q.52 Find the middle term in the expansion $\left(4x - \dfrac{x^3}{2}\right)^9$.

A. Both 1 and 2 $^9C_4 4^3 x^{17}$
B. $-{}^9C_5 2^3 x^{19}$
C. Both (A) and (B)
D. None of these

Q.53 Find the common factors of the given terms:

$12x^2 y, 18xy^2$

A. $6xy$ **B.** $6x^2 y$ **C.** $3xy$ **D.** $6x$

Q.54 Find the common factors of the given terms:

$4\,m^2, 6\,m^2, 8\,m^3$.

A. $6m^2$ **B.** $2m^2$ **C.** $2m$ **D.** $4m^2$

Q.55 A is the number of even factors of 7392 and B is the number of prime factors of 7392. Which of the following is true?

A. A = B   **B.** B = 5A   **C.** A = 5B   **D.** B = 2A

Q.56 Factorise the following:

$x^8 - y^8$

A. $(x^4 + y^4)(x^2 - y^2)(x + y)(x - y)$
B. $(x^4 - y^4)(x^2 + y^2)(x + y)(x - y)$
C. $(x^2 + y^4)(x^2 + y^2)(x + y)(x - y)$
D. $(x^4 + y^4)(x^2 + y^2)(x + y)(x - y)$

Q.57 What will come in the place of 'x' in the following question?

$$\sqrt{1600} - \sqrt[3]{8000} = (10)^x + 10$$

A. 10   **B.** 0.1   **C.** 1   **D.** 2

Q.58 What value can come in the place of the question mark (?) in the question below?

$$(10)^2 + (243)^{\frac{1}{5}} - 5 = -(7)^3 + (?)^2$$

A. 27   **B.** 29   **C.** 19   **D.** 21

Q.59 $4x^3 + 12x^2 - x - 3$ is divisible by:

[Indian Military Academy (IMA), 2021]

A. (2x + 1) only
B. (2x - 1) only
C. Both (2x + 1) and (2x - 1)
D. Neither (2x + 1) nor (2x - 1)

Q.60 Let XYZ be a 3-digit number. Let S = XYZ + YZX + ZXY. Which of the following statements is/are correct?

1. S is always divisible by 3 and (X + Y + Z)
2. S is always divisible by 9
3. S is always divisible by 37

Select the correct answer using the code given below:

A. 1 only   **B.** 2 only   **C.** 1 and 2   **D.** 1 and 3

// Smart Answer Sheet //

Correct   Indicates percentage of students who answered questions correctly.

Skipped   Indicates percentage of students who skipped questions.

Q.	Ans.	Correct / Skipped	Q.	Ans.	Correct / Skipped	Q.	Ans.	Correct / Skipped	Q.	Ans.	Correct / Skipped	Q.	Ans.	Correct / Skipped
1	C	51.51 % / 36.76 %	13	D	43.26 % / 52.36 %	25	C	45.68 % / 51.4 %	37	C	51.45 % / 35.61 %	49	A	49.66 % / 37.23 %
2	C	11.01 % / 69.29 %	14	C	21.08 % / 71.99 %	26	C	69.69 % / 30.17 %	38	C	63.98 % / 32.06 %	50	D	85.74 % / 12.65 %
3	C	68.93 % / 30.77 %	15	A	62.38 % / 36.74 %	27	B	50.72 % / 31.35 %	39	D	67.84 % / 30.25 %	51	D	51.79 % / 42.76 %
4	A	27.48 % / 70.06 %	16	A	45.5 % / 45.44 %	28	C	78.91 % / 17.93 %	40	A	56.32 % / 30.93 %	52	C	16.57 % / 68.69 %
5	A	25.2 % / 69.07 %	17	A	32.73 % / 67.0 %	29	B	46.42 % / 44.48 %	41	D	45.09 % / 50.87 %	53	A	61.17 % / 37.73 %
6	D	42.43 % / 40.01 %	18	C	52.02 % / 36.04 %	30	A	10.42 % / 73.06 %	42	B	64.85 % / 34.46 %	54	B	55.79 % / 33.51 %
7	A	85.81 % / 12.08 %	19	A	83.4 % / 10.02 %	31	B	62.88 % / 35.9 %	43	D	44.82 % / 36.5 %	55	C	59.77 % / 39.39 %
8	B	58.38 % / 39.02 %	20	D	68.13 % / 30.37 %	32	A	16.1 % / 74.56 %	44	C	54.13 % / 44.66 %	56	D	78.44 % / 21.21 %
9	A	16.22 % / 70.56 %	21	D	66.65 % / 30.18 %	33	A	62.72 % / 32.05 %	45	C	47.65 % / 34.4 %	57	C	56.64 % / 38.23 %
10	B	46.9 % / 40.38 %	22	B	48.18 % / 47.88 %	34	C	82.53 % / 12.94 %	46	B	58.83 % / 35.1 %	58	D	49.6 % / 48.85 %
11	D	66.55 % / 31.87 %	23	C	65.31 % / 33.7 %	35	C	53.96 % / 36.97 %	47	D	86.82 % / 11.55 %	59	C	81.58 % / 12.65 %
12	A	28.59 % / 69.27 %	24	C	45.28 % / 36.58 %	36	C	68.17 % / 30.87 %	48	B	54.07 % / 31.53 %	60	D	49.99 % / 32.58 %

Performance Analysis

Avg. Score (%)	46.67%
Toppers Score (%)	55.0%
Your Score	

//Hints and Solutions//

1. 7th term from the beginning is:

$$^nC_6(2)^{\frac{n-6}{3}}\left(\frac{1}{3}\right)^{\frac{6}{3}} \quad .....(\text{i})$$

7th term from the end is:

$$^nC_6\left(\frac{1}{3}\right)^{\frac{n-6}{3}}(2)^{\frac{6}{3}} \quad .....(\text{ii})$$

From equation (i) and (ii),

$$\Rightarrow \frac{^nC_6(2)^{\frac{n}{3}-2}\left(\frac{1}{3}\right)^2}{^nC_6 2^2\left(\frac{1}{3}\right)^{\frac{n}{3}-2}} = \frac{1}{6}$$

$$\Rightarrow (2)^{\frac{n}{3}-4}\left(\frac{1}{3}\right)^{4-\frac{n}{3}} = \frac{1}{6}$$

$$\Rightarrow (2\times3)^{\frac{n}{3}-4} = (2\times3)^{-1}$$

$$\Rightarrow n = 9$$

Hence, the correct option is (C).

2. As we know,

General term in the expansion of $(x+y)^n$ is given by,

$$T_{(r+1)} = {}^nC_r \times x^{n-r} \times y^r$$

The middle term is the expansion of $(x+y)^n$ depends upon the value of n.

If n is even, then total number of terms in the expansion of $(x+y)^n$ is $n+1$.

So there is only one middle term i.e., $\left(\frac{n}{2}+1\right)$th term.

If n is odd, then total number of terms in the expansion of $(x+y)^n$ is $n+1$.

So there are two middle terms i.e., $\left(\frac{n+1}{2}\right)^{\text{th}}$ and $\left(\frac{n+3}{2}\right)^{\text{th}}$.

Here $n = 5$ (n is odd number)

$$\therefore \text{Middle term} = \left(\frac{n+1}{2}\right)^{\text{th}} \text{ and } \left(\frac{n+3}{2}\right)^{\text{th}} = 3^{\text{rd}} \text{ and } 4^{\text{th}}$$

$$\therefore T_3 = T_{(2+1)} = {}^5C_2 \times (2x)^{(5-2)} \times \left(\frac{1}{x}\right)^2 \text{ and } T_4 =$$

$$T_{(3+1)} = {}^5C_3 \times (2x)^{(5-3)} \times \left(\frac{1}{x}\right)^3$$

$$\Rightarrow T_3 = {}^5C_2 \times (2^3 x) \text{ and } T_4 = {}^5C_3 \times 2^2 \times \frac{1}{x}$$

$$\Rightarrow T_3 = 80x \text{ and } T_4 = \frac{40}{x}$$

So, the middle terms in the expansion of $\left(2x+\frac{1}{x}\right)^5$ are $80x$ and $\frac{40}{x}$.

Hence, the correct option is (C).

3. According to Binomial expansion of $(x+a)^n = \sum_{r=0}^{n} x^{n-r}a^r$

$T_{r+1} = {}^nC_r.x^{n-r}.a^r$

For $\left(5+\frac{x}{7}\right)^n$

$$T_{r+1} = .5^{n-r}.\left(\frac{x}{7}\right)^r = 5^{n-r}.x^r.7^{-r}$$

Where $a = \frac{x}{7}$ and x = 5

Putting r = 10, we get

$T_{10+1} = T_{11} = {}^nC_{10}.5^{(n-10)}.x^{10}.7^{-10}$

Putting r = 11, we get

$T_{11+1} = T_{12} = {}^nC_{11}.5^{(n-11)}.x^{11}.7^{-11}$

Given condition is x^{10} and x^{11} are equal, so

$^nC_{10}.5^{(n-10)}.7^{-10} = {}^nC_{11}.5^{(n-11)}.7^{-11}$

$$\frac{.5^{(n-11)}.7^{-11}}{.5^{(n-10)}.7^{-10}} = 1$$

$$\frac{(n-10)}{11}.\frac{1}{5}.\frac{1}{7} = 1$$

$$\frac{(n-10)}{11\times5\times7} = 1$$

n-10 = 385

n = 385+10 = 395

Therefore, the value of n = 395

Hence, the correct option is (C).

4. Given expansion is:

$$\left(\sqrt{x}+\frac{1}{3x^2}\right)^{10}$$

Let r^{th} term is independent of x.

$$T_r = {}^nC_r x^r y^{n-r}$$

$$= {}^{10}C_r\left(\sqrt{x}\right)^r \left(\frac{1}{3x^2}\right)^{10-r}$$

$$= {}^{10}C_r\left(\frac{1}{3}\right)^{10-r}\left(\sqrt{x}\right)^r\left(\frac{1}{x^2}\right)^{10-r}$$

Equating the coefficient of x to zero

$$x^{\frac{r}{2}}x^{-2(10-r)} = x^0$$

$$\frac{r}{2} - 20 + 2r = 0$$

$\frac{5}{2}r = 20$

$r = 8$

Coefficient $= {}^{10}C_r \left(\frac{1}{3}\right)^{10-r}$

$= {}^{10}C_8 \left(\frac{1}{3}\right)^{10-8}$

$= \frac{10 \times 9}{2} \times \frac{1}{9}$

$= 5$

Hence, the correct option is (A).

5. As we know,

General term in the expansion of $(a+b)^n$ is given by,

$T_{(r+1)} = {}^nC_r \times a^{n-r} \times b^r$ or

$T_{(r+1)} = C_r a^{n-r} b^r$ ...(i)

In the given binomial expression $\left(x - \frac{1}{3x^2}\right)^9$, we have

$n = 9, a = x$ and $b = \frac{-1}{3x^2}$

Putting these values in (i), we get

$T_{r+1} = C_r (x)^{9-r} \left(\frac{-1}{3x^2}\right)^r$

$= {}^9C_r \left(\frac{-1}{3}\right)^r x^{9-3r}$

For the term to be independent of x, we must have $9 - 3r = 0$.

$\therefore r = 3$

So, the required term is ${}^9C_3 \left(\frac{-1}{3}\right)^3$.

Hence, the correct option is (A).

6. Given:

$\left(x^3 - \frac{1}{x^4}\right)^{13}$

$T_{r+1} = (-1)^r \times {}^{13}C_r \times (x^3)^{13-r} \times \left(\frac{1}{x^4}\right)^r$

$= (-1)^r \times {}^{13}C_r \times (x)^{39-3r} \times x^{-4r}$

$= (-1)^r \times {}^{13}C_r \times (x)^{39-7r}$ .....(i)

We need the coefficient of x^{11}

So, on equating power of x in (i) with 11, we get,

$11 = 39 - 7r$

$\Rightarrow 7r = 28$

$\Rightarrow r = 4$

$\Rightarrow r + 1 = 5$

Now, $T_5 = T_{(4+1)} = (-1)^4 \times {}^{13}C_4 \times x^{39-28}$

$= {}^{13}C_4 \times x^{11}$

$\therefore$ Cofficient of $x^{11} = {}^{13}C_4$

$= \frac{13 \times 12 \times 11 \times 10}{4 \times 3 \times 2 \times 1}$

$= 715$

Hence, the correct option is (D).

7. Given:

$\left(y^2 + \frac{c}{y}\right)^5$

$\left(y^2 + \frac{c}{y}\right)^5 = {}^5C_0 \left(\frac{c}{y}\right)^0 (y^2)^{5-0} + {}^5C_1 \left(\frac{c}{y}\right)^1 (y^2)^{5-1} +$
$\ldots + {}^5C_5 \left(\frac{c}{y}\right)^5 (y^2)^{5-5}$

$= \sum_{r=0}^{5} {}^5C_r \left(\frac{c}{y}\right)^r (y^2)^{5-r}$ .....(i)

We need coefficient of $y \Rightarrow 2(5-r) - r = 1$

$\Rightarrow 10 - 3r = 1$

$\Rightarrow r = 3$

Put $r = 3$ in (i),

$= {}^5C_3 \left(\frac{c}{y}\right)^3 (y^2)^2$

$= {}^5C_3 c^3 y$

So, coefficient of $y = {}^5C_3 \cdot c^3$

$= 10c^3$

Hence, the correct option is (A).

8. As we know,

${}^nC_r = \frac{n!}{(r!(n-r)!)}$

$(1+x)^n = {}^nC_0 \times 1^{(n-0)} \times x^0 + {}^nC_1 \times 1^{(n-1)} \times x^1 + {}^nC_2 \times 1^{(n-2)} \times x^2 + \ldots + {}^nC_n \times 1^{(n \cdot n)} \times x^n$

Given expansion is $(1+x)^{2n}$

$\Rightarrow {}^{2n}C_0 \times 1^{(2n-0)} \times x^0 + {}^{2n}C_1 \times 1^{(2n-1)} \times x^1 + \ldots + {}^{2n}C_{2n} \times 1^{(2n-2n)} \times x^{2n}$

First term $= {}^{2n}C_0 \times 1 \times 1 = 1$

Last term $= {}^{2n}C_{2n} \times 1 \times x^{2n} = 1 \times x^{2n} = x^{2n}$

$\Rightarrow$ Sum $= 1 + x^{2n}$

Coefficient of $1 = 1$, coefficient of $x^{2n} = 1$

$\therefore$ sum of the coefficients $= 1 + 1 = 2$.

Hence, the correct option is (B).

9. We have to find term independent of x in $\left(2x - \frac{1}{2x^2}\right)^{12}$.

We know that,

$$T_{(r+1)} = {}^nC_r \times x^{n-r} \times y^r$$

Here,

$$n = 12,$$

$$x = 2x$$

and, $y = -\dfrac{1}{2x^2}$

$$\Rightarrow T_{(r+1)} = {}^{12}C_r \times (2x)^{12-r} \times \left(\dfrac{-1}{2x^2}\right)^r$$

$$= (-1)^r \times {}^{12}C_r \times (2x)^{12-r} \times (2x^2)^{-r}$$

$$= (-1)^r \times {}^{12}C_r \times (2)^{12-r}(x)^{12-r} \times (2)^{-r}(x)^{-2r}$$

$$= (-1)^r \times {}^{12}C_r \times (2)^{12-2r}(x)^{12-3r}$$

For the term independent of x, power of x should be zero.

Therefore,

$$12 - 3r = 0$$

$$\Rightarrow r = 4$$

$$T_{(4+1)} = (-1)^4 \times {}^{12}C_4 \times (2)^{12-8} = {}^{12}C_4 \times (2)^4$$

Hence, the correct option is (A).

10. As we know, for expansion of $(a + b)^n$

$$T_{r+1} = {}^nC_r\, a^{n-r} b^r$$

Here $a = 2x^2$

$$b = \dfrac{-1}{3}x^2$$

$$r = 5$$

$$T_6 = {}^{10}C_5 (2x^2)^{10-5}\left(-\dfrac{1}{3x^2}\right)^5$$

$$= -{}^{10}C_5\left(\dfrac{2}{3}\right)^5 x^{10} \cdot \dfrac{1}{x^{10}}$$

$$= -{}^{10}C_5\left(\dfrac{2}{3}\right)^5$$

Hence, the correct option is (B).

11. Given:

A number 727X44

Concept used:

For a number divisible by 88, it has to be divisible by 11 and 8.

Divisibility rule of 8: If in any number, the last three digits are divisible by 8, then the whole number is divisible by 8.

Divisibility rule of 11: If the difference between the sum of digits at even places and the sum of digits at the odd places is divisible by 11, or it is 0, then the whole number is divisible by 11.

Calculation:

We have a number 727X44

The last three digits are X44

If the value of X = 1, 3, 5, 7 and 9, then the number 727X44 will be divisible by 8.

If X = 1

The number will be 727144 is divisible by 11.

At other values of X (3, 5, 7, 9) the number will not be divisible by 11.

∴ The value of X is 1.

Hence, the correct option is (D).

12. Given: $(585)^3 \times (1197)^{999} \times 2188$ is divided by 23.

Calculation:

Individual remainder When 585 is divided by 23, remainder will be 10.

When 1197 is divided by 23, remainder will be 1.

When 2188 is divided by 23, remainder will be 3.

Using remainder theorem,

$$(585)^3 \times (1197)^{999} \times \dfrac{2188}{23}$$

$$= \dfrac{[(10)^3 \times (1)^{999} \times 3]}{23}$$

$$= \dfrac{(1000 \times 3)}{23}$$

$$= \dfrac{3000}{23}, \text{ remainder will be } 10$$

∴ When dividing 3000 by 23, remainder will be 10.

Hence, the correct option is (A).

13. Given: $(77^{77} + 77)$ is divided by 78,

Calculation:

According to the question,

When 77 is divided by 78, the remainder will be (- 1).

Using remainder theorem,

$$\dfrac{[(77^{77} + 77)]}{78}$$

$$= \dfrac{[(-1)^{77} + (-1)]}{78}$$

$$= \dfrac{(-1 - 1)}{78}$$

$$= \dfrac{(-2)}{78}$$

$$= 76$$

∴ The reminder is 76.

Hence, the correct option is (D).

14. Given:

The number is $(2^{18} + 5)$ and the divisor is 9.

Concept used:

When a number is divided by another number then there are two remainder one is negative and other is positive.

Ex: $\dfrac{8}{9}$

Negative remainder = (8 - 9) = -1

And positive remainder = 8

Calculation:

The number is divided by 9.

$= (2^{18} + 5) \div 9$

$= \left(\dfrac{\left(2^3\right)^6 + 5}{9}\right)$

$= \left(\dfrac{\left(8^6 + 5\right)}{9}\right)$

$= \dfrac{\left((-1)^6 + 5\right)}{9}$

$= \dfrac{(1 + 5)}{9}$

$= \dfrac{6}{9}$

Remainder = 6

∴ The required remainder is 6.

Hence, the correct option is (C).

15. Given: p and q are positive integers and (p−q) is and even number.

Calculation:

From the concept of odd and even n umbers we know, if p−q is an even number,

- either both p and q are odd numbers, or,
- both p and q are even numbers.

There is no third possibility.

So it follows immediately that p+q also is an even number having a factor of 2.

Finally then, $p^2 - q^2 = (p−q)(p+q)$ will have two numbers of 2, that is, 4 as a factor.

Hence, the correct option is (A).

16. Given:

Numbers 11284 and 7655, when divided by a certain number of three digits, leave the same remainder.

One has to remember that each factor of the difference of two numbers gives the same remainder if those numbers are divided by it.

Now the difference here = 11284 − 7655 = 3629

Factors of 3629 are 1, 19, 191 and 3629

But we have to find the three digit number here, so 191 is the required number and their sum is 1+9+1 = 11

Hence, the correct option is (A).

17. Given:

Numbers from 200 to 800.

Total number from 200 and 800 = 800 − 200 + 1 = 601   ---- (including 200)

Total number from 1 to 200 (200 excluding) which are divisible by 5 = $\dfrac{199}{5} \approx 39$

Total number from 1 to 800 (800 including) which are divisible by 5 = $\dfrac{800}{5} = 160$

Total number from 200 to 800 which are divisible by 5 = 160 − 39 = 121

Total number from 1 to 200 (200 excluding) which are divisible by 7 = $\dfrac{199}{7} \approx 28$

Total number from 1 to 800 (800 including) which are divisible by 7 = $\dfrac{800}{7} \approx 114$

Total number from 200 to 800 which are divisible by 7 = 114 − 28 = 86

Similarly, Total number from 200 to 800 which are divisible by 35 = $\dfrac{800}{35} - \dfrac{200}{35} = 22 - 5 = 17$

Number neither divisible by 5 nor 7 = 601 − 121 − 86 + 17 = 411

∴ Number neither divisible by 5 nor 7 is 411.

Hence, the correct option is (A).

18. N = 64 × 3125 × 343 × 343 × 10000000 van be written as 26 × 55 × 73 × 73 × 107 = 26 × 55 × 76 × 107

The prime factorization of 26 × 55 × 76 × 107 is 213 × 512 × 76.

The total number of factors of N = 14 × 13 × 7

We need to find the total number of even factors. For this, let us find the total number of odd factors and then subtract this from the total number of factors. Any odd factor will have to be a combination of powers of only 5 and 7.

Total number of odd factors of 213 × 512 × 76 = (12 + 1) × (6 + 1) = 13 × 7

Total number of factors (T) = (13 + 1) × (12 + 1) × (6 + 1) = 14 × 13 × 7 = 1274

Total number of even factors (E) = 14 × 13 × 7 - 13 × 7

Number of even factors (E) = 13 × 13 × 7 = 1183

Desired Result = T + E = 1274 + 1183 = 2457

Hence, the correct option is (C).

19. We have,

$$10x^2 = 2 \times 5 \times x \times x$$

$$18x^3 = 2 \times 3 \times 3 \times x \times x \times x$$

$$14x^4 = 2 \times 7 \times x \times x \times x \times x \times x$$

The common factors of the three terms are $2, x$ and x.

Therefore,
$$10x^2 - 18x^3 + 14x^4 = (2 \times x \times x \times 5) - (2 \times x \times x \times 3 \times 3 \times x) + (2 \times x \times x \times 7 \times x \times x)$$

$$= 2 \times x \times x[(5 - (3 \times 3 \times x) + (7 \times x \times x))]$$

$$= 2x^2 \times (5 - 9x + 7x^2) = 2x^2(7x^2 - 9x + 5)$$

Hence, the correct option is (A).

20. Given,

$$= \frac{(x^2-25)+(x+5)}{(x-4)}$$

$$= \frac{(x+5)(x-5)+(x+5)}{(x-4)}$$

$$= \frac{(x+5)[(x-5+1)]}{(x-4)}$$

$$= \frac{(x+5)(x-4)]}{(x-4)}$$

$$= x + 5$$

Hence, the correct option is (D).

21. $x^2 - 22x + 120$

$$= x^2 - 12x - 10x + 120$$

$$= x(x - 12) - 10(x - 12)$$

$$= (x - 12)(x - 10)$$

Hence, the correct option is (D).

22. Given,

$$a^2 - (2a + 3b)^2 = a^2 - (2a + 3b)^2$$

$$= (a - 2a - 3b)(a + 2a + 3b)$$

$$= (-a - 3b)(3a + 3b)$$

$$= -3(a + 3b)(a + b)$$

Hence, the correct option is (B).

23. Given:

$$2a^2 + bc - 2ab - ac$$

We can further write it as

$$2a^2 + bc - 2ab - ac = 2a^2 - 2ab - ac + bc$$

By taking the common terms out

$$2a^2 + bc - 2ab - ac = 2a(a - b) - c(a - b)$$

So we get,

$$2a^2 + bc - 2ab - ac = (a - b)(2a - c)$$

Hence, the correct option is (C).

24. Given,

$$a^3 + 2a^2 - a - 2 = a^2(a + 2) - 1(a + 2)$$

$$a^3 + 2a^2 - a - 2 = (a^2 - 1)(a + 2)$$

$$a^3 + 2a^2 - a - 2 = (a - 1)(a + 2)(a + 1)$$
$$\left[\because a^2 - b^2 = (a + b)(a - b) \right]$$

Hence, the correct option is (C).

25. Given,

$$72m^2n - 50n^3$$

$$= 2n(36m^2 - 25n^2)$$

$$= 2n \times [(6m)^2 - (5n)^2]$$

As we know,

$$a^2 - b^2 - (a + b)(a - b)$$

$$= 2n(6m + 5n)(6m - 5n)$$

Hence, the correct option is (C).

26. Given:

$$\frac{1}{1+\sqrt{2}} + \frac{1}{\sqrt{2}+\sqrt{3}} + \frac{1}{\sqrt{3}+\sqrt{4}} + \cdots + \frac{1}{\sqrt{99}+\sqrt{100}}$$

As we know,

$$(a^2 - b^2) = (a + b)(a - b)$$

Now,

Rationalizing the denominator, we get

$$\frac{1}{(1+\sqrt{2})} \times \frac{(1-\sqrt{2})}{(1-\sqrt{2})} + \frac{1}{(\sqrt{2}+\sqrt{3})} \times \frac{(\sqrt{2}-\sqrt{3})}{(\sqrt{2}-\sqrt{3})} + \frac{1}{(\sqrt{3}+\sqrt{4})}$$
$$\times \frac{(\sqrt{3}-\sqrt{4})}{(\sqrt{3}-\sqrt{4})} \cdots + \frac{1}{(\sqrt{99}+\sqrt{100})} \times \frac{(\sqrt{99}-\sqrt{100})}{(\sqrt{99}-\sqrt{100})}$$

On canceling the negative and positive term, we get

$$\Rightarrow -\frac{(1-\sqrt{2})}{1} - \frac{(\sqrt{2}-\sqrt{3})}{1} - \frac{(\sqrt{3}-\sqrt{4})}{1} - \cdots \frac{(\sqrt{99}-\sqrt{100})}{1}$$

$$\Rightarrow \sqrt{2} - 1 + \sqrt{3} - \sqrt{2} + \sqrt{4} - \sqrt{3} \ldots + \sqrt{100} - \sqrt{99}$$

$$\Rightarrow \sqrt{100} - 1 = 9$$

Hence, the correct option is (C).

27. Let,

$$(25)^{7.5} \times (5)^{2.5} \div (125)^{1.5} = 5^x$$

Then,

$$\frac{\left(5^2\right)^{7.5} \times (5)^{2.5}}{(5^3)^{1.5}} = 5^x$$

$$\Rightarrow \frac{5^{(2 \times 7.5)} \times 5^{2.5}}{5^{(3 \times 1.5)}} = 5^x$$

$$\Rightarrow \frac{5^{15} \times 5^{2.5}}{5^{4.5}} = 5^x$$

$$\Rightarrow 5^x = 5^{(15 + 2.5 - 4.5)}$$

$$\Rightarrow 5^x = 5^{13}$$

$$\therefore x = 13$$

Hence, the correct option is (B).

28. Given,

$$\left(\frac{9^2 \times 18^4}{3^{16}}\right)$$

$$= \frac{9^2 \times (9 \times 2)^4}{3^{16}}$$

$$= \frac{\left(3^2\right)^2 \times \left(3^2\right)^4 \times 2^4}{3^{16}}$$

$$= \frac{3^4 \times 3^8 \times 2^4}{3^{16}}$$

$$= \frac{3^{(4+8)} \times 2^4}{3^{16}}$$

$$= \frac{3^{12} \times 2^4}{3^{16}}$$

$$= \frac{2^4}{3^{(16-12)}}$$

$$= \frac{2^4}{3^4}$$

$$= \frac{16}{81}$$

Hence, the correct option is (C).

29. Given:

$$(3^5)^x \div (9)^{2x-1} = 243$$

$$\Rightarrow (3)^{5x} \div (3^2)^{2x-1} = (3)^5$$

$$\Rightarrow (3)^{5x} \div (3)^{4x-2} = (3)^5$$

$$\Rightarrow (3)^{5x-4x+2\}} = (3)^5$$

$$\Rightarrow (3)^{x+2} = (3)^5$$

Equating powers,

$$\Rightarrow x + 2 = 5$$

$$\Rightarrow x = 5 - 2 = 3$$

Also, $(5)^{x-2y} \times (5)^{x+y} = 625$

$$\Rightarrow (5)^{(x-2y+x+y)} = (5)^4$$

$$\Rightarrow (5)^{2x-y} = (5)^4$$

Equating powers,

$$\Rightarrow 2x - y = 4$$

Substituting for 'x'

$$\Rightarrow 2(3) - y = 4$$

$$\Rightarrow y = 6 - 4 = 2$$

$$\therefore (x - y) = 3 - 2 = 1$$

Hence, the correct option is (B).

30. Given-

$$\sqrt{72 + \sqrt{72 + \sqrt{72 + \sqrt{72 + ---\infty}}}}$$

Let $\sqrt{72 + \sqrt{72 + \sqrt{72 + \sqrt{72 + ---\infty}}}} = a$

$$\Rightarrow a = \sqrt{72 + a}$$

$$\Rightarrow a^2 = 72 + a$$

$$\Rightarrow a^2 - a - 72 = 0$$

$$\Rightarrow a^2 - 9a + 8a - 72 = 0$$

$$\Rightarrow a(a - 9) + 8(a - 9) = 0$$

$$\Rightarrow (a - 9)(a + 8) = 0$$

$$\Rightarrow a = 9, -8$$

A square root value cannot be negative. So $a = -8$ is not possible.

$$\Rightarrow a = 9$$

$$\Rightarrow \sqrt{72 + \sqrt{72 + \sqrt{72 + \sqrt{72 + ---\infty}}}} = 9$$

Hence, the correct option is (A).

31. Given,

$$= \frac{1}{\left(1 + \frac{x^b}{x^a} + \frac{x^c}{x^a}\right)} + \frac{1}{\left(1 + \frac{x^a}{x^b} + \frac{x^c}{x^b}\right)} + \frac{1}{\left(1 + \frac{x^b}{x^c} + \frac{x^a}{x^c}\right)}$$

We know that,

$$= \frac{x^a}{(x^a + x^b + x^c)} + \frac{x^b}{(x^a + x^b + x^c)} + \frac{x^a}{(x^a + x^b + x^c)}$$

$$= \frac{(x^a + x^b + x^c)}{(x^a + x^b + x^c)}$$

$$= 1$$

Hence, the correct option is (B).

32. Given-

$$\sqrt{20 - \sqrt{20 - \sqrt{20 - \dots \infty}}}$$

Let $\sqrt{20 - \sqrt{20 - \sqrt{20 - \dots \infty}}} = x$

$\Rightarrow x = \sqrt{20 - x}$

$\Rightarrow x^2 = 20 - x$

$\Rightarrow x^2 + x - 20 = 0$

$\Rightarrow x^2 + 5x - 4x - 20 = 0$

$\Rightarrow x(x + 5) - 4(x + 5) = 0$

$\Rightarrow (x + 5)(x - 4) = 0$

$\Rightarrow x = -5, 4$

A square root value cannot be negative. So $x = -5$ is not possible.

$\Rightarrow x = 4$

$\Rightarrow \sqrt{20 - \sqrt{20 - \sqrt{20 - \dots \infty}}} = 4$

Hence, the correct option is (A).

33. Given,

$$\sqrt{4624} = 68$$

$\Rightarrow ? = \sqrt{46.24} + \sqrt{0.4624} + \sqrt{0.004624}$

$\Rightarrow ? = \sqrt{(4624 \times 10^{-2})} + \sqrt{(4624 \times 10^{-4})} + \sqrt{(4624 \times 10^{-6})}$

$\Rightarrow \frac{68}{10} + \frac{68}{100} + \frac{68}{1000}$

$\Rightarrow ? = 6.8 + 0.68 + 0.068$

$\therefore ? = 7.548$

Hence, the correct option is (A).

34. Given,

$$\left(\frac{4^{-2} \times 3^2}{4 \times 3^{-4}}\right)^{\frac{1}{3}} \times \frac{4^{-3} \times 3^3}{4^{-4} \times 3^6}$$

$= (4^{-3} \times 3^6)^{\frac{1}{3}} \times 4^1 \times 3^{-3}$

$= 4^{-1} \times 3^2 \times 4^1 \times 3^{-3}$

$= 4^0 \times 3^{-1}$

$= 1 \times \frac{1}{3}$

$= \frac{1}{3}$

$\therefore$ The required will be $\frac{1}{3}$.

Hence, the correct option is (C).

35. Given,

$$\sqrt{5} + \sqrt{12 - 2\sqrt{35}}$$

$= \sqrt{5} + \sqrt{(\sqrt{7})^2 + (\sqrt{5})^2 - 2(\sqrt{7} \cdot \sqrt{5})}$

$= \sqrt{5} + \sqrt{(\sqrt{7} - \sqrt{5})^2}$

$= \sqrt{5} + \sqrt{7} - \sqrt{5}$

$= \sqrt{7}$

$\therefore$ The value of the given expression is $\sqrt{7}$.

Hence, the correct option is (C).

36. Given:

Number = $28^{144} + 33^{168}$

Calculation:

28^{144} can be written as: $(28^4)^{36}$

33^{168} can be written as: $(33^4)^{42}$

We know that:

Unit digit of (Any even number)^{4n} = 6

Unit digit of (Any odd number)^{4n} = 1

Required unit digit = 6 + 1

= 7

Hence, the correct option is (C).

37. Given number is $(2023)^{2023}$

Unit digit of the given number (base) is 3, and its cyclicity 4. So,

Step 1: $\frac{2023}{4} \Rightarrow$ Remainder = 3

Step 2: $3^3 = 27$

Step 3: Unit digit of 27 is 7. So,

Unit digit of $(2023)^{2023}$ will be 7.

Hence, the correct option is (C).

38. Given:

$x = (433)^{24} - (377)^{38} + (166)^{54}$

Unit digit of x = Unit digit of $(433)^{24}$ – Unit digit of $(377)^{38}$ + Unit digit of $(166)^{54}$

$\Rightarrow$ Unit digit of $(433)^{(4 \times 5) + 4}$ – Unit digit of $(377)^{(4 \times 9) + 2}$ + 6 (as Unit digit of $(166)^{54}$)

Now,

$\Rightarrow$ Unit digit of $(433)^4 = 1$

$\Rightarrow$ Unit digit of $(377)^2 = 9$

$\Rightarrow$ Unit digit of $(166)^2 = 6$

So, Unit digit of x = $(1 - 9 + 6)$

$\Rightarrow x = (7 - 9)$

$\Rightarrow$ Or, x = $(17 - 9)$

$\Rightarrow x = 8$

$\therefore$ The required unit digit of x is 8.

Hence, the correct option is (C).

39. Unit digit of $(164)^{169} + (333)^{337} - (727)^{726}$

To check unit place divide power by 4

$4^{169} + 3^{337} - 7^{726}$

$\Rightarrow \dfrac{69}{4} = $ Reminder 1

$\Rightarrow \dfrac{37}{4} = $ Reminder 1

$\Rightarrow \dfrac{26}{4} = $ Reminder 2

$= 4^1 + 3^1 - 7^2$

$= 4 + 3 - 9$

$= 7 - 9$

or, $17 - 9$

$= 8$

So, the unit digit of number x is 8.

Hence, the correct option is (D).

40. Given:

The expression 67^{32}.

Calculation:

Unit digit of 67^{32} is 7^{32}

Now, $7^1 = 7$, $7^2 = 49$, $7^3 = 343$, $7^4 = 2401$, $7^5 = 16807$

Then unit digit is repeated here n = 4

7^{32} is written as $7^{28} \times 7^4 = 1 \times 1$

The unit digit of $7^{32} = 1 \times 1 = 1$

$\therefore$ The unit digit is 1.

Hence, the correct option is (A).

41. Given:

$(217)^{413} \times (819)^{547} \times (414)^{624} \times (342)^{812}$

Concept:

Cyclicity of 7 is 4

Cyclicity of 9 is 2

Cyclicity of 4 is 2

Cyclicity of 2 is 4

According to cyclicity theorem, dividing the powers by 4 and taking reminders (otherwise 4)

Calculation:

Unit digit of $(217)^{413} = 7^{413} = 7^{(4 \times 103) + 1} = 7^1 = 7$

Unit digit of $(819)^{547} = 9^{547} = 9^{(2 \times 273) + 1} = 9^1 = 9$

Unit digit of $(414)^{624} = 4^{624} = 4^{(2 \times 312)} = 4^4 = 6$

Unit digit of $(342)^{812} = 2^{812} = 2^{(4 \times 203)} = 2^4 = 6$

Unit digit of the this expression will be same as the unit digit of $7^{413} \times 9^{547} \times 4^{624} \times 2^{812}$

$= 7^1 \times 9^3 \times 4^4 \times 2^4$

For Unit digit: $7 \times 9 \times 6 \times 6$

$\therefore$ Unit Digit = 8

Hence, the correct option is (D).

42. Given conditions are a < b and c < b

If b = 9, a can take any numbers between 1 and 8 and c can take any numbers between 0 and 8

Total combination of such numbers = 8 × 9 = 72

If b = 8, a can take any numbers between 1 and 7 and c can take any numbers between 0 and 7

Total combination of such numbers = 7 x 8 = 56

Similarly add all combinations till b = 1

$= 8 \times 9 + 7 \times 8 + 6 \times 7 + 5 \times 6 + 4 \times 5 + 3 \times 4 + 2 \times 3 + 1 \times 2$

$= 240$

Hence, the correct option is (B).

43. We need to maximize each median in order to have the overall maximum median possible.

The highest possible median is 50 as they should be 5 numbers higher than the median in the group of 11. So, if we have a set that has a, b, c, d, e, 50, 51, 52, 53, 54, 55, the median will be 50. In this set, it is best not to waste any high values on a, b, c, d or e as these do not affect the median. So, a set that reads as 1, 2, 3, 4, 5, 50, 51, 52, 53, 54, 55 will also have median 50.

The next set can be 6, 7, 8, 9, 10, 44, 45, 46, 47, 48, 49. The median will be 44.

The medians of the 5 groups can be 50, 44, 38, 32, 26. The highest possible average of the medians will be 38.

Hence, the correct option is (D).

44. Given:

$n^2 + 5n + 6$

$(n + 2) (n + 3)$

$(n + 2)$ and $(n + 3)$ are two consecutive numbers.

One of $(n + 2)$ or $(n + 3)$ has to be even.

We need n such that $(n + 2) (n + 3)$ is a multiple of 3.

$(n + 2)$ or $(n + 3)$ should be a multiple of 3.

n leaves a remainder of 0 or 1 when divided by 3.

n could be 1, 3, 4, 6, 7, 9, 10, 12, 13, 15, 16, 18 ....

So, from among the first 99 natural numbers, N cannot take 2, 5, 8, 11, 14.......98.

There are 33 numbers in this list – we are effectively listing all numbers {3 × 0 + 2, 3 × 1 + 2, 3 × 3 + 2, ...3 × 32 + 2}.

So, N can take 99 – 33 = 66 values.

Hence, the correct option is (C).

45. Two digit numbers; The two digits can be 4 and 7: Two possibilities 47 and 74.

Three-digit numbers: The three digits can be 1, 4 and 7: 3! Or 6 possibilities.

We cannot have three digits as (2, 2, 7) as the digits have to be distinct.

We cannot have numbers with 4 digits or more without repeating the digits.

So, there are totally 8 numbers.

Hence, the correct option is (C).

46. For unit digit divide the power of any integer by 4 and the remainder is the cycle for unit digit of the number

∴ Unit digit of 541

$\Rightarrow \dfrac{41}{4} = 1$ is the remainder i.e. cycle of 1

$\Rightarrow 51 = 5$

Unit digit of 769

$\Rightarrow \dfrac{69}{4} = 1$ is the remainder

$\Rightarrow 71 = 7$

Unit digit of 357

$\Rightarrow \dfrac{57}{4} = 1$ is the remainder

$\Rightarrow 31 = 3$

∴ Unit digit of 541 × 769 × 357 = 5 × 7 × 3 = 105 or 5 is the unit digit

Hence, the correct option is (B).

47. Given:

$(144^{23} + 67^3)$

Formula:

Unit digit of a number is the digit in the one's place of the number.

Calculation:

Unit digit of 144^{23} = Unit digit of (4^{23}) = Unit digit of (4^3) = Unit digit of $(64) = 4$

Unit digit of 67^3 = Unit digit of (7^3) = Unit digit of $(343) = 3$

Unit digit of $(144^{23} + 67^3) = 4 + 3 = 7$

∴ Unit digit is 7.

Hence, the correct option is (D).

48. Considering the given number 5, 7, 8

LCM of (5, 7, 8) = 280

⇒ The number be 280n + 4

We can write this number as 273n + 7n + 4

Here, 273n will be completely divisible by 13 for all values of n

Now,

7n + 4 = 13 or any multiple of 13

⇒ n = 5 in order to get the least number divisible by 13

⇒ Number = 280 × 5 + 4 = 1404

But this number is not in option. So, next satisfying value of n = 18

∴ The required number will be 280 × 18 + 4 = 5044

Hence, the correct option is (B).

49. Given:

Number 42x73y is divisible by 72

72 = 8 × 9

So, the number is divisible by 8 and 9.

Concept:

Divisibility of 8 = last three digits of the number must be divisible by 8.

Here, 73y must be divisible by 8

⇒ y = 6 as 736 is divisible by 8

Divisibility of 9: if the sum of digits of the number is divisible by 9, then the number itself is divisible by 9.

⇒ 42x73y:

Sum = 4 + 2 + x + 7 + 3 + y = 16 + x + y

⇒ 16 + x + 6 = 22 + x

⇒ 22 + x; must be divisible by 9

⇒ x = 5 as 27 is divisible by 9

$\Rightarrow$ 5x - 3y = 5 × 5 − 3 × 6 = 25 - 18 = 7

Hence, the correct option is (A).

50. Sum of the odd place digits = 2 + 7 + 8 = 17

Sum of the even place digits = 5 + x

Difference between the sum of the odd place digits and sum of the even place digits,

= 17 − (5 + x)

= 12 − x

We can see only for x = 1, 12 − x = 11

Value of x = 1

∴ The value of x is 1.

Hence, the correct option is (D).

51. Concept:

We have

$(x + y)^n = {}^nC_0x^n + {}^nC_1x^{n-1} \cdot y + {}^nC_2x^{n-2} \cdot y^2 + \ldots + {}^nC_ny^n$

General term: General term in the expansion of $(x + y)^n$ is given by: $T_{(r+1)} = {}^nC_r \times x^{n-r} \times y^r$

Calculation:

We have to find term independent of x in $\left(x^2 - \dfrac{1}{x^3}\right)^{10}$

We know that,

$T_{(r+1)} = {}^nC_r \times x^{n-r} \times y^r$

$\Rightarrow T_{(r+1)} = {}^{10}C_r \times (x^2)^{10-r} \times \left(\dfrac{-1}{x^3}\right)^r$

$= (-1)^r \times {}^{10}C_r \times (x)^{20-2r} \times (x^3)^{-r}$

$= (-1)^r \times {}^{10}C_r \times (x)^{20-2r} \times (x)^{-3r}$

$= (-1)^r \times {}^{10}C_r \times (x)^{20-5r}$

For the term independent of x, power of x should be zero

Therefore, 20 − 5r = 0

$\Rightarrow$ r = 4

$T_{(4+1)} = (-1)^4 \times {}^{10}C_4 = {}^{10}C_4$

Hence, the correct option is (D).

52. Formula:

General Term in the expansion $(x - y)^n = T_{r+1} = (-1)^r \times {}^nC_r \times x^{n-r} \times y^r$

The number of terms in the expansion of $\left(4x - \dfrac{x^3}{2}\right)^9$ is 10 (even).

So, there are two middle terms. i.e. $\left(\dfrac{9+1}{2}\right)$th and $\left(\dfrac{9+3}{2}\right)$th terms.

They are given by T_5 and T_6.

$T_{r+1} = {}^nC_r x^{n-r} a^r$

Required term

$T_5 = T_{4+1} = {}^9C_4(4x)^5\left(-\dfrac{x^3}{2}\right)^4$

$\Rightarrow T_5 = {}^9C_4 4^5 x^5\left(\dfrac{1}{2^4}\right)x^{12}$

$\Rightarrow T_5 = {}^9C_4 4^3 x^{17}$

$T_6 = T_{5+1} = {}^9C_5(4x)^4\left(-\dfrac{x^3}{2}\right)^5$

$\Rightarrow T_6 = -{}^9C_5 4^4 x^4\left(\dfrac{1}{2^5}\right)x^{15}$

$\Rightarrow T_6 = -{}^9C_5\left(\dfrac{2^8}{2^5}\right)x^{19}$

$\Rightarrow T_6 = -{}^9C_5 2^3 x^{19}$

Hence, the correct option is (C).

53. The expansion of $12x^2y$ is $3 \times 2 \times 2 \times x \times x \times x \times y$

And that of $18xy^2$ is $3 \times 3 \times 2 \times x \times x \times y \times y$

By factorization, we see that the term $2, 3, x, y$ are common to both. So, the common factors of the given terms is $6xy$.

So, the correct option is (A).

54. We need to find common factors of $4\,m^2, 6\,m^2, 8\,m^3$

The factor of $4\,m^2 = 2 \times 2 \times m \times m$,

$6\,m^2 = 3 \times 2 \times m \times m$

and that of $8\,m^3 = 2 \times 2 \times 2 \times m \times m \times m$

Therefore, the common factors are $2 \times m \times m = 2\,m^2$.

Hence, the correct option is (B).

55. Concept:

N = a^p × b^q × c^r Where a and b are odd prime factors and c is even prime factor of N.

Number of factors of N = (p + 1) × (q + 1) × (r + 1)

Number of odd factors of N = (p + 1) × (q + 1)

Number of even factors of N = (p + 1) × (q + 1) × r

Number of prime factors = p + q + r

Calculation:

7392 = 3 × 7 × 11 × 32

= 2^5 × 3 × 7 × 11

Number of even factors = (1 + 1) × (1 + 1) × (1 + 1) × 5

= 2 × 2 × 2 × 5

$\Rightarrow$ A = 40

Number of prime factors = 5 + 1 + 1 + 1

$\Rightarrow$ B = 8

$\therefore$ A = 40 = 5B

Hence, the correct option is (C).

56. Given:

$$x^8 - y^8$$

$$[\because a^2 - b^2 = (a + b)(a - b)]$$

$$= (x^4)^2 - (y^4)^2$$

$$= (x^4 + y^4)(x^4 - y^4)$$

$$= (x^4 + y^4)[(x^2)^2 - (y^2)^2]$$

$$= (x^4 + y^4)(x^2 + y^2)(x^2 - y^2)$$

$$= (x^4 + y^4)(x^2 + y^2)(x + y)(x - y)$$

Hence, the correct option is (D).

57. Given:

$$\sqrt{1600} - \sqrt[3]{8000} = (10)^x + 10$$

$$\Rightarrow 40 - 20 = (10)^x + 10$$

$$\Rightarrow 20 = (10)^x + 10$$

$$\Rightarrow 20 - 10 = (10)^x$$

$$\Rightarrow 10 = (10)^x$$

On comparing powers,

$$\Rightarrow x = 1$$

$\therefore$ The value of x is 1.

Hence, the correct option is (C).

58. Given:

$$(10)^2 + (243)^{\frac{1}{5}} - 5 = -(7)^3 + (?)^2$$

According to the rule 'Brackets' should be solved first

$$\Rightarrow (10)^2 + (243)^{\frac{1}{5}} - 5 = (?)^2 - (7)^3$$

$$\Rightarrow 100 + 3 - 5 = (?)^2 - 343$$

$$\Rightarrow 103 - 5 + 343 = (?)^2$$

$$\Rightarrow 446 - 5 = (?)^2$$

$$\Rightarrow ? = \sqrt{441}$$

$$\Rightarrow ? = 21$$

$\therefore$ The required answer is 21.

Hence, the correct option is (D).

59. Let,

$$P(x) = 4x^3 + 12x^2 - x - 3$$

$$\Rightarrow P(x) = 4x^2(x + 3) - 1(x + 3)$$

$$\Rightarrow P(x) = (4x^2 - 1)(x + 3)$$

We know that, $(a^2 - b^2) = (a + b)(a - b)$

$$\Rightarrow P(x) = (2x - 1)(2x + 1)(x + 3)$$

We can see that, $(2x - 1) \& (2x + 1)$ are factor of polynomial.

$\therefore 4x^3 + 12x^2 - x - 3$ is divisible by both $(2x + 1)$ and $(2x - 1)$

Hence, the correct option is (C).

60. S = XYZ + YZX + ZXY

S = 100X + 10Y + Z + 100Y + 10Z + X + 100Z + 10X + Y

S = 111X + 111Y + 111Z

S = 111 (X + Y + Z)

We can observe here:

111 is divisible by 3 and 37.

So, S will be divisible by (X + Y + Z), 3 and 37 always.

$\therefore$ 1 and 3 are correct

On Checking statement 2:

take X = 1, Y = 2 & Z = 4

We get S = 111 (1 + 2 + 4) = 777

Which is not divisible by 9.

So, S will not be always divisible by 9.

$\therefore$ 2 is incorrect.

Hence, the correct option is (D).

Q.1 If x is a negative real number, then which of the following are not correct?

1. There is some natural number k such that $kx > 0$

2. $x^2 + x > 0$ always

3. $2x < x < -x$

4. x^2 is always a rational number

Select the correct answer using the code given below:

A. 1,2 and 3

B. 1,2 and 4

C. 1,3 and 4

D. 2,3 and 4

Q.2 The values of x satisfying $\frac{1}{2}\left(\frac{3}{5}x + 4\right) \geq \frac{1}{3}(x - 6)$ are:

A. $x \geq 120$

B. $x \leq 120$

C. $x \leq 12$

D. $x \geq 12$

Q.3 If $4 \leq 2x \leq 12$ and $6 \leq \frac{y}{2} \leq 14$, then find the maximum value of $\left(\frac{y}{x}\right)$

A. 14

B. 28

C. 7

D. 2

Q.4 If y is the smallest negative integer and m is any whole number, then which of the following statements are correct?

1. $ym \leq 0$

2. $y^2 - my - 1 \geq 0$

3. $2y \leq y \leq -my$

4. $y^2 \geq m$

Select the correct answer using the code given below:

A. 1,2 and 4

B. 2,3 and 4

C. 1,2 and 3

D. 1,3 and 4

Q.5 Find the value of x and y by solving given equations.

a) 3x + 6y = 159

b) 4x – 3y = 25

A. 17, 15

B. 19, 13

C. 15, 19

D. 19, 17

Q.6 A man gets Rs. 40 if he works for a day, and is fined 10% of this amount if he is absent for a day. After 60 days, if he receives a total of Rs. 1300, find the no. of days he was absent from work.

A. 25

B. 15

C. 10

D. 20

Q.7 Find the value of x + y + z, if x + y + xy = 3, y + z + yz = 8 and x + z + xz = 15.

A. $\frac{43}{6}$

B. $\frac{41}{6}$

C. $\frac{59}{6}$

D. $\frac{53}{6}$

Q.8 The parking charges of bike, car and bus are Rs. 20, Rs. 30 and Rs. 50 respectively. If total Rs. 4420 are collected from the parking and numbers of total vehicles are 159 then find the number of cars in the parking. Number of cars are 4 more than the twice the number of buses.

A. 48

B. 56

C. 44

D. 52

Q.9 On comparing the ratios $\frac{a_1}{a_2}, \frac{b_1}{b_2}$ and $\frac{c_1}{c_2}$, find out whether the following pairs of linear equations are consistent, or inconsistent.

$$2x - 3y = 8, 4x - 6y = 9$$

A. Consistent

B. Inconsistent

C. Ambiguous

D. Data insufficient

Q.10 If α and β are the zeros of the quadratic polynomial $f(x) = x^2 - 5x + 6$, find the value of $(\alpha^2\beta + \beta^2\alpha)$.

A. 20

B. 30

C. 50

D. 60

Q.11 If the roots of the equation $x^2 + bx + c = 0$ are two consecutive integers, then $b^2 - 4ac$ is equal to:

A. 0

B. 1

C. 2

D. 3

Q.12 If a is a perfect square, what is the value of a, given that $a^x = \frac{1}{8}$ and $x = \frac{3}{2}[(\log_2 a) - 3]$?

A. 2

B. 4

C. 16

D. 64

Q.13 Solve for x, if $\log_x[\log 5 \left(\sqrt{x + 5} + \sqrt{x}\right)] = 0$

A. 6

B. 5

C. 4

D. 7

Q.14 What is the value of $\log_3 5 \cdot \log_{25} 27$?

A. $\frac{1}{2}$

B. 2

C. $\frac{3}{2}$

D. 3

Q.15 What is the value of $\log_9 27 - \log_{27} 9$?

A. 1

B. $\frac{1}{2}$

C. $\frac{5}{6}$

D. $\frac{2}{3}$

Q.16 If $2\log_{10}(x + 1) = \log_{10}(7x + 1)$, then find the non-zero value of 'x'?

A. 4

B. 5

C. 6

D. 7

Q.17 If the function $f(x) = x^3 + e^{\frac{x}{2}}$ and $g(x) = f^{-1}(x)$, then the value of $g'(1)$ is:

A. 2

B. −2

C. 1

D. 0

Q.18 Given function $f(x) = \left(\frac{e^{2z}-1}{e^{2z}+1}\right)$ is:

A. Increasing

B. Decreasing

C. Even

D. None of the above

Q.19 Find the domain and range of following function

$$f(x) = \sqrt{25 - x^2}$$

A. [-5,5], [0,5]

B. [- 3,3], [- 3,3]

C. [-4,4], [4,0]

D. None of the above

Q.20 If $f(x) = x$ and $g(x) = \cos x$ then find the value of $g \circ f\left(\frac{\pi}{3}\right)$?

A. 1

B. - 1

C. $\frac{1}{2}$

D. $-\frac{1}{2}$

Q.21 The function f defined by $f(x) = x^3 - 3x^2 + 5x + 7$, is:

[JEE Main Advanced, 2017]

A. Increasing in R.
B. Decreasing in R.
C. Decreasing in $(0, \infty)$ and increasing in $(-\infty, 0)$
D. Increasing in $(0, \infty)$ and decreasing in $(-\infty, 0)$

Q.22 The domain of the function $f(x) = \sqrt{1 - \sqrt{1 - \sqrt{1 - x^2}}}$ is:

[UPSESSB TGT Mathematics, 2013]

A. $\{x \mid x < 1\}$
B. $\{x \mid x > -1\}$
C. $[0,1]$
D. $[-1,1]$

Q.23 If $f: R \to R$ is a function defined by $f(x) = [x - 1]\cos\left(\dfrac{2x-1}{2}\right)\pi$. where, [.] denotes the greatest integer function, then f is:

A. Discontinuous at all integral values of x except at $x = 1$
B. Continuous only at $x = 1$
C. Continuous for every real x
D. Discontinuous only at $x = 1$

Q.24 The function $f(x) = \dfrac{4x^3 - 3x^2}{6} - 2\sin x + (2x - 1)\cos x$:

A. Increases in $\left[\dfrac{1}{2}, \infty\right)$
B. Increases in $\left[-\infty, \dfrac{1}{2}\right)$
C. Decreases in $\left[\dfrac{1}{2}, \infty\right)$
D. Decreases in $\left(-\infty, \dfrac{1}{2}\right]$

Q.25 Find the real and imaginary part of the complex number $z = \dfrac{1-i}{i}$

A. 1 ,1
B. -1 ,1
C. 1 , -1
D. -1 , -1

Q.26 If rectangular form of complex number is shown as $z = \dfrac{5}{2} + \dfrac{5\sqrt{3}}{2}i$ then its polar form is represented as-

A. $5\left(\cos\left(\dfrac{2\pi}{3}\right) - i\sin\left(\dfrac{2\pi}{3}\right)\right)$
B. $5\left(\cos\left(\dfrac{\pi}{3}\right) - i\sin\left(\dfrac{\pi}{3}\right)\right)$
C. $5\left(\cos\left(\dfrac{2\pi}{3}\right) + i\sin\left(\dfrac{2\pi}{3}\right)\right)$
D. $5\left(\cos\left(\dfrac{\pi}{3}\right) + i\sin\left(\dfrac{\pi}{3}\right)\right)$

Q.27 The value of $\left(\dfrac{\cos\theta + i\sin\theta}{i\cos\theta + \sin\theta}\right)^4$ is:

[UPSESSB TGT Mathematics, 2013]

A. $\cos 4\theta + i\sin 4\theta$
B. $\cos 8\theta + i\sin 8\theta$
C. $\cos 8\theta - i\sin 8\theta$
D. $\cos 4\theta - i\sin 4\theta$

Q.28 If $iz^3 + z^2 - z + i = 0$, then the value of $|z|$ is:

[UPSESSB TGT Mathematics, 2013]

A. 1
B. -1
C. 2
D. 3

Q.29 If $2 + i$ is a root of the equation $x^2 - ax + 1 = 0$, then the value of a is:

[UPSESSB TGT Mathematics, 2013]

A. 2
B. 4
C. 1
D. 0

Q.30 Nature of the triangle formed by the points representing the complex numbers $3 + 4i, 8 - 6i$ and $13 + 9i$ is:

[UPSESSB TGT Mathematics, 2013]

A. Equilateral triangle
B. Right-angled triangle
C. Acute-angled triangle
D. Obtuse-angled triangle

Q.31 If $z = e^{i\theta}$, then the value of $\dfrac{z^2 - 1}{z^2 + 1}$ is:

[UPSESSB TGT Mathematics, 2013]

A. $i\tan\theta$
B. $\tan\theta$
C. $\cot\theta$
D. $i\sec^2\theta$

Q.32 $i^{1000} + i^{1001} + i^{1002} + i^{1003}$ is equal to: (where $i = \sqrt{-1}$)

A. 0
B. i
C. -i
D. 1

Q.33 If α, β are the different complex numbers with $|\beta| = 1$, then find $\left|\dfrac{\beta - \alpha}{1 - \overline{\alpha}\beta}\right|$?

A. 3
B. 2
C. 1
D. 0

Q.34 The number of non-zero integral solutions of the equation $|1 - 2i|^x = 5^x$ is:

A. 0
B. 1
C. 2
D. 3

Q.35 If $(p - x)(p - y) = 1$ and $(x - y = \sqrt{5})$, then, the value of $(p - y)^3 - \dfrac{1}{(p-y)^3}$ is -

A. $4\sqrt{5}$
B. $8\sqrt{5}$
C. $6\sqrt{7}$
D. $10\sqrt{5}$

Q.36 What is the value of $\log_9 27 + \log_8 32$?

A. $\dfrac{7}{2}$
B. $\dfrac{19}{6}$
C. 4
D. 7

Q.37 If 0 < a < 1, the value of log10 a is negative. This is justified by :

A. Negative power of 10 is less than 1
B. Negative power of 10 is between 0 and 1
C. Negative power of 10 is positive
D. Negative power of 10 is negative

Q.38 The value of $(\log_3 4)(\log_4 5)(\log_5 6)(\log_6 7)(\log_7 8)(\log_8 9)$ is:

[UPSESSB TGT Mathematics, 2016]

A. 2
B. 7
C. 8
D. 33

Q.39 If $x = 8 - 2\sqrt{15}$, then find the value of $\left(\dfrac{x+1}{\sqrt{x}}\right)^2$

A. $15 - \dfrac{3\sqrt{15}}{2}$
B. $17 - \dfrac{3\sqrt{15}}{2}$
C. $14 - \dfrac{5\sqrt{15}}{2}$
D. $12 - \dfrac{3\sqrt{15}}{2}$

Q.40 Consider the following inequalities:

1. $\dfrac{a^2-b^2}{a^2+b^2} > \dfrac{a-b}{a+b}$ where $a > b > 0$

2. $\dfrac{a^3+b^3}{a^2+b^2} > \dfrac{a^2+b^2}{a+b}$ only when $a > b > 0$ Which of the above is/are correct?

A. 1 only
B. 2 only
C. Both 1 and 2
D. Neither 1 nor 2

Q.41 If α and β are two real numbers such that $\alpha + \beta = -\dfrac{q}{p}$ and $\alpha\beta = \dfrac{r}{p}$, where $1 < p < q < r$, then which one of the following is the greatest?

A. $\dfrac{1}{\alpha+\beta}$
B. $\dfrac{1}{\alpha}+\dfrac{1}{\beta}$
C. $-\dfrac{1}{\alpha\beta}$
D. $\dfrac{\alpha\beta}{\alpha+\beta}$

Q.42 If $a = (0.05)^2$, $b = \dfrac{1}{(0.05)^2}$ and $c = 1 - (0.05)^2 - 0.995$, then which of the following is correct.

A. $a > b < c$
B. $a \geq c < b$
C. $a = c > b$
D. $a = c < b$

Q.43 Solve for x, if given, $4^{x+2} + 4^{2x+1} = 1280$.

A. 2
B. 4
C. 6
D. 8

Q.44 The minimum possible value of the sum of squares of the roots of the equation $x^2 + (a+3)x - (a+5) = 0$.

A. 1
B. 2
C. 3
D. 4

Q.45 What will be the range of the expression $\dfrac{x-2}{x^2+x+3}$, where x is real ?

A. $-1,\dfrac{1}{11}$
B. $[1,\dfrac{1}{11}]$
C. $(1,\dfrac{-1}{11}]$
D. $[-1,\dfrac{1}{11}]$

Q.46 The equation x² - 2x - 8 = 0 will have :

A. the numerically larger root as negative
B. the numerically larger root as positive
C. both roots as negative
D. both roots as positive

Q.47 If $x + \dfrac{1}{x} = \sqrt{2}$, then find $x^{80} + x^{76} + x^{72} + x^{68} + x^{64} + 4$:

A. 5
B. 6
C. 8
D. 4

Q.48 Find the quadratic equation whose roots are the reciprocals of the roots of 3x² − 8x + 4 = 0.

A. -4x² + 8x + 9 = 0
B. -8x² + 4x + 4 = 0
C. 4x² − 8x + 3 = 0
D. 8x² - 3x - 4 = 0

Q.49 If $20^{(\log_7 y)} = 800 - y^{(\log_7 20)}$ what is the value of $\log_{49} y$:

A. 0
B. 1
C. 2
D. 3

Q.50 If $\log_3 9 \times \log_9 27 \times \log_{27} 81 \times \ldots\ldots\times n^{\text{th}}$ term $= 21$, then the value of 'n' is:

A. 19
B. 20
C. 18
D. 21

Q.51 Given that $f(t) + f(2t) + f(3t) = g(t)$ and $g(t+6) = g(t-2) + 7$. If $g(8) = 22$, then what is the value of $f(0)$?

A. 10
B. 5
C. 8
D. 15

Q.52 The set of all real numbers x for which $x^2 - |x+2| + x > 0$:

A. $(-\infty, -2) \cup (\sqrt{2}, \infty)$
B. $(-\infty, -2) \cup (2, \infty)$
C. $(-\infty, -\sqrt{2}) \cup (\sqrt{2}, \infty)$
D. $(-\infty, -1) \cup (1, \infty)$

Q.53 If $\dfrac{x}{(y+z-x)} = \dfrac{y}{(z+x-y)} = \dfrac{z}{(x+y-z)} = r$, then r cannot take any value except :

A. $\dfrac{-1}{2}$
B. 1
C. 1 or $\dfrac{-1}{2}$
D. -1 or $\dfrac{1}{2}$

Q.54 Cost of 8 pencils, 5 pens and 3 erasers is Rs. 111. Cost of 9 pencils, 6 pens and 5 erasers is Rs. 130. Cost of 16 pencils, 11 pens and 3 erasers is Rs. 221. What is the cost (in Rs) of 39 pencils, 26 pens and 13 erasers?

A. 316
B. 546
C. 624
D. 482

Q.55 A piece of cloth costs Rs. 35. If the piece were 4 m longer and each meter was to cost Rs. 1 lesser, then the total cost would remain unchanged. How long is the piece of cloth?

A. 10 m
B. 14 m
C. 12 m
D. 8 m

A. B
B. D
C. C
D. A

Q.56 If $a + b + c = 9, ab + bc + ca = 26, a^3 + b^3 = 91, b^3 + c^3 = 72$ and $c^3 + a^3 = 35$, then what is the value of abc?

A. 48
B. 24
C. 36
D. 42

Q.57 What is $\dfrac{1}{\log_2 N} + \dfrac{1}{\log_3 N} + \dfrac{1}{\log_4 N} + \cdots + \dfrac{1}{\log_{100} N}$ equal to $(N \neq 1)$?

A. $\dfrac{1}{\log_{100!} N}$
B. $\dfrac{1}{\log_{99!} N}$
C. $\dfrac{99}{\log_{100!} N}$
D. $\dfrac{99}{\log_{99!} N}$

Q.58 X attempts 100 questions and gets 340 marks. If for every correct answer is 4 marks and wrong answer is negative one mark, then the number of questions wrongly answered by Mr. X is:

A. 14
B. 15
C. 12
D. 13

Q.59 If the system of equations 2x - 3y - 3 and -4x + qy $\dfrac{-p}{2}$ is inconsistent which of the following cannot be the value of p ?

A. -18
B. -24
C. -12
D. -36

Q.60 Jatin purchases 2 Mobile Phones and 1 Refrigerator for Rs. 50,000. Antim purchases 3 Mobile Phones and 2 Refrigerators for Rs. 85,000. Kanta wants to purchases 2 Mobile Phones and 2 Refrigerators. Then, he has to pay :

A. 50,000
B. 40,000
C. 70,000
D. 60,000

// Smart Answer Sheet //

Correct Indicates percentage of students who answered questions correctly.

Skipped Indicates percentage of students who skipped questions.

Q.	Ans.	Correct / Skipped
1	B	45.1 % / 49.25 %
2	B	57.72 % / 39.09 %
3	A	43.67 % / 46.79 %
4	C	54.21 % / 31.28 %
5	D	57.19 % / 32.3 %
6	A	76.12 % / 22.32 %
7	A	17.73 % / 74.45 %
8	D	50.18 % / 47.99 %
9	B	64.84 % / 34.82 %
10	B	85.68 % / 13.13 %
11	B	77.82 % / 19.59 %
12	B	27.61 % / 67.73 %

Q.	Ans.	Correct / Skipped
13	C	68.61 % / 30.42 %
14	C	40.42 % / 55.9 %
15	C	62.86 % / 35.7 %
16	B	30.04 % / 69.7 %
17	A	60.03 % / 30.07 %
18	A	48.1 % / 44.92 %
19	A	69.62 % / 30.27 %
20	C	66.77 % / 30.25 %
21	A	76.08 % / 15.36 %
22	D	40.87 % / 54.44 %
23	C	62.36 % / 32.88 %
24	A	24.71 % / 69.4 %

Q.	Ans.	Correct / Skipped
25	D	53.01 % / 35.46 %
26	D	54.03 % / 31.66 %
27	B	65.78 % / 30.49 %
28	A	50.87 % / 40.97 %
29	B	79.4 % / 12.89 %
30	B	67.25 % / 32.75 %
31	A	25.29 % / 67.54 %
32	A	80.84 % / 17.47 %
33	C	51.98 % / 47.16 %
34	A	46.0 % / 33.99 %
35	B	53.7 % / 45.75 %
36	B	19.25 % / 68.96 %

Q.	Ans.	Correct / Skipped
37	B	58.17 % / 38.24 %
38	A	62.57 % / 30.66 %
39	D	55.37 % / 35.8 %
40	A	55.03 % / 32.41 %
41	C	31.77 % / 67.28 %
42	D	55.89 % / 34.42 %
43	A	56.07 % / 34.01 %
44	C	44.2 % / 39.18 %
45	D	66.64 % / 30.58 %
46	B	69.77 % / 30.2 %
47	A	23.39 % / 74.45 %
48	C	89.75 % / 10.12 %

Q.	Ans.	Correct / Skipped
49	B	81.68 % / 15.99 %
50	B	44.98 % / 38.87 %
51	B	55.73 % / 40.31 %
52	C	44.55 % / 41.39 %
53	C	51.56 % / 46.25 %
54	B	84.79 % / 10.63 %
55	D	48.2 % / 44.28 %
56	B	29.35 % / 68.55 %
57	A	57.85 % / 39.14 %
58	C	84.82 % / 11.64 %
59	C	52.99 % / 34.45 %
60	C	64.58 % / 30.95 %

Performance Analysis	
Avg. Score (%)	46.11%
Toppers Score (%)	73.89%
Your Score	

//Hints and Solutions//

1. Given,

Condition is x is a negative real number

Case 1:

If we multiply a natural number with a negative real number we will always get a negative number eg. $1 \times -2 = -2$

So, Case 1 is wrong.

Case 2:

If we take $x = -1$

$(-1)^2 + (-1)$

$1 - 1 = 0$ which is not ≥ 0

So, Case 2 is also wrong.

Case 3:

If we take $x = -1$

$2 \times (-1) < (-1) < -(-1)$

$-2 < -1 < 1$

So, Case 3 is correct.

Case 4:

If we take real number $x = -3^{\frac{1}{4}}$ then we get $x^2 = 3^{\frac{1}{2}}$ which is not a rational number

So, Case 4 is also wrong.

Hence, the correct option is (B).

2. Given,

$$\frac{1}{2}\left(\frac{3}{5}x + 4\right) \geq \frac{1}{3}(x - 6)$$

$$\left(\frac{3x}{10} + 2\right) \geq \left(\frac{x}{3} - 2\right)$$

$$\left(\frac{3x}{10} - \frac{x}{3}\right) \geq (-2 - 2)$$

$$\Rightarrow \frac{9x - 10x}{30} \geq -4$$

$$\Rightarrow \frac{-x}{30} \geq -4$$

$$\Rightarrow -x \geq -120$$

Multiply with -1 on both sides, a sign of inequality will change.

$$\therefore x \leq 120$$

Hence, the correct option is (B).

3. Given,

$$4 \leq 2x \leq 12$$

Dividing by 2 each side

$$\Rightarrow 2 \leq x \leq 6 \quad - (1)$$

Also, $6 \leq \frac{y}{2} \leq 14$

Multiplying by 2 each side

$$\Rightarrow 12 \leq y \leq 28 \quad .... (2)$$

Now, to find the maximum value of $\frac{y}{x}$, the numerator i.e., y should be bigger and the denominator i.e., x should be smaller.

Now, the smallest value of $x = 2$

And, the biggest value of $y = 28$

$$\therefore \text{The maximum value of } \left(\frac{y}{x}\right) = \frac{28}{2} = 14$$

So, the required maximum value is 14.

Hence, the correct option is (A).

4. Given,

y is the smallest negative integer and m is any whole number

From statement (1)

We know that the product of negative integer and whole number is always less than or smaller than 0 .

So, $ym \leq 0$, it is correct

From statement (2)

We know that the square of negative is always positive and product of negative integer and positive integer is always negative

So, $y^2 - my - 1 \geq 0$ always

From statement (3)

Double of negative integer is smaller than integer negative of the product of negative integer and whole number is always greater than actual number

So, $2y \leq y \leq -my$ is also correct

From statement (4)

y and m is also different numbers so it is not true $y^2 \geq m$

$\therefore$ The required answer is 1,2 , and 3.

Hence, the correct option is (C).

5. Given:

3x + 6y = 159   ----(i)

4x – 3y = 25   ----(ii)

Calculations:

Now, to equate the equation, multiply equation (ii) by 2

(4x – 3y) × 2 = 25 × 2

$\Rightarrow 8x - 6y = 50$ ----(iii)

Now, adding equation (i) and (iii)

$3x + 6y + 8x - 6y = 159 + 50$

$\Rightarrow 11x = 209$

$\Rightarrow x = 19$

Now, putting value of x in equation (ii)

$4x - 3y = 25$

$\Rightarrow 4 \times 19 - 3y = 25$

$\Rightarrow 76 - 3y = 25$

$\Rightarrow 3y = 51$

$\Rightarrow y = 17$

$\Rightarrow x = 19$

∴ The value of x is 19 and value of y is 17

Hence, the correct option is (D).

6. Calculations:

Let the no. of days for which he was absent for work be x

No. of working days = 60 – x

Amount received for working = (60 – x)40

Amount charged for absent days = $\left(\dfrac{10}{100} \times 40\right) x = 4x$

Net amount = (60 – x)40 – 4x = 1300

$\Rightarrow 2400 - 44x = 1300$

$\Rightarrow 1100 = 44x$

$\Rightarrow x = 25$

∴ The numbers of days he was absent from work are of 25 days

Hence, the correct option is (A).

7. Given:

$x + y + xy = 3$

$y + z + yz = 8$

$x + z + xz = 15$

Calculations:

$x + y + xy = 3$

Adding 1 on both sides of the equation

$1 + x + y + xy = 4$

$\Rightarrow (1 + x) + y(1 + x) = 4$

$\Rightarrow (1 + x) (1 + y) = 4$ ----(1)

Similarly performing the same on other two equations,

$y + z + yz = 8$

$1 + y + z + yz = 9$

$\Rightarrow (1 + y) + z(1 + y) = 9$

$\Rightarrow (1 + y) (1 + z) = 9$ ----(2)

$x + z + xz = 15$

$1 + x + z + xz = 16$

$\Rightarrow (1 + x) + z(1 + x) = 16$

$\Rightarrow (1 + x) (1 + z) = 16$ ----(3)

Multiplying equations (1), (2) and (3)

$[(1 + x) (1 + y) (1 + z)]2 = [4 \times 9 \times 16]$

$\Rightarrow [(1 + x) (1 + y) (1 + z)] = [2 \times 3 \times 4]$ ......(4)

From equation (1) and (4)

$(1 + z) = 6$

$\Rightarrow z = 5$

Similarly, from equation (2) and (4)

$(1 + x) = \dfrac{8}{3}$

$\Rightarrow x = \dfrac{5}{3}$

Similarly, from equation (3) and (4)

$(1 + y) = \dfrac{3}{2}$

$\Rightarrow y = \dfrac{1}{2}$

∴ $x + y + z = \dfrac{5}{3} + \dfrac{1}{2} + 5 = \dfrac{43}{6}$

Hence, the correct option is (A).

8. Given:

The parking charges of bike, car and bus are Rs. 20, Rs. 30 and Rs. 50 respectively.

Total vehicles = 159

Total charges = 4420

Calculations:

Suppose the number of bike, car and bus are x, y and z respectively

∴ $y = 2z + 4$ ----(1)

And

$x + y + z = 159$

From equation (1)

$x + 2z + 4 + z = 159$

$\Rightarrow x + 3z = 155$ ----(2)

Since total Rs. 4420 are collected from the parking;

∴ $20x + 30y + 50z = 4420$

From equation (1)

20x + 60z + 120 + 50z = 4420

$\Rightarrow$ 20x + 110z = 4300

$\Rightarrow$ 2x + 11z = 430   ----(3)

From equation (2) and (3)

5z = 430 - 310 = 120

$\Rightarrow$ z = 24

$\therefore$ y = 48 + 4 = 52

$\therefore$ Number of cars = 52

Hence, the correct option is (D).

9. The given linear equation are:

$$2x - 3y - 8 = 0$$

On comparing with standard form of linear equation, we get

$$a_1 = 2, b_1 = -3, c_1 = -8$$

Similarly, for equation $4x - 6y - 9 = 0$ on comparing, we get

$$a_2 = 4, b_2 = -6, c_2 = -9$$

Now,

$$\frac{a_1}{a_2} = \frac{2}{4} = \frac{1}{2}$$

$$\Rightarrow \frac{b_1}{b_2} = \frac{-3}{-6} = \frac{1}{2}$$

$$\Rightarrow \frac{c_1}{c_2} = \frac{-8}{-9}$$

On comparing the ratios, we get

$$\frac{a_1}{a_2} = \frac{b_1}{b_2} \neq \frac{c_1}{c_2}$$

So, the following pairs of linear equations are inconsistent.

Hence, the correct option is (B).

10. Concept:

If α and β are the roots of equation, $ax^2 + bx + c = 0$

Sum of roots $(\alpha + \beta) = \dfrac{-b}{a}$

Product of roots $(\alpha\beta) = \dfrac{c}{a}$

$$(x + y)^2 = x^2 + y^2 + 2xy$$

Given: $f(x) = x^2 - 5x + 6$

Comparing $f(x)$ with $ax^2 + bx + c = 0$, we have, $a = 1, b = -5$ and $c = 6$

Now, sum of roots $= \alpha + \beta = \dfrac{-b}{a} = \dfrac{-(-5)}{1} = 5$

And product of roots $\alpha\beta = \dfrac{c}{a} = \dfrac{6}{1} = 6$

Now, $\alpha^2\beta + \beta^2\alpha = \alpha\beta(\alpha + \beta)$

$= 6 \times 5$

$= 30$

Hence, the correct option is (B).

11. Given:

$x^2 + bx + c = 0$

The roots of the equation are two consecutive integers.

Formula:

Quadratic equation = x^2 - (sum of roots)x + product of roots

Calculation:

$x^2 + bx + c = 0$ ---(1)

Let the roots are n, n + 1

So, a quadratic equation will be

x^2 - (n + n + 1)x + n(n + 1) = 0

$\Rightarrow x^2$ - (2n + 1)x + n(n + 1) = 0

So,

$\Rightarrow b^2$ - 4ac = $(2n + 1)^2$ - 4n(n+ 1)

$\because (a + b)^2 = a^2 + 2ab + b^2$

$\Rightarrow b^2$ - 4ac = $4n^2$ + 4n + 1 - $4n^2$ - 4n

$\Rightarrow b^2$ - 4ac = 1

Hence, the correct option is (B).

12. Given, $a^x = \dfrac{1}{8}$, $x = \dfrac{3}{2}[(\log_2 a) - 3]$

$\Rightarrow a^{\frac{3}{2}[(\log_2 a) - 3]} = \dfrac{1}{8}$

Applying log to base 2 in both sides, we get,

$$\frac{3}{2}\left[(\log_2 a) - 3\right]\log_2 a = \log_2\left(\frac{1}{8}\right)$$

$\Rightarrow \dfrac{3}{2}[(\log_2 a) - 3]\log_2 a$ = -3

Let $\log_2 a = x$

$\Rightarrow$ (x - 3) x = -2

$\Rightarrow x^2$ -3x + 2 = 0

$\Rightarrow$ (x - 1)(x - 2) = 0

$\Rightarrow$ x = 1 or 2

$\Rightarrow \log_2 a = 1$ or $\log_2 a = 2$

$\Rightarrow$ a = 2 or a = 4

As given 'a' is a perfect square $\Rightarrow$ a = 4

Hence, the correct option is (B).

13. Given,

$$\log_x\left[\log_5\left(\sqrt{x+5}+\sqrt{x}\right)\right] = 0$$

$$\Rightarrow \left[\log_5\left(\sqrt{x+5}+\sqrt{x}\right)\right] = x^0 = 1$$

$$\Rightarrow \left(\sqrt{x+5}+\sqrt{x}\right) = 5^1 = 5$$

$$\sqrt{x+5} = 5 - \sqrt{x}$$

$$\Rightarrow x + 5 = 25 + x - 10\sqrt{x}$$

$$\Rightarrow 10\sqrt{x} = 25 - 5$$

$$\Rightarrow \sqrt{x} = 2$$

$$\Rightarrow x = 4$$

Hence, the correct option is (C).

14. We know that $\log_a b = \dfrac{\log b}{\log a}$

$\therefore \log_3 5 \cdot \log_{25} 27 = \left(\dfrac{\log 5}{\log 3}\right) \times \left(\dfrac{\log 27}{\log 25}\right)$

$= \left(\dfrac{\log 5}{\log 3}\right) \times \left(\dfrac{\log 3^3}{\log 5^2}\right)$

$= \left(\dfrac{\log 5}{\log 3}\right) \times \left(\dfrac{3\log 3}{2\log 5}\right) = \dfrac{3}{2}$

Hence, the correct option is (C).

15. Given,

$\log_9 27 = m \Leftrightarrow 9^m = 27 \Leftrightarrow 3^{2m} = 3^3 \Leftrightarrow 2m = 3 = \dfrac{3}{2}.$

$\Rightarrow m = \dfrac{3}{2}$

And, $\log_{27} 9 = n \Leftrightarrow (27)n = 9 \Leftrightarrow 3^{3n} = 32 \Leftrightarrow 3n = 2$

$\Rightarrow n = \dfrac{2}{3}$

$\therefore \log_9 27 - \log_{27} 9 = \dfrac{3}{2} - \dfrac{2}{3} = \dfrac{(9-4)}{6}$

$\Rightarrow \dfrac{5}{6}$

Hence, the correct option is (C).

16. Considering the given equation

$2\log_{10}(x + 1) = \log_{10}(7x + 1)$

$\Rightarrow \log_{10}(x + 1)^2 = \log_{10}(7x + 1)$

After comparing:

$\Rightarrow (x + 1)^2 = (7x + 1)$

$\Rightarrow x^2 + 1 + 2x = 7x + 1$

$\Rightarrow x^2 - 5x = 0$

$\Rightarrow x(x - 5) = 0$

$x = 0$ and 5

$\therefore$ Non-zero value of 'x' = 5

Hence, the correct option is (B).

17. $f(x) = x^3 + e^{\frac{x}{2}}$

$$f'(x) = 3x^2 + \frac{1}{2}e^{\frac{x}{2}}$$

Given g is inverse of f

$$\Rightarrow g(f(x)) = x$$

Differentiating both sides with respect to x

$$g'(f(x)) \cdot f'(x) = 1$$

$$\Rightarrow g'(f(x)) = \frac{1}{f'(x)}$$

Clearly $f'(0) = \dfrac{1}{2}$

$$\therefore g'(1) = g'(f(0)) = \frac{1}{f'(0)} = 2$$

Hence, the correct option is (A).

18. $\Rightarrow f(x) = \dfrac{e^{2z}-1}{e^{2z}+1}$

$$\Rightarrow f(-x) = \frac{e^{-2z}-1}{e^{-2z}+1} = \frac{1-e^{2z}}{1+e^{2z}}$$

$$\Rightarrow f(x) = -\frac{e^{2x}-1}{e^{2x}+1} = -f(x)$$

$f(x)$ is an odd function.

Again

$$\Rightarrow f(x) = \frac{e^{2x}-1}{e^{2x}+1} \Rightarrow f'(x) = \frac{4e^{2x}}{(1+e^{2x})^2} > 0 \; \forall \, n \in R$$

$f(x)$ is an increasing function.

Hence, the correct option is (A).

19. $f(x) = \sqrt{25 - x^2}$

For the function to be defined, the expression inside the root must be greater than equal to 0.

$$25 - x^2 \geq 0$$

$$x^2 \leq 25$$

$$|x| \leq 5$$

$$-5 \leq x \leq 5$$

The domain of

$$f(x) = [-5,5]$$

When $x = \pm 5, f(x) = 0$

When $x = 0, f(x) = 5$, this is maximum value.

The range is $R = [0,5]$

Hence, the correct option is (A).

20. Given that,

$$f(x) = x \text{ and } g(x) = \cos x$$

As we know,

If $f: A \to B$ and $g: B \to C$ are functions then $g \circ f(x) = g(f(x))$ is a function from A to C.

$$\Rightarrow g \circ f\left(\frac{\pi}{3}\right) = g\left(f\left(\frac{\pi}{3}\right)\right)$$

$\because f(x) = x$

Therefore,

$$f\left(\frac{\pi}{3}\right) = \frac{\pi}{3}$$

$$\Rightarrow g \circ f\left(\frac{\pi}{3}\right) = g\left(\frac{\pi}{3}\right)$$

$\because g(x) = \cos x$

Then,

$$g\left(\frac{\pi}{3}\right) = \cos\left(\frac{\pi}{3}\right) = \frac{1}{2}$$

Therefore,

$$g \circ f\left(\frac{\pi}{3}\right) = \frac{1}{2}$$

Hence, the correct option is (C).

21. Given,

$$f(x) = x^3 - 3x^2 + 5x + 7$$

$$f'(x) = 3x^2 - 6x + 5$$

The discriminant of the above quadratic equations is

$$\Delta = 36 - 4(3)(5) = 36 - 60 < 0$$

$$\therefore f'(x) > 0 \forall x \in R^+,$$

Also $f'(x) > 0 \forall x \in R^-$

$\therefore f$ is increasing in R.

Hence, the correct option is (A).

22. Given,

$$f(x) = \sqrt{1 - \sqrt{1 - \sqrt{1 - x^2}}}$$

Here, $1 - x^2 \geq 0$

$$\Rightarrow x^2 - 1 \leq 0$$

$$\Rightarrow (x - 1)(x + 1) \leq 0$$

when, $x - 1 = 0 \Rightarrow x = 1$

when, $x + 1 = 0 \Rightarrow x = -1$

thus, domain of $x = [-1, 1]$

Hence, the correct option is (D).

23. Given:

$f: R \to R$ is a function defined by $f(x) = [x - 1]\cos\left(\frac{2x-1}{2}\right)\pi$

For $x = n, n \in Z$

$$\text{LHL} = \lim_{x \to n^-} f(x) = \lim_{x \to n^-}[x - 1]\cos\left(\frac{2x-1}{2}\right)\pi = 0$$

$$\text{RHL} = \lim_{x \to n^+} f(x) = \lim_{x \to n^+}[x - 1]\cos\left(\frac{2x-1}{2}\right)\pi = 0$$

$$f(n) = 0$$

$\Rightarrow$ LHL = RHL $= f(n)$

$\Rightarrow f(x)$ is continuous for every real x.

Hence, the correct option is (C).

24. Given:

$$f(x) = \frac{4x^3 - 3x^2}{6} - 2\sin x + (2x - 1)\cos x$$

$$f'(x) = (2x^2 - x) - 2\cos x + 2\cos x - \sin x(2x - 1)$$

$$= (2x - 1)(x - \sin x)$$

for $x > 0, x - \sin x > 0$

$x < 0, x - \sin x < 0$

for $x \in (-\infty, 0] \cup \left[\frac{1}{2}, \infty\right), f(x) \geq 0$

for $x \in \left[0, \frac{1}{2}\right], f'(x) \leq 0$

$\Rightarrow f(x)$ increases in $\left[\frac{1}{2}, \infty\right)$

Hence, the correct option is (A).

25. Concept:

Equality of complex numbers.

Two complex numbers $z_1 = x_1 + iy_1$ and $z_2 = x_2 + iy_2$ are equal if and only if $x_1 = x_2$ and $y_1 = y_2$

Or $Re(z_1) = Re(z_2)$ and $Im(z_1) = Im(z_2)$.

Calculations:

$$\Rightarrow z = \frac{1 - i}{i}$$

Multiplying numerator and denominator by i

$$\Rightarrow z = \frac{1 - i}{i} \times \frac{i}{i}$$

$$= \frac{i - i^2}{i^2}$$

$$= \frac{i + 1}{-1}$$

$$= -1 - i$$

$$Re(z) = -1$$

$$lm(z) = -1$$

Hence, the correct option is (D).

26. Given complex number is $z = \frac{5}{2} + \frac{5\sqrt{3}}{2}i$

$$r\cos\theta = \frac{5}{2}, r\sin\theta = \frac{5\sqrt{3}}{2}$$

By squaring and adding, we get -

$$r^2(\cos^2\theta + \sin^2\theta) = \frac{100}{4} = 25$$

$$\therefore r = 5$$

$$\Rightarrow \cos\theta = \frac{\frac{5}{2}}{r} = \frac{\frac{5}{2}}{5} = \frac{1}{2} \text{ and } \sin\theta = \frac{\frac{5\sqrt{3}}{2}}{r} = \frac{\frac{5\sqrt{3}}{2}}{5} = \frac{\sqrt{3}}{2}$$

Since it is in first quadrant, $\theta = \frac{\pi}{3}$

So, on comparing with $z = r(\cos\theta + i\sin\theta)$, we can write as:

$$5\left(\cos\left(\frac{\pi}{3}\right) + i\sin\left(\frac{\pi}{3}\right)\right)$$

Hence, the correct option is (D).

27. $\cos\theta + i\sin\theta = e^{i\theta} \qquad ....(1)$

$$\cos\theta - i\sin\theta = e^{-i\theta} \qquad ....(2)$$

We know that:

$$\cos\theta + i\sin\theta = e^{i\theta}$$

$$(i\cos\theta + \sin\theta)^4 = (\cos\theta - i\sin\theta)^4 \qquad ....(A)$$

Take, $\left(\frac{\cos\theta + i\sin\theta}{i\cos\theta + \sin\theta}\right)^4 = \left(\frac{e^{i\theta}}{e^{-i\theta}}\right)^4$

From equation (1), (2) and (A).

$$= \left(e^{2i\theta}\right)^4$$

$$\Rightarrow e^{8i\theta} = \cos 8\theta + i\sin 8\theta$$

Hence, the correct option is (B).

28. Given: $iz^3 + z^2 - z + i = 0$

$$\Rightarrow iz^3 + z^2 + (i^2)z + i = 0 \quad (i^2 = -1)$$

$$\Rightarrow iz^3 + i^2z + z^2 + i = 0$$

$$\Rightarrow iz(z^2 + i) + 1(z^2 + i) = 0$$

$$(z^2 + i)(iz + 1) = 0$$

$$(z^2 + i)i(z - i) = 0 \quad (-i^2 = 1)$$

$$z^2 = -i \text{ or } z = i$$

If $z = i$ then $|z| = |i| = 1$

If $z^2 = -i$ then $|z^2| = |-i| = 1$

$$\Rightarrow |z^2| = 1$$

$$\Rightarrow |z| = 1$$

Therefore, if $iz^3 + z^2 - z + i = 0$, then the value of $|z|$ is 1.

Hence, the correct option is (A).

29. If quadratic equation is $ax^2 + bx + c = 0$, then ....(1)

Sum of roots $(\alpha + \beta) = \frac{-b}{a}$

And product of roots $(\alpha \times \beta) = \frac{c}{a}$

Given equation $x^2 - ax + 1 = 0$, on comparing with equation (1) we get $a = 1, b = (-a)$ and $c = 1$.

Let $\alpha = (2 + i)$ then $\beta = (2 - i)$

Then Sum of roots $(\alpha + \beta) = \frac{-b}{a}$

$$\Rightarrow (2 + i) + (2 - i) = a$$

$$\Rightarrow 4 = a$$

$$\Rightarrow a = 4$$

Hence, the correct option is (B).

30. We have given three complex numbers $3 + 4i, 8 - 6i$ and $13 + 9i$.

Let A, B, C represent complex number $3 + 4i, 8 - 6i$ and $13 + 9i$.

$$AB = |(3 + 4i) - (8 - 6i)|$$

$$AB = |3 + 4i - 8 + 6i|$$

$$AB = |-5 + 10i| = \sqrt{(-5)^2 + (10)^2}$$

$$AB = \sqrt{25 + 100} = \sqrt{125}$$

$$BC = |(8 - 6i) - (13 + 9i)|$$

$$BC = |8 - 6i - 13 - 9i| = |-5 - 15i|$$

$$BC = \sqrt{(-5)^2 + (-15)^2}$$

$$BC = \sqrt{25 + 225} = \sqrt{250}$$

$$CA = |(13 + 9i) - (3 + 4i)|$$

$CA = |13 + 9i - 3 - 4i| = |10 + 5i|$

$CA = \sqrt{(10)^2 + (5)^2}$

$CA = \sqrt{100 + 25} = \sqrt{125}$

$\Rightarrow BC^2 = AB^2 + CA^2$

$\Rightarrow$ One of the angle is $90°$.

Thus, nature of the triangle formed by the points representing complex number $3 + 4i, 8 - 6i$ and $13 + 9i$ is right angled triangle.

Hence, the correct option is (B).

31. We know that, $z = e^{i\theta}$ $\quad$ .... (1)

and $e^{i\theta} = \cos\theta + i\sin\theta$ $\quad$ .... (2)

Given, $z = e^{i\theta}$

Take,

$\Rightarrow \dfrac{z^2-1}{z^2+1} = \dfrac{e^{2i\theta}-1}{e^{2i\theta}+1}$

$= \dfrac{\cos2\theta+i\sin2\theta-1}{\cos2\theta+i\sin2\theta+1}$

$= \dfrac{-1(1-\cos2\theta)+2i\sin2\theta\cos\theta}{(1+\cos2\theta)+2i\sin2\theta\cos\theta}$

$= \dfrac{-(1-1+2\sin^2\theta)+2i\sin2\theta\cos\theta}{(1+2\cos^2\theta-1)+2i\sin2\theta\cos\theta}$

$= \dfrac{(-2\sin^2\theta)+2i\sin\theta\cos\theta}{2\cos^2\theta+2i\sin\theta\cos\theta}$

$= \dfrac{-2\sin\theta(\sin\theta-i\cos\theta)}{2\cos\theta(\cos\theta+i\sin\theta)}$

$= -\tan\theta \times -i\left(\dfrac{\cos\theta+i\sin\theta}{\cos\theta+i\sin\theta}\right)$

$= -\tan\theta \times -i$

$\Rightarrow \dfrac{z^2-1}{z^2+1} = i\tan\theta$

Hence, the correct option is (A).

32. Given,

$i = \sqrt{-1}$

$\therefore i^2 = -1$

As we know,

$i^3 = -i \times i^2 = -i$

$i^4 = (i^2)^2 = (-1)^2 = 1$

So, $\dfrac{1000}{4} = 250$

Given,

$i^{1000} + i^{1001} + i^{1002} + i^{1003} = \left(i^4\right)^{250} + i \times \left(i^4\right)^{250} + i^2 \times \left(i^4\right)^{250} + i^3 \times \left(i^4\right)^{250}$

$= 1 + i + i^2 + i^3$

$= 1 + i + (-1) + (-i)$

$= 0$

Hence, the correct option is (A).

33. $\left|\dfrac{\beta-\alpha}{1-\alpha\beta}\right|^2 = \left(\dfrac{\beta-\alpha}{1-\overline{\alpha}\beta}\right)\left(\dfrac{\overline{\beta}-\overline{\alpha}}{1-\alpha\overline{\beta}}\right)$

$\Rightarrow \left|\dfrac{\beta-\alpha}{1-\alpha\beta}\right|^2 = \dfrac{\beta\overline{\beta}-\overline{\beta}\alpha-\alpha\overline{\beta}+\alpha\overline{\alpha}}{(1-\overline{\alpha}\beta)(1-\alpha\overline{\beta})}$

$\Rightarrow \left|\dfrac{\beta-\alpha}{1-\overline{\alpha}\beta}\right|^2 = \dfrac{|\beta|^2-\overline{\beta}\alpha-\alpha\overline{\beta}+|\alpha|^2}{1-\alpha\overline{\beta}-\overline{\alpha}\beta+|\alpha|^2|\beta|^2}$

$\Rightarrow \left|\dfrac{\beta-\alpha}{1-\alpha\beta}\right|^2 = \dfrac{|\alpha|^2-\overline{\beta}\overline{\alpha}-\alpha\overline{\beta}+1}{1-\alpha\overline{\beta}-\overline{\alpha}\beta+|\alpha|^{2'}}$ $\quad [\because |\beta| = 1]$

$\Rightarrow \left|\dfrac{\beta-\alpha}{1-\alpha\beta}\right| = 1$

Hence, the correct option is (C).

34. Giving, $|1 - 2i|^x = 5^x$

We need to find the value of x for which should be an integer but not zero.

Let first find value of $|1 - 2i|$

$|1 - 2i| = \sqrt{(1)^2 + (2)^2} = \sqrt{5}$

$\Rightarrow \left[\because z = x + iy \Rightarrow |z| = \sqrt{x^2 + y^2}\right]$

So,

$|1 - 2i|^x = 5^x$

$\Rightarrow \left(\sqrt{5}\right)^x = 5^x$

$\Rightarrow \left(\sqrt{5}\right)^x = \left(\sqrt{5}\right)^{2x}$

Comparing powers,

$\Rightarrow x = 2x$

$\Rightarrow x - 2x = 0$

$\Rightarrow -x = 0$

$\Rightarrow x = 0$

Hence, the correct option is (A).

35. Given:

(p-x)(p-y)=1

Also, $(x - y) = \sqrt{5}$

Formula Used:

$$(x - y)^3 = x^3 - y^3 - 3xy(x - y)$$

Calculation:

$$(p - x)(p - y) = 1$$

$$\Rightarrow (p - x) = \frac{1}{(p-y)} \quad \text{.........(1)}$$

$$\Rightarrow x - y = \sqrt{5} \quad \text{...............(2)}$$

Add and subtract 'p' in left side of eq. (2)

$$\Rightarrow -p + x + p - y = \sqrt{5}$$

$$\Rightarrow (p - y) - (p - x) = \sqrt{5} \quad \text{..........(3)}$$

Put the value of $(p - x)$ from eq. (1) to eq. (3)

$$\Rightarrow (p - y) - \frac{1}{(p-y)} = \sqrt{5}$$

Taking cube both sides, we have -

$$\Rightarrow (p - y)^3 - \frac{1}{(p-y)^3} - 3(\sqrt{5}) = 5\sqrt{5}$$

$$\therefore (p - y)^3 - \frac{1}{(p-y)^3} = 8\sqrt{5}$$

Hence, the correct option is (B).

36. Concept:

Logarithm properties

Product rule:

The log of a product equals the sum of two logs.

$$log_a(mn) = \log_a m + \log_a n$$

Quotient rule:

The log of a quotient equals the difference of two logs.

$$log_a \frac{m}{n} = \log_a m - \log_a n$$

Power rule:

In the log of power, the exponent becomes a coefficient.

$$\log_a m^n = n\log_a m$$

Change of base rule

$$\log_m n = \frac{\log_a n}{\log_a m}$$

If $m = n;$

$$\Rightarrow \log_m m = \frac{\log_a m}{\log_a m} = 1$$

Calculation:

$$\log_9 27 + \log_8 32$$

$$= \frac{\log 27}{\log 9} + \frac{\log 32}{\log 8}$$

$$= \frac{\log 3^3}{\log 3^2} + \frac{\log 2^5}{\log 2^3}$$

$$= \frac{3\log 3}{2\log 3} + \frac{5\log 2}{3\log 2}$$

$$= \frac{3}{2} + \frac{5}{3}$$

$$= \frac{9+10}{6} = \frac{19}{6}$$

Hence, the correct option is (B).

37. Calculation:

Given: $\log_{10}$ a is negative.

$$\Rightarrow \log_{10} a < 0$$

Let $\log_{10} a = -b$ (Here b is positive)

$$\Rightarrow a = 10^{-b}$$

Given a lies between 0 to 1

$$\Rightarrow 0 < a < 1$$

$$\Rightarrow 0 < 10^{-b} < 1$$

Hence it is negative power of 10 is between 0 and 1

Hence, the correct option is (B).

38. Formula used:

$$(\log_a b) = \frac{(\log b)}{(\log a)}$$

$$log a^b = b \log a$$

Calculation:

$$(\log_3 4)(\log_4 5)(\log_5 6)(\log_6 7)(\log_7 8)(\log_8 9)$$

$$\Rightarrow \frac{\log 4}{\log 3} \times \frac{\log 5}{\log 4} \times \frac{\log 6}{\log 5} \times \frac{\log 7}{\log 6} \times \frac{\log 8}{\log 7} \times \frac{\log 9}{\log 8}$$

$$\Rightarrow \frac{(\log 9)}{\log 3)} \quad (\because \text{Except } \log 9 \text{ and } \log 3 \text{ other terms cancelled out})$$

We can say $\log 9 = \log_{10} 9$

So, $\log 9 = \log 3^2 = 2\log 3$

$$\therefore \left(\frac{\log 9}{\log 3}\right) = \frac{2\log 3}{\log 3} = 2$$

Hence, the correct option is (A).

39. Given:

$$x = 8 - 2\sqrt{(15)}$$

Calculation:

$$x = (\sqrt{5})^2 + (\sqrt{3})^2 - 2\sqrt{(15)}$$

$$\Rightarrow x = (\sqrt{5} - \sqrt{3})^2$$

$$\Rightarrow \sqrt{x} = \sqrt{5} - \sqrt{3}$$

And $\dfrac{1}{\sqrt{x}} = \dfrac{\sqrt{5}+\sqrt{3}}{2}$

According to question,

$$\left(\sqrt{x} + \dfrac{1}{\sqrt{x}}\right)^2 = \left[\sqrt{5} - \sqrt{3} + \left(\dfrac{\sqrt{5}+\sqrt{3}}{2}\right)\right]^2$$

$$\Rightarrow \left[\dfrac{3\sqrt{5}-\sqrt{3}}{2}\right]^2$$

$$\Rightarrow \left[\dfrac{45+3-6\sqrt{15}}{4}\right]$$

$$\Rightarrow \dfrac{48-6\sqrt{15}}{4}$$

$$\Rightarrow 12 - \dfrac{3\sqrt{15}}{2}$$

Hence, the correct option is (D).

40. Calculation:

Statement:1 $\dfrac{a^2-b^2}{a^2+b^2} > \dfrac{a-b}{a+b}$ where $a > b > 0$

Let a = 2 and b = 1

$$\Rightarrow \dfrac{2^2-1^2}{2^2+1^2} > \dfrac{2-1}{2+1}$$

$$\Rightarrow \dfrac{3}{5} > \dfrac{1}{3} \text{ which is correct.}$$

This inequality also holds for a = 1 and b = 2 i.e.

Statement 2 is correct for b > a > 0 as well.

But according to statement 2, inequality will be correct only if a > b > 0

Hence, the correct option is (A).

41. Given, $(\alpha + \beta) = \dfrac{-q}{p}$ and $\alpha\beta = \dfrac{r}{p}$

Option $A \Rightarrow \dfrac{1}{(\alpha+\beta)} = \dfrac{1}{\left(\frac{-q}{p}\right)} = \dfrac{-p}{q}$

Option $B \Rightarrow \dfrac{1}{\alpha} + \dfrac{1}{\beta} = \dfrac{(\alpha+\beta)}{\alpha\beta} = \dfrac{\left(\frac{-q}{p}\right)}{\left(\frac{r}{p}\right)} = \dfrac{-q}{r}$

Option $C \Rightarrow \dfrac{-1}{\alpha\beta} = \dfrac{-1}{\frac{r}{p}} = \dfrac{-p}{r}$

Option $D \Rightarrow \dfrac{\alpha\beta}{(\alpha+\beta)} = \dfrac{\frac{r}{p}}{\frac{-q}{p}} = \dfrac{-r}{q}$

Now,

Option A > Option D

$\because q < r$

$\Rightarrow$ Option C > Option A

$\because p < q$

$\Rightarrow$ Option C > Option B

$\therefore$ Option C $\Rightarrow \dfrac{-1}{\alpha\beta}$ is the greatest

Hence, the correct option is (C).

42. Given:

$a = (0.05)^2, b = \dfrac{1}{(0.05)^2}$ and $c = 1 - (0.05)^2 - 0.995$

Calculation:

Considering the given values

$a = (0.05)^2$

$\Rightarrow 0.0025$

$b = \dfrac{1}{(0.5)^2}$

$\Rightarrow \dfrac{1}{0.25}$

$\Rightarrow \dfrac{100}{25}$

$\Rightarrow 4$

$c = 1 - (0.05)^2 - 0.995$

$\Rightarrow 1 - 0.0025 - 0.995$

$\Rightarrow 1 - 0.9975$

$\Rightarrow 0.0025$

$\therefore a = c < b$

Hence, the correct option is (D).

43. Given, $4^{x+2} + 4^{2x+1} = 1280$

$\Rightarrow (4^x)(4)^2 + (4^x)^2(4) = 1280$

$\Rightarrow (4^x)^2 + 4(4^x) = 320$

Let $4^x = y$

$\Rightarrow y^2 + 4y - 320 = 0 \Rightarrow (y + 20)(y - 16) = 0$

$\Rightarrow y = -20 \text{ or } 16$

$\therefore 4^x = -20 \text{ or } 16$

So, $x = 2$

Hence, the correct option is (A).

44. Let p and q be two roots of the equation

We have to find the minimum value of (p² + q²)

p² + q² = (p + q)² – 2pq   ----(i)

Some of the roots = -b/a

Therefore, p + q = -(a + 3)

Therefore, $p + q = -(a + 3)$

Product of the roots $\dfrac{c}{a}$

Therefore, $pq = -(a + 5)$

Substituting these values back in (i)

$\Rightarrow$ p² + q² = [-(a + 3)² + 2(a + 5)]

$\Rightarrow$ p² + q² = a² + 6a + 9 + 2a + 10

$\Rightarrow$ p² + q² = a² + 8a + 19

We have to find the minimum value of a² + 8a + 19.

By completion of squares, 19 can be split into 16 and 3

$\Rightarrow$ a² + 8a + 16 + 3

$\Rightarrow$ (a + 4)² + 3

$\Rightarrow$ The minimum possible value is 3 when a = -4.

Hence, the correct option is (C).

45. Let $f(x) = \dfrac{x-2}{x^2+x+3} = y$

$\Rightarrow yx^2 + yx + 3y - x + 2 = 0$

$\Rightarrow yx^2 + (y - 1)x + 3y + 2 = 0$

$f(x)$ can have any value y, provided the above equation in x has real roots.

$\therefore b^2 - 4ac \geq 0$

$\Rightarrow (y - 1)^2 - 4y(3y + 2) \geq 0$

$\Rightarrow -11y^2 - 10y + 1 \geq 0$

$\Rightarrow 11y^2 + 10y - 1 \leq 0$

$\Rightarrow (11y - 1)(y + 1) \leq 0$

$\Rightarrow -1 \leq y \leq \dfrac{1}{11}$

So, the range of y or $f(x)$ is $\left[-1, \dfrac{1}{11}\right]$

Hence, the correct option is (D).

46. Given the equation, x² - 2x - 8 =0   ...(1)

As we know, the sum of roots $= \dfrac{-b}{a}$ and, the product of roots $= \dfrac{c}{a}$

From equation (1), the sum of roots $= \dfrac{-(-2)}{1} = 2$

and, the product of roots $= -8$

Since the product of the roots is negative $\Rightarrow$ one of the roots is positive and the other is negative.

Since the sum of the roots is positive $\Rightarrow$ the positive root is numerically larger than the negative root.

So, The equation x² - 2x - 8 =0 will have the numerically larger root as positive.

Hence, the correct option is (B).

47. Given, $x + \dfrac{1}{x} = \sqrt{2}$

Squaring both sides, we get

$\Rightarrow x^2 + \dfrac{1^2}{x} + 2 = 2$

$\Rightarrow x^2 + \dfrac{1^2}{x} = 0$

$\Rightarrow x^4 = -1$

We have to find $x^{80} + x^{76} + x^{72} + x^{68} + x^{64} + 4$

$\Rightarrow (x^4)^{20} + (x^4)^{19} + (x^4)^{18} + (x^4)^{17} + (x^4)^{16} + 4$

$\Rightarrow (-1)^{20} + (-1)^{19} + (-1)^{18} + (-1)^{17} + (-1)^{16} + 4$

$\Rightarrow 1 - 1 + 1 - 1 + 1 + 4 = 5$

Hence, the correct option is (A).

48. The given equation is

3x² – 8x + 4 = 0   ---(1)

Let $\dfrac{1}{x} = y$

$\Rightarrow y = \dfrac{1}{x}$

If we express x in terms of y in (1) above, we will get an equation whose roots are y, the reciprocal of x.

$3\left(\dfrac{1}{y}\right)^2 \dfrac{-8}{y} + 4 = 0$

$\Rightarrow \dfrac{3}{y^2} \dfrac{-8}{y} + 4 = 0$

$\Rightarrow 4y^2 - 8y + 3 = 0$

Hence, the correct option is (C).

49. As we know,

$\Rightarrow a^{(\log_b c)} = c^{(\log_b a)}$

Calculation:

$\Rightarrow 20^{(\log_7 y)} = 800 - y^{(\log_7 20)}$

$\Rightarrow 2 \times 20^{(\log_7 y)} = 800$

$\Rightarrow 20^{(\log_7 y)} = 400$

$\Rightarrow 20^{(\log_7 y)} = 20^2$

$\Rightarrow \log_7 y = 2$

$\Rightarrow \frac{1}{2}\log_7 y = \frac{1}{2} \times 2$

$\Rightarrow \log_7^2 y = 1$

$\Rightarrow \log_{49} y = 1$

Hence, the correct option is (B).

50. CALCULATION:

Given that, $\log_3 9 \times \log_9 27 \times \log_{27} 81 \times \ldots\ldots \times n^{th}$ term $= 21$

Observing the pattern in the LHS of the above series, the nth term $= \log_{3^n} 3.3^n$

$\Rightarrow \log_3 9 \times \log_9 27 \times \log_{27} 81 \times \ldots\ldots \times \log_3 n3.3^n = 21$

$\Rightarrow$ Making the base same with 3 as the base,

$\Rightarrow \log_3 9 \times \left(\frac{\log_3 27}{\log_3 9}\right) \times \left(\frac{\log_3 81}{\log_3 27}\right) \times \ldots\ldots\ldots \times \left(\frac{\log_3 3.3^n}{\log_3 3^n}\right) = 21$

$\Rightarrow \log_3 3 \cdot 3^n = 21$

$\Rightarrow \log_3 3^{(n+1)} = 21$

$\Rightarrow n + 1 = 21$

$\Rightarrow n = 20$

Hence, the correct option is (B).

51. Given that,

f(t) + f(2t) + f(3t) = g(t) and g(t + 6) = g(t − 2) + 7 and g(8) = 22

Replacing t by 2 in g(t + 6) = g(t − 2) + 7

We get, g(8) = g(0) + 7

Therefore, g(0) = g(8) − 7 = 22 − 7 = 15

Now, Replacing t with 0 in f(t) + f(2t) + f(3t) = g(t)

We get, f(0) + f(0) + f(0) = g(0)

$\Rightarrow$ g(0) = 3f(0) = 15

$\Rightarrow f(0) = \frac{15}{3} = 5$

Hence, the correct option is (B).

52. The condition given in the question is x2 - |x + 2| + x > 0

$\Rightarrow$ Two cases are possible:

Case 1: When (x + 2) ≥ 0.

$\Rightarrow$ Therefore, x2 - x - 2 + x > 0

$\Rightarrow$ Hence, x2 − 2 > 0

$\Rightarrow$ So, either x < - √2 or x > √2.

$\Rightarrow$ Hence, x ∈ [-2, -√2) ∪ (√2, ∞)   ……. (1)

Case 2: When (x + 2) < 0

$\Rightarrow$ Then x2 + x + 2 + x > 0

$\Rightarrow$ So, x2 + 2x + 2 > 0

$\Rightarrow$ This gives (x+1)2 + 1 > 0 and this is true for every x

$\Rightarrow$ Hence, x ≤ -2 or x ∈ (-∞, -2)   ……… (2)

$\Rightarrow$ From equations (2) and (3) we get x ∈ (-∞, -√2) ∪ (√2, ∞).

Hence, the correct option is (C).

53. if x/(y + z − x) = r, then, x = r(y + z − x)   ----(i)

if y/(x + z − y) = r, then, y = r(x + z − y)   ----(ii)

if z/(x + y − z) = r, then, z = r(x + y − z)   ----(iii)

From equation (i) and (iii)

x + z = r(2y)   ----(iv)

Putting value of (iv) in (ii)

y = [r(2y)r − y]

$\Rightarrow$ 2yr2 − yr − y = 0

$\Rightarrow$ 2yr2 − 2yr + yr − y = 0

$\Rightarrow$ 2yr(r − 1) + y(r − 1) = 0

$\Rightarrow$ (2yr + y) (r − 1) = 0

$\Rightarrow r = 1$ and $r = \frac{-1}{2}$

Hence, the correct option is (C).

54. Let the price of single pencil, pen, and eraser be x, y, and z respectively

According to question,

8x + 5y + 3z = Rs. 111   ----(1)

9x + 6y + 5z = Rs. 130   ----(2)

16x + 11y + 3z = Rs. 221   ----(3)

Subtracting equation (1) from (3)

$\Rightarrow$ (16x + 11y + 3z) - (8x + 5y + 3z) = 221 - 111

$\Rightarrow$ 8x + 6y = 110

$\Rightarrow$ 4x + 3y = 55   ----(4)

Multiply the equation (2) by 3 and (3) by 5 and then subtracting equation (2) from (3)

$\Rightarrow$ (16x + 11y + 3z) × 5 - (9x + 6y + 5z) × 3 = 221 × 5 - 130 × 3

$\Rightarrow$ 80x + 55y + 15z - 27x - 18y - 15z = 1105 - 390

$\Rightarrow$ 53x + 37y = 715   ----(5)

Multiply the equation (4) by 53 and (5) by 4 and then subtracting equation (4) from (5)

$\Rightarrow$ 212x + 159y - 212x - 148y = 2915 - 2860

$\Rightarrow$ 11y = 55

$\Rightarrow y = 5$

By putting the value of y = 5 in equation (4)

$\Rightarrow 4x + 3 \times 5 = 55$

$\Rightarrow x = 10$

By putting the value of y = 5 and x = 10 in equation (1)

$\Rightarrow 8 \times 10 + 5 \times 5 + 3z = 111$

$\Rightarrow 80 + 25 + 3z = 111$

$\Rightarrow z = 2$

∴ Cost of 39 pencils, 26 pens and 13 erasers is 39x + 26y + 13z =39 × 10 + 26 × 5 + 13 × 2 = Rs. 546

Hence, the correct option is (B).

55. Let, length of the piece of cloth = x m

Cost of cloth = Rs. 35

∴ Cost of 1 m cloth = Rs. $\dfrac{35}{x}$

According to the question,

$\Rightarrow (x + 4)\ \dfrac{35}{x-1} = 35$

$\Rightarrow 35 - x + \dfrac{140}{x-4} = 35$

$\Rightarrow 35x - x^2 + 140 - 4x = 35x$

$\Rightarrow x^2 + 4x - 140 = 0$

$\Rightarrow x^2 + 14x - 10x - 140 = 0$

$\Rightarrow x(x + 14) - 10(x + 14) = 0$

$\Rightarrow (x + 14)\ (x - 10) = 0$

$\Rightarrow x = - 14$ or 10

Hence, the correct option is (D).

56. Using algebraic identities,

$(a + b + c)^2 = a^2 + b^2 + c^2 + 2ab + 2bc + 2ca$

By putting the respective values given in question,

$\Rightarrow (9)^2 = a^2 + b^2 + c^2 + 2(ab + bc + ca)$ [∵ ab + bc + ca = 26]

$\Rightarrow (9)^2 = a^2 + b^2 + c^2 + 2(26)$

$\Rightarrow a^2 + b^2 + c^2 = 81 - 52 = 29$

Given equations,

$a^3 + b^3 = 91$ ----(1)

$b^3 + c^3 = 72$ ----(2)

$c^3 + a^3 = 35$ ----(3)

On adding (1), (2) and (3)

$a^3 + b^3 + b^3 + c^3 + c^3 + a^3 = 91 + 72 + 35$

$\Rightarrow 2(a3 + b3 + c3) = 198$

$\Rightarrow a^3 + b^3 + c^3 = 99$

Using algebraic identities,

$a^3 + b^3 + c^3 - 3abc = (a + b + c)\ (a2 + b2 + c2 - ab - bc - ca)$

By putting the respective values,

$\Rightarrow 99 - 3abc = 9\ (29 - 26)$ [∵ ab + bc + ca = 26 and a + b + c = 9]

$\Rightarrow 3abc = 99 - 27$

$\Rightarrow abc = \dfrac{72}{3}$

Hence, the correct option is (B).

57. Concept:

Formula used:

- $\log_a b = \dfrac{1}{\log_b a}$

- $\log_a M + \log_a N = \log_a (MN)$

Factorial:

- $n! = 1 \times 2 \times 3 \times \cdots \times (n - 1) \times n$

Calculation:

Using $\log_a b = \dfrac{1}{\log_b a}$

$\dfrac{1}{\log_2 N} + \dfrac{1}{\log_3 N} + \ldots + \dfrac{1}{\log_{100} N} = \log_N 2 + \log_N 3 + \ldots + \log_N 100$

$= \log_N (2 \times 3 \times \cdots \times 100)$

$= \log_N (100!)$

$= \dfrac{1}{\log_{100!} N}$

Hence, the correct option is (A).

58. Let the wrong questions attempt by Mr. X be a then

Right question = (100 – a)

According to the question

$\Rightarrow (100 – a) \times 4 – a \times 1 = 340$

$\Rightarrow 400 – 4a – a = 340$

$\Rightarrow 5a = 400 – 340 = 60$

$\Rightarrow a = \dfrac{60}{5} = 12$

Hence, the correct option is (C).

59. Concept:

If a system has no solution, it is said to be inconsistent.

For a system of equations having no solution,

$a_1 x + b_1 y = c_1$ and $a_2 x + b_2 y = c_2$ we have, $\dfrac{a_1}{a_2} = \dfrac{b_1}{b_2} \neq \dfrac{c_1}{c_2}$

we have, $\dfrac{a_1}{a_2} = \dfrac{b_1}{b_2} \neq \dfrac{c_1}{c_2}$

Calculation:

The given equations are $2x - 3y - 3 = 0$ and $-4x + qy\dfrac{-p}{2} = 0$

So, here on comparing these equations with equation(1) and (2), we have

$$a_1 = 2, b_1 = -3, c_1 = -3$$

$$a_2 = -4, b_2 = q, c_2 = \dfrac{-p}{2}$$

Now, for a system to be inconsistent,.

we have, $\dfrac{a_1}{a_2} = \dfrac{b_1}{b_2} \neq \dfrac{c_1}{c_2}$

$$\Rightarrow \dfrac{2}{-4} = \dfrac{-3}{q} \neq \dfrac{-3 \times 2}{-p}$$

$$\Rightarrow \dfrac{2}{-4} \neq \dfrac{-3 \times 2}{-p}$$

$$\Rightarrow p \neq -12$$

Hence, the given system is inconsistent when $p \neq 12$.

Hence, the correct option is (C).

60. Given:

2 Mobile Phones and 1 Refrigerator for Rs. 50,000

3 Mobile Phones and 2 Refrigerators for Rs. 85,000

Calculation:

Let assume that cost of 1 Mobile Phone = Rs.x

And Cost of 1 Refrigerator = Rs.y

According to the question

$\Rightarrow$ 2x + y = 50,000   ....(i)

$\Rightarrow$ 3x + 2y = 85,000   ....(ii)

Multiply Equation (i) by 2

$\Rightarrow$ 2 × (2x + y = 50,000)

$\Rightarrow$ 4x + 2y = 1,00,000   ....(iii)

From Equation (ii) and Equation (iii)   ....(By Elimination Method)

x = 15,000

y = 20,000

Kanta has to pay = 2(15,000) + 2(20,000) = 70,000

Hence, the correct option is (C).

Q.1 The smallest interior angle is $100°$ and the common difference between two consecutive angles is $4°$ then find the number of sides of the polygon.

A. 5   **B.** 15   **C.** 18   **D.** 25

Q.2 If each interior angle of a regular polygon is $135°$, then find the number of diagonals of the polygon.

Q.3 If the sum of all interior angles of a regular polygon is twice the sum of all its exterior angles then the polygon is:

[Indian Military Academy (IMA), 2020]

A. Hexagon   **B.** Octagon   **C.** Nonagon   **D.** Decagon

Q.4 The ratio between the number of sides of two regular polygons is $1:2$ and the ratio between their interior angles is $2:3$. The number of sides of these polygons is respectively-

A. 6,12   **B.** 5,10   **C.** 4,8   **D.** 7,14

Q.5 In a triangle ABC, medians AD and BE are perpendicular to each other, and have lengths 12 cm and 9 cm, respectively. Then, the area of triangle ABC, in sq cm, is:

A. 80   **B.** 72   **C.** 78   **D.** 68

Q.6 Let $\triangle ABC \sim \triangle DEF$ and their areas be, respectively, 64 cm^2 and 121 cm^2. If $EF = 15.4$ cm, find BC.

A. $BC = 9.2$ cm   **B.** $BC = 10.2$ cm
C. $BC = 11.2$ cm   **D.** $BC = 15.2$ cm

Q.7 D, E and F are respectively the mid-points of sides AB, BC and CA of $\triangle ABC$. Find the ratio of the areas of $\triangle DEF$ and $\triangle ABC$.

A. $\frac{1}{3}$ **B.** $\frac{1}{4}$ **C.** $\frac{3}{5}$ **D.** $\frac{5}{3}$

Q.8 ABC and BDE are two equilateral triangles such that D is the midpoint of BC. Ratio of the areas of triangles ABC and BDE is:

Q.9 In $\triangle DEW, AB \parallel EW$. If $AD = 4$ cm, $DE = 12$ cm and $DW = 24$ cm, then find the value of DB.

A. 64 cm   **B.** 32 cm   **C.** 16 cm   **D.** 8 cm

Q.10 In the figure, $EF \parallel AC, BC = 10$ cm, $AB = 13$ cm and $EC = 2$ cm, find AF.

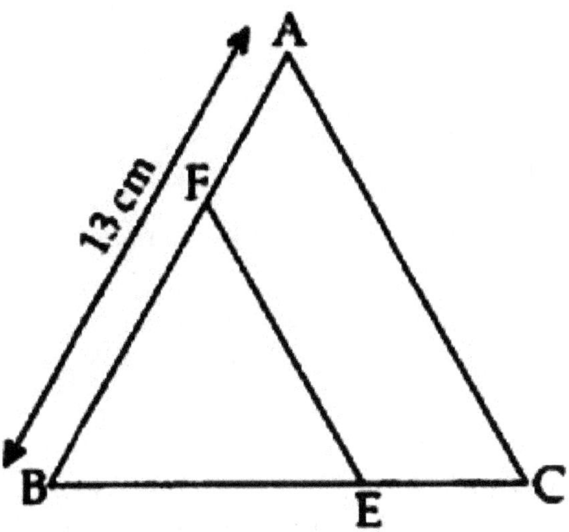

A. 2.6 cm   **B.** 3.6 cm   **C.** 4.6 cm   **D.** 5.6 cm

Q.11 If two tangents inclined at an angle $60°$ are drawn to a circle of radius 3 cm, then length of each tangent is equal to:

A. $\left(\frac{3}{2}\right)\sqrt{3}$ cm   **B.** 6 cm
C. 3 cm   **D.** $3\sqrt{3}$ cm

Q.12 If TP and TQ are the two tangents to a circle with centre O so that $\angle POQ = 110°$, then $\angle PTQ$ is equal to:

A. 60°   **B.** 70°   **C.** 80°   **D.** 90°

Q.13 In the figure below, the pair of tangents AP and AQ drawn from an external point A to a circle with centre O are perpendicular to each other and length of each tangent is 5 cm. Then the radius of the circle is:

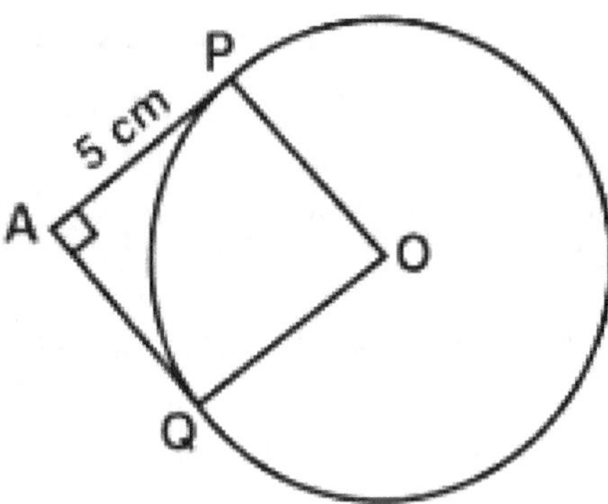

A. 10 cm   **B.** 7.5 cm   **C.** 5 cm   **D.** 2.5 cm

Q.14 In the figure, PQL and PRM are tangents to the circle with centre O at the points Q and R, respectively and S is a point on the circle such that $\angle SQL = 50°$ and $\angle SRM = 60°$. Then $\angle QSR$ is equal to:

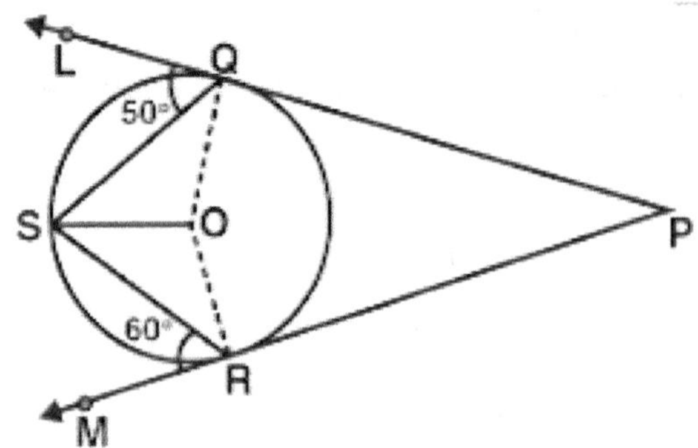

A. 40°   **B.** 60°   **C.** 70°   **D.** 80°

Q.15 Two circles touch each other externally at point X. PQ is a simple common tangent to both the circles touching the circles at point P and point Q. If the radii of the circles are R and r, then find PQ^2.

A. $\dfrac{3\pi Rr}{2}$ **B.** $4Rr$ **C.** $2\pi Rr$ **D.** $2Rr$

Q.16 In the given fig. O is the centre of the circle and $OP \parallel QR$, QR is tangent of the circle and OP $= 6$ cm, find the area of $\triangle OPR$.

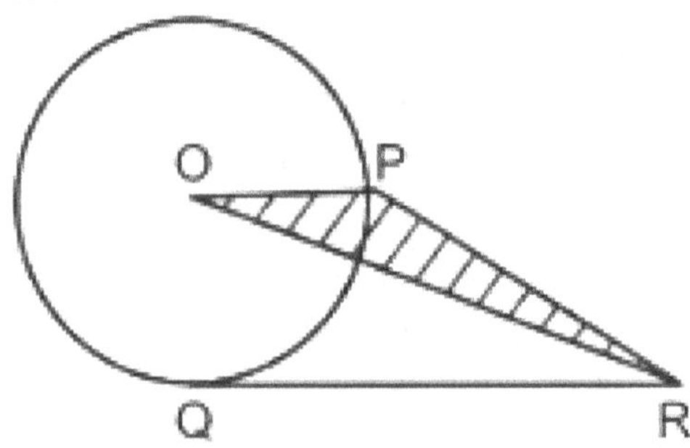

A. 14   **B.** 18   **C.** 26   **D.** 9

Q.17 If $cosec\theta - sin\theta = p^3$ and $sec\theta - cos\theta = q^3$, then what is the value of $tan\theta$?

[Indian Military Academy (IMA), 2020]

A. $\dfrac{p}{q}$ **B.** $\dfrac{q}{p}$ **C.** pq **D.** p^2q^2

Q.18 The value of
$$\frac{cos^4\theta + sin^4\theta + 2sin^2\theta cos^2\theta}{cosec\theta sec\theta (sin\theta + cos\theta - 1)(sin\theta + cos\theta + 1)}$$
is:

Q.19 If $sin(2\alpha + \beta) = 1$ and $sin(\alpha - 2\beta) = \dfrac{1}{2}$, then find the value of $(\alpha + \beta)$.

A. 76°   **B.** 36°   **C.** 48°   **D.** 56°

Q.20 If $4sec^2 a - 3tan^2 a = 7$, find the value of $cosec a$ if $cos a > 0$

A. $\dfrac{2}{\sqrt{3}}$ **B.** $\dfrac{3}{\sqrt{2}}$ **C.** $\sqrt{3}$ **D.** $\dfrac{1}{\sqrt{2}}$

Q.21 If sin α + cos α = p, then what is cos2 (2α) equal to?

A. p^2 **B.** $p^2 - 1$ **C.** $p^2(2 - p^2)$ **D.** $p^2 + 1$

Q.22 What is a $tan^{-1}\left(\dfrac{1}{4}\right) + tan^{-1}\left(\dfrac{3}{5}\right)$ equal to?

A. 0   **B.** $\dfrac{\pi}{4}$ **C.** $\dfrac{\pi}{3}$ **D.** $\dfrac{\pi}{2}$

Q.23 In the given figure rays P || Q || R || S and the ray I || m. find θ_1 and θ_2 respectively.

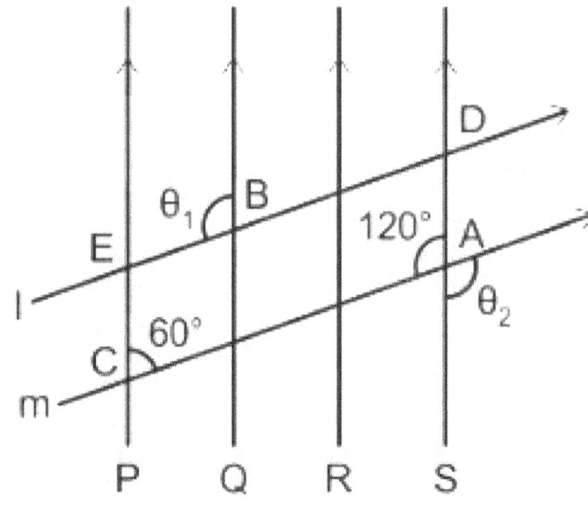

A. 120°, 140°   **B.** 120°, 120°
C. 160°, 150°   **D.** 60°, 120°

Q.24 The difference between two complementary angles is 15°. Find the ratio of greater and smaller angles.

A. 7 : 5   **B.** 6 : 5   **C.** 7 : 6   **D.** 5 : 4

Q.25 In given figure AC || EG, ∠DBC = 135° and ∠DFG = 145°, find the value of ∠BDF.

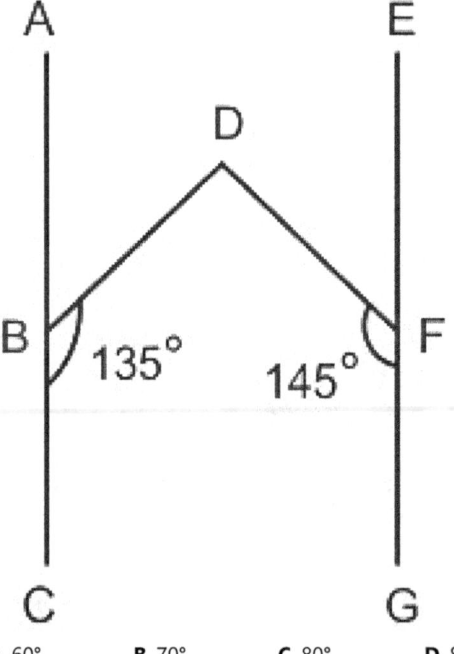

A. 60°   **B.** 70°   **C.** 80°   **D.** 85°

Q.26 In the given figure YZ bisects angle XYY' and YX bisects ∠ WXZ, then find the value of ∠ A'WX + ∠ YZX', if AA' || YY' || XX'

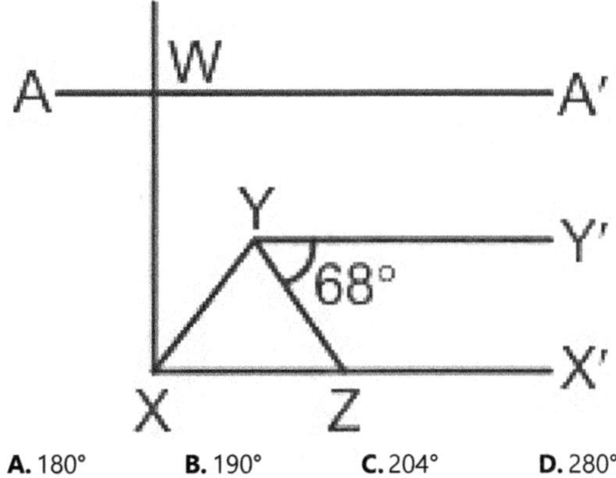

A. 180°   B. 190°   C. 204°   D. 280°

Q.27 In the given figure, AB is a straight line, the value of angle ∠AOC = (7a + 18)° and ∠BOC = (3a + 12)°. Find the value of ∠BOC.

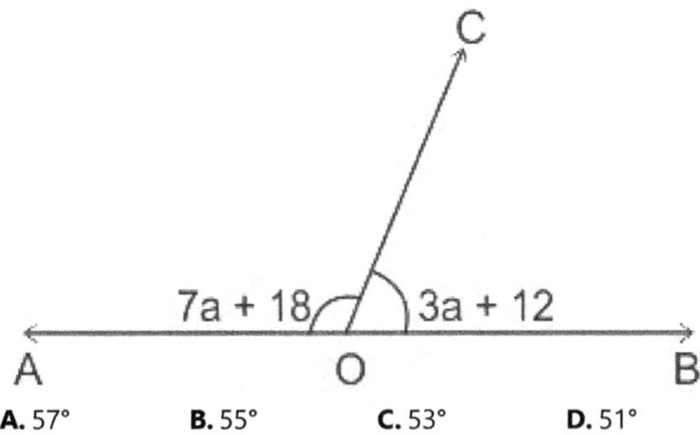

A. 57°   B. 55°   C. 53°   D. 51°

Q.28 If the value of ∠ABC is x°, then find the value of $\frac{3x}{4}$.

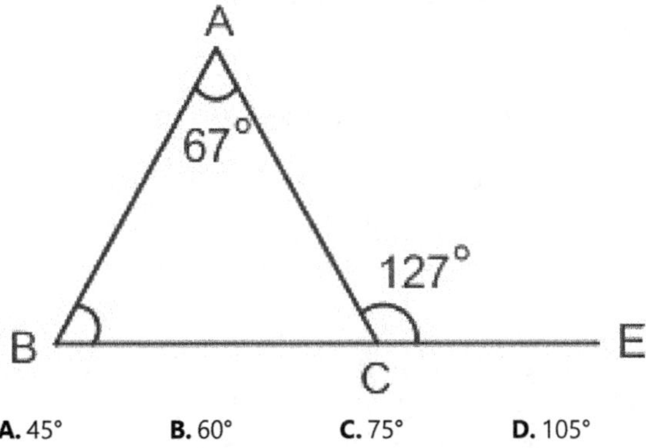

A. 45°   B. 60°   C. 75°   D. 105°

Q.29 In ∆ABC, the side AB is produced to E, and side AC is produced to D. If ∠BCD = 125° and ∠EBC = 110°, then which of the following is true?

[CTET Paper-II (Science & Mathematics), 2021]

A. Difference between ∠ABC and ∠ACB is 35°
B. Difference between ∠BAC and ∠ACB is 20°
C. ∆ABC is an isosceles triangle
D. AB > BC

Q.30 If the angles, in degrees, of a triangle, are x, 3x + 20, and 6x, the triangle must be:

Q.31 Area of a circle is 81π and the equations of the normal to the circle are $2y + 3x - 5 = 0$ and $2y - 3x + 5 = 0$. Find the equation of the circle.

A. $\left(x - \frac{5}{3}\right)^2 + y^2 = 9$

B. $\left(x - \frac{5}{3}\right)^2 + y^2 = 81$

C. $\left(x + \frac{5}{3}\right)^2 + y^2 = 81$

D. $\left(x + \frac{5}{3}\right)^2 + y^2 = 9$

Q.32 Find the equation of directrix of the parabola y² + 8y - 12x + 4 = 0 ?

A. x - 4 = 0   B. x + 4 = 0   C. x + 2 = 0   D. x - 2 = 0

Q.33 Let 'd' be the perpendicular distance from the centre of the ellipse $\frac{x^2}{a^2} + \frac{y^2}{b^2} = 1$ to the tangent drawn at a point P on the ellipse. If F_1 and F_2 are two foci of the ellipse, then $(PF_1 - PF_2)^2$ is equal to;

A. $4\left(1 - \frac{b^2}{d^2}\right)$

B. $4a^2\left(1 - \frac{b^2}{d^2}\right)$

C. $4b^2\left(1 - \frac{a^2}{b^2}\right)$

D. None of these

Q.34 If 4x² + py² = 45 and x² - 4y² = 5 cut orthogonally, then the value of p is:

A. 9   B. $\frac{1}{3}$ C. 3   D. 18

Q.35 The tangents to the hyperbola $x^2 - y^2 = 3$ are parallel to the straight line $2x + y + 8 = 0$ at the following points:

[UPSESSB TGT Mathematics, 2016]

A. (2, 1) or (1, 2)
B. (2, -1) or (-2, 1)
C. (-1, -2)
D. (-2, -1)

Q.36 Let the equation of a circle and a parabola be $x^2 + y^2 - 4x - 6 = 0$ and $y^2 = 9x$ respectively. Then:

A. $(1, -1)$ is a point on the common chord of contact.
B. The equation of the common chord is $y + 1 = 0$.
C. The length of the common chord is 6.
D. Both (A) and (C)

Q.37 The angle between the lines $\beta x + y + 9 = 0, y - 3x = 4$ is $45°$, then the value of β is:

A. 1
B. 2
C. $\frac{-1}{2}$
D. Both (B) and (C)

Q.38 The equation of circumcircle of an equilateral triangle is $x^2 + y^2 + 2gx + 2fy + c = 0$ and one vertex of the triangle is $(1,1)$. The equation of incircle of the triangle is:

A. $4(x^2 + y^2) = g^2 + f^2$

B. $4\left(x^2 + y^2\right) + 8gx + 8fy = (1 - g)(1 + 3g) + (1 - f)(1 + 3f)$

C. $4(x^2 + y^2) + 8gx + 8fy = g^2 + f^2$

D. $4\left(x^2 + y^2\right) + 8gx + 8fy = (2 - g)(1 + 3g) + (2 - f)(2 + 3f)$

Q.39 The $y - z$ plane divides the line joining the points $(3,1,5)$ and $(-2,-1,4)$ in the ratio $\frac{p}{q}$ then $p + q$ will be:

A. 0 **B.** 1 **C.** 5 **D.** 9

Q.40 What is the sum of the 10 angles marked in the given figure?

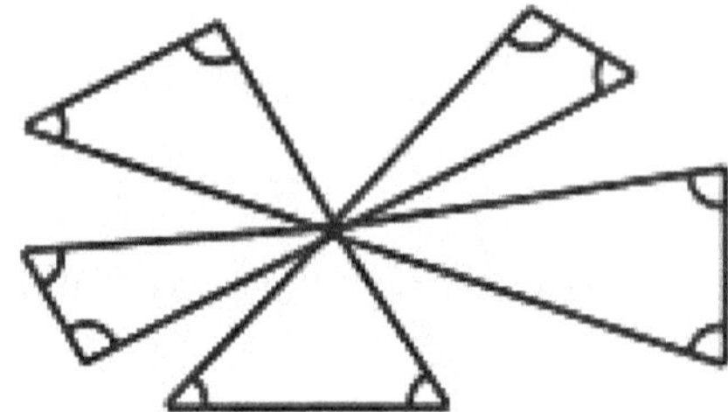

Q.41 Two regular polygons are such that the ratio between their number of sides is 4 : 3 and the ratio of measures of their interior angles is 3 : 2. Then the number of sides of each polygon are:

Q.42 ABCDEF is a regular hexagon. Find the value of $\angle DBC$ and $\angle FED$.

A. $30°, 130°$ **B.** $30°, 120°$
C. $30°, 110°$ **D.** $40°, 120°$

Q.43 In the following question, $ABCDE$ and HIJKL are regular pentagons and $AEFGHL$ is a regular hexagon. If $\angle LKB = \angle ABK$, then, what is the value of $\angle ABK$?

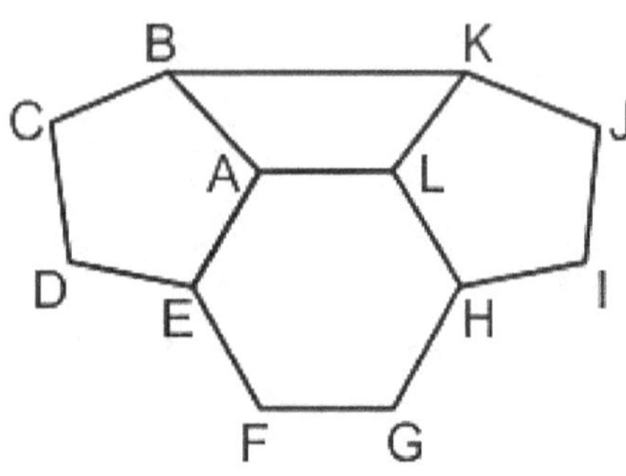

A. 96°   **B.** 48°   **C.** 35°   **D.** 52°

Q.44 In a right-angled triangle ABC. BE is a median and BD is an angle bisector. The lengths of DE, AD, and EC, in the same order, are in AP. If the length of AC is 10 cm and $AB < BC$, then what is the length of BC ?

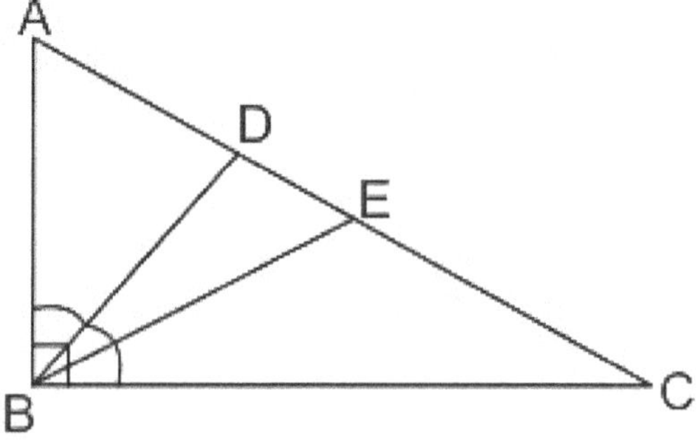

A. 3 cm **B.** $4\sqrt{5}$ cm **C.** $3\sqrt{5}$ cm **D.** 6 cm

Q.45 In the below figure, ABC is a right angled triangle with $AC = 30\ cm. AM = MN = NC$. Find the value of $BM^2 + B^2$.

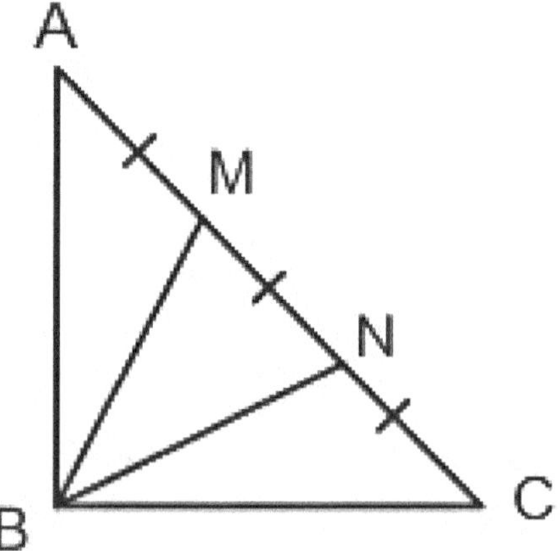

A. 600 cm^2 **B.** 500 cm^2 **C.** 800 cm^2 **D.** 400 cm^2

Q.46 A circle with centre O has a radius of 8 cm. PQ and PR are the two tangents to the circle and $\angle QPR = 60°$. If QR and PO intersect at point K, then, what is the value of KO?

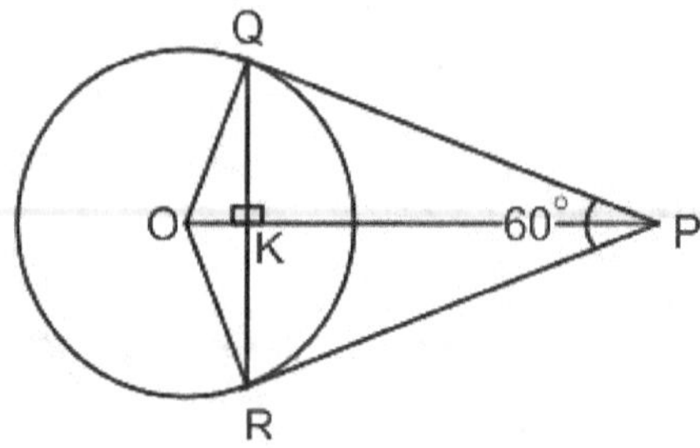

Q.47 In the figure given below there are two circles intersecting each other at points P and Q respectively. A and B are center of the circles, AP is tangent to smaller circle and $AP = 15\ cm$ and $AM = 9\ cm$, then what will the radius of smaller circle if OB is 2 cm less than ON ? (OB is perpendicular to MN.)

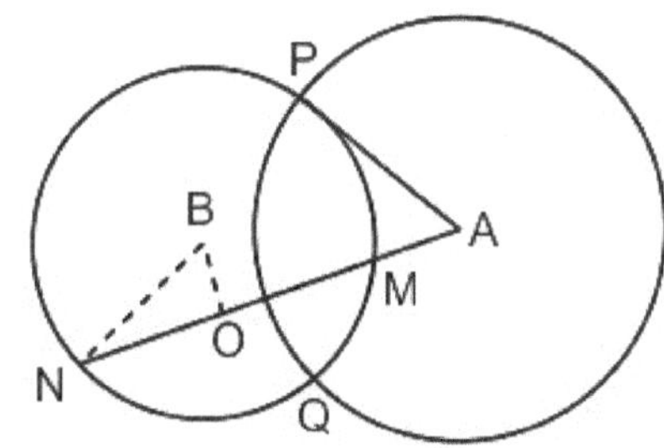

Q.48 If $\tan x + \cot x = 6$, then, find the value of
$$\frac{\left[\left(\frac{1}{\tan x}+\frac{1}{\cot x}\right)+\sin x\cos x\right]}{\sin 2x}$$

Q.49 $\cos^2 14x - \cos^2 18x =$?

A. $\{\sin(16x)\sin(4x)\}$ **B.** $\{\sin(32x)\sin(8x)\}$

C. $\{\sin(32x)\sin(4x)\}$ **D.** $\{\sin(16x)\sin(8x)\}$

Q.50 If $(\sin 3A - \sin 2A) = x\sin A$ and $(\cos 3A - \cos 2A) = y\cos A$, then find the value of $\sec A$.

Q.51 The sum of dimensions of a cuboid are $30\ cm$, and its diagonal is $2\sqrt{77}\ cm$. What is the total surface area of the cuboid?

Q.52 The internal length and breadth of a cuboidal store are $16\ m$ and $13\ m$ respectively and its height is $11\ m$. There is another cubical store whose internal length, breadth and height are $8\ m$ each. How many total cubical boxes each of side one metre can be placed in these two stores to a height of 7 metres?

Q.53 Two walls and a ceiling of a room meet at right angles at a point P. A fly is in the air $1\ m$ from one wall, $8\ m$ from the other wall and $9\ m$ from the point P. How many meters is the fly away from the ceiling?

Q.54 A solid metallic cuboid of dimensions $18\ cm \times 36\ cm \times 72\ cm$ is melted and recast into 8 cubes of the same volume. What is the ratio of the total surface area of the cuboid to the sum of the lateral surface areas of all 8 cubes?

A. $2:3$ **B.** $7:12$ **C.** $4:7$ **D.** $7:8$

Q.55 A metal spherical ball was melted and formed into three spherical balls, such that the radii of the two balls was 50% and 80% of the radius of the original ball. If 2% of the metal remained, then the radius of the third spherical ball is what percentage of the radius of the original ball?

Q.56 A solid sphere is cut into three parts, such that their volumes are in the ratio 4 : 5 : 2. From the largest part, a cube of side 20 cm is cut, such that its volume is (200/241) times the remaining portion of the largest part. Find the diameter of the sphere. Use $\pi = \dfrac{22}{7}$.

Q.57 The radius of lower base of a right circular cone is $10\ cm$ and the height is $10\ cm$. If a plane parallel to its base cuts the cone at a height of $6\ cm$ from the base and the volume of frustum of cone is $312\pi\,cm^3$ then, the radius on top of frustum of cone is,

Q.58 A vessel is in the form of an inverted cone. Its height is $12\ cm$ and the radius of its top, which is open, is $8\ cm$. It is filled with water up to the brim. When spherical lead shots of radius $0.5\ cm$ are dropped into the vessel, one-fourth of the water flows out. Find the number of lead shots dropped in the vessel.

Q.59 Ratio of base radius and height of cylinder of volume $2156\ cm^3$ is $1:2$. If the radius of cylinder is increased by $3\ cm$ and height is decreased by $3.5\ cm$, then what will be the change in the volume of cylinder?

A. $1144\ cm^3$ **B.** $1240\ cm^3$

C. $929\ cm^3$ **D.** $3344\ cm^3$

Q.60 The thickness of a cylinder is 1 foot, the inner radius of the cylinder is 3 feet and height is 7 feet. To paint the inner surface it requires one litre of a particular colour. How much quantity of the same colour is required to paint all the surfaces of the cylinder?

A. $\frac{7}{3}$ litre   **B.** $\frac{3}{2}$ litre   **C.** $\frac{8}{3}$ litre   **D.** $\frac{10}{3}$ litre

// Smart Answer Sheet //

Correct Indicates percentage of students who answered questions correctly.

Skipped Indicates percentage of students who skipped questions.

Q.	Ans.	Correct / Skipped
1	A	22.75 % / 76.51 %
2	#	44.71 % / 52.21 %
3	A	45.23 % / 44.1 %
4	C	67.26 % / 31.49 %
5	B	61.42 % / 31.77 %
6	C	47.08 % / 49.19 %
7	B	26.52 % / 69.3 %
8	#	66.04 % / 30.54 %
9	D	46.09 % / 40.59 %
10	A	66.84 % / 31.53 %
11	D	62.12 % / 36.34 %
12	B	57.68 % / 33.95 %

Q.	Ans.	Correct / Skipped
13	C	21.34 % / 73.79 %
14	C	86.85 % / 12.13 %
15	B	61.47 % / 30.04 %
16	B	14.03 % / 70.16 %
17	B	56.38 % / 32.54 %
18	#	30.03 % / 68.01 %
19	C	56.33 % / 34.82 %
20	A	56.35 % / 39.8 %
21	C	64.06 % / 30.6 %
22	B	42.39 % / 35.33 %
23	B	54.71 % / 37.11 %
24	A	18.16 % / 75.89 %

Q.	Ans.	Correct / Skipped
25	C	41.39 % / 36.28 %
26	C	14.58 % / 69.3 %
27	A	54.78 % / 32.89 %
28	A	61.14 % / 32.85 %
29	C	17.18 % / 80.73 %
30	#	40.39 % / 32.3 %
31	B	24.94 % / 73.91 %
32	B	27.52 % / 70.38 %
33	B	23.54 % / 68.47 %
34	A	20.01 % / 72.58 %
35	B	13.6 % / 74.2 %
36	D	26.17 % / 73.46 %

Q.	Ans.	Correct / Skipped
37	D	17.85 % / 78.46 %
38	B	28.32 % / 69.26 %
39	C	43.19 % / 41.0 %
40	720	25.65 % / 70.87 %
41	#	11.66 % / 88.19 %
42	B	24.65 % / 69.56 %
43	B	86.02 % / 12.89 %
44	B	18.25 % / 72.4 %
45	B	26.76 % / 67.8 %
46	#	16.94 % / 69.93 %
47	#	12.9 % / 69.97 %
48	#	26.86 % / 69.18 %

Q.	Ans.	Correct / Skipped
49	C	16.61 % / 82.98 %
50	#	14.12 % / 69.14 %
51	#	30.03 % / 67.12 %
52	#	10.9 % / 78.67 %
53	#	16.45 % / 68.34 %
54	D	69.25 % / 30.63 %
55	#	14.87 % / 80.26 %
56	#	32.25 % / 67.18 %
57	#	30.59 % / 69.14 %
58	#	17.6 % / 75.48 %
59	A	66.19 % / 30.54 %
60	C	65.35 % / 32.8 %

#

Q.	Answer
2	20
8	$4:1$
18	1
30	Obtuse angle
41	4, 3
46	4 cm
47	10 cm
48	37/2
50	$(y - x + 2)$

51	$592\ cm^2$
52	1904
53	4
55	70%
56	42 cm
57	$4\ cm$
58	384

Performance Analysis	
Avg. Score (%)	40.56%
Toppers Score (%)	63.89%
Your Score	

//Hints and Solutions//

1. Given:

The smallest interior angle is 100°

Formula Used:

$\text{Sumn} = \dfrac{n}{2} \times [2a + (n - 1)d]$

Calculation:

Let the polygon have n sides

Difference between two consecutive angles is 4°

⇒ Internal Angles are 100°, 104°, 108° ...... and so on.

⇒ External angles will be 80°, 76°...... and so on.

Thus the above series forms an arithmetic progression

∵ The sum of all the external angles of a polygon is 360°

And, $\text{Sum}_n = \dfrac{n}{2} \times [2a + (n - 1)d]$

⇒ $360 = \dfrac{n}{2} \times [160 + (n - 1) \times (-4)]$

⇒ $n^2 - 41n + 180 = 0$

⇒ $n^2 - 36n - 5n + 180 = 0$

⇒ $n(n - 36) - 5(n - 36) = 0$

⇒ $n = 36$ and 5

∴ Number of sides of the polygon = 5

Hence, the correct option is (A).

2. Each interior angle of a regular polygon is 135 ,

⇒ Exterior angle $= 180° -$ Interior angle $= 45°$

⇒ Number of sides of polygon $= \dfrac{360°}{\text{Exterior angle}} = 8$

∴ Number of diagonals $= \dfrac{n(n-3)}{2}$

$= 8 \times \dfrac{(8-3)}{2}$

$= 20,$

where n is the number of sides of a polygon.

Hence, the correct option is (D).

3. Given:

The sum of all interior angles of a regular polygon is twice the sum of all its exterior angles

We know that,

Sum of all interior angles of a regular polygon $=$
$(n - 2) \times 180°$

where $n =$ number of sides of polygon

Sum of all exterior angle of a regular polygon $= 360°$

According to question

$= 180°(n - 2) = 2 \times 360°$

$= n - 2 = 4$

$= n = 6$

∴ Number of sides of the polygon 6 (Hexagon).

Hence, the correct option is (A).

4. Given: Regular polygon

The Ratio of side $1 : 2$

Let sides be n and $2n$

We know for regular polygon interior angle is given by

$\dfrac{(n-2)180}{n}$

The ratio of interior angles $= \dfrac{2}{3}$

$\dfrac{\frac{(n-2)180}{n}}{\frac{(2n-2)180}{2n}} = \dfrac{2}{3}$

$\dfrac{(n-2)}{(n-1)} = \dfrac{2}{3}$

$3n - 6 = 2n - 2$

$n = 4$

Therefore, sides can be 4 and 8.

Hence, the correct option is (C).

5. Given:

Medians AD and BE are perpendicular to each other and have lengths 12 cm and 9 cm.

Calculation:

Draw a median from point C

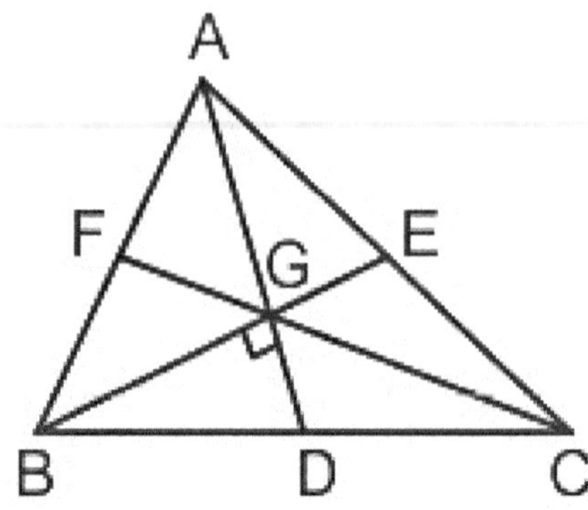

Now all three medians divide the Δ ABC into 6 triangles.

⇒ Area of Δ ABC = 6 × Any small triangle that is formed

Point G is centroid,

AG : GD = 2 : 1

AD = 12 cm

$\Rightarrow$ AG + GD = 12

$\Rightarrow$ 3 = 12

$\Rightarrow$ 1 = $\dfrac{12}{3}$

$\Rightarrow$ 1 = 4

$\Rightarrow$ AG = 2 × 4 = 8 cm

$\Rightarrow$ GD = 1 × 4 = 4 cm

Also BG : GE = 2 : 1,

BE = 9 cm

$\Rightarrow$ BG + GE = 9 cm

$\Rightarrow$ 2 + 1 = 9 cm

$\Rightarrow$ 3 = 9 cm

$\Rightarrow$ 1 = $\dfrac{9}{3}$

$\Rightarrow$ 1 = 3

$\Rightarrow$ BG = 2 × 3 = 6 cm

$\Rightarrow$ GE = 1 × 3 = 3 cm

Now, BE perpendicular to AD,

In Δ BGD, ∠ BGD = 90°

Area of Δ BGD = $\dfrac{1}{2}$ × BG × GD

$\Rightarrow$ Area of Δ BGD = $\dfrac{1}{2}$ × 6 × 4

$\Rightarrow$ Area of Δ BGD = 12 cm²

Area of Δ ABC = 6 × Area of Δ BGD

$\Rightarrow$ Area of Δ ABC = 6 × 12

$\Rightarrow$ Area of Δ ABC = 72 cm²

∴ The area of Δ ABC is 72 cm².

Hence, the correct option is (B).

6. Given:

$\triangle ABC \sim \triangle DEF$

ar $\triangle ABC = 64$ cm²

ar $\triangle DEF = 121$ cm²

$EF = 15.4$ cm

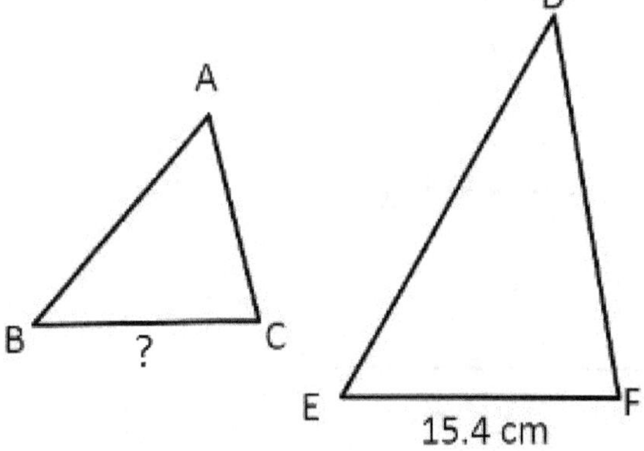

To find: BC

Since, $\triangle ABC \sim \triangle DEF$

We know that if two triangle are similar,

Ratio of areas is equal to square of ratio of its corresponding sides

So, $\dfrac{ar\triangle ABC}{ar\triangle DEF} = \left(\dfrac{BC}{EF}\right)^2$

Putting the values,

$\dfrac{64}{121} = \left(\dfrac{BC}{15.4}\right)^2$

$\dfrac{64}{121} = \dfrac{BC^2}{(15.4)^2}$

$\dfrac{64}{121} \times (15.4)^2 = BC^2$

$\left(\dfrac{8\times8}{11\times11}\right) \times (15.4)^2 = BC^2$

$\dfrac{8^2}{11^2} \times (15.4)^2 = BC^2$

$\left(\dfrac{8}{11} \times 15.4\right)^2 = BC^2$

$\dfrac{8}{11} \times 15.4 = BC$

$BC = \dfrac{8}{11} \times 15.4$

$BC = 8 \times 1.4$

$BC = 11.2$

So, $BC = 11.2$ cm

Hence, the correct option is (C).

7. Given:

$\triangle ABC$

and D, E, F mid-points of AB, BC and CA respectively

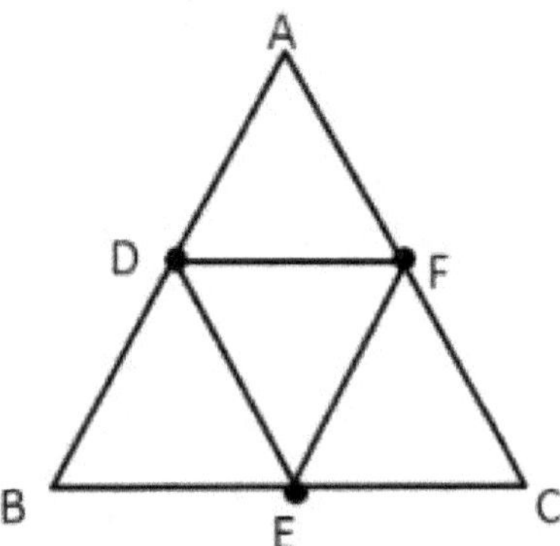

So, $\angle DFE = \angle ABC$ $\qquad ...\,...(3)$

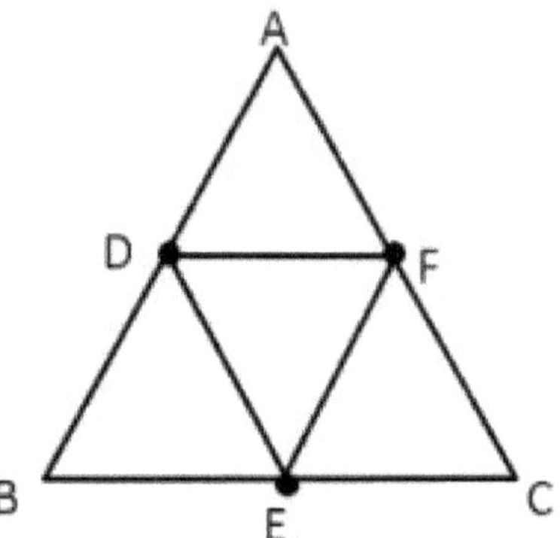

Note: Since we need to find ratio of area of $\triangle DEF$ and $\triangle ABC$. We first need to prove these triangles are similar.

We know that,

line joining mid-points of two sides of a triangle is parallel to the 3rd side.

Similarity,

We can prove $DECF$ is a parallelogram,

In a parallelogram, opposite angles are equal

So, $\angle EDF = \angle ACB$ $\qquad ...\,...(4)$

Now, in $\triangle EDF$ and $\triangle ABC$

$\angle DFE = \angle ABC$ and from 3,

$\angle EDF = \angle ACB$ and from 4,

By using AA similarity criterion,

$\triangle DEF \sim \triangle ABC$

We know that if two triangles are similar, the ratio of their area is always equal to the square of the ratio of their corresponding side.

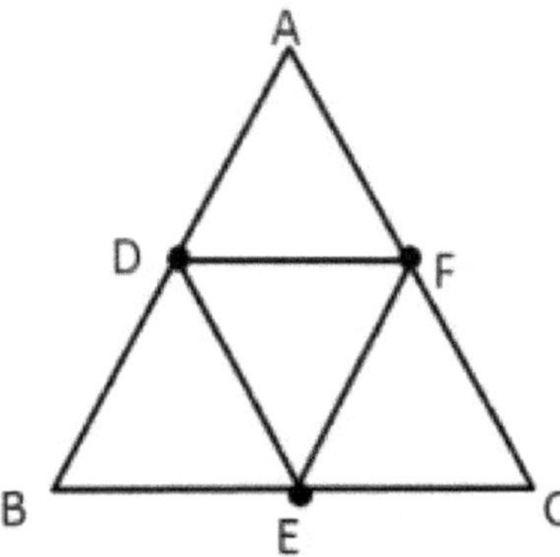

In $\triangle ABC$,

D and F are mid-points of AB and AC resp.,

$\therefore DF \parallel BC$

So, $DF \parallel BE$ also $\qquad ...\,...(1)$

Similarly,

E and F are mid-points of BC and AC resp.

$EF \parallel AB$

So, $EF| \, |DB$ $\qquad ...\,...(2)$

From (1) and (2),

$DF \parallel BE$ and $FE \parallel DB$

Therefore, opposite sides of quadrilateral is parallel.

$DBEF$ is a parallelogram,

$DBEF$ is a parallelogram

Now we know that,

in parallelogram, opposite angle are equal.

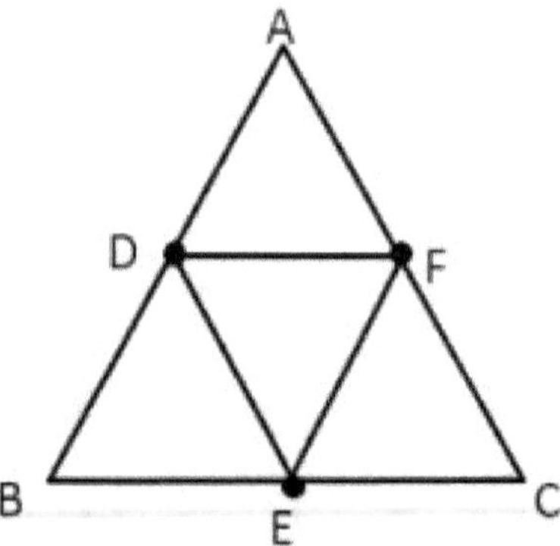

$\therefore \dfrac{ar\triangle DEF}{ar\triangle ABC} = \dfrac{DE^2}{AC^2}$

$\dfrac{ar\triangle DEF}{ar\triangle ABC} = \dfrac{FC^2}{AC^2}$ (Since $DECF$ is a parallelogram,

opposite sides are equal, i.e $DE = FC$.)

$\dfrac{\text{Area of } \triangle DEF}{\text{Area of } \triangle ABC} = \dfrac{\left(\frac{AC}{2}\right)^2}{(AC)^2}$ (As F is the mid-point of AC)

$$\frac{\text{Area of } \triangle DEF}{\text{Area of } \triangle ABC} = \frac{\frac{(AC)^2}{4}}{(AC)^2}$$

$$\frac{\text{Area of } \triangle DEF}{\text{Area of } \triangle ABC} = \frac{\frac{1}{4}}{1}$$

So, $\dfrac{\text{Area of } \triangle DEF}{\text{Arae of } \triangle ABC} = \dfrac{1}{4}$

Hence, the correct option is (B).

8. Given:

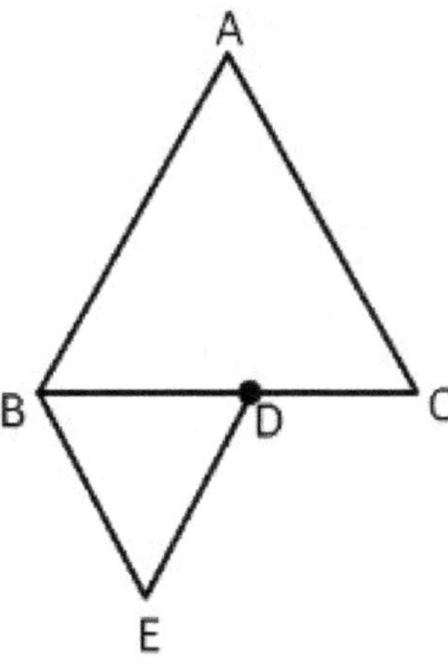

Given:

$\triangle ABC$ is equilateral

$\triangle BDE$ is equilateral

$BD = \dfrac{1}{2}BC$ as D is midpoint of BC

To find: $\dfrac{ar\triangle ABC}{ar\triangle BDE}$

Since, $\triangle ABC$ and $\triangle BDE$ are equilateral, Their sides would be in the same ratio

$$\frac{AB}{BE} = \frac{AC}{ED} = \frac{BC}{BD}$$

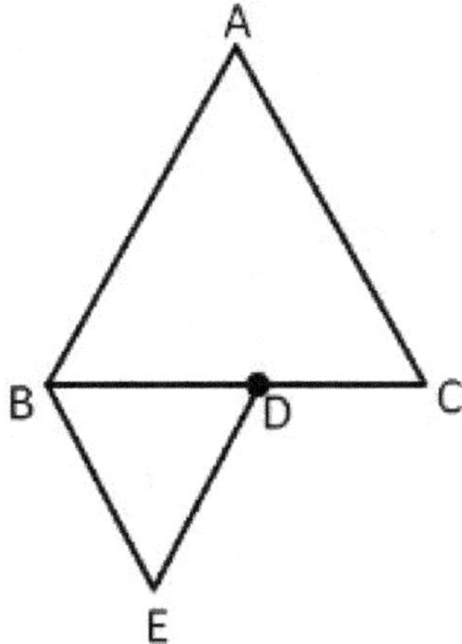

So, by SSS similarity

$$\triangle ABC \sim \triangle BDE$$

And, we know that ratio of area of triangle is equal To the ratio of square of corresponding sides.

So, $\dfrac{\text{area of } \triangle ABC}{\text{area of } \triangle BDE} = \dfrac{(BC)^2}{(BD)^2}$

$$= \frac{(BC)^2}{\left(\frac{BC}{2}\right)^2} \quad \left(\text{Since } BD = \frac{1}{2}BC\right)$$

$$= \frac{BC^2}{\frac{BC^2}{4}}$$

$$= \frac{4BC^2}{BC^2}$$

$$= \frac{4}{1}$$

So, $\dfrac{\text{area of } \triangle ABC}{\text{area of } \triangle BDE} = \dfrac{4}{1}$ i.e. $4:1$

Hence, the correct option is (C).

9. Given,

In $\triangle DEW, AB \parallel EW$,

$AD = 4$ cm, $DE = 12$ cm and $DW = 24$ cm

Let $BD = x$ cm

then $BW = (24 - x)$ cm

$AE = 12 - 4 = 8$ cm

In $\triangle DEW, AB \parallel EW$

$$\frac{AD}{AE} = \frac{BD}{BW}$$

(Thales' Theorem)

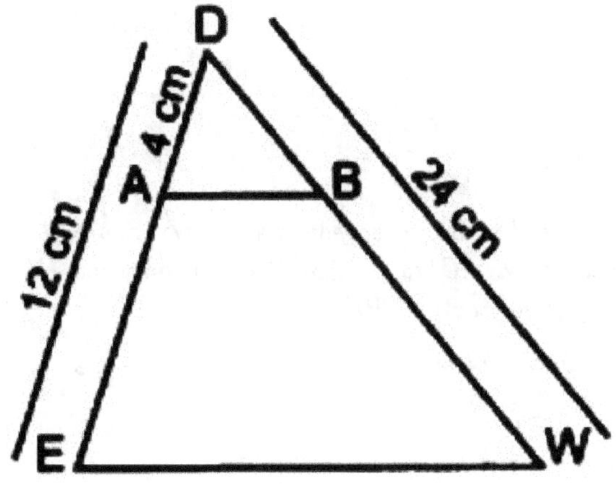

$$\frac{4}{8} = \frac{x}{24-x}$$

$$8x = 96 - 4x$$

$$\Rightarrow 12x = 96$$

$\Rightarrow x = \frac{96}{12} = 8$ cm

$\therefore DB = 8$ cm

Hence, the correct option is (D).

10. Given,

$BE = BC - EC = 10 - 2 = 8$ cm

Let $AF = x$ cm,

then $BF = (13 - x)$ cm

In $\triangle ABC, EF \parallel AC$

Given,

$\frac{BF}{FA} = \frac{BE}{EC}$

(Thales' theorem)

$\frac{13-x}{x} = \frac{8}{2}$

$\Rightarrow 4x = 13 - x$

$4x + x = 13$

$\Rightarrow \quad 5x = 13$

$x = \frac{13}{5} = 2.6$ cm

$\therefore AF = 2.6$ cm

Hence, the correct option is (A).

11.

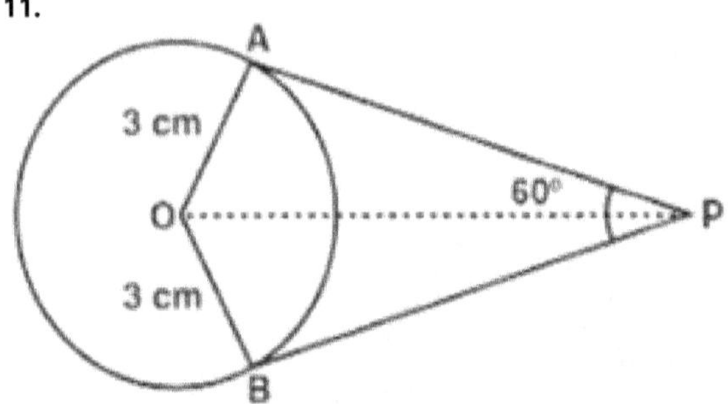

If PA and PB be the two tangents to a circle with centre O and radius 3, $\triangle AOP$ and $\triangle BOP$ are congruent and OP is the angle bisector of $\angle APB$.

$\therefore \angle APO = \angle BPO$

$= \frac{1}{2} \times \angle APB$

$= \frac{1}{2} \times 60°$

$= 30°$

Therefore, $\angle APO = \angle BPO = \frac{60°}{2} = 30°$

OA is perpendicular to AP.

In right triangle AOP,

$\tan 30° = \frac{OA}{AP}$

$\frac{1}{\sqrt{3}} = \frac{3}{AP}$

$AP = 3\sqrt{3}$

So, the length of the tangent is $3\sqrt{3}$ cm.

Hence, the correct option is (D).

12. As per the given question:

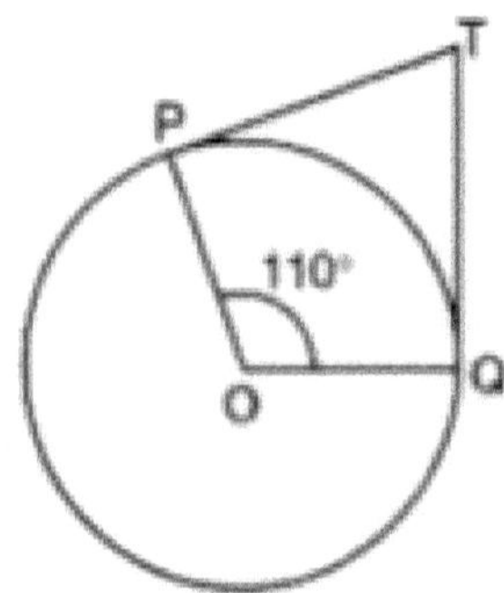

We can see, OP is the radius of the circle to the tangent PT and OQ is the radius to the tangents TQ.

SO, $OP \perp PT$ and $TQ \perp OQ$

$\therefore \angle OPT = \angle OQT = 90°$

Now, in the quadrilateral POQT, we know that the sum of the interior angles is $360°$

$So, \angle PTQ + \angle POQ + \angle OPT + \angle OQT = 360°$

Now, by putting the respective values, we get,

$\Rightarrow \angle PTQ + 90° + 110° + 90° = 360°$

$\Rightarrow \angle PTQ = 70°$

Hence, the correct option is (B).

13. Join OP and OQ,

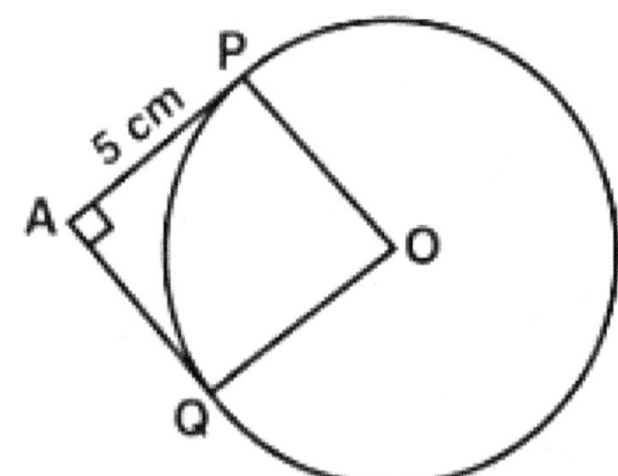

Tangents $AP = AQ$

In triangle APO and AQO,

$AP = AQ$

$AO = AO$ (Common)

$OP = OQ$ (radius of same circle)

Thus, $\triangle APO \sim \triangle AQO$.

If $\triangle APO$ and $\triangle AQO$ are congruent then we can say,

$OP = OQ = AP = AQ$

So, $AP = AQ = 5$ cm

And $AP = OP$

Therefore, radius $= OP = 5$ cm

Hence, the correct option is (C).

14.

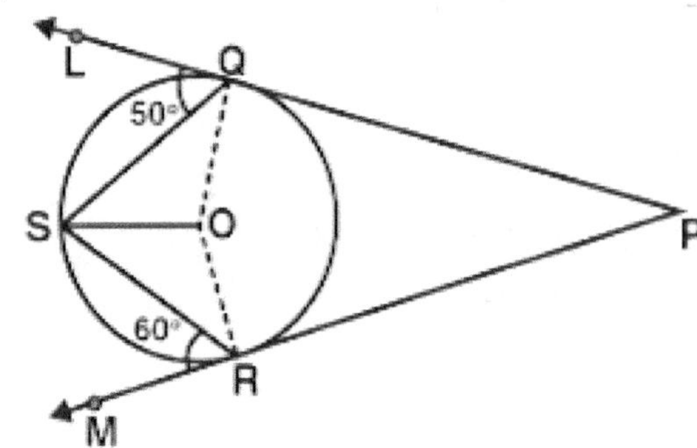

Step 1: Write the given angles referring to given diagram.

Given $\angle SRM = 60°, \angle SQ = 50°$.

Step 2: Use the geometric rules and property to find the value of $\angle QSR$.

If, $\angle SRM = 60°$

$\Rightarrow \angle SRM + \angle SRO = 90°$

$\therefore \angle SRO = 30°$

For $\triangle OSR$

$OS = OR$[radii of same circle]

$\angle OSR = \angle SRO = 30°$ [angles opposite to equal sides are equal]

As, $\angle SQL = 50°$

$\Rightarrow \angle SQL + \angle SQO = 90°$

$\therefore \angle SQO = 40°$

For $\triangle OSQ$,

$OS = OQ$[radii of same circle]

$\angle SQO = \angle OSQ = 40°$ [angles opposite to equal sides are equal]

$\therefore \angle QSR = \angle OSR + \angle OSQ$

$= 30° + 40°$

$= 70°$

The value of $\angle QSR$ is $70°$.

Hence, the correct option is (C).

15.

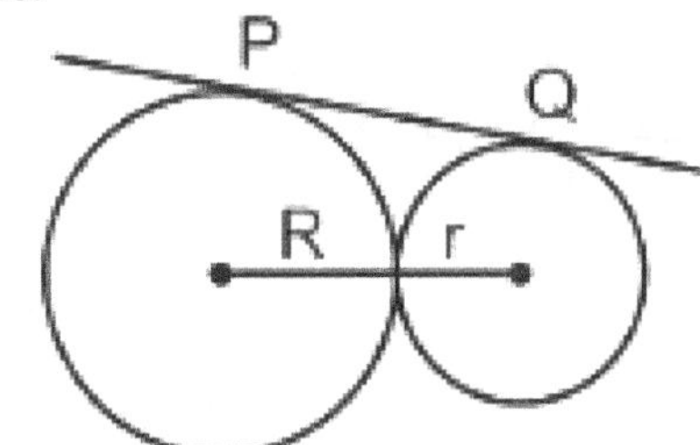

As we know that,

Length of direct common tangent $= \sqrt{[d^2 - (R - r)^2]}$

where d is the distance between the centers and R and r are the radii of the circles.

$PQ = \sqrt{[(R + r)^2 - (R - r)^2]}$

$\Rightarrow PQ = \sqrt{[R^2 + r^2 + 2Rr - (R^2 + r^2 - 2Rr)]}$

$\Rightarrow PQ = \sqrt{4Rr}$

$\Rightarrow PQ^2 = 4Rr$

Hence, the correct option is (B).

16.

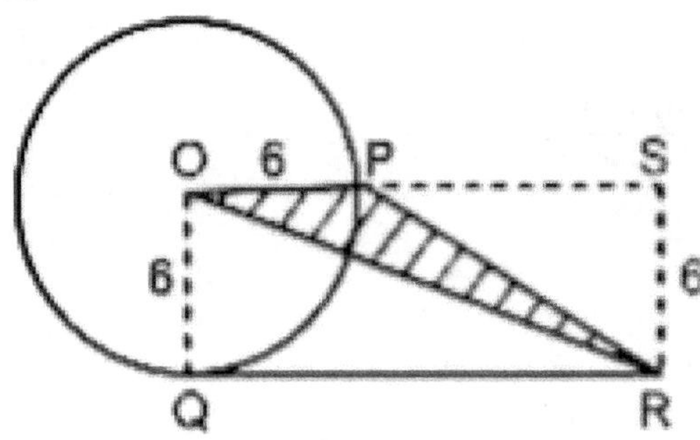

$OP \parallel QR$ (given)

$\Rightarrow$ Extend the point P to the point S such that $QR = OS$

Thus, rectangle QRSO is formed

$\Rightarrow OQ = SR = 6$ cm (Height of the $\triangle OPR$)

$\Rightarrow OP = 6cm =$ Base of the $\triangle OPR$

$\Rightarrow$ Area of $\triangle OPR = \frac{1}{2} \times 6 \times 6 = 18$ cm^2

Hence, the correct option is (B).

17. Given:

$cosec\theta - sin\theta = p^3$ and $sec\theta - cos\theta = q^3$

As we know,

$1 - sin^2\theta = cos^2\theta$

$1 - cos^2\theta = sin^2\theta$

Now,

$cosec\theta - sin\theta = \frac{1}{(sin\theta)} - sin\theta$

$= \frac{(1-sin^2\theta)}{sin\theta}$

$= \frac{(cos^2\theta)}{(sin\theta)}$

So,

$\frac{(cos^2\theta)}{(sin\theta)} = p^3 \quad ... (1)$

Now,

$sec\theta - cos\theta = \left(\frac{1}{cos\theta}\right) - cos\theta$

$= \frac{(1-cos^2\theta)}{cos\theta}$

$= \frac{(sin^2\theta)}{(cos\theta)}$

So,

$\frac{(sin^2\theta)}{(cos\theta)} = q^3 \quad ... (2)$

Divide equation (2) by (1)

$\frac{(sin^2\theta)}{(cos\theta)} \div \frac{(cos^2\theta)}{(sin\theta)} = \frac{q^3}{p^3}$

$\frac{sin^3\theta}{cos^3\theta} = \frac{q^3}{p^3}$

$tan\theta = \frac{q}{p}$

Hence, the correct option is (B).

18. Given,

$\dfrac{cos^4\theta+sin^4\theta+2sin^2\theta cos^2\theta}{cosec\theta sec\theta(sin\theta+cos\theta-1)(sin\theta+cos\theta+1)}$

Considering the given equation,

$\dfrac{cos^4\theta+sin^4\theta+2sin^2\theta cos^2\theta}{cosec\theta sec\theta(sin\theta+cos\theta-1)(sin\theta+cos\theta+1)}$

$\because (sin^4\theta + cos^4\theta = 1 - 2sin^2\theta cos^2\theta)$

$= \dfrac{(1-2sin^2\theta cos^2\theta+2sin^2\theta cos^2\theta)}{cosec\theta sec\theta[(sin\theta+cos\theta)^2-1]}$

$= \dfrac{1}{cosec\theta sec\theta[(sin^2\theta+cos^2\theta+2sin\theta cos\theta-1]}$

$= \dfrac{(sin\theta cos\theta)}{(1+2sin\theta cos\theta-1)}$

$= \dfrac{(sin\theta cos\theta)}{(2sin\theta cos\theta)} = \dfrac{1}{2}$

$\therefore$ The value of $\dfrac{cos4\theta+sin^4\theta+2sin^2\theta cos^2\theta}{cosec\theta sec\theta(sin\theta+cos\theta-1)(sin\theta+cos\theta+1)}$ is $\dfrac{1}{2}$.

Hence, the correct option is (A).

19. Given:

$\Rightarrow sin(2\alpha + \beta) = 1$

$\Rightarrow sin(2\alpha + \beta) = sin90°$

$\Rightarrow (2\alpha + \beta) = 90° \;.....(1)$

$\Rightarrow sin(\alpha - 2\beta) = \frac{1}{2}$

$\Rightarrow sin(\alpha - 2\beta) = sin30° \;.....(2)$

Multiply by 2 in equation (1)

$\Rightarrow (4\alpha + 2\beta) = 180° \;.....(3)$

Add equation (1) and equation (2)

$\Rightarrow 5a = 210°$

$\Rightarrow \alpha = 42°$

Put $a = 42°$ in equation (1)

$\Rightarrow 84° + \beta = 90°$

$\Rightarrow \beta = 6°$

$\therefore (\alpha + \beta) = 42° + 6° = 48°$

Hence, the correct option is (C).

20. Given:

$4sec^2a - 3tan^2a = 7$

We know that,

$cosec\alpha = \dfrac{1}{sin\alpha}$

$sec\alpha = \dfrac{1}{cos\alpha}$

$tan\alpha = \dfrac{sin\alpha}{cos\alpha}$

$4sec^2a - 3tan^2a = 7$

$$\Rightarrow \left(\frac{4}{\cos^2\alpha}\right) - 3\left(\frac{\sin^2\alpha}{\cos^2\alpha}\right) = 7$$

$$\Rightarrow 4 - 3\sin^2\alpha = 7\cos^2\alpha$$

$$\Rightarrow 4 - 3(1 - \cos^2\alpha) = 7\cos^2\alpha$$

$$\Rightarrow 4 - 3 = 7\cos^2\alpha - 3\cos^2\alpha$$

$$\Rightarrow 1 = 4\cos^2\alpha$$

$$\Rightarrow \cos^2\alpha = \frac{1}{4}$$

$$\Rightarrow \cos\alpha = \frac{1}{2}$$

$$\cos 60° = \frac{1}{2}$$

$$\Rightarrow \alpha = 60°$$

$$\Rightarrow cosec\,60° = \frac{2}{\sqrt{3}}$$

$\therefore$ Value of $cosec\,\alpha$ is equal to $\frac{2}{\sqrt{3}}$.

Hence, the correct option is (A).

21. We know that,

$$\sin^2 x + \cos^2 x = 1$$

$$\sin 2x = 2\sin x\cos x$$

Given: $\sin\alpha + \cos\alpha = p$

By squaring both the sides, we get

$$\Rightarrow \sin^2 a + \cos^2 a + 2\sin a\cos a = p^2$$

As we know that, $\sin^2 x + \cos^2 x = 1$ and $\sin 2x = 2\sin x\cos x$

$$\Rightarrow 1 + \sin 2a = p^2$$

$$\Rightarrow \sin 2a = p^2 - 1$$

As we can write $\cos^2 2a = 1 - \sin^2 2a$

$$\Rightarrow \cos^2 2a = 1 - (p^2 - 1)^2$$

$\therefore$ The value of $\cos^2 2a$ is $p^2(2 - p^2)$.

Hence, the correct option is (C).

22. Given:

$$\tan^{-1}\left(\frac{1}{4}\right) + \tan^{-1}\left(\frac{3}{5}\right)$$

On solving. we get-

$$= \tan^{-1}\left(\frac{\frac{1}{4} + \frac{3}{5}}{1 - \frac{1}{4} \times \frac{3}{5}}\right)$$

$$= \tan^{-1}\left(\frac{\frac{5+22}{20}}{\frac{20-3}{20}}\right) = \tan^{-1}\left(\frac{17}{17}\right) = \tan^{-1}(1)$$

$$= \tan^{-1}\left(\tan\frac{\pi}{4}\right) = \frac{\pi}{4}$$

Hence, the correct option is (B).

23. Given:

Rays P || Q || R || S and the ray l || m.

Calculation:

We are given that, ∠ECA = 60°

So, ∠IBQ = 60° (Opposite angles in a parallelogram are equal)

Now, ∠IBQ + θ_1 = 180° (Linear pairs)

$\Rightarrow \theta_1$ = 180° - 60°

$\Rightarrow \theta_1$ = 120°

Now, we know that vertically opposite angles are equal

$\therefore$ ∠CAD = θ_2 = 120°

$\therefore \theta_1$ = 120° and θ_2 = 120°

Hence, the correct option is (B).

24. Given:

The difference between two complementary angles is 15°

Calculation:

Let two complementary angles be ∠x and ∠y respectively.

∠x - ∠y = 15°   ----(i) (given)

∠x + ∠y = 90°   ----(ii) (Sum of complementary angles is 90°)

From (i), ∠y = 15 + ∠x   ----(iii)

From (ii), ∠y = 90 - ∠x   ----(iv)

On comparing the values of ∠y from (iii) & (iv) we get,

15 + ∠x = 90 - ∠x

$\Rightarrow$ 2∠x = 75

$\Rightarrow$ ∠x = 37.5

So, ∠y = 90 - 37.5 = 52.5

Since, ∠x = 37.5 and ∠y = 52.5

Therefore, Greater angle : Smaller angle = ∠y : ∠x

$\Rightarrow$ 52.5 : 37.5 = 7 : 5

$\therefore$ Required ratio is 7 : 5

Hence, the correct option is (A).

25. Given:

AC || EG

∠DBC = 135° and ∠DFG = 145°

Calculation:

We construct a PQ line parallel to AC and EG

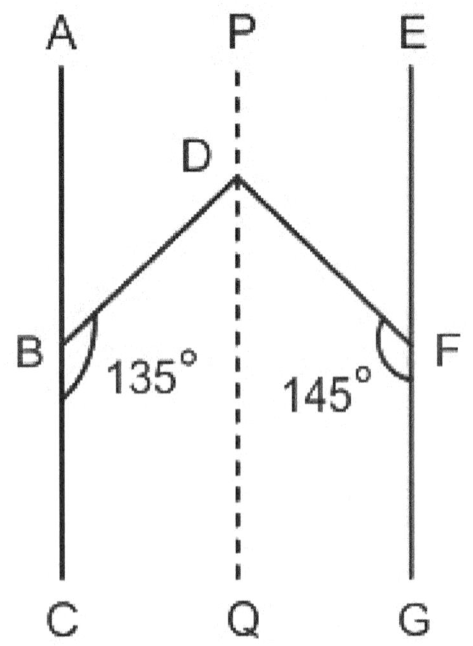

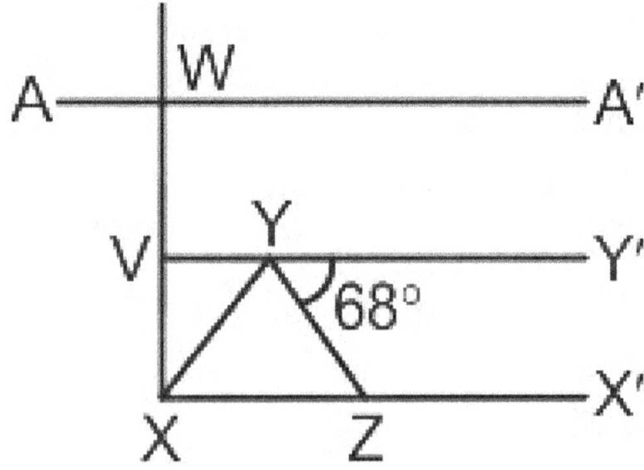

Now, AB || PQ || EG

We know that the sum of interior anngle formed on the same side of parallel lines is 180°

∠BDQ + ∠DBC = 180°

⇒ ∠BDQ + 135° = 180°

⇒ ∠BDQ = 45° -------(1)

Similarly, we have

∠QDF + ∠DFG = 180°

⇒ ∠QDF + 145° = 180°

⇒ ∠QDF = 35° -------(2)

Since, ∠BDF = ∠BDQ + ∠QDF

So on putting values of ∠BDQ and ∠QDF from -(1) & (2) we get,

∠BDF = 45° + 35° = 80°

∴ The value of ∠BDF is 80°

Hence, the correct option is (C).

26. Given :

AA' || YY' || XX'

YZ bisects ∠XYY'.

∠YXW = ∠YXZ

Calculations :

⇒ ∠XYZ = ∠ZYY'   (YZ bisects angle XYY')

⇒ ∠XYV + ∠ XYZ + ∠Y'YZ = 180°

⇒ ∠XYV + 68° + 68° = 180°

⇒ ∠XYV = 44°

⇒ ∠YXW = ∠YXZ   (given YX bisects ∠ WXZ)

⇒ ∠YXW + ∠YXZ = 44° + 44° = 88°

Now

⇒ ∠A'WX + ∠WXZ = 180° (sum of interior angles on the same side of transversal is 180°)

⇒ ∠ A'WX = 180° - 88°

⇒ 92°

Now

⇒ ∠ YZX' = ∠ZYX + ∠YXZ (exterior angle is equal to the sum of interior opposite angles)

⇒ 68° + 44°

⇒ 112°

Now

⇒ ∠A'WX + ∠YZX' = 112° + 92°

⇒ 204°

Hence, the correct option is (C).

27. Given:

AB is a straight line

∠AOC = (7a + 18)°

∠BOC = (3a + 12)°

Calculations:

According to the question, we have

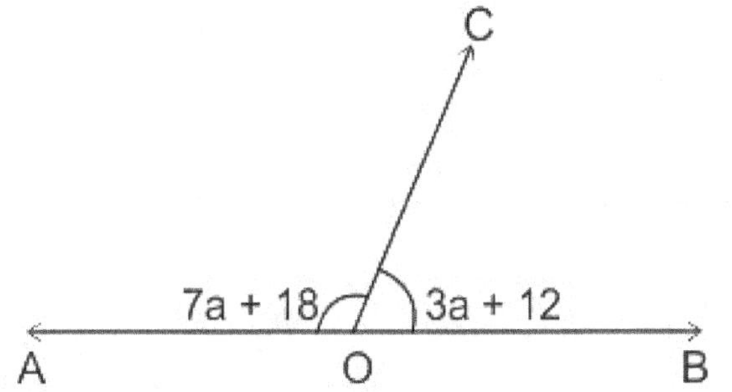

The sum of angle ∠AOC and ∠BOC is 180° [linear pair of angles]

∠AOC + ∠BOC = 180°

⇒ (7a + 18)° + (3a + 12)° = 180°

⇒ 10a + 30° = 180°

⇒ 10a = 180° - 30°

⇒ 10a = 150°

⇒ a = 15°

Thus, the value of ∠BOC is

∠BOC = (3a + 12)°

⇒ ∠BOC = (3 x 15° + 12)°

⇒ ∠BOC = 57°

∴ The value of ∠BOC is 57°.

Hence, the correct option is (A).

28. Given:

∠BAC = 67°

∠ACE = 127°

Calculation:

∠ACB = 180° - ∠ACE = 180° - 127° (The sum of an angle and its supplementary angle is 180°.)

⇒ ∠ACB = 53°

In △ABC,

∠ABC + ∠BAC + ∠ACB = 180° (The sum of all angles in a triangle is 180°.)

⇒ ∠ABC + 67° + 53° = 180°

⇒ ∠ABC = (180 - 120)°

⇒ ∠ABC = 60° = ∠ x°

Required value of $\dfrac{3x}{4} = \left(\dfrac{3}{4}\right) \times 60$

∴ The required value = 45°.

Hence, the correct option is (A).

29. Given:

∠BCD = 125° and ∠EBC = 110°

Calculation:

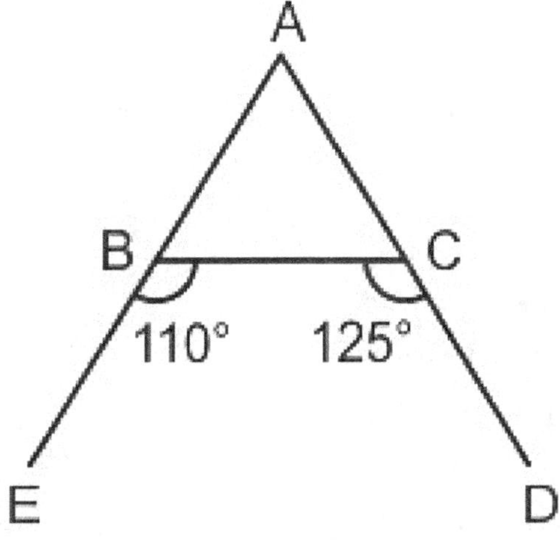

∠EBC + ∠ABC = 180°   ----(Linear pair)

⇒ 110° + ∠ABC = 180°

⇒ ∠ABC = 70°

And, ∠BCD + ∠ACB = 180°   ----(Linear pair)

⇒ 125° + ∠ACB = 180°

⇒ ∠ACB = 55°

Now, Sum of all the angles of the triangle is 180°

∠BAC + ∠ABC + ∠ACB = 180°

⇒ ∠BAC + 70° + 55° = 180°

⇒ ∠BAC = 55°

Checking option one by one,

A) ∠ABC - ∠ACB = 70° – 55° = 15° ≠ 35° so option (A) is wrong.

B) ∠BAC - ∠ACB = 55° – 55° = 0 ≠ 20° so the option (B) is wrong.

C) ∠BAC = ∠ACB then, Side BC is equal to side AB

Two sides of the triangle are equal then it is isosceles triangle so option (C) is correct.

D) AB = BC so option (D) is wrong.

∴ △ABC is an isosceles triangle.

Hence, the correct option is (C).

30. Calculation:

As we know,

Sum of all angles of triangles is 180.

According to the question,

x + 3x + 20 + 6x = 180°

⇒ 10x + 20 = 180°

⇒ 10x = 180° – 20°

⇒ 10x = 160°

⇒ x = $\dfrac{160}{10}$

$\Rightarrow$ x = 16°

First angle = x = 16°

Second angle = 3x + 20 = 3 × 16 + 20 = 48 + 20 = 68°

Third angle = 6x = 6 × 16 = 96°

Since, one angle is greater than 90° so given triangle is an obtuse angle triangle.

Hence, the correct option is (D).

31. Given normal to the circle are:

$2y - 3x + 5 = 0 \dots$ (i)

$2y + 3x - 5 = 0 \dots$ (ii)

Substracting (ii) from (I),

$-6x + 10 = 0$

$\Rightarrow x = \dfrac{5}{3}$

From equation (ii),

$2y + 3\left(\dfrac{5}{3}\right) - 5 = 0$

$y = 0$

$\therefore$ Coordinates of the centre are $\left(\dfrac{5}{3}, 0\right)$

Given the area of circle = 81π

$\pi r^2 = 81\pi$

$\Rightarrow r^2 = 81$

$\therefore$ The equation of circle is:

$(x - h)^2 + (y - k)^2 = r^2$

$\Rightarrow \left(x - \dfrac{5}{3}\right)^2 + (y - 0)^2 = 81$

$\Rightarrow \left(x - \dfrac{5}{3}\right)^2 + y^2 = 81$

$\therefore$ The equation for the circle is $\left(x - \dfrac{5}{3}\right)^2 + y^2 = 81.$

Hence, the correct option is (B).

32. Given,

Equation of parabola: $y^2 + 8y - 12x + 4 = 0$

$\Rightarrow y^2 + 8y + 16 - 16 - 12x + 4 = 0$

$\Rightarrow (y + 4)^2 - 16 - 12x + 4 = 0$

$\Rightarrow (y + 4)^2 = 12x + 16 - 4$

$\Rightarrow (y + 4)^2 = 12x + 12$

$\Rightarrow (y + 4)^2 = 12(x + 1)$

Let y + 4 = Y, x + 1 = X $\qquad$ ....(i)

$\therefore$ $Y^2 = 12X$

Comparing it with $Y^2 = 4aX$ we get

$\therefore$ a = 3 $\qquad$ .....(ii)

As we know that directrix of parabola $Y^2 = 4aX$ is given by X = - a.

From equation (i) and (ii)

x + 1 = - 3

$\Rightarrow$ x + 4 = 0

So, equation of directrix is x + 4 = 0

Hence, the correct option is (B).

33. Given:

'd' is the perpendicular distance from the centre of the ellipse

$\dfrac{x^2}{a^2} + \dfrac{y^2}{b^2}$ = 1 to the tangent drawn at a point P on the ellipse.

-- F_1 and F_2 are two foci of the ellipse.

We have to find the value of $(PF_1 - PF_2)^2$.

Consider,

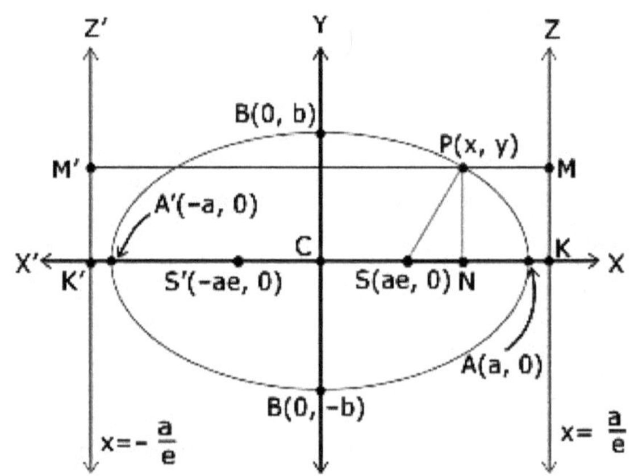

Let P(x, y) be any point on the ellipse $\dfrac{x^2}{a^2} + \dfrac{y^2}{b^2} = 1$ (As shown in Fig).

Then, by definition of ellipse, we have

SP = e PM and S'P = e PM'

$\Rightarrow$ S = e(NK) and S'P = e(NK')

$\Rightarrow$ SP = e(CK - CN) and S'P = e(CK' + CN)

$\Rightarrow$ SP = $e\left(\dfrac{a}{e} - x\right)$ and S'P = $e\left(\dfrac{a}{e} + x\right)$

$\Rightarrow$ SP = a - ex and S'P = a + ex

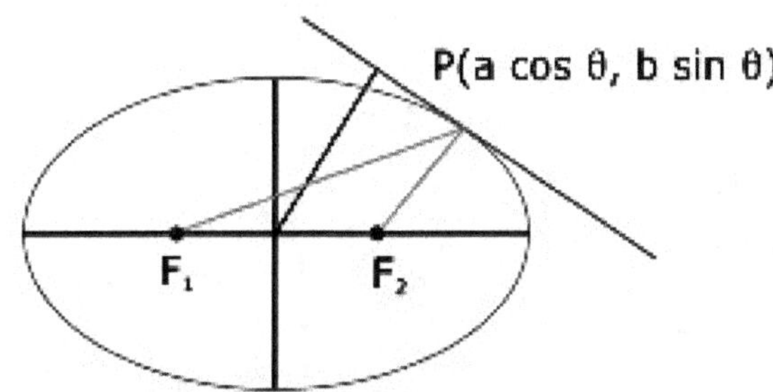

Consider, co-ordinate of point P in parametric form as (a cos θ, b sin θ).

Since $PF_1 = a + ex$ and $PF_2 = a - ex$, therefore

$PF_1 - PF_2 = 2ex = 2ea \cos θ$

∴ $(PF_1 - PF_2)^2 = 4a^2e^2\cos^2 θ$ .... (i)

Equation of tangent to ellipse at P(θ) is,

$$\frac{x}{a}\cos θ + \frac{y}{b}\sin θ = 1$$

$$\Rightarrow d = \frac{1}{\sqrt{\frac{\cos^2 θ}{a^2}+\frac{\sin^2 θ}{b^2}}}$$ [Using perpendicular distance of a line

from a point and trigonometric identities]

$$\Rightarrow \frac{1}{d^2} = \frac{\cos^2 θ}{a^2} + \frac{\sin^2 θ}{b^2}$$

$$\Rightarrow \frac{b^2}{d^2} = \frac{b^2}{a^2}\cos^2 θ + \sin^2 θ$$

Or

$$1 - \frac{b^2}{d^2} = 1 - \frac{b^2}{a^2}\cos^2 θ - \sin^2 θ = \cos^2 θ - \frac{b^2}{a^2}\cos θ$$
$$= \cos^2 θ \left(1 - \frac{b^2}{a^2}\right)$$

$$= \cos^2 θ \cdot e^2 \quad [\text{ Using eccentricity of ellipse }]$$

$$\Rightarrow 4a^2 \left(1 - \frac{b^2}{d^2}\right) = 4a^2\cos^2 θ \cdot e^2$$

$$(PF_1 - PF_2)^2 = 4a^2e^2\cos^2 θ = 4a^2\left(1 - \frac{b^2}{d^2}\right) \quad [$$

So, Using$(i)]$

Hence, the correct option is (B).

34. Given:

Equations of curves, $4x^2 + py^2 = 45$ and $x^2 - 4y^2 = 5$ cut orthogonally.

We have to find the value of p.

Consider,

$4x^2 + py^2 = 45$

Differentiating w.r.t x, we get

$$8x + 2\,py\,\frac{dy}{dx} =$$
$$0 \quad [\text{ Using standard derivatives- 1}]$$

$$\Rightarrow \frac{dy}{dx} = \frac{-4x}{py}$$

Similarly for $x^2 - 4y^2 = 5$

$$\frac{dy}{dx} = \frac{x}{4y}$$

Let $(α, β)$ be the point of contact.

Then, $4α^2 + pβ^2 = 45$...(i)

$α^2 - 4β^2 = 5$ ....(ii)

Multiplying (ii) by 4 and subtracting it from (i), we get

$$(p + 16)β^2 = 25$$

$$\Rightarrow β^2 = \frac{25}{p+16}...(iii)$$

Using (ii), we get

$$α^2 = 5 + 4 \cdot \frac{25}{p+16}$$

$$= \frac{5p+80+100}{p+16}$$

$$= \frac{5p+180}{p+16}$$

$$= \frac{5(p+36)}{p+16}$$

Dividing (iv) by (iii), we get

$$\frac{α^2}{β^2} = \frac{p+36}{5}$$

Now, using tangents and normals, we get

$$m_1 = \left(\frac{dy}{dx}\right)_{(α,β)} = \frac{4α}{pβ}$$

and $$m_2 = \left(\frac{dy}{dx}\right)_{(α,β)} = \frac{α}{4β}$$

: Both curves cut orthogonally, then

$$m_1 m_2 = -1$$
$$\Rightarrow \left(\frac{-4α}{pβ}\right) \cdot \frac{α}{4β} = -1$$
$$\Rightarrow \frac{1}{p}\left(\frac{p+36}{5}\right) = 1$$
$$\Rightarrow 5p = p + 36$$
$$\Rightarrow p = 9$$

Hence, the correct option is (A).

35. Slope of parallel lines are equal.

Slope of tangent is defined as $\frac{dy}{dx}$

Given hyperbola is $x^2 - y^2 = 3$

We know that slope of tangent is defined as $\frac{dy}{dx}$

Differentiating above equation wrt. x,

$$2x - 2y \cdot \frac{dy}{dx} = 0$$
$$\Rightarrow \frac{dy}{dx} = \frac{2x}{2y} = \frac{x}{y}$$

∴ Slope $= m_1 = \frac{dy}{dx} = \frac{x}{y}$

Now,

Equation of straight line $2x + y + 8 = 0$

Differentiating above equation with respect to x,

$$2 + \frac{dy}{dx} = 0$$

$$\Rightarrow -2 = \frac{dy}{dx}$$

$$\therefore \text{Slope} = m_2 = \frac{dy}{dx} = -2$$

We know that the slope of parallel lines are equal.

$$\Rightarrow m_1 = m_2$$

$$\Rightarrow \frac{x}{y} = -2$$

$$\Rightarrow x = -2y \text{........(i)}$$

Now put this value in the equation of the hyperbola.

$$x^2 - y^2 = 3$$

$$\Rightarrow (-2y)^2 - y^2 = 3$$

$$\Rightarrow 4y^2 - y^2 = 3$$

$$\Rightarrow 3y^2 = 3$$

$$\Rightarrow y = \pm 1$$

Now, at $y = +1$

$x = -2$ (Using equation (i))

And, at $y = -1$

$x = 2$ (Using equation (i))

$\therefore$ Points will be: $(2, -1)$ or $(-2, 1)$

Hence, the correct option is (B).

36.

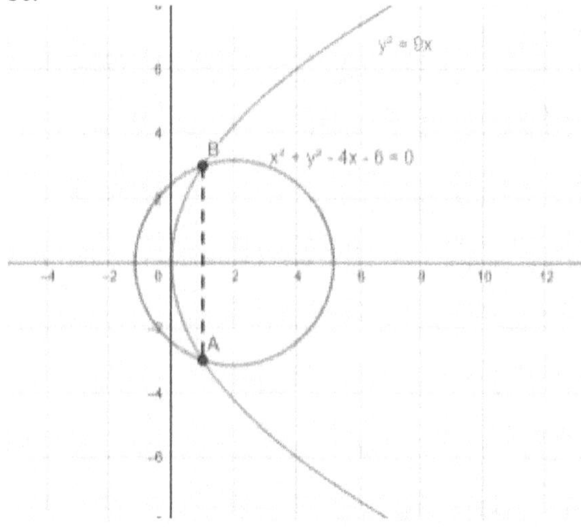

AB is the common chord.

Finding the coordinates of A and B:

A and B are the points of intersection of the curves $x^2 + y^2 - 4x - 6 = 0$ and $y^2 = 9x$.

Thus, we solve these equations simultaneously to get the coordinates of A and B.

Substituting the value of y^2 from the equation of the parabola in the equation of the circle, we get:

$$x^2 + 9x - 4x - 6 = 0$$

$$\Rightarrow x^2 + 5x - 6 = 0$$

We use the method of splitting the middle term to solve the quadratic equation.

We have $5 = 6 - 1$ and $6 \times 1 = 6$

Thus, we have

$$x^2 + 5x - 6 = 0$$

$$\Rightarrow x^2 + 6x - x - 6 = 0$$

Taking x common from the first two terms and -1 common from the last two terms, we get:

$$x(x + 6) - 1(x + 6) = 0$$

Taking $x + 6$ common from both the terms, we get:

$$(x + 6)(x - 1) = 0$$

Using zero product property, we have

$$x + 6 = 0 \text{ or } x - 1 = 0$$

Thus, we have

$$x = -6 \text{ or } x = 1$$

Since from the equation of the parabola, we have

$$y^2 = 9x$$

$$\Rightarrow 9x \geq 0$$

$$\Rightarrow x \geq 0$$

Thus, we have $x = -6$ is rejected.

Thus, we have $x = 1$

When $x = 1$, we have

$$y^2 = 9$$

$$\Rightarrow y = \pm 3$$

Thus, we have

$$B \equiv (1, 3) \text{ and } A \equiv (1, -3)$$

Now, we know that the equation of the line passing through points $A(x_1, y_1)$ and $B(x_2, y_2)$ is given by,

$$y - y_1 = \frac{y_2 - y_1}{x_2 - x_1}(x - x_1)$$

Thus, we have

$$(y - y_1)(x_2 - x_1) = (x - x_1)(y_2 - y_1)$$

Thus, the equation fo the line AB is $(y - 3)(1 - 1) = (x - 1)(-3 - 3)$.

$$\Rightarrow -6(x - 1) = 0$$

$$\Rightarrow x - 1 = 0$$

Therefore, the equation of the line AB is $x - 1 = 0$.

So, option (B) is incorrect.

Clearly, the point $(1, -1)$ lies on AB.

Thus, option (A) is correct.

Now, we know that the distance between the points $P(x_1, y_1)$ and $Q(x_2, y_2)$ is given by

$$PQ = \sqrt{(x_2 - x_1)^2 + (y_2 - y_1)^2}$$

So, we have

$$AB = \sqrt{(1-1)^2 + (-3-3)^2} = 6$$

Thus, the length of the common chord is 6.

So, option (C) is correct.

Thus, options (A) and (C) are correct.

Hence, the correct option is (D).

37. Given,

$$\beta x + y + 9 = 0 \ldots\ldots(1)$$

Slope of line $1(m_1) = -\dfrac{a}{b} = \dfrac{-\beta}{1} = -\beta$

And

$$-3x + y - 4 = 0 \ldots\ldots\ldots\ldots\ldots(2)$$

Slope of line $2(m_2) = 3$

We know that, $\tan\theta = \left|\dfrac{m_1 - m_2}{1 + m_1 m_2}\right|$

$$\Rightarrow \tan 45° = 1 = \left|\dfrac{-\beta - 3}{1 - 3\beta}\right|$$

$$\Rightarrow \dfrac{-(\beta+3)}{1-3\beta} = \pm 1$$

So either $\dfrac{-(\beta+3)}{1-3\beta} = 1$ or $\dfrac{-(\beta+3)}{1-3\beta} = -1$

First, consider $\dfrac{-(\beta+3)}{1-3\beta} = 1$

$$\Rightarrow -(\beta + 3) = 1 - 3\beta$$

$$\Rightarrow -\beta - 3 = 1 - 3\beta$$

$$\Rightarrow 2\beta = 4$$

$$\Rightarrow \beta = 2$$

Also $\dfrac{-(\beta+3)}{1-3\beta} = -1$

$$\Rightarrow -(\beta + 3) = -1 + 3\beta$$

$$\Rightarrow -4\beta = 2$$

$$\Rightarrow \beta = -\dfrac{1}{2}$$

So $\beta = 2$ or $\dfrac{-1}{2}$

Hence, the correct option is (D).

38. We have the equation of the circumcircle as $x^2 + y^2 + 2gx + 2fy + c = 0$.

We can write this equation as follows,

We can add $g^2 + f^2$ on both sides:

$$\Rightarrow x^2 + y^2 + 2gx + 2fy + g^2 + f^2 = g^2 + f^2 - c$$

Rearranging the equation, we get:

$$\Rightarrow (x^2 + 2gx + g^2) + (y^2 + 2fy + f^2) = g^2 + f^2 - c$$

Using the algebraic identity, $(a+b)^2 = a^2 + 2ab + b^2$ we get:

$$\Rightarrow (x + g)^2 + (y + f)^2 = g^2 + f^2 - c$$

Comparing this with the standard equation of the circle \x-h)^{2}+(y-k)^{2}=r^{2}\) with radius r and center (h, k), we get:

Center is $(-g, -f)$ and $r = \sqrt{g^2 + f^2 - c}$ $\quad\ldots.(1)$

We know that a circumcircle is a circle that passes through all the vertices of the triangle.

So, the point $(1,1)$ satisfies the equation of the circle.

$$\Rightarrow 1^2 + 1^2 + 2g(1) + 2f(1) + c = 0$$

$$\Rightarrow c = -2 - 2g - 2f \quad\ldots.(2)$$

We can substitute equation (2) in (1),

$$\Rightarrow r = \sqrt{g^2 + f^2 - (-2 - 2g - 2f)}$$

On opening the bracket we get,

$$\Rightarrow r = \sqrt{g^2 + f^2 + 2 + 2g + 2f} \quad\ldots (3)$$

For an equilateral triangle, the circumcenter and incircle have a common centre and radius of incircle is half the radius of circumcenter.

Let R be the radius of incircle.

$$\Rightarrow R = \dfrac{r}{2}$$

And center $(-g, -f)$.

Therefore, equation of the incircle is given by,

$$(x + g)^2 + (y + f)^2 = R^2$$

Substituting (3), we get,

$$(x + g)^2 + (y + f)^2 = \left(\dfrac{r}{2}\right)^2$$

On substituting (2), we get:

$$(x + g)^2 + (y + f)^2 = \left(\frac{\sqrt{g^2+f^2+2+2g+2f}}{2}\right)^2$$

Expanding the squares, we get,

$$\Rightarrow \left(x^2 + 2gx + g^2\right) + \left(y^2 + 2fy + f^2\right) = \frac{1}{4}\left(g^2 + f^2 + 2 + 2g + 2f\right)$$

Multiplying both sides with (4), we get,

$$\Rightarrow 4x^2 + 8gx + 4g^2 + 4y^2 + 8fy + 4f^2 = g^2 + f^2 + 2 + 2g + 2f$$

On rearranging, we get:

$$\Rightarrow 4x^2 + 4y^2 + 8gx + 8fy = g^2 - 4g^2 + f^2 - 4f^2 + 2 + 2g + 2f$$

On simplification, we get:

$$\Rightarrow 4x^2 + 4y^2 + 8gx + 8fy = -3g^2 - 3f^2 + 2 + 2g + 2f$$

$$\Rightarrow 4x^2 + 4y^2 + 8gx + 8fy = \left(-3g^2 + 2g + 1\right) + \left(-3f^2 + 2f + 1\right)$$

We can factorize the 2 terms of RHS.

$$\Rightarrow 4x^2 + 4y^2 + 8gx + 8fy = \left(-3g^2 + 3g - g + 1\right) + \left(-3f^2 + 3f - f + 1\right)$$

On taking terms common we get:

$$\Rightarrow 4x^2 + 4y^2 + 8gx + 8fy = \left(-3g(g - 1) - (g - 1\right) + \left(-3f(f - 1) - (f - 1\right)$$

On further simplification we get:

$$\Rightarrow 4x^2 + 4y^2 + 8gx + 8fy = g - 1)(-3g - 1 + f - 1)(-3f - 1$$

$$\Rightarrow 4\left(x^2 + y^2\right) + 8gx + 8fy = 1 - g)(1 + 3g + 1 - f)(1 + 3f$$

Therefore, the equation of the incircle is:

$$4\left(x^2 + y^2\right) + 8gx + 8fy = (1 - g)(1 + 3g) + (1 - f)(1 + 3f)$$

Hence, the correct option is (B).

39. Given,

$y - z$ plane divides the line joining the points $(3,1,5)$ and $(-2, -1, 4)$ in the ratio $\frac{p}{q}$.

We know that when the line segment is divided internally in the ratio $m : n$, we use the formula.

$$(x, y, z) = \left(\frac{mx_2 + nx_1}{m+n}, \frac{my_2 + ny_1}{m+n}, \frac{mz_2 + nz_1}{m+n}\right)$$

$$x = \frac{3p + (-2q)}{p + q}$$

But, in the $y - z$ plane, the x coordinate is zero.

$$\Rightarrow x = \frac{3p - 2q}{p + q} = 0$$

$$\Rightarrow 3p - 2q = 0$$

$$\Rightarrow \frac{p}{q} = \frac{2}{3}$$

Therefore, $y - z$ plane devices given line in ratio of $2 : 3$.

$$p + q = 2 + 3$$

$$p + q = 5$$

Hence, the correct option is (C).

40.

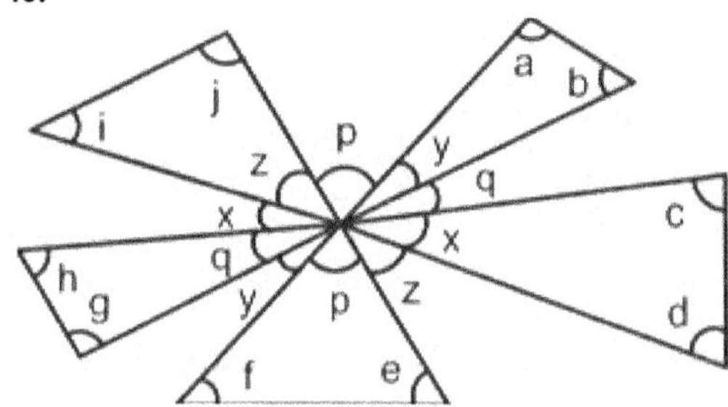

Concept Used:

angle around a point add up to $360°$

sum of all angles of a triangle is $180°$

Calculation:

$$\Rightarrow \angle y = 180° - (\angle a + \angle b) \quad \text{.........(i)}$$

$$\Rightarrow \angle X = 180° - (\angle C + \angle d) \quad \text{.........(ii)}$$

$$\Rightarrow \angle p = 180° - (\angle e + \angle f) \quad \text{.........(iii)}$$

$$\Rightarrow \angle q = 180° - (\angle h + \angle g) \quad \text{.........(iv)}$$

$$\Rightarrow \angle Z = 180° - (\angle i + \angle j) \quad \text{.........(v)}$$

also, $2(\angle y + \angle x + \angle p + \angle q + \angle Z) = 360°$

$$\Rightarrow (\angle y + \angle x + \angle p + \angle q + \angle z) = 180°$$

adding all equation we have

$$\Rightarrow (\angle y + \angle x + \angle p + \angle q + \angle Z) = 900° - (\angle a + \angle b + \angle C + \angle d + \angle e + \angle f + \angle g + \angle h + \angle i + \angle j)$$

$$\Rightarrow 180° = 900° - (\angle a + \angle b + \angle c + \angle d + \angle e + \angle f + \angle g + \angle h + \angle i + \angle j)$$

$$\Rightarrow (\angle a + \angle b + \angle C + \angle d + \angle e + \angle f + \angle g + \angle h + \angle i + \angle j) = 900° - 180° = 720°$$

$\therefore$ required value of angle $= 720°$

Hence, the correct answer is $720°$.

41. Given:

Ratio between number of sides of two polygons = 4 : 3

Ratio between their interior angles = 3 : 2

Formula:

$$\theta = \frac{2n-4}{n} \times 90$$

Where

θ = interior angle of polygon

n = Number of sides of polygon

Let $4n$ and $3n$ be the number of sides of the polygon respectively

$$\frac{\theta_1}{\theta_2} = \frac{\frac{2(4n)-4}{4n} \times 90}{\frac{2(3n)-4}{3n} \times 90}$$

$$\frac{3}{2} = \frac{8n-4}{6n-4} \times \frac{3}{4}$$

$$12n - 8 = 8n - 4$$

$$n = 1$$

∴ Number of sides of polygons are 4,3 respectively

Hence, the correct answer is 4, 3.

42. Given:

ABCDEF is a regular hexagon

Calculation:

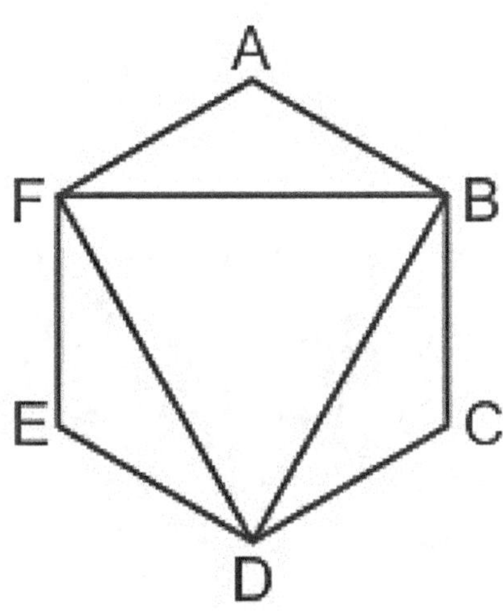

⇒ Angle of a polygon = $\dfrac{[(n-2)180°]}{n}$

⇒ Angle of hexagon = $\dfrac{(4 \times 180°)}{6}$ = 120°

⇒ ∠FED = 120°

In a triangle BCD,

⇒ BC = DC (∵ regular hexagon)

⇒ $\angle CDB = \angle DBC$

⇒ $\angle BCD = 120°$

⇒ $\angle BCD + \angle DBC + \angle CDB = 180°$

(∵ regular hexagon has equal internal angles)

⇒ $120° + 2\angle DBC = 180°$

⇒ $\angle DBC = 30°$

∴ Required answers are $\angle DBC = 30°$ and $\angle FED = 120°$.

Hence, the correct option is (B).

43. Given:

$\angle LB = \angle ABK$ and $ABCDE$ and $HIJKL$ are regular pentagons and $AEFGHL$ is a regular hexagon.

Formula used:

Sum of the interior angles of the polygon $= (n-2) \times 180°$

Each Interior angle = $\dfrac{[(n-2) \times 180°]}{n}$

Calculation:

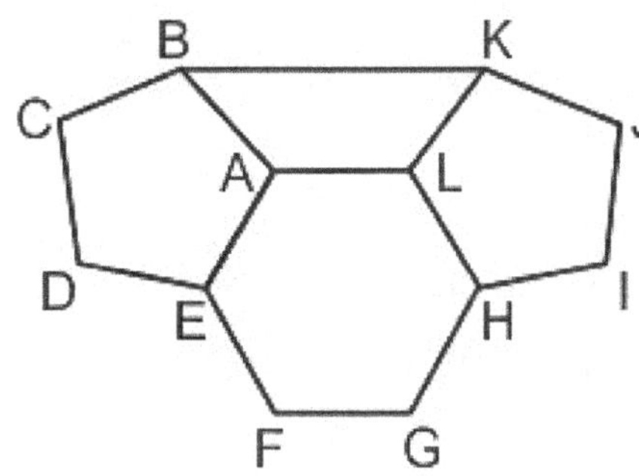

Each interior angle of pentagon = (5 - 2)× $\dfrac{180°}{5}$ = 108°

Each interior angle of hexagon = (6 - 2) × $\dfrac{180°}{6}$ = 120°

Now, $\angle BAE + \angle EAL + \angle BAL = 360°$

⇒ $108° + 120° + \angle BAL = 360°$

⇒ $228° + \angle BAL = 360°$

⇒ $\angle BAL = 132°$

Similarly, $\angle KLA = 132°$

Suppose, $\angle ABK = \angle LKB = x°$

⇒ $x° + x° + 132° + 132° = 360°$

⇒ $2x° + 264° = 360°$

⇒ $2x° = 96°$

$$\Rightarrow x° = \frac{96°}{2}$$

$$\Rightarrow x° = 48°$$

$$\therefore \angle ABK = 48°$$

Hence, the correct option is (B).

44. Calculation:

BE is the median, so $AE = EC = 5\ cm$.

Let the length of AD be ' x ' cm such that $DE = AE - AD = 5 - x \cdot As DE, AD$, and EC are in A.P. So,

$\Rightarrow x - (5 - x) = 5 - x$

$\Rightarrow 3x = 10$

$$\Rightarrow x = \frac{10}{3}$$

As BD is the angle bisector. So,

$$\frac{AD}{DC} = \frac{AB}{BC}$$

$$\Rightarrow \frac{\left(\frac{10}{3}\right)}{\left(5 + \frac{5}{3}\right)} = \frac{AB}{BC}$$

$$\Rightarrow \frac{AB}{BC} = \frac{1}{2}$$

$\Rightarrow BC = 2AB$

Apply pythagoras theorem in triangle ABC.

$$AB^2 + BC^2 = AC^2$$

$$\Rightarrow AB^2 + (2AB)^2 = 10^2$$

$$\Rightarrow 5AB^2 = 100$$

$$\Rightarrow AB^2 = 20$$

$$\Rightarrow AB = 2\sqrt{5}$$

As, $BC = 2AB$. Therefore, $BC = 4\sqrt{5}\ cm$

Hence, the correct option is (B).

45. Calculation:

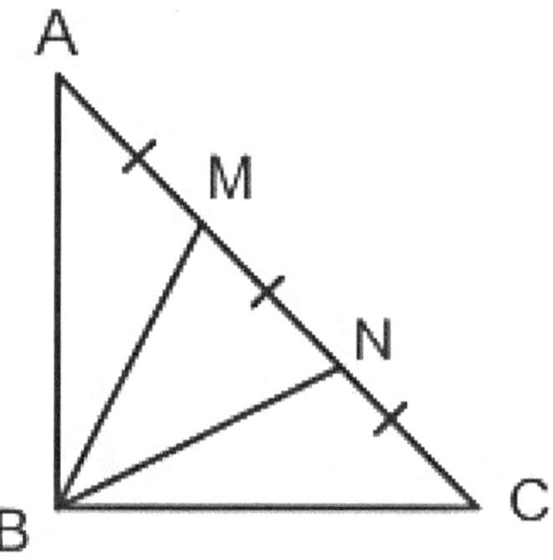

Using pythagoras theorem,

$$\Rightarrow AC^2 = AB^2 + BC^2$$

Then,

$\Rightarrow AM = MN = NC$

$\Rightarrow AM = MN = NC = \dfrac{30}{3} = 10\ cm$

M is the midpoint of AN and N is the midpoint of MC.

In ΔABN,

Using Apollonius's theorem,

$$\Rightarrow AB^2 + BN^2 = 2 \times (AM^2 + BM^2) \ \ldots\ldots(1)$$

Similarly in ΔMBC,

Using Apollonius's theorem,

$$\Rightarrow BM^2 + BC^2 = 2 \times (M^2 + BN^2) \ \ldots(2)$$

Adding (1) and (2),

$$\Rightarrow AB^2 + BC^2 + BN^2 + BM^2 = 2AM^2 + 2MN^2 + 2BN^2 + 2BM^2$$

$$\Rightarrow 30^2 = 4AM^2 + BN^2 + BM^2$$

$$\Rightarrow BM^2 + BN^2 = 900 - 4 \times 10^2$$

$$\therefore BM^2 + BN^2 = 500\ cm^2$$

Hence, the correct option is (B).

46.

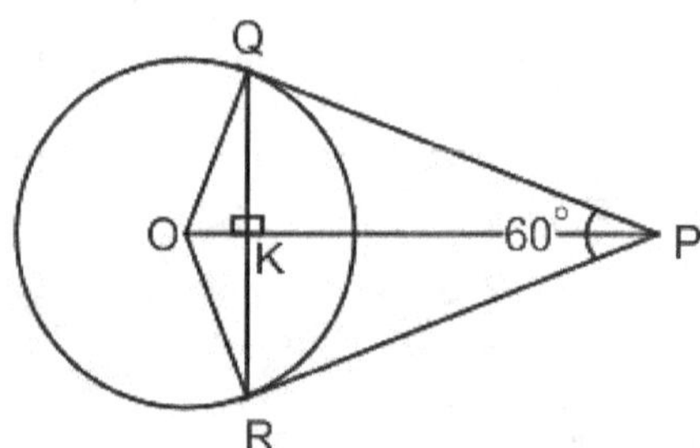

Given, $OQ = OR = 8\ cm$ and $\angle RPQ = 60°$

OP is the angle bisector of $\angle QPR$

$\angle OPQ = 30°$

$\angle OPQ = 90°$

In $\triangle POQ$

$\angle QOP + \angle QPO + \angle OQP = 180°$

$\Rightarrow \angle QOP = 180° - (30° + 90°) = 60°$

Now,

$\cos\angle POQ = \dfrac{OK}{OQ}$

$\Rightarrow \cos 60° = \dfrac{OK}{8}$

$\Rightarrow \dfrac{1}{2} = \dfrac{OK}{8}$

$\Rightarrow OK = 4\ cm$

Hence, the correct answer is 4 cm.

47.

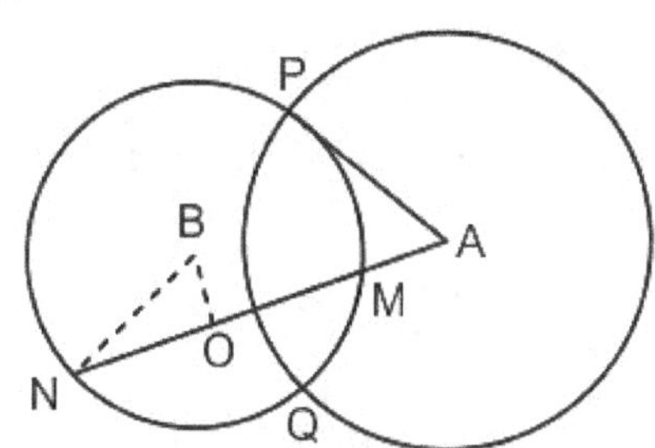

AP is tangent and AMN is secant to the smaller circle, then
$AP^2 = AM \times AN$

Let $MN = x$

$15^2 = 9 \times (9 + x)$

$225 = 9(9 + x)$

$(9 + x) = 25$

$x = 16$

ON $= \dfrac{MN}{2} = \dfrac{16}{2} = 8$ cm

OB $= 8 - 2 = 6$ cm

Now, in triangle BON:

$BN^2 = OB^2 + ON^2$

$BN^2 = 6^2 + 8^2$

$BN = 10\ cm$

Hence, the correct answer is 10 cm.

48. $\tan x + \cot x = 6$ ....(1)

$\Rightarrow \dfrac{\sin x}{\cos x} + \dfrac{\cos x}{\sin x} = 6$

$\Rightarrow \dfrac{(\sin^2 x + \cos^2 x)}{\cos x \sin x} = 6$

$\Rightarrow \dfrac{1}{\sin x \cos x} = 6$

$\Rightarrow \sin x \cos x = \dfrac{1}{6}$ ....(2)

$\Rightarrow \dfrac{\left[\left(\frac{1}{\tan x} + \frac{1}{\cot x}\right) + \sin x \cos x\right]}{\sin 2x}$

$\Rightarrow \dfrac{\left[\left(\frac{\cot x + \tan x}{\tan x \cot x}\right) + \sin x \cos x\right]}{2\sin x \cos x}$

$\Rightarrow \dfrac{\left[\frac{6}{1} + \frac{1}{6}\right]}{\frac{2}{6}}$

$\Rightarrow \dfrac{37}{6} \times \dfrac{6}{2}$

$\Rightarrow \dfrac{37}{2}$

Hence, the correct answer is $\dfrac{37}{2}$.

49. Formula used:

$\cos^2\theta = 1 - \sin^2\theta$

$\sin C + \sin D = \dfrac{2\sin(C+D)}{2} \dfrac{\cos(C-D)}{2}$

$\sin C - \sin D = \dfrac{2\cos(C+D)}{2} \dfrac{\sin(C-D)}{2}$

Calculations:

$\cos^2 14x - \cos^2 18x$

$\Rightarrow \{(1 - \sin^2 14x) - (1 - \sin^2 18x)\}$

$\Rightarrow \{1 - \sin^2 14x - 1 + \sin^2 18x\}$

$\Rightarrow \{\sin^2 18x - \sin^2 14x\}$

$\Rightarrow (\sin 18x + \sin 14x)(\sin 18x - \sin 14x)$

$\Rightarrow (2\sin 16x \cos 2x)(2\cos 16x \sin 2x)$

$\Rightarrow (2\sin 16x \cos 16x)(2\sin 2x \cos 2x)$

$\Rightarrow \sin 32x \sin 4x$

$\therefore \cos^2 14x - \cos^2 18x = \{\sin(32x)\sin(4x)\}$

Hence, the correct option is (C).

50. Given:

$(\sin 3A - \sin 2A) = x\sin A$ and $(\cos 3A - \cos 2A) = y\cos A$

Formula Used:

$$\sin 3A = (3\sin A - 4\sin^3 A) \,\&\, \sin 2A = 2\sin A \cos A$$

$$\cos 3A = (4\cos^3 A - 3\cos A) \,\&\, \cos 2A = (2\cos^2 A - 1)$$

Calculation:

$$3\sin A - 4\sin^3 A - 2\sin A \cos A = x\sin A$$

$$\Rightarrow 3 - 4\sin^2 A - 2\cos A = x$$

$$\Rightarrow 3 - 4(1 - \cos^2 A) - 2\cos A = x$$

$$\Rightarrow 3 - 4 + 4\cos^2 A - 2\cos A = x$$

$$\Rightarrow (4\cos^2 A - 2\cos A - 1) = x \,..........(1)$$

Similarly,

$$\Rightarrow 4\cos^3 A - 3\cos A - 2\cos^2 A + 1 = y\cos A$$

$$\Rightarrow \cos A(4\cos^2 A - 2\cos A - 3) + 1 = y\cos A$$

$$\Rightarrow \cos A(4\cos^2 A - 2\cos A - 1 - 2) + 1 = y\cos A$$

Substituting from (1), we get

$$\Rightarrow (x - 2)\cos A + 1 = y\cos A$$

$$\Rightarrow 1 = y\cos A - (x - 2)\cos A$$

$$\Rightarrow 1 = (y - x + 2)\cos A$$

$$\Rightarrow 1/\cos A = (y - x + 2)$$

$$\Rightarrow \sec A = (y - x + 2)$$

Hence, the correct answer is $(y - x + 2)$.

51. Given:

The sum of dimensions of a cuboid $= 30\ cm$.

Length of diagonal $= 2\sqrt{77}\ cm$

Formula used:

Diagonal of the cuboid $= \sqrt{(L^2 + B^2 + H^2)}$

Surface area of the cuboid $= 2(LB + BH + LH)$

Calculation:

Let Length be L, Breadth be B, and Height be C

According to the question,

Length $+$ Breadth $+$ Height $= 30\ cm$

$$L + B + H = 30\ cm$$

Squaring both the sides we get,

$$(L + B + H)^2 = (30\ cm)^2$$

$$\Rightarrow (L + B + H)^2 = 900 Cm^2$$

$$\Rightarrow L^2 + B^2 + H^2 + 2LB + 2BH + 2LH = 900$$
$$..........(1)$$

$$\Rightarrow \text{Diagonal of the cuboid} = \sqrt{(L^2 + B^2 + H^2)}$$

By the question,

$$\Rightarrow \sqrt{(L^2 + B^2 + H^2)} = 2\sqrt{77}$$

Thus,

$$L^2 + B^2 + H^2 = 308 \,........(2)$$

Putting the value of equation(2) in equation(1),

$$2LB + 2BH + 2LH + 308 = 900$$

$$\Rightarrow 2(LB + BH + LH) = 592$$

$\therefore$ The total surface area of the cuboid is $592\ cm^2$.

Hence, the correct answer is $592\ cm^2$.

52. Concept:

Volume of cuboid $=$ length $\times$ breadth $\times$ height

Volume of cube $=$ side ^{3}

Number of cubical boxes that can fit inside cuboidal/cubical store $=$ Volume of cuboidal/cubical store $\div$ Volume of one cubical box

Calculation:

Length and breadth of cuboidal store $= 16\ m$ and $13\ m$ respectively

Boxes are to be placed to a height of $7\ m$

so, height $= 7\ m$

Volume of cuboidal store $= 16 \times 13 \times 7 = 1456\ m^3$

Similarly, Length and breadth of cubical box $= 8\ m$ each and height $= 7\ m$

Volume of cubical store $= 8 \times 8 \times 7 = 448\ m^3$

Volume cubical box of side $1\ m = 1 \times 1 \times 1 = 1\ m^3$

Number of boxes to be placed $= (1456 \div 1) + (448 \div 1) = 1904$

So, the number of boxes $= 1904$.

Hence, the correct answer is 1904.

53. Given:

Distance of the fly from wall $1 = 1\ m$

Distance of the fly from wall $2 = 8\ m$

Distance of the fly from point $P = 9m$

Calculation:

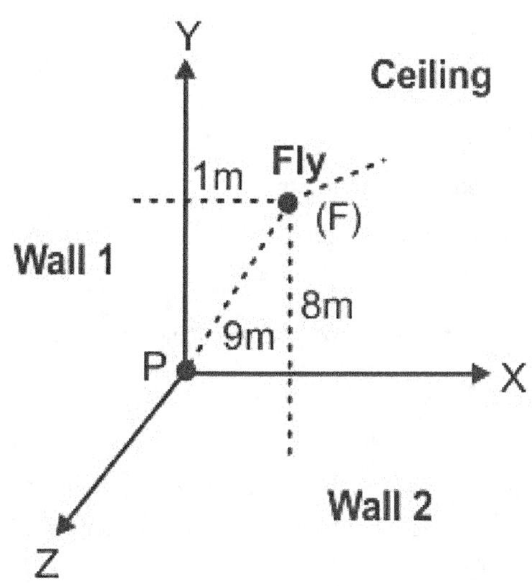

Let the ceiling be xy plane, wall 1 be the yz plane and wall 2 be the zx plane.

Then, point P will be $(0,0,0)$

To find the distance between the fly and the ceiling, we use distance formula:

$(x, y, z) = P = (0,0,0)$

$(x1, y1, z1) = (1, 8, z1)$

Distance of the fly from point $P = \sqrt{(x - x1)^2 + (y - y1)^2 + (z - z1)^2)}$

$9 = \sqrt{(0 - 1)^2 + (0 - 8)^2 + (0 - z1)^2)}$

Squaring both sides,

$81 = (-1)^2 + (-8)^2 + (-z1)^2$

$81 = 1 + 64 + z1^2$

$z1^2 = 81 - 65$

$z1^2 = 16$

$z1 = 4$

∴ The distance of the fly from the ceiling is $4\ m$

Hence, the correct answer is 4.

54. Given:

A solid metallic cuboid of dimensions $18\ cm \times 36\ cm \times 72\ cm$

where $I = 18\ cm,\ b = 36\ cm$ and $h = 72\ cm$

It is melted and recast into 8 cubes of the same volume.

Concept used:

The volume of cuboid $= lbh$

The total surface area of the cuboid $= 2(lb + bh + hl)$

Where $I = $ length, $b = $ breadth and $h = $ height

The volume of cube $= a^3$

The lateral surface area of cube $= 4 \times a^2$

Where a side of cube

Explanation:

according to the question,

$lbh = 8 \times a^3$

$\Rightarrow 18 \times 36 \times 72 = 8 \times a^3$

$\Rightarrow a^3 = 18 \times 36 \times 9$

$\Rightarrow a = \sqrt{(9 \times 2 \times 9 \times 2 \times 2 \times 9)}$

$\Rightarrow a = 18\ cm$

now,

according to the question,

$2(lb + bh + hl) : 8 \times 4 \times a^2$

$\Rightarrow 2(18 \times 36 + 36 \times 72 + 72 \times 18) : 8 \times 4 \times (18)^2$

$\Rightarrow 2 \times 18 \times 36(1 + 4 + 2) : 8 \times 4 \times 18 \times 18$

$\Rightarrow 36 \times 36 \times 7 : 32 \times 18 \times 18$

$\Rightarrow 7 : 8$

∴ The ratio is $7 : 8$.

Hence, the correct option is (D).

55. Given:

Radii of the two balls was 50% and 80% of the radius of the original ball

2% of the metal remained while forming

Formula used:

Volume of sphere $= \left(\dfrac{4}{3}\right)\pi \times (\text{radius})^3$

Calculation:

Let the radius of the original ball be R units and that of the third ball be $r\,cm$

$\Rightarrow$ Radii of two spherical balls formed is $0.5R$ and $0.8R$

∵ 2% of the metal remained,

$\Rightarrow$ Volume of three spherical balls $= 98\%$ of Volume of original ball

Now, Volume of sphere $= \left(\dfrac{4}{3}\right)\pi \times (\text{radius})^3$

$$\Rightarrow \left[\left(\tfrac{4}{3}\right)\pi \times (0.5\text{R})^3\right] + \left[\left(\tfrac{4}{3}\right)\pi \times (0.8\text{R})^3\right] + \left[\left(\tfrac{4}{3}\right)\pi \times (r)^3\right] = 98\%$$

of

$$\left[\left(\tfrac{4}{3}\right)\pi \times (R)^3\right]$$

$$\Rightarrow \left(\tfrac{5R}{10}\right)^3 + \left(\tfrac{8R}{10}\right)^3 + (r)^3 = 98\% \text{ of } (R)^3$$

$$\Rightarrow \frac{125R^3}{1000} + \frac{512R^3}{1000} + r^3 = \frac{98R^3}{100}$$

$$\Rightarrow \frac{637R^3}{1000} + r^3 = \frac{980R^3}{1000}$$

$$\Rightarrow r^3 = \frac{(980-637)R^3}{1000}$$

$$\Rightarrow r^3 = \frac{343R^3}{1000}$$

$$\Rightarrow r = \frac{7R}{10} = 0.7R$$

$$\Rightarrow r = 70\% \text{ of } R$$

Hence, the correct answer is 70%.

56. Given:

Side of cube cut = 20 cm

Ratio of volumes of 3 parts of sphere = 4 : 5 : 2

Volume of cube cut = $\left(\dfrac{200}{241}\right)$ times the remaining portion of the largest part

Area of cube $= (\text{ side })^3$

Volume of sphere = $\left(\dfrac{4}{3}\right)\pi \times (\text{radius})^3$

Calculation:

$\Rightarrow$ Volume of cube cut = $(20)^3$ = 8000 cm³

Given, volume of cube cut = $\left(\dfrac{200}{241}\right)$ × Volume of remaining portion of largest part

$\Rightarrow$ Volume of cube cut = $\left(\dfrac{200}{241}\right)$ × (Volume of largest part – Volume of cube cut)

$\Rightarrow$ 441 × Volume of cube cut = 200 × Volume of largest part

$\Rightarrow$ Volume of largest part = $\dfrac{(441 \times 8000)}{200}$ = 17640 cm³

But, the sphere was cut in the ratio 4 : 5 : 2,

$\Rightarrow$ Volume of largest part = $\dfrac{5}{11}$ × Volume of sphere

$\Rightarrow$ Volume of sphere = $\left(\dfrac{11}{5}\right)$ × 17640 = 38808 cm³

Now,

Volume of sphere = $\left(\dfrac{4}{3}\right)\pi \times (\text{radius})^3$

$\Rightarrow \dfrac{4}{3} \times \dfrac{22}{7} \times (\text{radius})^3$ = 38808 cm³

$\Rightarrow (\text{radius})^3 = (441 \times 21) = (21)^3$

$\Rightarrow$ Radius of sphere = 21 cm

$\therefore$ Diameter of sphere = 2(21) = 42 cm

Hence, the correct answer is 42 cm.

57. Concept:

In two similar triangles, the ratio of corresponding sides is equal.

Calculation:

Given:

Let's assume the height and radius of the top cone is h and r respectively and the height and radius of the original cone is H, and R respectively.

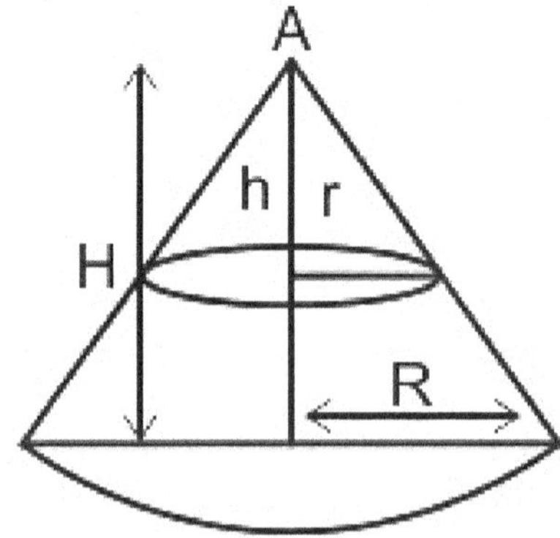

Then corresponding to h, the radius of top cone $= r$

where, $\dfrac{r}{h} = \dfrac{10}{10}$

$\dfrac{r}{h} = 1$

$h = r$ ....(1)

Now, we can write the volume of the frustum, V as

$$V = \frac{\pi \times 10^2 \times 10}{3} - \frac{\pi r^2 h}{3}$$

$$V = \frac{\pi \times 1000}{3} - \frac{\pi r^3}{3} \quad \text{..........fram equation (1)}$$

Volume is given as 312π

$$312\pi = \frac{\pi \times 1000}{3} - \frac{\pi r^3}{3}$$

$$r = 4\ cm$$

Hence, the correct answer is $4\ cm$.

58. $= \dfrac{1}{3}\pi r^2\, h = \dfrac{1}{3}\pi(8)^2 \times 12\ cm^3$

$= 256\pi\, cm^3$ Formula Used:

The volume of the cone $= \frac{1}{3}\pi r^2 h$

The volume of the sphere $= \frac{4}{3}\pi r^3$

Where r = radius of the cone and sphere, h = height of cone

Given:

Radius $= 8\ cm$, Height $= 12\ cm$

And, Radius of sphere $= 0.5\ cm$

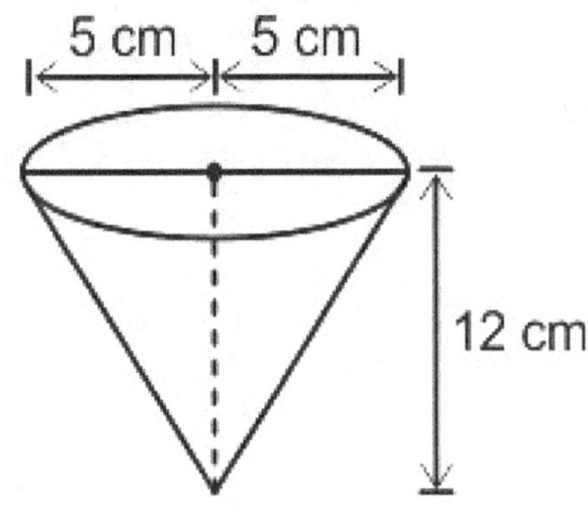

Calculation:

We know that,

The volume of cone = volume of water in the cone

$= \frac{1}{3}\pi r^2\ h = \frac{1}{3}\pi(8)^2 \times 12\ cm^3$

$= 256\pi\ cm^3$

Now,

The total volume of water overflown

$= \frac{1}{4} \times (256)\pi = 64\pi\ cm^3$

Now, the number of lead shots

The total volume of water overflown/ Volume of lead shot

$= \frac{64\pi}{\frac{1}{6}\pi}$

$= 64 \times 6 = 384$

$\therefore$ The number of lead shots dropped in the vessel is 384.

Hence, the correct answer is 384.

59. GIVEN:

Volume of cylinder $= 2156\ cm^3$

Ratio of base radius and height of cylinder $= 1:2$

CONCEPT:

Radius and height of cylinder are to be determined first.

FORMULA USED:

Volume of cylinder $= \pi r^2 h$

CALCULATION:

Let the radius and height of the cylinder is ' x ' and ' $2x$ ' respectively.

Volume of cylinder $= \pi r^2\ h$

$2156 = \left(\frac{22}{7}\right) \times x^2 \times 2x \Rightarrow x^3 = 343$

$\Rightarrow x = 7\ cm$

$\Rightarrow$ Radius $= 7\ cm$ and height $= 2x = 2 \times 7 = 14\ cm$

According to the question,

Increased radius of cylinder $= x + 3 = 10\ cm$

Decreased height of cylinder $= 2x - 3.5 = 10.5\ cm$

$\Rightarrow$ Volume of new cylinder $= \pi \times 10^2 \times 10.5 = 3300\ cm^3$

$\therefore$ Required change $= 3300 - 2156 = 1144\ cm^3$

Hence, the correct option is (A).

60. Given:

Inner radius $(r) = 3$ feet and thickness $= 1$ foot

Height $(h) = 7$ feet

Formula Used:

Surface area of whole cylinder $= 2\pi Rh + 2\pi rh + 2\pi(R^2 - r^2)$

Calculation:

Inner radius $(r) = 3$ feet and thickness $= 1$ foot

So, outer radius $(R) = 3 + 1 = 4$ feet

Surface area of whole cylinder $= 2\pi Rh + 2\pi rh + 2\pi(R^2 - r^2)$

$= 2\pi \times 4 \times 7 + 2\pi \times 3 \times 7 + 2\pi \times (4^2 - 3^2)$

$= 56\pi + 42\pi + 14\pi$

$= 112\pi$

It is given on the question that 'To paint the inner surface it requires one litre of a particular colour';

Area of inner surface $= 2\pi rh = 42\pi$

Paint required for 42π area $= 1$ litre

$\therefore$ Paint required for 112π area $= 1 \times \dfrac{112}{42} = \dfrac{8}{3}$ litre

Hence, the correct option is (C).

Q.1 A pair of dice is thrown. Find the probability of obtaining a sum of 8 or getting an even number on both the dice.

A. $\frac{2}{3}$ **B.** $\frac{1}{3}$ **C.** $\frac{11}{36}$ **D.** $\frac{5}{36}$

Q.2 Five letters are sent to different persons and addresses on the five envelopes are written lat random. The probability that all the letters do not reach the correct destiny is:

A. $\frac{44}{120}$ **B.** $\frac{1}{120}$ **C.** $\frac{1}{5}$ **D.** $\frac{5}{120}$

Q.3 If a leap year is selected at random, what is the chance that it will contain 53 Tuesdays?

A. $\frac{2}{7}$ **B.** $\frac{2}{5}$ **C.** $\frac{4}{7}$ **D.** $\frac{3}{7}$

Q.4 A die is thrown again and again until three sixes are obtained. Find the probability of obtaining the third six in the sixth throw of the die.

A. $\frac{625}{23328}$ **B.** $\frac{625}{23338}$ **C.** $\frac{625}{23438}$ **D.** $\frac{615}{23328}$

Q.5 How many times must a man toss a fair coin so that the probability of having at least one head is more than 90%?

Q.6 In a game, a man wins a rupee for a six and loses a rupee for any other number when a fair die is thrown. The man decided to throw a die thrice but to quit as and when he gets a six. Find the expected value of the amount he wins/loses.

A. $\frac{11}{206}$ **B.** $\frac{11}{236}$ **C.** $\frac{11}{216}$ **D.** $\frac{11}{226}$

Q.7 Find the probability of getting 5 exactly twice in 7 throws of a die.

A. 0.56 **B.** 0.24 **C.** 0.23 **D.** 0.29

Q.8 A factory has two machines A and B. Past record shows that machine A produced 60% of the items of output and machine B produced 40% of the items. Further, 2% of the items produced by machine A and 1% produced by machine B were defective. All the items are put into one stockpile and then one item is chosen at random from this and is found to be defective. What is the probability that it was produced by machine B?

A. $\frac{3}{4}$ **B.** $\frac{1}{3}$ **C.** $\frac{1}{2}$ **D.** $\frac{1}{4}$

Q.9 Two groups are competing for the position on the Board of directors of a corporation. The probabilities that the first and the second groups will win are 0.6 and 0.4 respectively. Further, if the first group wins, the probability of introducing a new product is 0.7 and the corresponding probability is 0.3 if the second group wins. Find the probability that the new product introduced was by the second group.

A. $\frac{2}{7}$ **B.** $\frac{2}{9}$ **C.** $\frac{3}{7}$ **D.** $\frac{2}{5}$

Q.10 Suppose a girl throws a die. If she gets a 5 or 6 , she tosses a coin three times and notes the number of heads. If she gets $1,2,3$ or 4 , she tosses a coin once and notes whether a

head or tail is obtained. If she obtained exactly one head, what is the probability that she threw $1,2,3$ or 4 with the die?

A. $\frac{8}{11}$ **B.** $\frac{7}{11}$ **C.** $\frac{5}{11}$ **D.** $\frac{9}{11}$

Q.11 Cards numbered from 107 to 1006 are put in a bag. A card is drawn from it at random. Find the probability that the number on the card is not divisible both by 11 and 37?

A. 0.998 **B.** 0.105 **C.** 0.107 **D.** 0.103

Q.12 There are 12 points in a plane out of which 5 are collinear. The number of triangles formed by the points as vertices are:

Q.13 A student is to answer 10 out of 13 questions in an examination such that he must choose at least 4 from the first five questions. The number of choices available to him is:

Q.14 10 students are to be seated in two rows equally for the Mock test in a room. There are two sets of papers, Code A and Code B. each of the two rows can have only one set of paper but different that from the other row. In how many ways these students can be arranged?

Q.15 If $5 \times {}^{n}P_3 = 4 \times {}^{(n+1)}P_3$, find n ?

Q.16 If bag A contains 4 red and 4 black balls while another bag B contains 2 red and 6 black balls. One of the two bags is selected at random and a ball is drawn from the bag and it is found to be red. Find the probability that it is drawn from bag A?

A. $\frac{2}{3}$ **B.** $\frac{1}{3}$
C. $\frac{2}{5}$ **D.** None of these

Q.17 Two dice are thrown simultaneously. What is the probability of getting two numbers whose product is even?

A. $\frac{1}{2}$ **B.** $\frac{3}{4}$ **C.** $\frac{3}{8}$ **D.** $\frac{5}{16}$

Q.18 A box contains 5 green pencils and 7 yellow pencils. Two pencils are chosen at random from the box without replacement. What is the probability they are both yellow?

A. $\frac{42}{234}$ **B.** $\frac{6}{11}$ **C.** $\frac{7}{12}$ **D.** $\frac{7}{22}$

Q.19 Write the set builder form for $D = \{-6, -4, -2, 0, 2, 4, 6\}$.

A. $\{x : x = 2n,$ where $n \in Z$ and $-2 \leq n \leq 3\}$
B. $\{x : x = 2n,$ where $n \in Z$ and $-4 \leq n \leq 4\}$
C. $\{x : x = 2n,$ where $n \in Z$ and $-3 \leq n \leq 3\}$
D. $\{x : x = 2n,$ where $n \in Z$ and $-3 \leq n \leq 4\}$

Q.20 Which of the following is the roster form of the set $A = \{4x^2 - x - 5 = 0 : x \in I\}$?

A. $\{1, -1.25\}$ **B.** $\{1\}$

C. $\{-1, 1.25\}$ **D.** $\{-1\}$

Q.21 Given the sets $A = \{2,3,4,5,6,7\}, B = \{6,7,8\}$ and $C = \{1,5,8,9\}$ then find $A \cap (B \cup C)$ and number of elements in $A \cap (B \cup C)$:

A. $\{6,7,8\}, 3$ **B.** $\{5,6,7\}, 3$
C. $\{4,5,6,7\}, 4$ **D.** $\{4,5,6\}, 3$

Q.22 Which of the following is not a finite set?
A. $\{x : x \in N \text{ and } x^2 < 36\}$
B. $\{x \in Z : 0 < x < 10\}$
C. $\{x : x \in N \text{ and } x^2 = x\}$
D. $\{x \in N : x \text{ is even }\}$

Q.23 A die is tossed thrice. Find the probability of getting an odd number at least once.

A. $\frac{1}{8}$ **B.** $\frac{5}{8}$ **C.** $\frac{3}{8}$ **D.** $\frac{7}{8}$

Q.24 6 men and 4 women are to be seated in a row so that no two women sit together. The number of ways they can be seated is:

A. 604800 **B.** 17280 **C.** 120960 **D.** 518400

Q.25 Two coins are tossed once, determine $P(E \mid F)$ where E: tail appears on one coin, F: one coin shows head.

A. $\frac{3}{4}$ **B.** $\frac{4}{3}$ **C.** 0.5 **D.** 1

Q.26 A fair die is rolled. Consider events $E = \{1,3,5\}$, and $F = \{2,3\}$. Find $P(E \mid F)$.

A. $\frac{2}{3}$ **B.** $\frac{1}{4}$ **C.** $\frac{1}{2}$ **D.** $\frac{1}{3}$

Q.27 Find the range of the function $f(x) = \sqrt{20 - x^2}$.
A. $[0, 2\sqrt{5}]$ **B.** $(0, 2\sqrt{5})$
C. $(-2\sqrt{5}, 2\sqrt{5})$ **D.** $(0, 2\sqrt{5}]$

Q.28 Let X be a non-empty set and let A, B, C be subsets of X, consider the following statements:

1. $A \subset C \Rightarrow (A \cap B) \subset (C \cap B), (A \cup B) \subset (C \cup B)$

2. $(A \cap B) \subset (C \cup B)$ for all sets $B \Rightarrow A \subset C$

3. $(A \cup B) \subset (C \cup B)$ for all sets $B \Rightarrow A \subset C$

Which of the above statements is/are correct?
A. 1 and 2 only **B.** 2 and 3 only
C. 1 and 3 only **D.** 1, 2 and 3

Q.29 If A = {x ∈ R: x² - 10x + 9 = 0}, B = {y ∈ R: y² - 3y + 2 = 0} and U = {z ∈ N: 1 ≤ z ≤ 10}. Find the set representing the shaded region.

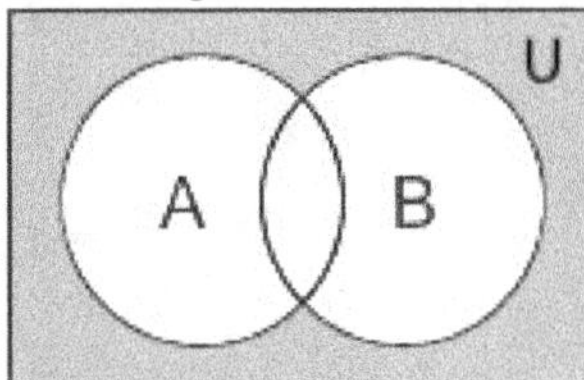

A. {3, 4, 5, 6, 7, 8, 10} **B.** {3, 4, 5, 6, 7, 8}

C. {3, 4, 5, 6, 7, 10} **D.** None of these

Q.30 If A = {x ∈ R: x is the sum of divisors of 2}, B = {x ∈ R: x² = 2} and C = {x ∈ R: x² - 5x + 6 = 0}. Find (A ∪ B) ∩ C.
A. $\{\sqrt{2}\}$ **B.** $\{\sqrt{2}, -\sqrt{2}\}$
C. $\{3\}$ **D.** None of these

Q.31 Let P = Set of all integral multiples of 3
Q = Set of all integral multiples of 4
R = Set of all integral multiples of 6
Consider the following relations:
I. P ∪ Q = R
II. P ⊂ R
III. R ⊂ (P ∪ Q)
Which of the relation(s) given above is/are correct?
A. Only I **B.** Only II **C.** Only III **D.** II and III

Q.32 Let x ∈ {2, 3, 4} and y ∈ {4, 6, 9, 10}. If A be the set of all order pairs (x, y) such that x is a factor of y. Then, how many elements does the set A contain.

Q.33 Consider the following statements:
I. A' ∪ B = (A ∩ B)'
II. (φ')' = U
III. A ∩ (B ∪ C) = (A ∩ B) ∪ (A ∩ C)
Which of the statement(s) given above is/are correct?
A. Only II **B.** I and III **C.** Only III **D.** II and III

Q.34 Which of the following is an empty set?
A. $\{x \in R : x^2 - 4x + 4\}$
B. $\{x \in R: x^3 = 1\}$
C. $\{x \in R: x^2 = -1\}$
D. None of these

Q.35 What is $C(n, r) + 2C(n, r + 1) + C(n, r + 2)$ equal to?
A. $C(n + 1, r)$ **B.** $C(n + 1, r + 2)$
C. $C(n + 2, r + 2)$ **D.** $C(n + 2, r + 3)$

Q.36 How many different words can be formed by using all the letters of the word, ALLAHABAD if both L's do not come together?

Q.37 There are 13 points in a plane of which 5 are collinear. Find the number of straight lines obtained by joining these points in pairs.

Q.38 If $^nC_r = {}^nC_{r-1}$ and $^nP_r = {}^nP_{r+1}$ then the value of r is:

Q.39 If a denotes the number of permutations of $x + 2$ things taken all at a time, b the number of permutations of x things being taken 11 at a time and c the number of permutations of $x - 11$ things taken all at a time such that $a = 182bc$, then the value of x is:

Q.40 If $^9P_5 + 5 \cdot {}^9P_4 = {}^{10}P_r$, then r is

Q.41 The total number of ways in which 5 toys of different colours can be distributed among 3 children, so that, each child gets at least one toy is:

Q.42 How many 5 letter code can be formed using the first 6 letters of the English alphabet if no letter can be repeated.

Q.43 A class has three teachers Mr. X, Ms. Y and Mrs. Z and six students A, B, C, D, E, F. A number of ways in which they can be seated in a line of 9 chairs, If between any two teachers there are exactly two students, is:

A. $18(6!)$ **B.** $12(6!)$ **C.** $24(6!)$ **D.** $6(6!)$

Q.44 A committee of 6 members is to be formed out of 6 men and 3 women. The number of committees that can be formed in which at least one woman is included is:

Q.45 A box contains 4 tennis balls, 6 season balls and 8 dues balls. 3 balls are randomly drawn from the box. What is the probability that the balls are different?

A. $\frac{4}{17}$ **B.** $\frac{3}{11}$ **C.** $\frac{2}{13}$ **D.** $\frac{5}{17}$

Q.46 In a box, 4 coins of ten rupees, 2 coins of five rupees, 2 coins of two rupees and 2 coins of one rupee are put. Now, three coins are taken out randomly. What is the probability that the amount drawn is 12 rupees?

A. $\frac{1}{\sqrt{5}}$ **B.** $\frac{1}{6}$ **C.** $\frac{6}{16}$ **D.** $\frac{1}{20}$

Q.47 A basket contains 2 white, 3 red and 4 black balls. Two balls are drawn at random. Find the probability of not any ball being drawn is black?

A. $\frac{10}{21}$ **B.** $\frac{5}{18}$ **C.** $\frac{9}{11}$ **D.** $\frac{7}{11}$

Q.48 A box contains 10 reds, 9 green and some blue balls. Find the probability of getting three different coloured balls when 3 balls are drawn from box at random if total number of balls in the box is 36 .

A. $\frac{2}{7}$ **B.** $\frac{3}{16}$ **C.** $\frac{1}{15}$ **D.** $\frac{3}{14}$

Q.49 A Bag contains 7 red, 8 white and 9 black balls. Four balls are drawn out at random. Find the probability that none of the balls drawn is White.

A. $\frac{130}{759}$ **B.** $\frac{237}{771}$ **C.** $\frac{110}{759}$ **D.** $\frac{37}{759}$

Q.50 A basket contains 6 blue, 2 red, 4 green and 3 yellow balls. If 5 balls are picked up at random, what is the probability that at least one is blue?

A. $\frac{18}{455}$ **B.** $\frac{9}{91}$ **C.** $\frac{137}{143}$ **D.** $\frac{2}{5}$

Q.51 What is the probability of solving a given problem if three students $(A, B$ and $C)$, try it independently, with respective probabilities $\frac{4}{7}, \frac{3}{8}$ and $\frac{1}{2}$?

A. $\frac{97}{112}$ **B.** $\frac{95}{112}$ **C.** $\frac{97}{111}$ **D.** $\frac{97}{125}$

Q.52 Probability of Ankit passing in Maths, English and Science is $\frac{5}{8}, \frac{7}{9}$ and $\frac{3}{5}$ respectively. Find the probability of him failing in atleast two subjects.

A. $\frac{92}{360}$ **B.** $\frac{88}{360}$ **C.** $\frac{24}{90}$ **D.** $\frac{27}{90}$

Q.53 In a class there are 16 boys and 10 girls. Three students are randomly selected. What is probability of selecting 1 boy and 2 girls?

A. $\frac{21}{73}$ **B.** $\frac{21}{73}$ **C.** $\frac{21}{73}$ **D.** $\frac{21}{73}$

Q.54 Let $A = \{x \in R : x^2 - 4x + 4 = 0\}$ and $B = \{x \in R : x^3 = 1\}$. Then A and B are:

A. Equal sets   **B.** Equivalent sets
C. Subsets   **D.** None of these

Q.55 What is the domain and range of the function $(x) =$ function

$$f(x) = \sqrt{(16 - x^2)}?$$

A. $[0,4], [0,4]$ **B.** $[0,4], [-4,4]$
C. $[-4,4], [0,4]$ **D.** $[-4,4], [-4,4]$

Q.56 Let $f : R \to R$ be a function defined as $f(x) = e^x$; for each $x \in R, R$ is being the set of real numbers. Which one of the following is correct?

A. f is one-one but not onto
B. f is onto but not one-one
C. f is both one-one and onto
D. f is neither one-one nor onto

Q.57 Let P = Set of all integral multiples of 3

Q = Set of all integral multiples of 4

R = Set of all integral multiples of 6

Consider the following relations:

I. $P \cup Q = R$

II. $P \subset R$

III. $R \subset (P \cup Q)$

Which of the relation(s) given above is/are correct?

A. Only I   **B.** Only II   **C.** Only III   **D.** II and III

Q.58 Let $x \in \{2,3,4\}$ and $y \in \{4,6,9,10\}$. If A be the set of all order pairs (x, y) such that x is a factor of y. Then, how many elements does the set A contain.

Q.59 Consider the following statements:

I. $A' \cup B = (A \cap B)'$

II. $(\phi')' = U$

III. $A \cap (B \cup C) = (A \cap B) \cup (A \cap C)$

Which of the statement(s) given above is/are correct?

A. Only II   **B.** I and III   **C.** Only III   **D.** II and III

Q.60 Which of the following is an empty set?

A. $\{x \in R : x^2 - 4x + 4\}$
B. $\{x \in R : x^3 = 1\}$
C. $\{x \in R : x^2 = -1\}$
D.   None of these

// Smart Answer Sheet //

Correct	Indicates percentage of students who answered questions correctly.
Skipped	Indicates percentage of students who skipped questions.

Q.	Ans.	Correct	Skipped
1	C	79.03 %	17.44 %
2	A	25.39 %	72.91 %
3	A	80.64 %	12.55 %
4	A	47.94 %	34.82 %
5	4	49.1 %	40.94 %
6	C	45.23 %	48.25 %
7	C	40.06 %	48.72 %
8	D	50.9 %	44.25 %
9	B	49.25 %	35.32 %
10	A	44.43 %	34.83 %
11	A	51.25 %	46.46 %
12	210	56.46 %	33.9 %

Q.	Ans.	Correct	Skipped
13	196	66.07 %	30.26 %
14	7257600	54.04 %	34.44 %
15	14	88.49 %	11.25 %
16	A	11.69 %	82.77 %
17	B	69.11 %	30.62 %
18	D	77.78 %	17.95 %
19	C	81.22 %	10.85 %
20	D	76.29 %	19.64 %
21	B	86.15 %	11.2 %
22	D	80.79 %	13.41 %
23	D	57.02 %	38.25 %
24	A	52.99 %	35.74 %

Q.	Ans.	Correct	Skipped
25	D	79.46 %	15.57 %
26	C	55.91 %	40.31 %
27	A	76.52 %	21.88 %
28	C	59.87 %	39.22 %
29	A	30.18 %	68.32 %
30	C	40.63 %	43.31 %
31	C	55.67 %	30.13 %
32	6	64.74 %	31.53 %
33	C	62.69 %	33.95 %
34	C	59.26 %	36.62 %
35	C	25.21 %	70.35 %
36	5880	13.5 %	81.81 %

Q.	Ans.	Correct	Skipped
37	69	41.78 %	33.02 %
38	2	31.25 %	67.22 %
39	12	24.94 %	68.22 %
40	5	51.89 %	35.58 %
41	150	49.9 %	35.04 %
42	720	59.76 %	30.39 %
43	A	46.11 %	33.5 %
44	83	49.25 %	35.78 %
45	A	64.35 %	33.48 %
46	D	48.93 %	51.06 %
47	B	48.79 %	36.4 %
48	D	23.19 %	72.04 %

Q.	Ans.	Correct	Skipped
49	A	52.13 %	44.96 %
50	C	40.93 %	30.86 %
51	A	42.27 %	36.65 %
52	A	60.84 %	38.1 %
53	D	55.37 %	30.26 %
54	B	62.29 %	36.06 %
55	C	44.9 %	40.71 %
56	A	64.21 %	33.06 %
57	C	23.02 %	67.74 %
58	6	51.69 %	41.92 %
59	C	22.81 %	74.85 %
60	C	59.27 %	37.55 %

Performance Analysis

Avg. Score (%)	54.44%
Toppers Score (%)	60.0%
Your Score	

//Hints and Solutions//

1. Let the events be defined as:

A: Obtaining a sum of 8

B: Getting an even number on both dice

Now cases favourable to A are $(3,5)(5,3)(2,6)(6,2)(4,4)$

So, $P(A) = \dfrac{5}{36}$

Cases favourable to B:
$(2,2),(2,4),(2,6),(4,2),(4,4),(4,6),(6,2),(6,4),(6,6)$

$P(B) = \dfrac{9}{36}$

Now, $(2,6)(6,2)$ and $(4,4)$ are common to both events A and B

So, $P(A \cap B) = \dfrac{3}{36}$

$\Rightarrow P(A \cup B) = \dfrac{5}{36} + \dfrac{9}{36} - \dfrac{3}{36}$

$\Rightarrow P(A \cup B) = \dfrac{11}{36}$

Hence, the correct option is (C).

2. Probability $= \left[\dfrac{\text{Number of Favorable Outcomes}}{\text{Number of Total Outcomes}}\right]$

Number of Total Outcomes = Total Number of ways in which 5 envelopes can be sent to 5 persons $= 5! = 120$

Number of Favorable Outcomes = When none of the letters reaches correct destiny

Unfavorable cases $=$ When all the five envelope reaches to their destiny $+$ When one of them reaches to its correct destiny $+$ Two of them reaches to its correct destiny $+$ Three of them reaches their correct place

$= {}^6C_1 \times$
$\left[4! - {}^4C_1 \times \left\{3! - \left({}^3C_1 \times 1 + 1\right)\right\} + {}^4C_2 \times 1 + 1\right]$
$+ {}^6C_2 \times \left\{3! - \left({}^3C_1 \times 1 + 1\right)\right\} + {}^6C_3 \times 1 + 1$

$\because$ Number of Favorable Outcomes $=$ Total Outcomes Unfavorable Outcomes

$= 120 - [5 \times 9 + 10 \times 2 + 10 + 1]$

$= 120 - 45 - 20 - 11$

$= 44$

$\therefore$ Probability $= \dfrac{44}{120}$

Hence, the correct option is (A).

3. We know that in a leap year there are a total of 366 days, 52 weeks, and 2 days

Now, in 52 weeks there are a total of 52 Tuesdays.

Therefore,

The probability that the leap year will contain 53 Tuesdays is equal to the probability of the remaining 2 days will be Tuesdays. Thus, the remaining two days can be:

(Monday and Tuesday), (Tuesday and Wednesday), (Wednesday and Thursday), (Thursday and Friday), (Friday and Saturday), (Saturday and Sunday), and (Sunday and Monday)

Therefore,

Total Number of cases = 7

Cases in which Tuesday can come = 2

So, probability (leap year having 53 Tuesdays) = $\dfrac{\text{Number of favourable outcomes}}{\text{Total number of outcomes}}$

$= \dfrac{2}{7}$

Hence, the correct option is (A).

4. Given,

Probability of getting a sir in a throw of die $= \dfrac{1}{6}$

And, probability of not getting a six $= \dfrac{5}{6}$

Let us assume, $p = \dfrac{1}{6}$ and $q = \dfrac{5}{6}$

Now, we have

Probability that the 2 sixes come in the first five throws of the die

$= {}^5C_2 \left(\dfrac{1}{6}\right)^2 \left(\dfrac{5}{6}\right)^3$

$= \dfrac{10 \times (5)^2}{(6)^5}$

Also, Probability that the six come in the sixth throw $= \dfrac{10 \times (5)^2}{(6)^4} \times \dfrac{1}{6}$

$= \dfrac{10 \times 125}{(6)^6}$

$= \dfrac{625}{23328}$

Hence, the correct option is (A).

5. Let us assume that, man tosses the coin n times. Thus, n tosses are the Bernoulli trials

Probability of getting head at the toss of the coin $= \dfrac{1}{2}$

Let us assume, $p = \dfrac{1}{2}$ and $q = \dfrac{1}{2}$

$P(X = x) = {}^nC_x p^{n-x} q^x$

$= {}^nC_x \left(\dfrac{1}{2}\right)^{n-x} \left(\dfrac{1}{2}\right)^x$

$$= {}^nC_x \left(\frac{1}{2}\right)^n$$

It is given in the question that,

Probability of getting at least one head $> \dfrac{90}{100}$

Therefore,

$$P(x \geq 1) > 0.9$$

$$1 - P(x = 0) > 0.9$$

$$1 - {}^nC_0 \cdot \frac{1}{2^n} > 0.9$$

$$\frac{1}{2^n} < 0.1$$

$$2^n > \frac{1}{0.1}$$

$$2^n > 10$$

So, the minimum value of n satisfying the given inequality $= 4$

∴ The man have to toss the coin 4 or more times.

Hence, the correct answer is 4.

6. Given,

Probability of getting a six in a throw of a die $= \dfrac{1}{6}$

Also, the probability of not getting a $6 = \dfrac{5}{6}$

Now, there are three cases from which the expected value of the amount which he wins can be calculated:

(i) First case is that, if he gets a six on his first through then the required probability will be $\dfrac{1}{6}$

∴ Amount received by him $=$ Rs. 1

(ii) Secondly, if he gets six on his second throw then the probability $= \left(\dfrac{5}{6} \times \dfrac{1}{6}\right)$

$$= \frac{5}{36}$$

∴ Amount received by him $= -$ Rs. $1 +$ Rs. 1

$$= 0$$

(iii) Lastly, if he does not get six in first two throws and gets six in his third throw then the probability $= \dfrac{5}{6} \times \dfrac{5}{6} \times \dfrac{1}{6}$

∴ Amount received by him $= -$ Rs. $1 -$ Rs. $1 +$ Rs. 1

$$= -1$$

So, expected value that he can win $= \dfrac{1}{6} - \dfrac{25}{216}$

$$= \frac{(36-25)}{216}$$

$$= \frac{11}{216}$$

Hence, the correct option is (C).

7. Let us assume X represent the number of times of getting 5 in 7 throws of the die

Also, the repeated tossing of a die are the Bernoulli trials

Thus, the probability of getting 5 in a single throw, $p = \dfrac{1}{6}$

And, $q = 1 - p$

$$= 1 - \frac{1}{6}$$

$$= \frac{5}{6}$$

Clearly, we have X has the binomial distribution where $n = 7$ and $p = \dfrac{1}{6}$

$$P(X = x) = {}^nC_x q^{n-x} p^x$$

$$= {}^7C_x \left(\frac{5}{6}\right)^{7-x} \left(\frac{1}{6}\right)^x$$

Probability of getting 5 exactly twice in a die $= P(X = 2)$

$$= {}^7C_2 \left(\frac{5}{6}\right)^5 \times \left(\frac{1}{6}\right)^2$$

$$= 21 \times \left(\frac{5}{6}\right)^5 \times \frac{1}{36}$$

$$= \left(\frac{7}{12}\right)\left(\frac{5}{6}\right)^5$$

$$= \left(\frac{7}{12}\right) \times \left(\frac{5}{6}\right)^5$$

$$= \left(\frac{7}{12}\right) \times \left(\frac{3125}{7776}\right)$$

$$= \left(\frac{21875}{93312}\right)$$

$$= 0.23$$

Hence, the correct option is (C).

8. Let E_1 be the event that item is produced by A, E_2 be the event that item is produced by B and X be the event that produced product is found to be defective.

Then $P(E_1) = 60\% = \dfrac{60}{100}$

$$= \frac{3}{5}$$

$$P(E_1) = 40\% = \frac{40}{100}$$

$$= \frac{2}{5}$$

Also $P\left(\dfrac{X}{E_1}\right) = P$ (item is defective given that it is produced by machine A) $= 2\% = \dfrac{2}{100}$

$= \dfrac{1}{50}$

And $P\left(\dfrac{X}{E_2}\right) = P$ (item is defective given that it is produced by machine B) $= 1\%$

$= \dfrac{1}{100}$

Now the probability that item is produced by B, being given that item is defective, is $P\left(\dfrac{E_2}{A}\right)$.

By using Bayes' theorem, we have

$$P\left(\dfrac{E_2}{A}\right) = \dfrac{P(E_2)\cdot P\left(\frac{X}{E_2}\right)}{P(E_1)\cdot P\left(\frac{X}{E_1}\right) + P(E_2)\cdot P\left(\frac{X}{E_2}\right)}$$

By substituting the values we get

$$= \dfrac{\frac{2}{5}\times\frac{1}{100}}{\frac{3}{5}\times\frac{2}{100}+\frac{2}{5}\times\frac{1}{100}}$$

$$= \dfrac{\frac{2}{5}\times\frac{1}{100}}{\frac{1}{500}(6+2)} = \dfrac{2}{8}$$

$$\Rightarrow P\left(\dfrac{E_2}{A}\right) = \dfrac{1}{4}$$

Hence, the correct option is (D).

9. Let E_1 be the event that first group wins the competition, E_2 be the event that that second group wins the competition and A be the event of introducing a new product.

Then $P(E_1) = 0.6$ and $P(E_2) = 0.4$

Also $P\left(\dfrac{A}{E_1}\right) = P$ (introducing a new product given that first group wins) $= 0.7$

And $P\left(\dfrac{A}{E_2}\right) = P$ (introducing a new product given that second group wins) $= 0.3$

Now the probability of that new product introduced was by the second group, being given that a new product was introduced, is $P\left(\dfrac{E_2}{A}\right)$.

By using Bayes' theorem, we have

$$P\left(\dfrac{E_2}{A}\right) = \dfrac{P(E_2)\cdot P\left(\frac{A}{E_2}\right)}{P(E_1)\cdot P\left(\frac{A}{E_1}\right) + P(E_2)\cdot P\left(\frac{A}{E_2}\right)}$$

Now by substituting the values we get

$$= \dfrac{0.4\times 0.3}{0.6\times 0.7 + 0.4\times 0.3}$$

$$= \dfrac{0.12}{0.42+0.12}$$

$$= \dfrac{0.12}{0.54}$$

$$= \dfrac{12}{54}$$

$$= \dfrac{2}{9}$$

$$P\left(\dfrac{E_2}{A}\right) = \dfrac{2}{9}$$

Hence, the correct option is (B).

10. Let E_1 be the event that the outcome on the die is 5 or 6, E_2 be the event that the outcome on the die is $1,2,3$ or 4 and A be the event getting exactly head.

Then $P(E_1) = \dfrac{2}{6}$

$= \dfrac{1}{3}$

$P(E_2) = \dfrac{4}{6}$

$= \dfrac{2}{3}$

As in throwing a coin three times we get 8 possibilities.

(HHH, HHT, HTH, THH, TTH, THT, HTT, TTT)

$\Rightarrow P\left(\dfrac{A}{E_1}\right) = P$ (obtaining exactly one head by tossing the coin three times if she get 5 or 6) $= \dfrac{3}{8}$

And $P\left(\dfrac{A}{E_2}\right) = P$ (obtaining exactly one head by tossing the coin three times if she get $1,2,3$ or 4) $= \dfrac{1}{2}$

Now the probability that the girl threw $1,2,3$ or 4 with a die, being given that she obtained exactly one head, is $P\left(\dfrac{E_2}{A}\right)$

By using Bayes' theorem, we have

$$P\left(\dfrac{E_2}{A}\right) = \dfrac{P(E_2)\cdot P\left(\frac{A}{E_2}\right)}{P(E_1)\cdot P\left(\frac{A}{E_1}\right) + P(E_2)\cdot P\left(\frac{A}{E_2}\right)}$$

Now by substituting the values we get

$$= \dfrac{\frac{2}{3}\cdot\frac{1}{2}}{\frac{1}{3}\cdot\frac{3}{8}+\frac{2}{3}\cdot\frac{1}{2}}$$

$$= \dfrac{\frac{1}{3}}{\frac{1}{8}+\frac{1}{3}}$$

$$= \dfrac{\frac{1}{3}}{\frac{3+8}{24}} = \dfrac{8}{11}$$

$$\Rightarrow P\left(\dfrac{E_2}{A}\right) = \dfrac{8}{11}$$

Hence, the correct option is (A).

11. Given,

Number between 107 to $1006 = 900$

Number of possible outcomes $= n(S) = 900$

Numbers from 107 to 1006 divisible by 11 and 37 both $= \{407, 814\}$

$= 2$

Numbers on cards not divisible by both 11 and $37 = 900 - 2 = 898$

$\therefore$ Probability $= \dfrac{n\ (\text{Favourable Events})}{n(\text{Possible outcomes})}$

$= \dfrac{898}{900}$

$= 0.998$

Hence, the correct option is (A).

12. Given,

There are 12 points in a plane out of which 5 are collinear.

For formation of a triangle we need 3 points if they are not collinear.

So,

Total number of triangles that can be formed with 12 points (if none of them are collinear) $= {}^{12}C_3$

With collinear points, we cannot make any triangle as they are in straight line.

Here 5 points are collinear. Therefore we need to subtract ${}^{5}C_3$ triangles from the above count.

As we know,

$${}^{n}C_k = \dfrac{n!}{k!(n-k)!}$$

Hence, required number of triangles $= {}^{12}C_3 - {}^{5}C_3$

$= \dfrac{12!}{3!(12-3)!} - \dfrac{5!}{3!(5-3)!}$

$= 220 - 10$

$= 210$

Hence, the correct answer is 210.

13. There are two cases:

Case: $1.$ When 4 is selected from the first 5 and rest 6 from remaining 8.

As we know,

$${}^{n}C_r = \dfrac{n!}{r!(n-r)!}$$

Total arrangement $= {}^{5}C_4 \times {}^{8}C_6$

$= 5 \times {}^{8}C_6$

$= \dfrac{5 \times (8 \times 7)}{(2 \times 1)}$

$= 5 \times 4 \times 7 = 140$

Case: $2.$ When all 5 is selected from the first 5 and rest 5 from remaining 8.

Total arrangement $= {}^{5}C_5 \times {}^{8}C_5$

$= 1 \times {}^{8}C_5$

$= \dfrac{(8 \times 7 \times 6)}{(3 \times 2 \times 1)}$

$= 8 \times 7 = 56$

Now, the total number of choices available $= 140 + 56 = 196$

Hence, the correct answer is 196.

14. Given,

Total number of students $= 10$

Number of ways 5 students can be seated out of 10 students ${}^{10}C_5$

$= \dfrac{10!}{5!(10-5)!}$

$= \dfrac{10 \times 9 \times 8 \times 7 \times 6 \times 5!}{5! \times (5!)}$

$= 252$

The remaining 5 will be seated in ${}^{5}C_5$

Students of each row can be arranged as $= 5! \times 5!$

Two sets of paper can be arranged themselves in $= 2!$

Thus,

Total arrangement $= {}^{10}C_5 \times 5! \times 5! \times 2$

$= 252 \times 120 \times 120 \times 2$

$= 7257600$

Hence the correct answer is 7257600.

15. We know that,

$${}^{n}P_r = \dfrac{n!}{(n-r)!}$$

$${}^{n}P_3 = n \times (n-1) \times (n-2)$$

$${}^{(n+1)}P_3 = (n+1) \times n \times (n-1)$$

Now,

$5 \times n \times (n-1) \times (n-2) = 4 \times (n+1) \times n \times (n-1)$

$\Rightarrow 5(n-2) = 4(n+1)$

$\Rightarrow 5n - 10 = 4n + 4$

$\Rightarrow 5n - 4n = 4 + 10$

$n = 14$

Hence, the correct answer is 14.

16. Let E_1 be the event of choosing bag A, E_2 be the event of choosing the bag B and X be the event of drawing a red ball.

$$P(E_1) = P(E_2) = \frac{1}{2}$$

$P(X \mid E_1) = P\text{ (Drawing a red ball from bag }A) = \frac{4}{8} = \frac{1}{2}$

Similarly,

$P(X \mid E_2) = P\text{ (Drawing a red ball from bag }B) = \frac{2}{8} = \frac{1}{4}$

Here, we have to find the probability of drawing a ball from bag A given that the ball is red in color i.e $P(E_1 \mid X)$

As we know that, according to bayes' theorem:

$$P(E_i \mid A) = \frac{P(E_i) \times P(A|E_i)}{\sum_{i=1}^{n} P(E_i) \times P(A|E_i)}, i = 1,2,\ldots,n$$

$$P(E_1 \mid X) = \frac{P(E_1) \times P(X|E_1)}{|P(E_1) \times P(X|E_1) + P(E_2) \times P(X|E_2)|}$$

$$P(E_1 \mid X) = \frac{\frac{1}{2} \times \frac{1}{2}}{\left[\frac{1}{2} \times \frac{1}{2} + \frac{1}{2} \times \frac{1}{4}\right]} = \frac{2}{3}$$

Hence, the correct option is (A).

17. In a simultaneous throw of two dice, we have

$n(S) = (6 \times 6) = 36$

Let E = event of getting two numbers whose product is even. Then,

$E =$

$(1,2), (1,4), (1,6), (2,1), (2,2), (2,3), (2,4), (2,5), (2,6),$

$(3,2), (3,4), (3,6), (4,1), (4,2), (4,3), (4,4), (4,5), (4,6),$

$(5,2), (5,4), (5,6), (6,1), (6,2), (6,3), (6,4), (6,5), (6,6)$

$\therefore n(E) = 27$

$\therefore P(E) = \frac{n(E)}{n(S)}$

$= \frac{27}{36} = \frac{3}{4}$

Hence, the correct option is (B).

18. Event A is choosing a yellow pencil first, and Event B is choosing a yellow pencil second.

Initially, there are 12 pencils, 7 of which are yellow.

Probability the first pencil is yellow $= P(A) = \frac{7}{12}$

If a yellow pencil is chosen, there will be 11 pencils left, 6 of which are yellow.

Probability the second pencil is yellow $= P(B) = \frac{6}{11}$

Given: Two pencils are chosen at random from the box without replacement.

So events are independent of each other.

Probability they are both yellow $= P(A \cap B) =$

$P(A) \times P(B) = \frac{7}{12} \times \frac{6}{11} = \frac{7}{22}$

Hence, the correct option is (D).

19. Given,

$D = \{-6, -4, -2, 0, 2, 4, 6\}$

As we can see that, all the element of D are even integers from -6 to 6.

So, the required set-builder form of set D will be:

$\{x : x = 2n, \text{where } n \in Z \text{ and } -3 \le n \le 3\}$.

Hence, the correct option is (C).

20. Given,

$A = \{4x^2 - x - 5 = 0 : x \in I\}$

$4x^2 - x - 5 = 0$

$\Rightarrow (x+1)(4x-5) = 0$

$\Rightarrow x = -1, 1.25$

For set $A, x \in I$

$\therefore$ Roster form of set A will be $\{-1\}$.

Hence, the correct option is (D).

21. Given,

$A = \{2,3,4,5,6,7\}, B = \{6,7,8\}$ and $C = \{1,5,8,9\}$

Let,

$P = (B \cup C)$

$= \{6,7,8\} \cup \{1,5,8,9\}$

$= \{1,5,6,7,8,9\}$

$\Rightarrow A \cap P = \{2,3,4,5,6,7\} \cap \{1,5,6,7,8,9\}$

$\Rightarrow A \cap (B \cup C) = \{5,6,7\}$

Therefore, number of elements $= 3$

Hence, the correct option is (B).

22. A set that has the finite number of elements is said to be a finite set.

Option (D): $\{x \in N : x \text{ is even }\}$

As we can see that, elements of $\{x \in N : x \text{ is even }\}$ are: $2,4,6,8, \ldots \ldots$

So, there are infinitely many elements in the set $\{x \in N : x \text{ is even}\}$

Thus, $\{x \in N : x \text{ is even }\}$ is not a finite set.

Option (A): $\{x : x \in N \text{ and } x^2 < 36\}$

As we can see that, elements of $\{x : x \in N \text{ and } x^2 < 36\}$ are: $1,2,3,4,5$

So, there are 5 elements in the set $\{x : x \in N \text{ and } x^2 < 36\}$

Thus, the set $\{x : x \in N \text{ and } x^2 < 36\}$ is a finite set.

Option (B): $\{x \in z : 0 < x < 10\}$

As we can see that, elements of $\{x \in z : 0 < x < 10\}$ are: $1,2,3, \ldots \ldots, 9$

So, there are 9 elements in the set $\{x \in z : 0 < x < 10\}$

Thus, the set $\{x \in z : 0 < x < 10\}$ is a finite set.

Option (C): $\{x : x \in N \text{ and } x^2 = x\}$

$\because x^2 = x$

$\Rightarrow x^2 - x = 0$

$\Rightarrow x(x - 1) = 0$

$\Rightarrow x = 0 \text{ or } 1$

But since $x \in N$.

So, $x = 0 \notin \{x : x \in N \text{ and } x^2 = x\}$

Therefore, only $x = 1 \in \{x : x \in N \text{ and } x^2 = x\}$

Thus, $\{x : x \in N \text{ and } x^2 = x\}$ is a finite set.

Hence, the correct option is (D).

23. Given a die is tossed thrice.

Then the sample space $S = \{1,2,3,4,5,6\}$

Let $P(A) =$ probability of getting an odd number in first throw.

$\Rightarrow P(A) = \dfrac{3}{6} = \dfrac{1}{2}$

Let $P(B) =$ probability of getting an even number.

$\Rightarrow P(B) = \dfrac{3}{6} = \dfrac{1}{2}$

Now, probability of getting an even number in three times $= \dfrac{1}{2} \times \dfrac{1}{2} \times \dfrac{1}{2} = \dfrac{1}{8}$

So, probability of getting an odd number at least once

$= 1$ - probability of getting an odd number in no throw

$= 1$ - probability of getting an even number in three times

$= 1 - \dfrac{1}{8}$

$= \dfrac{7}{8}$

$\therefore$ Probability of getting an odd number at least once $= \dfrac{7}{8}$

Hence, the correct option is (D).

24. Given,

6 men and 4 women are to be seated in a row so that no two women sit together.

6 men can sit as,

$\_ \times M \times M \times M \times M \times M \times M \times \_$

Now, there are 7 spaces and 4 women can sit as $= {}^7P_4$

As we know,

$${}^nP_r = \dfrac{n!}{(n-r)!}$$

$${}^7P_4 = \dfrac{7!}{(7-4)!}$$

$$= \dfrac{7!}{3!}$$

$$= \dfrac{7 \times 6 \times 5 \times 4 \times 3!}{3!} = 840$$

Now, total number of arrangement $= 6! \times 840$

$= 6 \times 5 \times 4 \times 3 \times 2 \times 1 \times 840$

$= 720 \times 840$

$= 604800$

Hence, the correct option is (A).

25. The sample space of the given experiment is $S = \{HH, HT, TH, TT\}$

Here, $E :$ tail appears on one coin

And $F :$ one coin shows head

$E = \{HT, TH\}$ and $F = \{HT, TH\}$

$E \cap F = \{HT, TH\}$

So, $P(E) = \frac{2}{4} = \frac{1}{2}, P(F) = \frac{2}{4} = \frac{1}{2}, P(E \cap F) = \frac{2}{4} = \frac{1}{2}$

Now, we know that by definition of conditional probability,

$$P(E \mid F) = \frac{P(E \cap F)}{P(F)}$$

Substituting the values we get,

$$\Rightarrow P(E \mid F) = \frac{\frac{1}{2}}{\frac{1}{2}}$$

$$\Rightarrow P(E \mid F) = 1$$

Hence, the correct option is (D).

26. The sample space for the given experiment is $S = \{1,2,3,4,5,6\}$

Given,

$E = \{1,3,5\}$

$F = \{2,3\}$

$P(E) = \frac{3}{6} = \frac{1}{2}$

$P(F) = \frac{2}{6} = \frac{1}{3}$

Now, $E \cap F = \{3\}$

$P(E \cap F) = \frac{1}{6}$

We know that by definition of conditional probability,

$$P(E \mid F) = \frac{P(E \cap F)}{P(F)}$$

$$P(E \mid F) = \frac{\frac{1}{6}}{\frac{1}{3}}$$

$$P(E \mid F) = \frac{1}{2}$$

Hence, the correct option is (C).

27. Given,

$$f(x) = \sqrt{20 - x^2}$$

It is defined only when $20 - x^2 \geq 0$

So, $y \geq 0$ ....(i)

Let, $y = f(x)$

$\Rightarrow y = \sqrt{20 - x^2}$

Squaring both sides, we get

$$y^2 = 20 - x^2$$

$$\Rightarrow x^2 = 20 - y^2$$

$$\Rightarrow x = \sqrt{20 - y^2}$$

It is defined only when $20 - y^2 \geq 0$

$$\Rightarrow y^2 \leq 20$$

$$\Rightarrow y^2 - 20 \leq 0$$

$$\Rightarrow (y - 2\sqrt{5})(y + 2\sqrt{5}) \leq 0$$

$$\Rightarrow y \in [-2\sqrt{5}, 2\sqrt{5}] \text{ ...(ii)}$$

From eq (i) and eq (ii), we get

$$y \in [0, 2\sqrt{5}]$$

Hence, the correct option is (A).

28. Given:

A, B, C be subsets of X

Statement 1: $A \subset C \Rightarrow (A \cap B) \subset (C \cap B), (A \cup B) \subset (C \cup B)$

Now, if $A \subset C$ then $(A \cap B) \subset (C \cap B), (A \cup B) \subset (C \cup B)$ is true.

Statement 1 is true.

Statement 2: $(A \cap B) \subset (C \cup B)$ for all sets $B \Rightarrow A \subset C$

Let $A = \{1,2,3\}, B = \{3,4,5\}$ and $C = \{1,6,7,8\}$

$\Rightarrow A \cap B = \{3\} \subset (C \cap B)$ but $A \subset C$ is not true.

Statement 2 is false.

Statement 3: $(A \cup B) \subset (C \cup B)$ for all sets $B \Rightarrow A \subset C$

This is true as $(A \cup B) \subset (C \cup B)$ for all sets $B \Rightarrow A \subset C$

Hence, the correct option is (C).

29. Given: A = {x ∈ R: x^2 - 10x + 9 = 0}, B = {y ∈ R: y^2 - 3y + 2 = 0} and U = {z ∈ N: 1 ≤ z ≤ 10}

$\Rightarrow$ x^2 - 10x + 9 = 0 (Given)

$\Rightarrow$ x^2 - x - 9x + 9 = 0

$\Rightarrow$ (x - 1) (x - 9) = 0

$\Rightarrow$ x = 1 or 9

$\Rightarrow$ A = {1, 9}

Similarly, y^2 - 3y + 2 = 0

$\Rightarrow$ y^2 - y - 2y + 2 = 0

$\Rightarrow$ (y - 1) (y - 2) = 0

$\Rightarrow$ y = 1 or 2

$\Rightarrow$ B = {1, 2}

U = {1, 2, 3, 4, 5, 6, 7, 8, 9, 10} -------(Given)

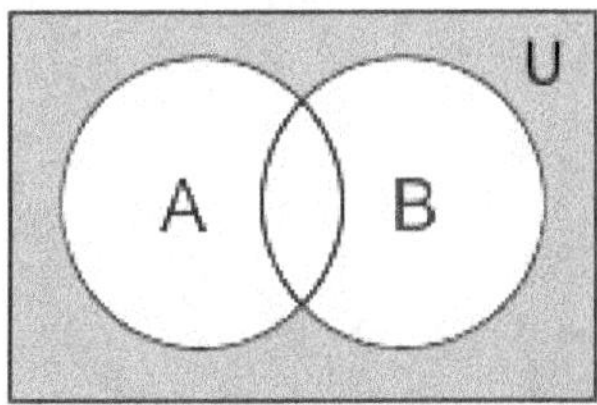

The shaded region represents (A ∪ B)'.

= A ∪ B = {1, 2, 9}

= (A ∪ B)' = U - (A ∪ B) = {3, 4, 5, 6, 7, 8, 10}

Hence, the correct option is (A).

30. Given: A = {x ∈ R: x is the sum of divisors of 2}, B = {x ∈ R: x^2 = 2} and C = {x ∈ R: $x^2 - 5x + 6 = 0$}

The divisors of 2 are: 1 and 2

∴ The sum of divisors of 2 is 3

⇒ A = {3}

∵ $x^2 - 2 = 0$

$$\Rightarrow x = \pm\sqrt{2}$$

$$\Rightarrow B = \{\sqrt{2}, -\sqrt{2}\}$$

Similarly, $x^2 - 5x + 6 = 0$

⇒ $x^2 - 2x - 3x + 6 = 0$

⇒ (x - 2) (x - 3) = 0

⇒ x = 2 or 3

⇒ C = {2, 3}

$$\Rightarrow (A \cup B) = \{\sqrt{2}, -\sqrt{2}, 3\}$$

$$\Rightarrow (A \cup B) \cap C = \{\sqrt{2}, -\sqrt{2}, 3\} \cap \{2,3\} = \{3\}$$

Hence, the correct option is (C).

31. Given:

P = Set of all integral multiples of 3

Q = Set of all integral multiples of 4

R = Set of all integral multiples of 6

Concept:

Set symbols:

Union: A ∪ B i.e. in A or B.

Proper Subset: A ⊂ B i.e. every element of A is in B.

Not a Subset: A ⊄ B i..e. A is not a subset of B.

Explanation:

P = Set of all integral multiples of 3

⇒ P = {3, 6, 9, 12, 15, 18, ...},

Q = Set of all integral multiples of 4

⇒ Q = {4, 8, 12, 16, 20, ...}

R = Set of all integral multiples of 6

⇒ R = {6, 12, 18, 24, 30, ...}

Considering the relation,

I. P ∪ Q = R

P ∪ Q = {3, 4, 6, 8, 9, 12, 15, 16,....} ≠ R

II. P ⊂ R

All the elements of P are not in R so P ⊄ R

III. R ⊂ (P ∪ Q)

P ∪ Q = {3, 4, 6, 8, 9, 12, 15, 16,....}

Therefore,

All the elements of R are in P ∪ Q

⇒ R ⊂ (P ∪ Q)

∴ Only (III) statement is correct.

Hence, the correct option is (C).

32. Given:

x ∈ {2, 3, 4} and,

y ∈ {4, 6, 9, 10}

To find the set of all ordered pairs (x,y) such that x is a factor of y.

Let, A = { (x,y) : x is a factor of y}

Here,

2 is a factor of 4 implies (2, 4) ∈ A

2 is a factor of 6 implies (2, 6) ∈ A

2 is a factor of 10 implies (2, 10) ∈ A

3 is a factor of 6 implies (3, 6) ∈ A

3 is a factor of 9 implies (3, 9) ∈ A

4 is a factor of 4 implies (4, 4) ∈ A

So,

A = {(2, 4), (2, 6), (2, 10), (3, 6), (3, 9), (4, 4) }

∴ Set A contains 6 elements.

Hence, the correct answer is 6.

33. Given:

Three statements,

I. A' ∪ B = (A ∩ B)'

II. (φ')' = U

III. A ∩ (B ∪ C) = (A ∩ B) ∪ (A ∩ C)

Concept:

De Morgan's law:

(A ∩ B)' = A' ∪ B'

Distributive law:

A ∩ (B ∪ C) = (A ∩ B) ∪ (A ∩ C)

Universal Law:

(φ)' = ∪

Explanation:

I. A' ∪ B = (A ∩ B)'

⇒ (A ∩ B)' = A' ∪ B' [by De Morgan's law]

So, statement (I) is not correct.

II. (φ')' = ∪

⇒ (φ)' = ∪ and (∪)' = φ [by universal law]

So, statement (II) is not correct.

III. A ∩ (B ∪ C) = (A ∩ B) ∪ (A ∩ C)

⇒ A ∩ (B ∪ C) = (A ∩ B) ∪ (A ∩ C) [by Distributive law]

∴ Statement (III) is correct.

Hence, the correct option is (C).

34. Option (A):

Given: $\{x \in R : x^2 - 4x + 4 = 0\}$

$x^2 - 4x + 4 = 0$

⇒ $x^2 - 2x - 2x + 4 = 0$

⇒ $(x - 2)(x - 2) = 0$

⇒ $x = 2$

So, 2 is an element of $\{x \in R : x^2 - 4x + 4 = 0\} \Rightarrow \{x \in R : x^2 - 4x + 4 = 0\}$ is not an empty set.

Option (B):

Given: $\{x \in R: x^3 = 1\}$

$x^3 = 1$

⇒ $x^3 - 1 = 0$

⇒ $(x - 1)(x^2 + x + 1) = 0$

⇒ $x = 1$ or ω or ω^2, where $\omega = \dfrac{-1+i\sqrt{3}}{2}$ and $\omega^2 = \dfrac{-1-i\sqrt{3}}{2}$

∵ $x \in R \Rightarrow$ only $x = 1$ is an element of $\{x \in R: x^3 = 1\}$

So, the given set $\{x \in R: x^3 = 1\}$ is not an empty set.

Option (C):

Given: $\{x \in R: x^2 = -1\}$

⇒ $x^2 = -1$

⇒ $x = \pm i \notin R$

So, the given set $\{x \in R: x^2 = -1\}$ is an empty set.

Hence, the correct option is (C).

35. The given problem can be written as,

$${}^nC_r + {}^nC_{r+1} + {}^nC_{r+1} + {}^nC_{r+2}$$

We know that:

$${}^nC_r = \frac{n!}{r!(n-r)!}$$

Therefore,

$${}^nC_r + {}^nC_{r+1} + {}^nC_{r+1} + {}^nC_{r+2}$$

$$= \frac{n!}{r!(n-r)!} + \frac{n!}{(r+1)!(n-r-1)!} + \frac{n!}{(r+1)!(n-r-1)!} + \frac{n!}{(r+2)!(n-r-2)!}$$

$$= \frac{n!}{r!(n-r-1)!}\left[\frac{1}{(n-r)} + \frac{1}{(r+1)}\right] + \frac{n!}{(r+1)!(n-r-2)!}\left[\frac{1}{(n-r-1)} + \frac{1}{(r+2)}\right]$$

$$= \frac{n!}{r!(n-r-1)!}\left[\frac{r+1+n-r}{(n-r)(r+1)}\right] + \frac{n!}{(r+1)!(n-r-2)!}\left[\frac{r+2+n-r-1}{(n-r-1)(r+2)}\right]$$

$$= \frac{n! \times (n+1)}{r! \times (r+1) \times (n-r-1) \times (n-r)} + \frac{n!}{(r+1)!(n-r-2)!} \times \frac{(n+1)}{(n-r-1)(r+2)}$$

$$= \frac{(n+1)!}{(r+1)!(n-r)!} + \frac{n! \times (n+1)}{(r+2)(r+1) \times (n-r-1)(n-r-2)}$$

$$= \frac{(n+1)!}{(r+1)!(n-r)!} + \frac{(n+1)!}{(r+2)!(n-r-1)!}$$

$$= \frac{(n+1)!}{(r+1)!(n-r-1)!}\left[\frac{1}{n-r} + \frac{1}{r+2}\right]$$

$$= \frac{(n+1)!}{(r+1)!(n-r-1)!}\left[\frac{n-r+r+2}{(r+2)(n-r)}\right]$$

$$= \frac{(n+2)(n+1)!}{(r+2)(r+1)!(n-r)(n-r-1)!}$$

$$= \frac{(n+2)!}{(r+2)!(n-r)!}$$

$$= {}^{n+2}C_{r+2}$$

$$= C(n+2, r+2)$$

Hence, the correct option is (C).

36. The word ALLAHABAD contains 9 letters, in which A occur 4 times, L occurs twice and the rest of the letters occur only once.

We know that:

Number of Permutations of ' n ' things taken ' r ' at a time:

$$p(n, r) = \frac{n!}{(n-r)!}$$

Number of Permutations of ' n ' objects where there are n_1 repeated items, n_2 repeated items, n_k repeated items taken ' r' at a time:

$$p(n, r) = \frac{n!}{n_1! n_2! n_1! \dots n_k!}$$

Therefore,

Number of different words formed by the word ALLAHABAD using all the letters.

$$= \frac{9!}{4! \times 2!}$$

$$= \frac{9 \times 8 \times 7 \times 6 \times 5 \times 4!}{4! \times 2}$$

$$= \frac{72 \times 7 \times 30}{2}$$

$$= 7560$$

Now, let us take both L together and consider (LL) as 1 letter.

Then, we will have to arrange 8 letters, in which A occurs 4 times and the rest of the letters occur only once.

So, the number of words having both L together will be:

$$= \frac{8!}{4!}$$

$$= \frac{8 \times 7 \times 6 \times 5 \times 4!}{4!}$$

$$= 1680$$

Therefore, the number of words with both L not occurring together will be;

$$= 7560 - 1680$$

$$= 5880$$

Hence, the correct answer is 5880.

37. We know that:

The number of ways to select r things out of n things is given by ^nC_r.

$$^nC_r = \frac{n!}{(n-r)! \times (r)!} = \frac{n \times (n-1) \times ... (n-r+1)}{r!}$$

Given that:

There are 13 points in a plane of which 5 are collinear.

We know that:

To form a line we have to select two points out of 13 points.

$\therefore$ Number of lines $= {}^{13}C_2$

$$= \frac{13 \times 12}{2 \times 1}$$

$$= 78$$

Also number of lines out of 5 points $= {}^5C_2$

$$= \frac{5 \times 4}{2 \times 1}$$

$$= 10$$

But, these 5 points are collinear, and only one line can be formed out of these points.

$\therefore$ The total number of straight lines obtained by joining these points in pairs.

$= 78 - 10 + 1$ (We add 1, as one line can be obtained out of 5 collinear points).

$$= 69$$

Hence, the correct answer is 69.

38. The formula of a combination of r objects out of n objects is given as follows:

$$^nC_r = \frac{n!}{r!(n-r)!}$$

The formula for permutation of r objects out of n objects is given as follows:

$$^nP_r = \frac{n!}{(n-r)!}$$

It is given that $^nC_r = {}^nC_{r-1}$ therefore, using a combination formula we can write:

$$^nC_r = {}^nC_{r-1}$$

$$\Rightarrow \frac{n!}{(n-r)!r!} = \frac{n!}{[n-(r-1)]!(r-1)!}$$

$$\Rightarrow \frac{[n-(r-1)] \cdot (r-1)!}{(n-r)r!} = 1$$

$$\Rightarrow \frac{(n-r+1)(n-r)!(r-1)!}{(r-1)(n-r)!(r)} = 1$$

$$\Rightarrow \frac{n-r+1}{r} = 1$$

$$\Rightarrow n = 2r - 1$$

Similarly, we know that, $^nP_r = {}^nP_{r+1}$ therefore, using the permutation formula:

$$^nP_r = {}^nP_{r+1}$$

$$\Rightarrow \frac{n!}{(n-r)!} = \frac{n!}{(n-(r+1))!}$$

$$\Rightarrow \frac{(n-r-1)!}{(n-r)!} = 1$$

$$\Rightarrow \frac{(n-r-1)!}{(n-r-1)!(n-r)} = 1$$

$$\Rightarrow n - r = 1$$

Now substitute $n = 2r - 1$ in the above equation.

$$n - r = 1$$

$$\Rightarrow (2r - 1) - r = 1$$

$$\Rightarrow r = 2$$

Therefore, the value of $r = 2$.

Hence, the correct answer is 2.

39. We know that the number of permutations of n things taken r at a time is given by, $^nP_r = \dfrac{n!}{(n-r)!}$

Given: a denotes the number of permutations of $x+2$ things taken all at a time.

$$\therefore a = {}^{x+2}P_{x+2} = (x+2)! \quad \dots (1)$$

b denotes the number of permutations of x things being taken 11 at a time.

$$\therefore b = {}^{x}P_{11} = \dfrac{x!}{(x-11)!} \quad \dots (2)$$

c denotes the number of permutations of $x-11$ things taken all at a time.

$$\therefore c = {}^{x-11}P_{x-11} = (x-11)! \quad \dots (3)$$

Given: $a = 182bc$

$$\Rightarrow (x+2)! = 182 \times \dfrac{x!}{(x-11)!} \times (x-11)! \quad [\text{Using}$$
$(1), (2)$ and $(3)]$

$$\Rightarrow (x+2)! = 182x!$$

$$\Rightarrow (x+2)(x+1)x! = 182x! \quad [\text{Using}$$
$(x+2)! = (x+2)(x+1)x!]$

$$\Rightarrow (x+2)(x+1) = 182$$

$$\Rightarrow x^2 + x + 2x + 2 = 182$$

$$\Rightarrow x^2 + 3x - 180 = 0$$

Now using factorization method to find the roots of equation,

$$\Rightarrow x^2 + (15-12)x - 180 = 0$$

$$\Rightarrow x^2 + 15x - 12x - 180 = 0$$

$$\Rightarrow x(x+15) - 12(x+15) = 0$$

$$\Rightarrow (x+15)(x-12) = 0$$

$$\Rightarrow x = -15 \text{ or } x = 12$$

$$\therefore x = 12$$

Hence, the correct answer is 12.

40. Given:

$$^9P_5 + 5 \cdot {}^9P_4 = {}^{10}P_r$$

As we know,

$$= {}^nP_r + r \times {}^nP_{r-1}$$

$$= \dfrac{n!}{(n-r)!} + r \times \dfrac{n!}{(n-r+1)!}$$

$$= \dfrac{n!}{(n-r)!} + r \times \dfrac{n!}{(n-r+1)\times(n-r)!}$$

$$= \dfrac{n!}{(n-r)!}\left(1 + \dfrac{r}{(n-r+1)}\right)$$

$$= \dfrac{n!}{(n-r)!}\left(\dfrac{n-r+1+r}{(n-r+1)}\right)$$

$$= \dfrac{(n+1)n!}{(n-r+1)(n-r)!} = \dfrac{(n+1)!}{(n-r+1)!} = {}^{n+1}P_r$$

$$\therefore P_r + r \times {}^nP_{r-1} = {}^{n+1}P_r$$

Now, $^9P_5 + 5.{}^9P_4 = {}^{10}P_r$

Compare with above results, we get

$$n = 9 \text{ and } r = 5$$

Hence, the correct answer is 5.

41. We know that:

Suppose a set of n objects has n_1 of one kind of object, n_2 of a second kind, n_3 of a third kind, and so, on with $n = n_1 + n_2 + n_3 + \cdots + n_k$ then the number of distinguishable permutations of the n objects is:

$$= \dfrac{n!}{n_1! \times n_2! \times n_1! \dots \dots n_k!}$$

If there are m ways to choose an object one and n ways to choose an object two then the number of ways of selecting objects one and two are given by $m \times n$.

If there are m ways to choose an object one and n ways to choose an object two then the number of ways of selecting objects one or two is given by $m + n$.

Given:

Total no. of toys $= 5$

Total no. of children $= 3$

Each should get one toy.

Selection can be done as follows: $(2,2,1)$ or $(1,1,3)$

$$= {}^5C_2 \times {}^3C_2 \times {}^1C_1 \times \dfrac{3!}{2!} + {}^5C_1 \times {}^4C_1 \times {}^3C_3 \times \dfrac{3!}{2!}$$

$$= (10 \times 3 \times 1 \times 3) + (5 \times 4 \times 1 \times 3)$$

$$= 90 + 60$$

$$= 150$$

Hence, the correct answer is 150.

42. The fundamental principal of multiplication:

Let us suppose there are two tasks A and B such that task A can be done in mifferent ways following which the second task B can be done in n different ways.

Then the number of ways to complete the task A and B in succession respectively is given by: $m \times n$ ways

Here, we have to form a 5 letter code using the first 6 letters of the English alphabet such that no letter is letter repeated.

Number of ways to choose 1st letter for the code $= 6$

Number of ways to choose 2nd letter for the code $= 5$

Number of ways to choose 3rd letter for the code $= 4$

Number of ways to choose 4th letter for the code $= 3$

Number of ways to choose 5th letter for the code $= 2$

The number of ways to form a 5 letter code using first 6 letters of english alphabet $= 6 \times 5 \times 4 \times 3 \times 2 = 720$.

Hence, the correct answer is 720.

43. For simplification let denote the teachers as ' T ' and students as 'S'.

Number of chairs $= 9$

Student $= A, B, C, D, E, F$

Now we will arrange according to the condition given in question.

TSS, TSS, TSS $= 3! \times 6!$

SST $, SST, SST = 3! \times 6!$

STS, STS,STS $= 3! \times 6!$

Now total number of ways = Sum of above three ways

$\Rightarrow 3! \times 6! + 3! \times 6! + 3! \times 6!$

$\Rightarrow 3 \times 3! \times 6!$

Now we will expand the factorial value.

$\Rightarrow 3 \times 3 \times 2 \times 6!$

$\Rightarrow 18(6!)$

Thus, the total number of arrangements that can be made if between any two teachers there are exactly two students is $18(6!)$

Hence, the correct option is (A).

44. Given:

Number of men $= 6$

Number of women $= 3$

Number of members in committee $= 6$ (at least 1 woman)

Formula used:

$$^{n}C_{r} = \frac{n!}{r!(n-r)!}$$

There are 3 cases we can consider

Case 1: 5 men and 1 woman in committee.

Number of ways $=$ (number of ways select 5 men from 6 men x number of way select 1 woman from 3 women)

$$\Rightarrow {}^{6}C_{5} \times {}^{3}C_{1} = 6 \times 3 = 18$$

Case 2: 4 men and 2 women in committee.

Number of ways $=$ (number of ways select 4 men from 6 men x number of way select 2 women from 3 women)

$$\Rightarrow {}^{6}C_{4} \times {}^{3}C_{2} = 15 \times 3 = 45$$

Case $3: 3$ men and 3 women in committee.

Number of ways $=$ (number of ways select 3 men from 6 men x number of way select 3 women from 3 women)

$$\Rightarrow {}^{6}C_{3} \times {}^{3}C_{3} = 20 \times 1 = 20$$

Total number of ways to select committee $= 18 + 45 + 20 = 83$

$\therefore$ The number of committee formed in 83 ways.

Hence, the correct answer is 83.

45. Given,

A box contains 4 tennis balls, 6 season balls and 8 dues balls

We know that,

$$\text{Probability} = \frac{\text{Favourable outcomes}}{\text{Total outcomes}}$$

Let us assume that all balls are unique.

There are a total of 18 balls.

Number of all combinations of n things, taken r at a time, is given by $^{n}C_{T} = \dfrac{n!}{(r)!(n-r)!}$

Total ways $= 3$ balls can be chosen in $^{18}C_{3}$ ways

$$= \frac{18!}{3! \times 15!}$$

$$= \frac{18 \times 17 \times 16}{3 \times 2 \times 1}$$

$$= 816$$

There are 4 tennis balls, 6 season balls and 8 dues balls, 1 tennis ball, 1 season ball and 1 dues Ball drawn.

Therefore, favorable ways $= 4 \times 6 \times 8 = 192$

$$\text{Probability} = \frac{192}{816}$$

$$= \frac{4}{17}$$

Hence, the correct option is (A).

46. Given,

There are 4 coins of ten rupees, 2 coins of five rupees, 2 coins of two rupees and 2 coins of one rupee.

Total coins $= 4 + 2 + 2 + 2 = 10$

Number of all combinations of n things, taken r at a time, is given by $^nC_r = \dfrac{n!}{(r)!(n-r)!}$

Total number of ways in which 3 coins can be taken out $= {}^{10}C_3$

$= \dfrac{10!}{3!7!} = \dfrac{10 \times 9 \times 8}{3 \times 2 \times 1}$

$= 120$

Amount drawn can be 12 rupees in the following cases:

(i). 1 coin of ten rupees and 2 coins of 1 rupee

This can be done in $^4C_1 \times {}^2C_2$ ways, i.e. $= \dfrac{4!}{1!3!} \times \dfrac{2!}{2!0!} =$ $4 \times 1 = 4$ ways.

(ii). 2 coins of five rupees and 1 coin of 2 rupees

This can be done in $^2C_2 \times {}^2C_1$ ways, i.e. $= \dfrac{2!}{220!} \times \dfrac{2!}{1!1!} =$ $1 \times 2 = 2$ ways.

Total number of ways in which 12 rupees can be drawn $= 4 + 2 = 6$

$\therefore$ Probability of drawing 12 rupees

$= \dfrac{\text{Total number of ways in which 12 rupees can be drawn in three coins}}{\text{Total number of ways in which 3 coins can be drawn}}$

$= \dfrac{6}{120}$

$= \dfrac{1}{20}$

Hence, the correct option is (D).

47. Given:

A basket contains 2 white, 3 red and 4 black balls, two balls are drawn at random.

Total number of balls $= 2 + 3 + 4 = 9$

We know that:

$\text{Probability} = \dfrac{\text{Favorable Outcome}}{\text{Total Outcome}}$

$P(E) = \dfrac{n(E)}{n(S)}$

Let S be the sample space.

Let $E =$ Event of drawing 2 balls, none of them is black

Number of all combinations of n things, taken r at a time is given by $^nC_r = \dfrac{n!}{(r)!(n-r)!}$

Total number of ways of drawing 2 balls out of 9 balls

$n(S) = {}^9C_2$

There are four black balls in the total nine balls. Total number of non-black balls $= 9 - 4 = 5$

Number of ways of drawing 2 balls out of 5 balls, if none of them is black

$n(E) = {}^5C_2$

$\Rightarrow P(E) = \dfrac{n(E)}{n(S)} = \dfrac{{}^5C_2}{{}^9C_2}$

$= \dfrac{\frac{[1}{2119}}{\frac{2}{2\pi}}$

$= \dfrac{\frac{5 \times 4 \times 3 \times 2 \times 1}{2 \times 1 \times 3 \times 2 \times 1}}{\frac{2 \times 8 \times \times 6 \times 5 \times 1 \times 3 \times 2 \times 1}{2 \times 1 \times 2 \times 6 \times 6 \times 1 \times 1 \times 3 \times 2 \times 1}}$

$= \dfrac{\left\{\frac{(5 \times 6)}{(2 \times 1)}\right\}}{\left\{\frac{(2 \times 8)}{(2 \times 1)}\right\}}$

$= \dfrac{10}{36}$

$= \dfrac{5}{18}$

$\therefore$ The probability of not any ball being drawn is black is $\dfrac{5}{18}$.

Hence, the correct option is (B).

48. Given,

The total number of balls in the box $= 36$

The number of green balls is $= 9$

The number of red balls is $= 10$

$\therefore$ The number of blue balls $= 36 - 10 - 9 = 17$

As we know,

Number of all combinations of n things, taken r at a time is given by $^nC_T = \dfrac{n!}{(r)!(n-r)!}$

The number of ways selecting three different coloured balls

$= {}^{10}C_1 \times {}^9C_1 \times {}^{17}C_1$

$= \dfrac{10!}{1!9!} \times \dfrac{9!}{1!8!} \times \dfrac{17!}{1!16!}$

$= \dfrac{10 \times 9!}{9!} \times \dfrac{9 \times 8!}{8!} \times \dfrac{17 \times 16!}{16!}$

$= 10 \times 9 \times 17$

$= 1530$

The total number of ways of selecting balls $= {}^{36}C_3$

$= \dfrac{36!}{3!33!}$

$= \dfrac{36 \times 35 \times 34 \times 33!}{3 \times 2 \times 1 \times 3!!}$

$$= \frac{36}{3} \times \frac{35}{2} \times \frac{34}{1}$$

$$= 7140$$

$$\text{Probability} = \frac{\text{Number of observation}}{\text{Total number of observation}}$$

$$= \frac{1530}{7140}$$

$$= \frac{3}{14}$$

$\therefore$ Required probability $= \dfrac{3}{14}$

Hence, the correct option is (D).

49. Given:

Total number of balls $= 7 + 8 + 9 = 24$

Number of all combinations of n things, taken r at a time, is given by $^nC_r = \dfrac{n!}{(r)!(n-r)!}$

Let S be the sample space.

$n(S) =$ Number of ways of drawing 4 balls from 24 balls $= {}^{24}C_4$

$$= \frac{24!}{(4)!(20)!}$$

$$= \frac{(24 \times 23 \times 22 \times 21)}{(4 \times 3 \times 2 \times 1)}$$

$$= 10626$$

Let E be the event that none of the drawn balls are white.

$$\therefore n(E) = {}^{16}C_4$$

$$= \frac{16!}{(4)!(12)!}$$

$$= \frac{(16 \times 15 \times 14 \times 13)}{(4 \times 3 \times 2 \times 1)}$$

$$= 1820$$

$$\therefore P(E) = \frac{n(E)}{n(S)}$$

$$= \frac{1820}{10626}$$

$$= \frac{910}{5313}$$

$$= \frac{130}{759}$$

Hence, the correct option is (A).

50. Given,

Total number of balls $= (6 + 2 + 4 + 3) = 15$

Number of all combinations of n things, taken r at a time, is given by $^nC_r = \dfrac{n!}{(r)!(n-r)!}$

Let E be the event of drawing 5 balls out of 9 non-blue balls.

$$\therefore n(E) = {}^9C_5$$

$$= {}^9C_{(9-5)}$$

$$= {}^9C_4$$

$$= \frac{9!}{(4)!(5)!}$$

$$= \frac{9 \times 8 \times 7 \times 6}{4 \times 3 \times 2 \times 1}$$

$$= 126$$

And,

$$n(S) = {}^{15}C_5$$

$$= \frac{15!}{(5)!(10)!}$$

$$= \frac{15 \times 14 \times 13 \times 12 \times 11}{5 \times 4 \times 3 \times 2 \times 1}$$

$$= 3003$$

$$\therefore P(E) = \frac{n(E)}{n(S)}$$

$$= \frac{126}{3003}$$

$$= \frac{6}{143}$$

$\therefore$ Required Probability $= \left(1 - \dfrac{6}{143}\right)$

$$= \frac{137}{143}$$

Hence, the correct option is (C).

51. Given,

$$P(A) = \frac{4}{7}, P(B) = \frac{3}{8} \text{ and } P(C) = \frac{1}{2}$$

We know that,

$$P(A \cup B \cup C) = P(A) + P(B) + P(C) - P(A \cap B) - P(B \cap C) - P(C \cap A) + P(A \cap B \cap C)$$

$$\Rightarrow P(A \cap B) = P(A) \times P(B)$$

So, the probability of the question getting solved is

$$P(A \cup B \cup C) = \frac{4}{7} + \frac{3}{8} + \frac{1}{2} - \left(\frac{4}{7} \times \frac{3}{8}\right) - \left(\frac{3}{8} \times \frac{1}{2}\right) - \left(\frac{1}{2} \times \frac{4}{7}\right) + \left(\frac{4}{7} \times \frac{3}{8} \times \frac{1}{2}\right)$$

$$\Rightarrow P(A \cup B \cup C) = \frac{4}{7} + \frac{3}{8} + \frac{1}{2} - \left(\frac{3}{14}\right) - \left(\frac{3}{16}\right) - \left(\frac{2}{7}\right) + \left(\frac{3}{28}\right)$$

$\Rightarrow P(A \cup B \cup C) = \frac{81}{56} - \left(\frac{3}{14}\right) - \left(\frac{3}{16}\right) - \left(\frac{2}{7}\right) + \left(\frac{3}{28}\right)$

$\Rightarrow P(A \cup B \cup C) = \frac{81}{56} + \frac{3}{28} - \left(\frac{24+21+32}{112}\right)$

$\Rightarrow P(A \cup B \cup C) = \frac{87}{56} - \frac{77}{112}$

$\Rightarrow P(A \cup B \cup C) = \frac{174-77}{112}$

$\Rightarrow P(A \cup B \cup C) = \frac{97}{112}$

Hence, the correct option is (A).

52. Given,

Probability of two or more incidents happening when they are not related to each other $= P_1 \times P_2 \times P_3$

We know that:

$P' = 1 - P$

P' is the probability of a thing not happening and P is of that happening.

Probability of Ankit failing in atleast two subject = Probability of him failing in 2 subject + Probability of him failing in 3 subjects.

Probability of failing in Maths $= 1 - \frac{5}{8} = \frac{3}{8}$

Probability of failing in English $= 1 - \frac{7}{9} = \frac{2}{9}$

Probability of failing in Science $= 1 - \frac{3}{5} = \frac{2}{5}$

Probability of him failing in 2 subject

$= \frac{3}{8} \times \frac{2}{9} \times \frac{3}{5} + \frac{5}{8} \times \frac{2}{9} \times \frac{2}{5} + \frac{3}{8} \times \frac{7}{9} \times \frac{2}{5}$

$= \frac{(18+20+42)}{360}$

$= \frac{80}{360}$

Probability of him failing in three subjects $= \frac{3}{8} \times \frac{2}{5} \times \frac{2}{9} = \frac{12}{360}$

Required probability $= \frac{80}{360} + \frac{12}{360}$

$= \frac{92}{360}$

Hence, the correct option is (A).

53. Given:

Total number of boys in a class $= 16$

Total number of girls in a class $= 10$

Selecting number of boy $= 1$

Selecting number of girls $= 2$

Total number of students $= (16 + 10) = 26$

Number of all combinations of n things, taken r at a time, is given by $^nC_r = \dfrac{n!}{(r)!(n-r)!}$

Number of ways to select three students

$= {}^{26}C_3 = \dfrac{26!}{23!3!} = \dfrac{26 \times 25 \times 24}{3 \times 2} = 2600$

Number of ways to select 1 boy $= {}^{16}C_1 = \dfrac{16!}{1!15!} = 16$

Number of ways to select 2 girls $= {}^{10}C_2 = \dfrac{10!}{218!} = \dfrac{10 \times 9}{2} = 45$

Probability of selecting 1 boy and 2 girls

$= \dfrac{\text{Number of ways to select 1 boy} \times \text{Number of ways to select 2 girls}}{\text{Number of ways to select three students}}$

$\therefore$ Probability of selecting 1 boy and 2 girls $= \dfrac{(16 \times 45)}{2600}$

$= \dfrac{720}{2600}$

$= \dfrac{18}{65}$

Hence, the correct option is (D).

54. Given: $A = \{x \in R : x^2 - 4x + 4 = 0\}$ and

$B = \{x \in R : x^3 = 1\}$

$x^2 - 4x + 4 = 0$

$\Rightarrow x^2 - 2x - 2x + 4 = 0$

$\Rightarrow (x - 2)(x - 2) = 0$

$\Rightarrow x = 2$

So, 2 is an element of the given set $\Rightarrow A = \{2\}$

Similarly, $x^3 = 1$ (Given) $\Rightarrow x^3 - 1 = 0 \Rightarrow$
$(x - 1)(x^2 + x + 1) = 0 \Rightarrow x = 1$ or ω or ω^2,
where $\omega = \frac{-1+i\sqrt{3}}{2}$ and $\omega^2 = \frac{-1-i\sqrt{3}}{2}$ $x \in R \Rightarrow B = \{1\}$

So, the cardinality of set A and B are same i.e $n(A) = n(B) = 1$ but there elements are not same.

Therefore, the given sets A and B are equivalent sets.

Hence, the correct option is (B).

55. Given function is $f(x) = \sqrt{(16 - x^2)}$

The domain of a function $f(x)$ is the set of all values for which the function is defined, and the range of the function is the set of all values that f takes.

For domain, $f(x) \geq 0$

$\Rightarrow 16 - x^2 \geq 0$

$\Rightarrow 16 \geq x^2$

$\Rightarrow x^2 \leq 16$

$\Rightarrow -4 \leq x \leq 4$

So, domain of $f(x) = [-4,4]$

For Range,

$f(x)$ is maximum at $x = 0$ i.e. $f(0) = 4$

$f(x)$ is minimum at $x = 4$ i.e. $f(4) = 0$

So, Range of $f(x) = [0,4]$

Therefore, the domain and range of the function $(x) =$ of the function $f(x) = \sqrt{(16 - x^2)}$ are $[-4,4], [0,4]$.

Hence, the correct option is (C).

56. $f: R \rightarrow R$, given by $f(x) = e^x$.

one-one:

Let x_1 and x_2 be any two elements in the domain (R), such that

$f(x_1) = f(x_2)$

$f(x_1):$

$\Rightarrow f(x_1) = e^{x_1}$

$f(x_2):$

$\Rightarrow f(x_2) = e^{x_2}$

Now, $f(x_1) = f(x_2)$

$\Rightarrow e^{x_1} = e^{x_2}$

$\Rightarrow x_1 = x_2$

$\therefore f$ is one-one function.

Onto:

We know that range of e^x is $(0, \infty) = R^+$

$\Rightarrow$ Co-domain $= R$

Both are not same.

$\therefore f$ is not onto function.

Hence, the correct option is (A).

57. Given:

$P =$ Set of all integral multiples of 3

$Q =$ Set of all integral multiples of 4

$R =$ Set of all integral multiples of 6

Concept:

Set symbois:

Union: $A \cup B$ i.e. in A or B.

Proper Subset: $A \subset B$ i.e. every element of A is in B.

Not a Subset: $A \not\subseteq B$ i..e. A is not a subset of B.

Explanation:

$P =$ Set of all integral multiples of 3

$\Rightarrow P = \{3,6,9,12,15,18, \ldots \ldots \}$,

$Q =$ Set of all integral multiples of 4

$\Rightarrow Q = \{4,8,12,16,20, \ldots \ldots \}$

$R =$ Set of all integral multiples of 6

$\Rightarrow R = \{6,12,18,24,30, \ldots \ldots \}$

Considering the relation,

I. $P \cup Q = R$

$P \cup Q = \{3,4,6,8,9,12,15,16, \ldots \} \neq R$

II. $P \subset R$

All the elements of P are not in R so $P \not\subseteq R$

$\Rightarrow P = \{3,6,9,12,15,18, \ldots \ldots \}$,

$Q =$ Set of all integral multiples of 4

$\Rightarrow Q = \{4,8,12,16,20, \ldots \ldots \}$

$R =$ Set of all integral multiples of 6

$\Rightarrow R = \{6,12,18,24,30, \ldots \ldots \}$

Considering the relation,

1. $P \cup Q = R$

$P \cup Q = \{3,4,6,8,9,12,15,16, \ldots \} \neq R$

II. $P \subset R$

All the elements of P are not in R so $P \not\subseteq R$

III. $R \subset (P \cup Q)$

$P \cup Q = \{3,4,6,8,9,12,15,16, \ldots \}$

Therefore,

All the elements of R are in $P \cup Q$

$\Rightarrow R \subset (P \cup Q)$

$\therefore$ Only (III) statement is correct.

Hence, the correct option is (C).

58. Given:

$x \in \{2,3,4\}$ and,

$y \in \{4,6,9,10\}$

To find the set of all ordered pairs (x, y) such that x is a factor of y.

Let, $A = \{(x, y) : x \text{ is a factor of } y\}$

Here,

2 is a factor of 4 implies $(2,4) \in A$

2 is a factor of 6 implies $(2,6) \in A$

2 is a factor of 10 implies $(2,10) \in A$

3 is a factor of 6 implies $(3,6) \in A$

3 is a factor of 9 implies $(3,9) \in A$

4 is a factor of 4 implies $(4,4) \in A$

So,

$A = \{(2,4), (2,6), (2,10), (3,6), (3,9), (4,4)\}$

$\therefore$ Set A contains 6 elements.

Hence, the correct answer is 6.

59. Given:

Three statements,

I. $A' \cup B = (A \cap B)'$

II. $(\phi')' = U$

III. $A \cap (B \cup C) = (A \cap B) \cup (A \cap C)$

Concept

De Morgan's law:

$(A \cap B)' = A' \cup B'$

Distributive law:

$A \cap (B \cup C) = (A \cap B) \cup (A \cap C)$

Universal Law:

$(\phi)' = U$

Explanation:

1. $A' \cup B = (A \cap B)'$

$\Rightarrow (A \cap B)' = A' \cup B'$ [by De Morgan's law]

So, statement (I) is not correct.

II. $(\phi')' = U$

$\Rightarrow (\phi)' = U$ and $(U)' = \phi$ [by universal law]

So, statement (II) is not correct.

III. $A \cap (B \cup C) = (A \cap B) \cup (A \cap C)$

$\Rightarrow A \cap (B \cup C) = (A \cap B) \cup (A \cap C)$ [by Distributive law]

$\therefore$ Statement (III) is correct.

Hence, the correct option is (C).

60. Option (A):

Given: $\{x \in R : x^2 - 4x + 4 = 0\}$

$x^2 - 4x + 4 = 0$

$\Rightarrow x^2 - 2x - 2x + 4 = 0$

$\Rightarrow (x - 2)(x - 2) = 0$

$\Rightarrow x = 2$

So, 2 is an element of $\{x \in R : x^2 - 4x + 4 = 0\} \Rightarrow \{x \in R : x^2 - 4x + 4 = 0\}$ is not an empty set.

Option (B):

Given: $\{x \in R : x^3 = 1\}$

$x^3 = 1$

$\Rightarrow x^3 - 1 = 0$

$\Rightarrow (x - 1)(x^2 + x + 1) = 0$

$\Rightarrow x = 1$ or ω or ω^2, where $\omega = \dfrac{-1+i\sqrt{3}}{2}$ and $\omega^2 = \dfrac{-1-i\sqrt{3}}{2}$

$\because x \in R \Rightarrow$ only $x = 1$ is an element of $\{x \in R : x^3 = 1\}$

So, the given set $\{x \in R : x^3 = 1\}$ is not an empty set.

Option (C):

Given: $\{x \in R : x^2 = -1\}$

$\Rightarrow x^2 = -1$

$\Rightarrow x = \pm i \notin R$

So, the given set $\{x \in R : x^2 = -1\}$ is an empty set.

Hence, the correct option is (C).

Ques (1-4):Direction: Study the given bar graph carefully and answer the questions given below.

The bar graph shows that 2 successive discounts are allowed on four different articles.

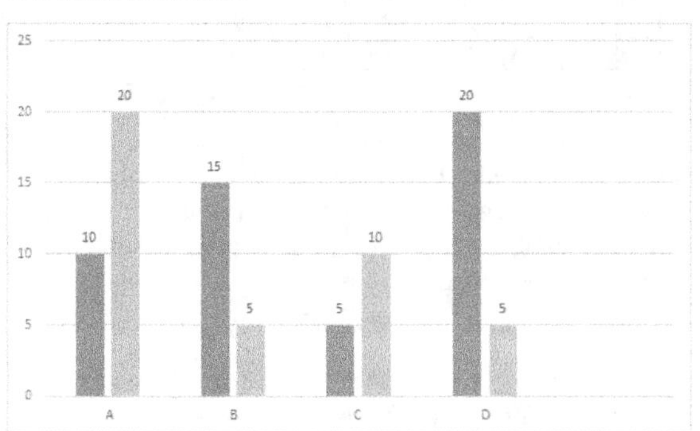

Q.1 Marked price of D is 20% less than that of A and sum of selling price of both the articles is 3984 and loss on D is 20% and profit on A is 20%. Find the ratio of cost price of D to that of A.

[IDBI Bank Assistant Manager, 2021]

A. 15 : 17   **B.** 17 : 10   **C.** 10 : 17   **D.** 19 : 15

Q.2 If the ratio of selling price of B to D is 5 : 8, then find the ratio of marked price of B to D.

[IDBI Bank Assistant Manager, 2021]

A. 578 : 176   **B.** 323 : 190
C. 109 : 177   **D.** 190 : 323

Q.3 The ratio of selling price of A to B is 5 : 2 and sum of marked price of both the article is Rs. 61000. Find the difference between the Selling price of both the articles.
A. 15500   **B.** 19480   **C.** 45700   **D.** 22600

Q.4 If the ratio of marked price of A to B is 2 : 3 and the difference between the selling price of both the article is 1198.65. Find the difference between marked price of articles A and B.
A. 820   **B.** 1220   **C.** 1020   **D.** 1100

Ques (5-8):Direction: Study the given bar graph carefully and answer the questions given below.

The given bar graph shows the number of students that appeared and those were selected in the placement interviews from six colleges A, B, C, D, E and F. Study the bar graph and answer the questions that follow.

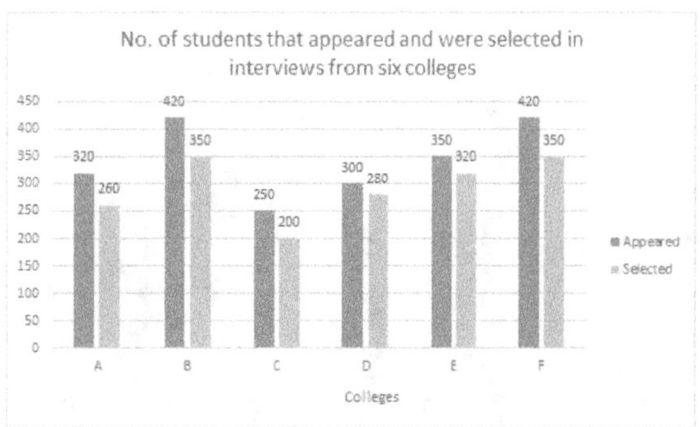

Q.5 The number of males that appeared in the interviews from college A is equal to the number of females that appeared from college B, such that the number of females appearing from college A and the number of males appearing from college B are in the ratio 6 : 11. If $\left(\dfrac{250}{3}\right)$ % of the females from college A and 85% of the females from college B were selected in the interviews, find the ratio of the males selected from college A to that from college B.

A. 7 : 8   **B.** 8 : 9   **C.** 9 : 10   **D.** 10 : 11

Q.6 The male to female ratio of the students that appeared from colleges C and D are equal. If 72% and 92% of the males and females were selected in the interview from the college C respectively, while 109 females were selected from college D, what percentage of the males were selected in the interview from the college D?
A. 75%   **B.** 80%   **C.** 85%   **D.** 95%

Q.7 40% and 25% of the students that appeared in the interviews from colleges E and F respectively were from the Science stream, such that 80% of the students from the Science stream that appeared from both the colleges were selected in the interview. If 35% of the students that got selected from college E were from the Science stream, what percentage of the selected students from college F were from the Science stream?
A. 12%   **B.** 18%   **C.** 24%   **D.** 30%

Q.8 The total number of students in the Science, Commerce and Arts stream in the six colleges are in the ratio 10 : 9 : 6, while the number of students in Science, Commerce and Arts stream in the six colleges that appeared in the interviews are in the ratio 2 : 2 : 1. If 80% of the students of the six colleges appeared in the interviews, then find the ratio of the students in the Science, Commerce and Arts stream in the six colleges that did not appeared in the interviews.
A. 2 : 1 : 2   **B.** 1 : 2 : 2   **C.** 2 : 1 : 1   **D.** 7 : 5 : 8

Ques (9-12):Direction: Study the given bar graph carefully and answer the questions given below.

The bar graph given below shows the data regarding the number of units of electricity consumed by five different houses (P, Q, R, S, and T) in two different months (June and July).

The electricity bill is charged in such a way that up to a certain limit of units of electricity the rate of charge (in Rs.) will be low, and on exceeding that limit the rate of charge will be high.

Note: Rate and limit for units remains unchanged for every month.

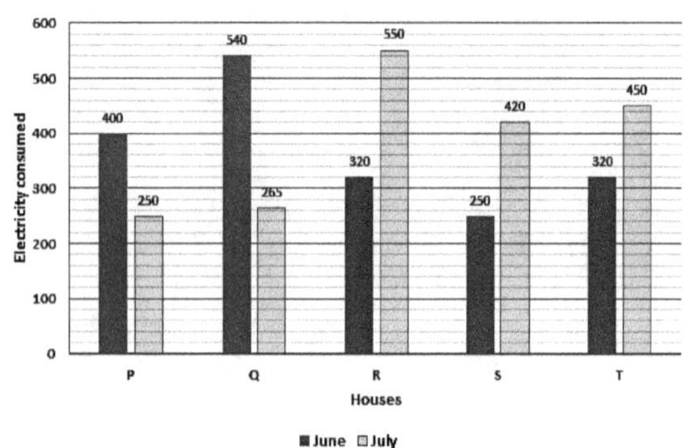

Q.9 In house S, the number of units of electricity used in the month of August is the average of the number of units of electricity used in the month of June and July. The initial 150 units of electricity used in August is charged at the rate of Rs. 3 per unit and the remaining units are charged at the rate of Rs. x per unit. If the total bill paid in August is Rs. 1745, then find the value of x.

A. 6 **B.** 5 **C.** 8 **D.** 7

Q.10 In the month of June, the rate up to the certain limit of units of electricity consumed by house P is Rs. 3 per unit, while the rate exceeding that limit is Rs. 5 per unit. If the total electricity bill for house P in June is Rs. 1600, then find the number of units of electricity which have the rate of charge is Rs. 3.

A. 150 **B.** 200 **C.** 180 **D.** 160

Q.11 For house Q, if the difference between the electricity bill of June and July is Rs.1650 and the initial number of units of electricity for which rate of charge is low is 120 units, then find the rate at which the electricity is charged for the exceeding limit of number of units of electricity.

A. Rs. 5.5 **B.** Rs. 7 **C.** Rs. 6 **D.** Rs. 6.5

Q.12 Find the average number of units of electricity consumed by each of the given houses in the month of July.

A. 387 units **B.** 367 units
C. 337 units **D.** 357 units

Ques (13-16):Direction: Study the given bar graph and answer the following questions accordingly

The bar graph shows the number of students from all three departments.

Number of students in four colleges

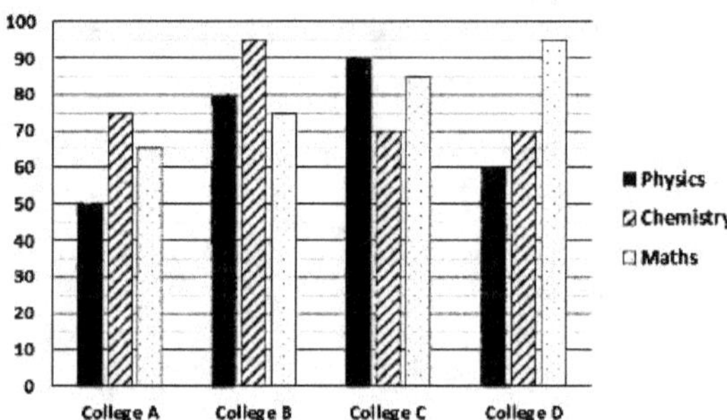

Q.13 Find the difference between the total number of students from the chemistry department from college B and college C and the total number of students from the physics department from college A and college D.

A. 45 **B.** 55 **C.** 65 **D.** 75

Q.14 Find the ratio between the students from physics and math from college A and the students from chemistry and math from college C.

A. $31:23$ **B.** $23:31$ **C.** $13:21$ **D.** $15:25$

Q.15 Find the average of all students from the physics department of all four colleges.

A. 70 **B.** 60 **C.** 50 **D.** 80

Q.16 The total number of students from college C is approximate what percentage more or less than that of college D?

A. 10% **B.** 8% **C.** 9% **D.** 11%

Ques (17-20):Directions: Read the following data carefully and answer the following questions.

The bar graph below shows the population of five different villages and the number of people who are literates in each of them.

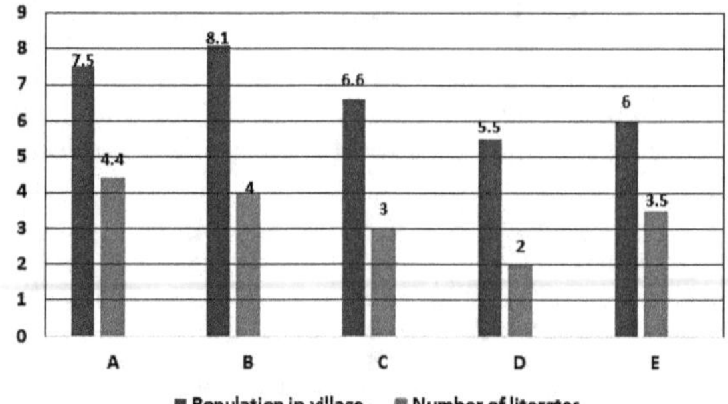

Note: all values are in thousands.

Q.17 In village A, if the literates are in the ratio of 1 : 4 : 6 of women, men, and children and out of which 40 percent of men and 30 percent of females go to cities for work, find the literates who stayed behind in the village.

A. 3,330 **B.** 4,530 **C.** 4,450 **D.** 3,640

Q.18 In village B and C, for promoting education, if, the government decided to introduce mid-day meals in schools, for

which they allotted Rs. 500 per student. If $22\left(\dfrac{2}{9}\right)\%$ of village population in B and half of $33\left(\dfrac{1}{3}\right)\%$ of village C are children, find the total amount received by both villages together for the execution of the plan.

A. Rs.14.5 lakh
B. Rs.15.5 lakh
C. Rs.16.5 lakh
D. Rs.18.5 lakh

Q.19 If the population in village F is 450% of the literates in D and the number of literates is one-third of the population in C, find the number of illiterates in F.

A. 6,300
B. 7,800
C. 5,800
D. 6,800

Q.20 In A, if out of the literates, 25% decided to go to the city to find a job, what percent of the total population decided to go?

A. $\dfrac{22}{3}\%$
B. $\dfrac{34}{5}\%$
C. $\dfrac{44}{3}\%$
D. $\dfrac{28}{5}\%$

Ques (21-24):Direction: Read the following bar graph carefully and answer the following questions

The following bar graph shows the number of Male and Female customers who visited a restaurant for 6 days of a week.

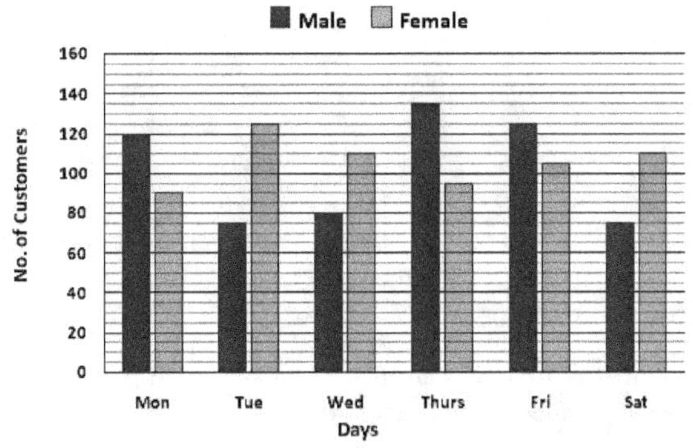

Q.21 Total number of males visiting the restaurant on Thursday and Saturday is what percent more or less than the number of females visiting the restaurant on Monday and Tuesday?
A. 5.66%
B. 3.45%
C. 2.33%
D. 1.5%

Q.22 What is the ratio between the number of Males visiting the restaurant on Tuesday, Thursday and Friday together and the number of females visiting the restaurant on the same days?
A. $68:63$
B. $63:68$
C. $67:65$
D. $61:59$

Q.23 What is the difference between the average number of Males and Females visiting the restaurant?
A. 5.85
B. 2.75
C. 3.24
D. 4.16

Q.24 The number of customers visiting the restaurant on Sunday is 30% more than the number of customers visiting the restaurant on Wednesday and the ratio of male and female is $8:5$, then the number of males visiting the restaurant on Sunday is what percent of Males visiting the restaurant on Monday?
A. 135.33%
B. 126.67%
C. 115.83%
D. 96.67%

Ques (25-28):Direction: Study the given bar graph carefully and answer the questions given below.

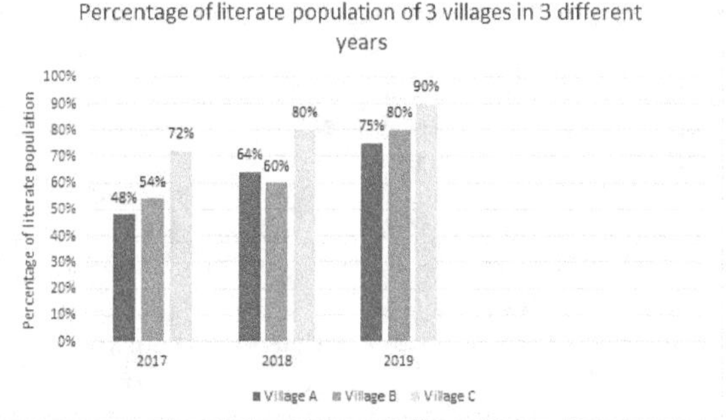

Q.25 If the population of the village B increased by 20% from 2016 to 2017, then by how much percentage did the literate population of the village B increased from 2016 to 2017?
A. 40%
B. 60%
C. 80%
D. 75%

Q.26 In the year 2015, the total number of literates in the three villages is 285000. If the population of village A and B in the year 2015 is 125000 and 150000 respectively, then what is the population of the village C in the year 2015?
A. 180000
B. 200000
C. 250000
D. 300000

Q.27 If the ratio of the literate population of the three villages in the year 2016 is $2:3:5$, then find the ratio of the total population of the three villages in the year 2016.
A. $3:5:6$
B. $4:6:9$
C. $5:8:10$
D. $6:10:15$

Q.28 In the year 2017, if the number of literate males in village A is 42000 more than the number of literate females, then find the ratio of the number of literate males to the number of literate females in village A in 2017.
A. $4:3$
B. $5:4$
C. $6:5$
D. Data insufficient

Ques (29-32):Direction: Study the following bar chart carefully and answer the questions given below.

Number of educational institutions in India

Q.29 Which of the following year has seen the maximum percentage growth in the number of upper primary institutions over the previous year?

A. 2000 – 01	**B.** 2001 – 02
C. 2002 – 03	**D.** 2003 – 04

Q.30 Which of the following statement is definitely true?

A. The increase in percentage share of Upper Primary Institutions in the year 2000 – 01 over the previous year is more than the decrease in percentage share of Primary Institutions in the same period

B. The decrease in percentage share of Upper Primary Institutions in the year 2004 – 05 over the previous year is less than the decrease in percentage share of Primary Institutions in the same period

C. The only year that has seen a decline in the percentage share of Primary Institutions over the previous year is 2001 – 02

D. The decrease in percentage share of Junior colleges in the year 2003 – 04 over the previous year is less than the decrease in percentage share of Primary Institutions in the same period

Q.31 What is the number of years in which the total number of Upper Primary schools and Junior Colleges were less than the total number of Primary schools?

A. 1	**B.** 2
C. 3	**D.** More than 3

Q.32 Which year has witnessed the highest percentage growth in the number of primary institutes over the previous years?

A. 2000 – 01	**B.** 2001 – 02
C. 2002 – 03	**D.** 2003 – 04

Ques (33-36):Direction: Study the following graph carefully & answer the questions given below it.

Value of imports and exports by company over the years (The value are in crore)

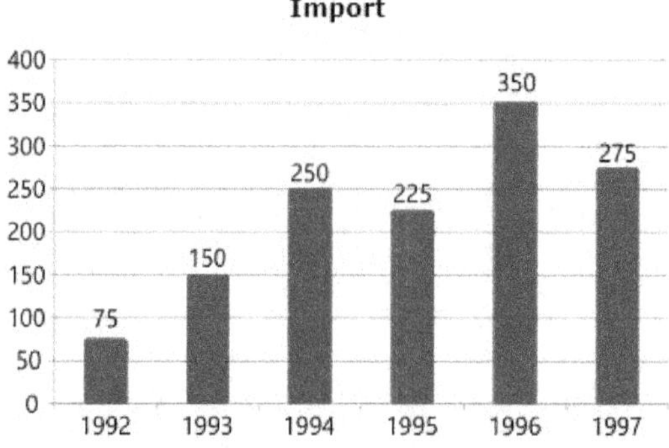

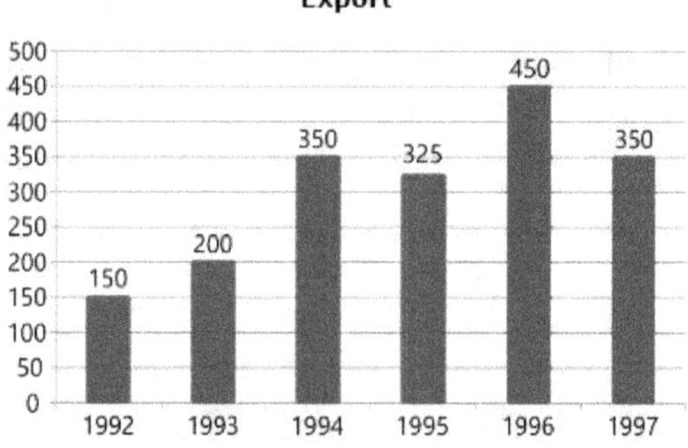

Q.33 The value of exports in 1996 was what percent of the average value of imports in the year 1994, 1995 and 1997?

A. 200	**B.** 100	**C.** 300	**D.** 180

Q.34 The value of exports in 1994 was exactly what percent of the value of imports in the same year?

A. 125	**B.** 160	**C.** 200	**D.** 140

Q.35 What was the approximate difference between the value of average exports and the value of average import of the given years?

A. Rs. 85 crores	**B.** Rs. 100 crores
C. Rs. 75 crores	**D.** Rs. 90 crores

Q.36 In which of the following years was the difference between the value of exports and the value of imports exactly Rs. 100 crores?

A. 1993	**B.** 1996
C. 1995	**D.** More than one year

Ques (37-40):Direction: Study the following bar chart carefully and answer the questions given beside.

The bar chart given below shows the number of students who cleared the two examinations, RRB Scale 1 and RRB Assistant over the years per every 1000 students who appeared in these exams.

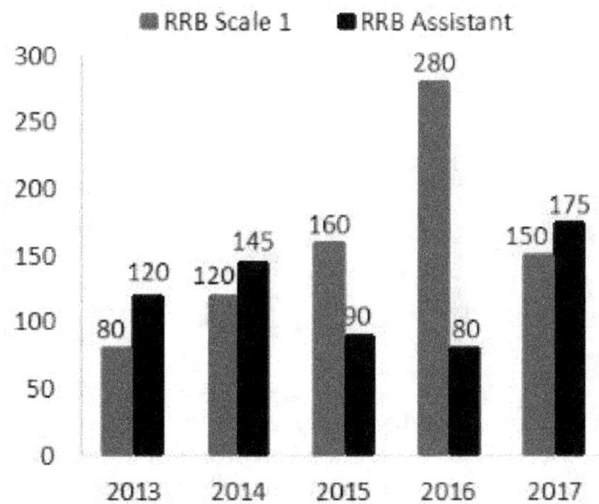

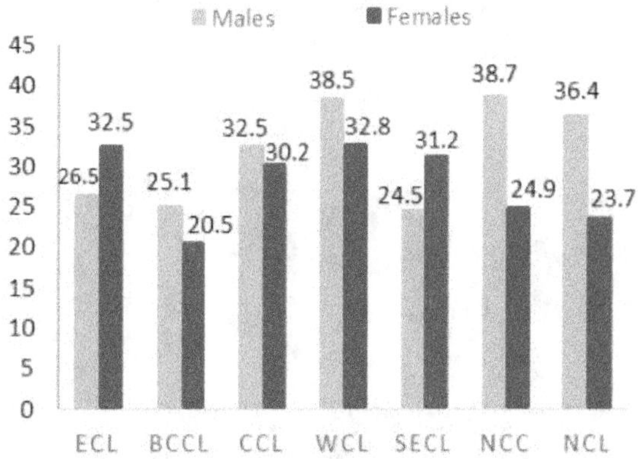

Q.37 If the total numbers of students appeared in RRB Scale I in 2016 was 2.5 lakhs then how many of them had cleared the RRB Scale I examination in 2016?

A. 65000 **B.** 75000 **C.** 60000 **D.** 70000

Q.38 The total number of students who cleared both the examinations together in 2014 is approximately what percent of the total number of students who cleared both the examination together in 2017? (Number of students who applied in 2014 is 50% less than the number of students who applied in 2017)

A. 40.77% **B.** 41.27% **C.** 38.28% **D.** 39.41%

Q.39 What is the respective ratio of the total number of students who cleared RRB Scale I examination over the years and the total number of students who cleared RRB Assistant examination over the years? (the total number of students applied for RRB Scale I examination over the years is 75% the total number of students applied for RRB Assistant examination over the years)

A. 79 : 61 **B.** 61 : 79
C. 237 : 244 **D.** 79 : 81

Q.40 The total number of students who applied in 2017 was 7.5 lakhs and the respective ratio of the number of students who applied RRB Scale I and RRB assistant $7 : 8$ then find the respective ratio of the number of students who cleared RRB Scale I examination in 2017 and the number of students who cleared RRB assistant examination 2017?

A. 4 : 5 **B.** 6 : 7 **C.** 3 : 4 **D.** 2 : 3

Ques (41-44):Direction: Study the following bar chart carefully and answer the questions given beside.

The graph below provides the number of male employees (in lakhs) and the number of female employees (in lakhs) in each of seven subsidiaries viz. ECL, BCCL, CCL, WCL, SCEL, NCC and NCL - of Coal India limited. The males and females in any subsidiary comprise the total workforce of that subsidiary and the total workforce population of the seven subsidiaries together is equal to the one fourth population of the country.

Q.41 For how many subsidiaries is the percentage of population of that subsidiary less than 14.5% of the one by fourth part of the country's population?

A. Zero **B.** One **C.** Three **D.** Four

Q.42 For how many subsidiaries is the ratio of the number of females to the number of males less than that for the one by fourth part of the country?

A. 1 **B.** 2 **C.** 3 **D.** 4

Q.43 If, in each subsidiary, exactly 60% of the males and 40% of the females are literate, which subsidiary has the third highest illiterate population?

A. ECL **B.** NCC **C.** WCL **D.** CCL

Q.44 If it is given that that there are no widows or widowers in the seven subsidiary then, For how many subsidiary is it possible that the population of the unmarried persons in the subsidiary is less than 10% of the population of the subsidiary?

A. 6 **B.** 4 **C.** 3 **D.** 2

Ques (45-48):Direction: Study the following graph carefully and answer the following questions given below.

Total Investment(in thousand) of Vikram and Deepa in six Savings Schemes

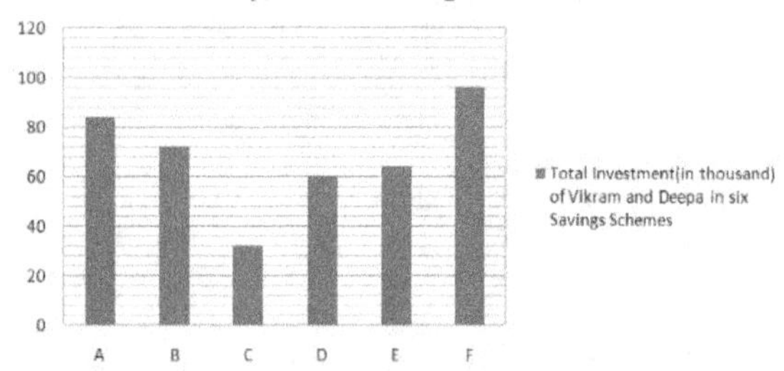

Percentage of Vikram's Investment out of total investment

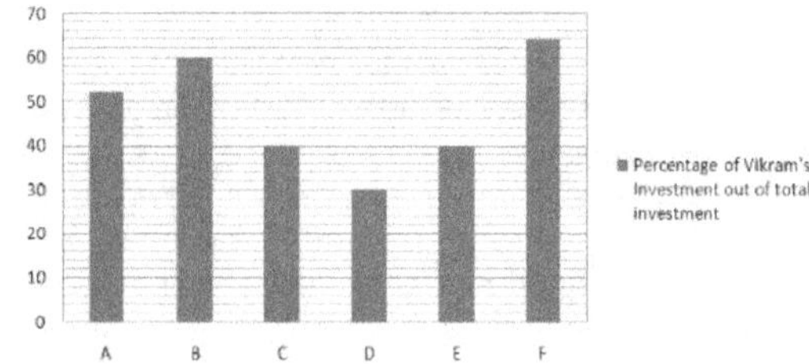

Time taken by the pipes to fill a tank/cistern (hours/minutes)

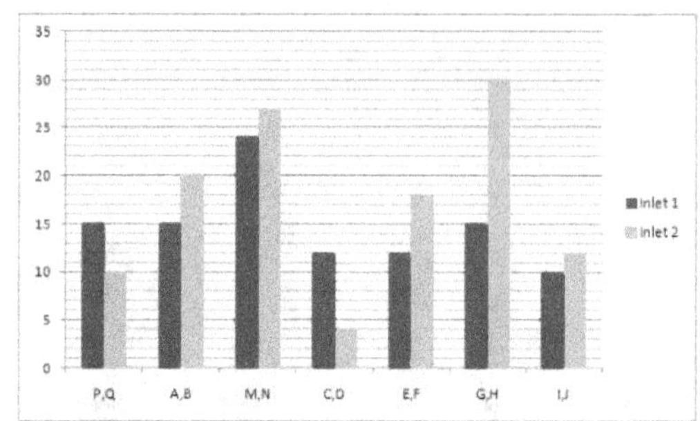

Q.45 Deepa invested in savings scheme F for 4 years. If the savings scheme F offers simple interest at the rate of 7 p.c.p.a. for the first two years and then compound interest at the rate of 10 p.c.p.a. (compounded annually) for the third and fourth year, what will be the interest earned by Deepa after 4 years?

A. 12364　　**B.** 12096　　**C.** 12242　　**D.** 12542

Q.46 If Scheme C offers compound interest (compounded annually) at the rate of 12 p.c.p.a., what is the difference between interests earned by Vikram and Deepa from scheme C after 2 years?

A. 1,628.16　　　　**B.** 1,584.38

C. 1,672.74　　　　**D.** 1,536.58

Q.47 What is the sum of the average amount invested in Savings schemes A, D and E by Vikram and the average amount invested in Savings schemes B, C and F by Deepa?

A. 54272　　**B.** 57614　　**C.** 54600　　**D.** 56613

Q.48 If the savings scheme D offers compound interest (compounded half yearly) at the rate of 16 p.c.p.a, what would be sum of interests earned by Vikram and Deepa from savings scheme D after one year?

A. Rs. 10,244　　　　**B.** Rs. 10,464

C. Rs. 9,872　　　　**D.** Rs. 9,984

Ques (49-52):Direction: Study the following graph carefully to answer the given questions.

Q.49 A large cistern can be filled by two pipes P and Q. How many minutes will it take to fill the Cistern from an empty state if Q is used for half the time and P and Q fill it together for the other half?

A. 6.5 minutes　　　　**B.** 7.5 minutes

C. 8.5 minutes　　　　**D.** 9.5 minutes

Q.50 Two pipes C and D can fill a cistern. If they are opened on alternate minutes and if pipe C is opened first, in how many minutes will the tank be full?

A. 4 minutes　　　　**B.** 5 minutes

C. 2 minutes　　　　**D.** 6 minutes

Q.51 Two pipes, A and B are opened simultaneously and it is found that due to the leakage in the bottom, $\frac{17}{7}$ minutes are taken extra to fill the tank. If the tank is full, in what approximate time would the leak empty it?

A. 27 minutes　　　　**B.** 32 minutes

C. 36 minutes　　　　**D.** 39 minutes

Q.52 A waste pipe, W can carry off 12 litre of water per minute. If all the pipes I, J and W are opened when the tank is full and it takes one hour to empty the tank. Find the capacity of the tank.

A. 30　　**B.** 45　　**C.** 60　　**D.** 75

Ques (53-56):Direction: The following bar graph shows expenditure (Rs. crore) and the second Bar graph shows the percentage of two companies over the years.

Expenditure

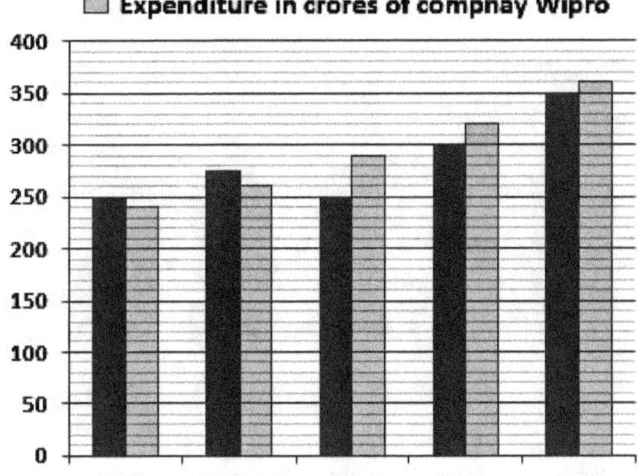

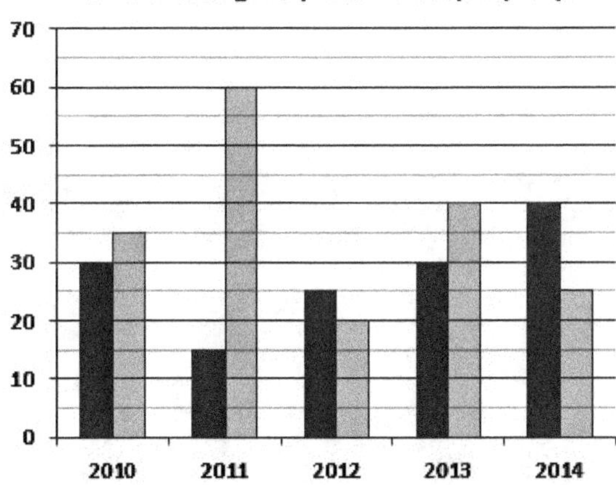

Q.53 What is the sum (Rs.) of the income of company HCL in the years 2010,2011 and 2012 together?

A. 953.75 crores   **B.** 978.50 crores

C. 789.45 crores   **D.** 579.45 crores

Q.54 If in the year 2013 the expenditure of company HCL is 50% more than the income of the company in 2010 and profit is 40%, then what is the income (in Rs.) of company HCL in 2013 ?

A. 953.751 crores   **B.** 658.125 crores

C. 789.435 crores   **D.** 579.452 crores

Q.55 What is the average income of company Wipro in the years 2011,2012 and 2013 together? (in Rs.)

A. 410   **B.** 408   **C.** 404   **D.** 420

Q.56 The income of Company HCL in 2012 is what percentage of the income of Company Wipro in 2010 ?

A. 95.78%   **B.** 65.89%   **C.** 78.98%   **D.** 96.45%

Ques (57-60):Direction: Study the following graph carefully to answer the given questions. Total investment in thousand of Gautam and Rudra in 6 schemes (M, N, O, P, Q and R)

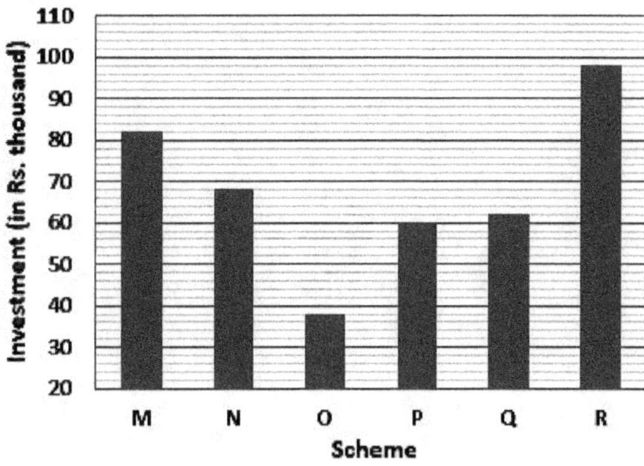

Percentage of Gautam's investment out of total investment:

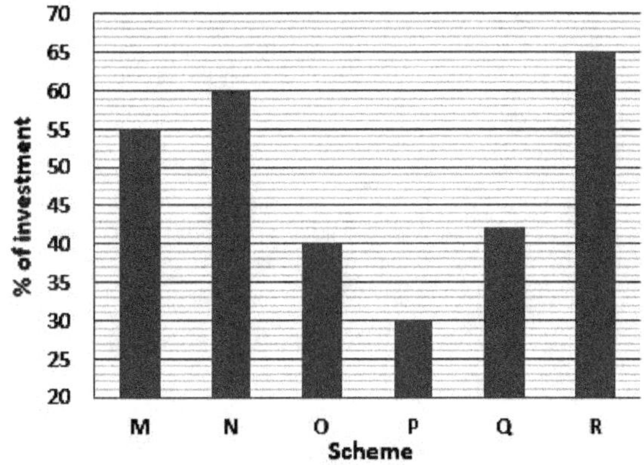

Q.57 Scheme R offers simple interest at a certain rate of interest per annum. If the difference between the interest earned by Gautam and Rudra from Scheme R after 3 years is Rs. 13,230, then what is the rate of interest?

A. 17.830   **B.** 18   **C.** 16.5   **D.** 15

Q.58 What is the approximate ratio of the total amount invested by Rudra in Schemes M and N together to the total amount invested by Gautam in the same Schemes together?

A. 0.50   **B.** 0.75   **C.** 1   **D.** 1.33

Q.59 Rudra invested in Scheme Q for 4 years. If Scheme Q offers simple interest @ 5% per annum for the first two years and then the amount is subjected to compound interest @ 10% per annum compounded annually for the 3rd and the 4th year, what will be the total approx. amount earned by Rudra after 4 years?

A. Rs. 46241   **B.** Rs. 46893

C. Rs. 47107   **D.** Rs. 47862

Q.60 The amount invested by Gautam in Scheme A is equal to the amount invested by him in Scheme P. The rate of interest of Scheme A and P are the same. The only difference is that Scheme A offers compound interest compounded annually while the Scheme P offers simple interest. If the difference between the interests earned by Gautam from both the Schemes after 2 years is Rs. 45 , what is the rate of interest?

A. 3%   **B.** 5%   **C.** 7%   **D.** 11%

// Smart Answer Sheet //

Correct Indicates percentage of students who answered questions correctly.

Skipped Indicates percentage of students who skipped questions.

Q.	Ans.	Correct / Skipped
1	D	53.6 % / 35.35 %
2	D	41.83 % / 39.12 %
3	B	69.2 % / 30.04 %
4	B	53.59 % / 46.04 %
5	B	15.52 % / 75.48 %
6	D	22.77 % / 68.1 %
7	C	26.78 % / 70.09 %
8	A	60.85 % / 37.93 %
9	D	69.49 % / 30.26 %
10	B	51.02 % / 32.85 %
11	C	85.35 % / 11.01 %
12	A	89.52 % / 10.44 %
13	B	64.96 % / 30.73 %
14	B	44.2 % / 33.03 %
15	A	87.71 % / 11.13 %
16	C	48.77 % / 45.91 %
17	D	67.61 % / 30.82 %
18	A	18.53 % / 74.3 %
19	D	55.51 % / 39.06 %
20	C	59.32 % / 34.44 %
21	C	64.27 % / 32.38 %
22	C	47.19 % / 46.78 %
23	D	58.87 % / 35.1 %
24	B	13.27 % / 80.86 %
25	B	62.89 % / 36.75 %
26	B	59.14 % / 40.4 %
27	C	40.47 % / 42.98 %
28	D	63.16 % / 31.98 %
29	C	49.17 % / 34.52 %
30	D	32.23 % / 67.29 %
31	D	65.03 % / 30.3 %
32	D	67.03 % / 31.69 %
33	D	58.27 % / 36.89 %
34	D	48.86 % / 46.76 %
35	A	58.4 % / 40.72 %
36	D	49.94 % / 30.3 %
37	D	52.65 % / 33.55 %
38	A	57.98 % / 40.39 %
39	C	59.26 % / 40.53 %
40	C	43.28 % / 46.3 %
41	D	51.11 % / 40.43 %
42	D	68.73 % / 31.11 %
43	B	55.72 % / 31.41 %
44	D	20.06 % / 67.95 %
45	B	47.01 % / 36.73 %
46	A	45.22 % / 39.2 %
47	D	50.56 % / 40.83 %
48	D	46.43 % / 38.03 %
49	B	50.35 % / 39.13 %
50	D	76.02 % / 23.82 %
51	D	68.42 % / 31.55 %
52	C	60.0 % / 39.13 %
53	A	22.19 % / 70.21 %
54	B	62.08 % / 35.68 %
55	C	59.0 % / 30.33 %
56	D	54.32 % / 32.91 %
57	D	24.19 % / 70.04 %
58	B	48.8 % / 34.67 %
59	D	61.98 % / 35.49 %
60	B	58.51 % / 35.42 %

Performance Analysis

Avg. Score (%)	70.0%
Toppers Score (%)	70.56%
Your Score	

//Hints and Solutions//

1. Let the marked price of A is $500x$.

Marked price of $D = 500x \times \dfrac{80}{100} = 400x$

Selling price of $A = 500x \times \dfrac{90}{100} \times \dfrac{80}{100} = 360x$

Selling price of $D = 400x \times \dfrac{80}{100} \times \dfrac{95}{100} = 304x$

Sum of selling price of both the articles $= 3984$

$\therefore 360x + 304x = 3984$

$\Rightarrow 664x = 3984$

$\Rightarrow x = \dfrac{3984}{664}$

$\Rightarrow x = 6$

Cost price of $A = 360 \times 6 \times \dfrac{5}{6} = 1800$

Cost price of $D = 304 \times 6 \times \dfrac{100}{80} = 2280$

Required Ratio $= \dfrac{2280}{1800} = \dfrac{19}{15} = 19:15$

Hence, the correct option is (D).

2. Let the marked price of B and D be x and y respectively.

Selling price of $B = x \times \dfrac{85}{100} \times \dfrac{95}{100} = \dfrac{8075x}{10000}$

Selling price of $D = y \times \dfrac{80}{100} \times \dfrac{95}{100} = \dfrac{7600y}{10000}$

The ratio of selling price of B to $D = 5:8$

$\therefore \dfrac{\frac{8075x}{10000}}{\frac{7600y}{10000}} = \dfrac{5}{8}$

$\Rightarrow \dfrac{8075x}{7600y} = \dfrac{5}{8}$

$\Rightarrow \dfrac{x}{y} = \dfrac{5 \times 7600}{8 \times 8075}$

$\Rightarrow \dfrac{x}{y} = \dfrac{190}{323}$

$\Rightarrow x:y = 190:323$

$\therefore$ The ratio of marked price of B to D is $190:323$.

Hence, the correct option is (D).

3. Let the marked price of A and B be Rs. a and Rs. b.

Selling price of $A = a \times \dfrac{90}{100} \times \dfrac{80}{100} = $ Rs. $0.72a$

Selling price of $B = b \times \dfrac{85}{100} \times \dfrac{95}{100} = $ Rs. $0.8075b$

According to question,

$\dfrac{0.72a}{0.8075b} = \dfrac{5}{2}$

$\Rightarrow \dfrac{a}{b} = \dfrac{5 \times 0.8075}{2 \times 0.72}$

$\Rightarrow \dfrac{a}{b} = \dfrac{45}{16}$

Let a be $45x$ and b be $16x$.

As, Sum of marked price of both the article $=$ Rs. 61000

$\therefore 45x + 16x = 61000$

$\Rightarrow 61x = 61000$

$\Rightarrow x = 1000$

Therefore, Marked price of $A = 45x = 45 \times 1000 = 45000$ and

Marked price of $B = 16x = 16 \times 1000 = 16000$

Selling price of $A = 45000 \times 0.72 = $ Rs. 32400

Selling price of $B = 16000 \times 0.8075 = $ Rs. 12920

$\therefore$ The difference between Selling price of both the articles $= 32400 - 12920 = $ Rs. 19480

Hence, the correct option is (B).

4. Given,

The ratio of marked price of A to $B = 2:3$

Let the marked price of the articles A and B is $200x$ and $300x$ respectively.

Selling price of the article $A = 200x \times \dfrac{90}{100} \times \dfrac{80}{100} = 144x$

Selling price of the articles $B = 300x \times \dfrac{85}{100} \times \dfrac{95}{100} = 242.25x$

The difference between the selling price of both the article $= 1198.65$

$\therefore 242.25x - 144x = 1198.65$

$\Rightarrow 98.25x = 1198.65$

$\Rightarrow x = 12.2$

Marked price of the article $A = 200x = 200 \times 12.2 = 2440$

Marked price of the article $B = 300x = 300 \times 12.2 = 3660$

$\therefore$ Difference between marked price of article A and $B = 3660 - 2440 = 1220$

Hence, the correct option is (B).

5. Let the number of males that appeared from college $A = $ number of females that appeared from college $B = x$

Total number of students that appeared from college $A = 320$

Total number of students that appeared from college $B = 420$

Given,

$$\frac{\text{Number of females that appeared form college A}}{\text{Number of males that appeared from college B}} = \frac{6}{11}$$

$$\therefore \frac{320-x}{420-x} = \frac{6}{11}$$

$$\Rightarrow 3520 - 11x = 2520 - 6x$$

$$\Rightarrow 5x = 1000$$

$$\Rightarrow x = \frac{1000}{5}$$

$$\Rightarrow x = 200$$

Now, $\left(\frac{250}{3}\right)\%$ of the females were selected from college A.

Number of females that appeared from college $A = 320 - x = 320 - 200 = 120$

Number of females that got selected from college $A = \left(\frac{250}{300}\right) \times 120 = 100$

But, total number of students selected from college $A = 260$

Number of males that got selected from college $A = 260 - 100 = 160$

Similarly, 85% of the females were selected from college B.

Number of females that appeared from college $B = x = 200$

Number of females that got selected from college $B = \left(\frac{85}{100}\right) \times 200 = 170$

But, total number of students selected from college $B = 350$

Number of males that got selected from college $B = 350 - 170 = 180$

$\therefore$ Ratio of males that got selected from college A to that from college $B = 160 : 180 = 8 : 9$

Hence, the correct option is (B).

6. Let the number of males that appeared from college C be x.

Total number of students that appeared from college $C = 250$

Number of females that appeared from college $C = (250 - x)$

Total number of students selected from college $C = 200$

$\therefore (72\% \text{ of } x) + [92\% \text{ of } (250 - x)] = 200$

$$\Rightarrow \frac{72x}{100} + \frac{92}{100} \times 250 - \frac{92x}{100} = 200$$

$$\Rightarrow \frac{18x}{25} + 230 - \frac{23x}{25} = 200$$

$$\Rightarrow 230 - 200 = \frac{23x}{25} - \frac{18x}{25}$$

$$\Rightarrow 30 = \frac{5x}{25}$$

$$\Rightarrow 30 = \frac{x}{5}$$

$$\therefore x = 150$$

Number of males that appeared from college $C = x = 150$

Number of females that appeared from college $C = (250 - x) = 250 - 150 = 100$

Male to female ratio of appeared students from college $D =$ Male to female ratio of appeared students from college $C = 150 : 100 = 3 : 2$

Now, Total number of students that appeared from college $D = 300$

Number of males that appeared from college $D = \frac{3}{5} \times 300 = 180$

Total number of students selected from college $D = 280$

Number of males selected from college $D = 280 - 109 = 171$

$\therefore$ Percentage of males selected from college $D = \frac{171}{180} \times 100 = 95\%$

Hence, the correct option is (D).

7. Total number of students that appeared from college $E = 350$

40% of the appearing students were from Science stream.

Number of students that appeared from Science stream from college $E = 40\%$ of $350 = \frac{40}{100} \times 350 = 140$

Similarly, Total number of students that appeared from college $F = 420$

25% of the appearing students were from Science stream.

Number of students that appeared from Science stream from college $F = 25\%$ of $420 = \frac{25}{100} \times 420 = 105$

Total number of students of Science stream that appeared from both colleges $= 140 + 105 = 245$

80% of the appearing students of Science stream from both colleges were selected.

Total number of students of Science stream selected from both colleges $= 80\%$ of $245 = \frac{80}{100} \times 245 = 196$ Now, Total number of students selected from college $E = 320$

35% of the students selected from college E were from Science stream.

Number of students of Science stream selected from college

$$E = 35\% \text{ of } 320 = \frac{35}{100} \times 320 = 112$$

Number of students of Science stream selected from college

$$F = 196 - 112 = 84$$

∵ Total no. of students selected from college $F = 350$

∴ Percentage of the selected students from college F that were from the Science stream $= \frac{84}{350} \times 100 = 24\%$

Hence, the correct option is (C).

8. Total number of students of six colleges that appeared in the interviews = 320 + 420 + 250 + 300 + 350 + 420 = 2060

Given,

Ratio of Science, Commerce & Arts students that appeared in interviews = 2 : 2 : 1

Number of Science students that appeared in interviews = $\frac{2}{5} \times$ 2060 = 824

Number of Commerce students that appeared in interviews = $\frac{2}{5} \times$ 2060 = 824

Number of Arts students that appeared in interviews = $\frac{1}{5} \times$ 2060 = 412

Now,

80% of the students from the six colleges appeared in the interviews.

Total number of students in six colleges = $\frac{2060}{0.8}$ = 2575

Given,

Ratio of total no. of Science, Commerce & Arts students in six colleges = 10 : 9 : 6

Total number of Science students in six colleges = $\frac{10}{25} \times$ 2575 = 1030

Total number of Commerce students in six colleges = $\frac{9}{25} \times$ 2575 = 927

Total number of Arts students in six colleges = $\frac{6}{25} \times$ 2575 = 618

∴ Ratio of number of students of Science, Commerce & Arts stream that did not appeared in the interviews = (1030 - 824) : (927 - 824) : (618 - 412)

= 206 : 103 : 206

= 2 : 1 : 2

Hence, the correct option is (A).

9. The number of units of electricity consumed by house S in June $= 250$

The number of units of electricity consumed by house S in July $= 420$

The number of units of electricity used in the month of August is the average of the number of units of electricity used in the month of June and July.

The number of units electricity consumed by house S in August $= \frac{250 + 420}{2} = 335$ units

The initial 150 units of electricity used in August is charged at the rate of Rs. 3 per unit.

The remaining units are charged at the rate of Rs. x per unit.

The total bill paid in August $=$ Rs. 1745

$$\therefore 150 \times 3 + (335 - 150) \times x = 1745$$

$$\Rightarrow 450 + 185x = 1745$$

$$\Rightarrow 185x = 1295$$

$$\Rightarrow x = 7$$

∴ The value of x is Rs. 7.

Hence, the correct option is (D).

10. As we know,

Total electricity bill = (Number of unit that rate of charge will low) $\times$ Rate $+$ (Number of unit that rate of charge will high) $\times$ Rate

The number of units electricity consumed by house P in June $= 400$

Let the number of unit that rate of charge is Rs. 3 be x.

Then, the number of unit that rate of charge is Rs. $5 = (400 - x)$

The total electricity bill for house P in June $=$ Rs. 1600

$$\therefore 3 \times x + 5 \times (400 - x) = 1600$$

$$\Rightarrow 3x + 2000 - 5x = 1600$$

$$\Rightarrow -2x + 2000 = 1600$$

$$\Rightarrow -2x = -400$$

$$\Rightarrow x = 200$$

∴ The number of units of electricity which have the rate of charge is Rs. 3 is 200 units.

Hence, the correct option is (B).

11. The initial number of units of electricity for which rate of charge is low = 120 units

The number of units of electricity consumed by house Q in June = 540

The number of units of electricity for which rate of charge is high in June = 540 - 120 = 420

The number of units of electricity consumed by house Q in July = 265

The number of units of electricity for which rate of charge is high in July = 265 - 120 = 145

Let the low rate of charge be x and the high rate of charge be y.

The electricity bill in June = 120x + 420y

The electricity bill in July = 120x + 145y

The difference between the electricity bill of June and July = Rs.1650

$\therefore$ 120x + 420y - (120x + 145y) = 1650

$\Rightarrow$ 120x + 420y - 120x - 145y = 1650

$\Rightarrow$ 275y = 1650

$\Rightarrow$ y = 6

$\therefore$ The rate at which the electricity is charged for the exceeding limit of number of units of electricity is Rs. 6 per unit.

Hence, the correct option is (C).

12. Total electricity consumed in July = 250 + 265 + 550 + 420 + 450 = 1935

The average number of units of electricity consumed = $\dfrac{1935}{5}$ = 387

$\therefore$The average number of units of electricity consumed is 387 units.

Hence, the correct option is (A).

Ques (13-16):Given:

College/subject	College A	College B	College C	College D
Physics	50	80	90	60
Chemistry	75	95	70	70
Maths	65	75	85	95

13. Number of students from chemistry department from college B = 95

Number of students from chemistry department from college C = 70

Number of students from physics department from college A = 50

Number of students from physics department from college D = 60

Total students from chemistry department from both college B and college C $= (95 + 70) = 165$

Total students from the physics department from both colleges A and college D $= (50 + 60) = 110$

So, the difference between the students from two departments $= (165 - 110) = 55$

$\therefore$ The difference between the total number of students from the chemistry department from college B and college C and the total number of students from the physics department from college A and college D is 55.

Hence, the correct option is (B).

14. Students from the physics department from college A $= 50$

Students from the math department from college A $= 65$

Students from chemistry department from college C $= 70$

Students from the math department from college C $= 85$

Total number of students from physics and math department from college A $= (50 + 65) = 115$

Total number of students from chemistry and math department from college C $= (70 + 85) = 155$

Now, the ratio between them $= 115 : 155$

$= 23 : 31$

$\therefore$ The ratio between them is $23 : 31$.

Hence, the correct option is (B).

15. Number of students from physics department from college A $= 50$

Number of students from physics department from college B $= 80$

Number of students from physics department from college C $= 90$

Number of students from physics department from college D $= 60$

$\text{Average} = \dfrac{\text{(Total sum of all numbers)}}{\text{(Total no. of the item in the set)}}$

Average of all students from physics department of all four colleges $= \left[\dfrac{(50+80+90+60)}{4}\right]$

$= \left[\dfrac{280}{4}\right]$

$= 70$

$\therefore$ The average of all students from the physics department of all four colleges is 70.

Hence, the correct option is (A).

16. Number of students from physics department from college C $= 90$

Number of students from chemistry department from college C $= 70$

Number of students from math department from college C $= 85$

Number of students from physics department from college D $= 60$

Number of students from chemistry department from college D $= 70$

Number of students from math department from college D $= 95$

Total number of students from college C $= (90 + 70 + 85) = 245$

Total number of students from college D $= (60 + 70 + 95) = 225$

Now, the total number of students from college C is more than that of college D

So, the difference between them $= (245 - 225) = 20$

So, the percentage $= \left(\frac{20}{225} \times 100\right)\% = \left(\frac{80}{9}\right)\% \approx 9\%$

∴ The students from college C are 9% more than that of college D.

Hence, the correct option is (C).

17. Given:

The ratio of women, men, and children who are literates = 1 : 4 : 6

Percentage of literate men who went to cities = 40%

Percentage of literate women who went to cities = 30%

Villages	Population in village	Number of literates
A	7.5	4.4
B	8.1	4
C	6.6	3
D	5.5	2
E	6	3.5

Calculation:

Number of literate women, men and children = x, 4x, and 6x

Total literates in village A = 4,400 = x + 4x + 6x

Or, x = 400

Number of literate men who went to cities = 40% × 4x = 40% × 4 × 400

Number of literate men who went to cities = 640

Number of literate women who went to cities = 30% × x = 30% × 1 × 400

Number of literate women who went to cities = 120

Literates who stayed in the village = total literates − (total men and women who went)

Literates who stayed in the village = 4,400 − (640 + 120) = 3,640

∴ The Number of literates who stayed in the village is 3,640.

Hence, the correct option is (D).

18. Given:

The amount allotted for each student in both villages = Rs.500

Percentage of children in village B $= 22\left(\frac{2}{9}\right)\% = \frac{2}{9}$

Percentage of children in village C $= \left(\frac{1}{2}\right) \times 33\left(\frac{1}{3}\right)\% = \left(\frac{1}{2}\right) \times \left(\frac{1}{3}\right) = \frac{1}{6}$

Villages	Population in village	Number of literates
A	7.5	4.4
B	8.1	4
C	6.6	3
D	5.5	2
E	6	3.5

Concept used:

Total amount received for the pan = number of students × amount allotted for each child

Calculation:

Total amount received by village B $= 8,100 \times \frac{2}{9} \times 500 =$ Rs. 9 lakh

Total amount received by village C $= 6,600 \times \frac{1}{6} \times 500 =$ Rs. 5.5 lakh

The total amount received by the villages = 9 + 5.5 = Rs. 14.5 lakhs

∴ The total amount received by the villages is 14.5 lakhs.

Hence, the correct option is (A).

19. Given:

The population of village F = 450% of literates in D

Number of literates in F $= \frac{1}{3}$rd of the population of village C

Villages	Population in village	Number of literates
A	7.5	4.4
B	8.1	4
C	6.6	3
D	5.5	2
E	6	3.5

Calculation:

Population of village F $= \frac{450}{100} \times 2,000 = 9,000$

Number of literates in F $= \frac{1}{3} \times 6,600 = 2,200$

Then, the number of illiterates in F = total population of village F – literates

Then, the number of illiterates in F = 9,000 – 2,200 = 6,800

∴ The number of illiterates in village F is 6,800.

Hence, the correct option is (D).

20. Given:

Villages	Population in village	Number of literates
A	7.5	4.4
B	8.1	4
C	6.6	3
D	5.5	2
E	6	3.5

Percentage of literates who decided to go to city = 25% of literates

Calculation:

Number of literates who stopped using $= \dfrac{25}{100} \times 4{,}400 = 1{,}100$

Percentage of people who went out of the who population = number of literates who went/ total population of village × 100

Percentage of people who went $= \dfrac{1{,}100}{7{,}500} \times 100 = \dfrac{44}{3}\%$

∴ Percentage of positive cases in the total population is $\dfrac{44}{3}\%$.

Hence, the correct option is (C).

21. Number of males visiting the restaurant on Thursday and Saturday $= 135 + 75 = 210$

Number of females visiting the restaurant on Monday and Tuesday $= 90 + 125 = 215$

∴ Required percentage $= \dfrac{215-210}{215} \times 100 = 2.325\% \approx 2.33\%$

∴ Total number of males visiting the restaurant on Thursday and Saturday is 2.33% less than the number of females visiting the restaurant on Monday and Tuesday.

Hence, the correct option is (C).

22. Number of Males visiting the restaurant on Tuesday and Thursday $= 75 + 135 + 125 = 335$

Number of Females visiting the restaurant on Tuesday and Thursday $= 125 + 95 + 105 = 325$

∴ Required ratio $= \dfrac{335}{325} = \dfrac{67}{65}$ or $67:65$

∴ The ratio between the number of Males visiting the restaurant on Tuesday, Thursday and Friday together and the number of females visiting the restaurant on the same days is $67:65$.

Hence, the correct option is (C).

23. Total number of males visiting the restaurant $= 120 + 75 + 80 + 135 + 125 + 75 = 610$

$\Rightarrow$ Average no. of males $= \dfrac{610}{6} = 101.67$

Total number of Females visiting the restaurant $= 90 + 125 + 110 + 135 + 95 + 105 + 110 = 635$

Average no. of males $= \dfrac{635}{6} = 105.833$

∴ Required difference $= 105.83 - 101.67 = 4.16$

Hence, the correct option is (D).

24. Number of customers visiting the restaurant on Sunday $= \dfrac{130}{100} \times (80 + 110) = 13 \times 19 = 247$

Ratio of Male to females $= 8:5$

∴ Number of males on Sunday $= \dfrac{8}{13} \times 247 = 152$

Number of males on Monday $= 120$

∴ Required percentage $= \dfrac{152}{120} \times 100 = 126.67\%$

Hence, the correct option is (B).

25. Let the population of village B in 2016 be x.

Literate population of village B in $2016 = 60\%$ of $x = 0.6x$

∵ The population of village B increased by 20% from 2016 to 2017.

∴ Population of village B in $2017 = 120\%$ of $x = 1.2x$

Literate population of village B in $2017 = 80\%$ of $1.2x = 0.96x$

Increase in literate population of village B from 2016 to $2017 = 0.96x - 0.6x = 0.36x$

∴ Percentage increase $= \dfrac{0.36x}{0.6x} \times 100 = 60\%$

Hence, the correct option is (B).

26. In the year 2015 , Number of literates in village A $= 48\%$ of $125000 = 60000$

Number of literates in village B $= 54\%$ of $150000 = 81000$

Now, Total number of literates in three villages $= 285000$

Number of literates in village C $= 285000 - (60000 + 81000) = 144000$

72% of total population of village C $= 144000$

$\therefore$ Total population of village C in $2015 = \dfrac{144000}{0.72} = 200000$

Hence, the correct option is (B).

27. Let the total population of the three villages A, B and C in 2016 be x, y and z respectively.

In the year 2016,

Literate population of village $A = 64\%$ of $x = \left(\dfrac{16}{25}\right)x$

Literate population of village $B = 60\%$ of $y = \left(\dfrac{3}{5}\right)y$

Literate population of village $C = 80\%$ of $z = \left(\dfrac{4}{5}\right)z$

Ratio of literate population of three villages $= 2:3:5$

$\therefore \left(\dfrac{16}{25}\right)x : \left(\dfrac{3}{5}\right)y : \left(\dfrac{4}{5}\right)z = 2:3:5$

$\Rightarrow 16x : 15y : 20z = 2:3:5$

$\Rightarrow x:y:z = 5:8:10$

$\therefore$ In 2016, the total populations of the three villages is in the ratio $5:8:10$.

Hence, the correct option is (C).

28. Considering village A in the year 2017,

Number of literate males = 42000 + Number of literate females

Number of literate males – Number of literate females = 42000...(1)

Also,

Number of literate males + Number of literate females = Total number of literates

Number of literate males + Number of literate females = 75% of the total population of village A

But, the total population of village A is not given.

$\therefore$ The data is insufficient to solve the question.

Hence, the correct option is (D).

29. Percentage growth in the number of upper primary institutions in 2000 – 01 $= \dfrac{206269-198004}{198004} = 4.17\%$

Percentage growth in the number of upper primary institutions in 2001 – 02 $= \dfrac{219626-206269}{206269} = 6.48\%$

Percentage growth in the number of upper primary institutions in 2002 – 03 $= \dfrac{245274-219626}{219626} = 11.68\%$

Percentage growth in the number of upper primary institutions in 2003 – 04 $= \dfrac{262286-245274}{245274} = 6.94\%$

Thus, the year 2002 – 03 has seen the maximum percentage growth in the number of upper primary institutions over the previous year.

Hence, the correct option is (C).

30. (A). Percentage share of Upper Primary Institutions in the year 1999 – 00

$= \dfrac{198004}{956519} \times 100 = 20.70\%$

Percentage share of Upper Primary Institutions in the year 2000 – 01

$= \dfrac{206269}{971054} \times 100 = 21.24\%$

The increase in percentage share of Upper Primary Institutions in the year 2000 - 01 over the previous year $= 21.24 - 20.70 = 0.54\%$

Percentage share of Primary Institutions in the year 1999 – 00

$= \dfrac{641695}{956519} \times 100 = 67.09\%$

Percentage share of Primary Institutions in the year 2000 – 01

$= \dfrac{638738}{971054} \times 100 = 65.78\%$

The decrease in percentage share of Primary Institutions in the year $2000 - 01$ over the previous year $= 67.09\% - 65.78\% = 1.31\%$ (False)

(B). Percentage share of Upper Primary Institutions in the year $2003 - 04 = 23.41\%$

Percentage share of Upper Primary Institutions in the year $2004 - 05 = 22.93\%$

The decrease in percentage share of Upper Primary Institutions in the year $2004 - 05$ over the previous year $= 0.48\%$

Percentage share of Primary Institutions in the year $2003 - 04 = 63.57\%$

Percentage share of Primary Institutions in the year $2004 - 05 = 63.89\%$

The increase in percentage share of Primary Institutions in the year $2004 - 05$ over the previous year $= 0.32\%$ (false)

(C). From option (A) we have already seen that the year $2001 - 02$ has also seen a decline in the percentage share of Primary Institutions. (False)

(D). Percentage share of Junior colleges in the year $2002 - 03 = 13.27\%$

Percentage share of Junior colleges in the year $2003 - 04 = 13.03\%$

The decrease in percentage share over the previous year $= 0.24\%$

Percentage share of Primary Institutions in the year $2002 - 03 = 63.00\%$

Percentage share of Primary Institutions in the year $2003 - 04 = 63.57\%$

The increase in percentage share over the previous year $= 0.57\%$ (True)

Hence, the correct option is (D).

31. In $1990 - 00$, the total number of Upper Primary schools and Junior Colleges was less than the total number of Primary schools by $(641695 - 198004 - 116820) = 326871$

In $2000 - 01$, the total number of Upper Primary schools and Junior Colleges was less than the total number of Primary schools by $(638738 - 206269 - 126047) = 306422$

In $2001 - 02$, the total number of Upper Primary schools and Junior Colleges was less than the total number of Primary schools by 310923.

In $2002 - 03$, the total number of Upper Primary schools and Junior Colleges was less than the total number of Primary schools by 268901.

In $2003 - 04$, the total number of Upper Primary schools and Junior Colleges was less than the total number of Primary schools by 303991.

In 2004 - 05, the total number of Upper Primary schools and Junior Colleges was less than the total number of Primary schools by 320740.

Therefore, required number of years $= 6$

Hence, the correct option is (D).

32. There is no growth in the number of Primary schools in $2000 - 01$ over previous year.

Percentage growth in the number of primary institutions in $2001 - 02 = 4\%$

There is no growth in the number of Primary schools in 2002 - 03 over previous year

Percentage growth in the number of primary institutions in $2003 - 04 = 9.3\%$

Percentage growth in the number of upper primary institutions in $2004 - 05 = 3.5\%$

Thus, the year $2003 - 04$ has seen the maximum percentage growth in the number of upper primary institutions over the previous year.

Hence, the correct option is (D).

33. Average value of imports in the year 1994,1995 and 1997

$= \frac{250+225+275}{3} = \frac{750}{3} = 250$

According to question,

Value of exports in $1996 - 450$

$\frac{450}{250} \times 100 = 180\%$

Hence, the correct option is (D).

34. The value of exports in 1994

$= \frac{350}{250} \times 100 = 140\%$

Hence, the correct option is (D).

35. Average of imports

$= \frac{75+150+250+225+350+275}{6}$

$= \frac{1325}{6} = 220.83$

Average of Exports

$= \frac{150+200+350+325+450+350}{6}$

$= \frac{1825}{6} = 304.16$

Difference $= 304.16 - 220.83$

$= 83.33 \approx 85$ crores

Hence, the correct option is (A).

36. The difference between the value of export and import in different years are:

$1992 - 150 - 75 = 75$

$1993 - 200 - 150 = 50$

$1994 - 350 - 250 = 100$

$1995 - 325 - 225 = 100$

$1996 - 450 - 350 = 100$

$1997 - 350 - 275 = 75$

In the year 1994, 1995 and 1996 the difference between export and import is 100 crores.

Hence, the correct option is (D).

37. The total numbers of students appeared in RRB Scale I in 2016 was 2.5 lakhs

In the question, it is given that 280 out of 1000 students cleared the RRB Scale I examination.

Then the total number of students out of 2.5 lakhs who cleared the examination

$= \frac{280 \times 250000}{1000} = 70000$

Hence, the correct option is (D).

38. Number of students who applied in 2014 is 50% less than the number of students who applied in 2017.

Let the total number of students who applied in $2017 = 2x$ thousands

Then the total number of students who applied in $2014 = 50\%$ less than $2x$ thousands $= 50\%$ of $2x$ thousands $= x$ thousands

The total number of students who cleared both the examination together in $2014 = (120 + 145)$ out of 2000

So out of x thousands $= 265 \times \dfrac{x}{2000}$

Similarly, The total number of students who cleared both the examination together in 2017

$$= (150 + 175) \times \dfrac{2x}{2000} = \dfrac{650x}{2000}$$

Required $\% = \dfrac{[\frac{265x}{2000}] \times 100}{[\frac{650x}{2000}]}$

$$= \dfrac{265 \times 100}{650} = 40.77\% \text{ approximately}$$

Hence, the correct option is (A).

39. Let the total number of students applied for RRB Assistant examination over the years $= 4x$ thousands

Then the total number of students applied for RRB Scale I examination over the years $= 75\%$ of $4x$ thousands $= 3x$ thousands

According to the question, the total number of students cleared RRB Scale I examination over the years $= 790$ out of 5000

So out of $3x$ thousands $= \dfrac{790 \times 3x}{5000}$ ....(i)

And, the total number of students cleared RRB assistant examination over the years $= 610$ out of 5000

So out of $4x$ thousands $= \dfrac{610 \times 4x}{5000}$ ....(ii)

Required ratio $= \dfrac{790 \times 3x}{5000} : \dfrac{610 \times 4x}{5000} = 237 : 244$

Hence, the correct option is (C).

40. The total number of students who applied in $2017 = 7.5$ lakhs

The respective ratio of the number of students who applied RRB Scale I and RRB assistant $7 : 8$

So, the number of students applied for RRB Scale I

$$= \dfrac{7 \times 7.5}{15} = 3.5 \text{ lakhs}$$

The number of students applied for RRB assistant

$$= \dfrac{8 \times 7.5}{15} = 4 \text{ lakhs}$$

the number of students who cleared RRB Scale I examination in $2017 = 150$ out of 1000

So out of 3.5 lakhs $= \dfrac{150 \times 3.5 \text{ lakhs}}{1000}$

Similarly, the number of students who cleared RRB Assistant examination

$$= \dfrac{175 \times 4 \text{ lakhs}}{1000}$$

Required ratio $= \dfrac{150 \times 3.5 \text{ lakhs}}{1000} : \dfrac{175 \times 4 \text{ lakhs}}{1000} = 3 : 4$

Hence, the correct option is (C).

41. The populations (in lakhs) of the subsidiary are tabulated below.

Subsidiary name	Populations (in lakhs)
ECL	(26.5 + 32.5) = 59.0
BCCL	(25.1 + 20.5) = 45.6
CCL	(32.5 + 30.2) = 62.7
WCL	(38.5 + 32.8) = 71.3
SCEL	(24.5 + 31.2) = 55.7
NCC	(38.7 + 24.9) = 63.6
NCL	(36.4 + 23.7) = 60.1
Total	418

The total population of the one by fourth part of the country $= 418$ lakhs

14.5% of the one by fourth part of the country's populations $= (0.145 \times 418) = 60.61$ lakhs

The subsidiary which have less than 14.5% of the one by fourth part of the country's population, i.e., which have less than 60.61 lakhs are are ECL, BCCL, SCEL and NCL.

Thus, number of subsidiary $= 4$

Hence, the correct option is (D).

42.

Subsidiary name	Number of males (in lakhs)	Number of females (in lakhs)	Number of females : Number of males
ECL	26.5	32.5	1.22
BCCL	25.1	20.5	0.81
CCL	32.5	30.2	0.92
WCL	38.5	32.8	0.85
SCEL	24.5	31.2	1.27
NCC	38.7	24.9	0.64
NCL	36.4	23.7	0.65
Total	222.2	195.8	0.88

The total number of males in the one by fourth part of the country $= 222.2$ lakhs

The total number of females in the one by fourth part of the country $= 195.8$ lakhs

Ratio of the number of females in the one by fourth part of the country to that of males $= 0.88$

We can observe from the table that for ECL and SCEL, the ratio is greater than 1

For CCL, the ratio is 0.92, which is greater than the required ratio.

For all the other subsidiary viz. BCCL, WCL, NCC and NCL, the ratio is less than 0.88

Thus, number of subsidiary which has less than the ratio of the number of females to the number of males are four.

Hence, the correct option is (D).

43. Number of illiterates in subsidiary ECL $= (0.4 \times 26.5 + 0.6 \times 32.5) = 30.1$

Number of illiterates in subsidiary BCCL $= (0.4 \times 25.1 + 0.6 \times 20.5) = 22.34$

Number of illiterates in subsidiary CCL $= (0.4 \times 32.5 + 0.6 \times 30.2) = 31.12$

Number of illiterates in subsidiary WCL $= (0.4 \times 38.5 + 0.6 \times 38.8) = 35.08$

Number of illiterates in subsidiary SCEL $= (0.4 \times 24.5 + 0.6 \times 31.2) = 28.52$

Number of illiterates in subsidiary NCC $= (0.4 \times 38.7 + 0.6 \times 24.9) = 30.42$

Number of illiterates in subsidiary NCL $= (0.4 \times 36.4 + 0.6 \times 23.7) = 28.78$

Thus, the third highest number of illiterates are in NCC.

Hence, the correct option is (B).

44. In Subsidiary ECL, since there are 26.5 lakhs males and 32.5 lakhs females, there can be a maximum of 26.5 lakhs married couples, a total of $(26.5 \times 2) = 53$ lakhs married persons.

Thus, the remaining $(32.5 - 26.5) = 6$ lakhs persons will be unmarried. This is the minimum number of persons who will be unmarried.

Now,

Subsidiary name	Number of males (in lakhs)	Number of females (in lakhs)	Minimum Number of unmarried person	10% population of the subsidiary
ECL	26.5	32.5	6.0	5.90
BCCL	25.1	20.5	4.6	4.56
CCL	32.5	30.2	2.3	6.27
WCL	38.5	32.8	5.7	7.13
SCEL	24.5	31.2	6.7	5.57
NCC	38.7	24.9	13.8	6.36
NCL	36.4	23.7	12.7	6.01
Total	222.2	195.8	26.4	41.8

Comparing the Minimum Number of unmarried persons with 10% population of the subsidiary of each subsidiary, we can conclude that only in subsidiary CCL and subsidiary WCL has the number of unmarried persons are less than that of 10% of the population of the subsidiary.

Hence, the correct option is (D).

45. The interest earned by Deepa after 4 years $=$
$$34560 \times 7 \times \frac{2}{100} + 34560\left(1 + \frac{10}{100}\right)^2 - 34560$$
$$= 34560 \times 7 \times \frac{2}{100} + 34560\left(\frac{121-100}{100}\right)$$
$$= \frac{34560}{100}(14 + 21)$$
$$= 12096$$

Hence, the correct option is (B).

46. Interest earned by Vikram $= 12800\left(1 + \frac{12}{100}\right)^2 - 12800$
$$= \text{Rs. } 3,256.32$$

Interest earned by Deepa $= 19200\left(1 + \frac{12}{100}\right)^2 - 19200$
$$= 19200\left(\frac{28}{25}\right)^2 - 19200$$
$$= \text{Rs. } 4,884.48$$

$\therefore$ Required difference $= 4884.48 - 3256.32$
$$= \text{Rs. } 1,628.16$$

Hence, the correct option is (A).

47. Average amount invested in schemes A, D and E by Vikram
$$= \frac{(43680+18000+25600)}{3} = \frac{87280}{3} = 29093$$

Average amount invested in schemes B, C and F by Deepa $=$
$$\frac{(28800+19200+34560)}{3} = \frac{82560}{3} = 27520$$

Sum $= 29093 + 27520 = 56613$

Hence, the correct option is (D).

48. Sum of interests earned by Vikram and Deepa $=$
$$60000\left(1 + \frac{8}{100}\right)^2 - 60000$$
$$= 600000 \times \left(\frac{27}{25}\right)^2 - 60000$$
$$= 60000 \times \frac{729}{625} - 60000$$

$=$ Rs. $9,984$

Hence, the correct option is (D).

49. Part filled by P and Q $= \dfrac{1}{15} + \dfrac{1}{10} = \dfrac{1}{6}$

Part filled by Q $= \dfrac{1}{10}$

$\dfrac{x}{2}\left(\dfrac{1}{6} + \dfrac{1}{10}\right) = \dfrac{2}{15} = \dfrac{15}{2} = 7.5$ minutes

Hence, the correct option is (B).

50. Pipe P can fill $= \dfrac{1}{12}$

Pipe Q can fill $= \dfrac{1}{4}$

For every two minutes, $\dfrac{1}{12} + \dfrac{1}{4} = \dfrac{1}{3}$ Part filled

Total $= 6$ minutes

Hence, the correct option is (D).

51. Total time taken by both pipes before the leak was developed $= \dfrac{60}{7}$ minutes

Now, leaks is developed which will take T time to empty the tank.

So, $\left(\dfrac{1}{15} + \dfrac{1}{20} - \dfrac{1}{T}\right) = \dfrac{1}{11}$

For T, we will get $\dfrac{660}{17}$ minutes $= 39$ minutes (approx.)

Hence, the correct option is (D).

52. Let the waste pipe take T time to empty the tank.

$\left(\dfrac{1}{10} + \dfrac{1}{12} - \dfrac{1}{T}\right) \times 60 = -1$

We will get $T = 5$ min

So capacity $= 5 \times 12 = 60$ litre

Hence, the correct option is (C).

53. Given:

HCL expenditure in $2010 = 250$

HCL expenditure in $2011 = 275$

and HCL expenditure $2012 = 230$

Percentage HCL in $2010 = 30\%$

percentage HCL in $2011 = 15\%$

and Percentage HCL in $2012 = 25\%$

Formula:

Total Income $=$ Income of HCL in $2010 +$ Income of HCL in $2011 +$ Income of HCL in 2012

According to the question,

Income of HCL in $2010 = 250 \times 130 \div 100 = 325$

Income of HCL in $2011 = 275 \times 115 \div 100 = 316.25$

Income of HCL in $2012 = 250 \times 125 \div 100 = 312.50$

Total Income $= 325 + 316.25 + 312.50$

Total Income $= 953.75$ crores

Hence, the correct option is (A).

54. Given:HCL expenditure in $2010 = 250$, Percentage $= 30\%$

Formula:

Total Income $=$ Income of HCL in $2010 +$ Income of HCL in $2011 +$ Income of HCL in 2012

Calculation:

Income in $2010 = 250 \times 130 \div 100 \times 150 \div 100$

Profit is 40% more, so

Income of HCL in $2013 =$ Expenditure $\times 140 \div 100$

Income of HCL in $2013 = 250 \times 130 \div 100 \times 150 \div 100 \times 135 \div 100$

The Income of HCL in $2013 = 658.125$ crores

Hence, the correct option is (B).

55. Given:

Company Wipro,

Expenditure in $2011 = 260$, Expenditure in $2012 = 290$, and Expenditure in $2013 = 320$

Profit in $2011 = 60\%$, Profit in $2012 = 20\%$ and profit in $2013 = 40\%$

Formula:

Average $=$ Total income $\div 3$

Calculation:

Income in $2011 = 260 \times 160 \div 100 = 416$

Income in $2012 = 290 \times 120 \div 100 = 348$

Income in $2013 = 320 \times 140 \div 100 = 448$

Total income $= 1212$

Average $=$ Total income $\div 3 = 1212 \div 3 = 404$

Hence, the correct option is (C).

56. Given:

Expenditure of HCL Company in $2012 = 250$

Profit Percentage $= 25\%$

Expenditure of Wipro Company in $2010 = 240$

Profit Percentage $= 35\%$

Formula:

Required Percentage $=$ Total income HCL company in $2012 \div$ Total income in Wipro Company in 2010×100

Calculation:

Required Percentage $= (250 \times 125 \div 100) \div (240 \times 135 \div 100)$

Required Percentage $= 96.45\%$

Hence, the correct option is (D).

57. Total investment of Rudra and Gautam in scheme R $=$ Rs. 98 thousand

Investment of Gautam $= 65\%$ of 98 thousand $= 63.7$ thousand

So, Investment of Rudra $= 98 - 63.7 = 34.3$ thousand

Formula of simple interest is: $\dfrac{PRT}{100}$ where $P =$ Principal, $R =$ Rate of interest and $T =$ Time period

Interest earned by Gautam $= \dfrac{63.7 \times 3 \times R}{100}$

Interest earned by Rudra $= \dfrac{34.3 \times 3 \times R}{100}$

$\Rightarrow \dfrac{63.7 \times 3 \times R}{100} - \dfrac{34.3 \times 3 \times R}{100} = \dfrac{13230}{1000}$

$R = 15\%$

Hence, the correct option is (D).

58. Total money invested in Scheme $M =$ Rs. 82000

Money invested by Gautam in Scheme $M = 55\%$ of $82000 =$ Rs. 45100

Money invested by Rudra in Scheme $M = 82000 - 45100 =$ Rs. 36900

Total money invested in Scheme N = Rs. $68,000$

Money invested by Gautam in Scheme N $= 60\% =$ Rs. 40800

Money invested by Rudra in Scheme N $= 68000 - 40800 =$ Rs. 27200

Total money invested by Gautam $= 45100 + 40800 =$ Rs. 85900

Total money invested by Rudra $= 36900 + 27200 =$ Rs. 64100

Ratio of money invested by Rudra to Gautam $= \dfrac{64100}{85900} = 0.75$

Hence, the correct option is (B).

59. Amount invested by Rudra in Scheme $Q = (100 - 42)\%$ of $62000 =$ Rs. 35960

For the first 2 years

Simple Interest $= \dfrac{35960 \times 2 \times 5}{100} =$ Rs. 3596

Total amount at end of 2 years $= 35960 + 3596 =$ Rs. 39556

This acts as Principal for the next years

$$A = P\left(1 + \dfrac{r}{100}\right)^n$$

Where A is the amount after adding compound interest, P is the Principal and n is the time period.

$$A = 39556\left(1 + \dfrac{10}{100}\right)^2$$

$= $ Rs. $47,862.76 \sim 47862$

Hence, the correct option is (D).

60. We know the formula for compound interest:

$$\Rightarrow CI = \left[P\left\{\left(1 + \dfrac{r}{100}\right)^t - 1\right\}\right]$$

Where,

$CI =$ Compound interest

$P =$ Principal

$R =$ Rate of interest

$T =$ Time period

Amount invested by Gautam in Scheme A and P each $= 30\%$ of $60000 =$ Rs. $18,000$

Difference in CI and $SI =$ Rs. 45

Let the rate of interest be $r\%$.

$$\Rightarrow SI = \dfrac{18000 \times 2 \times r}{100}$$

$$\Rightarrow CI = 18000\left(1 + \dfrac{r}{100}\right)^2 - 18000$$

$$\Rightarrow 18000\left(1 + \dfrac{r}{100}\right)^2 - 18000 - \left(\dfrac{18000 \times 2 \times r}{100}\right) = 45$$

Solving the above equation, we get $r = 5\%$

Hence, the correct option is (B).

Ques (1-5):Directions: Read the table and information given carefully and answer the following questions.

The following data is regarding the number of Pen of different colours with 4 friends Ram, Sita, Raj and Riya.

	Red	Yellow	Green	Blue	Total
Ram			4		
Sita				20	
Raj		5		2	
Riya					18
Total	18	16	14		

Four Friends Ram, Sita, Raj and Riya are studying in a group. Ram and Raj are boys. If all pens with all persons are put in a box then one pen is drawn, the probability that it will be a blue pen is $\frac{1}{4}$. Ratio of the number of Ram's pen to Raj pen is 7 : 6. The number of red pen with Ram is 3 times the number of Yellow pen at Ram. The yellow pens at Ram are 10% of the total pens at Sita. Number of red pens at Raj is 1 more than blue pen at Sita. The Ratio of Red, yellow and Green at Sita is 3 : 2 : 1. Probability of drawing a blue pen by Sita from her collection is $\frac{1}{10}$.

Q.1 All pens with Sita and Raj are put together in box A. If 2 pens are taken from box A, Find the probability that at least 1 pen is red.

A. $\frac{153}{248}$ **B.** $\frac{174}{248}$ **C.** $\frac{212}{248}$ **D.** $\frac{112}{237}$

Q.2 If 3 pens are drawn from the girls, what is the probability that all are blue?

A. $\frac{^{125}C_3}{^{38}C_3}$ **B.** $\frac{^{18}C_3}{^{38}C_3}$ **C.** $\frac{^{12}C_3}{^{38}C_3}$ **D.** $\frac{^{22}C_3}{^{38}C_3}$

Q.3 If 3 pens are picked randomly from Raj, what is the probability that they will be of different colours?

A. $\frac{19}{30}$ **B.** $\frac{17}{30}$ **C.** $\frac{13}{30}$ **D.** $\frac{23}{55}$

Q.4 Two pens are to be drawn From Green and blue pens that Riya have, Find the probability that Both are blue pens.

A. $\frac{3}{7}$ **B.** $\frac{4}{7}$ **C.** $\frac{5}{7}$ **D.** $\frac{6}{7}$

Q.5 Find the ratio of the probability of getting Sita's Red pen to the total red pen and Riya's Green pen to total green pen when a pen of each color is picked.

A. 5 : 7 **B.** 3 : 5 **C.** 5 : 3 **D.** 7 : 5

Ques (6-10):Directions: Read the data carefully and answer the following questions:

There are 4 wardrobes P, Q, R and S containing Brown, white and purple sarees. The total number of white sarees in all wardrobes together is 120. In wardrobe P, the probability of choosing a purple saree is $\frac{1}{6}$, a white saree is $\frac{4}{15}$, the number of brown sarees is 34 and the number of white sarees is 6 more than the number of purple sarees. In wardrobe Q, the probability of choosing a brown saree is $\frac{1}{4}$ and the number of purple sarees is $\left(\frac{3}{4}\right)^{th}$ of the number of white sarees which is 40% of the total number of white sarees. In wardrobe R, the total number of sarees is 120 and the ratio of brown and purple sarees is $9: 11$ and the probability of choosing a white saree is $\frac{1}{6}$. In wardrobe S, the total number of sarees is 157, the number of brown sarees is 20% more than the number of purple sarees and the number of white sarees is 25% less than that in wardrobe Q.

Q.6 Find the probability of choosing a brown saree from wardrobe R.

A. $\frac{1}{8}$ **B.** $\frac{1}{4}$ **C.** $\frac{3}{8}$ **D.** $\frac{1}{2}$

Q.7 If 10 white sarees are shifted from wardrobe Q to wardrobe S then, find the probability of purple sarees from wardrobe S.

A. $\frac{11}{167}$ **B.** $\frac{33}{167}$ **C.** $\frac{55}{167}$ **D.** $\frac{77}{167}$

Q.8 Find the difference between the probability of brown sarees from wardrobe P and the probability of purple sarees from wardrobe R.

A. $\frac{1}{4}$ **B.** $\frac{13}{120}$ **C.** $\frac{4}{15}$ **D.** $\frac{32}{120}$

Q.9 What is the probability of choosing a white saree from wardrobes Q and S each?

A. $\frac{108}{1100}$ **B.** $\frac{108}{1199}$ **C.** $\frac{108}{1109}$ **D.** $\frac{108}{1099}$

Q.10 If 2 sarees are chosen from wardrobe R then, what is the probability of getting 1 purple saree and 1 brown saree?

A. $\frac{163}{476}$ **B.** $\frac{165}{477}$ **C.** $\frac{167}{476}$ **D.** $\frac{165}{476}$

Ques (11-15):Directions: Read the data carefully and answer the following questions:

A journal plans to publish 18 research papers, written by eight authors (A, B, C, D, E, F, G, and H) in four issues of the journal scheduled in January, April, July and October. Each of the research papers was written by exactly one of the eight authors. Five papers were scheduled in each of the first two issues, while four were scheduled in each of the last two issues. Every author wrote at least one paper and at most three papers. The total number of papers written by A, D, G and H was double the total number of papers written by the other four authors. Four of the authors were from India and two each were from Japan and China. Each author belonged to exactly one of the three areas — Manufacturing, Automation, and Logistics. Four of the authors were from the Logistics area and two were from the Automation area. As per the journal policy, none of the authors could have more than one paper in any issue of the journal.

The following facts are also known.

1. F, an Indian author from the Logistics area, wrote only one paper. It was scheduled in the October issue.

2. A was from the Automation area and did not have a paper scheduled in the October issue.

3. None of the Indian authors were from the Manufacturing area and none of the Japanese or Chinese authors were from the Automation area.

4. A and H were from different countries, but had their papers scheduled in exactly the same issues.

5. C and E, both Chinese authors from different areas, had the same number of papers scheduled. Further, E had papers scheduled in consecutive issues of the journal but C did not.

6. B, from the Logistics area, had a paper scheduled in the April issue of the journal.

7. B and G belonged to the same country. None of their papers were scheduled in the same issue of the journal.

8. D, a Japanese author from the Manufacturing area, did not have a paper scheduled in the July issue.

9. C and H belonged to different areas.

Q.11 What is the correct sequence of number of papers written by B, C, E and G, respectively?

[CAT, 2021]

A. 1, 2, 2, 3 **B.** 1, 3, 3, 1 **C.** 3, 1, 1, 3 **D.** 1, 2, 2, 1

Q.12 How many papers were written by Indian authors?

[CAT, 2021]

Q.13 Which of the following statement(s) must be true?
Statement A: Every issue had at least one paper by author(s) from each country.
Statement B: Every issue had at most two papers by author(s) from each area.
A. Both the statements
B. Only Statement B
C. Only Statement A
D. Neither of the statements

Q.14 Which of the following statements is false?
A. Every issue had at least one paper by author(s) from Automation area
B. Every issue had exactly one paper by a Chinese author
C. Every issue had exactly two papers by authors from Logistics area
D. Every issue had exactly two papers by Indian authors

Q.15 Which of the following statements is false?
A. There were exactly two papers by authors from Manufacturing area in the January issue
B. There was exactly one paper by an author from Manufacturing area in the April issue
C. There was exactly one paper by an author from Logistics area in the October issue
D. There were exactly two papers by authors from Manufacturing area in the July issue

Ques (16-20):Directions: Read the table and information given carefully and answer the following questions.

Amudha, Bharatan, Chandran, Dhinesh, Ezhil, Fani and Gowtham are seven people in a town. Any pair of them could either be strangers, acquaintances, or friends. All relationships are mutual. For example, if Amudha is a friend of Bharatan, then Bharatan is also a friend of Amudha. Similarly, if Amudha is a stranger to Bharatan, then Bharatan is also a stranger to Amudha.

Partial information about the number of friends, acquaintances, and strangers of each of these people among them is given in the table below.

	No. of friends	No. of acquaintances	No. of strangers
Amudha		1	4
Bharatan			
Chandran		1	
Dhinesh			2
Ezhil			1
Fani	1		
Gowtham		3	2

The following additional facts are also known.

1. Amudha, Bharatan, and Chandran are mutual strangers.

2. Amudha, Dhinesh, and Fani are Ezil's friends.

3. Chandran and Gowtham are friends.

4. Every friend of Amudha is an acquaintance of Bharatan, and every acquaintance of Bharatan is a friend of Amudha.

5. Every friend of Bharatan is an acquaintance of Amudha, and every acquaintance of Amudha is a friend of Bharatan.

Q.16 Who are Gowtham's acquaintances?

[CAT, 2021]

A. Dhinesh, Ezhil and Fani
B. Amudha, Dhinesh and Fani
C. Bharatan, Dhinesh and Ezhil
D. Amudha, Bharatan and Fani

Q.17 Which of these pairs share the same type of relationship?

[CAT, 2021]

A. (Amudha, Gowtham) and (Ezhil, Fani)
B. (Bharatan, Chandran) and (Dhinesh, Ezhil)
C. (Chandran, Ezhil) and (Dhinesh, Gowtham)
D. (Bharatan, Ezhil) and (Fani, Gowtham)

Q.18 Who is an acquaintance of Amudha?

[CAT, 2021]

A. Dhinesh **B.** Fani
C. Gowtham **D.** Ezhil

Q.19 Who is an acquaintance of Chandran?

[CAT, 2021]

A. Dhinesh **B.** Fani **C.** Ezhil **D.** Bharatan

Q.20 How many friends does Ezhil have?

Ques (21-25):Directions: The following table represents the number of 6 hit by 5 players in three edition of IPL : 2006, 2007, and 2008. The pie player are Aaron finch, Gurkeeratsingh, Dale steyn, Parthivpatel and MS Dhoni. Each 6 fetches six run. Ratio of 6 hit by MS Dhoni in 2007 to 2008 is 6 : 5. Some of the data in the table is missing. Answer the question that Follow.

Players	2006	2007	2008	Total six	Run scored in six
Aaron finch	20		10		270
Gurkeeratsingh	18				
Dale steyn	15				354
Parthivpatel	20	10			
MS Dhoni					372
Total		81	75		1482

Q.21 What is the ratio of 6 hit by MS Dhoni in 2006, 2007 and 2008 respectively?

A. 9 : 12 : 13
B. 9 : 12 : 12
C. 9 : 12 : 10
D. 9 : 12 : 11

Q.22 What is the ratio of sixes hit by Aaron finch in 2006, 2007 and 2008 respectively?

A. 4 : 3 : 2 **B.** 5 : 4 : 3 **C.** 6 : 5 : 4 **D.** 3 : 2 : 1

Q.23 If Dale steyn hits 20 sixes in 2007, what is the ratio of sixes hit Gurkeeratsingh in 2007 to sixes hits by Dale steyn in 2008?

A. 1 : 2 **B.** 2 : 1 **C.** 2 : 3 **D.** 3 : 2

Q.24 If Parthivpatel hits 15 sixes in 2008, what is the difference of runs scored in sixes for 3 years by Dale steyn and by Gurkeeratshingh?

A. 11 **B.** 138 **C.** 116 **D.** 136

Q.25 What is the ratio of the difference in number of sixes hit by Aaron finch in 2006 and 2008 to the difference in number of sixes hit by MS Dhoni for the same 2 years?

A. 4 : 3 **B.** 4 : 1 **C.** 3 : 2 **D.** 5 : 1

Ques (26-30):Directions: Read the information carefully and answer the following questions:

Three major cities of Rajasthan – Jaipur, Jodhpur and Udaipur have been identified for the Covid-19 vaccination. A total of 1000 doses have reached in these three cities, which will be vaccinated in 3 categories 0-18 years old, 18-44 years old and Above 44 years old.

The number of vaccines in 18-44 years old category in Jaipur is 5/2 of that is above 44 years old category in Jodhpur. The total number of vaccines in Udaipur is equal to the total number of vaccines in Jodhpur. The number of vaccines in the 0-18 years old category in Jaipur is 25% of the total number of vaccines in Jaipur. The number of vaccines in above 44 years old category in Udaipur is 40% of the total vaccines in Udaipur. The total number of vaccines in 0-18 years old category in Jodhpur is 50% of the total number of vaccines in Jodhpur and the total number of vaccines in 18-44 years old category in jodhpur is 5% of the total vaccine in all the three cities. The total number

of vaccines in Udaipur is 300 and the total number of vaccines in category 0–18 years is 330.

Q.26 Find the total number of vaccines in Jaipur from all three categories.

A. 300 **B.** 350 **C.** 400 **D.** 450

Q.27 Which city and category have the highest number of vaccines respectively?

A. Jaipur and 18-44
B. Jaipur and Above 44
C. Udaipur and 0-18
D. Jodhpur and 0-18

Q.28 In Jaipur, the number of vaccines in 0-18 old years category is what percent of the number of vaccines in 18-44 old years category in Udaipur?

A. 120% **B.** 100% **C.** 150% **D.** 200%

Q.29 Find the ratio of the total number of vaccines in 0–18 years old category to the total number of vaccines in 18-44 year old category.

A. 3 : 4 **B.** 33 : 40 **C.** 40 : 27 **D.** 11 : 9

Q.30 Find the average number of vaccines in all the three cities in Above 44 years old category.

A. 270 **B.** 110 **C.** 90 **D.** 120

Ques (31-34):Directions: Read the table and information given carefully and answer the following questions.

The base exchange rate of a currency X with respect to a currency Y is the number of units of currency Y which is equivalent in value to one unit of currency X. Currency exchange outlets buy currency at buying exchange rates that are lower than base exchange rates, and sell currency at selling exchange rates that are higher than base exchange rates.

A currency exchange outlet uses the local currency L to buy and sell three international currencies A, B, and C, but does not exchange one international currency directly with another. The base exchange rates of A, B and C with respect to L are in the ratio 100:120:1. The buying exchange rates of each of A, B, and C with respect to L are 5% below the corresponding base exchange rates, and their selling exchange rates are 10% above their corresponding base exchange rates. The following facts are known about the outlet on a particular day:

1. The amount of L used by the outlet to buy C equals the amount of L it received by selling C.

2. The amounts of L used by the outlet to buy A and B are in the ratio 5:3.

3. The amounts of L the outlet received from the sales of A and B are in the ratio 5:9.

4. The outlet received 88000 units of L by selling A during the day.

5. The outlet started the day with some amount of L, 2500 units of A, 4800 units of B, and 48000 units of C.

6. The outlet ended the day with some amount of L, 3300 units of A, 4800 units of B, and 51000 units of C.

Q.31 How many units of currency A did the outlet buy on that day?

Q.32 How many units of currency C did the outlet sell on that day?

A. 22000   **B.** 19000   **C.** 6000   **D.** 3000

Q.33 What was the base exchange rate of currency B with respect to currency L on that day?

Q.34 What was the buying exchange rate of currency C with respect to currency L on that day?

A. 1.10   **B.** 0.95   **C.** 2.20   **D.** 1.90

Ques (35-38):Directions: Read the table and information given carefully and answer the following questions.

Sixteen patients in a hospital must undergo a blood test for a disease. It is known that exactly one of them has the disease. The hospital has only eight testing kits and has decided to pool blood samples of patients into eight vials for the tests. The patients are numbered 1 through 16, and the vials are labelled A, B, C, D, E, F, G, and H. The following table shows the vials into which each patient's blood sample is distributed.

Patient	Vials	Patient	Vials
1	B, D, F, H	9	A, D, F, H
2	B, D, F, G	10	A, D, F, G
3	B, D, E, H	11	A, D, E, H
4	B, D, E, G	12	A, D, E, G
5	B, C, F, H	13	A, C, F, H
6	B, C, F, G	14	A, C, F, G
7	B, C, E, H	15	A, C, E, H
8	B, C, E, G	16	A, C, E, G

If a patient has the disease, then each vial containing his/her blood sample will test positive. If a vial tests positive, one of the patients whose blood samples were mixed in the vial has the disease. If a vial tests negative, then none of the patients whose blood samples were mixed in the vial has the disease.

Q.35 Suppose vial C tests positive and vials A, E and H test negative. Which patient has the disease?

A. Patient 14   **B.** Patient 8
C. Patient 6   **D.** Patient 2

Q.36 Suppose vial A tests positive and vials D and G test negative. Which of the following vials should we test next to identify the patient with the disease?

A. Vial B   **B.** Vial E   **C.** Vial C   **D.** Vial H

Q.37 Which of the following combinations of test results is NOT possible?

A. Vials A and E positive, vials C and D negative
B. Vial B positive, vials C, F and H negative
C. Vials A and G positive, vials D and E negative
D. Vials B and D positive, vials F and H negative

Q.38 Suppose one of the lab assistants accidentally mixed two patients' blood samples before they were distributed to the vials. Which of the following correctly represents the set of all possible numbers of positive test results out of the eight vials?

A. {5,6,7,8}   **B.** {4,5,6,7}
C. {4,5,6,7,8}   **D.** {4,5}

Ques (39-42):Directions: Read the table and information given carefully and answer the following questions.

The game of Chango is a game where two people play against each other; one of them wins and the other loses, i.e., there are no drawn Chango games. 12 players participated in a Chango championship. They were divided into four groups: Group A consisted of Aruna, Azul, and Arif; Group B consisted of Brinda, Brij, and Biju; Group C consisted of Chitra, Chetan, and Chhavi; and Group D consisted of Dipen, Donna, and Deb.

Players within each group had a distinct rank going into the championship. The players have NOT been listed necessarily according to their ranks. In the group stage of the game, the second and third ranked players play against each other, and the winner of that game plays against the first ranked player of the group. The winner of this second game is considered as the winner of the group and enters a semi-final.

The winners from Groups A and B play against each other in one semi-final, while the winners from Groups C and D play against each other in the other semi-final. The winners of the two semi-finals play against each other in the final to decide the winner of the championship.

It is known that:

1. Chitra did not win the championship.

2. Aruna did not play against Arif. Brij did not play against Brinda.

3. Aruna, Biju, Chitra, and Dipen played three games each, Azul and Chetan played two games each, and the remaining players played one game each.

Q.39 Who among the following was DEFINITELY NOT ranked first in his/her group?

A. Dipen   **B.** Aruna   **C.** Brij   **D.** Chitra

Q.40 Which of the following pairs must have played against each other in the championship?

A. Deb, Donna   **B.** Azul, Biju
C. Donna, Chetan   **D.** Chitra, Dipen

Q.41 Who won the championship?

A. Chitra
B. Aruna
C. Brij
D. Cannot be determined

Q.42 Who among the following did not play against Chitra in the championship?

A. Aruna   **B.** Chetan   **C.** Dipen   **D.** Biju

Ques (43-46):Directions: Read the table and information given carefully and answer the following questions.

Ravi works in an online food-delivery company. After each delivery, customers rate Ravi on each of four parameters - Behaviour, Packaging, Hygiene, and Timeliness, on a scale from 1 to 9. If the total of the four rating points is 25 or more, then

Ravi gets a bonus of ₹20 for that delivery. Additionally, a customer may or may not give Ravi a tip. If the customer gives a tip, it is either ₹30 or ₹50.

One day, Ravi made four deliveries - one to each of Atal, Bihari, Chirag, and Deepak, and received a total of ₹120 in bonus and tips. He did not get both a bonus and a tip from the same customer.

The following additional facts are also known.

1. In Timeliness, Ravi received a total of 21 points, and three of the customers gave him the same rating points in this parameter. Atal gave higher rating points than Bihari and Chirag in this parameter.

2. Ravi received distinct rating points in Packaging from the four customers adding up to 29 points. Similarly, Ravi received distinct rating points in Hygiene from the four customers adding up to 26 points.

3. Chirag gave the same rating points for Packaging and Hygiene.

4. Among the four customers, Bihari gave the highest rating points in Packaging, and Chirag gave the highest rating points in Hygiene.

5. Everyone rated Ravi between 5 and 7 in Behaviour. Unique maximum and minimum ratings in this parameter were given by Atal and Deepak respectively.

6. If the customers are ranked based on ratings given by them in individual parameters, then Atal's rank based on Packaging is the same as that based on Hygiene. This is also true for Deepak.

Q.43 What was the minimum rating that Ravi received from any customer in any parameter?

Q.44 The COMPLETE list of customers who gave the maximum total rating points to Ravi is:

A. Atal   **B.** Bihari
C. Bihari and Chirag   **D.** Atal and Bihari

Q.45 What rating did Atal give on Timeliness?

Q.46 What BEST can be concluded about the tip amount given by Deepak?

A. Either or or
B. Either or
C.
D.

Ques (47-50):Directions: Read the following information carefully and answer the given questions.

In a company meeting there are eight employees named Girish, Sourav, Vestal, Richa, Saxena, Prashant, Vivek, and Sumit, who hold different positions - Managing Director (MD), Executive Director (ED), Chief General Manager (CGM), General Manager (GM), Assistant General Manager (AGM), Divisional Manager (DM), Marketing Officer (Mo) and Clerk but not necessarily in the same order. All the positions are in the increasing order where the clerk position is junior to all and MD position is senior to all.

Girish is not junior to Vestal. Richa is neither General manager nor Managing Director. Sourav is the Executive Director. Vestal is senior to Divisional Manager but junior to Managing Director. Saxena is senior to only three-person. Prashant is junior to Saxena. Prashant is not the most junior person. Vivek is just one position senior to Sumit.

Q.47 Who is the most junior among them?
A. Saxena   **B.** Prashant   **C.** Vivek   **D.** Sumit

Q.48 Who holds the Position of Divisional Manager?
A. Prashant   **B.** Vivek   **C.** Sourav   **D.** Richa

Q.49 Which post is held by Saxena?
A. MD   **B.** CGM   **C.** AGM   **D.** MO

Q.50 Four of the following five are alike in a certain way and hence they form a group. Which one of the following does not belong to that group?
A. Girish   **B.** Sourav   **C.** Richa   **D.** Prashant

Ques (51-55):Directions: Study the following information carefully and answer accordingly:

In a bank branch 300 employees working, and they speak three languages Hindi, Punjabi, English with fluency, 140 of employee speak fluently in Hindi, and 104 of them speak fluently in English, 126 of them speak fluently in Punjabi, 30 speak fluently in English and Punjabi both languages, which is 25% more than employees who fluent in both English and Hindi, 26 employees speak fluently both Punjabi and Hindi.

Q.51 What is the ratio of employees who fluent only in English to only in Punjabi?
A. 2 : 3   **B.** 4 : 3   **C.** 3 : 4   **D.** 3 : 2

Q.52 Fluent employee only in English is what percent less than who fluent only in Hindi?
A. 45%   **B.** 60%   **C.** 50%   **D.** 40%

Q.53 How many employees fluent in at least two of the languages?
A. 50 employees   **B.** 70 employees
C. 60 employees   **D.** 30 employees

Q.54 If certain number of employee join to bank and they fluent in all of the three language, and that number is 3.33% of employee who already work there, find new ratio of fluent in English : Punjabi : Hindi after join of new employee.
A. 68 : 57 : 75   **B.** 57 : 75 : 68
C. 75 : 68 : 57   **D.** 57 : 68 : 75

Q.55 Find number of employee who speak fluently only in single language.
A. 160 employees   **B.** 200 employees
C. 250 employees   **D.** 240 employees

Ques (56-60):Directions: Read the following table carefully and answer the given questions:

Following table shows total number of cars deal by different companies in India, percentage of SUV cars and percentage of MUV cars and ratio of petrol SUV cars to diesel MUV cars of six different companies in first quarter of year 2021.

Company	Number of cars (in thousands)	SUV car (%)	MUV car (%)	Ratio of petrol SUV cars to diesel MUV cars
Hyundai	110	40	30	3 : 4
Toyota	70	50	40	2 : 3
Mahindra	80	45	30	6 : 5
Tata motors	90	60	20	8 : 3
Maruti suzuki	120	40	40	11 : 6
Ford	100	60	30	5 : 1

Note:

Total cars deal by particular company = (Total SUV cars deal by particular company) + (Total MUV cars deal by particular company) + (Total XUV cars deal by particular company)

Total cars deal by particular company = (Total petrol cars deal by particular company) + (Total diesel cars deal by particular company)

Q.56 If number of diesel MUV cars deal by Hyundai is 24,000 and number of petrol SUV cars deal by Toyota is 14,000. Find the Number of diesel SUV cars deal by Hyundai and Toyota together.

A. 21,000 **B.** 40,000 **C.** 47,000 **D.** 22,000

Q.57 Number of XUV cars deal by Tata motors and Maruti suzuki together is what percent of petrol SUV cars deal by Ford, if number of petrol MUV cars deal by Ford is 20,000.

A. 48% **B.** 84% **C.** 96% **D.** 80%

Q.58 If number of diesel SUV cars deal by Mahindra and Tata motors is 12,000 and 14,000 respectively, find ratio of petrol SUV deal by Tata motors to Mahindra.

A. 3 : 2 **B.** 2 : 5 **C.** 3 : **D.** 5 : 3

Q.59 If ratio of Diesel MUV cars deal by Tata motors to Maruti suzuki is 5 : 4, and number of petrol SUV cars deal by Tata motors is 18,000 more than the petrol SUV cars deal by Maruti suzuki, find total diesel cars deal by Tata motors and Maruti suzuki in SUV and MUV segment.

A. 57,000 **B.** 65,000
C. 48,000 **D.** None of these

Q.60 Total number of XUV cars deal by all companies approximately what percent of the total number of MUV cars deal by all companies?

A. 58 **B.** 68% **C.** 51% **D.** 62%

// Smart Answer Sheet //

Correct Indicates percentage of students who answered questions correctly.

Skipped Indicates percentage of students who skipped questions.

Q.	Ans.	Correct / Skipped
1	A	53.58 % / 39.28 %
2	C	57.94 % / 31.78 %
3	D	19.07 % / 75.37 %
4	A	54.08 % / 33.95 %
5	D	44.06 % / 31.65 %
6	C	62.33 % / 35.63 %
7	C	47.06 % / 33.21 %
8	B	28.2 % / 69.37 %
9	D	47.22 % / 48.19 %
10	D	31.57 % / 67.82 %
11	A	51.72 % / 46.22 %
12	8	62.68 % / 33.43 %

Q.	Ans.	Correct / Skipped
13	C	25.71 % / 69.28 %
14	C	14.6 % / 73.67 %
15	D	59.37 % / 35.47 %
16	A	66.97 % / 32.55 %
17	D	24.67 % / 73.6 %
18	A	43.07 % / 46.23 %
19	B	59.77 % / 31.64 %
20	3	61.76 % / 33.89 %
21	C	48.46 % / 33.81 %
22	A	61.86 % / 30.88 %
23	A	68.41 % / 31.59 %
24	B	57.05 % / 30.69 %

Q.	Ans.	Correct / Skipped
25	D	51.39 % / 39.7 %
26	C	42.04 % / 38.57 %
27	A	46.36 % / 36.3 %
28	B	12.56 % / 73.14 %
29	B	59.91 % / 37.52 %
30	C	16.75 % / 74.1 %
31	1200	63.05 % / 32.21 %
32	B	51.17 % / 39.57 %
33	240	63.3 % / 30.33 %
34	D	51.19 % / 33.57 %
35	C	50.6 % / 36.92 %
36	B	42.46 % / 46.04 %

Q.	Ans.	Correct / Skipped
37	A	62.67 % / 34.15 %
38	C	30.63 % / 68.93 %
39	A	43.98 % / 38.93 %
40	D	56.93 % / 37.42 %
41	B	48.88 % / 30.28 %
42	D	45.78 % / 41.32 %
43	5	67.87 % / 30.68 %
44	C	67.27 % / 32.65 %
45	6	25.03 % / 67.36 %
46	B	59.91 % / 36.29 %
47	D	43.65 % / 50.96 %
48	A	49.5 % / 47.93 %

Q.	Ans.	Correct / Skipped
49	C	67.16 % / 32.09 %
50	D	52.03 % / 37.12 %
51	C	55.07 % / 32.98 %
52	D	48.08 % / 51.17 %
53	C	45.66 % / 36.89 %
54	D	48.76 % / 47.87 %
55	D	64.64 % / 30.0 %
56	C	58.5 % / 35.84 %
57	B	11.73 % / 74.53 %
58	D	66.65 % / 33.25 %
59	D	12.03 % / 74.98 %
60	D	19.6 % / 67.85 %

Performance Analysis

Avg. Score (%)	30.56%
Toppers Score (%)	56.67%
Your Score	

//Hints and Solutions//

Ques (1-5): Let the total number of blue pens be x.

Probability of one blue pen $= \dfrac{^xC_1}{^{(18+16+14+x)}C_1} = \dfrac{^xC_1}{^{(48+x)}C_1}$

$\Rightarrow \dfrac{x}{(48+x)} = \dfrac{1}{4}$

$\Rightarrow 3x = 48$

$\Rightarrow x = 16$

Total pen $= 18 + 16 + 14 + 16 = 64$

Ram's pen to Raj's pen $= 7:6$ (or $7y:6y$)

$7y + 6y + 20 + 18 = 64$

$\Rightarrow 13y + 38 = 64$

$\Rightarrow 13y = 64 - 38 = 26$

$\Rightarrow y = 2$

Ram's pen $= 7y = 7 \times 2 = 14$

Raj's pen $= 6y = 6 \times 2 = 12$

Red pen with Ram $= 3$ (Yellow pen with Ram)

Yellow pens with Ram $= 20 \times \dfrac{10}{100} = 2$

$\Rightarrow$ Red pens with Ram $= 2 \times 3 = 6$

$\Rightarrow$ Blue pens with Ram $= 14 - (6 + 2 + 4) = 2$

Let the number of blue pens with Sita be y.

$\Rightarrow \dfrac{y}{20} = \dfrac{1}{10}$

$\Rightarrow y = 2$

Let the number of red, yellow, and green pens with Sita be $3z, 2z,$ and z respectively

$\Rightarrow 3z + 2z + z = 20 - 2 = 18$

$\Rightarrow 6z = 18$

$\Rightarrow z = 3$

Number of red pens with Raj $= 2 + 1 = 3$

$\Rightarrow$ Green pens with Raj $= 12 - (3 + 5 + 2) = 2$

Pens with Riya,

$Red = 18 - (6 + 9 + 3) = 0$

Yellow $= 16 - (2 + 6 + 5) = 3$

Green $= 14 - (4 + 3 + 2) = 5$

Blue $= 16 - (2 + 2 + 2) = 10$

From all the data calculated above, we get

	Red	Yellow	Green	Blue	Total
Ram	6	2	4	2	14
Sita	9	6	3	2	20
Raj	3	5	2	2	12
Riya	0	3	5	10	18
Total	18	16	14	16	64

1. Total pens in box $= 20 + 12 = 32$

$\therefore$ Probability of at least 1 pen is Red $= 1 -$ (Probability of no pen is red)

$\Rightarrow 1 - \dfrac{^{20}C_2}{^{32}C_2}$

$\Rightarrow 1 - \dfrac{[(20 \times 19)]}{[(32 \times 31)]}$

$= 1 - \dfrac{95}{248} = \dfrac{153}{248}$

Hence, the correct option is (A).

2. Total pens with girls $= 20 + 18 = 38$

Blue pens with girls $= 2 + 10 = 12$

$\therefore$ Required probability $= \dfrac{^{12}C_3}{^{38}C_3}$

Hence, the correct option is (C).

3. Let R for Red, Y for yellow, G for green and B for blue.

Combination of different colours:
$(R \times Y \times G) + (Y \times G \times B) + (G \times B \times R) + (B \times R \times Y)$

$\therefore$ Required probability $=$
$\dfrac{(3 \times 5 \times 2) + (5 \times 2 \times 2) + (2 \times 2 \times 3) + (2 \times 3 \times 5)}{^{12}C_3}$

$= \dfrac{92}{^{12}C_3} = \dfrac{23}{55}$

Hence, the correct option is (D).

4. Green and blue pens with Riya $= 5 + 10 = 15$

$\therefore$ Probability that both drawn pens are blue $= \dfrac{^{10}C_2}{^{15}C_2}$

$= \dfrac{(10 \times 9)}{(15 \times 14)} = \dfrac{3}{7}$

Hence, the correct option is (A).

5. Probability of getting Sita's red pen $= \dfrac{9}{18} = \dfrac{1}{2}$

Probability of getting Riya's green pen $= \dfrac{5}{14}$

$\therefore$ Required ratio $= \dfrac{1}{2} : \dfrac{5}{14} = 7:5$

Hence, the correct option is (D).

Ques (6-10): Given:

The table shows the number, percentage of sarees and probability of one saree:

Wardrobe	Brown Saree	White Saree	Purple Saree	Total
P	34	$p = \left(\frac{4}{15}\right)$ and 6 more than purple saree	$p = \left(\frac{1}{6}\right)$	
Q	$p = \left(\frac{1}{4}\right)$	40% of total white saree	$\left(\frac{3}{4}\right)^{th}$ of white saree in Q	
R	9x	$p = \left(\frac{1}{6}\right)$	11x	120
S	20% more than purple sarees in S	25% less than white saree in Q		157
Total		120		

Formula:

Probability of favourable outcome $=$

$$\frac{\text{Number of favourable outcome}}{\text{Total outcome}}$$

Calculation:

Total probability in wardrobe $P = 1$

Probability of brown sarees from wardrobe $P = 1 - \left(\frac{1}{6}\right) - \left(\frac{4}{15}\right)$

$$= \frac{(30-5-8)}{30}$$

$$= \frac{17}{30}$$

Total number of sarees in wardrobe $P = 34 \times \left(\frac{30}{17}\right)$

$$= 60$$

Total number of white sarees in all wardrobe together $= 120$

Number of white sarees in wardrobe $Q = \left(\frac{40}{100}\right) \times 120 = 48$

Number of purple sarees in wardrobe $Q = \left(\frac{3}{4}\right) \times 48 = 36$

Probability of a white and a purple saree $= 1 - \left(\frac{1}{4}\right) = \frac{3}{4}$

So, the total number of sarees in wardrobe $Q =$

$$\left(\frac{3}{2}\right) \times (48 + 36)$$

$$= \left(\frac{4}{3}\right) \times 84$$

$$= 112$$

Probability of choosing white saree from wardrobe $Q = \frac{48}{112} = \frac{3}{7}$

and number of white sarees in wardrobe $S = [1 - \left(\frac{25}{100}\right)] \times 48$

$$= \left(\frac{75}{100}\right) \times 48$$

$$= 36$$

Let the number of brown and purple saree be $9x$ and $11x$.

Total number of sarees in wardrobe $R = 120$

probability of choosing white saree $= \frac{1}{6}$

$$\Rightarrow \frac{\text{Number of white sarees}}{\text{Total number of sarees}} = \frac{1}{6}$$

$$\Rightarrow \text{Number of white sarees} = 120 \times \left(\frac{1}{6}\right)$$

$$\Rightarrow \text{Number of white sarees} = 20$$

Then, $9x + 11x = 120 - 20$

$$\Rightarrow 20x = 100$$

$$\Rightarrow x = 5$$

Number of brown sarees $= 9 \times 5 = 45$

Number of purple sarees $= 11 \times 5 = 55$

Then, Let the number of purple sarees in wardrobe S be x.

Then, the number of brown sarees in the wardrobe $S = 1.2x$

Total number of white sarees in all wardrobe together $= 120$

Number of white sarees in wardrobe $Q = \left(\frac{40}{100}\right) \times 120$

$$= 48$$

Number of white sarees in wardrobe $S = [1 - \left(\frac{25}{100}\right)] \times 48$

$$= \left(\frac{75}{100}\right) \times 48$$

$$= 36$$

So, $1.2x + x = 157 - 36$

$$\Rightarrow 2.2x = 121$$

$$\Rightarrow x = 55$$

Now, the following table will be prepared:

Wardrobe	Brown Saree	White Saree	Purple Saree	Total
P	34	16	10	60
Q	28	48	36	112

R	45	20	55	120
S	66	36	55	157
Total	173	120	156	449

6. Now, required probability $= \dfrac{45}{120}$

$= \dfrac{3}{8}$

$\therefore$ The probability of choosing a brown saree from wardrobe R is $\dfrac{3}{8}$.

Hence, the correct option is (C).

7. Total number of all sarees together in wardrobe $S = 157 + 10 = 167$

Now, required probability $= \dfrac{55}{167}$

$\therefore$ The probability of purple sarees from wardrobe S is $\dfrac{55}{167}$.

Hence, the correct option is (C).

8. Probability of brown sarees from wardrobe $P = \dfrac{34}{60}$

Probability of purple sarees from wardrobe $R = \dfrac{55}{120}$

Now, required difference $= \dfrac{34}{60} - \dfrac{55}{120}$

$= \dfrac{(68-55)}{120}$

$= \dfrac{13}{120}$

$\therefore$ The difference between the probability of brown sarees from wardrobe P and the probability of purple sarees from wardrobe R is $\dfrac{13}{120}$.

Hence, the correct option is (B).

9. Probability of choosing white saree from wardrobe $Q = \dfrac{48}{112} = \dfrac{3}{7}$

Probability of choosing white saree from wardrobe $S = \dfrac{36}{157}$

Now, required probability $= \left(\dfrac{3}{7}\right) \times \left(\dfrac{36}{157}\right)$

$= \dfrac{108}{1099}$

$\therefore$ The probability of choosing a white saree from wardrobes Q and S each is $\dfrac{108}{1099}$.

Hence, the correct option is (D).

10. Number of favorable outcomes $= \left({}^{55}C_1 \times {}^{45}C_1\right)$

$= 55 \times 45$

$= 2475$

And total number of outcomes $= {}^{120}C_2$

$= \dfrac{(120 \times 119)}{(2 \times 1)}$

$= 7,140$

Now, required probability $= \dfrac{2475}{7140}$

$= \dfrac{165}{476}$

$\therefore$ The probability of getting 1 purple saree and 1 brown saree is $\dfrac{165}{476}$.

Hence, the correct option is (D).

Ques (11-15): In the information, it is provided that there are four authors in the logistics department, 2 authors in automation, and 2 authors in manufacturing. There are 4 Indian authors, 2 Chinese authors, and 2 Japanese authors.

The total issues publicized were 18 of which the publications done by A, D, G, H are twice the papers written by the other four authors. Hence A+D+G+H has written 12 papers in total and B+C+E+F has written 6 in total. Since an author can write a minimum of 4 papers and a maximum of 3 papers. Each of A, D, G, H must have written 3 papers each.

In statement 3 it was provided that none of the Indian authors were from the Manufacturing area and none of the Japanese or Chinese authors were from the Automation area.

Since none of the Japanese and Chinese authors belonged to automation. Hence the two automation authors must be from India. In statement 1 it was given that F an Indian author is from logistics.

Of the remaining 5 authors 3 from logistics and 2 from manufacturing, in statement 5 it is given that the two Chinese authors are from different areas and hence they must be from manufacturing and logistics.

Of the remaining 3 authors 2 in logistics and 1 in manufacturing, in statement 8 is given that a Japanese author belonged to manufacturing, and hence of the remaining 2 in logistics one of them was from India and the other from Japan.

Of the four Indian authors, 2 belonged to logistics and 2 automation. Of the two authors from Japan, one belonged to manufacturing and one logistics. Of the two Chinese authors, one of them belonged to logistics and the other manufacturing.

Five papers were scheduled in each of the January and April issues, while four were scheduled in each of July and October issues.

Using statement 1, F an Indian author wrote a single paper in logistics published in October.

Using statement 2, A was from Automation and did not have a paper scheduled in October. Since A wrote 3 papers in total he must have written in the other three months and since only

Indian authors worked in Automation he must have been from India.

Using statement 5, C, E are Chinese and wrote an equal number of papers. Since B+C+E+F have written a total of 6 papers. The two possibilities are 2+2+1+1 or 3+1+1+1.. Since it was given that E had papers scheduled in consecutive issues and C did not. So the only possible case is C = 2, E = 2, F = 1, B = 1.

Using statement 4, A and H were from different countries and wrote papers in the same months. Hence H must be Japanese and must have written in Jan, April, July.

Author	Country	Area of Interest	Publications	Months of publication
A	India	Automation	3	Jan, April, July
B			1	
C	Chinese		2	
D			3	
E	Chinese		2	
F	India	Logistics	1	October
G			3	
H	Japan		3	Jan, April, July

In statement 6, B, from the Logistics area, had a paper scheduled in the April issue of the journal.

In statement 7, B and G belonged to the same country. None of their papers were scheduled in the same issue of the journal. Since B and G belonged to the same country the only possibility is that both of them belonged to the same country and since they published Journals in different months. G must have published in January, July, and October.

In statement 8, D, a Japanese author from the Manufacturing area, did not have a paper scheduled in the July issue. Hence he must have had the three issues in Jan, April, Oct. The other Japanese author H must have written in logistics.

The fourth Indian author G must have written a paper in Automation.

In January, one more paper needs to be publicized, one in April, 1 in July, and one in October.

In statement 5, E had papers scheduled in consecutive issues of the journal but C did not.

So, C must have written in Jan and October, and E in April and July.

In statement 9, C and H belonged to different areas. Hence C must be from Manufacturing and E must be from Logistics.

Author	Country	Area of Interest	Publications	Months of publication
A	India	Automation	3	Jan, April, July
B	India	Logistics	1	April
C	China	Manufacturing	2	Jan, October
D	Japan	Manufacturin	3	Jan, April,
E	China	Logistics	2	April, July
F	India	Logistics	1	October
G	India	Automation	3	Jan, July, October
H	Japan	Logistics	3	Jan, April, July

11. Number of papers written by B, C, E and G are: 1, 2, 2, 3

Hence, the correct option is (A).

12. Indian authors wrote a total of 3+1+1+3 = 8 papers

Hence, the correct answer is 8.

13. The publication of April has three authors from logistics. So, false

Hence, the correct option is (C).

14. Option (C) is false in the issue of April there were three authors from logistics department.

Hence, the correct option is (C).

15. There are no authors from Manufacturing in the July issue and hence option (D) is false.

Hence, the correct option is (D).

Ques (16-20): Since A, B, C are mutual strangers,(B, C)are strangers for A, (A, C) are strangers for B, (A, B) are strangers for C.

Since the total number of strangers + acquaintances + friends for any among the 7 is 6.

The number of friends for Amudha is 1, the number of friends for Gowtham is 1.

Using statement 3 Chandran and Gowtham are friends.

Using statement 2: Amudha, Dinesh, and Fani are Ezil's friends. Similarly, Ezil is a friend of Amudha, Dhinesh, and Fani.

Using statement 4: Every friend of Bharatan is an acquaintance of Amudha, and every acquaintance of Amudha is a friend of Bharatan, Hence the number of acquaintances of Bharatan is equal to the number of friends of Amudha.

Using statement 5: Every friend of Amudha is an acquaintance of Bharatan, and every acquaintance Bharatan is a friend of Amudha, Hence the number of acquaintances of Amudha is equal to the number of friends of Bharatan.

So, Bharatan has one friend, 1 Acquaintance, 4 strangers.

For Amudha we are yet to find a relationship with Dhinesh, Fani, and Gowtham. Any among the three can be the stranger for Amudha, considering the three different cases.

Case 1:

Considering Fani as an acquaintance of Amudha, then Dhinesh and Gowtham are strangers to Amudha.

Every acquaintance of Amudha is a friend of Bharathan and since the friend and acquaintance of Bharatan are known the strangers are found for Bharatan.

Fani is an acquaintance of Amudha, hence Amudha is an Acquaintance of Fani, Fani is a friend of Bharathan and hence Bharathan is a friend of Fani. But Fani has only one friend and Ezhil is already a friend of Fani.

So, this case fails.

	No. of friends	No. of acquaintances	No. of strangers
Amudha	1, (E)	1, (F)	4, (B, C, D, G)
Bharatan	1, (F)	1, (E)	4, (A, C, D, G)
Chandran	G	1	(A, B)
Dhinesh	E		2
Ezhil	A, D, F		1
Fani	1, (E)		
Gowtham	1, (C)	3	2

Case 2:

Considering Gowtham as an acquaintance of Amudha, then Dhinesh and Fani are strangers to Amudha.

Every acquaintance of Amudha is a friend of Bharathan and since the friend and acquaintance of Bharatan are known the strangers are found for Bharatan. Since Gowtham is a friend of Bharatan, Bharatan must be a friend of Gowtham. But Gowtham can only have one friend and it already mentioned that Chandran is a friend of Gowtham and hence this case fails.

	No. of friends	No. of acquaintances	No. of strangers
Amudha	1, (E)	1, (G)	4, (B, C, D, F)
Bharatan	1, (G)	1, (E)	4, (A, C, D, F)
Chandran	G	1	(A, B)
Dhinesh	E		2
Ezhil	A, D, F		1
Fani	1, (E)		
Gowtham	1, (C)	3	2

Case 3:

Considering Dhinesh as an acquaintance of Amudha, then Fani and Gowtham are strangers to Amudha.

Every acquaintance of Amudha is a friend of Bharathan and since the friend and acquaintance of Bharatan are known the strangers are found for Bharatan.

Since Fani, Gowtham are strangers to Amudha, Bharatan. Amudha, Bharatan are strangers to Fani, Gowtham.

The 2 strangers to Gowtham and his only friend are known. So, his three acquaintances are (Dhinesh, Ezhil, Fani).

So, Gowtham is an acquaintance of Dhinesh, Ezhil, and Fani.

Dhinesh is an acquaintance of Amudha and hence Amudha must be an acquaintance of Dhinesh.

Dhinesh is a friend of Bharatan and hence Bharatan is a friend of Dhinesh.

	No. of friends	No. of acquaintances	No. of strangers
Amudha	1, (E)	1, (D)	4, (B, C, F, G)
Bharatan	1, (D)	1, (E)	4, (A, C, F, G)

Chandran	G	1	(A, B)
Dhinesh	E, B	G, A	2
Ezhil	A, D, F	G	1
Fani	1, (E)	G	A, B
Gowtham	1, (C)	3, (D, E, F)	2, (A, B)

Ezhil is an acquaintance of Bharatan and hence Bharatan is an acquaintance of Ezhil. The only stranger to Ezhil who is left is Chandran. So, Ezhil is a stranger to Chandran.

The two strangers to Dhinesh who are left are Chandran and Fani. Chandran is a stranger to Dhinesh and hence Dhinesh is a stranger to Chandran.

The only acquaintance of Chandran who is left is Fani.

The remaining relationships with Fani are Dhinesh and Chandran. Dhinesh is a stranger to Fani and Chandran is an acquaintance of Fani.

	No. of friends	No. of acquaintances	No. of strangers
Amudha	1, (E)	1, (D)	4, (B, C, F, G)
Bharatan	1, (D)	1, (E)	4, (A, C, F, G)
Chandran	1, (G)	1, (F)	4, (A, B, E, D)
Dhinesh	2, (E, B)	2, (G, A)	2, (C, F)
Ezhil	3, (A, D, F)	2, (G, B)	1, (C)
Fani	1, (E)	2, (G, C)	3, (A, B, D)
Gowtham	1, (C)	3, (D, E, F)	2, (A, B)

16. Gowtham's Acquaintances are Dhinesh, Ezhil, Fani.

Hence, the correct option is (A).

17. In the given options Bharatan and Ezhil are Acauaintances, Fani and Gowtham are acquaintances.

Hence, the correct option is (D).

18. Dhinesh is an acquaintance of Amudha

Hence, the correct option is (A).

19. Fani is an acquaintance of Chandran

Hence, the correct option is (B).

20. Ezhil has a total of 3 friends.

Hence, the correct answer is 3.

Ques (21-25): Total sixes hit by all players in 3 years $= \dfrac{1482}{6} = 247$

Sixes hit in 2006 = 247 − 81 − 75 = 91

Sixes hit by Msdhoni in 2006 = 91 − 20 − 18 − 15 − 20 = 18

Total sixes hit by Msdhoni in 3 years $= \dfrac{372}{6} = 62$

Ratio of sixes hit by Msdhoni is 2007 and 2008 is 6 : 5. Let them be 6a and 5a respectively.

∴ 18 + 6a + 5a = 62

⇒ 11a = 44

⇒ a = 4

Sixes hit by Msdhoni in 2007 and 2008 is 24 and 20 respectively.

Total sixes hit by Dale steyn in 3 years $= \dfrac{354}{6} = 59$

Total sixes hit by Aaron finch in 3 years $= \dfrac{270}{6} = 45$

Sixes hit by Aaron finch in 2007 = 45 – 20 – 10 = 15

We tabulate the data known:

Players	2006	2007	2008	Total six	Run scored in six
Aaron finch	20	15	10	45	270
Gurkeeratsingh	18				
Dale steyn	15		59	354	
Parthivpatel	20	10			
MS Dhoni	18	24	20	62	372
Total	91	81	75	247	1482

21. From the table,

Required ratio = 18 : 24 : 20 = 9 : 12 : 10

∴ Required ratio is 9 : 12 : 10

Hence, the correct option is (C).

22. From the table,

Required ratio = 20 : 15 : 10 = 4 : 3 : 2

∴ Required ratio is 4 : 3 : 2

Hence, the correct option is (A).

23. Sixes hit by Dale Steyn in 2007 = 20

Sixes hit by Dale Steyn in 2008 = (59 – 15 – 20) = 24

Sixes hit by Gurkeeratsingh in 2007 = (81 – 15 – 20 – 10 – 24) = 12

Required ratio = 12 : 24 = 1 : 2

∴ Required ratio is 1 : 2

Hence, the correct option is (A).

24. Parthivpatel hits 15 sixes in 2008.

Runs scored by Parthipatel in sixes for 3 years = (20 + 10 + 15) × 6 = 270

Runs scored by Gurkeeretsingh in sixes for 3 years = 1482 – 270 – 354 – 270 – 372 = 216

Required difference = 354 – 216 = 138

∴ Required difference is 138.

Hence, the correct option is (B).

25. Difference in number of sixes hit by Aaron finch in 2006 and 2008 = 20 – 10 = 10

Difference in number of sixes hit by MS Dhoni in 2006 and 2008 = 20 – 18 = 2

Required ratio = 10 : 2 = 5 : 1

∴ Required ratio is 5 : 1.

Hence, the correct option is (D).

Ques (26-30): Given:

We will collect the data scattered in the question step by step.

Calculation:

Let the number of vaccines in 18-44 years old category in Jaipur be 5x and the number of vaccines in Above 44 years old category in Jodhpur be 2x.

The number of vaccines in 0-18 years old category in Jaipur is 25% of the total number of vaccines in Jaipur, then the number of vaccines in Jaipur in 0-18 years old category = 400 × 25%

Let the total number of vaccines in Udaipur be 'y' = The total number of vaccines in Jodhpur is also 'y'.

= 100

The number of vaccines in Above 44 years old category in Udaipur is 40% of the total vaccines in Udaipur = 300 × 40%

= 120

Categories (In ages)	City			Total
	Jaipur	Jodhpur	Udaipur	
0 – 18				330
18 - 44	5x			
Above 44		2x	120	
Total		y	y	1000

The total number of vaccines in 0-18 years old category in Jodhpur is 50% of the total number of vaccines in Jodhpur = 300 × 50%

= 150

The total number of vaccines in 18-44 years old category in jodhpur is 5% of the total vaccines in all the three cities = 1000 × 5%

= 50

Value of 2x = 300 – (150 + 50)

⇒ 2x = 100

⇒ 5x = 250

Categories (In ages)	City			Total
	Jaipur	Jodhpur	Udaipur	
0 – 18		150		330
18 - 44	250	50		
Above 44		100	120	
Total		y	y	1000

The total number of vaccines in Udaipur is 300 and the total number of vaccines in 0–18 years old category is 330 then, all data can be filed easily:

Categories (In ages)	City			Total
	Jaipur	Jodhpur	Udaipur	
0 – 18	100	150	80	330
18 - 44	250	50	100	400

Above 44	50	100	120	270
Total	**400**	**300**	**300**	**1000**

As per the table,

26. The total number of vaccines in Jaipur from all the three categories = 100 + 250 + 50

= 400

∴ The total number of vaccines in Jaipur from all three categories is 400.

Hence, the correct option is (C).

27. The maximum number of vaccines is 250 in Jaipur and the 18-44 years old category.

∴ The maximum number of vaccines is 250 in Jaipur and the 18-44 years old category.

Hence, the correct option is (A).

28. The number of vaccines in 0-18 years old in Jaipur = 100

The number of vaccines in 18-44 years old in Udaipur = 100

$$= \frac{100}{100} \times 100$$

= 100%

∴ The number of vaccines in 0-18 years old category in Jaipur is 100% of the number of vaccines in 18-44 years old category in Udaipur.

Hence, the correct option is (B).

29. The total number of vaccines in category 0–18 = 100 + 150 + 80

= 330

The total number of vaccines in category 18–44 = 250 + 50 + 100

= 400

The ratio of the total number of vaccines in 0–18 years old category to the total number of vaccines in 18-44 year old category = 330 : 400

= 33 : 40

∴ The ratio of the total number of vaccines in 0–18 years old category to the total number of vaccines in 18-44 year old category is 33 : 40.

Hence, the correct option is (B).

30. The number of vaccines in all the three cities in Above 44 years old category = 50 + 100 + 120

= 270

Total number of Cities = 3

The average number of vaccines in all the three cities in Above 44 years old category $= \dfrac{270}{3}$

= 90

∴ The average number of vaccines in all the three cities in Above 44 years old category is 90.

Hence, the correct option is (C).

Ques (31-34): It is given that the base exchange rates of A, B and C with respect to L are in the ratio 100:120:1. Let us assume that base exchange rates are '100a', '120a' and 'a' in that order.

It is given that the buying exchange rates of each of A, B, and C with respect to L are 5% below the corresponding base exchange rates. Therefore, we can say that the buying exchange rates are 95a, 114a, 0.95a.

It is given that the selling exchange rates of each of A, B, and C with respect to L are 10% above their corresponding base exchange rates. Therefore, we can say that the selling exchange rates are 110a, 132a, 1.1a.

We know about the opening and closing units in stock for each currency. Let us draw the table accordingly.

Currency	Buying rate	Base rate	Selling rate	No. of units			
				Opening stock	Buy	Sell	Closing stock
A	95a	100a	110a	250			3300
B	114a	120a	132a	4800			4800
C	0.95	A		48000			51000

Let 'p', 'q' and 'r' be the number of units of currency A, B and C bought by the outlet on that day.

Then, we can say that the outlet sold 'p - 800', 'q' and 'r-3000' units of currency A, B and C respectively.

Currency	Buying rate	Base rate	Selling rate	No. of units			
				Opening stock	Buy	Sell	Closing stock
A	95a	100a	110a	250	p	p-800	3300
B	114a	120a	132a	4800	q	Q	4800
C	0.95	a	1.1a	48000	r	r-3000	51000

It is given that the amount of L used by the outlet to buy C equals the amount of L it received by selling C.

⇒ 0.95a×r = 1.1a×(r - 3000)

⇒ 0.15r = 3300

⇒ r = 22000

It is also given that the amounts of L used by the outlet to buy A and B are in the ratio 5 : 3.

$$\Rightarrow \frac{p \times 95a}{q \times 114a} = \frac{5}{3}$$

$$\Rightarrow p = 2q$$

Also, the amounts of L the outlet received from the sales of A and B are in the ratio 5:9.

$$\Rightarrow \frac{(p-800)\times 110a}{q\times 132a} = \frac{5}{9}$$

$$\Rightarrow \frac{(2q-800)\times 110a}{q\times 132a} = \frac{5}{9}$$

$\Rightarrow q = 600$

Therefore, p = 2q = 2×600 = 1200

It is given that the outlet received 88000 units of L by selling A during the day.

$\Rightarrow$ (p-800)×110a = 88000

$\Rightarrow$ (1200-800)×110a = 88000

$\Rightarrow$ 44000a = 88000

$\Rightarrow$ a = 2

We can fill the entire table and answer all the questions.

Curren cy	Buyi ng rate	Bas e rat e	Selli ng rate	Openi ng stock	Buy	Sell	Closi ng stock
				No. of units			
A	190	200	220	2500	120 0	400	330
B	228	240	264	4800	600	600	4800
C	1.9	2	2.2	48000	220 00	190 00	5100 0

31. From the table we can see that the currency outlet bought 1200 units of A.

Hence, the correct answer is 1200.

32. From the table we can see that the currency outlet sold 19000 units of currency C.

Hence, the correct option is (B).

33. From the table we can see that the base exchange rate of currency B with respect to currency L was 240.

Hence, the correct answer is 240.

34. From the table we can see that the buying exchange rate of currency C with respect to currency L was 1.9.

Hence, the correct option is (D).

35. The patients in

Vial A: 9,10,11,12,13,14,15,16

Vial B: 1,2,3,4,5,6,7,8

Vial C: 5,6,7,8,13,14,15,16

Vial D: 1,2,3,4,9,10,11,12

Vial E: 3,4,7,8,11,12,15,16

Vial F: 1,2,5,6,9,10,13,14

Vial G: 2,4,6,8,10,12,14,16

Vial H: 1,3,5,7,9,11,13,15

If vial C tests positive and vials A, E and H test negative then Patient 6 must have disease as all other patients in Vial C expect patient 6 are present in at least one of A, E, H.

Hence, the correct option is (C).

36. The patients in:

Vial A: 9,10,11,12,13,14,15,16

Vial B: 1,2,3,4,5,6,7,8

Vial C: 5,6,7,8,13,14,15,16

Vial D: 1,2,3,4,9,10,11,12

Vial E: 3,4,7,8,11,12,15,16

Vial F: 1,2,5,6,9,10,13,14

Vial G: 2,4,6,8,10,12,14,16

Vial H: 1,3,5,7,9,11,13,15

Suppose vial A tests positive and vials D and G test negative then the patient who tested positive must be one of patient 13 or 15.

Patient 13 or 15 are not present in vial B. So, A is not the answer.

Both patients present in vial C. Even if tested positive or negative we can't know who has got the disease. So, C is not the answer.

Both patients present in vial H. Even if tested positive or negative we can't know who has got the disease. So, H is not the answer.

Only patient 15 is present in vial E, if tested positive then patient 15 has the disease else patient 13 as disease.

Hence, the correct option is (B).

37. The patients in:

Vial A: 9,10,11,12,13,14,15,16

Vial B: 1,2,3,4,5,6,7,8

Vial C: 5,6,7,8,13,14,15,16

Vial D: 1,2,3,4,9,10,11,12

Vial E: 3,4,7,8,11,12,15,16

Vial F: 1,2,5,6,9,10,13,14

Vial G: 2,4,6,8,10,12,14,16

Vial H: 1,3,5,7,9,11,13,15

If vials C and D negative then no patient could test negative. Hence A is correct answer.

Hence, the correct option is (A).

38. Let one of the patients, patient 1 or patient 16 has the disease and his blood is mixed with other them all 8 vials will tests positive.

8 has to be one of the answers.

If patient 2 and patients 16's blood is mixed of one of them has the disease then 7 of the 8 vials will test positive. So 7 has to be there in the option.

If 1 has the disease and 1, 7 are mixed then 6 out the 8 vials tests positive.

IF 1 has the disease and 1,9 are mixed then 5 of the 8 vials tests positive,

Now, let us assume that patient 1 has the disease if his blood is not mixed, then 4 vials will definitely show positive.

Hence, the correct option is (C).

Ques (39-42): Group A:

Since Aruna played 3 games if she belongs to rank 2 or rank 3 in her group she must have reached the semifinals and lost in the semifinals. But for this case, she must play against rank 1 and rank 3 in her group. But she did not play against Arif from her group.

So Aruna was ranked 1 in her group, Among Azul and Arif one of them was ranked 2 and the other was ranked 3. Azul defeated Arif in the first round and in the second round lost to Aruna. Aruna played her first round with Azul and won the round and played against the winner from group B and defeated them and moved to the finals.

Group B:

Brij did not play against Brinda. Biju played three games, Brij and Brinda played one game each.

Since Brij and Brinda played only one game each one of them was ranked 1 and the other was ranked 2 and 3. Brij did not play against Brinda. We are aware that Aruna reached finals and hence the person from Group B did not reach the finals. Biju played three games and hence must have played with Brij/Brinda in the first round and won the round. Plays with Brij/ Brinda and wins the second round. Plays with Aruna and loses the third round.

Group A	Group B
Aruna vs Brij	
Azul vs Aruna	Brij vs Brinda/Biju
Azul vs Arif	Brij vs Brinda/Biju

Group C:

Chitra played 2 matches and Chetan played 2 matches. For Chitra to play 2 matches if she is rank 2 or rank 3 in her group. She must at least reach the semifinals. But in this case, Chetan will be defeated in his first round. So Chitra must be ranked 1 in her group and Chetan must be ranked 2 or rank 3 in his group. He defeats Chhavi in his first round and loses to Chitra in his second round. Chitra plays Chetan in her first round, wins over the winner of group D in her second round, and loses in the final against Aruna as per condition 1.

Group D:

The person from Group D did not reach the finals because Chitra reached the finals. In order for Dipen to play 3 matches before his finals. Dipen must be ranked 2 or rank 3 in his group and plays Deb and Donna in the first two rounds in any order and wins over both of them. Dipen loses to Chitra in his third round.

Group C	Group D
Aruna vs Dipen	

Chetan vs Chitra	Dipen vs Deb/Donna
Chetan vs Chitra	Dipen vs Deb/ Donna

Aruna plays Chitra in the finals and wins the final round.

39. Dipen was ranked 2 or 3 in his group

Hence, the correct option is (A).

40. Chitra and Dipen played in the semifinals

Hence, the correct option is (D).

41. Aruna is the winner.

Hence, the correct option is (B).

42. Brij was the player from group B who played Chitra. Aruna played in finals, Chetan in round 2, and Dipen in semi finals

Hence, the correct option is (D).

Ques (43-46): Using condition 1:

Ravi had a total of 21 points in timeliness. 3 of the four customers among Atal, Bihari, Chirag, and Deepak gave him the same ratings. Atal gave the highest rating in timeliness in comparison with Bihari and Chirag. Hence he must have given the distinct rating.

Using condition 2:

The possibilities are A - 9, B - 4, C - 4, D - 4.

A - 6, B - 5, C - 5, D - 5.

Ravi received a total of 29 points in the Packaging and for this, the possibility of the four scores are (5, 7, 8, 9) awarded by the four customers.

In Hygiene the sum of the ratings awarded was 26. This could possibly be awarded by considering the following cases:

A-(4,6,7,9) , B-(5,6,7,8), C-(4,5,8,9)

Using condition 4: Bihari gave the highest rating in packaging and thus Bihari must have given a 9 rating in the packaging.

Chirag gave the highest rating in Hygiene. In condition 3 it was mentioned that Chirag gave the same points for packaging and hygiene. Since 9 was rated by Bihari packaging it cannot be awarded by Chirag in packaging and hygiene. Since Chirag was awarded the highest in Hygiene. He must award 8 points in Hygiene and Packaging.

So, of the three possibilities among A, B, and C for Hygiene only B is the possible case with 8 as the maximum score.

In condition 5 it was mentioned that everyone awarded Ravi between 5 and 7 in Behaviour. Unique maximum and minimum ratings in this parameter were given by Atal and Deepak respectively.

So, Atal must have awarded 7, Deepak 6, Bihari, and Chirag 6 each in Behaviour.

The two possible cases are:

Case 1:

	Behaviour	Packaging	Hygiene	Timeliness

Atal	7			9
Bihari	6	9		4
Chirag	6	8	8	4
Deepak	5			4

Case 2:

	Behaviour	Packaging	Hygiene	Timeliness
Atal	7			6
Bihari	6	9		5
Chirag	6	8	8	5
Deepak	5			5

The ratings awarded by Atal and Deepak in Packaging are among 5 and 7.

The ratings awarded by Atal, Bihari, Deepak are among 5, 6 and 7.

Atal individual ranking in Packaging and Hygiene are the same. The same is true for Deepak.

Since Atal and Deepak can give the ranking among 3 and 4 in Packaging as Bihari is first and Chirag is second in this parameter.

They can rank 3 or 4 in the Hygiene parameter also. Hence Bihari must rate 7 points in Hygiene.

In both the possibilities Bihari and Chirag award a total of 26 points. Hence he wins 40 because the total ratings are greater than 25 received from Bihari and Chirag.

Since he gets a total of 120 in bonuses and tips. He must have 80 from Atal and Deepak.

This is possible if he gets a tip of 30 ad 50 from them respectively.

In case 1 irrespective of Atal standing at rank 3 or rank 4 in Hygiene and Packaging Atal total rating is greater than 25 which implies Ravi gets a tip from Atal but this is not a possible case because Ravi needs a total of Rs 80 from Atal and Deepak. From Atal if he gets Rs 20 as a bonus he cannot get a total of Rs 120 and hence this case fails.

So, case 1 fails.

In case 2 there are two possibilities:

Atal ranking 3 in both the parameters and Deepak 4th. Atal ranking 4th in both the parameters and Deepak 3rd

In the case where Atal ranks 3rd in Packaging and Hygiene the total score is 26 and is not a feasible case.

Case 2A:

	Behaviour	Packaging	Hygiene	Timeliness
Atal	7	7	6	6
Bihari	6	9	7	5
Chirag	6	8	8	5
Deepak	5	5	5	5

Case 2B:

	Behaviour	Packaging	Hygiene	Timeliness
Atal	7	5	5	6
Bihari	6	9	7	5
Chirag	6	8	8	5

Deepak	5	7	6	5

Case - 2A fails because Atal's total rating is greater than 25 which should not be the case.

43. The minimum rating awarded is 5.

Hence, the correct answer is 5.

44. Bihari and Chirag has given the highest ratings.

Hence, the correct option is (C).

45. Atal has given a rating of 6 in timeliness

Hence, the correct answer is 6.

46. Among Atal and Deepak, one of them gives a tip of 30 and the other gives a tip of 50. So, 30 or 50 any case is possible

Hence, the correct option is (B).

Ques (47-50): According to the given information,

There are eight company employees - Girish, Sourav, Vestal, Richa, Saxena, Prashant, Vivek, and Sumit.

Different Positions in company - Managing Director (MD), Executive Director (ED), Chief General Manager (CGM), General Manager (GM), Assistant General Manager (AGM), Divisional Manager (DM), Marketing Officer (Mo), and Clerk.

1) Saxena is senior to only three-person.

2) Prashant is junior to Saxena.

3) Prashant is not the most junior person.

So, two possible cases are here.

Positions	Employees case 1	Employees case 2
MD		
ED		
CGM		
GM		
AGM	Saxena	Saxena
DM	Prashant	
Mo		Prashant
Clerk		

4) Sourav is an Executive Director.

5) Vestal is senior to Divisional Manager but junior to Managing Director.

So, Again each case will have one subcases.

Positions	Employees case 1 - A	Employees case 1 - B	Employees case 2- A	Employees case 2 - B
MD				
ED	Sourav	Sourav	Sourav	Sourav
CGM	Vestal		Vestal	
GM		Vestal		Vestal
AGM	Saxena	Saxena	Saxena	Saxena
DM	Prashant	Prashant		
Mo			Prashant	Prashant

Clerk				

6) Vivek is just one position senior to Sumit. Here case 2 - A and case 2 - B gets eliminated because Vivek and Sumit can not be placed successively.

7) Richa is neither General Manager nor Managing Director. Here case 1 - A gets eliminated.

8) Girish is not a junior to Vestal.

Positions	Employees case 1 - B
MD	Girish
ED	Sourav
CGM	Richa
GM	Vestal
AGM	Saxena
DM	Prashant
Mo	Vivek
CLERK	Sumit

47. This will be our final arrangement.

So, Sumit is the correct answer.

Hence, the correct option is (D).

48. This will be our final arrangement.

So, Prashant is the correct answer.

Hence, the correct option is (A).

49. This will be our final arrangement.

So, AGM is the correct answer.

Hence, the correct option is (C).

50. This will be our final arrangement.

So, Prashant does not belong to that Group. Because all other people are in sequence from top.

Hence, the correct option is (D).

Ques (51-55): Given:

Total number of employee in bank = 300

140 of employee speak fluently in Hindi

104 of employee speak fluently in English

126 of employee speak fluently in Punjabi

30 speak fluently in English and Punjabi both languages

Who speak fluently in English and Punjabi both languages is 25% more than employee who fluent in both English and Hindi

Only 26 employee speak fluent in Punjabi and Hindi both.

Concept:

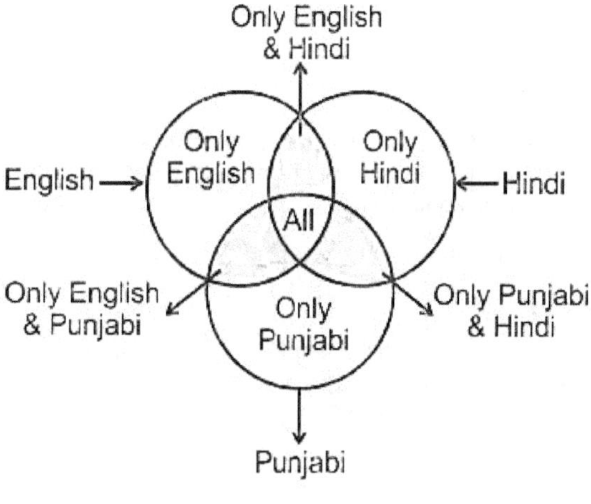

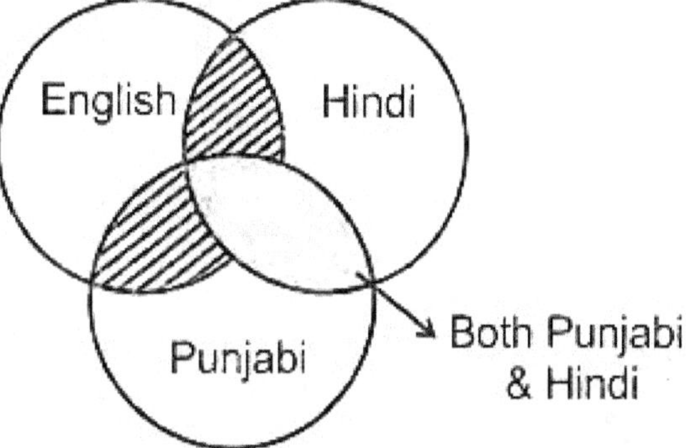

In Venn diagram, first try to find value of all which is here number of employee who speak fluently in all (Hindi, Punjabi, English) languages.

Employee fluent in speaking of all language = overall total employee – total employee fluent speak in (English + Punjabi + Hindi) + number of employee who speak fluently any of two language.

Calculation:

Let employee speak fluently in Hindi and English both = x employee

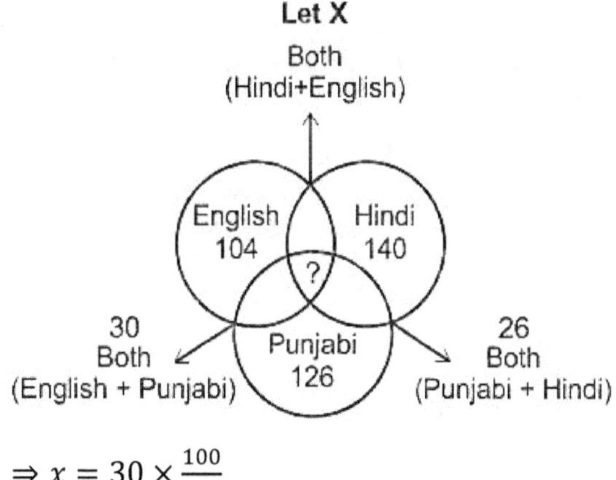

$$\Rightarrow x = 30 \times \frac{100}{125}$$

$\Rightarrow$ x = 24 employees

Employee fluent in speaking of all language = 300 – 104 – 140 – 126 + 30 + 24 + 26

= 10 employees

51. Only fluent in English = total of employee fluent in English – employee fluent in English and Hindi both – employee fluent in English and Punjabi both + fluent in all

Only fluent in English = 104 – 30 – 24 + 10

= 60 employee

Only fluent in Punjabi = total of employee fluent in Punjabi – employee fluent in English and Punjabi both – employee fluent in Hindi and Punjabi both + fluent in all

Only fluent in Punjabi = 126 – 30 – 26 + 10

= 80 employee

Employees who fluent only in English : Employees who fluent only in Punjabi = 60 : 80

= 3 : 4

∴ Ratio of employees who fluent only in English to only in Punjabi is 3 : 4.

Hence, the correct option is (C).

52. Only fluent in English = total of employee fluent in English – employee fluent in English and Hindi both – employee fluent in English and Punjabi both + fluent in all

Only fluent in English = 104 – 30 – 24 + 10

= 60 employee

Only fluent in Hindi = total of employee fluent in Hindi – employee fluent in English and Hindi both – employee fluent in Hindi and Punjabi both + fluent in all

Only fluent in Hindi = 140 – 26 – 24 + 10

= 100 employee

Fluent employee only in English is what percent less than who fluent only in Hindi $= \dfrac{100-60}{100} \times 100$

= 40%

∴ Employee who fluent only in English is 40% less than who fluent only in Hindi.

Hence, the correct option is (D).

53. Only fluent in English = total of employee fluent in English – employee fluent in English and Hindi both – employee fluent in English and Punjabi both + fluent in all

Only fluent in English = 104 – 30 – 24 + 10

= 60 employee

Fluent only in Hindi = total of employee fluent in Hindi – employee fluent in English and Hindi both – employee fluent in Hindi and Punjabi both + fluent in all

Fluent only in Hindi = 140 – 26 – 24 + 10

= 100 employee

Fluent only in Punjabi = total of employee fluent in Punjabi – employee fluent in Punjabi and Hindi both – employee fluent in English and Punjabi both + fluent in all

Fluent only in Punjabi = 126 – 30 – 26 + 10

= 80 employee

Employee fluent in at least two of languages = 300 – 60 – 80 – 100

= 60 employees

∴ 60 employees fluent in at least of two language.

Hence, the correct option is (C).

54. $\dfrac{1}{30}$ of 300 employee join to bank newly who fluent in all of three language

= 10 employee

After join, total number of employee fluent in English = 104 + 10

= 114 employee

After join, total number of employee fluent in Punjabi = 126 + 10

= 136 employee

After join, total number of employee fluent in Hindi = 140 + 10

= 150

New ratio of fluent in (English : Punjabi : Hindi) after join of new employee = 114 : 136 : 150 = 57 : 68 : 75

∴ New ratio of fluent in (English : Punjabi : Hindi) after join of new employee is 57 : 68 : 75.

Hence, the correct option is (D).

55. Fluent only in single language = Fluent only in English + Fluent only in Hindi + Fluent only in Punjabi

Fluent only in English = total of employee fluent in English – employee fluent in English and Punjabi both – employee fluent in Hindi and English both + fluent in all

Fluent only in English = 104 – 30 – 24 + 10

= 60 employees

Fluent only in Hindi = total of employee fluent in Hindi – employee fluent in English and Hindi both – employee fluent in Hindi and Punjabi both + fluent in all

Fluent only in Hindi = 140 – 26 – 24 + 10

= 100 employees

Fluent only in Punjabi = total of employee fluent in Punjabi – employee fluent in Punjabi and Hindi both – employee fluent in English and Punjabi both + fluent in all

Fluent only in Punjabi = 126 – 30 – 26 + 10

= 80 employees

Fluent only in single language = 60 + 80 + 100

= 240 employees

∴ 240 employees fluent only in single language.

Hence, the correct option is (D).

56. Number of SUV cars deal by Hyundai $= \dfrac{40}{100} \times 110000 = 44,000$

Number of diesel MUV cars deal by Hyundai = 24,000

Ratio of petrol SUV cars to diesel MUV cars deal by Hyundai = 3 : 4

Petrol SUV cars deal by Hyundai $= \dfrac{3}{4} \times 24000 = 18,000$

Diesel SUV cars deal by Hyundai = 44000 − 18000 = 26,000

Number of petrol SUV cars deal by Toyota = 14,000

Total number of cars deal by Toyota = 70,000

Number of SUV cars deal by Toyota $= \dfrac{50}{100} \times 70000 = 35,000$

Number of diesel SUV cars deal by Toyota = 35000 − 14000 = 21,000

Number of diesel SUV cars deal by Hyundai and Toyota together = 26000 + 21000 = 47,000

∴ Number of diesel SUV cars deal by Hyundai and Toyota together is 47,000.

Hence, the correct option is (C).

57. Total SUV cars deal by Tata motors $= \dfrac{60}{100} \times 90000 = 54,000$

Total MUV cars deal by Tata motors $= \dfrac{20}{100} \times 90000 = 18,000$

Total SUV cars deal by Maruti suzuki $= \dfrac{40}{100} \times 120000 = 48,000$

Total MUV cars deal by Maruti suzuki $= \dfrac{40}{100} \times 120000 = 48,000$

Total MUV cars deal by Ford $= \dfrac{30}{100} \times 100000 = 30,000$

Total diesel MUV cars deal by Ford = (Total MUV cars deal by Ford − Total petrol MUV cars deal by Ford)

Total diesel MUV cars deal by Ford = 30000 − 20000 = 10,000

Total petrol SUV cars deal by Ford $= \dfrac{5}{1} \times 10000 = 50,000$

Total cars deal by Tata motors = (Total SUV cars deal by Tata motors) + (Total MUV cars deal by Tata motors) + (Total XUV cars deal by Tata motors)

Total XUV cars deal by Tata motors = 90000 − (54000 + 18000) = 18,000

Total cars deal by Maruti suzuki = (Total SUV cars deal by Maruti suzuki) + (Total MUV cars deal by Maruti suzuki) + (Total XUV cars deal by Maruti suzuki)

Total XUV cars deal by Maruti suzuki = 120000 − (48000 + 48000) = 24,000

Total XUV cars deal by Tata motors and Maruti suzuki together = 24000 + 18000 = 42,000

Let total number of XUV cars deal by Tata motors and Maruti suzuki together is x% of total SUV petrol cars deal by Ford

$x\% = \dfrac{42000}{50000} \times 100 = 84$

∴ Total number of XUV cars deal by Tata motors and Maruti suzuki together is 84% of total SUV petrol cars deal by Ford.

Hence, the correct option is (B).

58. Total SUV cars deal by Mahindra $= \dfrac{45}{100} \times 80000 = 36,000$

Total SUV cars deal by Tata motors $= \dfrac{60}{100} \times 90000 = 54,000$

Total petrol SUV cars deal by Mahindra = (Total SUV cars deal by Mahindra − Total diesel SUV cars deal by Mahindra)

Total petrol SUV cars deal by Mahindra = (36000 − 12000) = 24,000

Total petrol SUV cars deal by Tata motors = (Total SUV cars deal by Tata motors − Total diesel SUV cars deal by Tata motors)

Total petrol SUV cars deal by Tata motors = (54000 − 14000) = 40,000

Ratio of petrol SUV deal by Tata motors to Mahindra = 40000 : 24000

= 5 : 3

∴ Ratio of petrol SUV deal by Tata motors to Mahindra is 5 : 3.

Hence, the correct option is (D).

59. Number of SUV cars deal by Tata motors $= \dfrac{60}{100} \times 90000 = 54,000$

Number of MUV cars deal by Tata motors $= \dfrac{20}{100} \times 90000 = 18,000$

Number of SUV cars deal by Maruti suzuki $= \dfrac{40}{100} \times 120000 = 48,000$

Number of MUV cars deal by Maruti suzuki $= \dfrac{40}{100} \times 120000 = 48,000$

Ratio of petrol SUV cars to diesel MUV cars deal by Tata motors = 8x : 3x

Ratio of petrol SUV cars to diesel MUV cars deal by Maruti suzuki = 11y : 6y

Number of diesel MUV cars deal by Tata motors/Number of diesel MUV cars deal by Maruti suzuki $= \dfrac{5a}{4a}$

Here, a represent multiple value or coefficient

$\Rightarrow \dfrac{3x}{6y} = \dfrac{5a}{4a}$

$\Rightarrow \dfrac{x}{y} = \dfrac{5a}{2a}$

Now, Ratio of petrol SUV cars to diesel MUV cars deal by Tata motors = 8 × 5a : 3 × 5a

= 40a : 15a

Ratio of petrol SUV cars to diesel MUV cars deal by Maruti suzuki = 11 × 2a : 6 × 2a

= 22a : 12a

(Petrol SUV cars deal by Tata motors) : (Diesel MUV cars deal by Tata motors) : (Petrol SUV cars deal by Maruti Suzuki) : (Diesel MUV cars deal by Maruti Suzuki) = 40a : 15a : 22a : 12a

Number of petrol SUV cars deal by Tata motors is 18,000 more than the petrol SUV cars deal by Maruti Suzuki

(40 − 22)a =18000

⇒ a = 1000

Number of petrol SUV cars deal by Tata motors = 40 × 1000 = 40,000

Number of diesel MUV cars deal by Tata motors = 15 × 1000 = 15,000

Number of petrol SUV cars deal by Maruti Suzuki = 22 × 1000 = 22,000

Number of diesel MUV cars deal by Maruti Suzuki = 12 × 1000 = 12,000

Number of diesel SUV cars deal by Tata motors = (Total number of SUV cars deal by Tata motors) − (Number of petrol SUV cars deal by Tata motors)

Number of diesel SUV cars deal by Tata motors = 54000 − 40000 = 14,000

Number of diesel SUV cars deal by Maruti suzuki = (Total number of SUV cars deal by Maruti suzuki) − (Number of petrol SUV cars deal by Maruti Suzuki)

Number of diesel SUV cars deal by Maruti suzuki = 48000 − 22000 = 26,000

Total diesel cars deal by Tata motors and Maruti suzuki = (26000 + 14000 + 12000 + 15000)

= 67,000

∴ Total diesel cars deal by Tata motors and Maruti suzuki is 67,000.

Hence, the correct option is (D).

60. Number of MUV cars deal by Hyundai $= \dfrac{30}{100} \times 110000 = 33,000$

Number of MUV cars deal by Toyota $= \dfrac{40}{100} \times 70000 = 28,000$

Number of MUV cars deal by Mahindra $= \dfrac{30}{100} \times 80000 = 24,000$

Number of MUV cars deal by Tata motors $= \dfrac{20}{100} \times 90000 = 18,000$

Number of MUV cars deal by Maruti suzuki $= \dfrac{40}{100} \times 120000 = 48,000$

Number of MUV cars deal by F $= \dfrac{30}{100} \times 100000 = 30,000$

Total MUV cars deal by all companies = (33000 + 28000 + 24000 + 18000 + 48000 + 30000) = 1,81,000

Percentage of XUV cars deal by Hyundai = 100 − (40 + 30) = 30%

Number of XUV cars deal by Hyundai $= \dfrac{30}{100} \times 110000 = 33,000$

Percentage of XUV cars deal by Toyota = 100 − (50 + 40) = 10%

Number of XUV cars deal by Toyota $= \dfrac{10}{100} \times 70000 = 7,000$

Percentage of XUV cars deal by Mahindra = 100 − (45+ 30) = 25%

Number of XUV cars deal by Mahindra $= \dfrac{25}{100} \times 80000 = 20,000$

Percentage of XUV cars deal by Tata motors = 100 − (60 + 20) = 20%

Number of XUV cars deal by Tata motors $= \dfrac{20}{100} \times 90000 = 18,000$

Percentage of XUV cars deal by Maruti suzuki = 100 − (40 + 40) = 20%

Number of XUV cars deal by Maruti suzuki $= \dfrac{20}{100} \times 120000 = 24,000$

Percentage of XUV cars deal by Ford = 100 − (60 + 30) = 10%

Number of XUV cars deal by Ford $= \dfrac{10}{100} \times 100000 = 10,000$

Total number of XUV cars deal by all companies = (33000 + 7000 + 20000 + 18000 + 24000 +10000) = 1,12,000

Let, Total number of XUV cars deal by all companies approximately x% of the total number of MUV cars deal by all companies

$$x\% = \frac{112000}{181000} \times 100 = 62\%$$

∴ Total number of XUV cars deal by all companies approximately 62% of the total number of MUV cars deal by all companies.

Hence, the correct option is (D).

Ques (1-4):Directions : Study the following table and bar chart carefully and answer the questions given beside.

Five teams - Green, Blue, Red, Yellow and White participate in a relay race of 400 m. In the relay race first 200 m are run by Starter and next 200 m are run by Finisher, the finisher starts running when the baton is passed on to him by the starter, after completing the first 200 m.The table below shows the players of each team

Team	Starter	Finisher
Green	J	K
Blue	M	N
Yellow	P	Q
Red	S	T
White	U	V

The chart given below shows the time the finisher of each team would take to complete the 400 m race alone as a percent of the time taken by his team when both starter and finisher are running their respective distance.

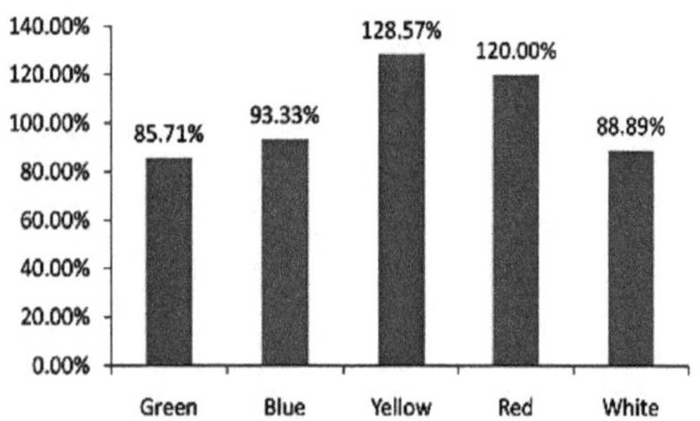

Team Blue takes 28.57% less time than team Green. The time taken by team Yellow is 200% of time taken by team Red. Time taken by team blue is 25% less that by team Red. Team White takes 12.5% more time than team yellow.

Q.1 The speed of starter of team Green is what percent of the speed of the finisher of team Red?

A. 75%   **B.** 100%
C. 125%   **D.** 114.28%

Q.2 The distance between P and Q when U reaches halfway his course is what percent of the distance between U and V when Q finishes the race?

A. 25%   **B.** 12.56%   **C.** 16.67%   **D.** 20%

Q.3 Team Red runs in the reverse direction, starts from the finish line and ends at the starting line. What will be the distance between T and N when J passes the baton to K?

A. $172\frac{11}{19}m$ **B.** $180\frac{20}{21}m$ **C.** $180\frac{17}{21}m$ **D.** $175m$

Q.4 S and K, M and V, and U and T are three pairs of players who replaced each other from their respective positions in their teams. The names of the team remain the same. The distance between K and U when Team green finishes the race, is what percent of the distance between T and M when baton is passed from starter to finisher in team Red?

A. 123.33%   **B.** 125.33%
C. 176%   **D.** 160.%

Q.5 Direction: Study the following table and bar chart carefully and answer the questions given below.

Two cities, namely Agra and Meerut, were tested for COVID-19 cases in three months March, April, and May.

 Both the cities have Urban and Rural areas, and the tests were conducted in both areas.

Outcomes of the tests were either positive or negative.

Month	Number of Tests in both the cities together	Negative outcomes out of total number of tests in both the cities
March	100	30%
April	200	35%
May	360	50%

The column chart below shows some other information about the tests.

P = Number of positive cases in Agra

Q = Number of negative cases in Meerut

R = Number of tests conducted in Urban area of Agra

S = Number of tests conducted in Urban area of Meerut.

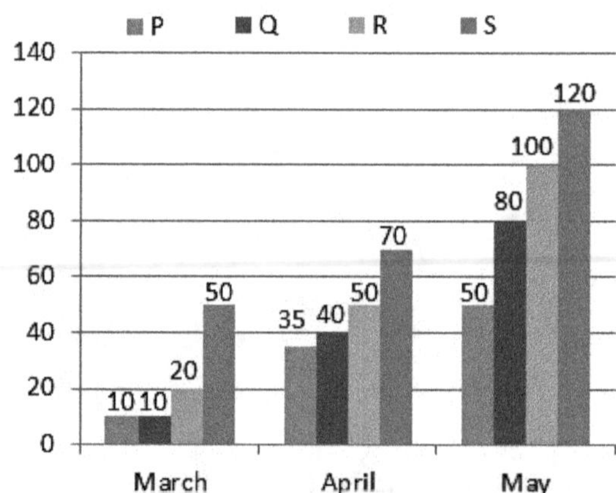

In a given month, it is also known that number of tests found negative in rural area is equal to the number of tests found negative in urban area (True for both the cities)

Find the difference between the total number of positive cases in Urban and Rural areas of Meerut in the three months together.

Find the difference between the total number of positive cases in Urban and Rural areas of Meerut in the three months together.

A. 55 **B.** 65 **C.** 70 **D.** 75

Ques (6-8):Direction: Study the following table and bar chart carefully and answer the questions given below.

Two cities, namely Agra and Meerut, were tested for COVID-19 cases in three months March, April, and May.

Both the cities have Urban and Rural areas, and the tests were conducted in both areas.

Outcomes of the tests were either positive or negative.

Month	Number of Tests in both the cities together	Negative outcomes out of total number of tests in both the cities
March	100	30%
April	200	35%
May	360	50%

The column chart below shows some other information about the tests.

P = Number of positive cases in Agra

Q = Number of negative cases in Meerut

R = Number of tests conducted in Urban area of Agra

S = Number of tests conducted in Urban area of Meerut.

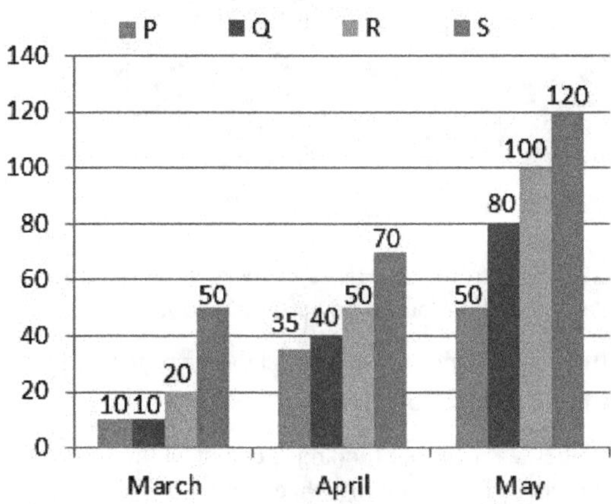

In a given month, it is also known that number of tests found negative in rural area is equal to the number of tests found negative in urban area (True for both the cities)

Find the difference between the total number of positive cases in Urban and Rural areas of Meerut in the three months together.

Q.6 Find the number of positive cases in April in the two cities together is what percent more than the number of negative cases in the two cities in March?

A. 120 **B.** 333.33 **C.** 233.33 **D.** 133.33

Q.7 In which case there was no positive test result:

A. Urban area of Meerut in March

B. Rural area of Meerut in all the three months

C. Rural area of Agra in May

D. Urban area of Agra in all the three months

Q.8 Find the average number of negative cases in the three months in Agra.

A. 50 **B.** 60 **C.** 120 **D.** 150

Ques (9-12):Direction: Study the following bar and table chart carefully and answer the questions given below.

A new kind of rocket is produced by ISRO. It uses many small propellers to push the weight. A rocket can have many propellers and each propels the weight one by one. Means, one propeller pushes the rocket up for some time, and when it is run out of fuel, the next propeller starts, and so on.

In an experimental test, five similar rockets are tested. Each of them can have different number of propellers.

It is not necessary that all the propellers will be consumed while the test. Those which will not be consumed, are called unused, will be reused for a new rocket.

It might be possible that not all the propellers will work properly, such propellers are called defected. Some of the defected propellers can be improved to be used for new rocket.

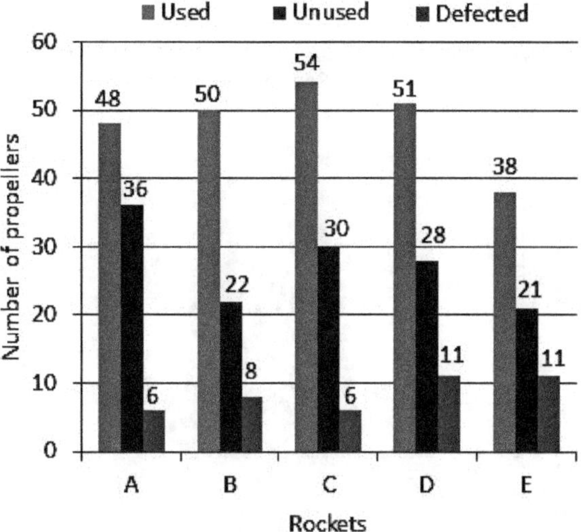

All propellers are identical, but the height they can push the weight of the rocket varies with the altitude above the earth surface.

Table gives information about the same.

Range of altitude above Earth Surface	Height pushed by one propeller
0– 10 km	0.4 km
10– 16 km	0.6 km
16– 20 km	1 km
above 20 km	1.2 km

Q.9 Find the average number of propellers in the five rockets that were fittedin the rockets for the experimental test.

A. 80   **B.** 84   **C.** 86   **D.** 88

Q.10 If 66.66% of the defected propellers are improved to be used again, how many rockets can be made again if all the unused propellers are used along with improved propellers if each rocket is fitted with 55 propellers?

A. 2   **B.** 3   **C.** 4   **D.** 5

Q.11 Find the maximum height that a rocket will go among the five rockets.

A. 20 km   **B.** 18 km   **C.** 32 km   **D.** 38 km

Q.12 A propeller pushes a rocket for 0.006 minutes. Find the average speed of rocket E before it starts falling down towards the earth from the maximum height.

A. $5000 kmph$ **B.** $500 kmph$
C. $4000 kmph$ **D.** $10000 kmph$

Ques (13-16): To test people for COVID- 19, a city was divided into six zones. Name of the zones was on the name of colours – Skyblue Zone, Yellow Zone, Green Zone, Red Zone, Blue Zone, and Black Zone as shown below in the bubble chart.

The bubble chart below shows the number of tests that were conducted for COVID- 19 and the number of positive outcomes in various zones.

The number of positive outcomes is shown on each bubble for the corresponding zone.

The numbers of tests are represented by small coloured circles (Blue, Green, Yellow, Skyblue, Red and Black) given on the x-axis.

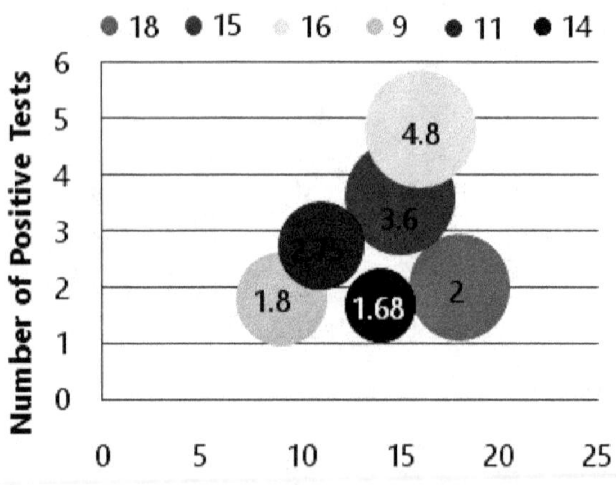

Q.13 Find what percent of people were found positive out of those who were tested in Yellow zone?

A. 10   **B.** 16   **C.** 3   **D.** 30

Q.14 Find the average number of people that were tested in Green Zone, Skyblue Zone, Red Zone and Black Zone.

A. 11550   **B.** 12250   **C.** 13125   **D.** 12500

Q.15 The number of people who were found positive in Yellow Zone was what percent more than the number of people who were found positive in Skyblue Zone?

A. $164\frac{2}{3}\%$ **B.** $166\frac{1}{3}\%$ **C.** $166\frac{2}{3}\%$ **D.** $136\frac{2}{3}\%$

Q.16 A number of new people, which is twice the already tested number of people, are tested in Blue Zone, and the numbers of positive outcomes are more than 50% of previous outcomes. Find approximately what percent people are found positive (old $+$ new positive) in Blue Zone out of total tests.

A. 7.8   **B.** 8.1   **C.** 9.2   **D.** 10

Ques (17-20):Direction: Study the following pie and table chart carefully and answer the questions given beside.

The pie-chart shows the percentage distribution of the total distance covered by five trains (A, B, C, D and E) from source to the destination. Let the source be point X and the destination be point Y for all trains.

Percentage of the distance covered

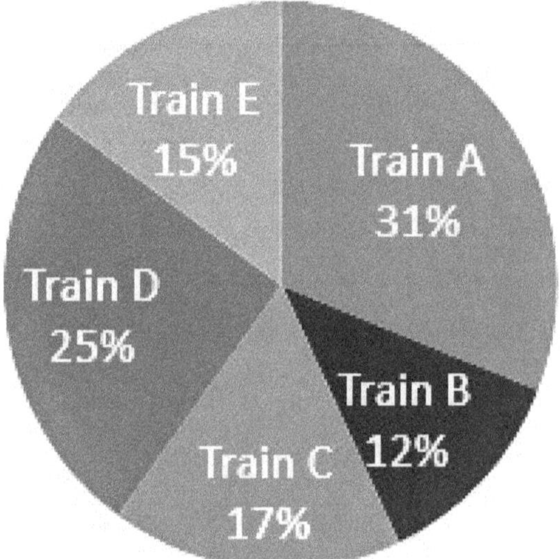

Each trains starts from X but takes a different route to reach Y and follows the same route when it returns to X from Y.

Note: The total distance covered by all the trains together to reach Y from X is 3100 km.

The table below shows the running speed of all the trains (excluding their stoppage time) while going from source (X) to destination (Y) and the ratio of the time taken (including stoppage time) by all the trains while going from X-to-Y to the time taken (including stoppage time) while returning from Y-to-X. The number of stoppages for each train on its route is given in the table and the average stoppage time taken at each stop is also given.

The respective number of stoppages and stoppage time for each train is same for its journey from X-to-Y and Y-to-X.

Note: Average speed of train for a journey = Distance of the journey ÷ Total time taken to complete the journey

Train	Running speed of train from X-to-Y (in km/hr)	Number of stoppages	The average time taken by the train on each stoppage (in minutes)	Time taken from X-to-Y: Time taken from Y-to-X
A	74.4	25	5	5 : 6
B	80	3	7	10 : 7
C	62	5	6	9 : 10
D	75	16	10	13 : 12
E	60	9	5	17 : 15

Q.17 For which two trains their average speeds for the journey from X-to-Y is the closest to each other?

A. Train A and Train B   **B.** Train C and Train E

C. Train D and Train E   **D.** Train C and Train D

Q.18 For which train, the difference between the running speed from X-to-Y and the running speed from Y-to-X is the second highest?

A. Train A   **B.** Train B   **C.** Train C   **D.** Train D

Q.19 While going from X-to-Y, if train D and train E passes a pole in 24 seconds and 27 seconds, respectively, then find the ratio of the length of train D to the length of train E.

A. $9 : 8$ **B.** $10 : 9$ **C.** $4 : 3$ **D.** $6 : 5$

Q.20 Running speed of train F from X-to-Y is 20 less than the running speed of train B from X-to-Y. The total time taken by train F, including stoppages, to cover 400 km is equal to the time taken by train C to cover 446.4 km from X-to-Y without stoppage. Find the number of stoppages train F stops at, if each stoppage is of 3 minutes.

A. 17   **B.** 21

C. 18   **D.** None of these

Ques (21-24):Direction: Study the following bar chart and table chart carefully and answer the questions given beside.

A water-tank T supplies 3000 litres of water. It supplies equal volume of water to the pipelines connecting the sub-stations $P, Q \& R$. Similarly, sub-stations $Q \& R$ supply equal volume of water to the pipelines connecting them to their respective mini-stations. Sub-station P supplies water such that equal volume of water is received at mini-stations $P_1 \& P_2$. The numbers indicate the length of the pipelines in km. It is observed that there is a loss of $x\%$ and $2x\%$ of water in the pipelines joining the tank to the sub-station and the pipelines joining the sub-stations to mini-stations respectively. (where x represents the length of the pipeline).

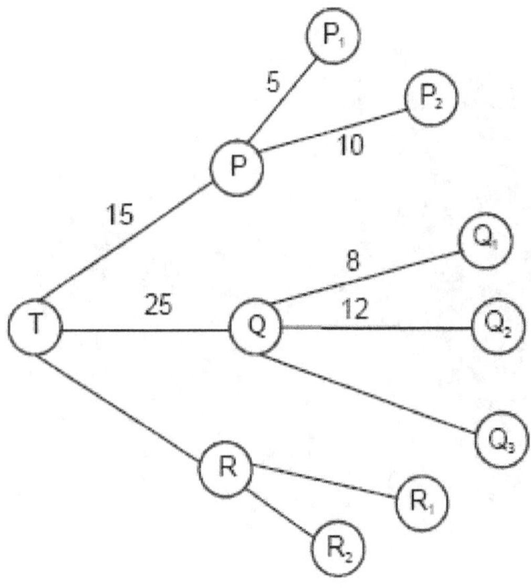

Q.21 How much water (in litres) is received at mini-station P_1?

Q.22 Find the length of pipe $Q \to Q_3$ (in km.) if the sum of the volume of water received at Q_1 and Q_3 is 380 litres.

Q.23 L_1 and L_2 are the lengths of $R \to R_1$ and $R \to R_2$ pipelines respectively. Also, it is known that $L_1 + L_2 = 25km$. The sum of the volume of water received at mini-stations R_1 and R_2 is 600 litres. Find the length of the pipeline $T \to R$.

A. $10km$ **B.** $30km$ **C.** $25km$ **D.** $20km$

Q.24 Due to scarcity of water at sub-station Q, a new pipeline is fitted between sub-station R and sub-station Q. A water loss of $5x\%$ is observed in the new pipeline where 'x' is the length of the pipeline (in km). Sub-station Q now supplies 300 litres of water in each pipeline to its mini-stations. Find the length of the new pipeline if R supplies equal volume of water to each pipeline. (Use data from the previous question if necessary)

A. $12.5km$ **B.** $11.25km$

C. $17.5km$ **D.** $8.75km$

Ques (25-28):Direction: Study the following pie and line chart carefully and answer the questions given beside.

The following pie chart gives information about the percentage breakup of the total assets of the family among four members of the family. The line graph given below gives the information about the percentage distribution of assets in three forms, Cash, Gold, and Fixed deposit of each member.

The total assets of each member $=$ Cash $+$ Gold $+$ Fixed deposit $+$ Others

The total assets of the family $=$ Rs. 75 lakhs

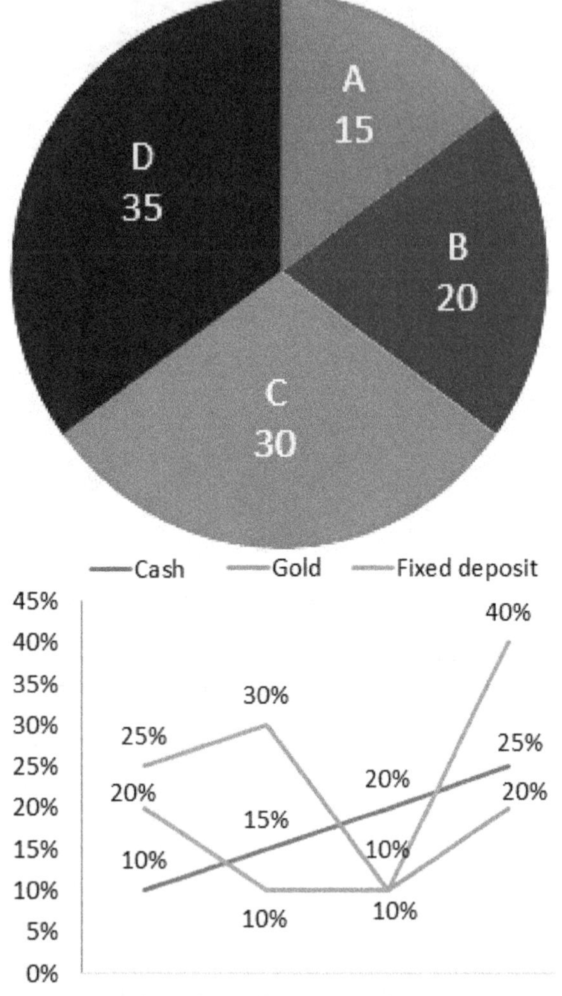

Q.25 What are the total assets of members C and B together in the form of Gold?

A. 7.25 lakhs

B. 7.75 lakhs

C. 6.75 lakhs

D. 6.25 lakhs

Q.26 The total assets of the members B and D together in the form of gold is how much more that of the members A and C together in the form of fixed deposit?

A. Rs. 5.50 lakhs

B. Rs. 5.75 lakhs

C. Rs. 6.25 lakhs

D. Rs. 5.25 lakhs

Q.27 What is the ratio of the total assets of the member B in the form of Cash to the total assets of the member D in the form of Gold?

A. $4:7$ **B.** $3:7$ **C.** $1:2$ **D.** $2:3$

Q.28 Which of the following member have highest assets in the form of Gold?

A. B   **B.** C   **C.** A   **D.** D

Ques (29-32):Direction: Study the following information carefully and answer the questions given beside.

There are 5600 students in KIIT University in the academic year 2017. The ratio of the boys to the girls in the University is $4:3$. All the students are enrolled in different extra-curricular activities (Singing, Dancing, Debating, Painting and Athletics) and one student is enrolled in only one extra-curricular activity. The number of boys enrolled in the Painting is 612. The ratio of the number of boys who enrolled in Singing to the number of boys who enrolled in Dancing is $72:89.32\%$ of the students are enrolled in Athletics. The number of boys enrolled in Debating is 12.5% to the total number of boys. The number of girls enrolled in Athletics is 570 which is 150 less than the number of girls enrolled in Dancing. The number of girls enrolled in Singing is 186 more than the number of boys enrolled in the same activity. The total number of students enrolled in Painting is 816.

Q.29 The difference in the number of boys and girls who are enrolled in Painting is what percentage of the total number of students who are enrolled in Debating?

A. 45%   **B.** 59%   **C.** 65%   **D.** 55%

Q.30 Find the percentage of students of the university who are enrolled in Singing.

A. 14   **B.** 24   **C.** 22.25   **D.** 8.75

Q.31 Find the ratio of the number of boys enrolled in Dancing to the number of girls enrolled in the same activity.

A. $7:11$ **B.** $117:139$

C. $89:120$ **D.** $57:71$

Q.32 Find the number of girls who are enrolled in Debating.

A. 304   **B.** 288   **C.** 324   **D.** 372

Ques (33-36):Direction: Study the following information carefully and answer the questions given beside:

There are five ISKCON temples in five different cities of India; Vrindavan, Ahmedabad, Anantpur, Baroda and Banglore. The total number of ISKCON devotees in the cities are 9000. The strength of Vrindavan temple is 20% and that of Ahmedabad is 35% of the total devotees of the cities. Baroda and Banglore have equal strength. 30% of the devotees of Vrindavan know only Sanskrit. 40% devotees of temple in Baroda know only Hindi.

There are 10 more devotees in Ahmedabad temple who know only Hindi than the number of devotees of Baroda temple who know only Hindi. The strength of Anantpur temple is 50% that of temple Vrindavan. Two-fifths of devotees of Ahmedabad temple know both the languages. 40% devotees of Vrindavan temple know both languages.

50% devotees of Anantpur temple know only Hindi and the number of devotees of Anantpur temple who know both the languages is equal to the number of devotees who know only Sanskrit. The number of devotees who know only Sanskrit from Banglore temple is equal to the number of devotees who know only Hindi from Baroda temple.

The number of devotees who know only Hindi from Banglore temple is 40 more than the number of devotees who know only Hindi from Anantpur temple. The number of devotees of Baroda temple who know only Sanskrit is 45 more than the number of devotees who know both the languages from Banglore temple. Each devotee knows at least one of the two languages. Sanskrit and Hindi.

Q.33 What is the percentage of the number of ISKCON devotees who know both the languages?

A. 24.5%   **B.** 34.5%   **C.** 28.5%   **D.** 36.5%

Q.34 What is the difference between the number of ISKCON devotees who know Sanskrit and those who know only Hindi?

A. 2500   **B.** 2800   **C.** 4000   **D.** 3500

Q.35 The number of Banglore ISKCON temple devotees who know only Sanskrit language is how many times of those who know both the languages from Vrindavan temple?

A. 2 times   **B.** 0.875 times
C. 2.58 times   **D.** 0.5 times

Q.36 What is the ratio of the total number of devotees who know both the languages from temple Vrindavan and temple Anantpur together to the total number of devotees from temple Baroda?

A. 2 : 1   **B.** 3 : 5   **C.** 4 : 3   **D.** 3 : 2

Ques (37-40):Direction: Study the following information carefully and answer the questions given beside.

The census officers provided the data regarding changes in population of three major towns for three years. Population of town A was 180600 in the third year and it increased 5% and 7.5% in second and third year respectively. Population of town B increased by 25% in second year and in the second year it was equal to 150% of the population of town A in first year. After taking population control measures, town B succeeds in controlling population as growth rate in third year was half of that of previous year. The area of town C is $1250km2$ and population density for second year was 250. Growth rate for town C was 11.11% and 10% for second and third year respectively.

Note: Population density is calculated as Total population $\div$ Total area.

Q.37 Population of town B in third year exceed by how much compare to population of town A in second year?

A. 10000   **B.** 107500   **C.** 102000   **D.** 105250

Q.38 The average population of town B for three years forms what percentage of average population of town C for three years?

A. 73.15   **B.** 74.88   **C.** 78.44   **D.** 76.28

Q.39 For town B, male to female ratio for the last two years was $7 : 5$ and literate male and illiterate male are in the ratio of $4 : 1$ for same years. Find the ratio between illiterate male in second year and literate male in third year.

A. 8 : 9   **B.** 4 : 9   **C.** 9 : 2   **D.** 2 : 9

Q.40 Refer the data provided in previous question, by what percentage the number of illiterate male in third year for town B less than female in third year for town B?

A. 72%   **B.** 75%   **C.** 69%   **D.** 70.50%

Ques (41-44):Direction: Study the following table charts carefully and answer the questions given beside.

Two movies Bahubali and Robot 2.0 are released in three theatres INOX, PVR and Galaxy. On Friday a total of 4500 people watched Bahubali and 4000 people watched Robot 2.0.

The table below shows the percent distribution of total viewers of a particular movie into three theatres.

Theatre	Bahubali	Robot 2.0
INOX	40%	35%
PVR	35%	25%
Galaxy	25%	40%

The viewers are classified on the basis of age as adults and children. The table below shows the percentage of children out of the total viewers in each theater for each movie.

Theatre % of Children	Bahubali	Robot 2.0
INOX	15%	20%
PVR	16%	18%
Galaxy	20%	17%

Q.41 What is the ratio of the number of children who watched Bahubali in PVR to the children who watched Robot in PVR?

A. 9 : 11   **B.** 7 : 13   **C.** 9 : 7   **D.** 7 : 5

Q.42 The number of children who watched Bahubali in INOX is what percent of the number of adults who watched Bahubali in Galaxy?

Q.43 What is the difference between the total viewers in INOX and PVR?

Q.44 What is the ratio of the sum of adults and children who watched Robot in INOX and PVR respectively to the sum of adults and children who watched Bahubali in Galaxy and INOX respectively?

A. 14 : 11   **B.** 11 : 9   **C.** 10 : 9   **D.** 13 : 7

Ques (45-48):Direction: Study the following table chart carefully and answer the questions given below.

Some blood samples of COVID-19 from three districts A, B and C were taken. District A, B and C had 160,200 and 240 villages, respectively and from each village of each district 100 blood samples were taken. Samples taken from were divided in 3 age groups which were below 20 years (20), 20 years to 40 years (20-40) and above 40 years (40). Out of total samples, 20%

were of category $20, 50\%$ were of category $20 - 40$ and rest were of category 40.

The samples were further divided in two groups based on whether the samples were tested in government hospital (GH) or private hospital (PH). The table below gives the number of samples from different categories which were tested in government hospital.

Districts	Category 20	Category 2 0-40	Category 40
A	2840	4200	3650
B	2450	6600	1800
C	800	4800	4250

It is also known that:

- 17.5% of total samples were of category 20 from C. From C, number of samples tested in PH for category 20-40 and number of samples tested in PH for category 40 were same.

- From A, for the category 40, number of samples tested in GH was 82.5% more than number of samples tested in PH.

- Ratio of number of samples tested for category 20 from A to number of samples tested for category 20 from B was 19: 20 .

Q.45 If out of samples tested for category 40 in PH from B, 20% were found positive. How many samples were negative for category 40 in PH from B?

Q.46 What was the ratio of total samples tested for category 20 from B to total samples tested for category 40 from A?
A. 40 : 93   **B.** 80 : 113   **C.** 65 : 111   **D.** 32 : 59

Q.47 Out of total samples tested for category 20-40 from C, 5175 samples were of females. Number of samples of males tested for category 20-40 from C is what percent of samples tested in PH for category 40 from A?
A. 280%   **B.** 220%   **C.** 300%   **D.** 250%

Q.48 Find the difference between number of samples tested in PH and number of samples tested in GH, for all three categories.

Ques (49-52):Direction: Read the table and information carefully and answer the following question.

The following table represents the number of sixes hit by five players in three formats of cricket: t20, test match, and one day. The 5 players are Dhoni, Pollard, Gayle, Hardik, and Finch. The ratio of sixes hit by Finch in Test and One day match is 9 : 2, some of the data in the table is missing.

Players	T20 match	Test match	One day match	Total sixes	Runs scored in sixes
Dhoni	20	- -	10	- -	270
Pollard	18	- -	- -	- -	
Gayle	15	- -	- -	- -	354
Hardik	20	10	- -	- -	
Finch	- -	- -	- -	- -	372
Total	- -	81	75	- -	1482

Q.49 What is the ratio of sixes hit by Finch in T20, Test match, and one day match?
A. 9 : 18 : 4   **B.** 5 : 8 : 9   **C.** 4 : 9 : 5   **D.** 9 : 4 : 18

Q.50 If Gayle hits 10 sixes in Test match. What is the ratio of sixes hit by Pollard in Test match to sixes hit by Gayle in One day match?
A. 9 : 5   **B.** 5 : 17   **C.** 4 : 9   **D.** 9 : 4

Q.51 If the ratio of total sixes hit by Pollard and Hardik is 4 : 5 respectively and Pollard hits 12 sixes in Test match, What is the difference between the runs scored only by sixes by Gayle in test match and Pollard in one day match?
A. 90   **B.** 54   **C.** 12   **D.** 36

Q.52 If Hardik hits 15 sixes in one day, What is the difference of runs scored by Gayle and by Pollard?
A. 190   **B.** 154   **C.** 112   **D.** 138

Ques (53-56):Direction: Read the data carefully and answer the questions that follow:
The following line graph shows the percentage of total employees working as a manager in Alexis Finance Limited, for the time period from the year 2003 to the year 2007.
(Note: Total number of employees = Managers + Workers)

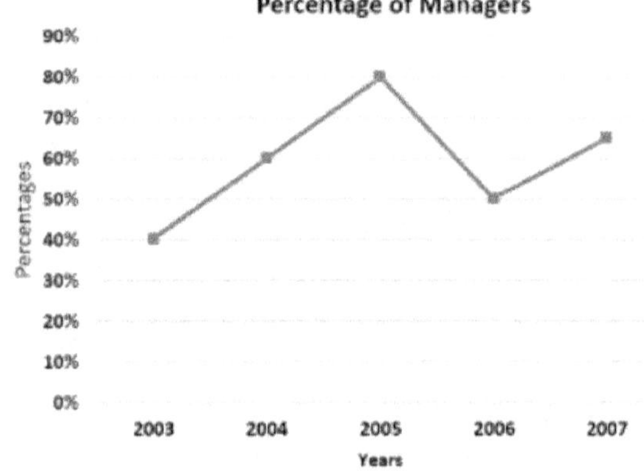

The table shows the ratio of the number of male to female managers within the company.

Year	Male : Female
2003	3:2
2004	2:1
2005	5:3
2006	2:3
2007	8:5

Q.53 If the total number of workers remains the same in the year 2005 and the year 2006, then find the ratio between the total number of male managers in these two years.

[IBPS PO, 2021]

A. 32 : 125   **B.** 10 : 13   **C.** 13 : 10   **D.** 25 : 4

Q.54 If the number of workers in the year 2008 is 1400, and the number of total workers in the company has doubled since

2007; then find the number of managers in the company in 2007.

[IBPS PO, 2021]

A. 1500 **B.** 1200 **C.** 1300 **D.** 1000

Q.55 If the number of male managers in the year 2003 is 480, and the number of female managers in the year 2005 is 450. Then find the ratio of the number of employees in the company in 2003 and that in the year 2005.

[IBPS PO, 2021]

A. 3 : 2 **B.** 4 : 3 **C.** 2 : 3 **D.** 3 : 4

Q.56 If the number of employees working in the company in 2005 is 1000. Also, it is known that the number of male workers is the same as the number of female workers in 2005. Then what is the difference between the number of female workers and the number of female managers in the year 2005?

[IBPS PO, 2021]

A. 400 **B.** 200 **C.** 100 **D.** 300

Ques (57-60):Direction: Read the following information carefully and answer the questions that follow.

There are four friends Rita, Gita, Mita and Sita. Time taken by Rita to complete the work alone is 14 days more than the time taken by Sita to complete the work alone. Sita start working and Gita joined sita after 11 days. Both works together and after 15 days they left and the remaining work is completed by Mita in 10 more days. The ratio of efficiency of Gita to Rita is $4:5$ and the ratio of the efficiency of Gita to Mita is $6:7$.

Q.57 Who amongst the following is most efficient?
A. Sita and Gita **B.** Gita and Rita
C. Sita only **D.** Mita and Sita

Q.58 In how many days Mita completes the work?
A. 56 days **B.** 60 days **C.** 68 days **D.** 72 days

Q.59 What is the ratio of efficiency of Rita to Sita?
A. 3 : 4 **B.** 4 : 3 **C.** 5 : 4 **D.** 4 : 5

Q.60 In how many days Sita and Gita together will finish the work?
A. 26.25 days **B.** 32.50 days
C. 20.25 days **D.** 18.50 days

// Smart Answer Sheet //

| Correct | Indicates percentage of students who answered questions correctly. |
| Skipped | Indicates percentage of students who skipped questions. |

Q.	Ans.	Correct / Skipped	Q.	Ans.	Correct / Skipped	Q.	Ans.	Correct / Skipped	Q.	Ans.	Correct / Skipped	Q.	Ans.	Correct / Skipped
1	B	29.63 % / 70.34 %	13	D	69.13 % / 30.19 %	25	C	54.46 % / 32.5 %	37	C	60.21 % / 38.83 %	49	A	64.25 % / 30.44 %
2	C	13.56 % / 67.63 %	14	B	78.54 % / 18.27 %	26	D	44.83 % / 30.15 %	38	B	45.38 % / 51.97 %	50	B	32.74 % / 67.23 %
3	B	19.18 % / 72.66 %	15	C	85.18 % / 11.94 %	27	B	44.22 % / 53.19 %	39	D	20.08 % / 78.96 %	51	C	26.16 % / 72.08 %
4	C	65.0 % / 30.39 %	16	C	78.99 % / 10.76 %	28	D	69.9 % / 30.06 %	40	A	60.22 % / 39.69 %	52	D	24.71 % / 67.17 %
5	B	30.63 % / 68.02 %	17	D	13.91 % / 82.77 %	29	B	30.78 % / 69.12 %	41	D	11.39 % / 76.12 %	53	D	23.02 % / 75.16 %
6	B	58.08 % / 38.18 %	18	A	61.15 % / 38.1 %	30	D	15.85 % / 75.4 %	42	30	20.35 % / 75.98 %	54	C	42.79 % / 52.37 %
7	C	63.3 % / 30.89 %	19	B	65.87 % / 30.12 %	31	C	12.36 % / 72.35 %	43	625	68.65 % / 30.4 %	55	B	31.82 % / 67.6 %
8	A	42.1 % / 43.0 %	20	D	57.08 % / 31.86 %	32	B	68.58 % / 31.31 %	44	C	52.19 % / 41.15 %	56	B	65.4 % / 31.2 %
9	B	51.31 % / 45.5 %	21	360	56.93 % / 38.22 %	33	B	21.96 % / 70.85 %	45	740	16.76 % / 76.06 %	57	C	23.58 % / 67.81 %
10	B	40.26 % / 58.53 %	22	16	44.43 % / 40.96 %	34	D	27.19 % / 69.56 %	46	B	15.72 % / 69.18 %	58	B	18.9 % / 75.99 %
11	D	63.15 % / 34.06 %	23	D	18.33 % / 73.0 %	35	B	28.37 % / 68.45 %	47	D	27.03 % / 72.8 %	59	A	66.15 % / 30.44 %
12	A	59.63 % / 36.74 %	24	D	32.36 % / 67.57 %	36	B	13.35 % / 77.76 %	48	28610	32.64 % / 67.24 %	60	A	25.46 % / 70.58 %

Performance Analysis

Avg. Score (%)	33.33%
Toppers Score (%)	61.67%
Your Score	

//Hints and Solutions//

1. From the chart,

In team green, starter is J and finisher is K

Time taken by K to finish $400\,m$ race $= 85.71\%$ (Time taken by team Green)

$$\frac{\text{Time } (K-400\,m)}{\text{Time (Green)}} = \frac{6}{7}$$

So, $\dfrac{\text{Time } (K-200\,m)}{\text{Time (Green)}} = \dfrac{3}{7}$

Time $(\text{Green}) = Time(J - 200) + \text{Time } (K - 200)$

$$\frac{Time(K-200)}{\text{Time } (J-200)} = \frac{3}{4}$$

So in team Green, $\dfrac{\text{Time } (K)}{\text{Time } (J)} = \dfrac{3}{4}$

Let the time taken by $J = 4\,g$ and that by $K = 3\,g$

Similarly we can find the time ratio of the players of each team,

Team	Green	Blue	Yellow	Red	White
Time ratio Starter/Finisher	$\frac{4}{3}$	$\frac{8}{7}$	$\frac{5}{9}$	$\frac{2}{3}$	$\frac{5}{4}$
Time Starter	J (4g)	M (8b)	P (5y)	S (2r)	U (5w)
Time Finisher	K (3g)	N (7b)	Q (9y)	T (3r)	V (4w)
Time Team	7g	15b	14y	5r	9w

Team Blue takes 28.57% less time than team Green

Time $(\text{Blue}) = \dfrac{5}{7} \times$ Time (Green)

$$15b = \frac{b}{g} = \frac{1}{3}$$

Time taken by team blue is 25% less that by team Red.

Time (Blue) $= \dfrac{3}{4} \times$ Time (Red)

$$15b = \frac{3}{4} \times 5r$$

$$\frac{b}{r} = \frac{1}{4}$$

The time taken by team Yellow is 200% of time taken by team Red.

Time (Yellow) $= 2 \times$ Time (Red)

$$14y = \frac{y}{r} = \frac{5}{7}$$

Team White takes 12.5% more time than team yellow.

Time (White) $= \dfrac{9}{8} \times$ Time (Yellow)

$$9w = \frac{9}{8} \times 14y$$

$$\frac{w}{y} = \frac{7}{4}$$

So, $g:b:y:r:w = 21:7:20:28:35$

Speed of starter of team Green as a percent of the finisher of team Red

Speed of $J = \dfrac{\text{Distance}}{\text{Time}} = \dfrac{200}{4\,g}$

Speed of $T = \dfrac{200}{3r}$

$$\frac{\text{Speed } (J)}{\text{Speed } (T)} = \frac{3r}{4g}$$

$$= \frac{3}{4} \times \frac{r}{g} = \frac{3}{4} \times \frac{28}{21} = 1:1$$

So, speed of J is 100% of speed of T

Hence, the correct option is (B).

2.

Team	Green	Blue	Yellow	Red	White
Time ratio Starter/Finisher	$\frac{4}{3}$	$\frac{8}{7}$	$\frac{5}{9}$	$\frac{2}{3}$	$\frac{5}{4}$
Time Starter	J (4g)	M (8b)	P (5y)	S (2r)	U (5w)
Time Finisher	K (3g)	N (7b)	Q (9y)	T (3r)	V (4w)
Time Team	7g	15b	14y	5r	9w

$$g:b:y:r:w = 21:7:20:28:35$$

Ratio of $\dfrac{y}{w} = \dfrac{20}{35} = \dfrac{4}{7}$

Let $y = 4t$ and $w = 7t$

Time of Team Yellow $\rightarrow P = 20t$ and $Q = 36t$

Time of Team White $\rightarrow U = 35t$ and $V = 28t$

U is halfway his course at $35t/2$

The distance covered by P in $\dfrac{35t}{2} = \dfrac{35t}{2 \times 20t} \times 200 = 175m$

So distance between P and $Q = (200 - 175) = 25m$

Q finishes the race at, $20t + 36t = 56t$, from the start

U passes the baton to V at $35t$ and when Q finishes, V has run for $(56t - 35t) = 21t$

Distance between U and $V = \dfrac{21t}{28t} \times 200 = 150m$

Reqd. $\% = \dfrac{25}{150} \times 100 = 16.67\%$

Hence, the correct option is (C).

3.

Team	Green	Blue	Yellow	Red	White
Time ratio Starter/Finisher	$\frac{4}{3}$	$\frac{8}{7}$	$\frac{5}{9}$	$\frac{2}{3}$	$\frac{5}{4}$
Time Starter	J (4g)	M (8b)	P (5y)	S (2r)	U (5w)
Time Finisher	K (3g)	N (7b)	Q (9y)	T (3r)	V (4w)
Time Team	7g	15b	14y	5r	9w

$g:b:y:r:w = 21:7:20:28:35$ $g:r:b = 21:28:7 = 3:4:1$

Let $g = 3t, r = 4t$ and $b = t$

Team red runs in the reverse direction, S starts from finish line and passes baton to T at the centre and T finishes at the starting line.

Time taken by players to complete $200m$

Green	J	12t	K	9t
Red	S	8t	T	12t
Blue	M	8t	N	7t

S and M reach and pass the baton to T and N respectively after $8t$.

J passes the baton to K at $12t$

So, when J and K meet, T and N have run for time $4t$

Distance between T and N in time $4t$

$$= \frac{4t}{12t} \times 200 + \frac{4t}{7t} \times 200 = \frac{19}{21} \times 200 = 180\frac{20}{21}m$$

Hence, the correct option is (B).

4.

Team	Green	Blue	Yellow	Red	White
Time ratio Starter/Finisher	$\frac{4}{3}$	$\frac{8}{7}$	$\frac{5}{9}$	$\frac{2}{3}$	$\frac{5}{4}$
Time Starter	J (4g)	M (8b)	P (5y)	S (2r)	U (5w)
Time Finisher	K (3g)	N (7b)	Q (9y)	T (3r)	V (4w)
Time Team	7g	15b	14y	5r	9w

$g:b:y:r:w = 21:7:20:28:35$

As there is no replacement in yellow, let us consider the other four only

$g:b:r:w = 21:7:28:35 = 3:1:4:5$

Let $g = 3z, b = 1z, r = 4z$ and $w = 5z$

Team	Green	Blue	Red	White
Time Starter	J (12z)	M (8z)	S (8z)	U (25z)
Time Finisher	K (9z)	N (7z)	T (12z)	V (20z)

After Replacement

Team	Green	Blue	Red	White
Time Starter	J (12z)	V (20z)	K (9z)	T (12z)
Time Finisher	S (\98\)z)	N (7z)	U (25z)	M (8z)
Time Team	20z	27z	34z	20z

The distance between K and U when Team green finishes the race,

Team green finishes race in $20z$, in that time K runs for $9z$ and

then U runs for $11z$,

The distance between U and K in $11z$

$$= \frac{11z}{25z} \times 200 = 88m$$

Distance between T and M when baton is passed from starter to finisher in team Red

Baton is passed in team Red at $9z$

Distance between T and M at $9z$

$$= \frac{1-9z}{12z} \times 200 = 50m$$

Reqd. $\% = \frac{88}{50} \times 100 = 176\%$

Hence, the correct option is (C).

5. From table- 3 of common explanation, we have

The number of positive cases in Urban Meerut $= 45 + 50 + 80 = 175$

The number of positive cases in Rural Meerut $= 15 + 45 + 50 = 110$

Difference $= 65$

So, option B is correct.

Common explanation :

Using the given table chart in the question, we find the following table.

(Table- 1)

Month	Positive ($+$ve)	Negative ($-$ve)
March	70	30
April	130	70
May	180	180

Using the values of P and Q from column chart, we have the following information.

(Table- 2)

Month	Positive ($+$ve)		Negative ($-$ve)	
	Agra	Meerut	Agra	Meerut
March	10	60	20	10
April	35	95	30	40
May	50	130	100	80

From this table, we have that total number of tests (Urban $+$ Rural) in Agra in

March $= 10 + 20 = 30$

April $= 35 + 30 = 65$

May $= 50 + 100 = 150$

From value of R in March, we have

Urban test in Agra $= 20$ ($+$ve and $-$ve both)

Rural test in Agra $= 10$

From value of R in April, we have

Urban test in Agra $= 50$

Rural test in Agra $= 15$

From value of R in May, we have

Urban test in Agra $= 100 (+$ ve and $-$ ve both$)$

Rural test in Agra $= 50$

Now, we have last information that in a given month, number of tests found negative in rural area is equal to the number of tests found negative in urban area.

Consider March of Agra.

Let the number of Rural test found positive/negative $= \dfrac{R^+}{R^-}$; and

Urban test found positive $= \dfrac{U^+}{U^-}$

So, we have been given that $R^- = U^-$

We have from the calculations above that

(March in Agra)

$U^+ + U^- = 20$

$R^+ + R^- = 10$

From table 1, we have

$R^- + U^- = 20$

$R^+ + U^+ = 10 \quad \cdots (iv)$

But since $R^- = U^- = Y$ (say), we have from (iii)

$R^- = U^- = 10$

Putting value of $R^- = U^- = 10$ in (i), (ii) and (iv), we get

$U^+ = 10$

$R^+ = 0$

Similarly we find for each month and both the cities.

We fill all the values in the table given below.

(Table- 3)

Agra					Meerut			
	Urban		Rural		Urban		Rural	
	$+v$e	$-v$e	$+v$e	$-v$e	$+v$e	$-v$e	$+v$e	$-v$e
March	10	10	0	10	45	5	15	5
April	35	15	0	15	50	20	45	20
May	50	50	0	50	80	40	50	40

Hence, the correct option is (B).

Ques (6-8): Using the given table chart in the question, we find the following table.

(Table- 1)

Month	Positive ($+$ve)	Negative ($-$ve)
March	70	30
April	130	70
May	180	180

Using the values of P and Q from column chart, we have the following information.

(Table- 2)

Month	Positive ($+$ve)		Negative ($-$ve)	
	Agra	Meerut	Agra	Meerut
March	10	60	20	10
April	35	95	30	40
May	50	130	100	80

From this table, we have that total number of tests (Urban + Rural) in Agra in

March $= 10 + 20 = 30$

April $= 35 + 30 = 65$

May $= 50 + 100 = 150$

From value of R in March, we have

Urban test in Agra $= 20$ ($+$ ve and $-$ ve both)

Rural test in Agra $= 10$

From value of R in April, we have

Urban test in Agra $= 50$

Rural test in Agra $= 15$

From value of R in May, we have

Urban test in Agra $= 100$ ($+$ve and $-$ve both)

Rural test in Agra $= 50$

Now, we have last information that in a given month, number of tests found negative in rural area is equal to the number of tests found negative in urban area.

Consider March of Agra.

Let the number of Rural test found positive/negative $= \dfrac{R^+}{R^-}$; and

Urban test found positive $= \dfrac{U^+}{U^-}$

So, we have been given that $R{-} = U{-}$

We have from the calculations above that

(March in Agra)

$U{+} + U{-} = 20 - - - - - - (i)$

$$R + +R- = 10 - - - - - - (ii)$$

From table 1, we have

$$R- +U- = 20 - - - - - - (iii)$$

$$R + +U+ = 10 - - - - - - (iv)$$

But since $R- = U- = Y$ (say), we have from (iii)

$$R- = U- = 10$$

Putting value of $R- = U- = 10$ in $(i), (ii)$ and (iv), we get

$$U+ = 10$$

$$R+ = 0$$

Similarly we find for each month and both the cities.

We fill all the values in the table given below.

(Table- 3)

	Agra				Meerut			
	Urban		Rural		Urban		Rural	
	+ve	−ve	+ve	−ve	+ve	−ve	+ve	−ve
March	10	10	0	10	45	5	15	5
April	35	15	0	15	50	20	45	20
May	50	50	0	50	80	40	50	40

6. From table- 2, we have

Number of positive cases in April $= 35 + 95 = 130$

Number of negative cases in March $= 20 + 10 = 30$

Percentage $= \dfrac{130-30}{30} \times 100 = 333.33\%$

Hence, the correct option is (B).

7. From table- 3, we see that the Rural area of Agra in May has zero case.

Hence, the correct option is (C).

8. From table- 2, we have

Total number of negative cases in the three months $= 20 + 30 + 100 = 150$

Average $= \dfrac{150}{3} = 50$

Hence, the correct option is (A).

Ques (9-12): Each rocket has 3 kind of propellers $=$ used $+$ unused $+$ defected We add the value for the three columns for each rocket to get the number of propellers used in each rocket.

Rockets	Used	Defected	Unused	Total
A	48	6	36	\(90\)

B	50	8	22	80
C	54	6	30	90
D	51	11	28	90
E	38	11	21	70
Total	241	42	137	420

9. From common explanation, we have

Average $= \dfrac{420}{5} = 84$

Hence, the correct option is (B).

10. Improved propellers $= 66.66\%$ of $42 = 28$

Total reusable propellers $=$ unused $+$ improved $= 137 + 28 = 165$

Number of rockets $= \dfrac{165}{55} = 3$

Hence, the correct option is (B).

11. It is obvious that the rocket which has maximum number of 'used' rocket will go maximum height. Rocket C is that rocket.

Now, to find the height, we use the information given in the table in question.

For $0 - 10$ km range, number of propellers required

$$= \dfrac{10km}{0.4km} = 25$$

For $10 - 16$ km range, number of propellers required

$$= \dfrac{6km}{0.6km} = 10$$

For $16 - 20$ km range, number of propellers required

$$= \dfrac{4km}{1km} = 4$$

Till now, we have 39 used propellers to reach height of 20 km, for above this, we have $54 - 39 = 15$ propellers.

Each of these 15 will go 1.2 km, so max height $= 20 + 15 \times 1.2 = 38$ km

Hence, the correct option is (D).

12. First we find out how high the rocket E can go. So,

For $0 - 10$ km range, number of propellers required

$$= \dfrac{10km}{0.4km} = 25$$

For $10 - 16$ km range, number of propellers required

$$= \dfrac{6km}{0.6km} = 10$$

From now, rocket E has only 3 propellers, so maximum height it can go $= 10 + 6 + 3 = 19km$

Total time $= 0.006$ minutes $\times 38$

$$= \frac{38 \times 0.006}{60} \text{ hours} = 0.0038 \text{ hours}$$

Average speed $= \dfrac{19km}{0.0038 \text{ hours}} = 5000 kmph$

Hence, the correct option is (A).

13. $16,000$ people were tested for COVID- 19 in yellow zone.

Now, 4.8 thousand $= 4800$ were found positive.

$$\text{Percent} = \frac{4800}{16000} \times 100 = 30\%$$

Hence, the correct option is (D).

14. Number of people tested in

Green Zone $= 15,000$

Skyblue Zone $= 9,000$

Red Zone $= 11,000$

Black Zone $= 14,000$

Average $= \dfrac{(15+9+11+14) \times 1000}{4} = 12250$

Hence, the correct option is (B).

15. The number of people who were found positive in Yellow Zone $= 4.8$ thousand

The number of people who were found positive in Skyblue Zone $= 1.8$ thousand

Percent $= \dfrac{(4.8-1.8)}{1.8} \times 100 = 166\frac{2}{3}\%$

Hence, the correct option is (C).

16. Number in previous tests $= 18$ thousand

Number of new tests $= 18 \times 2 = 36$ thousand

Total tests after new tests $= 54$ thousand

Positive outcome in previous tests $= 2$ thousand

Positive outcome in new tests $= 2 + 50\%$ of $2 = 3$ thousand

Total positive after new tests $= 5$ thousand

Percent $= \dfrac{5}{54} \times 100 = 9.2\%$

Hence, the correct option is (C).

Ques (17-20): Distance covered by train A from source (X) to destination $(Y) = 31\%$ of $3100 = 961$ km

Distance covered by train B from source (X) to destination $(Y) = 12\%$ of $3100 = 372$ km

Distance covered by train C from source (X) to destination $(Y) = 17\%$ of $3100 = 527$ km

Distance covered by train D from source (X) to destination $(Y) = 25\%$ of $3100 = 775$ km

Distance covered by train E from source (X) to destination $(Y) = 15\%$ of $3100 = 465$ km

Total time taken by train A going from X to Y

$$= \frac{961}{74.4} \times 60 + 25 \times 5 = 900 \text{ minutes} = 15 \text{ hours}$$

Total time taken by train B going from X to Y

$$= \frac{372}{80} \times 60 + 3 \times 7 = 300 \text{ minutes} = 5 \text{ hours}$$

Total time taken by train C going from X to Y

$$= \frac{527}{62} \times 60 + 5 \times 6 = 540 \text{ minutes} = 9 \text{ hours}$$

Total time taken by train D going from X to Y

$$= \frac{775}{75} \times 60 + 16 \times 10 = 780 \text{ minutes} = 13 \text{ hours}$$

Total time taken by train E going from X to Y

$$= \frac{465}{60} \times 60 + 9 \times 5 = 510 \text{ minutes} = 8.5 \text{hours}$$

Train	Distance travelled (in km)	Running speed of train from X-to-Y (in km/hr)	Number of stoppages	The average time taken by the train on each stoppage (in minutes)	Time taken from X-to-Y (in hours)
A	961	74.4	25	5	15
B	372	80	3	7	5
C	527	62	5	6	9
D	775	75	16	10	13
E	465	60	\99\	5	8.5

17. Average speed of train A going from X to $Y = \dfrac{961}{15} = 64.07$ km / hr

Average speed of train B going from X to $Y = \dfrac{372}{5} = 74.4$ km / hr

Average speed of train C going from X to $Y = \dfrac{527}{9} = 58.6$ km / hr

Average speed of train D going from X to $Y = \dfrac{775}{13} = 59.6$ km / hr

Average speed of train E going from X to $Y = \dfrac{465}{8.5} = 54.7$ km / hr

The average speeds of train C and train D are closest to each other.

Hence, the correct option is (D).

18. Running time of train A from Y to $X = 18 \times 60 - 25 \times 5 = 955$ minutes $= 15.9$ hours

Running time of train B from Y to $X = 3.5 \times 60 - 3 \times 7 = 189$ minutes $= 3.15$ hours

Running time of train C from Y to $X = 10 \times 60 - 5 \times 6 = 570$ minutes $= 9.5$ hours

Running time of train D from Y to $X = 12 \times 60 - 16 \times 10 = 560$ minutes $= 9.33$ hours

Running time of train E from Y to $X = 7.5 \times 60 - 9 \times 5 = 405$ minutes $= 6.75$ hours

Running speed of train A from Y to $X = \dfrac{961}{15.9} = 60.4$ km / hr

Running speed of train B from Y to $X = \dfrac{372}{3.15} = 118.1$ km / hr

Running speed of train C from Y to $X = \dfrac{527}{9.5} = 55.5$ km / hr

Running speed of train D from Y to $X = \dfrac{775}{9.33} = 83$ km / hr

Running speed of train E from Y to $X = \dfrac{465}{6.75} = 68.9$ km / hr

Train A: Difference $= 74.4 - 60.4 = 14$ km / hr (second highest)

Train B: Difference $= 118 - 80 = 38$ km / hr

Train C: Difference $= 62 - 55.5 = 6.5$ km / hr

Train D: Difference $= 83 - 75 = 8$ km / hr

Train E: Difference $= 68.9 - 60 = 8.9$ km / hr

Hence, the correct option is (A).

19. Running speed of train D going from X-to-Y

$$= 75 km/hr = \dfrac{125}{6} m/s$$

Running speed of train E going from X-to-Y

$$= 60 km/hr = \dfrac{50}{3} m/s$$

Length of train $D = \dfrac{125}{6} \times 24 = 500$ meters

Length of train $E = \dfrac{50}{3} \times 27 = 450$ meters

Required ratio $= 500 : 450 = 10 : 9$

Hence, the correct option is (B).

20. Running speed of train $F = 80\%$ of $80 = 64$ km / hr

Time taken by train F without stoppage to cover $400x$ km $= \dfrac{400}{64} = 6$ hours 15 minutes

Time taken by train C with stoppage to cover 446.4 km $= \dfrac{446.4}{62} = 7$ hours 12 minutes

Time taken by train F in all the stoppages together $= 45 + 12 = 57$ minutes

So, number of stoppages $= \dfrac{57}{3} = 19$ stops.

Hence, the correct option is (D).

21. As the water gets equally divided in the pipelines from the tank, water entering pipeline

$$T \to P = \dfrac{3000}{3} = 1000 \text{ litres}$$

Water received at sub-station $P = 85\%$ of 1000 litres $= 850$ litres

Let a and b represent the volume of water entering pipeline $P \to P_1$ and $P \to P_2$ respectively.

$$a + b = 850 \dots (1)$$

As mini-stations P_1 and P_2 receive equal volume of water,

$$90\% \text{ of } a = 80\% \text{ of } b$$

Therefore, $9a = 8b$

Therefore, $9a - 8b = 0$

Solving (1) and (2) simultaneously, we get $a = 400$ and $b = 450$

Hence, volume of water received at mini-station $P_1 = 400 \times 0.9 = 360$ litres

Therefore, the required answer is 360.

Hence, the correct answer is 360.

22. Let the length of pipe $Q \to Q_3$ be 'a' km.

Volume of water received by sub-station $Q = 75\%$ of 1000 litres $= 750$ litres.

Quantity of water received by mini-station $Q_1 = 84\%$ of $\left(\dfrac{750}{3}\right) = 210$ litres

Volume of water received by mini-station $Q_3 = \dfrac{750}{3} -$

$$\dfrac{750}{3} \times \dfrac{2a}{100} = 5(50 - a)$$

$$\Rightarrow 210 + 5(50 - a) = 380$$

$$\Rightarrow \quad (50 - a) = 170$$

$\Rightarrow (50 - a) = 34$

$\Rightarrow a = 16 km$

23. Let x represent the length of pipeline $T \to R$.

Therefore Volume of water received by sub-station

$$R = 1000 \frac{(100-x)}{100} = 10(100 - x)$$

Therefore Volume of water distributed by $R = \frac{10(100-x)}{2} = 5(100 - x)$

Volume of water received by mini-stations:

$$R_1 = 5(100 - x)\frac{(100-2L_1)}{100} \text{ and}$$

$$R_2 = 5(100 - x)\frac{(100-2L_2)}{100}$$

$$\to \frac{5(100-x)}{100}[200 - 2(L_1 + L_2)] = 600$$

$$\Rightarrow (100 - x)(200 - 50) = 12000$$

$$\Rightarrow (100 - x) = \frac{1200}{15} = 80$$

$$\Rightarrow x = 20 km$$

Hence, the correct option is (D).

24. Since sub-station Q distributes 300 litres of water to each of its mini-stations, it receives $300 \times 3 = 900$ litres of water.

As it receives 750 litres from T, it receives the remaining 150 litres from R.

Let the length of the new pipeline be ' a ' km.

At sub-station R, there are 3 pipelines. Thus, R distributes $\frac{800}{3}$ litres of water in each pipeline.

Volume of water received by $Q = \frac{800}{3} - \frac{800}{3} \times \frac{5a}{100} = 150$

$$\Rightarrow \frac{800}{3} \frac{(100-5a)}{100} = 150$$

$$\Rightarrow (100 - 5a) = \frac{150 \times 3}{8}$$

$$\Rightarrow 5a = 100 - \frac{150 \times 3}{8} = \frac{800-450}{8} = \frac{350}{8}$$

$$\Rightarrow a = 8.75 km$$

Hence, the correct option is (D).

25. The total assets of member $A = 15\%$ of $75 = 11.25$ lakhs

The total assets of member $B = 20\%$ of $75 = 15$ lakhs

The total assets of member $C = 30\%$ of $75 = 22.5$ lakhs

The total assets of member $D = 35\%$ of $75 = 26.25$ lakhs

The total assets of the members C and B together in the form of Gold $= 10\%$ OF 22.5 LAKHS $+30\%$ of 15 lakhs

$= .25 + 4.5 = 6.75$ lakhs

Hence, the correct option is (C).

26. The total assets of member $B = 20\%$ of $75 = 15$ lakhs

The total assets of member $D = 35\%$ of $75 = 26.25$ lakhs

The total assets of the members B and D together in the form of gold $= 30\%$ of 15 lakhs $+20\%$ of 26.25 lakhs

$= 4.5$ lakhs $+5.25$ lakhs $= 9.75$ lakhs

The total assets of member $A = 15\%$ of $75 = 11.25$ lakhs

The total assets of member $C = 30\%$ of $75 = 22.5$ lakhs

The total assets of the members A and C together in the form of fixed deposit $= 20\%$ of 11.25 lakhs $+10\%$ of 22.5 lakhs

$= 2.25 + 2.25 = 4.5$ lakhs

The required difference $= 9.75 - 4.5 = 5.25$ lakhs

Hence, the correct option is (D).

27. The total assets of member B in the form of cash $= 15\%$ of 15 lakhs $= 2.25$ lakhs

The total assets of member D in the form of gold $= 20\%$ of 26.25 lakhs $= 5.25$ lakhs

The required ratio $= 2.25 : 5.25 = 3 : 7$

Hence, the correct option is (B).

28. The total assets of member $A = 15\%$ of $75 = 11.25$ lakhs

In the form of gold $= 25\%$ of $11.25 = 2.8125$ lakhs

The total assets of member $B = 20\%$ of $75 = 15$ lakhs

In the form of gold $= 30\%$ of $15 = 4.5$ lakhs

The total assets of member $C = 30\%$ of $75 = 22.5$ lakhs

In the form of gold $= 10\%$ of $22.5 = 2.25$ lakhs

The total assets of member $D = 35\%$ of $75 = 26.25$ lakhs

In the form of gold $= 20\%$ of 26.25 lakhs $= 5.25$ lakhs

It is clear that the member D have highest assets in the form of gold.

Hence, the correct option is (D).

Ques (29-32): Total number of students $= 5600$

Number of boys $= \frac{4}{7} \times 5600 = 3200$

Number of girls $= 5600 - 3200 = 2400$

Number of boys enrolled in Painting $= 612$

Number of students enrolled in Athletics $= 32\%$ of $5600 = 1792$

Number of girls enrolled in Athletics $= 570$

Number of boys enrolled in Athletics $= 1792 - 570 = 1222$

Number of boys enrolled in Debating $= 12.5\%$ of $3200 = 400$

Number of girls enrolled in Dancing $= 570 + 150 = 720$

Number of students enrolled in Painting $= 816$

Number of girls enrolled in painting $= 816 - 612 = 204$

Number of boys enrolled in Singing and Dancing together $= 3200 - (400 + 612 + 1222) = 966$

Number of boys enrolled in singing $= \dfrac{72}{72+89} \times 966 = 432$

Number of girls enrolled in singing $= 432 + 186 = 618$

Number of boys enrolled in dancing $= 966 - 432 = 534$

Number of girls enrolled in debating $= 2400 - (618 + 720 + 204 + 570) = 288$

Activity	Number of Boys	Number of Girls	Total number of students
Singing	432	618	1050
Dancing	534	720	1254
Debating	400	288	688
Painting	612	204	816
Athletics	1222	570	1792

29. The difference in the number of boys and girls who are enrolled in Painting $= (612 - 204) = 408$

So, required percentage $= \dfrac{408 \times 100}{688} = 59.3 \approx 59\%$

Hence, the correct option is (B).

30. Required percentage $= \dfrac{1050}{5600} \times 100 = 18.75\%$

Hence, the correct option is (D).

31. Required ratio $= 534 : 720 = 89 : 120$

Hence, the correct option is (C).

32. The required number of girls who are enrolled in Debating $= 288$

Hence, the correct option is (B).

Ques (33-36): Following the given information we can create a table as follows:

Temples	Total	Only Sanskrit	Only Hindi	Both Sanskrit & Hindi
Vrindavan	20% of 9000 = 1800	30% of 1800 = 540	540	40% of 1800 = 720
Ahmedabad	35% of 9000 = 3150	1250	630 + 10 = 640	2/5 of 3150 = 1260
Anantpur	50% of 1800 = 900	225	50% of 900 = 450	225
Baroda	1575	455 + 45 = 500	40% of 1575 = 630	445
Banglore	1575	630	450 + 40 = 490	455

33. Total number of ISKCON devotees who know both languages $= 720 + 1260 + 225 + 445 + 455 = 3105$

Total number devotees in all the cities $= 9000$

$= \dfrac{3105}{9000} \times 100 = 34.5\%$

Hence, the correct option is (B).

34. Total number of devotees who know Sanskrit $= 540 + 1250 + 225 + 500 + 630 = 3145 + 3105$ (from both the languages $) = 6250$

Total number of devotees who know only Hindi $= 540 + 640 + 450 + 630 + 490 = 2750$

Required difference $= 6250 - 2750 = 3500$

Hence, the correct option is (D).

35. Total number of Banglore ISKCON temple devotees who know only Sanskrit $= 630$

Total number of Vrindavan ISKCON temple devotees who know both the languages $= 720$

Required answer $= \dfrac{630}{720} = 0.875$ times

Hence, the correct option is (B).

36. Total number of devotees from Vrindavan temple who know both the languages $= 720$

Total number of devotees from Anantpur temple who know both the languages $= 225$

$= 720 + 225 = 945$

Total number of devotees from Baroda temple $= 1575$

Reqd ratio $= \dfrac{945}{1575} = \dfrac{3}{5} = 3:5$

Hence, the correct option is (B).

37. Let the Population of Town A in first year be 100.

Thus, population of town A in third year $= 105\%$ of 107.50% of $100 = 112.875$ i.e. 180600 .

$\therefore$ Population of Town A in first year

$= \dfrac{180600 \times 100}{112.875} = 160000$

Thus, population of town A in second year $= 105\%$ of $160000 = 168000$

Population of town B in second year $= 150\%$ of $160000 = 240000$

As given, growth rate of population for town B in the second year was 25%, thus population in first year $= \dfrac{240000 \times 100}{125} = 192000$

As growth year became half of previous years' growth rate, Population of town B in third year $= 240000 + [240000 \times 12.50\%$ (half of 25%)$] = 240000 + 30000 = 270000$

For town C, population in second year = Population density $\times$ Area $= 250 \times 1250 = 312500$

As growth rate for town C was 11.11% and 10% for second and third year respectively, population of C in first year $= \dfrac{312500 \times 100}{111.11} = 281250$

Population of C in third year $= 110\%$ of $312500 = 343750$.

Thus, we can present above data in tabular form as follows:

Towns	Population		
	First Year	**Second Year**	**Third Year**
A	160000	168000	180600
B	192000	240000	270000
C	281250	312500	343750

Required difference = Population of town B in third year – Population of town A in second year

$= 270000 - 168000 = 102000$

Hence, the correct option is (C).

38. Average population of town B

$= \dfrac{192000 + 240000 + 270000}{3} = \dfrac{702000}{3} = 234000$

Average population of town C

$= \dfrac{281250 + 312500 + 343750}{3} = \dfrac{937500}{3} = 312500$

$\therefore$ Required $\% = \dfrac{234000}{312500} \times 100 = 74.88\%$

Hence, the correct option is (B).

39. Number of male in town B for Second year

$= \dfrac{7 \times 240000}{12} = 140000$

Number of male in town B for third year

$= \dfrac{7 \times 270000}{12} = 157500$

Number of illiterate male in second year

$= \dfrac{1 \times 140000}{5} = 28000$

Number of literate male in third year

$= \dfrac{4 \times 157500}{5} = 126000$

Thus, required ratio $= 28000 : 126000$ i.e. $2:9$

Hence, the correct option is (D).

40. Number of illiterate male in third year for town B

$= \dfrac{1 \times 157500}{5} = 31500$

Number of female in third year for town B

$= \dfrac{5 \times 270000}{12} = 112500$

$\therefore$ Reqd. $\% = \dfrac{112500 - 31500}{112500} \times 100 = 72\%$

Hence, the correct option is (A).

Ques (41-44): Bahubali viewers -4500 and Robot viewers -4000

Bahubali viewers' distribution in theaters

INOX $-40\% = 1800, PVR - 35\% = 1575$ and Galaxy $-25\% = 900$

In INOX, Children $= 15\%$ so, adults $= 85\%$

Children $= 15\%(1800) = 270$ and Adults $= 85\%(1800) = 1530$

Similarly calculating for every theatre and each show, we get

Movie →	Bahubali			Robot 2.0			Total
Theatre	Viewers	Adult	Children	Viewers	Adult	Children	Viewers
INOX	1800	1530	270	1400	1120	280	3200
PVR	1575	1323	252	1000	820	180	2575
Galaxy	1125	900	225	1600	1328	272	2725

Tota l	450 0	37 53	747	400 0	32 68	732	8500

41. Number of children who saw Bahubali in PVR $= 252$

Number of children who saw Robot in $PVR = 180$

Required ratio $= 252 : 180 = 7 : 5$

Hence, the correct option is (D).

42. The number of children who watched Bahubali in INOX $= 270$

The number of adults who watched Bahubali in Galaxy $= 900$

Required $\% = \dfrac{270}{900} \times 100 = 30\%$

43. Total viewers in INOX $= 3200$

Total viewers in $PVR = 2575$

Required difference $= 3200 - 2575 = 625$

44. Sum of adults and children who watched Robot in INOX and PVR $= 1120 + 180 = 1300$

Sum of adults and children who watched Bahubali in Galaxy and INOX $= 900 + 270 = 1170$

Required ratio $= 1300 : 1170 = 10 : 9$

Hence, the correct option is (C).

Ques (45-48): Sample taken from district $A = 160 \times 100 = 16000$

Sample taken from district B $= 200 \times 100 = 20000$

Sample taken from district $C = 240 \times 100 = 24000$

Total samples $= 16000 + 20000 + 24000 = 60000$

Total samples of category $20 = 20\%$ of $60000 = 12000$

Total samples of category $20 - 40 = 50\%$ of $60000 = 30000$

Total samples of category $40 = 30\%$ of $60000 = 18000$

Distr icts	Category 20			Category 20-40			Category 40			Gra nd Tot al
	G H	P H	Tot al	GH	P H	Tot al	G H	P H	Tot al	
A	28 40			420 0			36 50			160 00
B	24 50			660 0			18 00			200 00
C	80 0			480 0			42 50			240 00
Tota l	60 90		120 00	156 00		300 00	97 00		180 00	

From condition (1),

In C, total samples of category $20 = 17.5\%$ of $24000 = 4200$

Samples tested in PH for category 20 from $C = 4200 - 800 = 3400$

Rest samples from C which were tested in $PH = 24000 - 4200 - 4800 - 4250 = 10750$

Samples tested in PH for category 20-40 from C = Samples tested in PH for category 40 from C

$= \dfrac{10750}{2} = 5375$

From condition (2),

Since, from A, for the category 40 , number of samples tested in GH was 82.5% more than number of samples tested in PH.

Let samples tested for the category 40 from A in $PH = x$

Samples tested for the category 40 from A in $GH = 182.5\%$ of $x = 1.825x$

So, $1.825x = 3650$

$x = 2000$

Samples tested for the category 40 from A in $PH = 2000$

Total samples tested for the category 40 from A $= 3650 + 2000 = 5650$

From condition (3),

Number of samples tested for category 20 from A and number of samples tested for category 20 from B together $= 12000 - 4200 = 7800$ Samples tested for category 20 from A

$= \dfrac{7800}{39} \times 19 = 3800$

Samples tested for category 20 from B

$= \dfrac{7800}{39} \times 20 = 4000$

Samples tested in PH for category 20 from $A = 3800 - 2840 = 960$

Samples tested in PH for category 20 from $B = 4000 - 2450 = 1550$

After using all three conditions, table will be

Dist ricts	Category 20			Category 20-40			Category 40			Gr an d Tot al
	G H	P H	Tot al	GH	P H	Tot al	G H	P H	Tot al	
A	28 40	96 0	38 00	42 00			36 50	20 00	56 50	16 00 0
B	24 50	15 50	40 00	66 00			18 00			20 00 0
C	80 0	34 00	42 00	48 00	53 75	10 17 5	42 50	53 75	96 25	24 00 0
Tot al	60 90	59 10	12 00 0	19 60		30 00 0	97 00		18 00 0	

Total samples tested for category 40 from $B = 18000 - 5650 - 9625 = 2725$

Samples tested for category 40 in PH from $B = 2725 -$

$1800 = 925$

Total samples tested for category $20 - 40$ from $A =$
$16000 - 3800 - 5650 = 6550$

Samples tested for category $20 - 40$ in PH from $A =$
$6550 - 4200 = 2350$

Total samples tested for category $20 - 40$ from $B =$
$20000 - 4000 - 2725 = 13275$

Samples tested for category $20 - 40$ in PH from B $=$
$13275 - 6600 = 6675$

Final table :

Dist ricts	Category 20			Category 20-40			Category 40			Gr an d Tot al
	GH	PH	Tot al	GH	PH	Tot al	GH	PH	Tot al	
A	2840	960	3800	4200	2350	6550	3650	2000	5650	160000
B	2450	1550	4000	6600	6675	13275	1800	925	2725	200000
C	800	3400	4200	4800	5375	10175	4250	5375	9625	240000
Tot al	6090	5910	120000	15600	14400	300000	9700	8300	180000	

45. Samples found positive for category 40 in PH from B $=$
20% of $925 = 185$

Samples found negative for category 40 in PH from B $=$
$925 - 185 = 740$

46. Ratio $= 4000 : 5650 = 80 : 113$

Hence, the correct option is (B).

47. Number of samples of males tested for category $20 - 40$ from $C = 10175 - 5175 = 5000$

$$\text{Percent} = \frac{5000}{2000} \times 100 = 250\%$$

Hence, the correct option is (D).

48. Number of samples tested in $GH = 6090 + 15600 + 9700 = 31390$

Number of samples tested in $PH = 60000 - 31390 = 28610$

Hence the correct answer is 28610.

Ques (49-52): Total sixes hit by all players across all format $= \dfrac{1482}{6} = 247$

Sixes hit in T20 match = 247 - 81 - 75 = 91

Sixes hit by Finch in T20 = 91 - (20 + 18 + 15 + 20) = 18

Sixes hit by Finch in all format $= \dfrac{372}{6} = 62$

Ratio of sixes hit by Finch in Test and one day match = 9 : 2

Sixes hit by Finch in Test $= (62 - 18) \times \dfrac{9}{11} = 36$

Sixes hit by Finch in One day = 62 - (18 + 36) = 8

Total sixes hit by Gayle across all format $= \dfrac{354}{6} = 59$

Total sixes hit by Dhoni across all format $= \dfrac{270}{6} = 45$

Sixes hit by Dhoni in Test match = 45 - 20 - 10 = 15

Players	T20 match	Test match	One day match	Total sixes	Runs scored in sixes
Dhoni	20	15	10	45	270
Pollard	18	- -	- -	- -	- -
Gayle	15	- -	- -	59	354
Hardik	20	10		- -	- -
Finch	18	36	8	62	372
Total	91	81	75	247	1482

49. Required Ratio = 18 : 36 : 8

= 9 : 18 : 4

Hence, the correct option is (A).

50. Sixes hit by Gayle in Test match = 10

Sixes hit by Gayle in One day match = 59 - 15 - 10 = 34

Sixes hit by Pollard in Test match = 81 - 15 - 10 - 10 - 36 = 10

Required ratio = 10 : 34

= 5 : 17

Hence, the correct option is (B).

51. Let the total sixes hit by Pollard and Hardik be 4x and 5x respectively.

$\Rightarrow$ 45 + 4x + 59 + 5x + 62 = 247

$\Rightarrow$ 9x = 81

$\Rightarrow$ x = 9

Total sixes hit by Pollard and Hardik is 36 and 45 respectively

Pollard hits 12 sixes in Test match

$\Rightarrow$ Sixes hit by Polard in One day match = 36 - 18 - 12 = 6

$\Rightarrow$ Sixes hit by gayle in Test match = 81 - 15 - 12 - 10 - 36 = 8

$\therefore$ Difference of runs scored only in sixes = (8 - 6) × 6 = 12

Hence, the correct option is (C).

52. Hardik hits 15 sixes in One day,

$\Rightarrow$ Runs scored by Hardik = (20 + 10 + 15) × 6 = 270

$\Rightarrow$ Runs scored by Pollard = 1482 - 270 - 354 - 270 - 372 = 216

$\therefore$ Required difference = 354 - 216 = 138

Hence, the correct option is (D).

53. Let the total number of employees in the the year 2005 be x.

So, the total number of managers in $2005 = \dfrac{80}{100} \times x = 0.8x \Rightarrow$

Total number of workers in $2005 = x - 0.8x = 0.2x$

Thus, the number of male managers in $2005 = \dfrac{5}{8} \times 0.8x = 0.5x$

And the total number of employees in the the year 2006 be y.

Also, So, the total number of managers in $2006 = \dfrac{50}{100} \times y = 0.5y$

Total number of workers in $2006 = y - 0.5y = 0.5y$

Thus, the number of male managers in $2006 = \dfrac{2}{5} \times 0.5y = 0.2y$

As the number of workers is the same, we get:

$0.2x = 0.5y$

$\Rightarrow x = 2.5y \dots$ (i)

Using equation (i), the required ratio will become:

$\dfrac{(0.5 \times 2.5y)}{0.2y} = \dfrac{25}{4}$

$\therefore$ The required ratio between the number of male managers in 2005 and 2006 is $25 : 4$.

Hence, the correct option is (D).

54. Number of workers in $2008 = 1400$

As the number of total workers has doubled in 2008 from 2007,

Number of workers in $2007 = \dfrac{1400}{2} = 700$

Also, the percentage of the total employees working as managers in $2007 = 65\%$

Thus, the percentage of the total employees working as workers in $2007 = 100 - 65 = 35\%$

So, 35% of the total employees in $2007 = 700$

Total employees in $2007 = 700 \times \dfrac{100}{35} = 2000$

So, the number of managers in the year $2007 = 2000 - 700 = 1300$

Hence, the correct option is (C).

55. Ratio of male managers to female managers in $2003 = 3 : 2$

The number of male managers in $2003 = 480$

Thus, the number of female managers in $2003 = 480 \times \dfrac{2}{3} = 320$

So, the total number of managers in $2003 = 480 + 320 = 800$

Percentage of the total employees as managers in $2003 = 40\%$

So, $\dfrac{40}{100} \times$ total employees in $2003 = 800$

Total employees in $2003 = 800 \times \dfrac{100}{40} = 2000$

Similarly, we have:

Ratio of male managers to female managers in $2005 = 5 : 3$

The number of female managers in $2005 = 450$

Thus, the number of male managers in $2005 = 450 \times \dfrac{5}{3} = 750$

So, the total number of managers in $2005 = 450 + 750 = 1200$

Percentage of the total employees as managers in $2005 = 80\%$

So, $\dfrac{80}{100} \times$ total employees in $2005 = 1200$

Total employees in $2005 = 1200 \times \dfrac{100}{80} = 1500$

Thus, the required ratio $= 2000 : 1500 = 4 : 3$

Hence, the correct option is (B).

56. Number of employees in the company in $2005 = 1000$

So, total number of managers in $2005 = \dfrac{80}{100} \times 1000 = 800$

Thus, the number of workers $= 1000 - 800 = 200$

Now, the number of male and female workers is equal.

So, the number of female workers in $2005 = \dfrac{200}{2} = 100$

Also, the number of female managers $= \dfrac{3}{8} \times 800 = 300$

Thus, the required difference $= 300 - 100 = 200$

$\therefore$ The difference between the number of female workers and the number of female managers in the year 2005 is 200.

Hence, the correct option is (B).

Ques (57-60): Given:

Formula Used:

If time taken finish the work $= X$ days

$\therefore$ Part of work completed in one day $= \dfrac{1}{X}$

Efficiency $\propto \dfrac{1}{\text{Time}}$

Let the time taken by Sita alone to complete the work $= x$ days

$\therefore$ The time taken by Rita alone to complete the work $=$
$(x + 14)$ days

Now, The ratio of efficiency of Gita to Rita is $4:5$.

$\therefore$ Efficiency of Rita $= \dfrac{1}{(x+14)}$ and Efficiency of Gita $=$
$\dfrac{1}{(x+14)} \times \dfrac{4}{5}$

Also, efficiency of Gita to Mita is $6:7$

$\therefore$ Efficiency of Mita $= \dfrac{4}{[5(x+14)]} \times \dfrac{7}{6} = \dfrac{14}{[15(x+14)]}$

Then according to the question,

$\therefore \dfrac{11}{x} + \left\{ \dfrac{1}{x} + \dfrac{4}{5(x+14)} \right\} \times 15 + \left\{ \dfrac{14}{15(x+14)} \right\} \times 10 = 1$

$\Rightarrow \dfrac{11}{x} + \dfrac{15}{x} + \dfrac{12}{(x+14)} + \dfrac{28}{3(x+14)} = 1$

$\Rightarrow 3x^2 - 126x + 26x - 1092 = 0$

$\Rightarrow 3x(x - 42) + 26(x - 42) = 0$

$\Rightarrow (x - 42)(x + 26) = 0$

$\Rightarrow x = 42, x = -26$ So, $x = 42$

Time taken by Sita alone to complete the work $= 42$ days

Time taken by Rita alone to complete the work $=$
$(42 + 14) = 56$ days

Time taken by Gita alone to complete the work $= \dfrac{5(42+14)}{4} =$
70 days

Time taken by Mita alone to complete the work $=$
$\dfrac{15(42+14)}{14} = 60$ days

57. From the data formed above Sita completes the work in 42 days only.

$\therefore$ Sita is most efficient.

Hence, the correct option is (C).

58. Thus, Mita alone to complete the work in 60 days.

Hence, the correct option is (B).

59. Now the ratio of time taken by Rita to Sita $= 56:42 =$
$4:3$

$\therefore$ The ratio of their efficiency $= 3:4$

Hence, the correct option is (A).

60. $\therefore \dfrac{1}{42} + \dfrac{1}{70} = \dfrac{1}{D}$

$\Rightarrow D = 26.25$ days

Hence, the correct option is (A).

Ques (1-4):Direction: Read the following passage and answer the questions carefully. Certain words are printed in bold in order to help you locate them while answering some of the questions.

Global estimates published by the World Health Organization (WHO) indicate that about 1 in 3 (35%) women worldwide have experienced either physical and/or sexual intimate partner violence or non-partner sexual violence in their lifetime. Worldwide as many as 38% of murders of women are committed by a male intimate partner. What makes this worse for countries like India is the fact that intimate partner violence is the highest at 37.7% in the WHO South-East Asia region. As per figures released by WHO, the violence ranges from 23.2% in high-income countries and 24.6% in the WHO Western Pacific region to 37% in the WHO Eastern Mediterranean region.

"Violence against women — particularly intimate partner violence and sexual violence — is a major public health problem and a violation of women's human rights. WHO together with UN Women and other partners has developed a framework for prevention of violence against women called Respect which can be used by governments to counter this menace," noted WHO.

Meanwhile, healthcare professionals cautioned that violence can negatively affect a woman's physical, mental, sexual, and reproductive health, and may increase the risk of acquiring HIV in some settings. Explaining how gender-based violence is **perpetrated**, the global health organisation said that men are more likely to perpetrate violence if they have low education, a history of child maltreatment, exposure to domestic violence against their mothers, harmful use of alcohol, unequal gender norms, including attitudes accepting of violence, and a sense of entitlement over women.

Women are more likely to experience intimate partner violence if they have low education, exposure to mothers being abused by a partner, abuse during childhood, and attitudes accepting violence, male privilege and women's subordinate status. Warning that intimate partner violence causes serious short-and long-term problems for women and **adversely** affect their children besides leading to high social and economic costs for women, their families and societies, WHO said: "There is now evidence that advocacy and empowerment counselling interventions, as well as home visitation, are promising in preventing or reducing intimate partner violence against women."

Q.1 Which among the following is the main issue for women as highlighted in the information given in the passage?

A. Women have to go through a lot of hardships during pregnancy and that should be taken care of

B. The government is not serious about providing shelter to homeless women especially in under developed countries

C. The developing nations are yet to understand the problem of having too much male population

D. Women face a lot of events of violence in their intimate and sexual lives, especially in developing countries

Q.2 Which among the following correctly defines the position of India in the context of violence against women, as stated in the passage?

A. India is far better than the developed countries where the rate of such crimes is increasing day by day

B. India is at par with all the other countries of the world given the fact that it is same for women everywhere.

C. India is worse than most of the developed countries since the incidents of violence against women are more in the South Asian region of the world.

D. The WHO has not given any status report typical to India and its neighboring countries making it impossible to understand the Indian context

Q.3 Which among the following cannot be considered as an adverse effect of the violence against women, as described in the given passage?

A. The children of such couples suffer a lot due to such incidents of violence.

B. The families of the women suffer a lot due to the attacks on their children by their partners.

C. Society, as a whole, suffers a lot due to such incidents of violence against women.

D. None of the above

Q.4 Which among the following can be considered as a reason why men indulge in violence against women, as described in the passage?

A. The men have such upbringing where they must have observed their family members doing so.

B. The men who do such things are not educated enough to understand the adverse effects of such actions.

C. The men who do such things may have been treated badly during their own childhood.

D. All of the above

Ques (5-8):Direction: Read the passage carefully and select the best answer to the given question out of the given four alternatives.

RBI Governor Shaktikanta Das expressed optimism about the overall COVID-19 situation following the rollout of the vaccines and complimented all the SAARC central banks for their efforts in combating the pandemic, the central bank said in a statement on Tuesday. Das made these remarks in his opening speech at the 41st Meeting of the SAARCFINANCE Governors' Group in virtual format on Monday. Das chaired the meeting. Das led the discussions on progress made under the SAARCFINANCE initiatives, achieved with the all-round cooperation of the SAARC central banks and launched the maiden issue of the annual SAARCFINANCE e-Newsletter. While the Governors agreed that the pandemic had an adverse impact on their economies, they recognized the importance of leveraging technology to spur growth, the RBI said. The meeting was attended by the Governors from other SAARC central banks – Ajmal Ahmadi, Da Afghanistan Bank; Fazle Kabir, Bangladesh Bank; Dasho Penjore, Royal Monetary Authority of Bhutan; Ali Hashim, Maldives Monetary Authority; Maha Prasad Adhikari, Nepal Rastra Bank; Reza Baqir, State Bank of Pakistan; and W D Lakshman, Central Bank of Sri Lanka. With the RBI's tenure coming to a close, Governor Das handed over the SAARCFINANCE Chair (effective from April 01, 2021) to the Governor, Maldives Monetary Authority and assured him of the Reserve Bank's continued commitment to the SAARCFINANCE initiative. SAARCFINANCE is a network of central bank governors and finance secretaries of the SAARC region. The Reserve Bank of India is the present chair of the SAARCFINANCE from October 2019 to March 2021.

While inaugurating the SAARCFINANCE Governors' Symposium on Tuesday, Das emphasised the importance of effective, creative and prudent use of technology by central bankers, especially in the areas of big data, digital currencies, reg-tech, sup-tech and cyber security. The keynote address was delivered by Jermy Prenio, Senior Adviser, Financial Stability Institute, BIS on the topic 'Suptech use in central banks'. The Symposium also included a Panel Discussion on 'Cyber Security in Central Banks' and a presentation by the researchers of the SAARCFINANCE Collaborative Study on 'Comparison of Financial Sector Regulatory Regimes in the SAARC Region', the RBI's release added.

Q.5 Which of the following statements is false according to the passage?

SAARCFINANCE initiative is a network where the

A. Governors of banks and finance secretaries of the SAARC region exchange their ideas.

B. Prudent use of technology like digital currencies, sup-tech etc will stimulate growth.

C. 'Cyber Security in Central Banks' was also discussed in the 41st Meeting of the SAARCFINANCE Governors' Group.

D. The central bank governors are not hopeful about the overall covid situation.

Q.6 Why did the RBI Governor praise the SAARC central banks?

A. To praise their new schemes

B. To improve the economy of India

C. To improve the infrastructure of the RBI

D. To commend their efforts in combating the pandemic

Q.7 Which of the following statements is true according to the passage?

A. The keynote address of SAARCFINANCE initiative was on the topic of cyber security issues during covid 19.

B. The Reserve bank of India is the organizer of SAARCFINANCE Symposium.

C. Royal Monetary Authority of Bhutan is the present chair of the SAARCFINANCE.

D. Jermy Prenio, is the Senior Adviser of the Financial Stability Institute, BIS .

Q.8 Choose the synonym of the word 'Adverse'.

A. Lucrative   **B.** Productive

C. Hostile   **D.** Essential

Ques (9-12):Directions: Read the passage and answer the following questions.

Long-awaited Afghanistan's peace process is focused to empower the country people for sustainable development by addressing the core and utmost necessity to emerge as a successful nation. "We Want Peace!" and "No War!"- An urgency that enveloped the entire atmosphere in Afghanistan reflecting the Afghan people's quest for peace and stability. The Afghan people's **undaunted** spirit is appreciable that echoes 'the national movement will be strengthened and supported by the people in large numbers, Afghanistan has been witnessing bloodshed for over 40 years of conflict resulting in dismantling growth and prosperity. The emotional toll of the prolonged war is in immeasurable terms and more importantly, the increasing number of casualties reminds the grim picture of the state. Afghanistan's tremendous potential for trade, connectivity, geo-political strategic importance and people-to-people contact for inclusive development can take the country to trajectory level has been hampered by escalating challenges. Afghanistan is continuously persuading peace-building efforts for the people of the country that is reflective through bilateral ties, regional cooperation programmes and time to time working on Confidence Building Measures (CBM's). 'Afghan-led Afghan Owned' is President Ghani's approach for sustained peace. Therefore it is very important to strategize an efficient, unified and effective national security apparatus in establishing peace in the country. Corruption is the most pressing issue which the Government of Afghanistan is trying to bring down and it is spelt through President Ghani's initiative 'Corruption in recess, Peace in progress'. Afghanistan in the best possible way is seeking initiatives to fulfil the commitment of democracy. The upcoming election in Afghanistan is the reflection of the best practice of inclusive governance. With regard to the current situation, the component of peace in Afghanistan also depends on the regional countries stance for seeking collective action centred around **solidarity**- economic, cultural, political and social till Afghanistan attain stability. Emphasis on the cooperation by regional countries could **incentivize** to provide a tangible mechanism in establishing long-term peace in Afghanistan. The presence of the United States of America for the past 17 years in Afghanistan since the overthrow of the Taliban regime was a commitment to provide longer-term military support for uprooting terrorism in the country. The recent announcement of withdrawing of 7,000 US troops from Afghanistan this year by President Donald Trump will seem to have a detrimental effect at a crucial time of Afghanistan's Presidential elections slated to July 2019. US's stance for Afghanistan needs to be in continuation for achieving peace and curbing terrorism. For the upcoming elections, more forces are required in Afghanistan. The U.S must coordinate with Russia, Pakistan and Iran keeping in mind to work for the people of Afghanistan. Pakistan must take a firm step in curtailing terrorism from their soil. India has been extending assistance to Afghanistan mainly in the field of capacity building, education, training and the bilateral relation between the two nations have grown from strength to strength. The complementarities between the two countries obviously make them natural partners. "India firmly believes in the critical role that developmental assistance can play in transforming human lives". Regional countries must continue to push for Taliban factions to return to peace talks and pick up negotiations for a **cease-fire** from where they let off. The narrative of Afghanistan's development is much dependent on the planned economic agenda which is envisioned through the connectivity potential between Central and South Asia and can be a trade and energy hub in the region. In order to achieve this vision, a political consensus with regional cooperation can bring immense prosperity within and outside the country.

Q.9 Which of the following can be inferred from the passage?

A. Afghanistan has faced a stressed situation for a long time and initiatives have been taken by the Government recently to ensure peace in the country.

B. Afghanistan does not need any interference of the US government and the regional countries should help in the process.

C. India has been providing assistance to Afghanistan for its improvement but the terrorism activities prevalent in Pakistan have been impeding it.

D. B and C both

Q.10 Which of the following is/are needed to ensure peace in the country?

A. Pakistan must extend its assistance in terms of military support to curb the Taliban factions.

B. The military support that has been provided by the US government should continue especially for the successful occurrence of the elections.

C. Assistance from the regional countries is extremely important for improving the economic condition.

D. B and C both

Q.11 Which of the following are correct regarding the relationship that Afghanistan shares with the other countries?

A. India has been supportive of Afghanistan's development and has extended support to make the country financially more sound.

B. Afghanistan has co-ordinated with Russia and Pakistan for achieving peace and curbing terrorism.

C. USA has provided security to the country for curbing terrorism but is withdrawing some of its military support.

D. Both A and C

Q.12 Which of the following can be concluded from the passage?

A. Afghanistan is trying its best to ameliorate the situation and establish peace in the country by taking several steps.

B. Afghanistan has a strong potential of becoming a business hub due to its geo-political-strategic importance.

C. Terrorism in Pakistan is a threat to the peace and stability of Afghanistan thus it must be curtailed.

D. All the above

Ques (13-16):Direction: Read the passage given below and then answer the questions given below the passage. Some words may be highlighted for your attention. Read carefully.

There is a lot of talk these days, not so much among government circles as among the 'strategic community', about India being a major or even global power, with the capability, even responsibility, to play an 'important role' on the world stage as a balancing power between major powers and as a 'security provider' to others. We need to temper this **rhetoric**, be more realistic and less ambitious. The dividing line between national pride and national ego can be thin. India's first Prime Minister Jawaharlal Nehru was convinced that India was bound to play an increasing and beneficent part in world affairs. He had developed a zeal for diplomacy that was not backed by the needed military and economic hard power. He was banking on our moral high ground because he and the nation were proud of the non-violent manner in which we had achieved our independence. As early as 1948, he declared: "India had already become the fourth or fifth most influential country in the United Nations." This was a strange claim; just a year earlier, we were forced to withdraw our candidature for the Security Council when Ukraine, which was contesting the same seat, secured more votes than us in seven successive ballots in a single day. We have been afflicted with this malady ever since.

Over the decades, no doubt influenced by our experience in the early years in Kashmir and China, the idealist strain has diminished and eventually disappeared altogether; national interest alone would guide our policy. This is not necessarily an undesirable thing. The only caveat is that we have to be realists and check the **inexplicable** urge to play a big role in international relations. Leaders everywhere look for a role for themselves. They believe, perhaps genuinely, that an increased prestige for themselves will translate into more votes domestically and ipso facto bring benefits to their countries. The driving factor is prestige, status. Often the leaders do not realize that playing a role carries with it responsibilities which we may not be able or keen to accept but which we might be dragged into. These responsibilities would be defined by others and would invariably involve us into tasks and areas which we may not wish to get involved in. Recent events do not lend support to that view and the government was right in not paying heed to that rhetoric. India is without doubt the pre-eminent power in South Asia. However, given our firm commitment not to use force and to non-interference in internal affairs in other states, our neighbors do not feel threatened by us. We did make a huge effort in Sri Lanka to bring peace and stability to that country and we did so at the request of its lawful government. The venture ended in failure and eventually cost the life of a former prime minister. Small-scale interventions in the Maldives and the Seychelles in the 1980s were successful in stabilizing legitimate governments. To that extent, India was able to play a positive role in the region. In these examples, the motivating factor was not prestige, there were domestic factors at play. The resulting increase in our prestige was incidental. If intervention does not succeed, as in Sri Lanka, the ensuing loss of prestige more than offsets whatever prestige we might have gained in the other operations. Often, when a country gets involved in what might be assessed as a low cost foreign adventure, it remains bogged down even when the going gets tough precisely because it apprehends loss of face or prestige. It is easy to get in but difficult to get out.

Apart from protecting our people from adverse external factors and interventions, the principal criterion in the conduct of foreign policy for India ought to be lifting the poor from poverty. Whatever brings concrete benefits to our people should be encouraged. A mere wish to be praised as a global or even regional power should not be allowed to guide the policy. When other countries flatter us by describing us as a major power, it is invariably because they want to rope us into

some schemes of their own. It is best not to get too entangled in the chess moves of other countries. The principal interest of most of them is to sell very expensive military hardware to us. Our single minded focus should be on economic development. Without the necessary economic strength, we cannot strengthen our military. We do need a strong military but for that we need undisturbed double digit economic growth for a generation. Prime Minister Vajpayee's seasoned adviser Brajesh Mishra's advice was sound: do not provoke nor get provoked for two decades, concentrate on building the economy. Since we do have to think critically about allocating our scarce resources among alternative uses, and since we are a democratic polity with a multi-religious and multi-ethnic society with a large number of poor, we have to think more than twice about defense spending. Even when at some stage we acquire credible hard power, we must not allow ourselves to be seduced by the flattering and mostly insincere talk of others about India playing a global role. Other countries express their admiration, not so much for our economy or military, but for the orderly manner in which power is transferred from one party to another and for the largely **harmonious** and peaceful, integrated manner in which people of different faiths live together. An internally divided India cannot play any role externally. The 'strategic community' should concentrate on reinforcing this real soft power of India which is what the rest of the world appreciates and not lose time and resources in peripheral ventures that bring no lasting benefit.

Q.13 Which of the following are TRUE with reference to the context of the passage?

A. India's foreign policy should emphasis on extirpating poverty.

B. India needs a robust economy without which it cannot invigorate its military.

C. Leaders believe burgeoning prestige on global level may impede their vote bank domestically.

D. Both (A) and (B)

Q.14 According to the given passage, which of the following options is considered as a warning that need to focus for economic growth in the country?

A. We should be harmonious in the matter of contesting elections

B. Government should threaten neighboring countries by interfering in inter-states matters

C. It is necessary to be rationalist and not focus more on puzzling international relations

D. We can strengthen our country on the basis of strong military

Q.15 According to the passage, which of the following is the reason behind other countries' callousing India by describing it as major power?

A. To increase their prestige at global level

B. To invest in India's big companies

C. To be in business of military weapons and equipment

D. To gain more support in relief operations from India

Q.16 On the basis of your reading, choose an appropriate title for the passage.

A. Impact of India at global level

B. Importance of strong military

C. Liabilities associated with a leader

D. Soft power of India

Ques (17-20):Direction: Read the following passage carefully and answer the questions given below. Certain words are highlighted for your attention. Read carefully.

Credit is an important instrument for rural development. Most of the agricultural chores still depend on manual labour. It also involves techniques which are outdated and result in low outputs. The investment in rural areas has been on a low which effectively results in low output and productivity in all kinds of activities. A capital infusion for a jump in productivity in reference to both agricultural and non-agricultural activities can be achieved by reforming credit and banking system. During the gestation period between sowing and harvesting seasons, farmers need credit to make ends meet, their general needs, initial requirements etc. Additionally, they also need credit to venture into modern agricultural techniques, to buy cattle, land etc.

The difference in monetary activities of rural people relative to urban people led to the realization of NABARD (National Bank For Agricultural And Rural Development), in addition to the presence of RBI.

The post-independence period saw exploitation of rural poor in need of credit, by the hands of moneylenders and traders. Loans were granted at very high-interest rates which ultimately pulled defaulters into a debt trap, robbing them out of credit. To stop this exploitation NABARD was established to provide rural areas with easy credit. Although RBI is the national banking apex body, NABARD has been given powers that establish it as the apex banking body in rural India which regulates all the credit and banking activities of rural India. Although NABARD has been proving to be a step in the right direction, the problem with formal banking system is that some kind of collateral is required. The rural poor in need of urgent credit, don't generally possess any collateral. Consequently, they are ruled out of the formal banking system. To help such kind of people self-help groups (SHG) emerged on the scene. They are successfully bridging the gap between formal credit system and rural poor.

Such groups dispense small credit to the needy members, who need to provide a minimum sum to the pool initially. Then loans can be taken from the sum collected at very cheap interest rates. For this reason, by March-end 2003, more than seven lakh SHGS were reported operational. Such credit provisions are referred to as micro-credit programmes.

The banking and credit system in rural India has come a long way. With credit available at low-interest rates through operation of NABARD and microcredit generation by the various self-help groups, less poor are falling into the debt trap. After the advent of the green revolution, productivity in agriculture increased manifold. In essence modern techniques, high yielding variety seeds, sustainable activities etc. have been promoting productivity and output. But the formal banking system has been proving inadequate in lending to worthwhile borrowers and effective loan recovery. By and large, the number of loan defaulters is rising. The poor are forced to look in direction of informal moneylenders, who exploit them. Hence some changes are required.

The rural banks need to establish a banking relationship with the people and scrap away the image of just money lenders. The banking system in rural India needs a reform, considering the difference in livelihoods of urban and rural people. **Leniency** on the part of the government in the collection of taxes inculcated a habit of not repaying borrowed amounts among people which needs to be altered. Banks need to educate people about thrift generation and efficient utilization of financial resources to become feasible again.

Q.17 What is/are the reason(s) that make(s) the introduction of credit system important in rural areas?

A. Farmers can venture into modern agricultural techniques

B. To enhance the productivity of both the agricultural and non-agricultural activities

C. To meet the basic needs of farmers during the gestation period

D. All of these

Q.18 Which one of the following change is not suggested in the passage for the formal banking system in the rural sector?

A. Banks need to build a relationship with people while removing the image of just money lenders.

B. Banks need to formulate policies according to the difference in the livelihood of urban and rural people

C. Banks need to spread awareness about thrift generation and efficient utilization of financial resources

D. Banks need to lower the interest rates to increase the credit distribution among the people

Q.19 What was the justification to establish the Self-help groups for the rural poor?

A. SHGs provide long term institutional loans for the rural people.

B. SHGS provide the sum to repay the easy monthly installments for the loan.

C. A programme for credit was required at the proximity.

D. Rural poor didn't possess any collateral to mortgage for the urgent loan.

Q.20 What led to the establishment of NABARD for the rural sector?

A. To provide easy credit in the rural areas

B. Money lenders and traders used to charge high rate of interests to trap the defaulters into the debt trap

C. The difference in monetary activities of rural people as compared to urban people

D. All of the above

Q.21 Direction: Read the passage given below and answer the question.

In line with the proposed deal, Axis Bank NSE -0.78 % is likely to raise its stake in Max Life Insurance to about 20 percent over the next year, said the insurance company's CEO Prashant Tripathy. Currently, Axis Bank and its two subsidiaries -- Axis Capital Ltd and Axis Securities Ltd -- collectively own 12.99 percent in Max Life Insurance post-approval of the deal in April this year.

With this, Axis entities have now become co-promoters of Max Life with three board seats. "Axis Bank is to increase to 19.99 percent in tranches. Thirteen percent is already done over the next two quarters, we will seek approval for the balance of seven percent. So, it will reach about 20 percent and that will be the ownership of Axis Bank," Tripathy told. When asked about the timeline for the completion of the remaining stake transfer, he said: "It should happen in the next 12 to 18 months." Under the deal, the Axis entities also have the right to acquire an additional stake of up to seven percent in Max Life, in one or more tranches, subject to regulatory approvals.

Tripathy said there is no change in the brand but the tagline will have the name of Axis Bank as the joint venture partner. Talking about synergy, he said, "We are coming up with a new strategy for future growth. We are working together as a common team to ensure that Max Insurance life grows faster than the industry. We are working together to look at product mix to drive Axis channel so that the outcome is favourable for both customers and the company." Besides, he said working on analytics areas to leverage each other's capabilities. He said the company launched 14 products or product variants last year and increased the margin by 3.60 percent in 2020-21.

Max Life Insurance recorded a 22 percent rise in its total new business premium (individual and group) to Rs 6,826 crore in the financial year ending in March 2021.

The renewal premium income of the insurer rose 15 percent to Rs 12,192 crore, taking the gross premium to Rs 19,018 crore, up by 18 percent from a year ago. In terms of individual APE (adjusted premium equivalent), the company witnessed a growth of 19 percent to Rs 4,907 crore. Max Life's post-tax shareholders' profit fell six percent to Rs 523 crore in 2020-21 as compared to Rs 539 crore in the previous year.

What is the tone of the passage?

A. Nihilistic   **B.** Optimistic

C. Sarcastic   **D.** Sardonic

Ques (22-24):Direction: Read the passage given below and answer the question.

In line with the proposed deal, Axis Bank NSE -0.78 % is likely to raise its stake in Max Life Insurance to about 20 percent over the next year, said the insurance company's CEO Prashant Tripathy. Currently, Axis Bank and its two subsidiaries -- Axis Capital Ltd and Axis Securities Ltd -- collectively own 12.99 percent in Max Life Insurance post-approval of the deal in April this year.

With this, Axis entities have now become co-promoters of Max Life with three board seats. "Axis Bank is to increase to 19.99 percent in tranches. Thirteen percent is already done over the next two quarters, we will seek approval for the balance of seven percent. So, it will reach about 20 percent and that will be the ownership of Axis Bank," Tripathy told. When asked about the timeline for the completion of the remaining stake transfer, he said: "It should happen in the next 12 to 18 months." Under the deal, the Axis entities also have the right to acquire an additional stake of up to seven percent in Max Life, in one or more tranches, subject to regulatory approvals.

Tripathy said there is no change in the brand but the tagline will have the name of Axis Bank as the joint venture partner. Talking about synergy, he said, "We are coming up with a new strategy for future growth. We are working together as a common team to ensure that Max Insurance life grows faster than the industry. We are working together to look at product mix to drive Axis channel so that the outcome is favourable for both customers and the company." Besides, he said working on analytics areas to leverage each other's capabilities. He said the company launched 14 products or product variants last year and increased the margin by 3.60 percent in 2020-21.

Max Life Insurance recorded a 22 percent rise in its total new business premium (individual and group) to Rs 6,826 crore in the financial year ending in March 2021.

The renewal premium income of the insurer rose 15 percent to Rs 12,192 crore, taking the gross premium to Rs 19,018 crore, up by 18 percent from a year ago. In terms of individual APE (adjusted premium equivalent), the company witnessed a growth of 19 percent to Rs 4,907 crore. Max Life's post-tax shareholders' profit fell six percent to Rs 523 crore in 2020-21 as compared to Rs 539 crore in the previous year.

Q.22 According to Mr. Tripathy, when will the remaining stake transfer take place?

A. In 12-20 months   **B.** In 15-19 months

C. In 12-18 months   **D.** In 16-18 months

Q.23 Which of the following statement(s) is/are NOT TRUE according to the passage?

A. The company launched 14 products or product variants last year and increased the margin by 3.60 percent in 2020-21

B. In terms of individual APE (adjusted premium equivalent), the company witnessed a growth of 20 percent to Rs 4,907 crore.

C. Max Life Insurance recorded a 22 percent rise in its total new business premium (individual and group) to Rs 6,826 crore in the financial year ended March 2021.

D. Both (A) and (C)

Q.24 What is the antonym of the word 'Approval'?

A. Mandate   **B.** Repudiation

C. Imprimatur   **D.** Assent

Q.25 Direction: Read the passage and answer the questions that follow.

We now spend more time online each day than we do in sleep. But how does that affect our everyday lives? What effect does it have on how we communicate and interact, how we work and engage with the rest of the world? Well, we have some answers to these questions. But they're not black and white. What we've found is that there are as many positive implications and improvements to our everyday lives as there are potentially negative consequences. The key is to use them in ways that are beneficial. Seize the many opportunities digital media offers and avoid the risks that arise from overuse or maleficent use. A survey of 5,000 digital media users across five countries paints a positive picture: half of the respondents agreed that their digital media use had improved their overall quality of life –

both socially and professionally. Only one in seven respondents disagreed.

The most positive effects of digital media were found in the work sphere. Roughly two-thirds of survey respondents said that digital media use had improved their ability to learn and develop professionally. This included their ability to carry out their work, collaborate with colleagues and build relationships. New digital technologies offer the opportunity to work across boundaries of location and time, opening up job opportunities for remotely located workers and ensuring access to the best talent, no matter where it is located around the globe. Then there's online education: programmes such as Coursera offer online courses from different universities. Professional social networks such as LinkedIn allow for networking, while talent platforms like Upwork help to source the best contingent talent. However, digital media usage has to be managed well, especially when it comes to the extent of usage, the type of social interaction and the nature of the content accessed. According to the survey, the least positive effects were reported in the personal sphere. While roughly four out of 10 respondents reported positive effects on long-term memory, attention span, the ability to find a partner, stress and health, about one in 10 respondents found those same areas to be negatively affected.

The survey didn't just throw up differences between people, countries, too, returned varied results. While perceptions in emerging markets such as China and Brazil were largely positive (in China, two-thirds agree that digital media use has improved their quality of life), opinions in Germany and the United States were less enthusiastic. In Germany, for instance, only 30% agree (and 24% disagree) that digital media use has improved their quality of life. The differences are astonishing.

What is the central idea Digital media is the future?

A. Digital media is the future.

B. Digital media has as more negative aspects than positive.

C. To criticize the implications of digital media.

D. To discuss the pros and cons of digital media.

Q.26 Direction: Read the passage and answer the questions that follow.

We now spend more time online each day than we do in sleep. But how does that affect our everyday lives? What effect does it have on how we communicate and interact, how we work and engage with the rest of the world? Well, we have some answers to these questions. But they're not black and white. What we've found is that there are as many positive implications and improvements to our everyday lives as there are potentially negative consequences. The key is to use them in ways that are beneficial. Seize the many opportunities digital media offers and avoid the risks that arise from overuse or maleficent use. A survey of 5,000 digital media users across five countries paints a positive picture: half of the respondents agreed that their digital media use had improved their overall quality of life – both socially and professionally. Only one in seven respondents disagreed.

The most positive effects of digital media were found in the work sphere. Roughly two-thirds of survey respondents said that digital media use had improved their ability to learn and develop professionally. This included their ability to carry out their work, collaborate with colleagues and build relationships. New digital technologies offer the opportunity to work across boundaries of location and time, opening up job opportunities for remotely located workers and ensuring access to the best talent, no matter where it is located around the globe. Then there's online education: programmes such as Coursera offer online courses from different universities. Professional social networks such as LinkedIn allow for networking, while talent platforms like Upwork help to source the best contingent talent. However, digital media usage has to be managed well, especially when it comes to the extent of usage, the type of social interaction and the nature of the content accessed. According to the survey, the least positive effects were reported in the personal sphere. While roughly four out of 10 respondents reported positive effects on long-term memory, attention span, the ability to find a partner, stress and health, about one in 10 respondents found those same areas to be negatively affected.

The survey didn't just throw up differences between people, countries, too, returned varied results. While perceptions in emerging markets such as China and Brazil were largely positive (in China, two-thirds agree that digital media use has improved their quality of life), opinions in Germany and the United States were less enthusiastic. In Germany, for instance, only 30% agree (and 24% disagree) that digital media use has improved their quality of life. The differences are astonishing.

What can be inferred from the sentence 'but they are not black and white'?

A. The answers to the questions are clear.

B. The answers to the questions are not clear.

C. The answers pertaining to what effect does digital media have on our social life are clear.

D. The answers pertaining to what effect digital media has on our social life are not absolute.

Q.27 Direction: Read the passage and answer the questions that follow.

We now spend more time online each day than we do in sleep. But how does that affect our everyday lives? What effect does it have on how we communicate and interact, how we work and engage with the rest of the world? Well, we have some answers to these questions. But they're not black and white. What we've found is that there are as many positive implications and improvements to our everyday lives as there are potentially negative consequences. The key is to use them in ways that are beneficial. Seize the many opportunities digital media offers and avoid the risks that arise from overuse or maleficent use. A survey of 5,000 digital media users across five countries paints a positive picture: half of the respondents agreed that their digital media use had improved their overall quality of life – both socially and professionally. Only one in seven respondents disagreed.

The most positive effects of digital media were found in the work sphere. Roughly two-thirds of survey respondents said that digital media use had improved their ability to learn and develop professionally. This included their ability to carry out their work, collaborate with colleagues and build relationships.

New digital technologies offer the opportunity to work across boundaries of location and time, opening up job opportunities for remotely located workers and ensuring access to the best talent, no matter where it is located around the globe. Then there's online education: programmes such as Coursera offer online courses from different universities. Professional social networks such as LinkedIn allow for networking, while talent platforms like Upwork help to source the best contingent talent. However, digital media usage has to be managed well, especially when it comes to the extent of usage, the type of social interaction and the nature of the content accessed. According to the survey, the least positive effects were reported in the personal sphere. While roughly four out of 10 respondents reported positive effects on long-term memory, attention span, the ability to find a partner, stress and health, about one in 10 respondents found those same areas to be negatively affected.

The survey didn't just throw up differences between people, countries, too, returned varied results. While perceptions in emerging markets such as China and Brazil were largely positive (in China, two-thirds agree that digital media use has improved their quality of life), opinions in Germany and the United States were less enthusiastic. In Germany, for instance, only 30% agree (and 24% disagree) that digital media use has improved their quality of life. The differences are astonishing.

What has been referred to as 'that' in the sentence 'But how does that affect our everyday lives'?'

A. Online activity on Whats App

B. Less sleep due to media

C. Insomnia

D. Digital media

Q.28 Direction: Read the passage and answer the questions that follow.

We now spend more time online each day than we do in sleep. But how does that affect our everyday lives? What effect does it have on how we communicate and interact, how we work and engage with the rest of the world? Well, we have some answers to these questions. But they're not black and white. What we've found is that there are as many positive implications and improvements to our everyday lives as there are potentially negative consequences. The key is to use them in ways that are beneficial. Seize the many opportunities digital media offers and avoid the risks that arise from overuse or maleficent use. A survey of 5,000 digital media users across five countries paints a positive picture: half of the respondents agreed that their digital media use had improved their overall quality of life – both socially and professionally. Only one in seven respondents disagreed.

The most positive effects of digital media were found in the work sphere. Roughly two-thirds of survey respondents said that digital media use had improved their ability to learn and develop professionally. This included their ability to carry out their work, collaborate with colleagues and build relationships. New digital technologies offer the opportunity to work across boundaries of location and time, opening up job opportunities for remotely located workers and ensuring access to the best talent, no matter where it is located around the globe. Then there's online education: programmes such as Coursera offer online courses from different universities. Professional social networks such as LinkedIn allow for networking, while talent platforms like Upwork help to source the best contingent talent. However, digital media usage has to be managed well, especially when it comes to the extent of usage, the type of social interaction and the nature of the content accessed. According to the survey, the least positive effects were reported in the personal sphere. While roughly four out of 10 respondents reported positive effects on long-term memory, attention span, the ability to find a partner, stress and health, about one in 10 respondents found those same areas to be negatively affected.

The survey didn't just throw up differences between people, countries, too, returned varied results. While perceptions in emerging markets such as China and Brazil were largely positive (in China, two-thirds agree that digital media use has improved their quality of life), opinions in Germany and the United States were less enthusiastic. In Germany, for instance, only 30% agree (and 24% disagree) that digital media use has improved their quality of life. The differences are astonishing.

What can be inferred on reading the second paragraph of the passage?

A. It is criticising the positive aspects of digital media.

B. It is highlighting the best aspects of digital media.

C. It is portraying the good and bad aspect of digital media.

D. It is talking about the people's view on digital media.

Ques (29-32):Direction: Read the passage and answer the questions that follow.

Tokyo is donating more than one million doses of the AstraZeneca coronavirus vaccines to Taiwan, Japan's foreign minister announced Friday, as Taipei struggles to secure jabs, accusing China of interference.

The move is likely to stir controversy with Beijing, which views democratic and self-ruled Taiwan as its own territory and works to keep the island diplomatically isolated.

"We have received requests from various countries and areas for the provision of vaccines," Toshimitsu Motegi told reporters in Tokyo.

"At this point, we have finished the arrangement for the request from Taiwan. And we will deliver free of charge 1.24 million doses of the AstraZeneca vaccines that have been produced in Japan," he added.

He said the vaccine would be handled through the territory's embassy equivalent and would arrive in Taiwan later today. In a statement, Taiwan's foreign ministry welcomed the move, pointedly emphasizing that the neighbours "share the universal values of freedom and democracy."

It comes as Taiwan battles a sudden surge of cases after having one of the world's best pandemic responses. Infections have jumped in recent weeks to nearly 10,000 with 166 deaths after a cluster initially detected among airline pilots spread.

Taiwan wants to roll out mass inoculations in the next few months by setting up thousands of community vaccination

stations to administer one million shots weekly, but it is struggling to secure enough doses.

It has pre-order deals for around 30 million shots, but has so far received just 726,600 AstraZeneca doses and 150,000 Moderna shots for its population of 23.5 million. Taiwan is receiving doses through the Covax programme and is included in plans outlined by Washington this week to distribute 80 million doses globally.

But President Tsai Ing-wen has explicitly accused China of having "interfered" with efforts to secure Pfizer doses. Japan has secured AstraZeneca doses sufficient for its 60 million people, but is not administering the formula despite approving it, as concerns linger about rare blood clots.

Q.29 What problem could Beijing have with Taiwan receiving vaccines from Japan?

A. Beijing wants to receive the supply of vaccines for itself.

B. Beijing is the capital of China which considers Taiwan to a part of its country and thus wants to keep it separate from relations with other countries.

C. Beijing feels that the vaccines coming in from Japan leads to blood clots in the people it is administered to.

D. Beijing wants to be the one to supply Taiwan with vaccines.

Q.30 Why does Taiwan especially appreciate this move made by Japan to supply it with vaccines?

A. Japan is giving up vaccines for its own citizens to supply Taiwan with vaccines.

B. China is unwilling to help Taiwan with vaccines.

C. Japan seems to have similar ideologies when it comes to freedom and democracy.

D. Japan is a democratic country that has pledged to help them in their fight against China.

Q.31 What does 'inoculations' mean in the context of the passage?

A. Any variety of materials that are designed to reduce the flow of heat in and out of the body it is covering.

B. To attempt to counter the effects of something.

C. The introduction of an antigenic body in a person in order to build immunity to a specific disease.

D. To teach someone something by repeated instructing.

Q.32 Why does Japan not want to administer vaccines to its own citizens?

A. There are not enough vaccines for everyone and so Japan is waiting to have enough for everyone.

B. It wants to make sure that all its neighbors get the vaccine before it does, as a part of a peace deal.

C. There are (rare) reports of blood clotting in people who receive the vaccine and thus Japan is holding back from administering the vaccine just yet.

D. There are reports of people getting infected by the virus and dying despite having received the vaccine, so Japan is holding back.

Ques (33-36):Direction: Read the given passage carefully and select the best answer to the question out of the four given alternatives.

Young men are addicted to internet more than the young women in Hyderabad. Internet usage for the purpose of social networking is also higher among men as compared to women. These observations are from a research paper co-authored by M. Sarada Devi and Aprajita Raj from the Department of Human Development and Family Studies, Prof. Jayashankar, Telangana State Agricultural University. It was recently published in the Current Journal of Applied Science and Technology. With 30 male respondents and an equal number of females selected at random between ages 18 and 25 using Young's Internet Addiction Test, the research paper noted the mean Internet addiction score of men was at 54.9 as compared to 41.6 of women.

Half of the male respondents said they spend over two hours on the Internet for non-educational purposes, as compared to only 30% of women. According to Ms. Sarada Devi, non-educational activity implies internet for activity other than coursework. About 90% of male respondents stated they spend time in 'purposeless surfing'. In comparison, young women spent less time in this activity — 77%.

Social networking took a large part of the respondents' time. A comparison of activity revealed all male respondents use social media 'most of the time'. Around 87% women said they use social media most of the time. Touching upon levels of Internet addiction, the research paper stated a majority of respondents showed moderate Internet addiction. Speaking to The Hindu, Ms. Sarada Devi said, "When they are on the Internet for a large part of the time, it is natural to get secluded. They do not realise that they are addicted as the habit has been established."

Q.33 Which of the sentences below summarizes the theme of the passage?

A. 90% of young men respondents spend time in 'purposeless surfing' on the internet.

B. Men can feel secluded if they spend hours surfing on the internet.

C. Research paper on internet addiction published in Current Journal of Applied Science and Technology.

D. Research paper shows that internet addiction is higher among males than in females.

Q.34 Which of the following words is the most similar in meaning to the word "implies" as given in the passage?

A. Suggests

B. Elucidates

C. Deciphers

D. Construes

Q.35 Which of the following words is the most opposite in meaning to the word "purposeless" as given in the passage?

A. Inadvertent

B. Intentional

C. Onerous

D. Instinctive

Q.36 Which of the following can be correctly inferred from the passage?

A. 57% of male respondents said they spend their time on the Internet for socializing.

B. 40% of male respondents indulged in online gambling.

C. A larger number of female respondents spend more time on online shopping at 84%, as compared to 33% of male respondents.

D. Equal number of men and women were selected for the research paper using Young's Internet Addiction Test.

Ques (37-40):Direction: Read the passage given below and answer the questions that follow.

The Reserve Bank of India (RBI) is India's central bank, responsible for the issue and supply of the Indian rupee and the regulation of the Indian banking system. It also manages the country's main payment systems and works to promote its economic development.

Until the Monetary Policy Committee was established in 2016, it also had full control of monetary policy in India. It commenced its operations on 1 April 1935 in accordance with the Reserve Bank of India Act, 1934. The original share capital was divided into shares of 100 each fully paid. Following India's independence on 15 August 1947, the RBI was nationalised on 1 January 1949.

The overall direction of the RBI lies with the 21-member central board of directors, composed of: the governor; four deputy governors; two finance ministry representatives (usually the Economic Affairs Secretary and the Financial Services Secretary); ten government-nominated directors; and four directors who represent local boards for Mumbai, Kolkata, Chennai, and Delhi. Each of these local boards consists of five members who represent regional interests and the interests of co-operative and indigenous banks.

It is a member bank of the Asian Clearing Union. The bank is also active in promoting financial inclusion policy and is a leading member of the Alliance for Financial Inclusion (AFI). The bank is often referred to by the name 'Mint Street'.

The primary objective of RBI is to undertake consolidated supervision of the financial sector comprising commercial banks, financial institutions, and non-banking finance companies.

The board is constituted by co-opting four directors from the Central Board as members for a term of two years and is chaired by the governor. The deputy governors of the reserve bank are ex-officio members. One deputy governor, usually the deputy governor in charge of banking regulation and supervision, is nominated as the vice-chairman of the board. The board is required to meet normally once every month. It considers inspection reports and other supervisory issues placed before it by the supervisory departments.

BFS through the Audit Sub-Committee also aims at upgrading the quality of the statutory audit and internal audit functions in banks and financial institutions. The audit sub-committee includes deputy governor as the chairman and two directors of the Central Board as members. The BFS oversees the functioning of the Department of Banking Supervision (DBS), the Department of Non-Banking Supervision (DNBS) and the Financial Institutions Division (FID) and gives directions on the regulatory and supervisory issues.

The institution is also the regulator and supervisor of the financial system and prescribes broad parameters of banking operations within which the country's banking and financial system functions. Its objectives are to maintain public

confidence in the system, protect depositors' interest and provide cost-effective banking services to the public. The Banking Ombudsman Scheme has been formulated by the Reserve Bank of India (RBI) for effective addressing of complaints by bank customers. The RBI controls the monetary supply, monitors economic indicators like the gross domestic product and has to decide the design of the rupee banknotes as well as coins.

Q.37 What was the purpose behind the Banking Ombudsman Scheme formulated by the Reserve Bank of India (RBI)?

A. For the regulation of the Indian banking system.

B. For the issue and supply of the Indian rupee.

C. To upgrade the quality of the statutory audit and internal audit functions in banks and financial institutions.

D. For effective addressing of complaints by bank customers.

Q.38 What is the correct meaning of the word "inspection"?

A. The process of excluding or the state of being excluded

B. A whole formed by combining several separate elements

C. A careful examination or scrutiny

D. To keep safe from harm or injury

Q.39 With reference to the passage, which of the following statements is correct?

A. The audit sub-committee includes deputy governor as the chairman and two directors of the Central Board as members.

B. The Banking Ombudsman Scheme has been formulated by the Reserve Bank of India (RBI) for effective addressing of complaints by bank customers.

C. The RBI is often referred to by the name 'Mint Street'.

D. All of the above

Q.40 Which of the following is a synonym for the word "consolidate", with reference to the passage?

A. Combine   **B.** Scatter

C. Stabilize   **D.** Dissociate

Ques (41-44):Direction : Read the following passage carefully and answer the questions given below it. Certain words have been printed in the bold to help you locate them while answering some of the questions.

One of our largest infrastructure finance companies, Infrastructure Leasing and Financial Services (IL&FS), a "systemically important core investment company" registered with the Reserve Bank of India (RBI), began to implode. Starting with a default on its Rs 1,000 crore bond repayment to SIDBI, IL&FS and its non-banking finance subsidiaries have begun to renege on one repayment after another. Fears that mounting troubles in the IL&FS group might be symptomatic of larger problems in the non-banking finance company (NBFC) space and, in turn, pose a serious threat to financial stability saw markets plunge more than 1,100 points intra-day. The unstated fear was that thanks to its inter-linkages with the financial system IL&FS may drag the entire financial system and the larger macro-economy down with it.

For now the storm seems to have abated. Latest reports speak of Orix Corporation, the diversified Japanese financial services company and one of the largest shareholders in IL&FS, being

willing to up its stake; of government and RBI pitching in to help with speedy sale of IL&FS assets. But these are only band-aid solutions that cannot, and will not, last. We need to look deeper and address the cause, rather than the symptom, of the disease. The crisis at IL&FS has exposed a number of fault lines. To begin with, the ills of the financial sector go much beyond the much-maligned public sector banks. It is the familiar story of failure on multiple fronts: the regulator Reserve Bank of India (RBI), credit rating agencies who downgraded IL&FS much too late, auditors, and most importantly, the board of IL&FS.

Given that one of the biggest learnings of the 2008 crisis is of the dangers posed by shadow banks like IL&FS, one would have expected RBI to keep a close eye on IL&FS, particularly in view of its excessive leverage. But, sadly, it failed to do so! If RBI bears the main responsibility for the unfolding events at IL&FS, it is not the only one. Rating agencies have, again, been caught sleeping on the watch. Ratings have been rapidly downgraded; in many cases after the event. Rating agencies are technically under the Securities and Exchange Board of India (Sebi); but are not subject to close regulatory oversight. Worse, under the current rating model, fees are paid by the rated entities. There is, thus, a huge incentive to give generous ratings for fear of losing business. Until we address this basic flaw in the rating model, ratings must be taken for what they are worth: very little! Company auditors are no less culpable. The annual accounts of IL&FS and its close to 200 subsidiaries were audited by some of the biggest names in the profession. Yet none thought it fit to red flag the growing dependence on short term debt and the excessively high leverage. The biggest **opprobrium** must, however, be reserved for the board of IL&FS. IL&FS had a star-studded board. Yet Ravi Parthasarathy, CEO from 1989 till July 2018, seems to have run the company like his **fiefdom**. Since he was asked no questions, it seemed that he was handsomely rewarded for presiding the virtual destruction of IL&FS.

Each of these entities must share the blame and take corrective measures. But there is a larger factor at play that must be factored in while considering any kind of rescue package: the inherent flaw in the extant model of infrastructure financing. Infra projects have long gestation periods. They require long term funding that neither banks nor NBFCs can provide. Moreover, issues related to land acquisition, environmental clearance, policy flip-flop, political interference and rapidly changing external dynamics make infrastructure financing particularly risky. Cost and time overruns are inevitable. Unless we address these we will not be able to ring-fence either banks or NBFCs from the risk associated with financing infrastructure. It is imperative that before we consider any solution, especially bailout with taxpayer money, RBI must make an informed assessment of IL&FS's inter-connectedness (and, hence, risk of systemic failure). Remember, any solution will prove short lived unless we address fault lines all around, including underlying risks in infra financing.

Q.41 According to the author, in the statement "But these are only band-aid solutions that cannot, and will not, last," what does he referred to as "band-aid solutions"?

I. The quick and/or temporary solutions to a problem that do not address or resolve the underlying cause of said problem.

II. Orix Corporation of Japan is willing to acquire a majority stake in the infrastructure development and finance company.

III. The temporary solutions or short-term fix used until something better can be obtained.

IV. Government and RBI are pitching in to sell assets so that IL&FS will be able to get liquidity to repay debtors and creditors.

A. Both II and IV   **B.** Only II
C. I, II and IV   **D.** II, III and IV

Q.42 The passage supports which of the following inferences?

I. Public-sector banks are often criticized by people, but the criticism is unfair or exaggerated because they have good qualities too.

II. India's financial markets are in the throes of a bear hug.

III. Issues related to building permit and approvals, climate, unsolved finance, unrealistic plan and design changes are all marked as the five main sources of cost and time overruns.

IV. IL&FS has an opaque balance sheet with over 200 subsidiaries.

V. A red flag refers to a flag used as a sign of danger or a warning signal.

A. I, III and IV   **B.** II, III and V
C. III, IV and V   **D.** I, II, III and V

Q.43 Which of the following options is an assumption for the statement "Given that one of the biggest learnings of the 2008 crisis is of the dangers posed by shadow banks like IL&FS, one would have expected RBI to keep a close eye on IL&FS, particularly in view of its excessive leverage" of the passage?

A. The shadow banking system that had burgeoned in the run-up to the global financial crisis was one of the major causes of the global turmoil.

B. IL&FS, one of India's key shadow banks, is facing something of an existential threat.

C. Shadow bank refers to the non-bank financial intermediaries that provide services similar to traditional commercial banks.

D. IL&FS was not stringently regulated by RBI.

Q.44 Why rating agencies bear the responsibility for the unfolding events at IL&FS?

A. They have been caught sleeping on the watch.

B. Ratings of its debt have been rapidly downgraded from high investment grade ratings to default/junk ratings; in many cases after the events.

C. They are accountable for manipulation, inflated ratings, or even slacking in their analysis.

D. They are not subject to close regulatory oversight and Because their revenues flowed from rated entities, the agencies' primary allegiance was to these customers as their reputations, along with the future of their business, was at stake if they provided faulty predictions or ratings.

Ques (45-48):Direction : Read the following passage carefully and answer the questions given below it. Certain words have been printed in the bold to help you locate them while answering some of the questions.

Between a tenth and a third of the jobs in Britain are at risk of being automated away, depending on which survey or well-

informed guess you believe. Should social workers be among them? It might seem that the particular and personal skills of social work are of a nature that could never be replaced by a machine, but from the point of view of an economist they are part of the machinery to provide help in the most cost-effective way. This involves judgment: which families need what kind of help most urgently? And that kind of classification is one of the things that various forms of artificial intelligence promise to do better and more quickly than unaided human beings. It involves the ability to detect significance in a mass of confusing information, often in ways that are hard to explain – a faculty that in humans is called intuition. When computers do it, it is called machine learning. In neither case is it wholly reliable.

The augmentation or replacement of social workers with machine learning is the possibility raised by our report that five English councils are trialling software which will help to pick out families and children in need of intervention. It is not the only danger of the projects. There are obvious problems around informed consent: as far back as 2012, Dame Louise Casey took the view that demanding informed consent for the use of the relevant data damaged society as a whole and particularly its most vulnerable members. This is not what the Guardian believes. Nor, after the GDPR, is it what the law allows. Then there is the fallibility of the algorithms themselves: the way in which putting human prejudices into software makes AI "money laundering for bias". Beyond that is the further danger that even if this function of social workers and other professionals can be successfully augmented by machine learning, that might tend to make all the other things they do look less important when in fact they will become much more so.

Yet Ms Casey's argument has an intuitive force. We are all leaving increasingly large trails of data behind us as we move through life. At the moment it is mostly analysed in order to sell us things more efficiently. It would be absurd for society not to make use of it for more valuable purposes. If informed consent could be obtained from everyone within a council's area, there are no doubt interesting and useful things that could be discovered. But that kind of analysis would have to involve all citizens. The more data these algorithms have, the better the results will be. Importantly, this must not just be data on "problem" families. We cannot know how they differ from the norm without a great deal of data from the families who will never trouble social work departments. This is unlikely to be politically as popular as the idea of automating hard-pressed social services departments. None of this happens in a vacuum. Technology is not bestowed on us by **benevolent** gods. It is deployed in response to pre-existing social and economic pressures. Why might local government want to invest in this kind of thing, and why might central government want to believe in it? To ask the question is to answer it. The technology appears to promise a magical way to slip out of the vice of rising costs, demand and expectation on the one side, and shrinking revenues on the other. But there is no magic escape here. In some cases the **enthusiastic** deployment of technology can make a bad situation very much worse. The good intentions of local councils will only be rewarded if they are properly funded from the centre.

Q.45 What peril is faced by the people of Britain as mentioned in the passage?

A. Meeting the social welfare department.

B. Introduction of machine based social work.

C. Automation of jobs.

D. Introduction of GDPR law.

Q.46 What is the correct antonym of the given word 'enthusiastic'?

A. Dispassionate   **B.** Eager

C. Ardent   **D.** Warm

Q.47 Which of the following is the most suitable title for the given passage?

A. Do algorithms have all the answers?

B. Jobs decline in Britain.

C. How to classify social issues?

D. Is technology the way to societal improvement?

Q.48 In the context of the passage, what is machine learning?

A. An instinctual role based on short term statistics.

B. Deducing relevant information from layers and layers of data available.

C. Unbiased approach in solving a problem

D. Educating the masses about better possible ways of approaching a problem.

Ques (49-52):Direction : Read the following passage carefully and answer the questions given below it.

Today Indian economy is considered as the fastest growing economies in the world. Contributing to its high growth are many critical sectors, amongst which 'financial services sector' is unarguably one of the most distinguished sectors of Indian economy. The role of financial sector in shaping fortunes for Indian economy has been even more critical, as India since independence lacked prowess of a resilient industrial sector. This prompted India to depend on other sectors for its sustenance. These other sectors mostly constituted of 'financial service sector and 'agricultural sector'. India's watershed decision to nationalize 14 commercial banks in 1969 validated how critical was 'financial sector'. Its importance after economic reforms of 1992 has grown only manifolds to the extent that today it presently contributes to over 6% of India's GDP. It is the dynamic growth of financial services sector during post reform age that has helped it in assuming such an important place in Indian economy. Unlike in past when financial services sector mainly constituted of banking sector, today financial sector has broaden its reach to include sectors like insurance services, non-banking financial services, co-operatives, pension funds, mutual funds, capital market etc. Financial sector's contribution comes across even more strong when we look at sheer number of employment and tax revenue it generates. Especially employment generated by banking and insurance sector every year runs in millions. Equally revenue generation through tax and dividend collection by the government surpasses billions of rupees every year. While revenue and employment generation are two very important contributions, successfully maintaining healthy credit line to industrial sector as well as to overall economy is another important contribution of financial sector. Banks and non-banks in India have been

discharging credit in billions to big, medium/small industries, entrepreneurs etc every financial year. With improved availability of credit, the Indian economy during past two decades has managed to march towards higher economic growth. Reforms within banking sector during post liberalization era have especially proven to be prudent for credit disbursement in the country. The advent of private sector banks in particular opened a new chapter for Indian economy. The enormous success of private sector banks helped large corporate paving the way for consolidated growth in industrial sector encompassing MSME.Over past few years government has taken many reformative steps to make financial sector even more robust. Although it will take quite a few years to see positive impact of these reforms, there is a general consensus that these reforms will rewrite a chapter in Indian economy.

More specifically, these reforms will open new stream of revenue and employment generation for the economy. Last year in 2015, RBI took unprecedented step by opening up the much anticipated 'payment bank' sector. It awarded payment bank licenses to 11 entities. Along with redefining consumer experience, these 11 payment banks are expected to give further boost to growth of financial sector as well as to overall Indian economy. To make banks more 'credit friendly', RBI has allowed banks to raise funds via long-term bonds for financing the critical infrastructure sector. This means banks no longer have to meet cash reserve ratio, statutory liquidity ratio or priority sector norms to disburse credit for big infrastructure projects. In a welcome step, in 2015 Indian government raised the cap of FDI in insurance sector by 49%. Thereby making way for more foreign direct investment in insurance as well as financial sector. Following this decision, many foreign insurance companies operating in India have already raised their stake to 49% in their joint venture with Indian insurance companies. In 2015, Indian government started Mudra Scheme, under which Indian banks will be providing cheap and affordable credit to new & small entrepreneurs. With the above mentioned reforms, road ahead for financial sector indeed looks very bright. According to joint report prepared by KPMG-Confederation of Indian Industry (CII), Indian banking sector is poised to become fifth largest by 2020. The report also states that bank credit is expected to grow at a compound annual growth rate of 17 per cent in coming years. As for insurance sector, it is expected to touch US$ 350-400 billion by 2020.

India's life insurance sector will continue to remain world's largest life insurance sector in coming decades. The road ahead for other sectors like pension funds, mutual sector, non-banking financial etc looks equally very promising. In the midst of all these bright projection, there is a growing concern about increasing NPAs in banking sector. Many analysts, however, feel that some tough steps by RBI coupled with 'special financial stimulus' to banks is necessary to overcome the incremental issue of NPAs. Over all, the impressive figures and projection highlighted above only means that financial services contribution to Indian economy is going to improve in coming years, thereby adding to India's GDP growth rate.

Q.49 Which of the following has been the major contribution of the financial services?

A. Employment.

B.   Revenue collection with unbalanced credit line

C.   Growth of industrial sector

D.   Both A and C

Q.50 What made the banks more credit-friendly?

A.   Payment banks' contribution in boosting up the economy generated by financial services.

B.   RBI's decision to issue license for 11 entities have increased the peer pressure.

C.   Funds generation from the long-term bonds for financing the infrastructure.

D.   Economic boost occurring in India making money more available.

Q.51 Based on your understanding the passage, which of the following can be regarded as a fact?

A.   Foreign investments have increased in India due to the financial services.

B.   Economic boost in India is making more money available in India.

C.   Revenue generation through taxes is the most remarkable contribution of the financial services.

D.   Indian banks will be providing cheap and affordable credit to new & small entrepreneurs.

Q.52 How would the insurance sector continue to be the largest in the world?

A.   Due to increased revenue generation from this sector more investment would be made in this direction.

B.   Increased FDI post reforms is the key

C.   RBI's leverage given towards the insurance sector of the financial services.

D.   As the other sectors are not performing that well as for now, more emphasis would be laid on the insurance sector.

Ques (53-56):Direction : Read the following passage carefully and answer the questions given below it.

"India's growth is expected to increase to 7.3% in 2018 and to 7.4% in 2019 [slightly lower than in the April 2018 World Economic Outlook (WEO) for 2019, given the recent increase in oil prices and the tightening of global financial conditions], up from 6.7% in 2017," the IMF said in its latest World Economic Outlook report. This acceleration, the world body said, reflected a rebound from transitory shocks (the currency exchange initiative and implementation of the national Goods and Services Tax), with strengthening investment and robust private consumption. India's medium-term growth prospects remain strong at $\left(7\frac{3}{4}\%\right)$, benefiting from ongoing structural reform, but have been marked down by just under $1\frac{1}{2}$ percentage point relative to the April 2018 WEO, it said. If projections are true, then India would regain the tag of fastest growing major economies of the world, crossing China with more than 0.7 percentage point in 2018 and an impressive 1.2 percentage point growth lead in $2019.$

China was the fastest growing economy in 2017 as it was ahead of India by 0.2 percentage points. For the record, the IMF has lowered the growth projections for both India and China by

0.4% and 0.32%, respectively, from its annual April's World Economic Outlook. Released in Bali during the annual meeting of the IMF and the World Bank, the IMF's flagship World Economic Outlook said its 2019 growth projection for China is lower than in April, given the latest round of US tariffs on Chinese imports, as are its projections for India. In China, growth is projected to moderate from 6.9% in 2017 to 6.6% in 2018 and 6.2% in 2019, reflecting a slowing external demand growth and necessary financial regulatory tightening, the report said. The 0.2 percentage point downgrade to the 2019 growth forecast is attributable to the negative effect of recent tariff actions, assumed to be partially offset by policy stimulus, it said. Over the medium term, growth is expected to gradually slow to 5.6% as the economy continues to make the transition to a more sustainable growth path with continued financial de-risking and environmental controls, it noted.

"Owing to these changes, our international growth projections for both this year and next are downgraded to $3.7\%, 0.2$ percentage point below our last assessments and the same rate achieved in 2017," the report said. The growth rate of United States for 2018 is 2.9% and that of 2019 has been powered to 2.5%. In India, the report said, important reforms have been implemented in the recent years, including the Goods and Services Tax, the inflation-targeting framework, the Insolvency and Bankruptcy Code, and steps to liberalise foreign investment and make it easier to do business.

Q.53 Why is China's growth projection for 2019 showing a downgrade?

A.   Unfavourable tariff actions

B.   Financial de-risking and environmental controls

C.   Low internal demand

D.   Only A and B

Q.54 The World Economic Outlook is carried out by whom?

A. World Bank   B. IMF

C. The US   D. B and C both

Q.55 Which of the following is true as per the context of the passage?

A.   India is looking forward to being amongst the fastest growing major economies of the world.

B.   Medium term growth of china is gradually picking up.

C.   Growth projections for two years are downgraded to 5.6%.

D.   All A, B, and C are correct

Q.56 What would be the most appropriate title for the passage?

A.   Synopsis of the World Economic Outlook

B.   The highs and lows of the World Economy

C.   Analysis of growth projections of India and China

D.   Impact of important reforms on the economy

Ques (57-60):Direction : Read the following passage carefully and answer the questions given below it. Certain words have been printed in the bold to help you locate them while answering some of the questions.

Tourism is often about seeking deeper emotional and personal connections with the world around us. It's a **quintessential** part of the "experience economy", creating memories that can be recalled, re-lived and re-shared for a lifetime. But not all travel experiences take place in the real world. With the evolution of virtual reality (VR) technology, tourism is increasingly a mash-up of physical and virtual worlds. VR can even remove the need to travel entirely. Excessive tourism, or over-tourism, in popular destinations can degrade heritage sites, the quality of life of host communities, and the experience of visitors. Virtual reality not only offers alternative forms of access to threatened locations, it also recreates historical experiences and provides virtual access to remote locations you might not make it to otherwise. Our brains seem to have an inbuilt VR-like mechanism that enables us to live imagined experiences. Much of our waking life is spent thinking about either the past (retrospection) or the future (prospection). This is known as **mind** wandering.

During these events we're not paying attention to the current world around us. Instead, we're recalling memories, or creating and processing imagined futures. When we're engaged in mind **wandering**, our brains process and appraise mental images via the same neutral pathways they use to receive stimuli from the real world. So, the imagined past or future can evoke emotions and feelings similar to how we react to everyday life. VR can **elicit** these same feelings. Virtual worlds use sensory stimulation and vivid imagery to generate authentic experiences. Immersion in these environments can lead to a deeper understanding of a place or event than simply reading about it or looking at pictures. There is evidence that virtual reality can create absorption, or a state of attention, leading to a sense of "presence" or "being there". After a tourism VR experience of the Great Barrier Reef, for example, participants reported experiencing a sense of relaxation, similar to that gained from travel in real life.

Immersive videos of Australian holiday destinations created by Tourism Australia have been viewed more than 10.5 million times over the past two years. Research conducted by Tourism Australia shows that almost 20% of consumers have used VR to choose a holiday destination, while about 25% plan to use VR to choose a future destination. There is evidence VR can sometimes surpass reality, potentially leading the participant to choose an alternate destination.

In March, Thai authorities closed sections of the famous Maya Bay (which featured in Hollywood movie The Beach) because over-tourism threatened coral reefs. VR could offer experiences of locations like this without impacting the natural environment. It could also help support capacity management at "bucket list" destinations, such as Machu Picchu. But if VR is too effective at reducing visitation, alternate forms of income for local people need to be developed to support economic viability. In 2018, the Australian War Memorial brought the Battle of Hamel to virtual life using 3D and 360 degree video. Designers of the A$100 million Sir John Monash Centre in Villers-Bretonneux, France used immersive video, interactive touch screens and historical relics to recreate the soldiers' experience on the Western Front during WWI. Similar work is being completed in regional Australia to recreate life on a US

Airbase on "the Brisbane Line" – Australia's controversial last point of defense in WWII.

Wildlife watching can elicit feelings of empathy, surprise, novelty, even fear. It can also generate excitement, stimulation, entertainment and learning. But government regulation, cost, remoteness and seasonality of migratory patterns may limit opportunities for people to encounter some of the awe-inspiring creatures on our planet. Virtual immersion can offer alternatives that support conservation goals and provide transformative visitor experiences. VR tourism could also help to increase health and well-being. Long working hours can lead to anxiety and depression. Research demonstrates immersion in the outdoors encourages relaxation, rejuvenation, expectation, surprise, trust in oneself, and improved self-esteem that can contribute to reduced symptoms. Short breaks using tourism-based VR experiences can mirror these effects and improve health. New possibilities for VR applications – both practical and pleasurable – are emerging as the technology evolves. And as travellers seek new and novel experiences, combining virtual with real world experiences may become a common feature of tourism in the future.

Q.57 Which of the following features Virtual Reality Tourism offers over the conventional tourism?

A. Access to a remote location which a traveler might not visit.

B. Recreation of historical experience which is not possible in the present.

C. Excessive tourists at the popular tourist destinations.

D. Only A and B

Q.58 With which of the following reasons, a person who is skeptical about VR Tourism will agree the most?

A. VR tourism gives a similar sense of relaxation as experienced in conventional tourism.

B. VR tourism allows reliving the lives which would have been in the past.

C. VR tourism can eventually kill the multi-billion dollar Tourism Industry.

D. VR tourism can never give the similar information regarding different cultures and traditions which an actual journey can give.

Q.59 Which of the following statements regarding Tourism Australia is correct?

A. Around 15% customers have chosen Virtual Reality (VR) to choose a future destination.

B. Video of Great Barrier reef has been most viewed video on YouTube till date.

C. Interactive videos of Australian Holiday Destinations have garnered more than 10 million views in the past two years.

D. Close to 40% customers plan to choose Virtual Reality (VR) in the near future.

Q.60 A person choosing VR Tourism will justify his choice with which of the following reasons?

A. It gives access to remote areas.

B. It gives multiple options in choosing a destination.

C. It helps in enhancing health and wellbeing.

D. All the options are true

// Smart Answer Sheet //

Correct — Indicates percentage of students who answered questions correctly.

Skipped — Indicates percentage of students who skipped questions.

Q.	Ans.	Correct / Skipped
1	D	89.66 % / 10.11 %
2	C	78.87 % / 12.68 %
3	D	76.01 % / 16.89 %
4	D	81.01 % / 10.3 %
5	D	40.8 % / 32.15 %
6	D	41.71 % / 56.49 %
7	D	52.79 % / 38.13 %
8	C	46.96 % / 32.19 %
9	A	31.3 % / 67.78 %
10	D	65.55 % / 30.39 %
11	D	49.83 % / 39.65 %
12	D	55.51 % / 31.7 %

Q.	Ans.	Correct / Skipped
13	D	43.34 % / 54.78 %
14	C	47.28 % / 34.54 %
15	C	43.65 % / 47.55 %
16	D	40.61 % / 41.43 %
17	D	62.59 % / 36.61 %
18	D	66.71 % / 31.04 %
19	D	47.21 % / 52.11 %
20	D	52.6 % / 31.62 %
21	B	40.63 % / 36.39 %
22	C	57.07 % / 31.7 %
23	B	89.01 % / 10.32 %
24	B	53.51 % / 44.24 %

Q.	Ans.	Correct / Skipped
25	D	58.45 % / 31.42 %
26	D	45.42 % / 47.89 %
27	D	49.37 % / 32.29 %
28	C	69.36 % / 30.39 %
29	B	66.48 % / 30.24 %
30	C	48.19 % / 38.8 %
31	C	43.42 % / 49.38 %
32	C	40.66 % / 57.04 %
33	D	41.56 % / 50.58 %
34	A	55.96 % / 40.1 %
35	B	58.11 % / 35.47 %
36	D	64.53 % / 31.34 %

Q.	Ans.	Correct / Skipped
37	D	67.34 % / 32.14 %
38	C	11.25 % / 75.33 %
39	D	65.45 % / 32.73 %
40	A	64.76 % / 34.9 %
41	C	48.76 % / 50.84 %
42	B	14.56 % / 83.67 %
43	D	45.87 % / 34.25 %
44	C	55.02 % / 31.17 %
45	C	63.87 % / 35.46 %
46	A	60.26 % / 35.99 %
47	A	41.74 % / 51.02 %
48	B	66.76 % / 32.05 %

Q.	Ans.	Correct / Skipped
49	D	62.29 % / 35.0 %
50	C	48.97 % / 41.08 %
51	A	43.37 % / 31.2 %
52	B	42.54 % / 53.72 %
53	D	57.36 % / 41.55 %
54	B	62.81 % / 33.63 %
55	A	86.55 % / 13.05 %
56	C	68.44 % / 30.04 %
57	D	58.45 % / 36.51 %
58	D	67.32 % / 30.13 %
59	C	49.79 % / 38.06 %
60	D	63.27 % / 34.19 %

Performance Analysis

Avg. Score (%)	**65.56%**
Toppers Score (%)	**70.0%**
Your Score	

//Hints and Solutions//

1. If we go through the whole passage it is clear that the author is mainly concerned regarding the violence towards women by their intimate partners and they are attracted to doing so because of their socio-economic status and upbringing.

Among the given options, (A), (B) and (C) do not follow from the passage whereas Option (D) highlight the main issue among women and that also in the countries such as India.

Hence, the correct option is (D).

2. Refer to, "Worldwide as many as 38% of murders of women are committed by a male intimate partner. What makes this worse for countries like India is the fact that intimate partner violence is the highest at 37.7% in the WHO South-East Asia region."

It is clear from the above lines that the incidents of violence against women are more in India as compared to the other areas of the world, be it developed or otherwise and that is why the option that states this will be our pick for the correct answer.

Among the given options, only Option C is there that underlines the actual condition of India and the problems that women face in India whereas other options do not follow from the passage and can be ruled out from consideration.

Hence, the correct option is (C).

3. Refer to, "Warning that intimate partner violence cause serious short-and long-term problems for women and adversely affect their children besides leading to high social and economic costs for women, their families and societies."

It is clear from the above lines that the children of the couples where the women are tortured by their partners, the families of such women and the society, as a whole, suffer due to the attacks on women. Therefore all of these are adverse effects of violence against women.

Hence, the correct option is (D).

4. Refer to, "Explaining how gender-based violence is perpetrated, the global health organisation said that men are more likely to perpetrate violence if they have low education, a history of child maltreatment, exposure to domestic violence against their mothers, harmful use of alcohol, unequal gender norms, including attitudes accepting of violence, and a sense of entitlement over women."

It is clear from the above lines that men who may not have been properly educated or have seen the history of violence at their own homes may indulge in violence against women during their own internal lives. On the other hand, troubled childhood for men can also be a reason why they may indulge in violence against women. Therefore all the given reasons are correct in this context.

Hence, the correct option is (D).

5. Option (A) is true. According to the passage, "Das led the discussions on progress made under the SAARCFINANCE initiatives, achieved with the all-round cooperation of the SAARC central banks and launched the maiden issue of the annual SAARCFINANCE e-Newsletter."

Option (B) is true. According to the passage, "SAARCFINANCE is a network of central bank governors and finance secretaries of the SAARC region."

Option (C) is true. According to the passage, "While inaugurating the SAARCFINANCE Governors' Symposium on Tuesday, Das emphasised the importance of effective, creative and prudent use of technology by central bankers, especially in the areas of big data, digital currencies, reg-tech, sup-tech and cyber security."

Option (D) is false. According to the passage, "The Symposium also included a Panel Discussion on 'Cyber Security in Central Banks' and a presentation by the researchers of the SAARCFINANCE Collaborative Study on 'Comparison of Financial Sector Regulatory Regimes in the SAARC Region', the RBI's release added."

Hence, the correct option is (D).

6. The following lines are mentioned in the passage:

"RBI Governor Shaktikanta Das expressed optimism about the overall COVID-19 situation following the rollout of the vaccines and complimented all the SAARC central banks for their efforts in combating the pandemic".

It is clear that the governor of RBI praised the SAARC central banks for their efforts in combating the pandemic.

Hence, the correct option is (D).

7. Option (A) is a false statement. According to the passage, "The keynote address was delivered by Jermy Prenio, Senior Adviser, Financial Stability Institute, BIS on the topic 'Suptech use in central banks'."

Option (B) is a false statement. According to the passage, "SAARCFINANCE is a network of central bank governors and finance secretaries of the SAARC region."

Option (C) is a false statement. According to the passage, "The Reserve Bank of India is the present chair of the SAARCFINANCE from October 2019 to March 2021."

Option (D) is true. According to the passage, "The keynote address was delivered by Jermy Prenio, Senior Adviser, Financial Stability Institute".

Hence, the correct option is (D).

8. The meaning of the word 'Adverse' is 'unfavourable or harmful'.

The meaning of the 'Hostile' is 'unfriendly'.

Therefore, the word 'Hostile' is the synonym of the word 'Adverse'.

Hence, the correct option is (C).

9. Option A is correct as it can be clearly inferred from the passage that Afghanistan has been undergoing turmoil for a long time and the people have been craving for peace and stability.

The government is trying to incur these in the country with help from other countries as well as certain measures of its own.

Statement B is incorrect as the country does need assistance from the US government in order to control the disruptions of the terrorist groups and local militants.

Statement C is incorrect as it is not mentioned in the passage.

Hence, the correct option is (A).

10. Reading the passage we find that:

Option A is incorrect as it is not mentioned anywhere in the passage.

Option B is correct as it is mentioned in the passage.

- "US's stance for Afghanistan needs to be in continuation for achieving peace and curbing terrorism. For the upcoming elections, more forces are required in Afghanistan."

Option C is correct as we can infer from the lines:

- "The U.S must coordinate with Russia, Pakistan and Iran keeping in mind to work for the people of Afghanistan. Pakistan must take a firm step in curtailing terrorism from their soil. India has been extending assistance to Afghanistan mainly in the field of capacity building, education, training and the bilateral relation between the two nations have grown from strength to strength."

Thus we find that the correct answer is Both B and C.

Hence, the correct option is (D).

11. Reading the passage we find that:

Option A is correct as we can see from the lines:

- "India has been extending assistance to Afghanistan mainly in the field of capacity building, education, training and the bilateral relation between the two nations have grown from strength to strength. The complementarities between the two countries obviously make them natural partners."

Option C is correct as we can see from the lines:

- "The presence of the United States of America for the past 17 years in Afghanistan since the overthrow of the Taliban regime was a commitment to provide longer-term military support for uprooting terrorism in the country. The recent announcement of withdrawing of 7,000 US troops from Afghanistan this year by President Donald Trump will seem to have a detrimental effect at a crucial time of Afghanistan's Presidential elections slated to July 2019."

Option B is incorrect as it is not mentioned anywhere in the passage.

Thus we find that Statements A and C are mentioned in the passage.

Therefore the correct answer is Both A and C

Hence, the correct option is (D).

12. Reading the passage we find that:

All three statements are correct as they are mentioned in the passage.

- Afghanistan is continuously persuading peacebuilding efforts for the people of the country that is reflective through bilateral ties, regional cooperation programmes and time to time working on Confidence Building Measures (CBM's).

- Afghanistan's tremendous potential for trade, connectivity, geo-political strategic importance and people-to-people contact for inclusive development can take the country to trajectory level.

- Pakistan must take a firm step in curtailing terrorism from their soil.

From these three statements of the options from the passage, we can conclude that all the given statements are valid.

Thus the correct answer is All of the above.

Hence, the correct option is (D).

13. The above given passage explains that India should focus on its military and economic power rather than get influenced by countries who consider India as a leading global power.

(A). The word "extirpating" means eradicating or destroying. It is mentioned in the passage that the principal criterion in the conduct of foreign policy for India ought to be lifting the poor from poverty. So, extirpating poverty. So, (A) is true.

(B). "Invigorate" means strong and powerful. It is given that India without the necessary economic strength, we cannot strengthen our military. So, (B) is true.

(C) "Burgeoning" means begin to grow or increase rapidly; flourish and "impede" means to hinder or destroy. Now, it is given in the passage that an increased prestige for themselves will translate into more votes domestically. So, (C) is untrue.

Hence, the correct option is (D).

14. It is given in the passage that the only caveat(warning) is that we have to be realistic and check the correct understanding to play a big role in international relations.

Thus, option (C) gives the most appropriate answer.

Hence, the correct option is (C).

15. The word 'callousing' means showing or having an insensitive and cruel disregard for others. It is given that other countries deceive India by describing us as a major power. They do so because the principal interest of most of them is to sell very expensive militCry hardware to India. That is to be in the business of military weapons and equipment.

Hence, the correct option is (C).

16. The starter of the passage explains how India is considered as a global power and it plays an 'important role' on the world stage as a balancing power between major powers and as a 'security provider' to others. Though, India is a developing country, it is helping other nations in case of crisis. So, "soft power of India" can be an appropriate title.

Hence, the correct option is (D).

17. All the given options are mentioned in the first paragraph of the passage signifying the importance of credit system in the rural sector. Refer to the lines of first paragraph, Most of the agricultural chores still depend on manual labour. It also involves techniques which are outdated and result in low outputs. A capital infusion for a jump in productivity in reference to both agricultural and non-agricultural activities can be achieved by reforming credit and banking system. During the gestation period between sowing and harvesting seasons, farmers need credit to make ends meet, their general needs, initial requirements etc. Additionally, they also need credit to venture into modern agricultural techniques, to buy cattle, land etc.

Hence, the correct option is (D).

18. Among the given sentences, option (D) is not suggested in the paragraph. Refer to the last paragraph 'The rural banks need to establish a banking relationship with the people and scrap away the image of just money lenders. The banking system in rural India needs a reform, considering the difference in livelihoods of urban and rural people. Leniency on the part of the government in the collection of taxes inculcated a habit of not repaying borrowed amounts among people which needs to be altered. Banks need to educate people about thrift generation and efficient utilization of financial resources to become feasible again.' However, it is nowhere mentioned in the given passage that the banks need to lower the interest rates to increase the credit distribution among lower the interest rates to increase the credit distribution among the people.

Hence, the correct option is (D).

19. Refer to the 9th line of the 2nd paragraph 'The rural poor in need of urgent credit, don't generally possess any collateral. Consequently, they are ruled out of the formal banking system. To help such kind of people self-help groups (SHG) emerged on the scene'. All the other options are irrelevant in the context of the passage.

All the other options are related to the working of SHGs.

Hence, the correct option is (D).

20. NABARD was established for all the reasons given above. Refer to the second paragraph 'The difference in monetary activities of rural people relative to urban people led to the realization of NABARD (National Bank For Agricultural And Rural Development), in addition to the presence of RBI.' However, it does not mention about punishing the culprits who were ill practicing regarding the distribution of loan.

So, option D is the most suitable answer choice.

Hence, the correct option is (D).

21. The tone of the passage is optimistic.

Optimistic: conveying a sense of hope, and a positive outlook for the future.

Nihilistic: rejecting all religious and moral principles in the belief that life is meaningless

Sarcastic: marked by or given to using irony in order to mock or convey contempt

Sardonic: grimly mocking or cynical

Hence, the correct option is (B).

22. The answer can be found in this line from the passage- When asked about the timeline for the completion of the remaining stake transfer, he said: "It should happen in the next 12 to 18 months."

Hence, the correct option is (C).

23. In terms of individual APE (adjusted premium equivalent), the company witnessed a growth of 20 percent to Rs 4,907 crore- this statement is not true according to the passage.

Option (A) has been given in the passage- "He said the company launched 14 products or product variants last year and increased the margin by 3.60 percent in 2020-21."(third paragraph)

Option (C) has been given in the passage- "Max Life Insurance recorded a 22 percent rise in its total new business premium (individual and group) to Rs 6,826 crore in the financial year ended March 2021."(third paragraph)

Option (B) talks about a growth of 20 percent, while the passage states- "In terms of individual APE (adjusted premium equivalent), the company witnessed a growth of 19 percent to Rs 4,907 crore."

Thus we can see that only option (B) is incorrect as per the passage.

Hence, the correct option is (B).

24. The antonym of the word 'Approval is repudiation.

Approval: the action of approving something

Repudiation: the rejection of a proposal or idea

Mandate, Imprimatur and Assent are all synonyms or near-synonyms of 'approval'.

Hence, the correct option is (B).

25. The passage is clearly talking about the implications of digital media, both positive and negative.

The only option in line with this context is (D). The passage not only condemns the digital media but also praises it.

Hence, the correct option is (D).

26. The passage is clearly stating that the answers to the questions on the impact and effect of digital media cannot be seen in definite terms, i.e. they are neither completely beneficial nor completely harmful.

So the only option that follows is option (D).

Hence, the correct option is (D).

27. The passage is talking about digital media.

Online activity or not getting enough sleep is just a small fragment and gives no clear picture. It is saying how digital media is having an impact on our everyday activity. Insomnia is a condition where a person experiences sleeplessness. It is an effect, not a cause that can affect anyone's life.

Hence, the correct option is (D).

28. On reading the second paragraph of the passage, it is evident that the passage is talking about people's review on digital media which is both positive and negative. It is talking about how people are happy because of its impact on their professional development. They are also saying that there is not much development at the personal front.

All this accounts for the good and bad side of digital media and its effect on people or sample review and study.

Hence, the correct option is (C).

29. 'Beijing is the capital of China which considers Taiwan to a part of its country and thus want to keeps it separate from relations with other countries.'

The passage talks about how Taiwan is set to receive vaccines against the COVID virus from Japan as China is accused of stopping Taiwan from getting access to vaccines.

The first paragraph of the passage talks about how Taiwan is set to receive vaccines from Japan as Taipei (the capital of Taiwan) is unable to access enough vaccines.

The second paragraph then explains that this move may not sit well with Beijing (the capital of China) as China considers self-ruling Taiwan a part of its country.

It then makes sense to understand that since China wants Taiwan to be a part of itself it would not prefer Taiwan managing anything on its own (without China's help), including securing vaccines for itself.

Thus, China does not want Taiwan to have fruitful relations with any other country.

Hence, the correct option is (B).

30. 'Japan seems to have similar ideologies when it comes to freedom and democracy.'

The passage talks about how Taiwan is set to receive vaccines against the COVID virus from Japan as China is accused of stopping Taiwan from getting access to vaccines.

The fifth paragraph of the passage talks about a statement given by the foreign ministry of Taiwan.

It also mentions that Japan has assured that the vaccine would reach Taiwan that very day.

The statement by the ministry states that the move of Japan to provide them with vaccines was welcome and that they were glad that they shared the same values of freedom and democracy as their neighbors that are present across the world.

Hence, the correct option is (C).

31. 'The introduction of an antigenic body in a person in order to build immunity to a specific disease.'

The passage talks about how Taiwan is set to receive vaccines against the COVID virus from Japan as China is accused of stopping Taiwan from getting access to vaccines.

The word 'inoculations' is mentioned in the seventh paragraph of the passage in the plural form of the noun 'inoculation'.

The entire passage is about the COVID-19 vaccination in Taiwan. So it makes sense that the word mentioned in the question is also related to the same.

In order to prevent people from getting a disease, they have to be given a vaccine. A vaccine is basically something that is introduced to the body of a person in order to ensure that they build immunity against that specific disease.

The paragraph also mentions that Taiwan plans to set up vaccination stations, to administer these 'inoculations'.

This process of adding a foreign body to prepare one's immunity is called 'inoculation'.

Hence, the correct option is (C).

32. The passage talks about how Taiwan is set to receive vaccines against the COVID virus from Japan as China is accused of stopping Taiwan from getting access to vaccines.

The last paragraph of the passage talks about how Japan has enough vaccines for its population of 60 million.

It also mentions that the vaccine has been approved for inoculation (the Astrazeneca vaccine) but for some reason, they are not administering it just yet.

The last phrase of the last line mentions the reason, there have been reports (rare) of people getting blood clots due to the vaccine. The government is Japan fears a similar reaction in its population and thus is holding off until further research is conducted.

Hence, the correct option is (C).

33. Research paper shows that internet addiction is higher among males than in females.

In a research paper co-authored by M. Sarada Devi and Aprajita Raj from the Department of Human Development and Family Studies, Prof. Jayashankar Telangana State Agricultural University it was shown that Internet addiction among young males is higher than young females in Hyderabad.

With 30 male respondents and an equal number of females selected at random between ages 18 and 25 using Young's Internet Addiction Test, the research paper noted the mean Internet addiction score of men was at 54.9 as compared to 41.6 of women.

Options A, B and C are only mentioned briefly in the passage and are not the themes.

Hence, the correct option is (D).

34. The word that is most similar in meaning to this is "Suggests: to state something indirectly."

Implies means "indicate the truth or existence of (something) by suggestion rather than explicit reference."

In the above passage, it is mentioned that according to Ms. Sarada Devi who wrote a research paper with others, non-educational

activity implies internet for activity other than coursework.

Hence, the correct option is (A).

35. The word that is the most opposite in meaning to this is "Intentional: done on purpose; deliberate."

Purposeless means "done or made with no discernible point or purpose."

In the above passage, it is said that about 90% of young men respondents stated they spend time in 'purposeless surfing'

Hence, the correct option is (B).

36. Only 5 is correct since in the above passage it is mentioned that 30 male respondents and an equal number of females selected at random between ages 18 and 25 using Young's Internet Addiction Test, and the research paper by Sarada Devi and others noted the mean Internet addiction score of men was at 54.9 as compared to 41.6 of women.

The rest of the options are not mentioned in the passage and we don't have enough information to correctly infer them.

Hence, the correct option is (D).

37. 'For effective addressing of complaints by bank customers'.

Let's refer to the last paragraph of the passage:

The institution is also the regulator and supervisor of the financial system and prescribes broad parameters of banking operations within which the country's banking and financial system functions. Its objectives are to maintain public confidence in the system, protect depositors' interest and provide cost-effective banking services to the public. The Banking Ombudsman Scheme has been formulated by the Reserve Bank of India (RBI) for effective addressing of complaints by bank customers. The RBI controls the monetary supply, monitors economic indicators like the gross domestic product, and has to decide the design of the rupee banknotes as well as coins.

Hence, the correct option is (D).

38. 'A careful examination or scrutiny'.

The correct meaning of the word **"inspection"** is careful examination or scrutiny, investigation, assessment.

Let's look at the words with meanings given in the other options:

- Exclusion: The process of excluding or the state of being excluded
- Aggregate: A whole formed by combining several separate elements
- Protect: To keep safe from harm or injury

Hence, the correct option is (C).

39. All the statements given in the options are correct.

The correct statements are:

- The audit sub-committee includes deputy governor as the chairman and two directors of the Central Board as members.
- The Banking Ombudsman Scheme has been formulated by the Reserve Bank of India (RBI) for effective addressing of complaints by bank customers.
- The RBI is often referred to by the name 'Mint Street'.

- The RBI is also active in promoting financial inclusion policy and is a leading member of the Alliance for Financial Inclusion (AFI).

Hence, the correct option is (D).

40. The word "consolidate" means to combine (a number of things) into a single more effective or coherent whole or make (something) physically stronger or more solid.

Let's refer to the passage:

The primary objective of RBI is to undertake consolidated supervision of the financial sector comprising commercial banks, financial institutions, and non-banking finance companies.

From the above line, we can say that the correct synonym of "consolidate" in the context of the passage is "combine".

Hence, the correct option is (A).

41. A band-aid solution refers to a temporary solution that does not deal with the cause of a problem. Also, the passage states "For now the storm seems to have abated. Latest reports speak of Orix Corporation, the diversified Japanese financial services company and one of the largest shareholders in IL&FS, being willing to up its stake; of government and RBI pitching in to help with a speedy sale of IL&FS assets. But these are only band-aid solutions that cannot, and will not, last."

From the above-mentioned paragraph, one can say that the author meant statements I, II and IV but not statement III.

A stop-gap measure is a temporary measure or short-term fix used until something better can be obtained.

Hence, the correct option is (C).

42. The passage supports II, III and V.

An inference is a piece of information which can be logically deduced from the given statement.

Statement I: The passage states "To begin with, the ills of the financial sector go much beyond the much-maligned public-sector banks." If you describe someone or something as much-maligned, you mean that they are often criticized by people, but you think the criticism is unfair or exaggerated because they have good qualities too. It is clearly stated in the passage.

Statement II: "In the throes" means in the midst of, especially of a difficult struggle. A bear hug refers to the action of putting your arms around someone very tightly and quite roughly. The statement trying to say that India's financial markets are in the midst of a difficult situation or struggle which has enfolded the markets in very tightly and roughly manner. This can be inferred from the passage, especially from the first paragraph.

Statement III: The passage states "Moreover, issues related to land acquisition, environmental clearance, policy flip-flop, political interference and rapidly changing external dynamics make infrastructure financing particularly risky. Cost and time overruns are inevitable." This means that when infrastructure financing becomes risky then cost and time overruns are inevitable. So, the given statement can be inferred from the passage.

Statement IV and V: The passage states "The annual accounts of IL&FS and its close to 200 subsidiaries were audited by some of the biggest names in the profession. Yet none thought it fit to red flag the growing dependence on short-term debt and the excessively high leverage." Statement IV is clearly stated in the passage, but one can infer what the red flag means in these lines.

Hence, the correct option is (B).

43. An assumption is something supposed or taken for granted.

Option A: It is inferred from the statement, not assumed.

Option B: From the statement, we can't assume that IL&FS is facing something of an existential threat.

Option C: Again, from the statement, we can't assume this statement.

Option D: It can't be assumed from the statement.

Hence, the correct option is (D).

44. From "Ratings have been rapidly downgraded; in many cases after the event. Rating agencies are technically under the Securities and Exchange Board of India (Sebi); but are not subject to close regulatory oversight. Worse, under the current rating model, fees are paid by the rated entities. There is, thus, a huge incentive to give generous ratings for fear of losing business. Until we address this basic flaw in the rating model, ratings must be taken for what they are worth: very little!..," one can clearly decipher that option C is the most appropriate answer.

Hence, the correct option is (C).

45. As mentioned in the passage "Between a tenth and a third of the jobs in Britain are at risk of being automated away, depending on which survey or well-informed guess you believe."

Hence, the correct option is (C).

46. The correct antonym of the given word is 'Dispassionate'.

Enthusiastic: full of excitement and interest in something

Dispassionate: not influenced by strong emotion, and so able to be rational and impartial.

The other options are the Synonyms of the word 'Enthusiastic'.

Hence, the correct option is (A).

47. Option B and C are easily rejected as there is just a mention of the two. The passage revolves around the question that despite providing efficient solutions for many things whether Machines can replace human intuition and cater to all the problems arising in the society. Is their judgement justified at all times. This makes option A as the most suitable solution.

Hence, the correct option is (A).

48. As mentioned in the passage.

"It involves the ability to detect significance in a mass of confusing information, often in ways that are hard to explain – a faculty that in humans is called intuition. When computers do it, it is called machine learning. "

Hence, the correct option is (B).

49. The major contribution of the financial services was employment as well as the growth of the industrial sector. So option D is the best suited answer.

"Financial sector's contribution comes across even more strong when we look at sheer number of employment and tax revenue it generates. Especially employment generated by banking and insurance sector every year runs in millions"

Hence, the correct option is (D).

50. To make the banks credit-friendly, abundant funds were provided to them which they got after RBI allowed them to generate funds from the long term bond investments financing infrastructure. Hence, option C is the best suited answer.

Hence, the correct option is (C).

51. Option B is irrelevant to the passage.

Options C and D are supporting statements to the fact that financial services have proven to be beneficial for India.

Option A is a fact as stated in the passage that In a welcome step, in 2015 Indian government raised the cap of FDI in insurance sector by 49%. Thereby making way for more foreign direct investment in insurance as well as financial sector. Following this decision, many foreign insurance companies operating in India have already raised their stake to 49% in their joint venture with Indian insurance companies. Thus option A is the correct answer.

Hence, the correct option is (A).

52. The insurance sector would grow and maintain its first position only if it gets more and more investment which was boosted as the FDI was increased up to 49%. Hence option B is the only fit answer.

"In a welcome step, in 2015 Indian government raised the cap of FDI in insurance sector by 49%. Thereby making way for more foreign direct investment in insurance as well as financial sector"

Hence, the correct option is (B).

53. The answer is given in the 4th paragraph of the passage. 'In China, growth is projected to moderate from 6.9% in 2017 to 6.6% in 2018 and 6.2% in 2019, reflecting a slowing external demand growth and necessary financial regulatory tightening, the report said'.

Hence, the correct option is (D).

54. As per the 3rd paragraph of passage, 'Released in Bali during the annual meeting of the IMF and the World Bank, the IMF's flagship World Economic Outlook'.

Hence, the correct option is (B).

55. Option A is mentioned in the 2nd paragraph of the passage, ' If projections are true, then India would regain the tag of fastest growing major economies of the world, crossing China'.

Hence, the correct option is (A).

56. World Economic Outlook is covered in only 2nd paragraph of the passage. Option d is also partially true. Amongst options c and d, c is the more correct answer as the passage gives

projections as well the basis of it and tries to reach a conclusion. Thus, C is the right option.

Hence, the correct option is (C).

57. As per the passage, VR Tourism prevents over-crowding at popular Tourists destinations. Other two statements are true. From the passage, "Virtual reality not only offers alternative forms of access to threatened locations, it also recreates historical experiences and provides virtual access to remote locations you might not make it to otherwise."

Hence, the correct option is (D).

58. The person who is having second thoughts on VR Tourism can't agree with options A and B. Out of options C and D, he will strongly agree with option D. C is the viewpoint of the business community not of an individual. As the passage mention 'Virtual worlds use sensory stimulation and vivid imagery to generate authentic experiences. Immersion in these environments can lead to a deeper understanding of a place or event than simply reading about it or looking at pictures.', it is clear that person skeptical about VR tourism will never believe in the things mentioned above.

Hence, the correct option is (D).

59. There is no information regarding options B and D in the passage. Australian Holiday Destinations video has been viewed more than 10.5 million times which is certainly greater than 10 million. Data in options A is totally wrong.

Hence, the correct option is (C).

60. As per the passage, all the given options are the advantages of choosing the technology based tourism.

Hence, the correct option is (D).

Q.1 Direction: The following sentences form a paragraph. The sentence are numbered as P, Q, R, S and T. These five parts are not given in their proper order. Arrange them in the correct order to make the paragraph meaningful and then answer the questions given below.

P. Alaska's national parks offer a unique opportunity to explore glacial environments. The part that once connected the two land masses is now underwater, beneath the Bering Strait.

Q. It used to connect East Asia and North America. This bridge was the primary pathway used by the original colonists of the Americas some 15,000 to 20,000 years ago.

R. And hence the name 'Bering Land Bridge'.

S. They are nestled in a wilderness so wild you'll need to arrange for a boat or a plane to get there.

T. The Bering Land Bridge National Preserve, located in northwestern Alaska, near Nome, is one of the most popular of these parks.

What is the correct sequence of the sentences?

Q.2 Direction: Read the following group of sentences. The sentence are numbered P,Q,R,S. Arrange these four sentences in proper order to form a meaningful paragraph/sentence.

P. Vijay jumped down from the tree and took to his heels. The watchman chased them furiously.

Q. After what seemed ages, he seemed to have slowed down.

R. Sanjay and Farhan were far ahead and Vijay ran faster.

S. As he ran the guavas started falling out of his pockets. By this time the other workers had also started chasing them.

What is the correct sequence of the sentences?

Q.3 Direction: Read the following group of sentences. The sentence numbered P,Q,R,S. Arrange these four sentences in proper order to form a meaningful paragraph/sentence.

P. Optimism is not a deep complicated philosophy. In some persons it is an inborn trait.

Q. In fact, it is always taking a positive and bright view of life.

R. It is more of a general attitude of life.

S. They are tuned that way by nature and temperament. However, in most cases it is an acquired and nurtured habit.

What is the correct sequence of the sentences?

A. RQPS   **B.** QRPS   **C.** PSRQ   **D.** PSQR

Q.4 Direction: Read the following group of sentences. The sentences are numbered P,Q,R,S. Arrange these four sentences in proper order to form a meaningful paragraph/sentence.

P. We frisked about cheerfully over a path that led to a guava orchard. There was a mud wall around it.

Q. I smacked my lips at the sight of the luscious green guavas in the orchard.

R. Ajit also followed him without a second's thought.

S. Saransh was the first one to leap over the wall to get the guavas. However I was scared that the watchman will catch us.

What is the correct sequence of the sentences?

A. RQSP   **B.** SQRP   **C.** PSQR   **D.** PSRQ

Q.5 Direction: Read the following group of sentences. The sentences are numbered P,Q,R,S. Arrange these four sentences in proper order to form a meaningful paragraph/sentence.

P. Slowly she started walking out of the house towards the lake in the park. She could only stay and experience the numbness straying out into the dark around her.

Q. Usually at this time the park remained silent and isolated.

R. She sat on the bench closest to the lake and tried to feel the cold breeze sweeping against her body.

S. Darkness gave her comfort;it was a means of escape to solace where she had to think less. The chill and the darkness provided a cover for her mostly a cover of protection from the world.

What is the correct sequence of the sentences?

A. QRPS   **B.** QSPR   **C.** PSQR   **D.** SRQP

Q.6 Direction: Read the following group of sentences. The sentences are numbered P,Q,R,S. Arrange these four sentences in proper order to form a meaningful paragraph/sentence.

P. Plato's 'Republic' has exercised tremendous influence. He states that statesmen should

Q. on human thought and intelligence.

R. integrity, because he felt that, only such men

S. be men of supreme intelligence and impeccable. could enlighten the darker side of human nature into a positive.

What is the correct sequence of the sentences?

A. PRSQ   **B.** SQPR   **C.** RSQP   **D.** QPSR

Q.7 Direction: Read the following group of sentences. The sentences are numbered P,Q,R,S. Arrange these four sentences in proper order to form a meaningful paragraph/sentence.

P. Youths are the assets and hope of a nation in making India a great

Q. Steeped in old cultural values

R. They can play a vital role

S. democratic, progressive and prosperous country. But equipped with modern scientific knowledge.

What is the correct sequence of the sentences?

A. SPRQ   **B.** PRSQ   **C.** RPSQ   **D.** QPRS

Q.8 Direction: Read the following group of sentences. The sentences are numbered P,Q,R,S. Arrange these four sentences in proper order to form a meaningful paragraph/sentence.

P. Civilization is based on a clearly defined and widely accepted yet often unarticulated hierarchy. Violence done by those lower on the hierarchy to those higher is unthinkable

Q. Violence done by those higher on the hierarchy to those lower is nearly always invisible, that is, unnoticed.

R. When it is noticed, it is fully rationalized.

S. When it does occur it is regarded with shock, horror, and the fetishization of the victims. The classification in society is a menace to mankind.

What is the correct sequence of the sentences?

A. QSPR   **B.** QRPS   **C.** SRQP   **D.** PSRQ

Q.9 Direction: Rearrange the following five sentences/group of sentences (A), (B), (C), (D), and (E) in the proper sequence to form a meaningful paragraph; then answer the questions given below them.

(A). The IAS is a part of the permanent bureaucracy of the nation, and is an inseparable part of the executive of the Government of India.

(B). Upon confirmation of service, an IAS officer serves a probationary period as a sub-divisional magistrate.

(C). The Indian Administrative Service (IAS) is the administrative arm of the All India Services.

(D). Completion of this probation is followed by an executive administrative role in a district as a district magistrate and collector which lasts several years.

(E). IAS officers may enter the IAS by passing the Civil Services Examination.

What is the correct sequence of the sentences?

A. (A),(C),(E),(D),(B)   **B.** (A),(C),(E),(B),(D)

C. (A),(C),(E),(B),(D)   **D.** (C),(A),(E),(B),(D)

Ques (10-13):Direction: In this question, each item consists of six sentences of passage. The first and sixth sentences are given in the beginning as S1 and S6. The middle four-sentence in each have been jumbled up and labelled as P, Q, R and S. You are required to find the proper sequence of the five sentences.

Q.10 S1: The British rule in India has brought about the moral, material, cultural and spiritual ruination of this great country.

S6: We are not to kill anybody but it is our dharma to see that the curse of this Government is blotted out.

P: I regard this rule as a curse.

Q: Sedition has become my religion

R: Ours is a non-violent battle

S: I am out to destroy this system of Government.

[UPSC NDA, 2019]

A. S P R Q   **B.** P S Q R   **C.** Q R P S   **D.** S R P Q

Q.11 S1: Mr. Sherlock Holmes and Doctor Watson were spending a weekend in a University town.

S6: It was clear that something very unusual happened.

P: One evening they received a visit from an acquaintance, Mr. Hilton Soames.

Q: On that occasion, he was in a state of great agitation.

R: They were staying in furnished rooms, close to the library.

S: Mr. Soames was a tall, thin man of a nervous and excitable nature.

The proper sequence should be:

A. P R S Q   **B.** R P S Q   **C.** P Q R S   **D.** R P Q S

Q.12 S1: The machines that drive modern civilisation derive their power from coal and oil.

S6: Nuclear energy may also be effectively used in this respect.

P: But they are not inexhaustible.

Q: These sources may not be exhausted very soon.

R: A time may come when some other sources have to be tapped and utilised.

S: Power may, of course, be obtained in future from forests, water, wind and withered vegetables.

The proper sequence should be:

A. P Q R S   **B.** Q P R S   **C.** S R Q P   **D.** S P Q R

Q.13 S1: The body can never stop.

S6: It comes from food.

P: To support this endless activity, the body needs all the fuel for action.

Q: Sometimes it is more active than at other times, but it is always moving.

R: Even in the deepest sleep we must breathe.

S: The fuel must come from somewhere.

The proper sequence should be:

A. P Q R S   **B.** P R Q S   **C.** Q R P S   **D.** S R Q P

Ques (14-21):Direction: Given below are sentences which have been presented in a random order. Arrange the following sentences in a proper sequence to form a meaningful paragraph and identify the correct sequence.

Q.14 A. This is because your witness will be called upon to testify in court if the will is ever challenged.

B. Lawyers advise people to use witnesses who are younger than they and are likely to outlive them.

C. You can make a will as simple as you want. You will need to sign the document in the presence of two witnesses, who will then have to put the signature on it.

D. It helps if a doctor is a witness or the document is signed in his presence.

E. This is because he could be called upon to testify to the stability of your mental condition when you drew up the will.

A. ABCDE   **B.** CBADE   **C.** DCBAE   **D.** CDBAE

Q.15 A. For years, the singles competition was judged according to two categories.

B. Secondly, the compulsory - figures category required each skater to perform three or six repetitions of three figures drawn from a possible 41 patterns.

C. Figure skating is primarily a sport of amateurs, contests are held for singles and for pairs.

D. Firstly, the free-skating category judged a skater's ability to perform jumps, spins, spirals, and skating coordinated with music.

E. All figures are based on a figure - eight pattern or variations thereof.

A. BCADE   **B.** CADBE   **C.** CDBAE   **D.** ABCDE

Q.16 A. They are the oligarchy.

B. Next are the rule takers, the companies that pay homage to the industrial "lords."

C. IBM, CBS, United Airlines, Sears, Coca – Cola, and the like are the creators and procreators of industrial orthodoxy.

D. First are the rule makers, the incumbents that built the industry.

E. Fujitsu, ABC, US Air, Smith Barney, J.C. Penny and numerous others are peasants.

F. Look at any industry and you will see three kinds of companies.

A. FDCABE
B. DFCBAE
C. FCBDAE
D. FBCADE

Q.17 A. In India, in the last 4 - 5 years, some US funds have entered.

B. US funds like draper and Walden have played an important role in kick-starting the venture capital industry in India.

C. Draper in particular played a pioneering role.

D. This was the second wave of venture capital.

E. The third wave is people coming back from the US and moving into venture capital - like myself.

F. Venture capital started about 15 years ago, with some government – backed funds.

A. BFACDE
B. FDABEC
C. FABCDE
D. CDBAEF

Q.18 A. The first is retained by employers to find specific people for specific jobs.

B. They are the consultants who advertise in this newspaper.

C. The other type of recruitment company – or agency to be precise – works on a contingency basis.

D. There are essentially two types of recruitment companies.

E. They are paid by the employer only when someone is appointed.

A. BCDEA
B. DABCE
C. DBEAC
D. ACBDE

Q.19 A. Living is not important - living with excellent health throughout is more meaningful.

B. It is non - invasive and without side - effects.

C. But the quality of life of such persons may not be as good as one would like it to be.

D. Exercise, yogic exercise, is the only tool that can maintain health in a cellular sense.

E. However, practice of asana and pranayama needs what modern thought calls motivation.

F. Many people do not exercise and yet live to a ripe old age.

A. EADBCF
B. CFEDBA
C. AFCDBE
D. FDABCE

Q.20 A. Electronic transactions are happening in closed group networks and Internet. Electronic commerce is one of the most important aspects of Internet to emerge.

B. Cash transactions offer both privacy and anonymity as it does not contain information that can be used to identify the parties nor the transaction history.

C. To support e-commerce, we need effective payment systems and secure communication channels and data integrity.

D. The whole structure of traditional money is built on faith and so will electronic money have to be.

E. Moreover, money is worth what it is because we have come to accept it.

A. BEDAC
B. ABECD
C. DEABC
D. DCEBA

Q.21 A. Merchants soon grew rich as the demand for products increased.

B. Trade started from person to person but grew to involve different towns in different lands.

C. Eventually, people got a greater variety of things to choose from.

D. People found work in transporting the goods or selling them.

A. BDAC
B. BADC
C. DABC
D. DBAC

Q.22 Directions: The following sentences form a paragraph. The sentences are numbered as P, Q, R, S, and T. These five parts are not given in their proper order. Arrange them in the correct order to make the paragraph meaningful and then answer the questions given below.

P. A team of scientists has observed for the first time the decay of one such nucleus, the xenon-124 nuclei. This duration is, however, tiny compared with the time taken for physical processes such as the radioactive decay of some nuclei.

Q. The universe is almost 14 billion years old.

R. This decay then gives information for further investigations on neutrinos, the lightest of all elementary particles whose nature is still not understood fully. The half-life measured thus for the xenon-124 decay process, called double electron capture, is about one trillion times longer than the age of the universe.

S. Half-life is the time over which half of the radioactive nuclei present in a sample decay.

T. It was observed using the dark matter detector XENON1T at the Gran Sasso National Laboratory of the National Institute for Nuclear Physics, Italy.

What is the correct sequence of the sentences?

Which of the following should be the THIRD sentence in the correct order?

A. QPTSR
B. QTPSR
C. QPTRS
D. PQTSR

Q.23 Direction: Rearrange the following five sentences/group of sentences (A), (B), (C), (D), and (E) in the proper sequence to form a meaningful paragraph; then answer the questions given below them.

(A) Globalization has accelerated due to advances in transportation and communication technology.

(B) However, disputes and diplomacy are also large parts of the history of globalization, and of modern globalization.

(C) Globalization is the process of interaction and integration among people, companies, and governments worldwide.

(D) Globalization is also an economic process of interaction and integration that is associated with social and cultural aspects.

(E) This increase in global interactions has caused a growth in international trade and the exchange of ideas and culture.

What is the correct sequence of the sentences?

Which of the following should be the LAST sentence after rearrangement?

Q.24 Direction: Rearrange the following six sentences 1, 2, 3, 4, 5 and 6 in the proper sequence to form a meaningful paragraph, then answer the question given below them.

1. The group desired to enhance the learning experience in schools with an interactive digital medium that can be used within and outside the classrooms.

2. Then the teacher can act on the downloaded data rather than collect it from each and every student and thereby save his time and effort.

3. Editor, decided by the group of engineers, all alumni of the Indian Institute of Technology when they founded Editor Technologies in August 2009.

4. They can even take tests and submit them digitally using the same tablets and teachers in turn can download the tests using the company's cloud services.

5. With this desire they created a solution that digitalizes the school text books and other learning material so that students no longer need to carry as many books to school and back as before, but can access their study material on their touch screen tablets.

6. A mechanic works on motors and accountant has his computer. Likewise, if a student has to work on a machine of the device, what should it be called?

What is the correct sequence of the sentences?

Q.25 Direction: Rearrange the following six sentences/ group of sentences (A), (B), (C), (D), (E), and (F) in the proper sequence to form a meaningful paragraph; then answer the questions given below them.

A. Most of the time I had been pacing up and down the platform, browsing at the book-stall

B. I think I was about twelve at the time and my parents considered me old enough to travel alone

C. Or feeding broken biscuits to stray dogs; trains came and went, and the platform would be quiet for a while and then

D. I had arrived by bus at Ambala early in the evening: now there was a wait till midnight before my train arrived

E. It was my second year at boarding-school, and I was sitting on platform no. 8 at Ambala station waiting for the northern bound train

F. When a train arrived, it would be an inferno of heaving, shouting, agitated human bodies

What is the correct sequence of the sentences?

A. EBDCAF   **B.** CAFEBD

C. EBCAFD   **D.** AFEBDC

Q.26 Direction: The following sentences form a paragraph. The sentences of the paragraph are numbered as P, Q, R, S and T. These five parts are not given in their proper order. Arrange them in the correct order to make the paragraph meaningful and then answer the questions given below.

P. Alaska's national parks offer a unique opportunity to explore glacial environments. The part that once connected the two land masses is now underwater, beneath the Bering Strait.

Q. It used to connect East Asia and North America. This bridge was the primary pathway used by the original colonists of the Americas some 15,000 to 20,000 years ago.

R. And hence the name 'Bering Land Bridge'.

S. They are nestled in a wilderness so wild you'll need to arrange for a boat or a plane to get there.

T. The Bering Land Bridge National Preserve, located in northwestern Alaska, near Nome, is one of the most popular of these parks.

What is the correct sequence of the sentences?

A. TSQRP   **B.** TSQPR   **C.** STQPR   **D.** STPQR

Q.27 Direction: The following sentences form a paragraph. The sentences are numbered as P, Q, R, S and T. These parts are not given in their proper order. Read the sentences and choose the alternative that arranges them in correct order.

P. Its small companion is the subject of a great deal of study, as well.

Q. It shows a classic spiral shape and a curious little companion that appears to be attached to one of the spiral arms.

R. The Whirlpool also has a fascinating structure, with its spiral arms and central black hole region.

S. It is showing astronomers how galaxies interact with each other and how stars form within them.

T. The Whirlpool is a neighboring galaxy to the Milky Way. For amateur observers, the Whirlpool is a joy to observe.

What is the correct sequence of the sentences?

After the rearrangement, which of the following sentence should be FIRST?

A. TSPRQ   **B.** TSRPQ   **C.** STRQP   **D.** TSRQP

Q.28 Direction: In the following question, sentences of a paragraph have been jumbled and labeled as A, B, C and D. You are required to rearrange the jumbled sentences of the paragraph and mark your response accordingly by selecting the correct option.

A. Before the 12th century, It is to be identified as Carnatic classical music.

B. And has been evolving since the 12th century.

C. It is a tradition that originated in Vedic ritual chants.

D. Shastriya Sangeet is the classical music of North India.

A. DCBA   **B.** DCAB   **C.** ABCD   **D.** ABDC

Q.29 Direction: The following sentences form a paragraph. The sentences are numbered as P, Q, R, S and T. These five parts are not given in proper order. Read the sentences and choose the alternative that arranges them in the correct order.

P. A fleet of Hellenistic, Roman, early Islamic and Ottoman wrecks that were lost some two kilometers below the waves

Q. For wrecks that sank along antiquity's mighty shipping lanes

R. Of the Levantine Basin between the 3rd century BC and the 19th century

S. For almost seven decades archaeologists have searched the eastern Mediterranean in vain

T. Now, though, a British-led team can reveal a spectacular discovery

What is the correct sequence of the sentences?

A. SQTRP   **B.** SQTRP   **C.** QSTPR   **D.** SQTPR

Q.30 Direction: Rearrange the following five sentences/ group of sentences (A), (B), (C), (D), and (E) in the proper sequence to form a meaningful paragraph; then answer the questions given below them.

(A) The Modi administration routinely issued formal responses, but closer scrutiny raises questions about whether India has adopted a policy of silence about China's transgressions along the border.

(B) While the Indian Army has deployed additional troops in response, one such face-off with the PLA, in the Bhutanese territory of Doklam in 2017, had led to a shift in the status quo in China's favour.

(C) The centre had maintained a studied silence despite previous incursions being raised in Parliament.

(D) The ongoing border dispute between India and China, following incursions by the People's Liberation Army into regions in Ladakh and Sikkim in early May, marked the third major transgression in four years by the Chinese armed forces without facing significant pushback from the Narendra Modi government.

(E) Since then, the Indian government has also ignored several incursions into Arunachal Pradesh, according to a parliamentarian and local politicians.

What is the correct sequence of the sentences?

A. DBECA   **B.** DBECA   **C.** BDEAC   **D.** DBEAC

Q.31 Direction: The question consists of five statements labelled A, B, C, D and E which when logically ordered form a coherent passage. Choose the option that represents the most logical order.

A. In simpler terms, it is the Indian version of the Razzies.

B. The 3rd Golden Kela Awards will be hosted by Cyrus Broacha this year.

C. It was created in order to ridicule the bad performances and as a revenge for wasting our precious time and money on such idiotic films.

D. The Golden Kela is held each year where awards are given for the year's worst in Bollywood.

E. It was created by Random magazine, India's longest running humor magazine in the year 2009.

What is the correct sequence of the sentences?

A. DAECB   **B.** BACDE   **C.** ACEDB   **D.** CEADB

Q.32 Direction: The question consists of five statements labelled A, B, C, D and E which when logically ordered form a coherent passage. Choose the option that represents the most logical order.

A. Despite the strong performance of the economy in 2010-11, the outlook for 2011-12 is clouded by stubborn and persistently high inflation, and rising external risks.

B. The three key macroeconomic concerns before the Union Budget 2011-12 were high inflation, high current account deficit (CAD), and fiscal consolidation.

C. Additionally, there was an expectation that the government would restart the reform process.

D. While the Budget sets a lower nominal gross domestic product (GDP) growth target of 14%, we believe that the real GDP growth target of 9% factored in the Budget is on the optimistic side.

E. The Budget has made an attempt to address all these issues, albeit through small steps.

What is the correct sequence of the sentences?

A. BCEAD   **B.** CBAED   **C.** DACEB   **D.** ADCEB

Q.33 Direction: The question consists of five statements labelled A, B, C, D and E which when logically ordered form a coherent passage. Choose the option that represents the most logical order.

A. These were mainly bulwarks against winter, the hoarded dregs of more plentiful seasons.

B. The first were the earliest mince pies, which saw cooked, shredded meat, dried fruits, alcohol with its preservative qualities and perhaps a few spices or herbs, all encased in large pies.

C. Subsequently, people baked this into a kind of pie, adding bread-crumbs for bulk, eggs to bind it, and upping the dried fruits and called it 'plum pudding'.

D. The pudding seems to have had two principal forerunners.

E. The second main pudding was a pottage or soup called frumenty, a fast dish involving cracked wheat, currants and almonds which was ladled out at the start of a meal.

What is the correct sequence of the sentences?

A. ECDAB   **B.** BAECD   **C.** DACEB   **D.** DBAEC

Q.34 Direction: The question consists of five statements labelled A, B, C, D and E which when logically ordered form a coherent passage. Choose the option that represents the most logical order.

A. In a bid to placate the associate members, the ICC has decided to increase the number of participating teams to 16 in the Twenty20 World Cup, as the game's governing body feels these countries will have a greater chance of competing on an equal footing in cricket's shortest format.

B. It is convenient just now to forget that in the last edition of the tournament, considerable criticism was heaped on the governing body for the inordinate length of the tournament, thanks in large part to the presence of the associates.

C. To be fair to the ICC, criticism of the move to restrict the number of teams in the next edition of the Cup is a case of damned if you do, damned if you don't.

D. The ICC's decision to restrict the number of teams in the 2015 World Cup has evoked mixed responses, with opinion divided among players of the full member teams.

E. Not surprisingly, the associate members aren't too thrilled about the idea of being kept out of cricket's showpiece event.

What is the correct sequence of the sentences?

A. ECDAB   **B.** BAECD   **C.** DACEB   **D.** DEACB

Q.35 Direction: The question consists of five statements labelled A, B, C, D and E which when logically ordered form a coherent passage. Choose the option that represents the most logical order.

A. Environment Education unit of Centre for Science & Environment has always been working towards providing easy to understand reading material.

B. Their new publication on this subject is an attempt to lend teachers a helping hand.

C. It unfolds in two sections: Climate change: how to make sense of it all

D. And natural resources how to share & care.

E. However, they are introduced to students not as a paragraph to memorize but as an activity to do.

What is the correct sequence of the sentences?

A. ACEBD   **B.** DBCAE   **C.** ABCDE   **D.** BECAD

Q.36 Direction: The question consists of five statements labelled A, B, C, D and E which when logically ordered form a coherent passage. Choose the option that represents the most logical order.

A. A famous Japanese rock garden is at Ryoan-Ji in Northwest Kyoto, Japan.

B. The rocks of various sizes are arranged on small white pebbles in five groups, each comprising five, two, three, two, & three rocks.

C. The garden is 30 meters long from East to West & 10 meters from north to south.

D. The garden contains 15 rocks arranged on the surface of white pebbles in such a manner that visitors can see only 14 of them at once from whichever angle the garden is viewed.

E. There are no trees, just 15 irregularly shaped rocks of varying sizes, some arranged by gravel/sand that is raked everyday.

What is the correct sequence of the sentences?

A. ACEBD   **B.** CAEDB   **C.** DEABC   **D.** BADEC

Q.37 Direction: The question consists of five statements labelled A, B, C, D and E which when logically ordered form a coherent passage. Choose the option that represents the most logical order.

A. When they gathered together, the Buddha was completely silent & some speculated that perhaps the Buddha was tired or ill.

B. It is said that Gautam Buddha gathered his disciples one day for a Dharma talk.

C. One of the Buddha's disciples, Mahakasyapa, silently gazed at the flower & broke into a broad smile.

D. The origin of Zen Buddhism is ascribed to the Flower Sermon, the earliest source which comes from the 14th century.

E. The Buddha silently held up & twirled a flower and twinkled his eyes, several of his disciples tried to interpret what this meant though none of them was correct.

What is the correct sequence of the sentences?

A. EBDAC   **B.** DBAEC   **C.** BCDEA   **D.** CADBE

Q.38 Direction: The question consists of five statements labelled A, B, C, D and E which when logically ordered form a coherent passage. Choose the option that represents the most logical order.

A. The post-election crisis in Kenya remains unresolved.

B. The damage being done to the country's economy is severe: tourism, horticulture, and other industries that depend on trade beyond the Kenyan border are reeling.

C. Many countries responded, providing essential humanitarian assistance and logistical support. For this, I and many other Kenyans are very grateful.

D. Thousands of livelihoods, along with investments throughout the region, are threatened and collapsing.

E. As the situation in Kenya escalated with murders, rapes, burning of property, looting, and the displacement of thousands of people throughout the country - the international community was urged to help.

What is the correct sequence of the sentences?

A. AEDBC   **B.** ABCED   **C.** ACDEB   **D.** ABDEC

Q.39 Direction: The question consists of five statements labelled A, B, C, D and E which when logically ordered form a coherent passage. Choose the option that represents the most logical order.

A. The US market will continue to be the dominant one in the foreseeable future. The rupee could become even stronger.

B. A greater recourse to hedging as well as striving for multi-currency revenue streams automatically suggests itself.

C. Already one company, TCS, by resorting to these methods extensively has turned in an above - average performance during the first quarter.

D. Most IT companies have been grappling with more mundane problems such as a high level of attrition amidst rising wage costs and inability to secure the right type and number of American visas.

E. The BPO industry and many medium-sized software exporters are reportedly operating on thin margins.

What is the correct sequence of the sentences?

A. BCADE   **B.** ABCDE   **C.** DCBAE   **D.** EDABC

Q.40 Direction: The question consists of five statements labelled A, B, C, D and E which when logically ordered form a coherent passage. Choose the option that represents the most logical order.

A. Last March, I was invited to present a paper on the topic of whether the mistakes of the 20th century would be repeated in the 21st century as well.

B. The economic crisis hadn't become grave then.

C. But today the world is in the midst of the biggest economic crisis since 1929.

D. The key difference between then and now is that the old power structures have finally disappeared.

E. Now even the US is pleading for financial help from China.

What is the correct sequence of the sentences?

A. BCADE   **B.** ABCDE   **C.** CDEAB   **D.** DEABC

Q.41 Direction: The question consists of five statements labelled A, B, C, D and E which when logically ordered form a coherent passage. Choose the option that represents the most logical order.

A. Thus, despite India's huge population, we have not done well in Olympic Games.

B. During the British period also, cricket remained popular in India.

C. Cricket has been an extremely popular game in India for quite some time now.

D. It is time our government and corporate fraternity pay due attention to other games/sports and we redeem our national pride in Olympic Games.

E. However, due to this reason, other games/sports did not receive the required attention they deserve.

What is the correct sequence of the sentences?

A. EACDB   **B.** BDACE   **C.** CBEAD   **D.** DCEAB

Q.42 Direction: The question consists of five statements labelled A, B, C, D and E which when logically ordered form a coherent passage. Choose the option that represents the most logical order.

A. People started fearing a famine.

B. Monsoon turned out to be unusually abundant and the danger was averted.

C. The monsoon failed and water tanks became almost empty.

D. So, no grain could be sown by the farmers in their fields.

E. Farmers looked anxiously for the next monsoon.

What is the correct sequence of the sentences?

A. CADBE   **B.** CDAEB   **C.** AEDCB   **D.** DABCE

Q.43 Direction: The question consists of five statements labelled A, B, C, D and E which when logically ordered form a coherent passage. Choose the option that represents the most logical order.

A. Economists all over the world have expressed anxiety in this regard.

B. As a result, Indian people have been subjected to high cost of living and inflation.

C. Indian economy has not shown desirable growth in the recent years.

D. Grim global economic scenario has also contributed to this problem and it seems a quick fix solution is yet far away.

E. But, one of the primary reasons for such a situation has been Indian government's inability to take tough decisions.

What is the correct sequence of the sentences?

A. CDAEB   **B.** ACDBE   **C.** DEABC   **D.** EADCB

Q.44 Direction: The question consists of five statements labelled A, B, C, D and E which when logically ordered form a coherent passage. Choose the option that represents the most logical order.

A. They fled to the higher ground.

B. Soon the floods retired and the villagers were able to return.

C. The river overflowed its banks.

D. The rain fell steadily for several days.

E. The terrified villagers abandoned their homes.

What is the correct sequence of the sentences?

A. CEBAD   **B.** DEBCA   **C.** DCEAB   **D.** EDABC

Q.45 Direction: Given below are four sentences in jumbled order. Select the option that gives their correct order.

A. This flight takes place on a hot summer day.

B. It has a pair of wings but bites them off after its 'wedding' flight.

C. In the heat, the queen leaves the nest and goes out to meet a drone, high up in the air.

D. The queen is the mother of the entire population of a colony of ants.

What is the correct sequence of the sentences?

A. DBAC   **B.** BACD   **C.** CABD   **D.** ACBD

Q.46 Direction: Given below are four sentences in jumbled order. Pick the option that gives their correct order.

A. Someone had been smart enough to remove it before I went on the rampage.

B. My hands had been itching to tear down that collage from my bedroom wall.

C. But I found the wall bare.

D. So, I entered my room in a hurry.

What is the correct sequence of the sentences?

A. DABC   **B.** CBAD   **C.** ABCD   **D.** BDCA

Q.47 Direction: In the following question, sentences of a paragraph have been jumbled and labelled as A, B, C, and D. You are required to rearrange the jumbled sentences of the paragraph and mark your response accordingly by selecting the correct option.

A: The Bihar Legislative Assembly election will be held to elect members of the Legislative Assembly of the Indian State of Bihar.

B: Finally, he results will be announced on 10 November 2020.

C: The elections will be conducted amid the COVID-19 pandemic with the necessary guidelines issued by the Election Commission of India.

D: The election will be held in three phases for a total of 243 seats.

What is the correct sequence of the sentences?

A. ACDB   **B.** CABD   **C.** DCAB   **D.** ADCB

Q.48 Direction: Sentences of a paragraph are given below in jumbled order. Arrange the sentences in the right order to form a meaningful and coherent paragraph.

A. But the eagle, in wrath, gave the beetle a flap of his wing, and straightaway seized upon the hare and devoured him.

B. The beetle, therefore, interceded with the eagle, begging of him not to kill the poor suppliant, and pleaded with him not to kill so small an animal.

C. When the eagle flew away, the beetle flew after him, to learn where his nest was.

D. A hare, being pursued by an eagle, took himself for refuge to the nest of a beetle, whom he begged to save him.

What is the correct sequence of the sentences?

A. ACDB   **B.** DCAB   **C.** CBAD   **D.** DBAC

Q.49 Direction: Given below are four jumbled sentences. Out of the given options, pick the one that gives their correct order.

A. Judy reached out one hand and laid it on the soft neck of the fawn.

B. He moved forward on all fours until he was close to it.

C. He put his arms around its body.

D. The touch made him delirious.

What is the correct sequence of the sentences?

A. ADBC   **B.** BACD   **C.** BDAC   **D.** ABDC

Q.50 Direction: In the following question, sentences of a paragraph have been jumbled and labelled as A, B, C and D. You are required to rearrange the jumbled sentences of the paragraph and mark your response accordingly by selecting the correct option.

A: According to BCCI, the 2015 IPL season contributed ₹11.5 billion (US$160 million) to the GDP of the Indian economy.

B: The Indian Premier League (IPL) is a Twenty20 cricket league in India contested by eight teams representing eight different cities or states in India.

C: The IPL has an exclusive window in ICC Future Tours Programme.

D: The league was founded by the Board of Control for Cricket in India (BCCI) in 2008.

What is the correct sequence of the sentences?

A. BACD   **B.** ACDB   **C.** BDCA   **D.** CBDA

Q.51 Direction: In the following question, sentences of a paragraph have been jumbled and labelled as A, B, C and D. You are required to rearrange the jumbled sentences of the paragraph and mark your response accordingly by selecting the correct option.

A: Thirdly, printing helped in the dissemination of knowledge in a permanent form.

B: However, all these are passive media.

C: Speech was the first means of conveying ideas followed by writing as a means for storing information.

D: Computer is the only medium that cannot only store but analyze information to make decisions—therefore it is called the fourth information revolution.

What is the correct sequence of the sentences?

A. ACDB   **B.** CABD   **C.** BDCA   **D.** DACB

Q.52 Direction: The question below comprises four scattered segments of a paragraph. Identify from among the four choices the sequences that correctly assemble the segments and complete the paragraph.

A. However, engineers and developers have voiced apprehensions about building the underwater arena as it poses many challenges which, at the moment, seem impossible to overcome.

B. Polish architect Krysztof Kotala has proposed to build an underwater tennis complex located offshore, between the Burj al Arab and the Palm Jumeirah islands.

C. After boasting of a tennis court high up in the air built atop the 1,000-foot-tall Burj al Arab hotel, Dubai has wooed an architect to test the waters for an underwater tennis court.

D. Designed with a massive curved roof, the undersea complex will spread out to hold seven courts. The sports arena will also

double up as an aquarium with a rooftop coral reef, which will put on display an abundance of sea life for spectators as well as players.

What is the correct sequence of the sentences?

A. ACDB   **B.** BDCA   **C.** CADB   **D.** CBDA

Q.53 Direction: Given below are four jumbled sentences. Select the option that gives their correct order.

A. Far below he saw green meadows and in their midst a village.

B. He sat down and rested in the shadow of a rock.

C. Nunez was in a pass between the mountains.

D. He slowly climbed down the precipices and about midday came to the plain, stiff and tired out.

What is the correct sequence of the sentences?

A. ADBC   **B.** CADB   **C.** CDAB   **D.** ABDC

Q.54 Direction: The question below comprises four scattered segments of a paragraph. Identify from among the four choices the sequences that correctly assemble the segments and complete the paragraph.

A. Mr D Gautam's personality sets him apart the rest.

B. Nothing is too small for his attention

C. He has a fanatical devotion to detail.

D. This is what makes him a different guy.

What is the correct sequence of the sentences?

A. ACBD   **B.** ABCD   **C.** BDCA   **D.** DCBA

Q.55 Direction: Given below are four jumbled sentences. Select the option that gives their correct order.

A. However, the rate of population increase is another important factor to consider.

B. This change can be expressed in two ways.

C. Growth of population refers to the change in the number of inhabitants of a country.

D. First, in terms of absolute numbers and second, in terms of percentage change.

What is the correct sequence of the sentences?

A. CBDA   **B.** CADB   **C.** BDCA   **D.** BADC

Ques (56-60):Direction: In the following question, sentences of a paragraph have been jumbled and labeled as A, B, C and D. You are required to rearrange the jumbled sentences of the paragraph and mark your response accordingly by selecting the correct option.

Q.56 A. "It is mine. I saw it first," claimed one cat.

B. Suddenly they spotted a loaf of bread lying beneath a tree.

C. Once upon a time, two cats were passing through a street.

D. Both pounced upon it and caught the loaf at the same time.

A. ADBC   **B.** BADC   **C.** DBCA   **D.** CBDA

Q.57 A. It is one of the most popular pastimes.

B. Finding fault with others is the most common human folly.

C. But while railing at others, we hardly realize that we have the same faults in ourselves.

D. We like to sit in idle groups and rail about the shortcomings of others.

A. DBCA   **B.** CBDA   **C.** BADC   **D.** ADBC

Q.58 A. She understood my signs, and I could make her do as I wished.

B. My constant companion was Martha, our cook's daughter.

C. We even helped in feeding the hens which crowded around the kitchen steps.

D. This pleased me greatly and we spent a lot of time together.

A. BADC   **B.** CBDA   **C.** DCAB   **D.** ADCB

Q.59 A. The forest and trees filter the air and absorb harmful gases.

B. The environment gives us countless benefits that we can't repay our entire life.

C. Plants purify water, reduce the chances of a flood, maintain a natural balance, and many more.

D. As they are connected with the forest, trees, animals, water, and air.

A. CDAB   **B.** BDCA   **C.** ABCD   **D.** BDAC

Q.60 A: Hence, they are the most useful members of any society.

B: No one can deny that farmers form the backbone of any nation

C: They grow food for the whole country.

D: Yet they don't get the profit and recognition which they deserve.

A. ADCB   **B.** CADB   **C.** DCBA   **D.** BCAD

// Smart Answer Sheet //

Correct   Indicates percentage of students who answered questions correctly.

Skipped   Indicates percentage of students who skipped questions.

Q.	Ans.	Correct / Skipped
1	#	60.59 % / 34.92 %
2	#	68.15 % / 30.73 %
3	A	64.39 % / 30.73 %
4	D	66.31 % / 30.38 %
5	B	28.29 % / 67.45 %
6	D	53.47 % / 44.44 %
7	C	19.21 % / 80.27 %
8	B	27.33 % / 71.64 %
9	D	56.84 % / 36.86 %
10	B	45.92 % / 46.24 %
11	B	44.31 % / 52.94 %
12	B	87.76 % / 10.77 %

Q.	Ans.	Correct / Skipped
13	C	15.04 % / 74.12 %
14	B	60.78 % / 32.91 %
15	B	52.4 % / 39.99 %
16	A	31.06 % / 67.52 %
17	C	51.8 % / 43.44 %
18	B	25.46 % / 67.57 %
19	C	23.07 % / 71.22 %
20	A	65.51 % / 30.93 %
21	A	31.91 % / 67.92 %
22	A	32.06 % / 67.73 %
23	#	63.78 % / 32.02 %
24	#	21.67 % / 73.31 %

Q.	Ans.	Correct / Skipped
25	A	45.91 % / 50.34 %
26	C	11.06 % / 74.17 %
27	D	48.63 % / 44.92 %
28	A	86.06 % / 10.08 %
29	D	11.0 % / 69.27 %
30	D	64.86 % / 30.64 %
31	A	62.44 % / 35.93 %
32	A	44.84 % / 35.48 %
33	D	55.94 % / 41.88 %
34	D	45.86 % / 44.37 %
35	C	81.58 % / 14.76 %
36	A	48.46 % / 39.1 %

Q.	Ans.	Correct / Skipped
37	B	56.17 % / 38.06 %
38	D	41.44 % / 51.97 %
39	D	51.8 % / 31.46 %
40	B	84.91 % / 10.74 %
41	C	69.23 % / 30.39 %
42	B	42.74 % / 36.41 %
43	A	57.76 % / 39.53 %
44	C	40.88 % / 58.79 %
45	A	58.25 % / 33.21 %
46	D	52.95 % / 46.78 %
47	D	50.98 % / 39.02 %
48	D	59.43 % / 34.83 %

Q.	Ans.	Correct / Skipped
49	A	31.09 % / 68.91 %
50	C	59.31 % / 35.64 %
51	B	81.17 % / 10.74 %
52	D	49.52 % / 46.72 %
53	B	65.55 % / 32.96 %
54	A	69.03 % / 30.48 %
55	A	66.82 % / 32.77 %
56	D	49.71 % / 47.96 %
57	C	84.56 % / 12.75 %
58	A	76.6 % / 13.32 %
59	D	44.71 % / 43.43 %
60	D	60.42 % / 37.99 %

#

Q.	Answer
1	STQPR
2	RSPQ
23	(C),(A),(E),(D),(B)
24	631542

Performance Analysis

Avg. Score (%)	47.22%
Toppers Score (%)	70.56%
Your Score	

//Hints and Solutions//

1. The correct order is: STQPR.

- The first sentence of a paragraph introduces a topic. The second sentence usually provides more information about the first.

- Here, the first sentence talks about Alaska's national parks. Only sentence S refers to them with the pronoun 'they', suggesting it must directly follow the first sentence.

- So, S must be the second sentence.

- The fourth sentence is given; so the third must be a preamble to it. Here, the fourth sentence uses the phrase 'this bridge', indicating that the third sentence must have introduced some bridge.

- This is only given by sentence T. So, T must be the third sentence.

- The fifth must follow further from the fourth sentence. This is only given by sentence Q, which uses the pronoun 'it' to refer to the bridge.

- So, Q must be the fifth sentence.

- Sixth and seventh sentences would follow the earlier sentences, with the last giving some kind of conclusion to the above.

- Out of the remaining sentences P and R, P refers to 'the two land masses' given earlier in Q. R seems like a fitting conclusion.

- So, P must be the sixth sentence while R is the last sentence of the paragraph.

The ordered paragraph is: Alaska's national parks offer a unique opportunity to explore glacial environments. They are nestled in a wilderness so wild you'll need to arrange for a boat or a plane to get there. The Bering Land Bridge National Preserve, located in northwestern Alaska, near Nome, is one of the most popular of these parks. This bridge was the primary pathway used by the original colonists of the Americas some 15,000 to 20,000 years ago. It used to connect East Asia and North America. The part that once connected the two land masses is now underwater, beneath the Bering Strait. And so the name 'Bering Land Bridge'.

Hence, the correct answer is (STQPR).

2. The ordered paragraph is: Vijay jumped down from the tree and took to his heels. Sanjay and Farhan were far ahead and Vijay ran faster. As he ran the guavas started falling out of his pockets. The watchman chased them furiously. After what seemed ages, he seemed to have slowed down. By this time the other workers had also started chasing them.

R is a continuation of 1. S states a consequence of Vijay's running faster. P follows S as it talks on a separate topic of the watchman chasing them furiously. Q follows P as it is related to it.

Hence, the correct answer is (RSPQ).

3. The second sentence should have a direct reference to the 1st sentence and most certainly it should start with a pronoun referring to optimism. So, R follows 1. The author continues to

define optimism. So, Q is next. If we now read the two sentences that are left, we see that S starts with 'they' So, it can't come next. So, the next sentence is P followed by S.

So, the correct order is RQPS.

Hence, the correct option is (A).

4. The first statement must be P as it describes the orchard. S must follow P as Saransh was the first person. R must follow S as the verb 'followed' is mentioned here. Q must be the fourth statement as it completes the sequence.

The completes sequence is: We frisked about cheerfully over a path that led to a guava orchard. There was a mud wall around it. Saransh was the first one to leap over the wall to get the guavas. Ajit also followed him without a second's thought. I smacked my lips at the sight of the luscious green guavas in the orchard. However, I was scared that the watchman will catch us.

So, the correct order is PSRQ.

Hence, the correct option is (D).

5. The first statement must be Q as the rest of the sentences are linked to one another. S must follow Q as it begins to state how darkness was peaceful for her. P describes it further.

The completes sequence is: Slowly she started walking out of the house towards the lake in the park. Usually at this time the park remained silent and isolated. Darkness gave her comfort;it was a means of escape to solace where she had to think less. She could only stay and experience the numbness straying out into the dark around her. She sat on the bench closest to the lake and tried to feel the cold breeze sweeping against her body. The chill and the darkness provided a cover for her mostly a cover of protection from the world.

So, the correct order is QSPR.

Hence, the correct option is (B).

6. The first question that comes to our mind is, on whom or what has Plato's 'Republic' exercised tremendous influence upon? Now if we string them together they make complete sense. Also Q ends in a 'full-stop'. So, the next part should be the beginning of a new sentence. So, P follows Q. What did he state about statesmen? That they should be of supreme intelligence and impeccable integrity. So, S comes next in the sequence followed by R.

The completes sequence is: Plato's 'Republic' has exercised tremendous influence on human thought and intelligence. Plato's 'Republic' has exercised tremendous influence be men of supreme intelligence and impeccable integrity, because he felt that, only such men could enlighten the darker side of human nature into a positive.The first statement must be Q as the rest of the sentences are linked to one another. S must follow Q as it begins to state how darkness was peaceful for her. P describes it further. R must precede 6 as it talks about the chill of the breeze which is mentioned in P.

The completes sequence is: Slowly she started walking out of the house towards the lake in the park. Usually at this time the park remained silent and isolated. Darkness gave her comfort;it was a means of escape to solace where she had to think less. She could only stay and experience the numbness straying out into the dark around her. She sat on the bench closest to the lake and tried to feel the cold breeze sweeping against her body. The chill and the darkness provided a cover for her mostly a cover of protection from the world.

So, the correct order is QPSR.

Hence, the correct option is (D).

7. The given sentence is complete. So the next sentence is either a new sentence or starts with a conjuction. Here we see R is the starting of a new sentence, So, follows 1. But they can play a vital role in what? In making India a great, democratic, progressive and prosperous country. So P comes next in the sequence followed by S. The youths of our country should not only have cultural values but also modern scientific knowledge. So, Q comes last in the sequence.

So, the correct order is RPSQ.

Hence, the correct option is (C).

8. Q must be the first statement and must be followed by R as it mentions the consequence of bad treatment inflicted on the lower ones. P must come after it as 'those' is mentioned in it. Finally, S states the consequence.

The complete sequence is: Civilization is based on a clearly defined and widely accepted yet often unarticulated hierarchy. Violence done by those higher on the hierarchy to those lower is nearly always invisible, that is, unnoticed. When it is noticed, it is fully rationalized. Civilization is based on a clearly defined and widely accepted yet often unarticulated hierarchy. When it does occur it is regarded with shock, horror, and the fetishization of the victims. The classification in society is a menace to mankind.

So, the correct order is QRPS.

Hence, the correct option is (B).

9. The first sentence is (C) as it informs us what the IAS is.

The second sentence is (A). This sentence informs us about the IAS elaborately.

The third sentence is (E). It informs us about the process to become an IAS officer.

The fourth sentence is (B). From this sentence, we can understand what happens after an IAS officer receives the confirmation of service.

The last sentence is (D) as it concludes the passage by stating what happens at the end of the probation period which is mentioned in the previous sentence.

So the correct sequence is (C),(A),(E),(B),(D).

Hence, the correct option is (D).

10. The passage is in points about how the British rule has ruined the country.

The first line tells us that the rule is a curse as it destroys. It then explains about our non-violent battle and the intention of destroying the government. The last line sarcastically explains

that our dharma is to see that the curse of this Government is blotted out.

The correct sequence is:

S1: The British rule in India has brought about moral, material, cultural and spiritual ruination of this great country.

P: I regard this rule as a curse.

S: I am out to destroy this system of Government.

Q: Sedition has become my religion.

R: Ours is a non-violent battle.

S6: We are not to kill anybody but it is our dharma to see that the curse of this Government is blotted out.

So, the correct answer is (P S Q R).

Hence, the correct option is (B).

11. Since the introductory part is already there, R will be the 1st statement as it takes the story forward by talking about the place where Mr. Sherlock Holmes and Doctor Watson were staying.

The next statement will be P as tells us about the visit by someone who was known to them.

Now the statement P must be followed by S as it narrates how Mr. Soames looked like.

And the concluding statement will be Q.

So the correct order will be: R-P-S-Q.

Hence, the correct option is (B).

12. Since the introductory part is already there, Q will be the 1st statement as it tells us more about the idea of exhaustion of sources of power.

The next statement will be P as it further states that the sources are exhaustible.

Now the statement P must be followed by R as it makes us explore other sources of power as well.

And the concluding statement will be S.

So the correct order will be: Q-P-R-S.

Hence, the correct option is (B).

13. Since the introductory part is already there, Q will be the 1st statement as it furthers the statement in S1.

The next statement will be R as it takes us to another aspect of body movement mentioned as 'breathing'.

Now the statement R must be followed by P as it talks about the idea of catalyst needed for an activity.

And the concluding statement will be S.

So the correct order will be: Q-R-P-S.

Hence, the correct option is (C).

14. The first sentence here should be C, as it introduces us to the idea of will mentioned in the paragraph.

Thus, we can eliminate option (A) and (C).

The next sentence should be B as it introduces the views of a lawyer.

Following B, should be A because it tells us the reason why lawyer suggested young people as witness.

The next sentence should be D as it tells us that it would be helpful if doctor is a witness.

The last sentence should be E.

The correct sequence should be "CBADE".

Hence, the correct option is (B).

15. The first sentence should be C as it is the introductory statement about the sport of figure-skating.

The next sentence should be A as it tells us about the two categories.

The connective word 'Firstly' and 'Secondly' used in sentence D and B suggest their sequence. So, the next sentence should be D followed by B.

The last sentence should be E.

The correct sequence should be "CADBE".

Hence, the correct option is (B).

16. Here, the opening sentence should be F, as it introduces us to the idea of kinds of companies present.

The second sentence should be D as it tells us about the first type of company.

Next sentence should be C, as it tells us the names of the first type of companies.

Followed by A, as the pronoun 'they' is used for the companies mentioned in sentence C.

Next sentence should be B, as it tells us about the second type of company.

The last sentence should be E.

The correct sequence should be "FDCABE".

Hence, the correct option is (A).

17. Chronological sequence can be seen in this paragraph.

The first sentence should be F, as it tells us that 15 years ago, Venture Capital started.

Next sentence should be A, as it deals with situation of last 4-5 years.

Following A should be B, as A ends with 'US funds' and B begins with 'US funds'

The next sentence that logically follows B is C as C speaks of Draper connecting it to sentence B.

Here, the next sentence should be D and the last sentence should be sentence E.

The correct sequence should be "FABCDE".

Hence, the correct option is (C).

18. In this paragraph, the central theme is introduced by sentence D. So, it should be the first sentence.

Next should be A as it tells us about the first type of company. The keyword here is 'First' for the type of company mentioned.

Sentence A should be followed by B as B describes the company mentioned in sentence A.

The next sentence should be C as it tells us about the other type of recruitment company.

The last sentence here should be E.

The correct sentence should be "DABCE".

Hence, the correct option is (B).

19. The first sentence of this paragraph should be A, as it opens the discussion of living long vs. living healthy.

The second sentence should be F as it describes the other side of the story followed by C which describes about the quality of life of the people mentioned in sentence F.

D should be next sentence as it gives the solution to improve the health and quality of life. B should be the next sentence as it describes about the qualities of yogic exercise mentioned in the previous sentence.

The last sentence should be E.

The correct sequence here should be "AFCDBE".

Hence, the correct option is (C).

20. This paragraph is about cash transaction and electronic commerce. The observation on cash transaction should precede e-commerce.

Therefore, the paragraph must start with B.

Followed by the concept mentioned in sentence E, it should be the next sentence.

E must be followed by D, as it speaks about transition of structure from traditional money to electronic money.

This brings our sequence to 'BED'

The correct sequence should be "BEDAC".

Hence, the correct option is (A).

21. Before, trade started to grow internationally; it must have started in its basic form as selling of goods from one person to another. Hence B would come before D.

Thus, B is the opening sentence followed by D.

When trade grew to involve different lands then merchants would grow rich, So, A should be the next sentence.

The last sentence left is C.

Therefore, the correct sequence should be "BDAC."

Hence, the correct option is (A).

22. The first sentence of a paragraph introduces a topic. The second sentence usually provides more information about the first.

Here, the second sentence talks about 'duration' of something large. Given this, the only befitting first sentence can be Q, talking about 14 billion years.

So, Q must be the first sentence.

The third sentence must logically follow from the second sentence. Only P refers to the 'nuclei' mentioned in the second sentence by 'one such nucleus'.

So, P must be the third sentence.

The fourth sentence must logically follow the third. Only sentence T uses the phrase 'it was observed', which refers to the observation made in P.

So, T must be the fourth sentence.

The sixth and seventh sentences would follow the earlier sentences, with the last giving some kind of conclusion to the above sentences.

Out of the remaining sentences, S directly follows the fifth sentence, referring to the 'half-life'; while R refers to 'this decay used for further information', following S.

So, S must be the sixth sentence while R is the last sentence of the paragraph.

The correct order is: QPTSR.

Hence, the correct option is (A).

23. The given passage is about globalization.

The first sentence is (C) because it defines the word 'globalization'. Thus the topic is introduced.

The second sentence is (A) because it informs us about the process(globalization) which has accelerated due to the advancement of transportation and communication technology.

The next sentence is (E) because it informs us how the international trade expanded due to the increase in global interactions.

The fourth sentence should be (D) because it mentions another important fact about globalization. It informs us that globalization is also an economic process of interaction and integration.

The last sentence is (B) because it concludes the passage by stating that disputes and diplomacy are also large parts of this process. Therefore, it is not just a process of interaction and integration.

The correct sequence is (C),(A),(E),(D),(B).

The following paragraph is formed after arranging the five sentences in proper sequence:

Globalization is the process of interaction and integration among people, companies, and governments worldwide. Globalization has accelerated due to advances in transportation and communication technology. This increase in global interactions has caused a growth in international trade and the exchange of ideas and culture. Globalization is also an economic process of interaction and integration that is associated with social and cultural aspects. However, disputes and diplomacy are also large parts of the history of globalization, and of modern globalization.

Hence, the correct answer is (C),(A),(E),(D),(B).

24. The correct sequence is 631542.

First sentence: On glancing the jumbled passage, we find that it is based on a educational startup Edutor, the motive and details of which have been provided in the passage. The first sentence should be the principle declaration of the passage. A self-sufficient statement which is devoid of any pronoun or a connector. The opening statement should introduce the idea of the passage and perhaps the idea behind the evolution of Edutor. On analyzing the sentences, we find that sentences 6 and 3 are devoid of such pronouns and connectors. However, it must be noted that one of them must be the first and second sentence respectively. Now, a question is generally asked to seek a relevant answer. It asks what should be a student working on device or machine be called? Now, we know, rest of the statements provide description regarding Edutor, which IS the platform for students to work on the device or machine (answer to the question). Hence, statement 6 will be the first sentence.

Second sentence: The relevance of the second statement has been duly brought out in the previous description. This sentence should bring forth the relevant (specifications) details associated with Edutor. So, statement 3 will be the second sentence.

Third sentence: A group of engineers from IIT have been talked about in the second sentence. So, a sentence containing a description about 'the group' shall be used here. On analyzing the remaining sentences, we find that sentence 1 aptly describes the motive of 'the group' behind the development of Edutor i.e. to enhance the learning experience by an interactive machine interface. Hence, statement 1 shall be the third sentence.

Fourth sentence: Out of the remaining sentences, we find that the 'downloaded data' has not been introduced yet to us and hence, can be eliminated here. On further interrogation, we are left with sentences 4 and 5, each with pronoun 'they'. Here, it important to note the person(s) for whom 'they' has been used. Now, we are introduced neither to students nor to teachers and it is a obvious fact that 'they' used in sentence 4 (they can even take tests) shall be for the students. Similarly, 'they' in sentence 5 shall be used for the group of engineers, which have been duly discussed in the previous statement and thus, forms the chain. Moreover, students, too, have been introduced in this sentence, which makes sense to used pronoun for them in the next sentence. Hence, statement 5 is the fourth sentence.

Fifth sentence: This statement shall discuss the test taking facility for the students, as highlighted in the previous statement. Hence, statement 4 is the fifth sentence.

Sixth sentence: Now, it is a common-sense fact that the tests performed by the students need to be checked by the teachers. In Edutor, the tests are performed by students online, which can be 'downloaded' by the teachers as per their convenience, thereby, saving time. So, statement 2 shall be the sixth sentence.

Hence, the correct answer is (631542).

25. Finding first sentence itself in this passage might be tricky. But that sentence is E. If we read all the sentences individually, we come to know that the author is describing the atmosphere around a station. It is only sentence E that gives us the vital information of date, time venue etc. 'Second year serves as the time, Ambala station serves as the venue the last part of the sentence tells us the reason.' The second sentence should be B. Because naturally after reading the first sentence the first question that may come to a reader's mind is 'what is a boarding school student doing at the station alone?' So the author answers this question. Third sentence is D. Now the author is describing the whole scenario as to how he had reached the station and all such details. From here on it is quite easy to arrange the sentences. The fourth sentence must be A because it is the only sentence that starts a new subject i.e. what was the author doing during that long wait?' Next sentence is C which starts with C linking it to sentence A. And the last sentence is F.

The correct sequence of the sentence is: EBDCAF

Hence, the correct option is (A).

26. The first sentence of a paragraph introduces a topic. The second sentence usually provides more information about the first.

Here, the first sentence talks about Alaska's national parks. Only sentence S refers to them with the pronoun 'they', suggesting it must directly follow the first sentence.

So, S must be the second sentence.

The fourth sentence is given; so the third must be a preamble to it. Here, the fourth sentence uses the phrase 'this bridge', indicating that the third sentence must have introduced some bridge.

This is only given by sentence T. So, T must be the third sentence.

The fifth must follow further from the fourth sentence. This is only given by sentence Q, which uses the pronoun 'it' to refer to the bridge.

So, Q must be the fifth sentence.

Sixth and seventh sentences would follow the earlier sentences, with the last giving some kind of conclusion to the above.

Out of the remaining sentences P and R, P refers to 'the two land masses' given earlier in Q. R seems like a fitting conclusion.

So, P must be the sixth sentence while R is the last sentence of the paragraph.

The correct order is: STQPR.

The ordered paragraph is: Alaska's national parks offer a unique opportunity to explore glacial environments. They are nestled in a wilderness so wild you'll need to arrange for a boat or a plane to get there. The Bering Land Bridge National Preserve, located in northwestern Alaska, near Nome, is one of the most popular of these parks. This bridge was the primary pathway used by the original colonists of the Americas some 15,000 to 20,000 years ago. It used to connect East Asia and North America. The part that once connected the two land masses is now underwater, beneath the Bering Strait. And so the name 'Bering Land Bridge'.

Hence, the correct option is (C).

27. The first sentence in a passage usually introduces a topic. Here, sentence T introduces the galaxy 'Milky way'. So, T must be the first sentence.

The second sentence provides more information about the first sentence. Here, sentence S talks about its impact on astronomers. So, S must be the second sentence.

The sentences P and Q show connection, as both talk about the 'little companion'. But, R introduces this visual description; so it must come before them. So, R must be the third sentence.

Out of P and Q, Q talks about the 'little companion', while P uses the word 'as well'. This shows that Q must come before P.

So, Q must be the fourth sentence and P is the fifth sentence.

The correct sequence is: TSRQP

Hence, the correct option is (D).

28. The sentence 'D' is independent of any other sentence as it is giving general information about the noun "Shastriya Sangeet". Therefore, the sentence 'D' is the first part.

The pronoun 'It' mentioned in the sentence 'C' refers back to the noun 'Shastriya Sangeet' mentioned in the sentence 'D'. Therefore, D follows C.

The sentence 'B' haven't any subject, The pronoun 'It' mentioned in the sentence 'C' act as the subject for the sentence 'B'. Therefore, B is the third part.

The sentence 'A' is the concluding sentence. Therefore, it is the last part.

Thus, the correct sequence is: DCBA.

Hence, the correct option is (A).

29. The passage is about a Mediterranean shipwreck.

We should go through the sentences in the following ways:

- The first sentence is S. This sentence introduces the topic and mentions the beginning of the search.
- The second sentence is Q. It is the continuation of the previous sentence. Here, what is being searched for is mentioned.
- The third sentence is T. Here what a British-led team can do is mentioned.
- The fourth sentence is P. This sentence informs what the British-led team may discover.
- The fifth sentence is R. It mentions the location of the wrecked ships.

Therefore, the correct chronological order of the passage is: SQTPR

Hence, the correct option is (D).

30. E should be the THIRD sentence after rearrangement.

- The FIRST sentence is (D) as it introduces one of the main subjects of the passage, i.e., the dispute between India and China, and also provides the backstory as well as the other subject, i.e., the Narendra Modi Government.

- The SECOND sentence is (B) as it details the recent developments that have reignited the issue again, and also brings to our attention the fact that the situation has been shifted in China's favour.

- Sentence (E), which is the THIRD sentence is in continuation of 'B', as it talks about the similar incursions that are insinuated in 'B' that resulted in the face-off with China.

- The FOURTH sentence is (A) as it talks about the government's response to the aforementioned issue, and also highlights the writer's criticism regarding the Narendra Modi government, which we knew was coming.

- Sentence (C) comes LAST, as it talks about the same silence being talked about in Sentence (A); Sentence (C) also talks about the incursions already introduced in Sentences (B) and (E), thereby concluding the passage.

Thus, the correct sequence is DBEAC.

Hence, the correct option is (D).

31. The paragraph talks about Golden Kela Awards. D introduces the Golden Kela awards, so it is the opening sentence (INTRO)

A explains what the awards are. So, A follows D. (keywords: in simpler terms) (EXPLANATION OF TOPIC)

E is dependent on A as it continues the intro of kela awards by telling about its creation. (HISTORY)

C statement tells the purpose of these awards. (PURPOSE)

B statement talks about the present that is why it is the closing sentence

The correct sequence of the sentences is: DAECB

Hence, the correct option is (A).

32. B is the opening sentence. it is independent and introduces three main problems

The word Additionally means that there must be something before sentence C. These issues in E are the issues mentioned in B and C. B will be followed by C, which will be followed by E. Thus, BCE is the mandatory pair.

The correct sequence of the sentences is: BCEAD

Hence, the correct option is (A).

33. The passage talks about puddings which is introduced in sentence D.Sentence D talks about two types of puddings.

Sentence B talks about the first type of pudding .It is dependent on sentence D .The keyword is ' FIRST'

In A 'these' is referring to the ingredients like shredded meat, fruits and alcohal etc and also preservatives which save the food from getting spoiled (bulwarks mean defense)

E follows A because it is referring to the second main pudding. Keyword is SECOND

C is dependent sentence which follows E because it talks about the same pudding.

The correct sequence of the sentences is: DBAEC

Hence, the correct option is (D).

34. The paragraph talks about the ICC's decision to restrict the number of teams and the response that it evoked.The decision is introduced in sentence D.

On one hand the ICC was criticized because of the inordinate length of the tournament and now it is criticized when it wants to reduce the number of teams. Hence, DEAC forms a logical sequence.

Sentence C will be followed by B as B shows the other side of the coin.

The correct sequence of the sentences is: DEACB

Hence, the correct option is (D).

35. A introduces the topic 'Environment Education Unit'

The pronoun 'their' in sentence 'B' refers to the same.

C and D form a mandatory pair as both of them tell the two topics discussed in the new publication. Also 'And' in D makes it ovious that it will follow C

In E , 'however' concludes the paragraph

The correct sequence of the sentences is: ABCDE

Hence, the correct option is (C).

36. A introduces the topic 'Japanese rock garden'.

C further defines the structure of the garden. So, AC.

E and B both define the structure of rocks...these are pairs but E will come first.

D is a concluding sentence here, it will follow.

The correct sequence of the sentence is: ACEBD

Hence, the correct option is (A).

37. D introduces the topic i.e., 'Origin of Zen Buddhism' ascribes to the flower sermon.

B logically tells about the first event in the story.

In A, 'they' refers to the disciples mentioned in B.

After this E as the question was asked by the Gautam Buddha.

Finally C will come as one of his disciples was able to figure out the answer.

The correct sequence of the sentences is: DBAEC

Hence, the correct option is (B).

38. E mentions the international community was ready to help.

C follows elaborating on the help.

The EC link is only present in the option (D).

The correct sequence of the sentences is: ABDEC

Hence, the correct option is (D).

39. E is the most independent sentence among all these sentences, so it will mark the opening of the paragraph.The problems are listed in E, D and A.

B which gives a course of action should follow them. BC will form a pair.

The correct sequence of the sentences is: EDABC

Hence, the correct option is (D).

40. BC shows a contrast and forms a pair

CD forms a pair as D elaborates C

A is the opening sentence as it is independent and complete..

try to solve this question according to chronology.

The correct sequence of the sentences is: ABCDE

Hence, the correct option is (B).

41. The opener will be sentence C as it highlights the stratus of cricket in India and is the topic of the discussion.

After this B will come as it further tells about the popularity of cricket during British time.

After this E will come as it tells the reason that why other games have not been given attention and it clear with the phrase 'due to this reason'.

Because of this reason, we are not able to do well in Olympic games.

So it is high time to our government and sports fraternity to take care of all the games.

The correct sequence of the sentences is: CBEAD

Hence, the correct option is (C).

42. The paragraph clearly identifies 3 ways:

The Para starts with failing monsoon and because of which tanks became empty.

This fear led to no sowing of the grains by the farmers.

This led to fear of famine

After this farmers again became anxious for the next monsoon.

After this speculation something opposite happened and monsoon fared well and danger was averted.

The correct sequence of the sentences is: CDAEB

Hence, the correct option is (B).

43. A will not start the arrangement as it uses "this regard" which means there has to be something before this sentence.

D says "this problem", this cannot start the arrangement as well.

E says "such situation" this too cannot start the arrangement.

So, the opener will be C as it introduces the topic of the discussion, which is Indian economy not showing the desirable growth in recent years. 'After this D will come as it citing another reason for Indian economy not showing desirable growth. Economists all the world are worried about this trend.

After this E will come as it is telling the real reason, which is Indian government's inability to take the tough decisions. Finally B will conclude as it tells the outcome of slowdown in the economy i.e. people are subjected to high cost of living etc.

The correct sequence of the sentences is: CDAEB

Hence, the correct option is (A).

44. D is the best opening sentence as the event mentioned in this s sentence is starting the whole story.

Because it rained continuously for several days the river overflowed.

Thus D-C form a logical pair.

Overflowing of the river terrified the villagers. 'THEY', villagers fled to higher ground.

The concluding sentence is B as it talks about the situation returning to normal.

The correct sequence of the sentences is: DCEAB

Hence, the correct option is (C).

45. The sentence 'D' is independent of any other sentence as it is giving general information about "the queen of ants". Hence, 'D' is the first part.

Sentence B will come after D because it explains what the queen of ants does with the pair of wings.

Sentence A will come after B because it explains when the wedding flight takes place.

The sentence 'C' is the concluding part because it mentions what the queen of ants does in the heat.

The correct sequence of the sentences is: DBAC

Hence, the correct option is (A).

46. The given sentence is an example of Sentence Jumble.

We know that the first statement of a sentence jumbled question is usually an independent general statement, a noun, a universal fact, starting of an incident, or it starts with 'most' or 'once'.

Part B will be the first sentence because it is the starting of an incident.

Part D will be used next because Part B talks about 'tearing down' of the collage and Part D further tell what the author did to tear down that collage.

Part C will be used next because it further explains what the author found when he entered that room.

Lastly, Part A will be used to give a possible explanation the author thinks of the wall being bare.

The correct sequence of the sentences is: BDCA

Hence, the correct option is (D).

47. Sentence 'A' is independent of any other sentences as it is giving general information about the "Bihar Legislative Assembly election". Hence, 'A' is the first sentence.

The 'election' mentioned in the sentence 'D' refers back to the "Bihar election" in the sentence 'A' and is further describing the election. Hence, 'D' follows 'A'.

Sentence 'C' talks about the conduction of the elections according to the guidelines and it follows D.

Sentence 'B' concludes the paragraph by starting with 'finally' and by giving some additional information about the election. It talks about the results. Thus, 'C' makes the last sentence.

The correct sequence of the sentences is: ADCB

Hence, the correct option is (D).

48. The sentence 'D' is independent of any other sentence as it is giving general information about "a hare". Hence, 'D' is the first part.

Sentence B will come after D because it explains how the beetle requested or pleaded with the eagle to not kill the hare.

Sentence A will come after B because it explains whether the eagle killed the hare or not.

The sentence 'C' is the concluding part because it explains what the beetle has done finally when the eagle flew away.

The correct sequence of the sentences is: DBAC

Hence, the correct option is (D).

49. While rearranging the given sentences, we should look for some grammatical or contextual connections between the sentences-

A will be the first sentence as it is an independent sentence that is introducing the subject 'Judy'.

D will be the second sentence as it means that Judy became overjoyed as he touched the soft neck of the fawn.

B will be the third sentence. 'move on all fours' is a phrase that means 'with hands, knees and feet on the ground.' It says that Judy moved close to the fawn.

C will be the last sentence as it means that Judy put his arms around the body of the fawn after moving closer to it.

Therefore, according to the given explanation, option A is the correct answer.

The correct sequence of the sentences is: ADBC

Hence, the correct option is (A).

50. Sentence 'B' is independent of any other sentences as it is giving general information about the "Indian Premier League". So, 'B' is the first sentence.

The 'league' mentioned in the sentence 'D' refers back to the "Indian Premier League" in sentence 'B' and is further describing the 'IPL'. So, 'D' follows 'B'.

Sentence 'C' is further describing the 'IPL' and is linked with the sentence 'D'. So, 'C' follows 'D'.

Sentence 'A' concludes the paragraph by giving some additional information about the revenue generated from the IPL. So, 'A' makes the last sentence.

The correct sequence of the sentences is: BDCA

Hence, the correct option is (C).

51. Sentence C establishes the subject matter i.e. the various ways through which information can and has been stored. Hence, it will be the first sentence after rearrangement.

A follows C because in C, we talk about the two modes 'speech' and 'writing'. The third mode is introduced in sentence 'A'.

B connects with A through 'however' which is used to introduce something that contrasts with what is previously said.

D is the concluding sentence of the paragraph as it talks about the 'fourth information revolution'.

The correct sequence of the sentences is: CABD

Hence, the correct option is (B).

52. The first sentence is C as it introduces the topic, which is Dubai's proposed underwater tennis court.

The next sentence is B which provides more detail on the topic introduced, such as the architect who proposed the idea, and the location of the court.

The next sentence is D which provides more information on the tennis court, information which is not as important and directly follows from the previous sentence.

The last sentence A provides an argument against the above proposition, by questioning the feasibility of the idea.

The correct sequence of the sentences is: CBDA

Hence, the correct option is (D).

53. The sentence 'C' is independent of any other sentences as it is giving general information about "Nunez". So, 'C' is the first part.

The pronoun "he" mentioned in the sentence 'A' refers back to the noun "Nunez" mentioned in the sentence 'C'. So, 'A' follows 'C'.

The phrase 'came to the plain' mentioned in the sentence 'D' is linked with the phrase 'he saw green meadows' mentioned in the sentence 'A'. So, 'D' follows 'A'.

The sentence 'B' is the concluding sentence. So, 'B' is the last sentence.

The correct sequence of the sentences is: CADB

Hence, the correct option is (B).

54. The introduction is obviously the first sentence, and then the detail has been talked about making sentence C the second one

followed by the sentence continuing the usage of the attention and the detail. And finally, what makes him different from the rest.

The correct sequence of the sentences is: ACBD

Hence, the correct option is (A).

55. The first statement, C introduces us to the topic at hand - the definition of growth, this is followed by statement B which explains the change that is referred to in statement C. Then comes statement D which then goes into deeper detail about the changes mentioned in the previous statements. Then comes the final statement, A which talks there is another factor that has to be taken into consideration.

The correct sequence of the sentences is: CBDA

Hence, the correct option is (A).

56. Sentence C introduces us to the subject 'two cats'. It is the introductory sentence and will be put in the first place.

Sentence B tells us about the instance of the cats spotting a loaf of bread. It will be put in second place.

Sentence D tells us the reaction of the cats after seeing the loaf of bread. It will be put in third place.

The last sentence is A as it mentions the conviction of one of the cats that the loaf was hers as she first spotted it.

Thus, the correct sequence is: CBDA.

Hence, the correct option is (D).

57. The sentence 'B' is independent of any other sentences as it is giving general information about "Finding fault with others". Therefore, 'B' is the first part.

The pronoun "It" mentioned in the sentence 'A' refers back to 'finding fault with others' mentioned in the sentence 'B'. Therefore, 'A' follows 'B'.

The phrase "sit in idle groups and rail" mentioned in the sentence 'D' is linked with the "most popular pastimes" mentioned in the sentence 'A'. Therefore, 'D' follows 'A'.

The sentence 'C' is the concluding sentence. Therefore, 'C' is the last sentence.

Thus, the correct sequence is: BADC.

Hence, the correct option is (C).

58. The sentence 'B' is independent of any other sentences as it is giving general information about the noun "Martha". Therefore, 'B' is the first part.

The pronoun "She" mentioned in the sentence 'A' refers back to the noun 'Martha' mentioned in the sentence 'B'. Therefore, 'A' follows 'B'.

The pronoun "we" mentioned in the sentence 'D' refers back to the "author and Martha" mentioned in the sentence 'A'. Therefore, 'D' follows 'A'.

The sentence 'C' is the concluding sentence. Therefore, 'C' is the last sentence.

Thus, the correct sequence is: BADC.

Hence, the correct option is (A).

59. The given paragraph is related to the importance of the environment. So, sentence 'B' will be the first sentence after rearrangement as it establishes the subject matter. The word 'they' in the sentence 'D' is used for 'countless benefits' mentioned in sentence 'B' so it will be followed by sentence 'D'. Sentence 'A' follows 'D' as it talks about the 'benefits of trees and forests' and is in the continuation of 'D'. Sentence 'C' is the logical successor of 'A' as it further explains the 'benefits of plants'.

Thus, the correct arrangement is BDAC.

Hence, the correct option is (D).

60. B is the sentence that introduces the topic- farmers. So, it will be the first sentence after rearrangement.

C follows B as it gives the reason for what is mentioned in B.

A follows C as it starts with 'hence' showing that it is indeed right to say that farmers are the most useful members of society.

D follows A as it connects with it by yet. 'Yet' signifies 'still'. Farmers are the most useful members of society, still, they don't get much profit or recognition.

Thus, the correct arrangement is: BCAD.

Hence, the correct option is (D).

Q.1 Direction: The passage given below is followed by four alternate summaries. Choose the option that best captures the essence of the passage.

McGurk and MacDonald (1976) reported a powerful multisensory illusion occurring with audio-visual speech. They recorded a voice articulating a consonant 'ba-ba-ba' and dubbed it with a face articulating another consonant 'ga-ga-ga'. Even though the acoustic speech signal was well recognized alone, it was heard as another consonant after dubbing with incongruent visual speech i.e., 'da-dada'. The illusion, termed as the McGurk effect, has been replicated many times, and it has sparked an abundance of research. The reason for the great impact is that this is a striking demonstration of multisensory integration, where that auditory and visual information is merged into a unified, integrated percept.

[CAT, 2021]

A. Visual speech mismatched with auditory speech can result in the perception of an entirely different message: this illusion is known as the McGurk effect.

B. When the quality of auditory information is poor, the visual information wins over the auditory information.

C. The McGurk effect which is a demonstration of multisensory integration has been replicated many times.

D. When the auditory speech signal does not match the visual speech movements, the acoustic speech signal is confusing and integration of the two is imperfect.

Q.2 Direction: The passage given below is followed by four alternate summaries. Choose the option that best captures the essence of the passage.

Foreign peacekeepers often exist in a bubble in the poor countries in which they are deployed; they live in posh compounds, drive fancy vehicles, and distance themselves from locals. This may be partially justified as they are outsiders, living in constant fear, performing a job that is emotionally draining. But they are often despised by the locals, and many would like them to leave. A better solution would be bottom-up peacebuilding, which would involve their spending more time working with communities, understanding their grievances and earning their trust, rather than only meeting government officials.

[CAT, 2021]

A. Peacekeeping duties would be more effectively performed by local residents given their better understanding, knowledge and rapport with their own communities.

B. The environment in poor countries has tended to make foreign peacekeeping forces live in enclaves, but it is time to change this scenario.

C. Extravagant lifestyles and an aloof attitude among the foreigners working as peacekeepers in poor countries have justifiably make them the target of local anger.

D. Peacekeeping forces in foreign countries have tended to be aloof for valid reasons but would be more effective if they worked more closely with local communities.

Q.3 Direction: The passage given below is followed by four alternate summaries. Choose the option that best captures the essence of the passage.

Developing countries are becoming hotbeds of business innovation in much the same way as Japan did from the 1950s onwards. They are reinventing systems of production and distribution, and experimenting with entirely new business models. Why are countries that were until recently associated with cheap hands now becoming leaders in innovation? Driven by a mixture of ambition and fear they are relentlessly climbing up the value chain. Emerging-market champions have not only proved highly competitive in their own backyards, they are also going global themselves.

[CAT, 2021]

A. Competition has driven emerging economies, once suppliers of cheap labour, to become innovators of business models that have enabled them to move up the value chain and go global.

B. Innovations in production and distribution are helping emerging economies compete with countries to which they once supplied cheap labour.

C. Developing countries are being forced to invent new business models which challenge the old business models, so they can remain competitive domestically.

D. Production and distribution models are going through rapid innovations worldwide as developed countries are being challenged by their earlier suppliers from the developing world.

Ques (4-5):Direction: The passage given below isfollowed by four alternate summaries.Choose the option that best captures theessence of the passage.

Q.4 For nearly a century most psychologists have embraced one view of intelligence. Individuals are born with more or less intelligence potential (I.Q.); this potential is heavily influenced by heredity and difficult to alter; experts in measurement can determine a person's intelligence early in life, currently from paper-and-pencil measures, perhaps eventually from examining the brain in action or even scrutinizing his/her genome. Recently, criticism of this conventional wisdom has mounted. Biologists ask if speaking of a single entity called "intelligence" is coherent and question the validity of measures used to estimate heritability of a trait in humans, who, unlike plants or animals, are not conceived and bred under controlled conditions.

[CAT, 2020]

A. Biologists have started questioningpsychologists' view of 'intelligence' as ameasurable immutable characteristic of anindividual.

B. Biologists have questioned the view that'intelligence' is a single entity and the waysin which what is inherited.

C. Biologists have questioned the longstanding view that 'intelligence' is a singleentity and the attempts to estimate itsheritability.

D. Biologists have criticised thatconventional wisdom that

individuals areborn with more or less intelligencepotential.

Q.5 For years, movies and television serieslike Crime Scene Investigation (CSI) paintan unrealistic picture of the "science ofvoices." In the 1994 movie Clear andPresent Danger an expert listens to a briefrecorded utterance and declares that thespeaker is "Cuban, aged 35 to 45, educatedin the eastern United States." The recording is then fed to a supercomputerthat matches the voice to that of a suspect,concluding that the probability of correctidentification is 90%. This sequence sumsup a good number of misimpressions aboutforensic phonetics, which have led toerrors in real-life justice. Indeed, thatmovie scene exemplifies the so-called "CSIeffect"—the phenomenon in which judgeshold unrealistic expectations of thecapabilities of forensic science.

[CAT, 2020]

A. Movies and televisions have led to thebelief that the use of forensic phonetics inlegal investigations is robust and foolproof.

B. Voice recognition as used in manymovies to identify criminals has been usedto identify criminals in real life also.

C. Although voice recognition is oftenpresented as evidence in legal cases, itsscientific basiscan be shaky.

D. Voice recognition has started to featureprominently in crime-scene intelligenceinvestigations because of movies andtelevision series.

Q.6 Direction: The passage given below isfollowed by four alternate summaries.Choose the option that best captures theessence of the passage.

As Soviet power declined, the worldbecame to some extent multi polar, andEurope strove to define an independentidentity. What a journey Europe hasundertaken to reach this point. It had in every century changed its internalstructure and invented new ways ofthinking about the nature of internationalorder. Now at the culmination of an era,Europe, in order to participate in it, feltobliged to set aside the politicalmechanisms through which it hadconducted its affairs for three and a halfcenturies. Impelled also by the desire tocushion the emergent unification ofGermany, the new European Unionestablished a common currency in 2002and a formal political structure in 2004. Itproclaimed a Europe united, whole, andfree, adjusting its differences by peacefulmechanisms.

[CAT, 2020]

A. Europe has consistently changed inkeeping with the changing world order andthat has culminated in a united Europe.

B. The establishment of a formal politicalstructure in Europe was hastened by theunification of Germany and the emergenceof a multi polar world.

C. Europe has chosen to lower political andeconomic heterogeneity, in order to adaptitself to an emerging multi-polar world.

D. Europe has consistently changed itsinternal structure to successfully adapt tothe changing world order.

Q.7 Direction: Read the following passage carefully and answer the question.

'Brevity is the soul of wit' is one of the countless maxims coined by William Shakespeare. It is relevant to speaking as well as writing. Brevity or Concision is the cutting out of unnecessary words while conveying an idea. It aims to enhance communication by eliminating redundancy without omitting important information. Summary Writing is one of its kind that has been described as one of the elementary principles of writing. To speak what is required and to write what is necessary is a requisite towards the development of language skills.

'Brevity is the soul of wit' is one of the countless maxims coined by ____________.

A. William Shakespeare

B. Mamang Dai

C. Douglas Malloch

D. None of these

Ques (8-60):Direction: The passage given below is followed by four alternate summaries. Choose the option that best captures the essence of the passage.

Q.8 Totalitarianism is not always operated by diktat. It can be insinuated by suggestion and replication. Dissent does not have to be banned if it is countered by orchestrated mass promo rallies and hypnotizing oratory. Despotic establishments do not need to turn Hitlerian; all they need to do is to let the Reich chemistry work. Self-regulation and self-censorship will click in. Then any dissident who wants to retain his intellectual liberty will find himself thwarted by the general drift of society rather than by active persecution.

A. Totalitarianism is generally operated by undermining freedom of expression through active persecution and censorship.

B. Hypnotizing oratory and promo rallies can effectively counter dissent and lead to persecution of the masses.

C. Self-regulation and self-censorship in societies stifle freedom of expression.

D. Intellectual liberty does not have to be repressed by authority if there are self-appointed vigilantes to bully it into silence.

Q.9 Modern history abounds with violence fueled by apocalyptic myths, not always explicitly religious in nature. The aim of the Jacobin terror in revolutionary France was the creation of a modern state. If the violent suppression of the peasant revolt in the Vendée is included, the casualties ran into the hundreds of thousands. The myths that possessed these anarchists in their campaigns of assassination were secular myths of social transformation. Lenin avowedly followed the Jacobin example when he used the Cheka to create a modern state in Russia. One of the factors that distinguished Nazism and fascism from conventional tyrannies was the belief that a new society could be fashioned by the systematic use of terror. Violent jihadism has more in common with these modern totalitarian movements than is commonly supposed.

A. Violent jihadism is justified on the secular myth of social transformation, rather than the idea of religious apocalypse.

B. The myth of social transformation has underpinned many totalitarian movements in modern history, and violent jihadism too exploits this.

C. Although it is believed that violence is fueled by religion, the reality is that it is unleashed on the premise of the creation of a modern state.

D. Modern history illustrates that it is a myth that societies can be transformed by the systematic use of terror.

Q.10 When a language seems especially telegraphic (that is, requiring less to be actually said to put a sentence together), it is usually because enough adults learnt it at a certain stage in its history that, given the difficulty of learning a new language after childhood, it became a kind of stripped-down "schoolroom" version of itself. Because all languages, are, to some extent, busier than they need to be, this streamlining leaves the language thoroughly complex and nuanced, just lighter on the bric-a-brac that so many languages pant under. For example, Indonesian, one of the most economical languages in the world, is a first language to only one in four of its speakers; the language has been used for many centuries as a lingua franca in a vast region, imposed on speakers of several hundred languages. This means that while other languages can be like overgrown lawns, Indonesian's grammar has been regularly mowed, such that especially the colloquial forms are tidier.

A. When a language has been used for many centuries as the lingua franca in a vast region, it becomes especially telegraphic.

B. Languages become less "busy" and more nuanced when imposed over long periods of time on new people, who learn it as adults.

C. When more adults who are non-native speakers are forced, over time, to learn a language, its colloquial forms become cryptic.

D. In languages that have been spoken for centuries over vast regions, time and repetition wear words out, and what wears away is often a nugget of meaning.

Q.11 Nineteenth-century liberals recognized that democracy comes in various forms, and dreaded the version advocated by Rousseau, in which an inspired lawgiver interprets and implements the will of the people. Nowadays such fears are dismissed as elitist. But the old-fashioned liberals grasped a vital truth: popular government has no necessary connection with the freedom of individuals or minorities. Of course, liberals today will say this can be remedied by installing the rule of constitutional rights. Such systems are fragile, however, and count for nothing when large sections of society are indifferent or actively hostile to liberal values. Where this is the case, democracy means not much more than the tyranny of the majority.

A. Inspired lawgivers in liberal democracies are better equipped to interpret and implement the will of the people than in illiberal democracies.

B. Nineteenth-century liberals believed that democracy means not much more than the tyranny of the majority.

C. Constitutional rights are fragile and ineffective in ensuring protection of the freedom of individuals in any democracy.

D. Popular governments in illiberal democracies use the power of the majority to clamp down on the freedom of minorities.

Q.12 Cheapness and its cinematic markers, such as hand-held camera work and low or high-contrast light, aren't themselves guarantors of a tone of artistic authenticity. In fact, they're often misused by filmmakers short of inspiration as badges of sincerity that take the place of actual artistry. The theatrical realism of many older, ostensibly classic movies have dated terribly and reflect the very exclusions and compromises of the system that produced them. Only the ingenious exertions and inventions of a slender minority of great filmmakers could circumvent and override them. Yet, critics fetishize the styles of studio-era movies and take them for an enduring and immutable aesthetic standard – as if, with an appreciation of Shakespeare came a comparable fixation on lesser Elizabethans and a disdain for latter-day dramatists for not writing in iambic pentameter.

A. Nostalgia for movies as they were made in the past converges to nostalgic exaltation of their production methods.

B. Rather than imitating the styles of studio-era movies in a bid to achieve artistic authenticity, filmmakers need to focus on inventive ideas and realistic themes.

C. Only the brilliance and resourcefulness of small minority of great filmmakers could overcome the hurdles posed by budget constraints in studio-era movies.

D. The veneration of the styles and production methods of low-budget movies of the studio-era as the ideal aesthetic standard is misguided.

Q.13 A recent study, published in the Proceedings of the National Academy of Sciences, has shown that high-level mathematical reasoning rests on a set of brain areas that do not overlap with the classical left-hemisphere regions involved in verbal semantics. Instead, all domains of mathematics tested (algebra, analysis, geometry, and topology) recruit a bilateral network, of prefrontal, parietal, and inferior temporal regions, which is also activated when mathematicians or non-mathematicians recognize and manipulate numbers mentally. These results suggest that high-level mathematical thinking makes minimal use of language areas and instead recruits circuits initially involved in space and number. This result may explain why knowledge of number and space, during early childhood, predicts mathematical achievement.

A. High-level mathematical expertise and basic number sense share common roots in a non-linguistic brain circuit.

B. Regardless of domain- algebra, analysis,geometry or topology- mathematicians recognize and manipulate numbers mentally.

C. Classic left-hemisphere regions involved in verbal semantics are not as well developed in mathematicians as the brain areas involving number and space.

D. The mathematical achievement of an individual can be predicted based on his knowledge of number, space and language during childhood.

Q.14 Since the Holocaust is an axial event of modern history, its misunderstanding turns our minds in the wrong direction. When the Holocaust is blamed on the modern state, the weakening of state authority appears salutary. On the political right, the erosion of state power by international capitalism seems natural; on the political left, rudderless revolutions portray themselves as virtuous. In the 21st century, anarchical protest movements join in a friendly tussle with global oligarchy, in which neither side can be hurt since both see the real enemy as the state. Both the left and the right tend to fear order rather than its destruction or absence.

A. The Holocaust was a result of an all-powerful state, which forced order through fear and crushed dissent from both the political right and the political left.

B. Following the Holocaust, the power of the state has been systematically eroded by international capitalism and rudderless revolutions, as both the right and the left fear order more than its absence.

C. The weakened state is the fundamental reason for disorder in the world, be it anarchical uprisings, global oligarchy or the Holocaust.

D. The Holocaust is not to be blamed on the modern state, but on the tussle between the political right and the political left.

Q.15 Journalism may never have been as public-spirited an enterprise as editors and writers liked to think it was. Yet the myth mattered. It pushed journalism to challenge power; it made journalists loath to bend to the whims of their audience; it provided a crucial sense of detachment. The new generation of media giants that dominates journalism today has no patience for the old ethos of detachment. It's not that these companies don't have aspirations toward journalistic greatness. BuzzFeed, Vice, and the Huffington Post invest in excellent reporting and employ first-rate journalists—and they have produced some of the most memorable pieces of investigative journalism in this century. But in the pursuit of audience, they have allowed the endless feedback loop of the web to shape their editorial sensibility and determine their editorial investments.

A. The belief that editorial insight can be engineered with the help of audience feedback loops has eroded the very nature of journalism.

B. The ethos of detachment and social-consciousness that marked journalism earlier has been progressively eroded by the relentless pursuit of the audience by media giants.

C. By playing to the audience, media giants that have engulfed journalism today have shattered the myth of detachment and compromised editorial sensibility.

D. The steady rise in the role of media giants in journalism and their strategic pursuit of the audience has had a damaging effect on the quality of journalism and its ethos.

Q.16 Much has rightly been made of the problem of political polarisation, but not nearly as much has been said about the problem of political homogenisation. Both are toxic to public discourse. While the former makes for awkward conversations at the family dinner table, the latter buries difficult conversations. Where agreement is sought without a decent discussion, opinion corridors form, limiting the range of ideas tolerated in public discourse. Where all views are not heard in appropriate discussion, the only alternative is inappropriate discussion. And populist rhetoric cuts through this muffled discussion culture like a hot knife through butter, as the pent-up need to be heard surfaces.

A. Political ambivalence is as harmful to public discourse as political polarisation.

B. By subduing discussion, political homogenisation can lead to the rise of populism.

C. When opinion across the political spectrum is not heard, public discourse is crippled.

D. Political homogenisation is as much a cause for rise of populism as political polarisation.

Q.17 Though they do not involve burning dirty fossil fuels, hydropower projects are not emissions free. Often, large dams flood vast vegetated areas. As a result, the vegetation rots under water. Eventually, this leads to the release of methane, a greenhouse gas 34 times as potent as carbon dioxide. In some cases, large dams can result in even more lifetime greenhouse gas emissions than equivalent conventional sources. And this does not even include the emissions resulting from the construction of such dams – cement and equipment-heavy projects that usually take several years to build.

A. Large hydropower projects contribute more to climate change than fossil fuels plants of equivalent generating capacity.

B. As large dams result in significant greenhouse gas emissions, hydropower cannot be regarded as a clean source of energy.

C. Hydropower projects cause flooding, leading to significant greenhouse gas emissions from rotting organic material.

D. In terms of greenhouse gas costs, hydropower is comparable to more conventional sources of energy.

Q.18 An ignorant mind is precisely not a spotless, empty vessel, but one that's filled with the clutter of irrelevant or misleading life experiences, theories, facts, intuitions, strategies, algorithms, heuristics, metaphors, and hunches that regrettably have the look and feel of useful and accurate knowledge. This clutter is an unfortunate by-product of one of our greatest strengths as a species. We are unbridled pattern recognizers and profligate theorizers. Often, our theories are good enough to get us through the day, or at least to an age when we can procreate. But our genius for creative storytelling, combined with our inability to detect our own ignorance, can sometimes lead to situations that are embarrassing, unfortunate, or downright dangerous—especially in a technologically advanced, complex democratic society that occasionally invests mistaken popular beliefs with immense destructive power (See: crisis, financial; war, Iraq).

A. The ability to recognize patterns and creatively formulate theories is both the greatest strength and the greatest weakness of our species.

B. The clutter in our minds that stems from our storytelling ability, along with our inability to perceive our own ignorance, hampers our judgement.

C. Our ignorance is compounded by our tendency to create stories around inaccurate, irrelevant and misleading information that clutters our minds.

D. Our tendency to weave theories out of the clutter of information stored in our minds can often lead us to truly dangerous situations.

Q.19 The most momentous development of our era, precisely, is the waning of the nation state: its inability to withstand countervailing 21st-century forces, and its calamitous loss of influence over human circumstance. National political authority is in decline, and, since we do not know any other sort, it feels like the end of the world. This is why a strange brand of apocalyptic nationalism is so widely in vogue. The current appeal of machismo as political style, the wall-building and xenophobia, the mythology and race theory, the fantastical promises of national restoration – these are not cures, but symptoms of what is slowly revealing itself to all: nation states everywhere are in an advanced state of political and moral decay from which they cannot individually extricate themselves.

A. Apocalyptic nationalism is on the rise because the nation state is on the decline.

B. Buffeted by countervailing 21st century forces, nation states have lost political authority.

C. Xenophobia and apocalyptic nationalism have led to the waning of the nation state.

D. The political and moral decay of nation states is the most significant development of our era.

Q.20 There may be a plethora of ways to define a "classic", but for me, a "classic" means a work that challenges the notion of its contemporaries and was is inspire the common people to look at things from a different perspective. A work is classical by reason of it being universal, by virtue of its ability to stir human emotions in a revolutionary way. Most of the classical works can be considered revolutionary given the changes they could inspire over the course of time. The classic is what gives birth to radically different forms of human consciousness for any generation of its viewers. A classical work nurtures an alternate reality among the masses and transcends barriers of culture, society, geography, age, etc.

A. A classic is able to stir the human condition and hence appeal directly to the human consciousness

B. A classical work seeks to resist contemporary trends and instead focus on a common humanity thereby producing novel and revolutionary work

C. A classic is a work going beyond the contemporary, and henceforth striking a chord with the audience given its novelty and revolutionary nature

D. A classic is a revolutionary piece of work which helps to develop human consciousness by transcending various social and cultural barriers

Q.21 Julius Ceaser is considered one of the most important works of William Shakespeare. However, even after centuries, connoisseurs of literature are divided as to who was the hero of the play. Many claim that even though the title of the play is Julius Ceaser, the actual hero of the play is Brutus. Brutus not only occupies more screentime than Caesar, but he also drives the theme of the play. Much like Othello, Brutus is the tragic hero who even though noble, falls prey to his own honesty. Another important point is that throughout the play it is through Brutus' dialogues that one gets to understand the essence of the Roman Kingdom. Even though Ceaser was the king, it was Brutus who imbibed the true Roman spirit. Hence the titular hero may be Julius Ceaser, but surely it is Brutus who is the real tragic hero of the magnum opus Julius Ceasar.

A. Brutus is the real hero of the play Julius Caesar as helps the viewer to visualize Rome and dominates other characters

B. Brutus is the tragic hero of the play Julius Caesar as he drives the entire play as evident by his screen time and his dialogues

C. Brutus helps the viewers to visualize Rome and hence is the tragic hero of the play Julius Caesar just like Othello

D. Brutus' enhanced on-screen presence drives the play and helps the viewers to visualize Rome, making him the tragic hero of the play

Q.22 Memories are not only essential functions for survival but are also major components of who we are—of our very identity. Also, they significantly contribute to many of our brain functions. In my lab, we have been studying the biological mechanisms of memory formation using adult rodents as models, but, at one point, It became clear to me that we couldn't understand how memory systems work if we did not understand how they develop. It's a question that, at the mechanistic level, has been largely overlooked. The study of biological mechanisms underlying early life memory formation has been mostly limited to models of stressful or traumatic experiences; very few investigations have been done to address the nature of the biology of learning and memory in normal development.

A. The insights we have obtained about the memories formed in early development have been very exciting and have taken us into a completely new way of thinking

B. Addressing the nature of biology is fundamental to understand how memories work throughout life, as well as to gain new insights into biological mechanisms of memory

C. The question of addressing the nature of biology is essential to understanding how memories work and gaining new insights into how neurodevelopmental disorders may occur

D. We will not be able to understand how memory systems work and how they develop their functions unless we understand the full complexity of rodents

Q.23 As school districts around the country are rolling out – and sometimes immediately rolling back – plans for the Fall 2020 semester in light of the current Covid-19 pandemic, many parents are carefully weighing their options. A growing number of epidemiologists and medical experts have suggested that schools should continue distance learning programs come August and September. But the American Academy of Paediatrics stunned many in both the medical and educational realms when it recommended that children return to school this fall, as they "learn best when they are in the classroom." Within days, the organization walked the controversial statement back, adding that "science and community circumstances" must guide when, where, and how schools safely reopen given the rising number of cases.

A. Online learning can be effective since emotional connections with students, even when they are not present, are critical to success

B. There may very well be a learning loss if there isn't the right technology or training to make the programs work online as children learn best when they are in the classroom

C. There may be a learning loss if the right technology or training is not available to make the programs work online, so children learn best in the classroom

D. Given the ever-changing situation regarding the novel coronavirus, it's likely that medical experts and educators will continue to debate the pros and cons of remote education initiatives for sometime to come

Q.24 Strategy is the creation of a unique value position, involving different sets of activities. Strategic positioning attempts to achieve a sustainable competitive advantage by preserving what is distinct about a company. It means performing different activities from rivals or performing similar activities in different ways. A good strategy involves trade-offs and being flexible. Just like you cannot paint an entire industry with the same color, similarly, you can't use the same strategy all the time. It would be prudent to mention that strategy doesn't mean efficiency. Strategy is a process that makes you efficient as well as effective. It is something which cannot be compared in entirety by the competitors and hence helps a company to differentiate itself.

A. A good strategy involves thinking out of the box and helps the company to differentiate itself from the rivals

B. A good strategy is one that is flexible can't be copied and thus helps the company to establish a point of differentiation from its rivals

C. A good strategy is one that is dynamic and makes the company more efficient and effective in its processes thus making it different from its rivals

D. A good strategy is one that is continuously evolving and hence helps a company to differentiate itself from its rivals

Q.25 Scientists have been trying to figure out various ways to make human clones. Artificial embryo twinning, one of the relatively low-tech ways to make clones, is gaining traction in recent days. As the name suggests, this technique involves mimicking the natural process that creates identical twins inside a women's uterus. In the natural course of events, twins form very early when the embryo splits in two. Twinning usually happens in the first days after the egg is fertilized by the and sperm, while the embryo is made of just a small number of unspecialized cells still undergoing rapid transformation. Each half of the embryo then continues to divide on its own, ultimately developing into separate, complete individuals. The resulting individuals are genetically identical as they are developed from the same fertilized egg.

A. Artificial embryo twinning is low-tech and mimetic of the natural development of genetically identical twins from the embryo after fertilization

B. Artificial embryo twinning is low-tech unlike the natural development of identical twins from the embryo after fertilization

C. Artificial embryo twinning is just like the natural development of twins, where during fertilization twins are formed and is low-tech

D. Artificial embryo twinning is low-tech and is close to the natural development of twins where the embryo splits into two identical twins

Q.26 A translator of literary works needs to have a good hold upon the two languages involved, supported by a good degree of familiarity with the two cultures. An effective translation of texts should ensure that the information, as well as the spirit behind the information, is clearly translated. Since the primary purpose of language is to ensure the exchange of ideas, it becomes imperative the idea is not lost while the scripts are being translated into different languages. Moreover, a translator should be aware of the cultural intricacies as certain phrases which can are considered as a symbol of appreciation in one language might turn out to be a source of sarcasm in another. Hence translation is an art as well as a science.

A. For a translation to be purposeful, it should have the context of the original text in the translated language apart from being grammatically accurate

B. A translator's job is to read between the lines and understand the cultural effect on language to ensure that the translation is accurate both in terms of letter and spirit

C. A translator's apart from being adept at grammatical syntax, should also understand the context and cultural habits so as to ensure accuracy in translation

D. A successful translation is one in which ideas can be accurately exchanged and understood by everyone

Q.27 North American walnut sphinx moth caterpillars (Amorpha juglandis) look like easy meals for birds, but they have a trick up their sleeves they produce whistles that sound like bird alarm calls, scaring potential predators away. At first, scientists suspected birds were simply startled by the loud noise. But a new study suggests a more sophisticated mechanism: the caterpillar's whistle appears to mimic a bird alarm call, sending avian predators scrambling for cover. When pecked by a bird, the caterpillars whistle by compressing their bodies like an accordion and forcing air out through specialized holes in their sides. The whistles are impressively loud they have been measured at over 50 dB from 5 cm away from the caterpillar considering they are made by a two-inch long insect.

A. North American walnut sphinx moth caterpillars will whistle periodically to ward off predator birds - they have a specialized vocal tract that helps them whistle.

B. North American walnut sphinx moth caterpillars can whistle very loudly; the loudness of their whistles is shocking as they are very small insects.

C. The North American walnut sphinx moth caterpillars, in a case of acoustic deception, produce whistles that mimic bird alarm calls to defend themselves.

D. North American walnut sphinx moth caterpillars, in. a case of deception and camouflage, produce whistles that mimic bird alarm calls to defend themselves.

Q.28 Both Socrates and Bacon were very good at asking useful questions. In fact, Socrates is largely credited with coming up with a way of asking questions, 'the Socratic method,' which itself is at the core of the 'scientific method,' popularised by Bacon. The Socratic method disproves arguments by finding exceptions to them, and can therefore lead your opponent to a point where they admit something that contradicts their original position. In common with Socrates, Bacon stressed it was as important to disprove a theory as it was to prove one — and real-world observation and experimentation were key to achieving both aims. Bacon also saw science as a collaborative affair, with scientists working together, challenging each other.

A. Both Socrates and Bacon advocated clever questioning of the opponents to disprove their arguments and theories.

B. Both Socrates and Bacon advocated challenging arguments and theories by observation and experimentation.

C. Both Socrates and Bacon advocated confirming arguments and theories by finding exceptions.

D. Both Socrates and Bacon advocated examining arguments and theories from both sides to prove them.

Q.29 A fundamental property of language is that it is slippery and messy and more liquid than solid, a gelatinous mass that changes shape to fit. As Wittgenstein would remind us, "usage has no sharp boundary." Oftentimes, the only way to determine the meaning of a word is to examine how it is used. This insight is often described as the "meaning is use" doctrine. There are differences between the "meaning is use" doctrine and a dictionary-first theory of meaning. "The dictionary's careful fixing of words to definitions, like butterflies pinned under glass, can suggest that this is how language works. The definitions can seem to ensure and fix the meaning of words, just as the gold standard can back a country's currency." What Wittgenstein found in the circulation of ordinary language, however, was a free-floating currency of meaning. The value of each word arises out of the exchange. The lexicographer abstracts a meaning from that exchange, which is then set within the conventions of the dictionary definition.

A. Dictionary definitions are like 'gold standards' — artificial, theoretical and dogmatic. Actual meaning of words is their free-exchange value.

B. Language is already slippery; given this, accounting for 'meaning in use' will only exasperate the problem. That is why lexicographers 'fix' meanings.

C. Meaning is dynamic; definitions are static. The 'meaning in use' theory helps us understand that definitions of words are culled from their meaning in exchange and use and not vice versa.

D. The meaning of words in dictionaries is clear, fixed and less dangerous and ambiguous than the meaning that arises when words are exchanged between people.

Q.30 To me, a "classic" means precisely the opposite of what my predecessors understood: a work is classical by reason of its resistance to contemporaneity and supposed universality, by reason of its capacity to indicate human particularity and difference in that past epoch. The classic is not what tells me about shared humanity — or, more truthfully put, what lets me recognize myself as already present in the past, what nourishes in me the illusion that everything has been like me and has existed only to prepare the way for me. Instead, the classic is what gives access to radically different forms of human consciousness for any given generation of readers, and thereby expands for them the range of possibilities of what it means to be a human being.

A. A classic is able to focus on the contemporary human condition and a unified experience of human consciousness.

B. A classical work seeks to resist particularity and temporal difference even as it focuses on a common humanity.

C. A classic is a work exploring the new, going beyond the universal, the contemporary, and the notion of a unified human consciousness.

D. A classic is a work that provides access to a universal experience of the human race as opposed to radically different forms of human consciousness.

Q.31 A translator of literary works needs a secure hold upon the two languages involved, supported by a good measure of familiarity with the two cultures. For an Indian translating works in an Indian language into English, finding satisfactory equivalents in a generalized western culture of practices and symbols in the original would be less difficult than gaining fluent control of contemporary English. When a westerner works on texts in Indian languages the interpretation of cultural elements will be the major challenge, rather than control over the grammar and essential vocabulary of the language

concerned. It is much easier to remedy lapses in language in a text translated into English, than flaws of content. Since it is easier for an Indian to learn the English language than it is for a Briton or American to comprehend Indian culture, translations of Indian texts is better left to Indians.

A. While translating, the Indian and the westerner face the same challenges but they have different skill profiles and the former has the advantage.

B. As preserving cultural meanings is the essence of literary translation Indians' knowledge of the local culture outweighs the initial disadvantage of lower fluency in English.

C. Indian translators should translate Indian texts into English as their work is less likely to pose cultural problems which are harder to address than the quality of language.

D. Westerners might be good at gaining reasonable fluency in new languages, but as understanding the culture reflected in literature is crucial, Indians remain better placed.

Q.32 For each of the past three years, temperatures have hit peaks not seen since the birth of meteorology, and probably not for more than 110,000 years. The amount of carbon dioxide in the air is at its highest level in 4 million years. This does not cause storms like Harvey — there have always been storms and hurricanes along the Gulf of Mexico — but it makes them wetter and more powerful. As the seas warm, they evaporate more easily and provide energy to storm fronts. As the air above them warms, it holds more water vapor. For every half a degree Celsius in warming, there is about a 3% increase in atmospheric moisture content. Scientists call this the Clausius-Clapeyron equation. This means the skies fill more quickly and have more to dump. The storm surge was greater because sea levels have risen 20 cm as a result of more than 100 years of human-related global warming which has melted glaciers and thermally expanded the volume of seawater.

A. The storm Harvey is one of the regular, annual ones from the Gulf of Mexico; global warming and Harvey are unrelated phenomena.

B. Global warming does not breed storms but makes them more destructive; the Clausius-Clapeyron equation, though it predicts potential increase in atmospheric moisture content, cannot predict the scale of damage storms might wreck.

C. Global warming melts glaciers, resulting in seawater volume expansion; this enables more water vapour to fill the air above faster. Thus, modern storms contain more destructive energy.

D. It is naive to think that rising sea levels and the force of tropical storms are unrelated; Harvey was destructive as global warming has armed it with more moisture content, but this may not be true of all storms.

Q.33 Production and legitimation of scientific knowledge can be approached from a number of perspectives. To study knowledge production from the sociology of professions perspective would mean a focus on the institutionalization of a body of knowledge. The professions-approach informed earlier research on managerial occupation, business schools and management knowledge. It however tends to reify institutional power structures in its understanding of the links between knowledge and authority. Knowledge production is restricted in the perspective to the selected members of the professional community, most notably to the university faculties and professional colleges. Power is understood as a negative mechanism, which prevents the non-professional actors from offering their ideas and information as legitimate knowledge.

A. Professions-approach aims at the institutionalization of knowledge but restricts knowledge production as a function of a select few.

B. The study of knowledge production can be done through many perspectives.

C. Professions-approach focuses on the creation of institutions of higher education and disciplines to promote knowledge production.

D. The professions-approach has been one of the most relied upon perspective in the study of management knowledge production.

Q.34 Artificial embryo twinning is a relatively low-tech way to make clones. As the name suggests, this technique mimics the natural process that creates identical twins. In nature, twins form very early in development when the embryo splits in two. Twinning happens in the first days after egg and sperm join, while the embryo is made of just a small number of unspecialized cells. Each half of the embryo continues dividing on its own, ultimately developing into separate, complete individuals. Since they developed from the same fertilized egg, the resulting individuals are genetically identical.

A. Artificial embryo twinning is low-tech and mimetic of the natural development of genetically identical twins from the embryo after fertilization.

B. Artificial embryo twinning is low-tech unlike the natural development of identical twins from the embryo after fertilization.

C. Artificial embryo twinning is just like the natural development of twins, where during fertilization twins are formed.

D. Artificial embryo twinning is low-tech and is close to the natural development of twins where the embryo splits into two identical twins.

Q.35 The conceptualization of landscape as a geometric object first occurred in Europe and is historically related to the European conceptualization of the organism, particularly the human body, as a geometric object with parts having a rational, three-dimensional organization and integration. The European idea of landscape appeared before the science of landscape emerged, and it is no coincidence that Renaissance artists such as Leonardo da Vinci, who studied the structure of the human body, also facilitated an understanding of the structure of landscape. Landscape which had been a subordinate background to religious or historical narratives, became an independent genre or subject of art by the end of sixteenth century or the beginning of the seventeenth century.

A. Landscape became a major subject of art at the turn of the sixteenth century

B. The three-dimensional understanding of the organism in Europe led to a similar approach towards the understanding of landscape

C. The study of landscape as an independent genre was aided by the Renaissance artists

D. The Renaissance artists were responsible for the study of landscape as a subject of art

Q.36 The early optimism about sport's deterrent effects on delinquency was premature as researchers failed to find any consistent relationships between sports participation and deviance. As the initial studies were based upon cross-sectional data and the effects captured were short-term, it was problematic to test and verify the temporal sequencing of events suggested by the deterrence theory. The correlation between sport and delinquency could not be disentangled from class and cultural variables known. Choosing individuals to play sports in the first place was problematic, which became more acute in the subsequent decades as researchers began to document just how closely sports participation was linked to social class indicators.

A. Sports participation is linked to class and cultural variables such as education, income, and social capital

B. Contradicting the previous optimism, latter researchers have proved that there is no consistent relationship between sports participation and deviance

C. Statistical and empirical weaknesses stand in the way of inferring any relationship between sports participation and deviance

D. There is a direct relationship between sport participation and delinquency but it needs more empirical evidence

Q.37 A Japanese government panel announced that it recommends regulating only genetically modified organisms that have had foreign genes permanently introduced into their genomes and not those whose endogenous genes have been edited. The only stipulation is that researchers and businesses will have to register their modifications to plants or animals with the government, with the exception of microbes cultured in contained environments. Reactions to the decision are mixed. While lauding the potential benefits of genome editing, an editorial opposes across-the-board permission. Unforeseen risks in gene editing cannot be ruled out. All genetically modified products must go through the same safety and labeling processes regardless of method.

A. A government panel in Japan says transgenic modification and genome editing are not the same.

B. Excepting microbes cultured in contained environments from the regulations of genome editing is premature.

C. Exempting from regulations the editing of endogenous genes is not desirable as this procedure might be risk-prone.

D. Creating categories within genetically modified products in terms of transgenic modification and genome editing advances science but defies laws.

Q.38 Should the moral obligation to rescue and aid persons in grave peril, felt by a few, be enforced by the criminal law? Should we follow the lead of a number of European countries and enact bad Samaritan laws? Proponents of bad Samaritan laws must overcome at least three different sorts of obstacles. First, they must show the laws are morally legitimate in principle, that is, that the duty to aid others is a proper candidate for legal enforcement. Second, they must show that this duty to aid can be defined in a way that can be fairly enforced by the courts. Third, they must show that the benefits of the laws are worth their problems, risks and costs.

A. A number of European countries that have successfully enacted bad Samaritan laws may serve as model statutes.

B. Everyone agrees that people ought to aid others, the only debate is whether to have a law on it.

C. If bad Samaritan laws are found to be legally sound and enforceable they must be enacted.

D. Bad Samaritan laws may be desirable but they need to be tested for legal soundness.

Q.39 A distinguishing feature of language is our ability to refer to absent things, known as displaced reference. A speaker can bring distant referents to mind in the absence of any obvious stimuli. Thoughts, not limited to the here and now, can pop into our heads for unfathomable reasons. This ability to think about distant things necessarily precedes the ability to talk about them. Thought precedes meaningful referential communication. A prerequisite for the emergence of human-like meaningful symbols is that the mental categories they relate to can be invoked even in the absence of immediate stimuli.

A. Thoughts are essential to communication and only humans have the ability to think about objects not present in their surroundings.

B. The ability to think about objects not present in our environment precedes the development of human communication.

C. Displaced reference is particular to humans and thoughts pop into our heads for no real reason.

D. Thoughts precede all speech acts and these thoughts pop up in our heads even in the absence of any stimulus.

Q.40 Physics is a pure science that seeks to understand the behaviour of matter without regard to whether it will afford any practical benefit. Engineering is the correlative applied science in which physical theories are put to some specific use, such as building a bridge or a nuclear reactor. Engineers obviously rely heavily on the discoveries of physicists, but an engineer's knowledge of the world is not the same as the physicist's knowledge. In fact, an engineer's know-how will often depend on physical theories that, from the point of view of pure physics, are false. There are some reasons for this. First, theories that are false in the purest and strictest sense are still sometimes very good approximations to the true ones, and often have the added virtue of being much easier to work with. Second, sometimes the true theories apply only under highly idealized conditions which can only be created under controlled experimental situations. The engineer finds that in the real world, theories rejected by physicists yield more accurate predictions than the ones that they accept.

A. The relationship between pure and applied science is strictly linear, with the pure science directing applied science, and never the other way round.

B. Though engineering draws heavily from pure science, it contributes to knowledge, by incorporating the constraints and conditions in the real world.

C. The unique task of the engineer is to identify, understand, and interpret the design constraints to produce a successful result.

D. Engineering and physics fundamentally differ on matters like building a bridge or a nuclear reactor.

Q.41 Vance Packard's The Hidden Persuaders alerted the public to the psychoanalytical techniques used by the advertising industry. Its premise was that advertising agencies were using depth interviews to identify hidden consumer motivations, which were then used to entice consumers to buy goods. Critics and reporters often wrongly assumed that Packard was writing mainly about subliminal advertising. Packard never mentioned the word subliminal, however, and devoted very little space to discussions of "subthreshold" effects. Instead, his views largely aligned with the notion that individuals do not always have access to their conscious thoughts and can be persuaded by supraliminal messages without their knowledge.

A. Packard argued that advertising as a 'hidden persuasion' understands the hidden motivations of consumers and works at the subliminal level, on the subconscious level of the awareness of the people targeted.

B. Packard argued that advertising as a 'hidden persuasion' works at the supraliminal level, wherein the people targeted are aware of being persuaded, after understanding the hidden motivations of consumers and works.

C. Packard held that advertising as a 'hidden persuasion' builds on peoples' conscious thoughts and awareness, by understanding the hidden motivations of consumers and works at the subliminal level.

D. Packard held that advertising as a 'hidden persuasion' understands the hidden motivations of consumers and works at the supraliminal level, though the people targeted have no awareness of being persuaded.

Q.42 Language is an autapomorphy found only in our lineage, and not shared with other branches of our group such as primates. We also have no definitive evidence that any species other than Homo sapiens ever had language. However, it must be noted straightaway that 'language' is not a monolithic entity, but rather a complex bundle of traits that must have evolved over a significant time frame.... Moreover, language crucially draws on aspects of cognition that are long established in the primate lineage, such as memory: the language faculty as a whole comprises more than just the uniquely linguistic features.

A. Language, a derived trait found only in humans, has evolved over time and involves memory

B. Language evolved with linguistic features building on features of cognition such as memory

C. Language is not a single, uniform entity but the end result of a long and complex process of linguistic evolution

D. Language is a distinctively human feature as there is no evidence of the existence of language in any other species

Q.43 Privacy-challenged office workers may find it hard to believe, but open-plan offices and cubicles were invented by architects and designers who thought that to break down the social walls that divide people, you had to break down the real walls, too. Modernist architects saw walls and rooms as downright fascist. The spaciousness and flexibility of an open plan would liberate homeowners and office dwellers from the confines of boxes. But companies took up their idea less out of a democratic ideology than a desire to pack in as many workers as they could. The typical open-plan office of the first half of the 20th century was a white-collar assembly line. Cubicles were interior designers' attempt to put some soul back in.

A. Wall-free office spaces did not quite work out the way their utopian inventors intended, as they became tools for exploitation of labor.

Wall-free office spaces could have worked out the way

B. their utopian inventors intended had companies cared for workers' satisfaction.

C. Wall-free office spaces did not quite work out as desired and therefore cubicles came into being.

D. Wall-free office spaces did not quite work out as companies don't believe in democratic ideology.

Q.44 Social movement organizations often struggle to mobilize supporters from allied movements in their efforts to achieve critical mass. Organizations with hybrid identities—those whose organizational identities span the boundaries of two or more social movements, issues, or identities—are vital to mobilizing these constituencies. Studies of the post-9/11 U.S. antiwar movement show that individuals with past involvement in non-anti-war movements are more likely to join hybrid organizations than are individuals without involvement in non-anti-war movements. In addition, they show that organizations with hybrid identities occupy relatively more central positions in inter-organizational contact networks within the antiwar movement and thus recruit significantly more participants in demonstrations than do nonhybrid organizations.

A. Post 9/11 studies show that people who are involved in non anti-war movements are likely to join hybrid organizations.

B. Movements that work towards social change often find it difficult to mobilize a critical mass of supporters.

C. Hybrid organizations attract individuals that are deeply involved in anti-war movements.

D. Organizations with hybrid identities are able to mobilize individuals with different points of view.

Q.45 For years, movies and television series like Crime Scene Investigation (CSI) paint an unrealistic picture of the "science of voices." In the 1994 movie Clear and Present Danger an expert listens to a brief recorded utterance and declares that the speaker is "Cuban, aged 35 to 45, educated in the [...] eastern United States." The recording is then fed to a supercomputer that matches the voice to that of a suspect, concluding that the probability of correct identification is 90%. This sequence sums up a good number of misimpressions about forensic phonetics, which have led to errors in reallife justice. Indeed, that movie scene exemplifies the so-called "CSI effect"—the phenomenon in which judges hold unrealistic expectations of the capabilities of forensic science.

A. Although voice recognition is often presented as evidence in legal cases, its scientific basis can be shaky.

B. Movies and televisions have led to the belief that the use of forensic phonetics in legal investigations is robust and fool proof.

C. Voice recognition as used in many movies to identify criminals has been used to identify criminals in real life also.

D. Voice recognition has started to feature prominently in crime-scene intelligence investigations because of movies and television series.

Q.46 With the Treaty of Westphalia, the papacy had been confined to ecclesiastical functions, and the doctrine of sovereign equality reigned. What political theory could then explain the origin and justify the functions of secular political order? In his Leviathan, published in 1651, three years after the Peace of Westphalia, Thomas Hobbes provided such a theory. He imagined a "state of nature" in the past when the absence of authority produced a "war of all against all." To escape such intolerable insecurity, he theorized, people delivered their rights to a sovereign power in return for the sovereign's provision of security for all within the state's border. The sovereign state's monopoly on power was established as the only way to overcome the perpetual fear of violent death and war.

A. Thomas Hobbes theorized the emergence of sovereign states based on a transactional relationship between people and sovereign state that was necessitated by a sense of insecurity of the people.

B. Thomas Hobbes theorized the voluntary surrender of rights by people as essential for emergence of sovereign states.

C. Thomas Hobbes theorized the emergence of sovereign states as a form of transactional governance to limit the power of the papacy.

D. Thomas Hobbes theorized that sovereign states emerged out of people's voluntary desire to overcome the sense of insecurity and establish the doctrine of sovereign equality.

Q.47 All humans make decisions based on one or a combination of two factors. This is either intuition or information. Decisions made through intuition are usually fast, people don't even think about the problem. It is quite philosophical, meaning that someone who made a decision based on intuition will have difficulty explaining the reasoning behind it. The decision-maker would often utilize her senses in drawing conclusions, which again is based on some experience in the field of study. On the other side of the spectrum, we have decisions made based on information. These decisions are rational — it is based on facts and figures, which unfortunately also means that it can be quite slow. The decision-maker would frequently use reports, analyses, and indicators to form her conclusion. This methodology results in accurate, quantifiable decisions, meaning that a person can clearly explain the rationale behind it.

A. We make decisions based on intuition or information on the basis of the time available.

B. It is better to make decisions based on information because it is more accurate, and the rationale behind it can be explained.

C. Decisions based on intuition and information result in differential speed and ability to provide a rationale.

D. While decisions based on intuition can be made fast, the reasons that led to these cannot be spelt out.

Q.48 The rural-urban continuum and the heterogeneity of urban settings pose an obvious challenge to identifying urban areas and measuring urbanization rates in a consistent way within and across countries. An objective methodology for distinguishing between urban and rural areas that is based on one or two metrics with fixed thresholds may not adequately capture the wide diversity of places. A richer combination of criteria would better describe the multifaceted nature of a city's function and its environment, but the joint interpretation of these criteria may require an element of human judgment.

A. The difficulty of accurately identifying urban areas means that we need to create a rich combination of criteria that

can be applied to all urban areas.

B. With the diversity of urban landscapes, measurable criteria for defining urban areas may need to be supplemented with human judgement.

C. Current methodologies used to define urban and rural areas are no longer relevant to our being able to study trends in urbanisation.

D. Distinguishing between urban and rural areas might call for some judgement on the objective methodology being used to define a city's functions.

Q.49 Brown et al. (2001) suggest that 'metabolic theory may provide a conceptual foundation for much of ecology just as genetic theory provides a foundation for much of evolutionary biology'. One of the successes of genetic theory is the diversity of theoretical approaches and models that have been developed and applied. A Web of Science (v. 5.9. Thomson Reuters) search on genetic* + theor* + evol* identifies more than 12000 publications between 2005 and 2012. Considering only the 10 most-cited papers within this 12000 publication set, genetic theory can be seen to focus on genome dynamics, phylogenetic inference, game theory and the regulation of gene expression. There is no one fundamental genetic equation, but rather a wide array of genetic models, ranging from simple to complex, with differing inputs and outputs, and divergent areas of application, loosely connected to each other through the shared conceptual foundation of heritable variation.

A. Genetic theory has a wide range of theoretical approaches and applications and Metabolic theory must have the same in the field of ecology.

B. Genetic theory has evolved to spawn a wide range of theoretical models and applications but Metabolic theory need not evolve in a similar manner in the field of ecology.

C. Genetic theory has a wide range of theoretical approaches and application and is foundational to evolutionary biology and Metabolic theory has the potential to do the same for ecology.

D. Genetic theory provides an example of how a range of theoretical approaches and applications can make a theory successful.

Q.50 The dominant hypotheses in modern science believe that language evolved to allow humans to exchange factual information about the physical world. But an alternative view is that language evolved, in modern humans at least, to facilitate social bonding. It increased our ancestors' chances of survival by enabling them to hunt more successfully or to cooperate more extensively. Language meant that things could be explained and that plans and past experiences could be shared efficiently.

A. From the belief that humans invented language to process factual information, scholars now think that language was the outcome of the need to ensure social cohesion and thus human survival.

B. Since its origin, language has been continuously evolving to higher forms, from being used to identify objects to ensuring human survival by enabling our ancestors to bond and cooperate.

C. Most believe that language originated from a need to articulate facts, but others think it emerged from the need to promote social cohesion and cooperation, thus enabling

human survival.

D. Experts are challenging the narrow view of the origin of language, as being merely used to describe facts and label objects, to being necessary to promote more complex interactions among humans.

Q.51 Aesthetic political representation urges us to realize that 'the representative has autonomy with regard to the people represented' but autonomy then is not an excuse to abandon one's responsibility. Aesthetic autonomy requires cultivation of 'disinterestedness' on the part of actors which is not indifference. To have disinterestedness, that is, to have comportment towards the beautiful that is devoid of all ulterior references to use – requires a kind of aesthetic commitment; it is the liberation of ourselves for the release of what has proper worth only in itself.

A. Disinterestedness is different from indifference as the former means a non-subjective evaluation of things which is what constitutes aesthetic political representation.

B. Aesthetic political representation advocates autonomy for the representatives manifested through disinterestedness which itself is different from indifference.

C. Disinterestedness, as distinct from indifference, is the basis of political representation.

D. Aesthetic political representation advocates autonomy for the representatives drawing from disinterestedness, which itself is different from indifference.

Q.52 Eternal peace is a chimera. Whatever pains we may take to avoid war, there always comes a moment when tradition and interest, passion and affection clash and bring to pass the shock which we desired to avoid, a shock which, in the conditions within which civilisation evolves, appears not merely inevitable, but salutary. So we see that philosophers and historians have generally spoken of war as a necessary evil.

A. Eternal peace is a myth since war brings about some positive changes and philosophers and historians consider war to be a necessary evil.

B. A clash due to conflict of interests is an integral part of how a civilization evolves and hence, philosophers and historians consider war to be a necessary evil.

C. The inevitability of a war due to conflict of interests renders the idea of eternal peace imaginary.

D. Though wars due to conflict of interests in a civilization are inevitable and unpleasant, war carries some positive effects with it.

Q.53 Our conscious thoughts, observations, wishes, aversions are important, because they represent inchoate, nascent activities. They fulfill their destiny in issuing, later on, into specific and perceptible acts. And these inchoate, budding organic readjustments are important because they are our sole escape from the dominion of routine habits and blind impulse. They are activities having a new meaning in process of development. Hence, normally, there is an accentuation of personal consciousness whenever our instincts and ready formed habits find themselves blocked by novel conditions.

A. Personal consciousness, which is stirred by novel conditions, is comprised of conscious thoughts, observations, wishes, and aversions. This consciousness is important because it leads to new acts which are our only escape from habitual actions.

The importance of our conscious thoughts, observations, wishes, aversions cannot be ignored because they are

B. responsible for accentuating our personal consciousness and they also help us in dealing with routine habits and blind impulse.

Our conscious thoughts, observations, wishes, aversions are important because they are nascent activities in the

C. process of development of personal consciousness and organic readjustments and they help to escape routine habits and blind impulse.

When faced with novel conditions, our personal consciousness accentuates which leads to the generation

D. of conscious thoughts, observations, wishes and aversions helping us to escape routine habits and blind impulse.

Q.54 It's been argued that artworks can be the equivalent of 'speech acts' - that is, they can be used to do things, such as protest or endorse something. If artworks can be speech acts, then presumably they can be harmful acts too, such as in straightforward hate speech - in racist, misogynistic or homophobic language. The utterance of 'Blacks are not permitted to vote' by a legislator during apartheid subordinates Black people. In parallel to this are the statues of slave traders and white supremacists. These public memorials don't just represent a particular person - they literally put them on a pedestal. Through various aesthetic conventions, statues commemorate and glamorise the person and their actions and, in doing this, they rank people of colour as inferior, legitimising racial hatred.

A. Speech and artworks are important means of expression, which should not be used to legitimise hateful actions or people.

B. Artworks that express hatred towards a particular community and endorse the transgression of individual freedom must be censored.

C. Artworks, like speech, express meaning and can similarly be harmful if they glorify hateful actions and people.

D. Artworks can be used as a medium to instigate acts of discrimination against people of colour and validate those committing them.

Q.55 That Nicholson would have carried out his intention if the council had come to a different conclusion I have not the slightest doubt, and I quite believe that his masterful spirit would have effected its purpose and borne down all opposition. Whether his action would have been right or wrong is another question, and one on which there is always sure to be great difference of opinion. At the time it seemed to me that he was right. The circumstances were so exceptional and the consequences of any delay would have been calamitous and far-reaching, that even now, after many years have passed, and after having often thought over Nicholson's intended action and discussed the subject with other men, I have not changed my opinion.

A. Nicholson and the council were not on the same page with respect to the issue. The author's view that Nicholson was right in disregarding the commands of the council has managed to remain unchanged over the years.

B. Nicholson and the council reached the same conclusion. The author feels that Nicholson would have overridden the orders of the council had they reached different conclusions and has always been approving of such a scenario.

C. Nicholson and the council differed in their opinion about the course of action that needed to be taken. The author is supportive of Nicholson's decision to override the command since he felt that it was the need of the hour.

D. Nicholson and the council agreed to go ahead with the same course of action. Had they differed in their opinion, Nicholson would have prevailed over the council. The author was approving of such a scenario back then but his views have changed over the years.

Q.56 Anxiety is not the same as fear. Although people experiencing anxiety are often afraid of both the anxiety and what they presume to be its cause, these two states have different triggers. Anxiety, unlike real fear, is always caused by uncertainty. It is caused, ultimately, by predictions in which you have little confidence. When you predict that you will be fired from your job and you are certain the prediction is correct, you don't have anxiety about being fired. You might have anxiety about the things you can't predict with certainty, such as the ramifications of losing the job. Predictions in which you have high confidence free you to respond, adjust, feel sadness, accept, prepare, or to do whatever is needed.

A. Anxiety is caused by uncertainty and lack of confidence in predictions; Better predictions free a person from anxiety and allow them to respond appropriately.

B. Anxiety, unlike fear, is always caused by uncertainty; when we have little confidence in our predictions, we suffer from anxiety which prevents us from responding to the situation.

C. Anxiety can be eliminated by focusing on a decision's known aspects rather than being worried about the uncertain aspects.

D. Anxiety precedes fear; anxiety, caused by the fear of uncertainty, can be reduced by improving our prediction, thus increasing our certainty.

Q.57 Many argue that health sciences, economics, mathematics, and geography related professions are enterprising because their industries have been established already and those professions are well paid and as such highly respected. Moreover, they are pursued by academically giants and gurus who had higher grading points. Though somehow true, these professions are no better than the arts. A retrospection into the renaissance age stresses this assertion

A. Many people nowadays consider artistic professions less enterprising than professions involving health sciences, economics, mathematics and geography despite the fact that artistic professions were given more importance during the renaissance period.

B. Professions related to health sciences, economics, mathematics, and geography are considered to be superior than art by many. Though this is partially true, this was not always the case as indicated by the renaissance period

C. The renaissance age valued professions involving art as more enterprising than those involving health sciences, economics, mathematics, and geography

D. Even though professions related to health sciences, economics, mathematics, and geography are considered to be more enterprising by many, they are not in any way superior to professions involving art as indicated by the renaissance age

Q.58 After almost a month of protests and people living in the streets, rocks being thrown, blood being spilled, and many injured, Egyptian President Mubarak finally resigns. There was partying and cheers from the streets all night. The people had spoken and the people had won.

A. Unfortunately there was bloodshed and deaths.

B. The basis of any democracy is a government for the people and by the people.

C. Are we starting to see a domino effect with these uprisings?

D. Now we come back to today, and right after the Egyptian conflict, the Iranian people are back in the streets and they are wanting a change.

Q.59 Like many thought experiments, the Veil of Ignorance could never be carried out in the literal sense, nor should it be. Its purpose is to explore ideas about justice, morality, equality, and social status in a structured manner. Behind the Veil of Ignorance, no one knows who they are. They lack clues as to their class, their privileges, their disadvantages, or even their personality. They exist as an impartial group, tasked with designing a new society with its own conception of justice. As a thought experiment, the Veil of Ignorance is powerful because our usual opinions regarding what is just and unjust are informed by our own experiences. We are shaped by our race, gender, class, education, appearance, sexuality, career, family, and so on. On the other side of the Veil of Ignorance, none of that exists. Technically, the resulting society should be a fair one.

A. The Veil of Ignorance thought experiment enables us to envision a fair society where ideas about justice, morality, equality, and social status are unambiguous and unbiased.

B. The Veil of Ignorance thought experiment encourages us to explore the true meaning of ideas about justice, morality, equality, and social status.

C. The Veil of Ignorance thought experiment allows us to examine ideas about justice, morality, equality, and social status for fairness without prejudice or bias.

D. The Veil of Ignorance thought experiment helps us formulate decisions on justice, morality, equality, and social status by leveraging the right social factors.

Q.60 Social scientists have been asking for decades whether boastful, self-aggrandising beliefs and behaviours are beneficial to those who make such claims. According to one school of thought, claiming to be better than others feels good, and when we feel good, we are happier and better adjusted. This argument suggests that bragging to others can satisfy the motive to craft and maintain a positive self-image. According to another line of research, however, consistently viewing oneself as superior entails a distortion of reality. Inaccurate individuals with low self-knowledge have weaker relationships and a tendency to make riskier decisions than their accurate, self-aware counterparts.

A. Bragging can make us feel good in the short run but distorts our reality and leads us to make risky decisions in the long run.

B. While some believe that bragging can make us feel good by projecting a positive self-image, others believe it distorts our reality.

C. One must strike a balance while bragging as it can make us feel good, happy, and adjusted but at the same time distorts our reality.

D. Social scientists believe that though bragging can help us maintain a positive self-image, it can also distort our reality, leading to risky decisions.

// Smart Answer Sheet //

Correct — Indicates percentage of students who answered questions correctly.

Skipped — Indicates percentage of students who skipped questions.

Q.	Ans.	Correct / Skipped
1	A	43.73 % / 54.05 %
2	D	49.67 % / 42.37 %
3	A	55.31 % / 35.59 %
4	C	51.21 % / 47.12 %
5	A	57.17 % / 32.77 %
6	C	56.8 % / 31.33 %
7	A	44.97 % / 31.47 %
8	D	53.1 % / 31.7 %
9	B	44.82 % / 53.63 %
10	B	32.79 % / 67.21 %
11	D	54.98 % / 38.12 %
12	D	42.02 % / 36.76 %
13	A	40.92 % / 37.42 %
14	C	56.18 % / 38.18 %
15	C	28.08 % / 71.91 %
16	B	60.31 % / 35.15 %
17	B	64.97 % / 33.64 %
18	B	13.9 % / 81.81 %
19	A	42.65 % / 43.19 %
20	C	43.79 % / 55.46 %
21	D	44.3 % / 50.95 %
22	B	13.97 % / 78.33 %
23	D	26.88 % / 69.66 %
24	B	62.75 % / 35.13 %
25	A	28.66 % / 67.32 %
26	C	59.68 % / 35.8 %
27	C	29.63 % / 68.56 %
28	D	51.17 % / 44.63 %
29	C	63.06 % / 35.43 %
30	C	63.33 % / 30.38 %
31	C	44.18 % / 35.76 %
32	C	19.6 % / 76.77 %
33	A	19.4 % / 72.69 %
34	A	57.69 % / 31.54 %
35	B	59.84 % / 33.93 %
36	C	62.03 % / 35.85 %
37	C	23.41 % / 69.6 %
38	D	66.74 % / 30.29 %
39	B	65.57 % / 33.09 %
40	B	19.28 % / 72.76 %
41	D	45.79 % / 46.21 %
42	B	51.1 % / 44.84 %
43	A	65.47 % / 32.4 %
44	D	47.13 % / 33.54 %
45	B	12.32 % / 74.99 %
46	A	53.63 % / 36.67 %
47	C	27.7 % / 69.72 %
48	B	43.64 % / 49.98 %
49	C	69.56 % / 30.14 %
50	C	61.11 % / 30.26 %
51	D	53.88 % / 30.47 %
52	D	48.31 % / 43.84 %
53	A	16.79 % / 70.56 %
54	C	67.77 % / 31.83 %
55	B	46.94 % / 52.61 %
56	A	40.11 % / 54.86 %
57	D	52.81 % / 38.93 %
58	B	50.35 % / 40.31 %
59	C	15.13 % / 83.07 %
60	B	65.4 % / 33.43 %

Performance Analysis

Avg. Score (%)	51.67%
Toppers Score (%)	61.67%
Your Score	

//Hints and Solutions//

1. The paragraph given explains the McGurk effect" the merging of auditory and visual information into a unified integrated percept. Where there is a mismatch of audio and video signals, the message perceived is completely different from either of the signals. Option (A) summarises the paragraph well.

- Option (B) is incorrect too, as there is no 'winning' signal.

- What option (C) states is true, but it does not summarise the main idea of the paragraph.

- Option (D) is incorrect, as it says that the 'acoustic speech signal is confusing and integration of the two is imperfect'. The integration of the signals is not imperfect and both speech and audio signals are perceived differently in case of a mismatch.

Hence, the correct option is (A).

2. The paragraph given states that while foreign peacekeepers, due to some valid reasons, tend to live in a bubble in the poor countries where they are deployed, a bottom-up peacebuilding approach working in concert with the locals would be more effective. Option (D) summarises the paragraph well.

- Option (B) does not touch upon the idea of bottom-up peace building. So, it is incorrect.

- The paragraph does not say locals would be better at peacekeeping; (A) is incorrect.

- The paragraph also does not say local anger against foreign peacekeepers makes them 'the target of local anger'. Option (C) is also incorrect.

Hence, the correct option is (D).

3. The main idea of the given paragraph is that driven by ambition and fear, developing countries are becoming leaders in innovation and are highly competitive both domestically and globally. Option (A) touches upon all key ideas of the paragraph.

- Option (B) is true but is not as comprehensive a summary as option (A).

- Option (C) states that developing countries have invented new business models solely to remain competitive domestically. This is incorrect.

- Option (D) states that production and distribution models are going through innovations 'worldwide'. The paragraph given only talks about developing countries innovating and transforming.

Hence, the correct option is (A).

4. The main ideas include:

- It has been believed for long that individuals are born with intelligence potential which is influenced by heredity and difficult to alter.

- Intelligence can be measured by paper-and-pencil measures, examining the brain and even studying the genome.

- Recently this approach has been criticized and biologists have questioned if considering intelligence a single entity is logical.

- Also they question validity of measures used to estimate heritability of intelligence in humans who are not kept under controlled environments during study.

Option (A) brings in an outside idea. It calls intelligence as immutable while the passage calls it difficult to alter and it therefore gets dismissed. Option (B) serves as a blend of correct and incorrect information. The latter half of the option talks about questioning "the ways in which intelligence is inherited" instead of questioning the "validity of measures used to estimate heritability of intelligence". So, it gets dismissed. Option (D) conveys something which is beyond the scope of the passage and therefore dismissed. Option (C) best captures all the key ideas well and is therefore the correct answer.

Hence, the correct option is (C).

5. The main ideas are:

- For years movies and televisionseries have painted an unrealisticpicture around "science of voices."

- Supercomputers declared that theprobability of correct identificationis 90%. This sequence is an example of agood number of misimpressionsabout forensic phonetics, whichhave led to errors in real-life justice.

- This movie sequence somewhere isa specimen of the "CSI effect" inwhich judges hold unrealisticexpectations of the "capabilities offorensic science."

Options (B) and (D) do not bring out thedemerit of the placing reliance on thecapabilities of forensic science. So, they getdismissed.

Option (C) limits itself to "voicerecognition" alone and not to the forensicscience in general. Also, it fails to cover therole played by movies and television series.

So, it gets dismissed. Only option (A) captures all main ideas properly and istherefore the best answer.

Hence, the correct option is (A).

6. The key ideas are:

- After the decline of the Sovietpower Eurpoe strived to establishits independent identity.

- Europe took measures to change itsinternal structure and inventednew ways of thinking about thenature of international order.

- In order to be a part of theculmination era Europe decided toput aside its political mechanismsthrough which it had conducted itsaffairs for three and a halfcenturies.

- Also driven by the desire tomitigate the effects generated bythe unification of Germany, thenew European Union established acommon currency in 2002 and aformal political structure in 2004.

- It proclaimed a Europe united,whole, and free, adjusting itsdifferences by peacefulmechanisms.

Options (A), (B) and (D) do not capture allpoints ,they do not mention that Europedid away with the political mechanismsthrough which it had conducted its affairsfor three and a half centuries. So, they getdismissed. Option (C) best captures the mainidea, that it in order to be a part of theculmination era, it put away the politicalmechanisms, and projected itself as aunited ,whole, and free Europe adjustingits differences by peaceful mechanisms.

Hence, the correct option is (C).

7. 'Brevity is the soul of wit' is one of the countless maxims coined by William Shakespeare.

It appears in his play, Hamlet, in the second act, where Polonius says, "Since brevity is the soul of wit / And tediousness the limbs and outward flourishes, I will be brie." However, doubt about the creation of this phrase lurks among literary circles.

Hence, the correct option is (A).

8. Intellectual liberty does not have to be repressed by authority if there are self-appointed vigilantes to bully it into silence.

Clearly, this option summarizes the paragraph best. Dissent does not need to be put down by authority. By clever insinuation, despotic establishments can steer the society towards self-regulation and self-censorship. Any opposing ideas are bullied into silence by these self-appointed vigilantes.

Hence, the correct option is (D).

9. The myth of social transformation has underpinned many totalitarian movements in modern history, and violent jihadism too exploits this.

This, clearly, is the main idea of the paragraph. Many totalitarian movements in modern history have been fueled by the myth of social transformation. Violent jihadism also draws on this idea. Option B summarizes the paragraph well.

Hence, the correct option is (B).

10. Languages become less "busy" and more nuanced when imposed over long periods of time on new people, who learn it as adults.

When a language has been used for many centuries as the lingua franca in a vast region, it becomes especially telegraphic. This is not the idea of the paragraph. The paragraph tells us that when a language is forced over a long period of time on non-native speakers who are adults, it becomes telegraphic. It does not get telegraphic simply because it is the lingua franca of a vast region.

Hence, the correct option is (B).

11. Popular governments in illiberal democracies use the power of the majority to clamp down on the freedom of minorities.

This option sums up the main idea of the paragraph best. In illiberal democracies, where the majority is indifferent or actively hostile to liberal values, popular governments use the power of majority to clamp down on the freedom of minorities.

Hence, the correct option is (D).

12. The veneration of the styles and production methods of low-budget movies of the studio-era as the ideal aesthetic standard is misguided.

The whole point of the paragraph is to say that the undue fetish for the styles and production of low-budget movies of the studio-era and the idea that this is the immutable artistic standard is misguided. So this is the right option to sum up the paragraph.

Hence, the correct option is (D).

13. High-level mathematical expertise and basic number sense share common roots in a non-linguistic brain circuit.

This option seems to convey all the three key ideas in the paragraph, summarising it well. High level mathematical thinking uses a non-linguistic circuit, and shares common roots with basic number sense.

Hence, the correct option is (A).

14. The weakened state is the fundamental reason for disorder in the world, be it anarchical uprisings, global oligarchy or the Holocaust.

This option sums up the paragraph well. Anarchical uprisings and global oligarchy are possible only in the absence of order that a strong state can command. Weakening of state authority led to the Holocaust.

Hence, the correct option is (C).

15. By playing to the audience, media giants that have engulfed journalism today have shattered the myth of detachment and compromised editorial sensibility.

The paragraph given argues that though journalism may have never been as public-spirited as it believed itself to be, the myth of detachment mattered, as it encouraged journalistic ideals such as standing up to power and not bending to the whims of the audience. In contrast, the guiding ethos of media giants that dominate journalism today is not detachment or editorial sensibility, but the relentless pursuit of the audience.

Hence, the correct option is (C).

16. By subduing discussion, political homogenisation can lead to the rise of populism.

The paragraph argues that political homogenisation is as toxic to public discourse as political polarisation. To support this, the paragraph puts forth two main points. The first one is that where agreement is sought without a "decent" or "appropriate" discussion, there are "opinion corridors". The ideas tolerated in public discourse get limited and discussion is subdued. The second point the paragraph makes is that when a culture buries difficult conversations, it sets the stage for the rise of populism as populist rhetoric resonates with those segments of the population that have a pent up need to be heard.

Hence, the correct option is (B).

17. As large dams result in significant greenhouse gas emissions, hydropower cannot be regarded as a clean source of energy.

Large dams result in significant greenhouse gas emissions. As to hydropower not being a "clean" source of energy, the paragraph does state that while hydropower projects do not involve burning "dirty" fossil fuels, they are not emissions free. The implication is that hydropower is not a clean source of energy. So, of the given options, (B) summarizes the given paragraph best.

Hence, the correct option is (B).

18. This paragraph tells us that the ignorant mind is filled with a clutter of misleading theories and facts. The clutter is a by-product of our ability, as a species, to recognize patterns and theorize based on these. But this very same genius for storytelling, along with our inability to recognize our own ignorance, can put us in undesirable situations.

Option (B) captures all the key ideas of the paragraph: (a) our mental clutter- a by-product of our storytelling ability, (b) our ignorance of our own ignorance, and (c) how this can hamper our judgement, leading us to undesirable situations.

Hence, the correct option is (B).

19. Apocalyptic nationalism is on the rise because the nation state is on the decline.

This paragraph states that the nation state has weakened considerably in the 21st century. The decline of national political authority, in turn, has led to a strange brand of "apocalyptic nationalism" characterized by political machismo, xenophobia and the like.

Hence, the correct option is (A).

20. A classic is a work going beyond the contemporary and henceforth striking a chord with the audience given its novelty and revolutionary nature.

To answer such questions, we need to find the central idea of the passage.

The passage talks about how the author thinks a "classic" should be defined

According to the author, classical work is revolutionary and different from the contemporaries

Hence given its novelty and revolutionary nature, a classical work appeals to the masses and stirs the human consciousness over any period of time.

Hence, the correct option is (C).

21. Brutus' enhanced on-screen presence drives the play and helps the viewers to visualize Rome, making him the tragic hero of the play.

The passage talks about how according to the author Brutus is the real hero of the play Julius Caesar

Brutus has more screen time and helps the viewers to feel the spirit of Rome

Just like Shakespeare's other works like Othello, Brutus meets a tragic end and hence is the tragic hero of the play.

Hence, the correct option is (D).

22. 'Addressing the nature of the biology is fundamental to understand how memories work throughout life, as well as to gain new insights into biological mechanisms of memory.'

In the passage, it is given that "It became clear to me that we couldn't understand how memory systems work if we did not understand how they develop. It's a question that, at the mechanistic level, has been largely overlooked." and "very few investigations have been done to address the nature of the biology of learning and memory in normal development."

From these lines, we can understand that the passage is emphasizing that if we do not understand how the memory system develops or the nature of biology, we cannot understand how memory systems work.

From the given explanation we can conclude that option (B) best summarizes the given paragraph as it says that "understanding the nature of biology is important for understanding how memories work throughout life and gaining new insights into biological mechanisms of memory."

Hence, the correct option is (B).

23. Given the ever-changing situation regarding the novel coronavirus, it's likely that medical experts and educators will continue to debate the pros and cons of remote education initiatives for sometime to come.

In the given passage, it is mentioned that medical experts have suggested that schools should continue distance learning programs, and later an organization says that children should return to school as they "learn best when they are in the classroom". Later, the organization retracts this statement and also referred to it as 'controversial'. From this, we can understand that various organizations and experts have differences of opinions regarding online learning or learning in schools.

Hence, the correct option is (D).

24. A good strategy is one that is flexible can't be copied and thus helps the company to establish a point of differentiation from its rivals.

The passage talks about how a good strategy is one which is flexible and involves doing something different

A good strategy helps a company to differentiate itself from its rivals by making it efficient as well as effective.

The passage highlights how a good stargey can't be entirely copied.

Hence, the correct option is (B).

25. Artificial embryo twinning is low-tech and mimetic of the natural development of genetically identical twins from the embryo after fertilization.

The passage talks about how artificial embryo twinning that is a low-tech process that tries to replicate the process that happens in the uterus while creating twins naturally.

The passage then highlights the process of twinning and hence how the twins are genetically identical.

Hence, the correct option is (A).

26. A translator's apart from being adept at grammatical syntax, should also understand the context and cultural habits so as to ensure accuracy in translation.

The passage talks about how a good translator should be adroit at the technical aspect of the languages as well as be aware of the two cultures.

Cultural awareness will help the translator to understand the context and tone of the text he/she is about to translate.

Due to cultural differences, the same phrases can have different meanings in different languages.

Hence, the correct option is (C).

27. The North American walnut sphinx moth caterpillars, in a case of acoustic deception, produce whistles that mimic bird alarm calls to defend themselves.

Hence, the correct option is (C).

28. Both Socrates and Bacon advocated clever questioning of the opponents to disprove their arguments and theories. Both Socrates and Bacon advocated challenging arguments and theories by observation and experimentation.

Hence, the correct option is (D).

29. Meaning is dynamic; definitions are static. The 'meaning in use' theory helps us understand that definitions of words are culled from their meaning in exchange and use and not vice versa.

Hence, the correct option is (C).

30. A classic is a work exploring the new, going beyond the universal, the contemporary, and the notion of a unified human consciousness.

Hence, the correct option is (C).

31. Indian translators should translate Indian texts into English as their work is less likely to pose cultural problems which are harder to address than the quality of language.

Indians have better knowledge of their culture. A westerner might be fluent in the language but will find it hard to relate to the culture. Indians, on the other hand, might be less fluent in the language but will be able to preserve the culture when a text is translated. Therefore, Indians should translate Indian texts.

Hence, the correct option is (C).

32. Global warming melts glaciers, resulting in seawater volume expansion; this enables more water vapour to fill the air above faster. Thus, modern storms contain more destructive energy.

Global warming does not cause storms but make them more powerful. Due to the increase in the temperature, the air can absorb more moisture. This relationship (the change in the ability to absorb water with the increase in the temperature) is given by the ClausiusClapeyron equation.

Option (C) precisely explains the mechanism through which global warming makes the modern storms more destructive.

Hence, the correct option is (C).

33. Professions-approach aims at the institutionalization of knowledge but restricts knowledge production as a function of a select few.

The first sentence says that scientific knowledge can be approached from a number of perspectives. Studying something from the perspective of a particular profession would lead to institutionalization of that knowledge. Though it helps, it restricts knowledge production to a domain of few, which results in power centered in the hands of few, preventing the non-professional actors from offering their ideas.

Hence, the correct option is (A).

34. Artificial embryo twinning is low-tech and mimetic of the natural development of genetically identical twins from the embryo after fertilization.

This is a slightly tricky question in which we have to pick the options after carefully comparing them with the others. The first sentence says that artificial embryo twinning is low-tech. The second sentence says that it mimics the natural process that creates identical twins.

Hence, the correct option is (A).

35. The three-dimensional understanding of the organism in Europe led to a similar approach towards the understanding of landscape.

Landscape became an independent genre of art of form, while the option says it became a major subject of art. This is a distortion of the fact given in the passage.

Hence, the correct option is (B).

36. Statistical and empirical weaknesses stand in the way of inferring any relationship between sports participation and deviance.

The passage focuses on delinquency and sports participation, suggesting that deviation from delinquency and sports participation is not yet confirmed, as there are many hindrances to arriving at the right conclusion.

Hence, the correct option is (C).

37. Exempting from regulations the editing of endogenous genes is not desirable as this procedure might be risk-prone.

The paragraph speaks about the Japanese government's recommendation. The recommendation is the key idea of the passage. The recommendation is about regulating only genetically modified organisms, and leaving the rest. The reactions are mixed, however the author cautions about the unforeseen risks.

Hence, the correct option is (C).

38. Bad Samaritan laws may be desirable but they need to be tested for legal soundness.

The passage starts with a few questions. The answer is nowhere given by the author. After the questions, the author says that proponents of bad Samaritan laws must overcome three obstacles, and further goes on to elaborate what those obstacles are. These obstacles are the test which must be overcome as per the author.

Hence, the correct option is (D).

39. The ability to think about objects not present in our environment precedes the development of human communication.

Option (B) is succinct and does not have any distortions or misrepresentations.

Hence, the correct option is (B).

40. Though engineering draws heavily from pure science, it contributes to knowledge, by incorporating the constraints and conditions in the real world.

The passage broadly talks about the difference between purse science and applied science, i.e. engineering. Further the author says that engineers might find even those theories of physics useful that from the point of view of pure physics are false. Option (B) precisely captures that. It says that engineering incorporates the constraints and conditions of physics in the real world.

Hence, the correct option is (B).

41. Packard held that advertising as a 'hidden persuasion' understands the hidden motivations of consumers and works at the supraliminal level, though the people targeted have no awareness of being persuaded.

There is a clear difference between the choices with respect to supraliminal and subliminal. The passage clearly tells us that Packard believed in supraliminal images, not subliminal.

Hence, the correct option is (D).

42. Language evolved with linguistic features building on features of cognition such as memory.

It says that it is a human trait, but not a derived trait (a derived trait would be something that was missing in the common ancestor).

Hence, the correct option is (B).

43. Wall-free office spaces did not quite work out the way their utopian inventors intended, as they became tools for exploitation of labor.

This is moderate difficulty question. The passage has two parts, the first speaks of the dismantling of the walls to overcome all divisions, the second speaks of how something else resulted from it because of selfish business interest.

Option (A) is the best choice; it says that the intention was to make things democratic, but by putting in as many people as possible in cubicles, it became a tool of exploitation of labour.

Hence, the correct option is (A).

44. Organizations with hybrid identities are able to mobilize individuals with different points of view.

The passage mentions hybrid organizations and says that it is easy for hybrid organizations to attract people, than it is for non-hybrid organizations.

Hence, the correct option is (D).

45. Movies and televisions have led to the belief that the use of forensic phonetics in legal investigations is robust and fool proof.

The most important critical element is "forensic phonetics in movies and television", and "these have led to errors in real-life justice, with unrealistic expectations of the capabilities of forensic science".

Hence, the correct option is (B).

46. Thomas Hobbes theorized the emergence of sovereign states based on a transactional relationship between people and sovereign state that was necessitated by a sense of insecurity of the people.

The passage has three important keywords: sovereign equality, sense of insecurity, and what was done to overcome that insecurity. The passage tells us that people delivered their rights to a sovereign power in return for the sovereign's provision of security. This was the only way to overcome the fear of insecurity. After all there is a give and take happening, and therefore there is a transaction.

Hence, the correct option is (A).

47. Decisions based on intuition and information result in differential speed and ability to provide a rationale.

In the passage the author compares the two factors based on which humans make decisions. The first is intuition and the other is information. The author seems to be comparing the two without any preference.

Hence, the correct option is (C).

48. With the diversity of urban landscapes, measurable criteria for defining urban areas may need to be supplemented with human judgement.

There are three important keywords in this paragraph: the challenge posed by rural-urban continuum, the objective methodology with one or two metrics may not be enough to capture the wide diversity, it may require an element of human judgement.

Hence, the correct option is (B).

49. Genetic theory has a wide range of theoretical approaches and application and is foundational to evolutionary biology and Metabolic theory has the potential to do the same for ecology.

In this paragraph the author uses two broad keywords "genetic theory and metabolic theory. The genetic theory was successful because of the diversity of genetic models, and the same might happen for metabolic theory, which would provide a conceptual foundation for much of ecology."

Hence, the correct option is (C).

50. Most believe that language originated from a need to articulate facts, but others think it emerged from the need to promote social cohesion and cooperation, thus enabling human survival.

There are two views pertaining to the evolution of language. One view believes in sharing of factual information as the reason,

whereas the other view believes in social bonding as the reason. The former being the dominant view, while the latter being the less dominant.

Hence, the correct option is (C).

51. Aesthetic political representation advocates autonomy for the representatives drawing from disinterestedness, which itself is different from indifference.

The author seems to prefer disinterestedness for aesthetic political representation.

Hence, the correct option is (D).

52. Though wars due to conflict of interests in a civilization are inevitable and unpleasant, war carries some positive effects with it.

The main idea the paragraph conveys is that 'war is not only inevitable, it is salutary'. 'Salutary' means some unpleasant event bringing some positive effects with it. Only option (D) captures all the main points - war is inevitable, unpleasant but has some positive effects as well.

Hence, the correct option is (D).

53. Personal consciousness, which is stirred by novel conditions, is comprised of conscious thoughts, observations, wishes, and aversions. This consciousness is important because it leads to new acts which are our only escape from habitual actions.

The main points of the paragraph are - when we face new conditions, our personal consciousness arises. This consciousness - that is our conscious thoughts, observations, wishes, aversions - produces new actions and hence it is important because it is the only way we can break old habits.

Hence, the correct option is (A).

54. Artworks, like speech, express meaning and can similarly be harmful if they glorify hateful actions and people.

In the passage, the author draws a parallel between artworks and speech acts- speech acts drive action, like a call for protest or the endorsement of a particular idea. And these artistic expressions can be harmful too. The author cites the example of statues and figurines of slave traders and white supremacists to suggest that the artistic expression can result in the endorsement of an idea, in this case, the "supposed" inferior nature of people of colour, and this could affect the lives of the individuals concerned.

Hence, the correct option is (C).

55. Nicholson and the council reached the same conclusion. The author feels that Nicholson would have overridden the orders of the council had they reached different conclusions and has always been approving of such a scenario.

From the first line of the paragraph, we can infer that Nicholson and the council agreed to go ahead with the same course of action. The author is describing a hypothetical scenario in the paragraph given. He is reasonably certain that had the council disagreed, Nicholson would have gone ahead to establish his intentions disregarding the orders of the council.

Hence, the correct option is (B).

56. Anxiety is caused by uncertainty and lack of confidence in predictions; Better predictions free a person from anxiety and allow them to respond appropriately.

In the passage, the author states that anxiety and fear are different and are triggered differently. Anxiety is always caused by uncertainty, i.e., predictions that we have very little confidence in. When we have confidence in our predictions, we are freed from anxiety and then we can respond and adjust to the situation.

Hence, the correct option is (A).

57. Even though professions related to health sciences, economics, mathematics, and geography are considered to be more enterprising by many, they are not in any way superior to professions involving art as indicated by the renaissance age.

The main purpose of the passage is to make the point that professions involving art are not inferior to professions involving health sciences, economics etc.

In the passage, the example of the Renaissance age is not used to express that there was a period in which Art was considered important but to contradict the argument of people that professions involving health sciences, economics etc are more enterprising than art.

Hence, the correct option is (D).

58. The basis of any democracy is a government for the people and by the people.

From the paragraph, we can see that Egypt's current government has been toppled and the people are rejoicing their new got freedom. An apt conclusion to the preceding events should be a statement describing the constituents of a real people's government.

Hence, the correct option is (B).

59. According to the passage, the Veil of Ignorance thought experiment should be not be taken in its literal sense; it is not about being ignorant - instead, the purpose of the experiment is to explore or examine the ideas about justice, morality, equality, and social status, without prejudice or bias (or influence from other innate/accumulated factors). The author highlights how, as a consequence, the resulting society would be a fair one, and in this regard, the exercise is essentially a test of perception associated with the aforementioned ideals.

Hence, the correct option is (C).

60. While some believe that bragging can make us feel good by projecting a positive self-image, others believe it distorts our reality.

In the paragraph, the author explores whether boastful, self-aggrandising beliefs and behaviours are beneficial to those who make such claims.

He presents the views of two schools of thought. One group believes that bragging to others can satisfy the motive to craft and maintain a positive selfimage, which makes us happy.

The other group believes that consistently viewing oneself as superior entails a distortion of reality.

Hence, the correct option is (B).

Ques (1-12):Direction: Five jumbled-up sentences, related to a topic, are given below. Four of them can be put together to form a coherent paragraph. Identify the odd one out and key in the number of the sentence as your answer:

Q.1 1. It has cleared the land, dried the marshes, pierced the forests, made roads; it has been building, inventing, observing, reasoning; it has created a complex machinery, wrested her secrets from Nature, and finally, it has made a servant of steam.

2. And this capital enables him to acquire, merely by his own labour, combined with the labour of others, riches surpassing the dreams of the Orient, expressed in the fairy tales of the Thousand and One Nights.

3. And the result is, that now the child of the civilized man finds ready, at its birth, to his hand an immense capital accumulated by those who have gone before him.

4. It is because, taking advantage of alleged rights acquired in the past, these few appropriate today two-thirds of the products of human labour, and then squander them in the most stupid and shameful way.

5. During the agitated times which have elapsed since, and which have lasted for many thousand years, mankind has nevertheless amassed untold treasures.

Q.2 1. Hume's ethical theory continues to be relevant for contemporary philosophers and psychologists interested in topics such as metaethics, the role of sympathy and empathy within the moral evaluation and moral psychology, as well as virtue ethics.

2. Although David Hume is commonly known for his philosophical skepticism, and empiricist theory of knowledge, he also made many important contributions to moral philosophy.

3. Consequently, when the person we are sympathizing with shares these similarities we will form a stronger conception of their feelings, and when such similarities are absent our conception of their feeling will be comparatively weaker.

4. As a central figure in the Scottish Enlightenment, Hume's ethical thought variously influenced, was influenced by, and faced criticism from, thinkers such as Shaftesbury, Francis Hutcheson, Adam Smith, and Thomas Reid.

5. Hume's ethical thought grapples with questions about the relationship between morality and reason, the role of human emotion in thought and action, the nature of moral evaluation, human sociability, and what it means to live a virtuous life.

Q.3 1. Because of its angular letter forms, however, and because early runic inscriptions were written from right to left like the earliest alphabets, runic writing seems to belong to a more ancient system.

2. The Scandinavian languages were even richer in sounds than Old English; but, instead of adding letters to the futhark to represent the new sounds, the users of the Nordic script compounded the letter values, using the same letter to stand for more than one sound.

3. Runic alphabet, also called futhark, writing system of uncertain origin used by Germanic peoples of northern Europe, Britain, Scandinavia, and Iceland from about the 3rd century to the 16th or 17th century AD.

4. Scholars have attempted to derive it from the Greek or Latin alphabets, either capitals or cursive forms, at any period from the 6th century BC to the 5th century AD.

5. Runic writing appeared rather late in the history of writing and is clearly derived from one of the alphabets of the Mediterranean area.

Q.4 1. In July 1992, two Danish birders visiting Patagonia, Arizona reported the first-ever, mega-rare cinnamon hummingbird in the United States

2. In this case, a couple of other out-of-towners—a birder from Mississippi and another from Nebraska—saw the species.

3. Scientists use eBird's open-access data to study the evolution and movement of invasive species and to highlight the importance of public lands in conservation.

4. Back then, reporting rare birds required phoning in observations to a "rare bird phone tree," usually via the nearest payphone—and hoping that word got out.

5. The Nebraskan photographed the hummingbird, flew home, developed the slide film, and snail-mailed photos to the Arizona committee in charge of validating unusual sightings but it was too late: the hummingbird was gone, and Arizona birders missed it.

Q.5 1. However, the needed acceleration in productivity growth is hampered by the degradation of natural resources, the loss of biodiversity, and the spread of transboundary pests and diseases of plants and animals, some of which are becoming resistant to antimicrobials.

2. Food losses and waste claim a significant proportion of agricultural output, and reducing them would lessen the need for production increases.

3. Although agricultural investments and technological innovations are boosting productivity, the growth of yields has slowed to rates that are too low for comfort.

4. While reducing losses to crops and rangelands, it minimizes pesticide use and negative environmental impacts and requires less investment.

5. The decline in the share of agriculture in total production and employment is taking place at different speeds and poses different challenges across regions.

Q.6 1. One of the biggest debates humans have is whether city life is better than village life or vice versa.

2. Each year, millions of people migrate to urban centers in search of greener pastures.

3. Each area represents the opposite of the other and the advantages of one are actually the disadvantages of the other.

4. A number of tribes, interspersed all over the country, enjoy their lives in forests as they experience pristine nature.

5. While village life has many advantages, including less noise, beautiful natural landscapes, less pollution, fresh air, and less congestion, the statistics do not favor the village folks worldwide.

Q.7 1. Exploring madness, heartbreak, postwar culture, racist pseudoscience, and cryptozoology in a game that's equal parts existential philosophy and absurdist nonsense, Disco Elysium was like nothing we've seen before.

2. With small rewrites, full silky voice acting that delivers every line in a set of gloriously European accents, and new political vision quests, Disco Elysium has been fully realized.

3. However, as ZA/UM had indicated to investors that this was to be a game that spanned a larger world, they found the need to spread beyond that single location, forcing them to delay the game's release, along with the name change to Disco Elysium.

4. Disco Elysium, if you didn't play it when it came out in 2019, is a narrative-focused gem that emphasizes a vast story, worldbuilding, and themes, which over-delivers on its promise to leave you stunned, and perhaps changed, by the game's conclusion.

5. After its initial release, the game saw a puzzlingly free update, Disco Elysium: The Final Cut, which overhauls what you already purchased and adds new content you didn't know you were desperate for.

Q.8 1. A small, but a meaningful blessing in Going Medieval is its intuitive menus.

2. The only frustration comes from Going Medieval's verticality—players can build up as it is harder than it should be to toggle a birds-eye view between resources inside a storehouse and the storehouse roof.

3. There's no digging through tabs to find one specific stat or resource, no immersion-breaking UX disasters.

4. By offering the game to a larger audience before its completion essential feedback can be achieved to help them balance out the experience and make the final game the best it can possibly be.

5. The game doesn't harshly punish you for missing an important menu (or system) early on, allowing you to incrementally appreciate new gameplay loops.

Q.9 1. The Boston Digital Arm is a recent artificial limb that has taken advantage of these more advanced processors.

2. Advancements in the processors used in myoelectric arms have allowed developers to make gains in fine-tuned control of the prosthetic.

3. The research of Robotic legs has made some advancements over time, allowing exact movement and control.

4. Recently the I-LIMB Hand, invented in Edinburgh, Scotland, by David Gow has become the first commercially available hand prosthesis with five individually powered digits.

5. The arm allows movement in five axes and allows the arm to be programmed for a more customized feel.

Q.10 1. The quarantine has led many of us into the kitchen to cook meals three (or more) times a day.

2. While some people find cooking therapeutic and thoroughly enjoy doing it, for many others the experience is not as exciting.

3. The recipe, for which you will need raw mango is not only easy to make, it is also tangy and good for health.

4. But there may be times when you end up cooking extra and are left wondering what to do with it the next day.

5. Just give yourself a break and tweak the leftover food to make a new dish for your next meal.

Q.11 1. There is a growing interest among people who study children's language spend regarding how newborns react to the speech when they hear.

2. One of the methods to study this is by making films of adults and babies while they are interacting with each other to determine how the babies react to speech from the moment they are born.

3. It is believed that babies react to speech from the moment they take birth.

4. However, these signs are very subtle - sometimes the baby's pupils dilate or there is a slight movement of the hand.

5. These movements won't be noticeable if you were just looking at the baby and hence there is a need to watch the recording over and over again.

Q.12 1. The only certainty in the VUCA world is the increase in the flow of data and the one who can draw meaning out of data will reign supreme.

2. The use of data analytics will lead to disruption and bring a new set of challenges and opportunities.

3. Moreover, since the flow of data is not confined to geographical boundaries, data analytics will form the backbone of global operations.

4. So if petrodollars ruled the past, it would be data dollars that would become the buzzword in the currency circles in the future.

5. Data analytic can be used to interpret data for any function and thus smash the window ceilings of productivity.

Q.13 Direction: Four jumbled-up sentences, related to a topic, are given below. Three of them can be put together to form a coherent paragraph. Identify the odd one out and key in the number of the sentence as your answer:

1. By Ptolemy V's reign in 205 BC, Egypt was in open revolt and the Rosetta stone was one of many that Ptolemy commissioned as a piece of political propaganda in 196 BC, to state publicly his claim to be the rightful pharaoh of Egypt.

2. These Greek rulers could neither speak the language of the people nor read hieroglyphs, and this fuelled resentment amongst the population.

3. Beginning with the conquest of Alexander the Great in 332 BC, Greek was the language of the governing elite in Egypt.

4. Without the Rosetta stone, we would know nothing of the ancient Egyptians, and the details of their three thousand years of history would remain a mystery.

Ques (14-60):Direction: Four jumbled-up sentences, related to a topic, are given below. Three of them can be put together to form a coherent paragraph. Identify the odd one out:

Q.14 1. The biggest fallout of NPA accumulation, particularly in the public sector banks, is that industrial credit growth rate has plunged in the last few years.

2. Without doubt, there are cases of bad loans where the debt repayment problems have been caused by diversion of funds.

3. Non-performing assets (NPAs) or bad loans in the Indian banking system have arisen primarily for reasons beyond the control of public sector bank management.

4. But the bulk of the problem has been caused by unexpected changes in the economic environment: timetables, exchange rates, and growth rate assumptions going wrong.

Q.15 A. As every language has evolved in a specific geocultural niche, it has different ways of talking of and codifying the world.

B. To learn another language, we must suspend our habit of glossing over differences, which distorts our understanding of others and of ourselves.

C. The work of learning new ways of talking – new sounds, grammars and storytelling techniques – stretches and builds the mind.

D. Therefore, it is not possible to achieve fluency in another language without learning its speakers' perspectives.

Q.16 A. Moreover, as temperatures rise, information technologies will work less efficiently, starting off a vicious cycle.

B. As much of the physical infrastructure that undergirds the internet is right next to the coast, rising seas can seriously imperil the internet.

C. The world's data centers already have roughly the same carbon footprint as the global aviation industry.

D. The internet, the primary vector of information about climate change, is increasingly a vector of the problem itself.

Q.17 A. Coastal wetlands can even grow in height as sea level rises, protecting communities further inland.

B. Salt marshes and mangrove forests store flood waters and protect coasts from hurricanes and storms.

C. Continuously removing and storing atmospheric carbon, wetlands act as 'carbon sinks' that help mitigate climate change.

D. In addition, wetlands make ecosystems and human communities more resilient in the face of climate change.

Q.18 A. Additionally, many native species are only found in the snag forest habitat of dead and dying trees created by high-severity wildfire.

B. Decades of science have shown that forest fires are an essential part of Western U.S. forest ecosystems and create highly biodiverse wildlife habitat.

C. Despite this steadily accumulating evidence, the government has posited that more active management of forests could help prevent future fires.

D. Many native animals thrive in the years and decades after large intense fires, including deer, bats, woodpeckers, and songbirds as well as spotted owls.

Q.19 A. Expertise is not an isolated event: rather, it changes when the social context changes.

B. Even exceptional players who find themselves in a different team with many other exceptional players, may find themselves playing below par.

C. In team sports, this includes supporting staff such as physical therapists and managers.

D. A network of high performing athletes and support staff provides a rich social platform for professional excellence.

Q.20 A. The political nature of the target modifies the standard economic constraints, encouraging local governments to generate whatever additional economic activity is required so that, along with the economic activity of the private and real-estate sectors, the target is reached.

B. The fact is that Chinese GDP will be unaffected by a trade war with the U.S., no matter how severe, because the government will do whatever it takes to meet its growth targets. To see the conflict's true toll, one should look at rising Chinese debt instead.

C. Thus, while GDP numbers may tell us something about the government's priorities, they're a poor measure of the underlying performance of the economy, for, as long as China has debt capacity, and the government is willing to use it, China can achieve any GDP growth target it wants.

D. In China, the government sets the GDP growth rate early in the year at a level thought adequate to accommodate its social and political objectives, among which is to keep unemployment low.

Q.21 A. Researchers found that the stone tools of H. erectus were made from stones lying around at the bottom of a hill, for instance, rather than from the better-quality stones found uphill.

B. In contrast, H. sapiens and Neanderthals, who came later, put in the effort to find good stone for the tools they made and even transported these stones over long distances.

C. Excavations from the Arabian Peninsula indicate that the species Homo erectus failed to put in enough effort to create good quality stone tools which were crucial to their survival.

D. This lackadaisical attitude, coupled with the inability to adapt to a changing environment, was what, according to these researchers, contributed to the population's demise.

A. A   **B.** B   **C.** C   **D.** D

Q.22 A. In its "I Want to Be Recycled" campaign, Keep America Beautiful urges consumers to reduce their plastic footprint by imagining the reincarnation of shampoo bottles and boxes post recycling.

B. Keep America Beautiful has, for decades, publicly opposed or marketed against legislation that would increase producer responsibility for plastic waste management.

C. In fact, its greatest success has been to shift the onus of environmental responsibility onto the public while simultaneously becoming a trusted name in the environmental movement.

D. A corporate greenwashing front, it has built public support for a legal framework that punishes individual litterers, while imposing almost no responsibility on plastic manufacturers.

A. A **B.** B **C.** C **D.** D

Q.23 A. In laughing along, the target of the joke shows that he's a good sport, thereby completing the ritual.

B. Ridicule can actually reinforce a group when the target is confident of their in-group status.

C. By laughing together at each other and at themselves, the rest of the group show their membership.

D. Laughing at someone is among the strongest markers of social exclusion in human connection.

A. A **B.** B **C.** C **D.** D

Q.24 A. Letters let us write words while emoji let us write gestures.

B. Emoji are so widely used that they are rightly called the lingua franca of the world.

C. They are the equivalent of gesticulating to add emphasis.

D. While they convey a writer's intentions, emoji are not a language in themselves.

A. A **B.** B **C.** C **D.** D

Q.25 A. On the sliding scale of attribution that art historians use – painted by; hand of; studio of; circle of; style of; copy of – each step takes the artist farther from the painting.

B. If a fake is so expert that even after the most thorough examination its authenticity is still open to doubt, is it not as satisfactory a work of art as if it were genuine?

C. Leaving straight forgeries aside, any discussion about the "authenticity" of an artwork opens suddenly, like a trapdoor, into the murk of semantics.

D. Added to this is the unease about overpainting: Salvator Mundi had been worked over so many times and so heavily, critics argue, that it is less by Da Vinci than by his restorers.

A. A **B.** B **C.** C **D.** D

Q.26 A. In fact, compared to other mammals, humans are actually naturally adapted for a relatively low protein intake, requiring protein to make up just 10% of our daily calorie requirement.

B. Over the past 50 years, research has consistently found that whenever we tinker with our natural protein needs, it can have adverse consequences, at all phases of our lives.

C. This became associated with an increased risk of developing chronic diseases such as cancer in later life, forcing the formula to be adapted to have a lower protein content.

D. Human breast milk is quite low in protein: when cow's milk formula was first used to create an artificial replacement for breast milk, the excessive protein content was found to cause accelerated growth rates in early life.

A. A **B.** B **C.** C **D.** D

Q.27 A. Many of those who are racked with self-doubt often seek confirmation of their distorted self-perception.

B. This seems logical as those with a negative self-image would be just the ones who would want to overcompensate.

C. The reason for their behaviour is the desire for coherence: if others respond in a way that confirms their self-image, then the world is as it should be.

D. In some cases, individuals actually provoke others to respond negatively to them, in order hear their own bleak view of themselves.

A. A **B.** B **C.** C **D.** D

Q.28 A. The stereotype that creativity is enhanced by a mood disorder is dangerous, both for those with mood disorders and those pursuing creativity: it could keep them from seeking treatment if they believe treatment would diminish their creative ability.

B. However, there are differences that might vary systematically between the groups: for instance, people who have achieved real creative success typically face the stress of being in the public eye, while the average person does not.

C. Most people chosen to be included in the creative groups are successful writers or artists, while those in the less-creative group are typically average people living nearby to wherever the study is taking place.

D. Just that component could account for any number of differences in the instance of mood disorder, given that stress is a major cause for the onset of mood disorders.

A. A **B.** B **C.** C **D.** D

Q.29 A. In the breakneck pace of decolonization, nations were thrown together in months; often their alarmed populations fell immediately into violent conflict to control the new state apparatus and the power and wealth that came with it.

B. If there are so few formerly colonized countries that are now peaceful, affluent, and democratic, it is not, as the west often pretends, because "bad leaders" somehow ruined otherwise perfectly functional nations.

C. On the premise that the colonial epoch had not permitted the growth of indigenous economic institutions, the new states were encouraged, largely by the West, to entrust economic modernization to parastatal corporations administered by inexperienced bureaucrats.

D. Many infant states were held together only by strongmen who entrusted the system to their own tribes or clans, maintained power by stoking sectarian rivalries and turned ethnic or religious differences into super-charged axes of political terror.

A. A **B.** B **C.** C **D.** D

Q.30 A. Museums are not neutral spaces, where objects exist without context; they do more than allow us to engage with history and art.

B. They are forms in and of themselves, which, to varying degrees, enable and propagate missions and legacies through design and architecture.

C. Try as some museums might to go unnoticed as simply the pedestal or wall on which history and art work hangs, there is no escaping the weight of the objects and stories told within their architecture.

D. A museum of modern art in Cologne isn't so different from a museum of modern art in Chicago – you see the same major-canon artists, arranged in more or less the same way.

A. A **B.** B **C.** C **D.** D

Q.31 A. Commonwealth enthusiasts believe that the Commonwealth has supposedly vast potential, which could be augmented further with a little additional funding, yet membership will always remain cheaper than the EU, and not only in terms of the UK's direct financial contribution.

B. But given the fact that there are huge variations in the levels of trade conducted by individual member states, it is difficult to see what we can actually learn from an average figure for "Commonwealth advantage" between two notional Commonwealth states.

C. In this light, the Commonwealth is the international relations equivalent of a homeopathic remedy – a cadre of staff so small as to be almost invisible when dissolved across a body comprising 2.4 billion people, which nevertheless does or could achieve miraculous results.

D. Somehow, this Commonwealth of the future will cost less than the EU in terms of the vast number of hours required to negotiate its treaties and other formal agreements; it will not require members to make significant concessions in return for some collective good; and it will have only the most rudimentary of mechanisms to enforce its will.

A. A   **B.** B   **C.** C   **D.** D

Q.32 A. If the regions, peoples, and nations currently demanding more freedom seem to be driven by "cultural nationalism", that in turn is driven by technological change plus global competition.

B. Information-rich societies reward the development of human capital; so, the ability to study in your first language, participate in rich national culture and create unique local selling points for incoming foreign investment is more important than ever.

C. The mixture of austerity, corruption, and political sclerosis at the center has limited the reality of regional democracy and pushed autonomous regions such as Catalonia to fight for self-determination.

D. Above the problems of economic failure and racial polarization, the positive factor driving progressive nationalism, from Scotland to Catalonia, is technological change.

A. A   **B.** B   **C.** C   **D.** D

Q.33 A. Sprinters cock the lead knee high and drive the foot into the track with a stiffened ankle—a punch delivered with high velocity and a sudden stop.

B. The swiftest runners achieve top speed by swinging their legs more rapidly than slow runners while repositioning their limbs between takeoff and landing.

C. What faster runners do better is apply a more powerful force to the ground through their foot, and, just as critically, do this in a briefer contact period.

D. Both swift runners and slow runners take roughly the same time when airborne to move their legs back into position for the next stride.

A. A   **B.** B   **C.** C   **D.** D

Q.34 A. Inflation, which increases nominal but not real wages, is assumed to trick workers into accepting a lower remuneration for their services; it is thus an indirect wage cut that helps prevent an increase in unemployment.

B. An economic concept that serves as the linchpin for monetary policymakers is that wages are quite inflexible in a market economy, so unemployment is bound to shoot up whenever workers refuse to accept lower wages.

C. The stagflation of the 1970s proved quite convincingly that high unemployment and high inflation can very well co-exist, and given that wages may not be as rigid as many economists assume, any effort to micromanage the economy may well be a fool's errand.

D. While framing monetary policies, central bank chiefs keep this inverse relationship in mind, trying to maintain a non-accelerating inflation rate of unemployment, which is the unemployment rate at which inflation too is just under control.

A. A   **B.** B   **C.** C   **D.** D

Q.35 A. Since Plato at least, we have held that subduing our passions to the iron rule of reason is our supreme aspiration; it is the ideal for human cognition.

B. If human beings can indeed be described as rational animals, it is due to the fact that humans, of all animals, are the only ones capable of irrational thoughts and action.

C. Ironically, we think that the more we are like Star Trek's unfeeling alien Mr. Spock, the more human we really are.

D. We delight in pretending that our most prized and most humanly attribute is our forebrain, which houses, we also pretend, our capacity for rational thought.

A. A   **B.** B   **C.** C   **D.** D

Q.36 A. Party politics is all too often merely the surf, spray and scum of the ocean that is society – it's the prevailing undercurrents, the slow shifting of tectonic plates, that count in the long run.

B. Emmanuel Macron's victory in France's legislative elections is the consummation of a political revolution which started with his triumph in the recent presidential election.

C. While on the surface the dominance of Macron's party – founded less than two years ago – is a huge transformation of the political landscape in France, the low turnout suggests that this is skin deep.

D. In France, growing abstention is the powerful current that risks, eventually, pulling the country under.

A. A   **B.** B   **C.** C   **D.** D

Q.37 A. Sea ice acts as a blanket on top of the ocean, protecting the water from incoming solar energy and atmospheric heat.

B. This effect accelerates overall warming, which in turn melts more land ice and drives up sea levels.

C. Although the sea ice is shrinking, it does not add to water levels as it melts because it is already part of the ocean's mass.

D. As that frozen coating disappears, its white surface is no longer there to reflect sunlight back into the atmosphere—so the ocean absorbs much more solar energy.

A. A   **B.** B   **C.** C   **D.** D

Q.38 A. The imaginary worlds of fiction serve as means to escape the ties and the ennui of the real world and indulge vicariously in an alternate reality.

B. Reading fiction trains people in this domain, just as reading nonfiction books about, say, genetics or history builds expertise in those subject areas.

C. The defining characteristic of fiction is not that it is made-up but that it is about human, or humanlike beings and their intentions and interactions.

D. The solitary act of holing up with a book is actually an exercise in human interaction.

A. A   **B.** B   **C.** C   **D.** D

Q.39 A. Though the "mother of all laws", the Constitution is external to society and has a largely exhortatory relationship to it.

B. This is not a defect — the Constitution is required to reflect the republic in the best possible light, and is at its most majestic when doing so.

C. However, this also means that the Constitution is unable to directly confront obstinate realities like caste that flout its fundamental tenets because acknowledging caste amounts to confessing that the republic is more desire than reality.

D. Right from the Preamble, where it presumes that "we, the people" are indeed a unified and homogenous collectivity, the Constitution treats hoped-for outcomes as though they were established facts.

A. A   **B.** B   **C.** C   **D.** D

Q.40 A. German scientists analyzing the 3300-year-old bust have found evidence suggesting that a royal sculptor at the time may have smoothed creases around the mouth and fixed a bumpy nose to depict the 'Beauty of the Nile' in a better light.

B. The new rendering at the entrance of the Egyptian city of Samalut attempts to re-create the strangeness of the Amarna style. That is probably best done in a museum instead of on a highway, where it might scare people.

C. The miracle of the Nefertiti bust in Berlin is that it combines the realism of the Amarna style, as it is known, with a feel for grace and harmony to create one of the world's great icons of beauty.

D. By getting the colossally awful sculpture of the ancient queen pulled down, Egyptians have shown the way forward. We need to topple art that's an insult to our public spaces.

A. A   **B.** B   **C.** C   **D.** D

Q.41 A. Farmers need to be encouraged to grow more pulses not simply because demand is projected to rise by roughly 50 per cent between now and 2024.

B. The Subramanian committee has rightly noted that the worst case scenario for farmers is weak government procurement combined with continuation of stock-holding and export restrictions.

C. Volatility in production and prices of pulses, the committee's report has shown, is far higher than that for cereals, and this is neither in the interests of the producers nor the consumers.

D. Pulses also help in soil rejuvenation and naturally fixing atmospheric nitrogen, without consuming much water.

A. A   **B.** B   **C.** C   **D.** D

Q.42 A. Automotive interests have consciously shaped a vision of the streets as places where cars belong.

B. Indeed, the twenty-first century's apex predator is the automobile.

C. A fatal collision is an everyday phenomenon— the kind of death, it seems, that is always expected.

D. Cars prowl the streets, growling in revving ravenousness.

A. A   **B.** B   **C.** C   **D.** D

Q.43 A. India is self-sufficient in strategic armaments – nuclear weapons and delivery systems, including advanced and accurate ballistic and cruise missiles, and nuclear-powered submarines.

B. By focusing militarily on Pakistan and ignoring China's challenge, India inspires little confidence about its judgment, resolve, and prospects as a consequential power in the extended region.

C. While India wishes to stand up to China and emerge as the other nodal power in Asia, this ambition is undermined by diffidence and skewed capabilities.

D. But paradoxically, India has become the world's largest importer of conventional weaponry, leaving its foreign policy hostage to the whims and interests of vendor states.

A. A   **B.** B   **C.** C   **D.** D

Q.44 A. As global warming speeds up the melting of these glaciers, this weight is lifting, and the surface slowly is springing back.

B. Though the average hiker wouldn't notice, the Alps and other mountain ranges have experienced a gradual growth spurt over the past century or so.

C. These glaciers are giant scrapers that carve out valleys and carry away rock debris on ice conveyor belts, sculpting mountains.

D. For thousands of years, the weight of the glaciers atop these mountains has pushed against the Earth's surface, causing it to depress.

A. A   **B.** B   **C.** C   **D.** D

Q.45 A. If we are not to make grievous mistakes in the name of good things such as fighting corruption or tackling crime, then we, the people, must reflect.

B. The problem is not of manipulation or political ambition; it is the willingness with which otherwise sensible citizens allow themselves to follow the Piper.

C. If we realize that it is our sentiments that are disturbed, not our security, perhaps we will see the issue with greater equanimity.

D. It is in the nature of democratic politics for ambitious politicians to use emotions to climb up the ladder of power.

A. A   **B.** B   **C.** C   **D.** D

Q.46 A. There are few more emotional ways to view history than through the lens of a camera.

B. To take photographs is to hold one's breath when all faculties converge in a face of fleeing reality.

C. They are not about dialing for quotes or quick sound bites.

D. Photographs convey the ultimate journalistic credo: to be present at the site of action at the right time, and alive to capture the fleeting moments that transform our lives.

A. A   **B.** B   **C.** C   **D.** D

Q.47 A. Muhammad Ali's rejection of the Vietnam War was thus a rejection of war itself as a viable means of solving human problems, real or perceived.

B. In refusing the draft, Ali thus also refused to believe that national boundaries somehow categorically divided human beings into "us" and "them".

C. Violence is the tool of the hegemon; by eschewing it you are already challenging the means through which hegemony is legitimized.

D. The best way to stand up to power and injustice is to be steadfast in your resistance while shunning violence.

A. A   **B.** B   **C.** C   **D.** D

Q.48 A. We don't actually do two, or three or 10 things at once, we just switch from one to another to another.

B. Multitasking makes us demonstrably efficient, increasing cognitive performance.

C. Each time we shift attention, there is a metabolic cost we pay in glucose.

D. Some brain activities are more expensive than others, and switching attention is among the most expensive.

A. A   **B.** B   **C.** C   **D.** D

Q.49 A. Since birds are the modern descendants of dinosaurs, they are likely to have once had teeth instead of beaks.

B. However, 100 million years ago a diverse range of non-avian dinosaurs spouted all manner of plumage, and like modern birds, doubtless made a great deal of use of them, even if they could not fly.

C. This fact became known way back in 1861 when paleontologists discovered a bird fossil, about 150 million years old, now classified as Archaeopteryx, which had teeth.

D. Researchers have now published details of how avian edentulism occurred in one common bird ancestor more than 100 million years ago.

A. A   **B.** B   **C.** C   **D.** D

Q.50 A. Consumers prefer reliability when it's available, and giving the state's imprimatur to legalized gambling goes a long way toward ensuring that.

B. Legalizing gambling would only ramp up the incentive to find new ways to fix games.

C. In Britain, betting shops were legalized in 1961, and giant gambling companies, like William Hill and Ladbrokes, watch out for suspiciously prescient bets.

D. Taking gambling into the light makes the marketplace more hostile to cheaters.

A. A   **B.** B   **C.** C   **D.** D

Q.51 A. Rowling's declarations on Twitter on what she "always thought" of a particular character are not only newsworthy but a cause for pride.

B. Rowling seems eager to retain an influence on how we understand her books by revealing ostensibly new information about her characters.

C. Rowling's chances for being a diverse author lie in the future, not the past.

D. Whether these character points were announced to readers via Twitter or alluded to within the Potter books, however, the meanings that we as a diverse international community of readers wish to take from them trump Rowling's intentions as an author.

A. A   **B.** B   **C.** C   **D.** D

Q.52 A. A mixture of vagueness and sheer incompetence is the most marked characteristic of modern English prose, and especially of any kind of political writing.

B. It follows that any struggle against the abuse of language is a sentimental archaism, like preferring candles to electric light or hansom cabs to aeroplanes.

C. Prose consists less and less of words chosen for the sake of their meaning, and more and more of phrases tacked together like the sections of a prefabricated hen-house.

D. As soon as certain topics are raised, the concrete melts into the abstract and no one seems able to think of turns of speech that are not hackneyed.

A. A   **B.** B   **C.** C   **D.** D

Q.53 A. In 400 BC, Leonidas' 300 Spartans died at Thermopylae in Greece while their countrymen vied at Olympia.

B. Troops were forbidden to enter the sacred Olympic precinct; but they were there in 420 B.C. when a Spartan attack was feared. Spartans had been banned from competing.

C. And yet, Spartan-like, America was represented at the Games while she was still fighting in Vietnam.

D. Civilization has advanced since then and—commendably — Olympiads of 1916, 1940 and 1944 were cancelled due to worldwide conflagration.

A. A   **B.** B   **C.** C   **D.** D

Q.54 A. There is a special intimacy to poetry because, in this idea of the art, the medium is not an expert's body, as when one goes to the ballet: in poetry, the medium is the audience's body.

B. In such movement the image fully becomes an intellectual and emotional complex because it dramatically exists both in the space of description and in the time of musical structure.

C. The luminous details in poetry must not only be precise, they must also be rendered so as to elicit and reward a dynamic sense of movement.

D. Poetry is a centaur. The thinking word-arranging, clarifying faculty must move and leap with the energizing, sentient, musical faculties.

A. A   **B.** B   **C.** C   **D.** D

Q.55 A. Forecasts say that in just two years, the total quantum of e-waste generated around the world will be 50 million tonnes.

B. In China, for instance, 73.9 million computers, 0.25 billion mobile phones and 56.6 million televisions were sold in 2011.

C. Close to 90 percent of the world's electronic waste — worth nearly $19 billion — is illegally traded or dumped each year, to destinations half way across the world.

D. While Europe and North America are by far the largest producers of e-waste, Asia's cities are fast catching up as consumers of electronic goods and as generators of e-waste.

A. A   B. B   C. C   D. D

Q.56 A. In China, for example, World Bank money has not been so important quantitatively, yet the Chinese generally credit the bank for having helpful blueprints and information.

B. While most of the US$800 billion invested in infrastructure in developing countries each year comes from domestic sources, the provision of infrastructure financing by multilateral development institutions globally is important.

C. By contrast, their greatest failures have come from funding grandiose projects that benefit the current elite, but do not properly balance environmental, social, and development priorities.

D. Multilateral development institutions have had their most consistent success when they serve as "knowledge" banks, helping to share experience, best practices, and technical knowledge across regions.

A. A   B. B   C. C   D. D

Q.57 A. Besides generating buzz, a season-based reality show does as well as a top-five show in terms of viewership.

B. The key, then, is for channels to find bankable reality formats and milk them till the cows come home.

C. Then again, they have realized that the easier way to gain ad revenue to cover costs is by luring advertisers to a fail-proof, steady-TRP format like reality TV.

D. The nearly 15% year-on-year rise in production cost levels for reality shows has networks rattled.

A. A   B. B   C. C   D. D

Q.58 A. In the entire body of Harappan and other Indus art and sculpture there are no monuments erected to glorify warfare and no depictions of war or conquered enemies.

B. It is speculated that the rulers might have been wealthy merchants, or powerful landlords or spiritual leaders, who showed their power and status through the use of seals and fine jewelry.

C. Decorated with animal motifs, many of the seals, the most commonly found objects in Harappan cities, are inscribed with short pieces of the Indus script.

D. It appears that the Harappan and other Indus rulers governed their cities through the control of trade and religion, not by military might.

A. A   B. B   C. C   D. D

Q.59 A. What we call "fundamentalism" has always existed in a symbiotic relationship with a secularization that is experienced as cruel, violent and invasive.

B. Historically, wherever secular governments were established to separate religion and politics, a counter-cultural movement developed in response, determined to bring religion back into public life.

C. In the developing world, secularization usually came with colonial rule; it was hence seen as a foreign import and rejected as profoundly unnatural.

D. All too often an aggressive secularism has pushed religion into a violent riposte.

A. A   B. B   C. C   D. D

Q.60 A. Cognitive science, however, tells us that students need to develop these different ways of thinking by means of extended, focused mental effort.

B. NO matter what happens in the relatively brief period students spend in the classroom, there is not enough time to develop the long-term memory structures required for subject mastery.

C. A traditional science instructor concentrates on teaching factual knowledge, with the implicit assumption that expert-like ways of thinking about the subject are already present.

D. To ensure that the necessary extended effort is made, teachers need to engage students in thinking deeply about the subject at an appropriate level, monitor that thinking and guide it to be more expert-like.

A. A   B. B   C. C   D. D

// Smart Answer Sheet //

Correct   Indicates percentage of students who answered questions correctly.

Skipped   Indicates percentage of students who skipped questions.

Q.	Ans.	Correct / Skipped	Q.	Ans.	Correct / Skipped	Q.	Ans.	Correct / Skipped	Q.	Ans.	Correct / Skipped	Q.	Ans.	Correct / Skipped
1	4	24.19 % / 68.97 %	13	4	69.57 % / 30.12 %	25	B	42.12 % / 48.57 %	37	C	87.4 % / 12.33 %	49	B	44.1 % / 30.81 %
2	3	22.73 % / 76.72 %	14	1	64.62 % / 33.77 %	26	A	66.5 % / 32.09 %	38	A	52.3 % / 41.96 %	50	B	64.34 % / 35.33 %
3	2	10.4 % / 82.25 %	15	#	66.87 % / 32.58 %	27	B	64.11 % / 34.69 %	39	A	64.77 % / 35.22 %	51	A	77.5 % / 11.82 %
4	3	10.92 % / 73.21 %	16	#	40.83 % / 49.92 %	28	A	41.34 % / 47.25 %	40	A	53.15 % / 38.36 %	52	B	58.01 % / 33.73 %
5	4	11.84 % / 67.04 %	17	#	69.02 % / 30.37 %	29	C	63.97 % / 30.88 %	41	B	58.54 % / 38.96 %	53	B	65.94 % / 32.12 %
6	4	10.14 % / 68.1 %	18	#	53.85 % / 36.1 %	30	D	46.16 % / 44.34 %	42	A	49.55 % / 35.72 %	54	A	44.43 % / 52.55 %
7	3	15.73 % / 71.74 %	19	#	80.44 % / 19.04 %	31	B	46.35 % / 33.69 %	43	B	56.03 % / 39.57 %	55	C	46.16 % / 37.95 %
8	4	23.81 % / 73.29 %	20	#	31.6 % / 68.17 %	32	C	28.87 % / 67.34 %	44	C	63.81 % / 34.19 %	56	B	45.23 % / 51.16 %
9	3	22.94 % / 72.34 %	21	B	57.96 % / 39.25 %	33	B	42.39 % / 50.51 %	45	C	52.46 % / 46.31 %	57	A	48.05 % / 50.01 %
10	3	68.69 % / 30.77 %	22	A	24.16 % / 74.4 %	34	C	50.88 % / 36.9 %	46	A	69.47 % / 30.48 %	58	C	58.27 % / 34.46 %
11	3	30.54 % / 68.45 %	23	D	84.92 % / 11.88 %	35	B	61.77 % / 34.17 %	47	B	52.75 % / 32.28 %	59	C	62.23 % / 34.57 %
12	4	66.37 % / 31.15 %	24	B	89.03 % / 10.24 %	36	B	49.55 % / 47.56 %	48	B	40.03 % / 58.83 %	60	B	67.62 % / 32.33 %

#

Q.	Answer
15	C
16	B
17	C
18	C
19	B
20	B

Performance Analysis

Performance Analysis	
Avg. Score (%)	56.67%
Toppers Score (%)	67.78%
Your Score	

//Hints and Solutions//

1. 5 is the first sentence as it is introducing the topic of mankind and the treasure accumulated by it.

1 is the second sentence as it how mankind has destroyed nature in order to accumulate treasures.

3 is the third sentence as it tells about how the next generation is enjoying the treasure accumulated by their ancestors.

2 is the last sentence as it concludes how it is utilizing other people to gather more capital.

Thus, the correct order is 5132.

- 5: During the agitated times which have elapsed since, and which have lasted for many thousand years, mankind has nevertheless amassed untold treasures.

- 1: It has cleared the land, dried the marshes, pierced the forests, made roads; it has been building, inventing, observing, reasoning; it has created a complex machinery, wrested her secrets from Nature, and finally, it has made a servant of steam.

- 3: And the result is, that now the child of the civilized man finds ready, at its birth, to his hand an immense capital accumulated by those who have gone before him.

- 2: And this capital enables him to acquire, merely by his own labour, combined with the labour of others, riches surpassing the dreams of the Orient, expressed in the fairy tales of the Thousand and One Nights.

- From the given explanation, it can be understood that all the above sentences are related to the capital acquisition by mankind.

- Sentence 4 seems odd as it is telling about the misuse of capital acquired.

Therefore, sentence 4 is the odd sentence.

Hence, the correct option is 4.

2. 2 is the first sentence as it is introducing the topic of David Hume his specialization.

5 is the second sentence as it explains about Hume's ethical thought deals with the relationship between morality and reason.

4 is the third sentence as it tells about Hume's thought was both influenced and criticized.

1 is the last sentence as it concludes where Hume's ethical theory is relevant.

Thus, the correct order is 2541.

- 2: Although David Hume is commonly known for his philosophical skepticism, and empiricist theory of knowledge, he also made many important contributions to moral philosophy.

- 5: Hume's ethical thought grapples with questions about the relationship between morality and reason, the role of human emotion in thought and action, the nature of moral evaluation, human sociability, and what it means to live a virtuous life.

- 4: As a central figure in the Scottish Enlightenment, Hume's ethical thought variously influenced, was influenced by, and faced criticism from, thinkers such as Shaftesbury, Francis Hutcheson, Adam Smith, and Thomas Reid.

- 1: Hume's ethical theory continues to be relevant for contemporary philosophers and psychologists interested in topics such as metaethics, the role of sympathy and empathy within moral evaluation and moral psychology, as well as virtue ethics.

- From the given explanation, it can be understood that all the above sentences are related to David Hume and his theory.

- Sentence 3 seems odd as it is telling about the general condition when we are sympathizing with somebody and the bond developed during that time.

Therefore, sentence 3 is the odd sentence.

Hence, the correct option is 3.

3. 3 is the first sentence as it is introducing the topic Runic alphabet (writing system) used by Germanic peoples.

5 is the second sentence as it explains the later formation of runic writing from these alphabets.

1 is the third sentence as it tells about how the writing system seems to belong to earlier ancient systems.

4 is the last sentence as it concludes by stating when scholars tried to derive it and how they tried.

Thus, the correct order is 3514.

- 3: Runic alphabet, also called futhark, writing system of uncertain origin used by Germanic peoples of northern Europe, Britain, Scandinavia, and Iceland from about the 3rd century to the 16th or 17th century AD.

- 5: Runic writing appeared rather late in the history of writing and is clearly derived from one of the alphabets of the Mediterranean area.

- 1: Because of its angular letter forms, however, and because early runic inscriptions were written from right to left like the earliest alphabets, runic writing seems to belong to a more ancient system.

- 4: Scholars have attempted to derive it from the Greek or Latin alphabets, either capitals or cursive forms, at any period from the 6th century BC to the 5th century AD.

- From the given explanation, it can be understood that all the above sentences are related to Runic writing.

- Sentence 2 seems odd as it is comparing Scandinavian languages with Old English languages which is out of the context of other sentences given.

Therefore, sentence 2 is the odd sentence.

Hence, the correct option is 2.

4. 1 is the first sentence as it is introducing the topic reporting of cinnamon hummingbirds in the United States.

4 is the second sentence as it explains what birders used at that time to report rare birds

2 is the third sentence as it tells about what happened when birders report.

5 is the last sentence as it concludes by stating that it was too late till the photos reached the Arizona committee.

Thus, the correct order is 1425.

- 1: In July 1992, two Danish birders visiting Patagonia, Arizona reported the first-ever, mega-rare cinnamon hummingbird in the United States.

- 4: Back then, reporting rare birds required phoning in observations to a "rare bird phone tree," usually via the nearest payphone—and hoping that word got out.

- 2: In this case, a couple of other out-of-towners—a birder from Mississippi and another from Nebraska—saw the species.

- 5: The Nebraskan photographed the hummingbird, flew home, developed the slide film, and snail-mailed photos to the Arizona committee in charge of validating unusual sightings but it was too late: the hummingbird was gone, and Arizona birders missed it.

- From the given explanation, it can be understood that all the above sentences are related to hummingbird spotting.

- Sentence 3 seems odd as it is generally stating what is generally used by birders to spot the bird.

Therefore, sentence 3 is the odd sentence.

Hence, the correct option is 3.

5. 5 is the first sentence as it is introducing the topic-decline in production and employment contributed by agriculture.

3 is the second sentence as it explains in spite of technological advancements the yield is not up to the mark.

2 is the third sentence as it tells about what is contributing to the decline in agriculture share in spite of increment in production due to technological advancement.

1 is the last sentence as it concludes by adding on the role of natural resources degradation in the decline.

Thus, the correct order is 5321.

- 5: The decline in the share of agriculture in total production and employment is taking place at different speeds and poses different challenges across regions.

- 3: Although agricultural investments and technological innovations are boosting productivity, the growth of yields has slowed to rates that are too low for comfort.

- 2: Food losses and waste claim a significant proportion of agricultural output, and reducing them would lessen the need for production increases.

- 1: However, the needed acceleration in productivity growth is hampered by the degradation of natural resources, the loss of biodiversity, and the spread of transboundary pests and diseases of plants and animals, some of which are becoming resistant to antimicrobials.

- From the given explanation, it can be understood that all the above sentences are related to the decline in agriculture and the reasons behind it.

- Sentence 4 seems odd as it is explaining something related that is done to minimize the loss of crops.

Therefore, sentence 4 is the odd sentence.

Hence, the correct option is 4.

6. 1 introduces the topic of debate.

3 mentions that there are advantages and disadvantages of both city life and village life.

5 Talks about the advantages of village life.

2 mentions why people are migrating to urban centers.

On a careful reading of the sentences, we find that 4 is out of context as it specifically talks about tribes and the associated tribal life. The rest of the sentences talk about which of the two, city life or village life, is better. So, the theme of 4 is completely different from the rest of the sentences.

Thus, the correct sequence is 1352.

- 1: One of the biggest debates humans have is whether city life is better than village life or vice versa.

- 3: Each area represents the opposite of the other and the advantages of one are actually the disadvantages of the other.

- 5: While village life has many advantages, including less noise, beautiful natural landscapes, less pollution, fresh air, and less congestion, the statistics do not favor the village folks worldwide.

- 2: Each year, millions of people migrate to urban centers in search of greener pastures.

Hence, the correct option is 4.

7. 4 is the first sentence as it is introducing the Disco Elysium which was launched in 2019 on what it is based.

1 is the second sentence as it explains what all a player will discover while playing the game.

5 is the third sentence as it tells about the new update in the game which provided it another edge.

2 is the last sentence as it concludes by telling all about the update featuring full voice acting and new content.

Thus, the correct order is 4152.

- 4: Disco Elysium, if you didn't play it when it came out in 2019, is a narrative-focused gem that emphasizes a vast story, worldbuilding, and themes, which over-delivers on its promise to leave you stunned, and perhaps changed, by the game's conclusion.

- 1: Exploring madness, heartbreak, postwar culture, racist pseudoscience, and cryptozoology in a game that's equal parts existential philosophy and absurdist nonsense, Disco Elysium was like nothing we've seen before.

- 5: After its initial release, the game saw a puzzlingly free update, Disco Elysium: The Final Cut, which overhauls what you already purchased and adds new content you didn't know you were desperate for.

- 2: With small rewrites, full silky voice acting that delivers every line in a set of gloriously European accents, and new political vision quests, Disco Elysium has been fully realized.

- From the given explanation, it can be understood that all the above sentences are related to Disco Elysium and its new update.

- Sentence 3 seems odd as it is explaining the reason for the delay in the launch which is nowhere discussed in other sentences.

Therefore, sentence 3 is the odd sentence.

Hence, the correct option is 3.

8. 1 is the first sentence as it is introducing the Going Medieval a game that has easily understandable and usable commands or facilities displayed on the screen.

3 is the second sentence as it explains how this menu is acting as blessing as it avoids looking through tabs to find the resource.

5 is the third sentence as it says even if you miss the important menu, you will appreciate step-by-step instructions that are repeated until you get what you have been looking for.

2 is the last sentence as it concludes the only drawback in this is it is difficult to change the view from between resources inside a storehouse and the storehouse roof.

Thus, the correct order is 1352.

- 1: A small, but a meaningful blessing in Going Medieval is its intuitive menus.

- 3: There's no digging through tabs to find one specific stat or resource, no immersion-breaking UX disasters.

- 5: The game doesn't harshly punish you for missing an important menu (or system) early on, allowing you to incrementally appreciate new gameplay loops.

- 2: The only frustration comes from Going Medieval's verticality—players can build up as it is harder than it should be to toggle a birds-eye view between resources inside a storehouse and the storehouse roof.

- From the given explanation, it can be understood that all the above sentences are related to the menus of Going Medieval.

- Sentence 4 seems odd as it says about the profit the launcher of this game gets by offering it to a larger audience.

Therefore, sentence 4 is the odd sentence.

Hence, the correct option is 4.

9. 2 introduces the topic of prosthetic arms.

1 denotes recent developments of the technology

5 Talks about the arm mentioned in 1 and 4 talks about another recent discovery.

All sentences except 3 talk about artificial or prosthetic arms while 3 talk about the robotic leg; Thus 3 is the odd sentence.

Thus, the correct sequence is 2154

- 2: Advancements in the processors used in myoelectric arms have allowed developers to make gains in fine-tuned control of the prosthetic.

- 1: The Boston Digital Arm is a recent artificial limb that has taken advantage of these more advanced processors.

- 5: The Boston Digital Arm is a recent artificial limb that has taken advantage of these more advanced processors.

- 4: Recently the I-LIMB Hand, invented in Edinburgh, Scotland, by David Gow has become the first commercially available hand prosthesis with five individually powered digits.

Hence, the correct option is 3.

10. 1 is the introductory sentence as it lays context.

2 talks about how the experience is different for different people.

4 and 5 talks about a particular situation and how to resolve it.

All except 3 talks about quarantine experience with cooking and what to do if you cook more than required while 3 talks about a random recipe; Thus 3 is the odd sentence.

Thus, correct order is: 1245

- 1: The quarantine has led many of us into the kitchen to cook meals three (or more) times a day.

- 2: While some people find cooking therapeutic and thoroughly enjoy doing it, for many others the experience is not as exciting.

- 4: But there may be times when you end up cooking extra and are left wondering what to do with it the next day.

- 5: Just give yourself a break and tweak the leftover food to make a new dish for your next meal.

Hence, the correct option is 3.

11. The correct answer is 3 i.e. the Statement It is believed that babies react to speech from the moment they take birth is the odd one.

1. The passage talks about how newborns react to speech and how this whole process is monitored.

2. Hence statements 2, 4, and 5 are interlinked as they talk about newborn and their responses to speech.

3. Statement 1 and Statement 3 are outliers compared to the rest of the statements.

4. However, Statement 1 touches upon the idea of speech in newborn babies.

So, Statement 3 is the odd one out.

Hence, the correct option is 3.

12. The correct answer is Statement 4 i.e. 'So if petrodollars ruled the past, it would be data dollars that would become the buzzword in the currency circles in the future.'

1. The central idea of the passage is how the use of data analytics would have long-lasting implications in the future.

2. Hence Statements 2, 3, and 5 are connected as all of them explain data analytics and its usages and benefits.

3. Statement 1 talks about the flow of data and data interpretation which is an explanation of data analytics in laymen's terms. Hence it is connected with the central theme of the passage.

Statement 4 talks about data dollars which is not the central theme of the passage. Also, the comparison of petrodollars with data dollars is a big deviation from the central theme of the passage.

Hence, the correct option is 4.

13. Sentences 3 and 2 go together, as do 1 and 4.

3 refers to the fact that Greek was the language of the governing elite, hinting that the language of the governed was something else. 2 says "Greek rulers could neither speak the language of the people? elaborating on the same theme.

1 and 4 both talk of the Rosetta Stone.

There is a link between 2 and 1 as well. 2 talks of fueling resentment while 1 elaborates on this by stating "Egypt was in open revolt".

Greece and Greek rulers are the common links between sentences 3, 2 and 1 which make sense when placed in sequence.

Therefore, sentence 4 is the odd sentence.

Hence, the correct option is 4.

14. The statement to be eliminated is 1, which talks of the effect of NPA accumulation – a plunge in industrial credit growth rate. None of the other sentences relate to this.

1 is slightly tricky to place right away, so let's look at 3 and 4.

3 states that NPAs have arisen in the Indian banking system due to reasons beyond the control of public sector banks. So what are the reasons for this problem? 4 provides the answers. So, 4 follows 3.

Now, according to 2, there are cases of bad loans where the repayment problems have been caused by "diversion of funds". Clearly, 2 relates to the idea in 3 and 4, as it talks of why loans turn bad. 2 concedes that some bad loans are caused by diversion of funds. 4, on the other hand, states the reasons for the bulk of the problem. So, 4 follows 2.

324 makes a cogent paragraph.

Hence, the correct answer is 1.

15. B states that we must suspend our habit of "glossing over" differences if we want to learn another language. A explains what these differences are– every language has different ways of codifying the world as it has evolved in a specific geocultural niche. So, BA is a link.

Now, looking at C and D, we see that C relates to how learning to talk a new language stretches our mind. This does not fit well with the idea in B and A.On the other hand, D adds to A. As different languages have different ways of codifying the world, it is not possible to achieve fluency in another language without learning its speakers' perspectives.

BAD makes a cogent paragraph.

Hence, the correct answer is C.

16. D states that the internet is a vector of climate change, that is, it contributes to the problem. C adds to this, stating that the world's data centers have the same carbon footprint as the aviation industry. DC is a unit.

Both A and B are about how climate change affects the internet. This is the exact opposite of what C and D are about (how the internet brings about climate change).

So where do AB and CD overlap?

B talks only of how rising seas imperil the internet. A, on the other hand, talks of a 'vicious cycle' that information technologies set off. What could this be? A states that with a rise in temperature, information technologies work less efficiently. C and D state that the internet contributes to global warming. So, with a rise in temperature, information technologies consume more energy, which in turn causes a further rise in temperature.

DCA is a unit.

Hence, the correct answer is B.

17. Statement A states that coastal wetlands help protect communities inland by growing in height as the sea level rises. Statement B, too, talks of wetlands such as marshes and mangrove forests. These help to protect coasts from hurricanes and storms by storing flood waters. The common thread between A and B is that wetlands help to protect coastal communities from hurricanes, storms and sea level rise.

Statements C and D talk of climate change. C states that wetlands help to mitigate climate change acting as carbon sinks, while D explains that wetlands make ecosystems and human communities more resilient in the face of climate change.

Let us look for an idea that overlaps AB and CD.

Like A and B, statement D talks of the impact of wetlands on human communities. D states that wetlands make these communities more resilient in the face of climate change—an idea that is substantiated by examples in A and B. DBA makes a cogent paragraph.

On the other hand, C talks of how wetlands help to mitigate or reduce the impact of climate change. This is a slightly different idea.

Hence, the correct answer is C.

18. A states in the "snag forest habitat" created by high-severity wildfire, many native species are found. Now, D too talks of native animals which thrive in the years following intense fires. DA is a unit—A follows D, as it begins with "additionally".

B explains that scientific studies over the years have established that forest fires are an essential part of Western U.S. forest ecosystems, as they create a biodiverse habitat. C follows B quite well : despite the evidence, the government has called for measures to prevent future fires. BC is a unit.

Now, considering DA and BC, we find one idea that is common to both groups—forest fires help in creating a biodiverse habitat. Sentence B links well to the unit DA. Note that even though A seems to introduce a new term (snag forest habitat), it explains what this is right away— a snag forest habitat is composed of dead and dying trees created by high-severity wildfire. BDA makes a cogent paragraph.

It is not clear from C what more "active management of forests" entails and none of the other sentences relate to this.

Hence, the correct answer is C.

19. Statement A states that expertise changes when "the social context" changes. What is the social context referred to here? It could apply equally well to the context mentioned in B (a different team with many other exceptional players) or to the one mentioned in D (a network of high performing athletes and support staff). So, both AB and AD make sense.

Now, looking at C, we see that this only fits with AD and not AB. Both C and D talk of the importance of support staff in team sports. ACD makes a cogent paragraph.

Hence, the correct answer is B.

20. Statement A, which talks of the "political nature" of "the target", is a bit vague. So, let's consider the other options. All of these relate to China's GDP.

B explains why Chinese GDP will be "unaffected" by a trade war with the US: the Chinese government will borrow to meet its growth targets.

C states that China's GDP numbers tell us about the "government's priorities" but are a "poor measure" of the performance of the economy as China will use it's debt capacity to achieve GDP growth. This relates to the point made in B.

D states that the Chinese government sets the GDP growth rate with "social and political objectives" in mind. This relates to C, which states that China's GDP numbers reflect the "government's priorities". In a paragraph, C would follow D.

So, does DCB make a cogent paragraph? It doesn't. B talks of the China-US trade war, while C and D do not mention this.

Now, let's have a look at A. In the given context, "the target" that A refers to is, clearly, the Chinese GDP figure, which, according to D is set early in the year, keeping social and political objectives in mind. Statement A explains how this target is achieved: local governments are encouraged to generate the economic activity that is necessary to achieve the GDP target. The sum total of this

and the economic activity of the private and real-estate sectors is made to add up to the GDP target. So, option A provides the link between D and C.

DAC is a cogent paragraph.

Hence, the correct answer is B.

21. Option (C) states that H erectus did not put in enough effort in finding good quality stones to make their tools. Option (A) adds to this point with an example. CA is a strong link.

Now, option B states that H sapiens and Neanderthals tried harder to make good quality stone tools, while D states that their "lackadaisical" attitude, combined with their inability to adapt to a changing environment, led to the "population's" demise.

Which of these relates best to the idea in CA? Both C and A talk of H erectus and their laziness, so to say. C mentions that the tools were crucial to the survival of the species. Clearly, D draws a conclusion based on the facts in C and A. CAD makes a cogent paragraph.

How other species made their stone tools does not fit in here: B would probably be the starting point of the next paragraph.

Hence, the correct option is (B).

22. Option (A) talks of a plastic recycling campaign by Keep America Beautiful which urges consumers to reduce their plastic footprint. None of the other three sentences refer to this campaign. However, the point of the campaign--making consumers assume responsibility for their plastic footprint-- is echoed in option (C), which talks of shifting "the onus of environmental responsibility onto the public".

Option (B) states that Keep America Beautiful has opposed legislation that would increase producer responsibility for plastic waste. Option (D) too talks of a legal framework and responsibility on plastic manufacturers. Clearly, D adds to the point in B, about Keep America Beautiful being against increasing the responsibility on plastic manufacturers, who are the producers of the waste.

We have two ideas relating to plastic footprint here: one relating to consumer responsibility and another relating to producer responsibility. Which sentence provides a common link?

Option (C), which states that "its greatest success" is in "shifting the onus of environmental responsibility onto the public" while "simultaneously becoming a trusted name in the environmental movement", fits the bill. This relates to the point made in D: Keep America Beautiful has built public support for punishing individual litterers, while "greenwashing" and ignoring the environmental responsibility of plastic manufacturers.

BCD makes a cogent paragraph.

Hence, the correct option is (A).

23. Option (A) talks of a "ritual" that the target of a joke completes when he laughs along. What ritual? Option B seems to offer a clue: ridicule can reinforce a group when the target of the joke is confident of his status within the group.

Option (C), which refers to the rest of the group "showing their membership" by laughing at each other and at themselves, seems to relate to the idea of a group ritual as well.

BCA makes a cogent paragraph.

Option (D) states that laughing at someone is among "the strongest markers of social exclusion". This is a completely different idea. Whereas the unit BCA talks of how laughter can strengthen a group, D talks of how laughter excludes one from a group.

Hence, the correct option is (D).

24. Option (A) states that emoji help us "write" gestures. Option (C) mentions "gesticulating": it states that emoji are the equivalent of making gestures to add emphasis. AC is a link.

Now, options (B) and (D) are clearly at odds with each other. While option B refers to emoji as the "lingua franca" (common language) of the world, D states that emoji are "not a language in themselves".

The sentence group AC only states that emoji help in communication by adding emphasis. In other words, they add to written language rather than replace it. Option (D) takes forward the idea in A and C.

Hence, the correct option is (B).

25. Sentence A talks of a "sliding scale of attribution" art historians use. When a painting is 'painted by' an artist, the degree of association between the artist and painting is obviously higher than if the painting merely showed the 'hand of' the artist. The other terms 'studio of', 'circle of', 'style of' and 'copy of' are clearly arranged in decreasing order of association between the artist and the painting.

Sentence B is rhetorical. The point it makes is that an expert fake is as satisfactory a work of art as a genuine one. This is a new idea. It is not clear right away how B relates to A, if at all.

Sentence C talks of 'the murk of semantics' that any discussion about the 'authenticity' of an art work opens. Now, sentence A too relates to semantics, as it discusses terms used by art historians to associate an artist with a painting. Also, both C and A relate to the idea of authenticity of an artwork, about how much the artwork can be associated with the artist. CA is a link. One more point to note here is that C does not include 'straight forgeries' in the discussion about the authenticity of an artwork. Sentence B, which talks of fakes i.e forgeries, is unlikely to be part of a paragraph which includes C.

Sentence D talks of the 'unease' about 'overpainting'. It declares that Savator Mundi has been worked over too many times and is so heavily overpainted that it is 'less by Da Vinci than by his restorers'. D clearly relates to the idea in A about how closely a painting can be attributed to an artist. In a paragraph, D would follow A as it adds to the point made in A.

Hence, the correct option is (B).

26. Both sentences A and B seem to be loosely related, as they talk of our protein needs--A, about how our relatively low protein requirement compared to mammals, and B, about the adverse consequences of tinkering with our natural needs.

There is also an obvious link between sentences C and D, in that both relate to formula milk. D talks of how cow's milk formula containing excessive protein was found to cause rapid growth rate in early life, and C relates the effect of this in later life. DC is a strong link.

Now, sentence A compares our protein needs to that of other mammals. Though cows are mammals and the sentence group DC compares human milk to cow's milk, ADC does not make a cogent paragraph, as the focus of A is on how small a percentage of protein we need to make up our calorie requirement.

However, sentence B, which speaks of the adverse consequences of tinkering with our natural protein needs fits right in with the message in the sentence group DC. BDC makes a cogent paragraph.

Hence, the correct option is (A).

27. Option (A) states that those who lack confidence in themselves "often seek confirmation" of this.

We see that option (D) relates to the same idea: some even go to the extent of provoking others to confirm their negative self-image.

Option (C) states the reason for this behaviour--the desire for "coherence".

ADC makes a cogent paragraph.

Option (B) talks about those who have a negative self-image wanting to "overcompensate". This does not relate to any of the other sentences.

Hence, the correct option is (B).

28. Option (A) explains why the stereotype that mood disorder enhances creativity is dangerous: it could stop people from seeking medical attention.

Option (B) talks of 'differences that may vary systematically' between 'the groups'. What groups People who achieve creative success and 'the average' person. According to B, these groups differ in that those who achieve creative success face the stress of being in the public eye, while the average person does not.

There is no obvious link between B and A.

Now, option (C) talks of groups too-- those in 'creative groups', which include successful writers and artists, and those in the 'less-creative' group, which includes the 'average' people living in the area where the study takes place.

It's clear that B and C have a common thread, and that C will precede B in a paragraph.

Option (D) states that 'just that component' could account for differences in cases of mood disorder. What is this 'component'? D states that stress is a major cause for the onset of mood disorders.

Now, option (B) also refers to stress, about this being one of the differences between those who achieve creative success and the 'average' person.

CBD forms a cogent paragraph. The main idea of this paragraph is that creative people are subject to the stress of being in the public eye and stress, by itself, is a cause for mood disorder.

None of the other sentences relate to the danger of thinking that creativity is enhanced mood disorder.

Hence, the correct option is (A).

29. Option (A) describes the chaotic cobbling together of nation states in the "breakneck" pace of decolonization and violent conflict that followed.

Option (B) posits that it is not the fault of "bad leaders" that few of the formerly colonized countries are now peaceful, affluent, and democratic. This relates to the idea in option A, that the rapid pace of decolonization contributed to violent conflict in the newly formed nations.

Option (C) talks about economic institutions in the new states. This is at odds with A and B, which relate to the political chaos resulting from decolonization.

Option (D) explained how 'strongmen' held infant states together by stoking sectarian rivalries. This too relates to the ideas in A and B, of the after-effects of decolonization on the political apparatus of the newly formed nations.

BAD makes a cogent paragraph.

Hence, the correct option is (C).

30. Sentence A talks of the "supposedly vast Sentence A posits that museums are not 'neutral spaces' that house objects without context. Sentence B expands on this idea, stating that museums propagate missions and legacies 'through design and architecture'. The point that these statements make is that the form of the museum--its design and architecture-- matters as much as the objects in it, for this adds context to the objects showcased in the space. Sentence C reiterates this, stating that 'there is no escaping the weight of the objects and stories told within their architecture'. ABC makes a cogent paragraph.

Sentence D states a diametrically opposite view to the one in the other sentences, declaring that one museum isn't so different from another, as it displays 'the same major-canon artists, arranged in more or less the same way'.

Hence, the correct option is (D).

31. Sentence A talks of the "supposedly vast potential" of the Commonwealth, and it always remaining "cheaper than EU", and that too, not just in terms of UK's direct financial contribution.

We see that sentence D carries forward this idea--the belief that the cost of the Commonwealth, in terms of the hours to be put in to negotiate treaties, the concessions to be given and the mechanisms to be put in place to make it work, will be less than the cost of EU.

D explains phrase "not only in terms of UK's direct financial contribution" in A. So, D follows A.

Sentence C sums up the ideas in A and D, of the Commonwealth being thought of as a miraculous remedy that would somehow achieve extraordinary results though terribly understaffed.

ADC makes a cogent paragraph.

Sentence B talks of trade between the member states of the Commonwealth, and "an average figure for Commonwealth advantage". These are new ideas, and the other sentences do not refer to these.

Hence, the correct option is (B).

32. Sentence A attributes "cultural nationalism" to technological change and global competition. Sentence B takes this idea forward, explaining how "information-rich societies" reward cultural uniqueness and the development of human capital. We see that sentence D, too, talks of technological change as an important factor driving nationalism.

DAB makes a cogent paragraph.

Sentence C, on the other hand, reasons that the mixture of austerity, corruption, and political sclerosis at the center is responsible for the rise in the fight for self-determination. This is a different idea and does not fit in the given paragraph.

Hence, the correct option is (C).

33. Sentence A talks of the 'punch' delivered by sprinters when they drive the foot into the track. That is, sprinters strike the ground with great force as they run. We see that sentence C, too, ties in with this idea. A follows C, as it explains how the 'force' mentioned in C is generated.

Now, looking at sentences B and D, we see that they are at odds with each other. Sentence B declares that the swiftest runners achieve top speed by swinging their legs faster while they reposition their limbs in air. Sentence D, on the other hand, states that all runners take roughly the same time when airborne to reposition their legs for the next stride. Only one of these can be true.

The primary idea in sentences A and C is that the speed of a sprinter is determined by the force and speed with which he strikes the ground. Neither of these makes a reference to the time taken to swing the leg or reposition it in the air.

Also note that sentence C begins with 'what faster runners do better...'. The sentence that links to this is not likely to attribute the reason sprinters achieve top speed to some other factor other than the force with which they strike the ground.

So, the sentence that does not fit in is sentence B, as it ties a sprinter's speed to his speed of repositioning his legs while airborne.

DCA makes a cogent paragraph.

Hence, the correct option is (B).

34. The link between sentences A and B is the reference to lower wages/remuneration in each.

Sentence A states that inflation "is assumed to trick workers into accepting a lower remuneration" and calls inflation "an indirect wage cut that helps prevent an increase in unemployment". That is, an increase in inflation prevents an increase in unemployment.

Sentence B too refers to wages, noting that they are inflexible in a market economy. Unemployment goes up when there is a situation where workers have to accept lower wages.

A follows B. Wages are inflexible. Unemployment goes up when wages have to be reduced. However, inflation tricks workers into accepting lower wages for their services, thereby preventing an increase in unemployment.

Now, sentence C declares any effort to micromanage the economy as a "fool's errand", based on two points. One is that the stagflation of the 1970s proved that both high unemployment and high inflation can co-exist. Two, wages may not be as rigid as many economists assume. The ideas put forth in sentence C do not seem to relate to sentences B and A, both of which refer to inflation as a possible means of preventing an increase in unemployment.

Sentence D, on the other hand, talks of "this inverse relationship" that central banks keep in mind while framing monetary policies.

BAD makes a cogent paragraph.

Hence, the correct option is (C).

35. The tone of sentence A suggests that subduing our passions to the iron rule of reason is not necessarily ideal for human cognition.

We can see that sentence D is in a similar, mocking vein. It implies our 'most prized' and 'most humanly' attribute is not our forebrain, and that it is not the forebrain that aids rational thinking.

Now, of the two remaining sentences B and C, we see that sentence C fits in with the idea in sentences A and D, both in terms of the derisive tone it uses as well as the message it conveys. We aspire to become more rational by subduing our emotions, and ironically, the more we are like Star Trek's unfeeling alien Mr. Spock, the more 'human' we think we are.

DAC makes a cogent paragraph.

Sentence B relates to a different idea—the paradox that humans can be described as rational animals only because humans are the only animals capable of being irrational.

Hence, the correct option is (B).

36. Both sentences B and C refer to Macron's victory in the French elections. Let us look at how they relate to each other. Sentence B declares Macron's victory to be the "consummation of a political revolution". Sentence C, however, posits the idea that the so-called transformation of the political landscape might be only skin deep, as the turnout was low. These are two different ideas.

Now, let us look at sentences A and D. Sentence A is a general statement, that party politics merely skims the surface of the ocean that is the society, and that it is the undercurrents that are of significance in the long run. Sentence D, too, makes a reference to a "powerful current" — growing abstention— declaring that this risks "pulling the country under". These are related ideas—while sentence A makes a generalized observation, sentence D cites a specific example, the case of France, where

abstention, or low voter turnout, is a strong undercurrent that could have a powerful impact in the long run. So, D follows A.

Does sentence B or C relate to the idea in sentences A and D? On close observation, we can see that sentence C does, referring to the low turnout and suggesting that what looks like a huge transformation of the political landscape on "the surface" might actually be only skin deep. Note that the reference to "the surface" ties in with the imagery in sentences A and D, to the surf, scum, spray, and undercurrents.

Therefore, sentence B is the odd sentence.

Hence, the correct option is (B).

37. Sentence A explains how sea ice serves as a blanket on top of the ocean, protecting the water from solar heat. We see that sentence D too refers to this idea, talking of how the melting of this frozen coating leads to the warming of the oceans. Sentence B concludes the paragraph, saying that this leads to the melting of land ice and driving up sea levels. So, ADB forms a cogent paragraph.

Option (C), which talks of the melting sea ice not adding to the ocean's mass and it discusses a completely unrelated idea.

Therefore, sentence C is the odd sentence.

Hence, the correct option is (C).

38. Sentence A labels fiction as a 'means of escape' from social ties and reality. Sentence D, the other hand, says that the act of reading is actually an 'exercise in human interaction'. As these are two opposing points of view, it is clear that either A or D is the sentence to be eliminated.

Sentence B is difficult to place without context, as it talks of reading training people in 'this domain'. What expertise reading fiction builds is not clear just by reading this sentence.

Now, sentence C declares that the 'defining characteristic of fiction' is not that it is something fabricated, but that it is about human intentions and interactions. Clearly, this is in line with the idea expressed in sentence D. We can now see that DCB makes a cogent paragraph.

Therefore, sentence A is the odd sentence.

Hence, the correct option is (A).

39. Sentence A declares that the Constitution is "external to society" and has only an advisory relationship with it. None of the other sentences carries forward or links to this idea.

On the other hand, we see right away that sentences C and D relate to the same idea—that the Constitution presumes "the people" to be a unified and homogenous collectivity and is hence unable to acknowledge "obstinate realities" like caste, as this is tantamount to confessing that the republic is not a reality.

Sentence B talks about something not being a "defect", as the Constitution is required to put the people in the best light. What is being referred to here? The fact mentioned in sentence D – that the Constitution treats what it hopes to achieve as if it was already an established fact – is the only one that fits with this statement.

To summarize, the Constitution presumes "the people" to be one unified unit, thereby treating what it hopes to achieve as an established fact. Nevertheless, this cannot be called a defect, as the Constitution is, after all, supposed to put the country in the best possible light. Yet, this also makes it difficult for the Constitution to directly confront divisive realities such as caste. DBC makes a cogent paragraph.

Therefore, sentence A is the odd sentence.

Hence, the correct option is (A).

40. Sentence C talks of the Nefertiti bust in Berlin being 'one of the world's great icons of beauty'. We can see that sentence A too talks of this sculpture, and evidence found to suggest that the sculptor might have made adjustments to depict the 'Beauty of the Nile' in better light.

Now sentence B and D seem to form a unit, both referring to a new rendering i.e. a replica at the entrance of the Egyptian city of Samalut, which is "colossally awful" and "might scare people".

While neither sentence B nor D fits with A and C to form a cogent unit, we can see that CBD does form a logical sequence. Sentence C talks of the Nefertiti bust in Berlin made in the Amarna style. Sentence B talks of a new rendering that attempts, unsuccessfully, to re-create this style. Sentence D talks of this ugly replica being pulled down by Egyptians as the 'way forward' to 'topple art that's an insult to our public spaces'.

Therefore, sentence A is the odd sentence.

Hence, the correct option is (A).

41. Let us look at the links between the sentences. Both sentences B and C talk about the Subramanian committee. Now, sentence B states that the committee has rightly noted that the "worst scenario for farmers" is the weak government procurement policy combined with restrictions on exports and stock-holding. Sentence C talks of the volatility in production and prices of pulses being shown by the report as higher than that of cereals. These sentences talk of two different ideas. Does A or D provide a link? Neither sentence A, which talks of the projected demand nor sentence D which talks of how pulses help in soil rejuvenation seem to fit in with C and B.

Now, sentence C tells us that the volatility in production and prices is "neither in the interests of the producers nor the consumers". Sentence A clarifies why this is not in the interest of the consumers. The demand is set to rise dramatically. Also, sentence A says that farmers need to be encouraged to grow more pulses "not simply" because of the projected demand. What other reason exists for encouraging farmers to grow pulses? Sentence D answers this question. Pulses help in soil rejuvenation and fix atmospheric nitrogen, without consuming much water. So it is also in the interest of the producers to grow more pulses. CAD forms cogent paragraph. The idea is that growing pulses is beneficial to both producers and consumers.

Sentence B talks about procurement and export/stock-holding restrictions.

Hence, the correct option is (B).

Therefore, sentence B is the odd sentence.

42. Sentence A talks about automotive interests, which have carefully planted the idea in our minds that streets are where cars belong. We find a reference to cars and streets in sentence D, which says that "cars prowl the streets". However, neither sentence B, which describes the automobile as the 21st century's "apex predator" nor sentence C, which talks of fatal collisions becoming an everyday phenomenon, is related to this idea.

Now, let's consider the interesting description of the automobile in Sentence B declares as "the twenty-first century's apex predator". Why apex predator? An apex predator is one that sits on top of the food chain. This comparison of automobiles to apex predators draws our attention to automobiles as killers, the cause of fatal collisions on roads. Sentence C too talks of fatal collisions. So the link between sentences B and C is clear.

Now between sentences A and D, we see that D relates to the idea of cars as predators. It describes cars prowling streets, "growling in revving ravenousness". Indeed, D adds to sentence B in the description of cars as apex predators. BDC forms a cogent paragraph.

Therefore, sentence A is the odd sentence.

Hence, the correct option is (A).

43. We can see straight away that both sentences B and C talk about India and its relations with its neighbors. Sentence B talks about India's military focus on Pakistan over China "inspiring little confidence in its judgment, resolve, and prospects as a consequential power in the extended region". Sentence C talks of India's ambition to emerge as the other major power in Asia being undermined by its "diffidence and skewed capabilities".

Again, the link between sentences A and D is obvious. Sentence A talks about India's self-sufficiency in strategic armaments and sentence D about India's dependence on other countries for conventional weaponry. It is also clear that D follows A, as it starts by observing the paradoxical nature of the situation.

So which sentence among these 2 groups has a common link with the other?

We see that sentence B refers to India's military focus. Both sentences A and D talk of India's military capabilities. However, a logical connection between these fails to emerge. If sentence B were to precede A and D, then the paragraph would start by saying that India's military focus on Pakistan and ignoring China shows poor judgment. But the sentence group A and D do not add to this: they talk instead of India's capabilities, and do not substantiate the focus of sentence B, i.e. how the military stance is affecting India's image in the world stage. What if B were to follow AD? Sentence D ends with a note on how India's dependence on imports for conventional weaponry leaves "its foreign policy hostage to the whims and interests of vendor states". There is nothing in sentence B to substantiate or add to this. In fact, sentence B goes on to talk of a totally different idea. So it does not make a good option to follow D.

Now, sentence C talks of India's strategic ambitions being undermined by its "diffidence and skewed capabilities". The word "skewed" provides a key link between this sentence and the sentence group AD. Clearly, sentences A and D talk about India's

asymmetrical capabilities in areas of strategic armaments and conventional weaponry. CAD makes a logical paragraph.

Therefore, sentence B is the odd sentence.

Hence, the correct option is (B).

44. Both sentences A and D talk about the "weight of the glaciers". Sentence D tells us that this weight has pushed against the Earth's surface, causing it to depress, and sentence A tells us that thanks to this weight being lifted, due to the melting of the glaciers, the surface is bounding back.

Now, we see that sentence B relates to the idea of the surface springing back. It tells us that mountain ranges such as the Alps have experienced a gradual "growth spurt" over the last century.

When placed in the order BDA, these sentences make a cogent paragraph.

Sentence C talks about glaciers "sculpting mountains" by carving out valleys and carrying away rock debris. This does not relate to the other sentences, which talk of the growth or rebounding of mountains due to the melting of glaciers.

Therefore, sentence C is the odd sentence.

Hence, the correct option is (C).

45. There is a common idea in sentences B and D: both refer to politics. Sentence D talks of politicians manipulating people by using emotions to grab power. Sentence B declares that this is not the problem. The problem is that people who are otherwise sensible allow themselves to be led blindly.

Again, sentences A and C seem related. Both talk of what the people must do. Sentence A calls upon the people to reflect, warning that if we don't, we are likely to make mistakes in the name of good things such as fighting corruption and tackling crime. Sentence C states that we might be able to approach "the issue" with greater level-headedness by understanding that our security is not under attack; it is our sentiments that are offended.

What is "the issue" referred to in sentence C that stirs up our emotions and makes us fear that our security is under threat? Sentence A makes a reference to fighting corruption and tackling crime. It doesn't specifically state one issue that makes us feel our security is threatened. Neither B nor D helps us pinpoint what "the issue" is.

On the other hand, we see that sentence A urges people to think deeply and reflect so that they do not commit "grievous" mistakes without proper deliberation. This continues the idea in sentence B that otherwise sensible citizens allow themselves to be led on by emotions stirred up by politicians. So DBA makes a cogent paragraph.

Sentence C does not fit, as it talks of a specific "issue" that the rest of the sentences cannot explain.

Therefore, sentence C is the odd sentence.

Hence, the correct option is (C).

46. Sentence A declares that the most emotional way to view history is through photographs.

Sentence B talks of what taking a photograph involves.

Sentence C says what "they" are not about- quotes or sound bites.

Sentence D states that photographs convey the ultimate journalistic credo of being in action at the right place at the right time.

So what ideas link the given sentences?

Sentences B and D share a common idea that photographs capture "fleeting moments" and "fleeing reality".

Both sentences C and D relate to photojournalism. Sentence D talks of photographs conveying the "ultimate journalistic credo" of being at the site of action at the right time to capture moments that though short-lived, are life-changing. Sentence C clarifies what kind of journalism photos are not about- they aren't about getting quotes or quick comments.

We see a common thread emerging here. In a paragraph, we could order sentence D first, as it talks of photos conveying the ideal of journalism, and then sentence C which talks about what kind of journalism photos aren't about, and follow it up with sentence B, which talks of what taking photographs involves. DCB makes a cogent paragraph.

Sentence A is the only one that voices a completely different idea- photos as emotional ways of looking back at history.

Therefore, sentence A is the odd sentence.

Hence, the correct option is (A).

47. The best way to approach sentence elimination questions is to figure out which three of the four sentences given form a cogent paragraph. The sentence that does not fit in is the one to be eliminated.

Now, looking at sentences A and B, it is clear that they share a link -Ali's rejection of the Vietnam War. Sentence A tells us that by rejecting war, Ali showed that he believed that war could not solve human problems. Sentence B talks of Ali's refusal to base national boundaries as lines demarcating humans into "us" and "them". Each sentence, thus, conveys a distinct idea that answers the question, "What does Ali's rejection of the Vietnam War show?". Also, note that both sentences A and B have the word "thus" in them. In a paragraph, some other idea is likely to have preceded both these sentences.

Now looking at sentences C and D, we see that these two sentences to share a common idea-that of shunning violence while standing up to injustice. Sentence C argues that violence is used to legitimize hegemony or dominance and not resorting to it is the best way to challenge it. Sentence D too echoes this idea. If these sentences were to be rearranged in a paragraph, how would they be ordered? Sentence D declares that the "best way" to stand up to power and injustice is to be unyielding, while at the same time avoiding violence. Sentence C explains why this is so. It declares that violence is often used as a tool to authorize or establish dominance, and by avoiding it you are already challenging the hegemon. So C follows D.

Now which sentence from the two groups AB and CD shares a common idea with the other group?

We see that sentence A shares a common idea with D and C. The main idea of sentence A is that Ali rejected the Vietnam War as he believed war/violence is not the solution to human problems. If these sentences were to form a paragraph, they would be ordered DCA.

Sentence B, on the other hand, talks of a completely new idea- of national boundaries dividing humans into opposing factions. It does not fit with either D or C.

Therefore, sentence B is the odd sentence.

Hence, the correct option is (B).

48. Sentence A declares that we don't do many activities at once, but just switch from one to the other. Sentence C talks about the cost of switching attention. C follows A.

Sentence B talks of multi-tasking, saying that it makes us demonstrably efficient, and increases our cognitive performance.

Sentence C, however, states that every time we switch attention, we "pay" a metabolic cost in glucose, suggesting that switching attention is a drain on our physical resources.

Sentence D asserts that switching attention is an "expensive" brain activity. This ties in with sentence C. D possibly follows C.

We also see that B contradicts D. D suggests switching attention is an "expensive" brain activity, while B states that multitasking increases cognitive performance.

ACD makes a paragraph.

Therefore, sentence B is the odd sentence.

Hence, the correct option is (B).

49. Sentence A tells us that birds are modern descendants of dinosaurs and hence they are likely to have once had teeth.

Sentence C also talks of teeth, stating that "this fact" became known in 1861 with the discovery of Archaeopteryx, which had teeth. The fact referred to here is the one stated in sentence A, that birds once had teeth. So C follows A.

We now need to find the third sentence that fits in with C and A.

Sentence B says that non-avian dinosaurs sprouted feathers 100 million years ago.

Sentence D declares that researchers have discovered that avian edentulism, or loss of teeth, occurred in one common bird ancestor 100 million years ago.

It is clear that CAD makes a cogent paragraph.

Therefore, sentence B is the odd sentence.

Hence, the correct option is (B).

50. Sentence A declares that by legalizing gambling, consumers are assured of reliability, something they prefer when it is available.

Sentence D also favors legalized gambling, stating that it makes the market more hostile to cheaters. Sentence C supports this idea with the example of Britain.

The only sentence that argues against legalized gambling is sentence B, which states that it could lead to new ways of fixing games.

Therefore, sentence B is the odd sentence.

Hence, the correct option is (B).

51. Sentence B notes that Rowling wishes to influence how readers understand her books by revealing new information about her characters.

Sentence A talks of Rowling's declarations on characters as being newsworthy and a "cause for pride".

Sentence D too talks of Rowling alluding to the characters in her books. However, it states that the meanings the international community of readers draws from the books trump or prevail over Rowling's intentions as an author.

This ties in with sentence C which declares that Rowling's chances of being a "diverse" author lie in the future, not in the past.

BDC makes a paragraph.

Therefore, sentence A is the odd sentence.

Hence, the correct option is (A).

52. Sentence A talks of modern prose being a mix of vagueness and incompetence.

Sentence D elaborates on the idea of "vagueness" talked of in sentence A, stating that in certain topics, the concrete melts into the abstract, and oft-used expressions abound.

Sentence C declares that prose is becoming less about words chosen for their meaning, and more about piling up pretentious phrases.

ADC makes a paragraph.

Sentence B starts off with "it follows that" and states that any struggle against the abuse of language is dismissed as sentimental and old-fashioned. None of the statements given offers a thought that would fit with the "it follows that" beginning of sentence B.

Therefore, sentence B is the odd sentence.

Hence, the correct option is (B).

53. Three sentences- A, B and C- mention Sparta. It is important, however, to understand the context to see which sentence is to be eliminated.

Sentence A tells us that though Spartans were at war with Greece and dying, some of their countrymen were competing at that time at the Olympia.

Sentence C talks of how America, like Sparta, was represented at the Games while still fighting in Vietnam.

We see that there is a link between sentences A and C. Both talk of warring countries still competing at the Olympic Games. C follows A, as it compares America to Sparta.

Now we need to look at a third sentence that will fit with these to form a paragraph.

Sentence B tells that while troops were normally not allowed in the Olympic precinct, they were there in 420 BC, as war with Sparta was thought to be imminent. Sentence B provides an example of an exception made to the Olympic rules at a time war was expected.

Sentence D talks of the cancellation of Olympiads in 1926, 1940 and 1944 due to world wars.

Of the two sentences above, we see that sentence D fits in with the idea of competing at Olympic Games while at war, discussed in sentences A and C. ADC forms a cogent paragraph.

Therefore, sentence B is the odd sentence.

Hence, the correct option is (B).

54. Sentence C talks of the details in poetry- that they should not only be precise but also elicit and reward a "sense of movement".

We have two other sentences that relate to the sense of movement. Sentence B talks of the "image"? of poetry existing both in space and time in "such movement". Sentence A also relates to movement. It talks of the "special intimacy" poetry has because the medium of poetry is the audience's body.

We see that sentence B develops the idea presented in sentence C . B follows C.

Sentence D describes poetry as a "centaur", where the thinking faculty must "move and leap" with the sentient and musical faculties. Again, we see the key idea that poetry involves a sense of movement in sentence D. In fact, sentence C builds on the same idea as sentence D. C follows D.

Sentence A is one that talks about a new idea- the medium of poetry not being the expert's body but the audience's.

Therefore, sentence A is the odd sentence.

Hence, the correct option is (A).

55. Sentence A talks about the amount of e-waste generated around the world.

Sentence D talks about the largest producers of e-waste and how Asian cities are catching up. Sentence B substantiates this point, giving the example of China as a huge consumer of electronic goods and hence generator of e-waste. So ADB make a paragraph.

Only sentence C, which talks about illegal dumping of e-waste, does not fit in with the rest.

Therefore, sentence C is the odd sentence.

Hence, the correct option is (C).

56. Sentence A cites the example of China, where the World Bank has been important not "quantitatively" but as a source of "blueprints and information".

Sentence B tells us that multilateral development institutions play an important role in global infrastructure financing.

Sentence C talks of their greatest failures springing from "funding grandiose projects" that benefit those countries considered the current "elite".

Sentence D tells us that multilateral development institutions have been most successful as knowledge banks, sharing expertise.

We can see that sentences A and D are of the same idea. The example of China substantiates the point made by sentence D that multilateral development institutions are most successful as knowledge banks.

So which is the third sentence that fits in with A and D- B or C?

Sentence D talks of the greatest successes of multilateral development banks and sentence C tells us of their greatest failures.

Sentence B on the other hand stresses the importance of infrastructure financing by multilateral development banks, which does not relate to the main idea of the other two sentences- that the role of these institutions is more significant with regard to knowledge transfer.

DCA make a paragraph.

Therefore, sentence B is the odd sentence.

Hence, the correct option is (B).

57. Sentence A talks about how well a reality show does in terms of viewership. Sentence B seems to carry forward that thought, stating that the "key" is for channels to find bankable reality formats.

Sentence C is unrelated to the idea that A and B share. Firstly it starts with a "then, again" and talks of "they" realized that an easy way to gain ad revenue is to lure advertisers to reality TV.

Sentence D tells us that the year-on-year increase in production costs for reality shows has rattled networks. We see right away that D and C are related and that C follows D.

Sentence B which talks of bankable reality formats provides the third sentence to complete the paragraph, in the order DCB.

Therefore, sentence A is the odd sentence.

Hence, the correct option is (A).

58. This sentence elimination question is tricky.

Sentence B tells us that it is thought that the Harappan rulers were wealthy merchants or landlords or religious leaders who used seals and jewelry to show their power. Sentence C describes the seals referred to in sentence B. So B and C go together.

Sentence A talks of Harappan and other Indus art and sculpture not having any depictions of warfare. Sentence D also contains a reference to war. It states that the Harappan rulers governed their cities not using military muscle but through control of trade and religion. So, A and D go together.

Which idea is common to both sets of sentences? If the paragraph is about Harappan seals, either A or D should fit in as the third sentence, joining B and C to make a paragraph. Sentence A is clearly not the choice, as it is about the Indus art and culture not depicting warfare. Sentence D is about how Harappan cities were governed. Neither fits in.

Sentence D talks of Harappan rulers possibly governing their cities through control of trade and religion. Sentence B too refers to Harappan rulers, speculating that they might have been wealthy tradesmen or religious leaders. We have already seen the link between A and D.

Sentences DAB makes sense when placed in order, the key idea being Harappan rulers. It appears that the Harappan rulers governed through control of trade, not military might. Sentence A substantiates this, stating that there are no monuments or artifacts depicting warfare. So it is speculated that the Harappan rulers were wealthy merchants, who demonstrated their power, not by military muscle but by demonstration of wealth- fine jewelry and status symbols- seals.

Therefore, sentence C is the odd sentence.

Hence, the correct option is (C).

59. The key ideas of the sentences are summarized as follows:

A - Fundamentalism and secularization always coexist. The secularization is seen as "violent, cruel and invasive" by the other side.

B- Historically, wherever an attempt was made to separate religion and politics, a counter-cultural movement sprung up.

C- Secularization came with colonial rule and was hence rejected in the developing world.

D- "Aggressive" secularism instigates a violent reply from religion.

It is clear from the above that while A, B, and D only talk of secularism and fundamentalism, option C stands out as the one with a different idea- linking secularism with colonial rule.

The paragraph makes sense when put in the order ABD.

Therefore, sentence C is the odd sentence.

Hence, the correct option is (C).

60. To find out which sentence needs to be eliminated, we have to frame a paragraph with the other three and see if it is cogent. We can look out for keywords or thoughts that link all sentences together with one main idea.

Sentence A talks of developing "these different ways of thinking" by "extended, focused mental effort".

Sentence B talks of the "relatively brief period" students spend in a classroom, and the "long-term memory structures" required for subject mastery.

Sentence C talks of how a traditional science instructor teaches by assuming "expert-like ways of thinking" are already present.

We can see right away that C and A go together, with the "way of thinking" being the key idea repeated in both sentences.

Sentence D talks of how the "necessary extended effort" can be made by students with some help from teachers.

Sentence A also talked of the "extended mental effort" students need to put in to develop expert-like thinking.

So D ties in with A. The paragraph makes sense when arranged in the sequence CAD.

Looking at B, we can reconfirm that it is indeed the sentence to be eliminated as it talks of "memory structure". This idea is not explained by any of the other sentences.

Therefore, sentence B is the odd sentence.

Hence, the correct option is (B).

// Notes //

// Notes //